Man
And The
Cosmos

Man
And The
Cosmos

by Gerald E. Tauber

GREENWICH HOUSE
New York

TO THE MEMORY OF
PAUL NADAN
WITHOUT WHOM THIS BOOK WOULD NOT HAVE BEEN POSSIBLE
AND
TO MY PARENTS
WHO INSTILLED IN ME THE LOVE FOR TRUTH

Copyright © 1979 by Crown Publishers, Inc.

This 1982 edition is published by Greenwich House,
a division of Arlington House, Inc.,
distributed by Crown Publishers, Inc., by arrangement with
Crown Publishers, Inc.

Previously published as *Man's View of the Universe:
A Pictorial History*

Manufactured in the United States of America

Library of Congress Cataloging in Publication Data
Tauber, Gerald E.
Man and the cosmos.

Reprint. Originally published: Man's view of the universe. New York :
Crown Publishers, c1979.
Bibliography: p.
Includes index.
1. Astronomy—History.   2. Cosmology—History.
I. Title.
[QB15.T38   1982]   520.9   82-6126
AACR2

ISBN: 0-517-387697
h g f e d c b a

Contents

Acknowledgments

It is the author's pleasure to express his appreciation to the large number of individuals, institutions, observatories, and publishers who assisted in the preparation of this book by providing illustrations, granting permission for their use, and reading the manuscript. Special mention should be made of the following persons for their help in obtaining illustrations:

Dr. William A. Blanpied, Head, Division of Public Sector Program, American Association for the Advancement of Science; Linda A. Chaffee, Photo Permissions Secretary, Hale Observatories; Miss Helen Dukas, The Institute of Advanced Studies, Princeton; Prof. Owen Gingerich, Center for Astrophysics, Cambridge; M. Leibovitz, photographer, Tel Aviv University; Paul Adolf Kirchvogel, Oberkustos i.R., Staatliche Kunstsammlung, Kassel; Prof. Martin J. Klein, Eugene Higgins Professor of the History of Physics, Yale University; Dr. Patrick Moore, O.B.E., Farthings; Dr. Otto Nathan, Trustee, Estate of Albert Einstein; Prof. Jerzy Neyman, Director, Statistical Laboratory, University of California; Prof. O. Neugebauer, School of Historical Studies, The Institute of Advanced Studies, Princeton; Ruth M. Olson, secretary to Dr. H. Friedman, Naval Research Laboratory, Washington, D.C.; Dr. Gian Carlo Oli, scientific attaché, Italian Embassy, Tel Aviv; Dr. Marta Bucciarelli Poggesi, Curator, Museo Zoologico de "La Specola," Florence; Prof. Guglielmo Righini, Director, Osservatorio Astrofisico Arcetri, Florence; Rudolf Thiel, Kulturhistoriker, Darmstadt; Prof. Dr. H. H. Voigt, Director, Universitäts-Sternwarte, Göttingen; Prof. Dr. G. Walterspiel, Munich; Joan N. Warnow, Associate Director, Center for the History of Physics, American Institute of Physics.

Special thanks are also due to the following for reading part of the manuscript and offering their comments and suggestions. (The author bears the full responsibility for any unintentional errors that might still remain.)

Prof. Ben Zion Koslovsky, Department of Physics and Astronomy, Tel Aviv University; Dr. E. Leibovitz, Department of Physics and Astronomy, Tel Aviv University; Prof. J. Otterman, Department of Geophysics and Planetary Science, Tel Aviv University; Prof. G. Shaviv, Chairman, Dept. of Physics and Astronomy, Tel Aviv University; Prof. N. Rosen, Department of Physics, Technion, Haifa.

However, it is to Paul Nadan, late senior editor at Crown Publishers, that the author is most indebted. Mr. Nadan was devoted to this project from its very beginning and nurtured it along for many years, advising, correcting, challenging, and encouraging the author. It was he who taught me the meaning of "glossies" and how to make the most efficient use of them. It is with great sadness that I can only acknowledge his help posthumously, since he died shortly before this book was completed and thus did not live to see the completion of a work to which he devoted so much time and effort.

Preface

Man has always been interested in the world in which he lives, in his neighbors the planets, and in the universe as a whole. It is the aim of the present book to trace the history of that interest—which we call astronomy—from its earliest expression in constructions such as Stonehenge up to the present age of space exploration, in which our knowledge about the origins of the universe has been greatly expanded. The book is richly illustrated with a variety of materials—paintings, photographs, charts, and diagrams—to give the reader a full and vivid picture of how man has viewed his world.

In addition to examining the development of astronomy, in both words and pictures, the book describes specific scientific discoveries that have contributed to that development, including the most recent ones, such as quasars, pulsars, and black holes. The descriptions are nontechnical and are accompanied by numerous diagrams and other illustrations (many never before available to the general public) to enhance the reader's understanding.

The lives of important contributors to the advancement of astronomy are covered in biographical sketches, also illustrated, that elucidate their scientific theories and achievements and set the men and their work in the context of their times. Included are such scientists as Copernicus, Tycho Brahe, Johannes Kepler, Galileo Galilei, Isaac Newton, Albert Einstein, and other, lesser-known figures who also made important contributions in their field.

Man and the Cosmos was written for the general reader both as an introduction to the science of astronomy and as an examination of how it developed. It is hoped that it will provide the reader not only with specific information but also with a deeper appreciation of our present efforts to understand the universe we inhabit.

I · INTRODUCTION

In the beginning God created
the heaven and the earth.

(GEN. 1:1)

1. Mankind and the Heavens

For centuries man has concerned himself with a study of
the heavens and marveled at the wonders of the stars, the
sun, the moon, and the planets. The daily and yearly
motion of the planets (literally "wanderers") has piqued
his curiosity throughout the ages and given rise to
different theories, with which we shall be concerned later
on. Yet these heavenly bodies form only a minute part of
the vast expanse seen in the sky. The beauty and splendor
of the night sky is as intriguing, and as inexplicable to us
as it was to primitive man.

At first, man was content to use the stars as markers in
his travels and forage for food and to use the apparent
motion of the sun to mark the seasons and days. He soon
learned that certain times in the year were more suited
than others for seeding, while fruits and corn ripened at
other times. These natural divisions became the seasons, a
succession of which formed a year. The length and
direction of the sun's shadow served as a convenient way
to measure time and marked these seasons. Man noted
that the length of the shadow cast by a long pole varied
during the day and changed at different seasons also. This
awareness led to the first sundial, and undoubtedly, many
of the obelisks served this purpose. Later he devised more
intricate sundials, some of which are used even today. But
as beautiful as they are, they have the disadvantage of
being fixed in place, a feature not shared by the shadow
watch.

To observe the transit, or passing, of stars, man had to
introduce the notion of angles. A sighting rod was
directed at the star and a second rod, some distance away,
aligned vertically with the help of a plumb line until the
star could be seen through the hole, thus fixing the line

Part of an ornate calendar commissioned by the Duc de Berry in 1409 and
executed by the Flemish painter Pol de Limbourg. The picture depicts summer.
Above, the sun-god Phoebus is riding his fiery chariot, and concentric circles
indicate the phases of the moon. The astrological signs of the Crab (Cancer) and
the Lion (Leo) above govern the month of July.

8

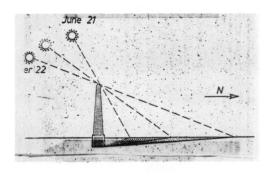

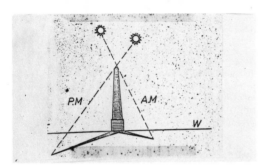

A sixteenth-century Chinese instrument, called a Kuei-pî, used for astronomical sighting.

Top

The length of the sun's shadow at noon can be used to mark the seasons and acts as a calendar. During the summer months the sun is higher in the sky than in the winter months and therefore its shadow is shorter. It is shortest on June 21, when the sun is at its highest point, and it reaches its maximum length on December 21. (Those dates refer to the Northern Hemisphere of the earth's surface; in the area below the equator the opposite holds true.)

Above

The direction and length of the sun's shadow act as the hour hand of a clock. In the morning (A.M.) the shadow points in a westerly direction and then moves during the day—first decreasing, then changing direction and increasing—until it reaches its most easterly direction in the evening (P.M.).

A portable Egyptian shadow watch built before the eighth century B.C. The shadow of a rod placed in the holes at the right falls on the hour scale on the handle. The scale includes five hour-markings in addition to the noon point.

This modern sundial includes a gnomon, or pointer (parallel to the earth's axis), which casts a shadow on the inner side of a ring. The ring is parallel to the earth's equator and has gradations showing the hours, just as on an ordinary clock.

A movable sundial, which also served as an ornament or piece of jewelry, is this gold and silver Saxon sundial, used in England during the tenth century. Supported by a gold chain, it was held in the hand while a gold peg was inserted in one of the three holes on either side—each hole corresponding to two months. The shadow of the peg was measured by dots or impressions marking the four parts of the day, called tides.

The *pi* (pronounced "pea") is an old Chinese astronomical instrument dating from ca. 1000 B.C. This one is made entirely of jade and probably was used to sight and measure relative diameters (and thus distances).

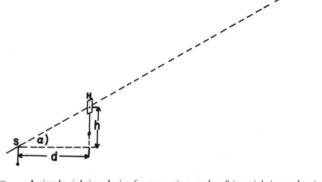

A simple sighting device for measuring angles. *S* is a sighting rod pointing at the star. A hole *H* in a second rod is moved until it coincides with the line of sight. Since a straight line is fixed by two points, this determines the direction of the star. Both rods are equipped with plumb lines to keep them in the vertical. The distance *d* between the two devices and their relative elevation *h* is measured, from which the angle α can then be determined.

The merkhet consists of a sighting rod and two plumb lines, which were used as in the simple device shown in the illustration above. The Egyptians employed it in observing the transit of stars. The pieces seen here are from the sixth century B.C.

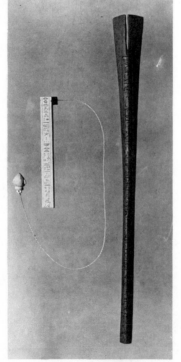

of sight. Knowing the distance between the two rods and the elevation of the hole (with respect to the sighting rod) is sufficient to determine the angle the line of sight makes with the horizontal. This, in principle, was the method used for the Egyptian merkhet.

Not only the sun and the stars but also the varying phases of the moon provided means of fixing time. A complete cycle, from new moon to new moon, constituted

The daily phases of the moon (indicated by Roman numbers), from a seventeenth-century German engraving. The two spirals show the dates of the various phases, which are indicated on the periphery.

a month as designated by the Babylonians. It was Aristotle who recognized (although he was probably not the first) that the various phases of the moon, i.e., its apparent change of shape during the month, resulted from the fact that the moon itself is not luminous but reflects the light from the sun. Because of its spherical shape, only half of the moon is illuminated by the sun at any particular time, namely that half turned toward the sun. The apparent shape of the moon as seen on Earth, then, simply depends on how much of that illuminated half sphere is turned toward us. Not only was the moon used for timekeeping, but it was endowed with various influences over man, some imagined—such as its effect on the weather—but others associated with definite cycles, such as the tides.

The daily and yearly motion of the sun, as well as the cycles of the moon, formed the materials from which

The various positions of the moon during a complete revolution are shown as it moves around the earth. Depending on its relative position to the earth, only part of its illuminated surface—always the half facing the sun—appears to an observer on Earth. These different phases are indicated next to the actual position as they appear to an observer in the Northern Hemisphere. (The phases of the moon have nothing to do with the shadow cast by the earth, as is often erroneously assumed.)

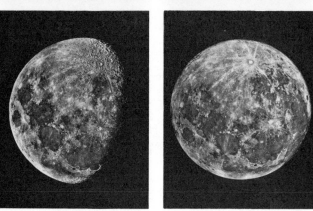

A series of photographs showing the various phases of the moon, starting from new moon to full moon, as seen by an observer in the Northern Hemisphere: (1) the new moon, age 4 days; (2) first quarter, age 7 days; (3) third quarter, age 10 days; (4) full moon, age 14 days.

The moon is believed to influence human lives. This seventeenth-century engraving depicts the moon's rays affecting the minds of women. It is, of course, known that menstruation follows the phases of the moon. ▼

In this calendar devised by the Portuguese Diegus Homē in 1559, the months are listed in the outer rings, under which are given the appearance of the new moon. In the 4 corners, other dates, such as religious holidays, are given. The calendar is a perpetual one, since all entries are for a 19-year cycle, after which both solar and lunar years repeat themselves.

This Aztec calendar, based on the Mayan system, was carved more than 100 years before our calendar was adopted. The year is divided into 18 months of 20 days each (shown here for a particular month on the inner circle) to which were added 5 "unlucky" days, resulting in 365 days. Fifty-two such years constituted a "century" and 73 centuries formed a "millennium." Obviously, this involved complicated calculations, but despite them the Mayan calendar was quite precise.

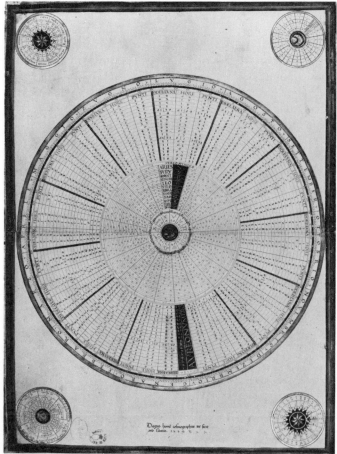

calendars were created, to remind us of the passing of another day, another month, another year.

A glance at the star-studded sky shows that not all the stars are distributed at random; many appear to form certain patterns or groupings—the constellations. We now know that stars forming any given constellation are not necessarily close to one another; some may be relatively close to us and others much farther off, but they appear to us to be in the same region of the sky. For this reason we use the constellations to denote approximate locations in the sky, much as we use the names of the countries to locate places on the earth. Certain constellations can be seen only in the Northern Hemisphere, while others appear only to an observer in the Southern Hemisphere, the two regions of the earth's surface being divided by the terrestrial equator.

Probably the best-known and most easily recognizable grouping of stars is the Big Dipper, which can be used to locate the North Star, Polaris. It not only shows us where north is but defines an imaginary axis around which the constellations seem to revolve, once in 24 hours. Strictly speaking, the Big Dipper is not one of the 88 recognized constellations but part of a larger grouping, Ursa Major, the Great Bear. To the ancient astronomers the various forms of the constellations may have suggested shapes of animals or figures taken from their particular mythology. More likely, however, a large number of the constellations were named not because they resembled actual people or animals, but rather in honor or memory of mythological figures—a practice similar to the present one of naming some of our buildings and places after famous people. Of the 88 constellations, 48 were identified by the Greeks and formed the subject of artistic drawings of the Map of Heavens.

Two views of a celestial brass globe, inlaid with silver and illustrating the constellations; Indo-Persian, about 1630. Shown here are the constellations near the North Pole *(left)* and those seen when facing west *(right)*. The ecliptic appears as a band crossing the celestial equator.

A decorative map of the heavens made in 1660 by Andreas Cellarius. It shows the constellations with biblical and Christian characters, such as Noah's Ark, King David, Abraham and Isaac, Pope Sylvester, and others.

Ursa Major (the Great Bear) is a typical contour constellation, in a comparatively empty region of the sky. One star represents the eye, others the claws of the feet, and the handle of the Big Dipper forms a rather long tail.

Above left

Map of Heavens—Northern Hemisphere. In this map the constellations appear together with the persons and objects they are said to represent, such as Ursa Major, Draco, Andromeda, and others found in the Northern Hemisphere. The names are taken from mythology, and in many cases the star pattern only faintly resembles the object or person it is supposed to represent.

Above right

Map of Heavens—Southern Hemisphere. In this map, also by Cellarius, the constellations of the southern sky are shown, such as the Southern Cross, Apus, Pavo, Argo Navis (here again identified with Noah's Ark). Astronomers with telescope and quadrant are shown at the lower corners.

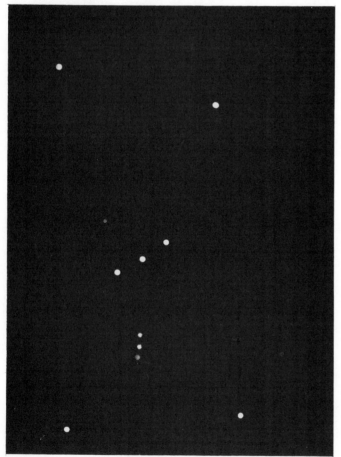

A photograph taken by an ordinary camera of the constellation Orion. Note the stars Betelgeuse at the upper left and Rigel at the lower right.

Orion against its starry background, photographed with a 10-inch-focus lens. ➤

inset

An idealized drawing of Orion, son of Neptune. According to mythology, he was slain in error by Diana, the virgin moon-goddess and huntress, and after his death was raised to heaven to form the constellation bearing his name. Note the 3 bright stars forming his belt; they also serve to locate the constellation in the sky.

Different cultures used different heroes for their constellations, as in this artistic conception of Perseus, the son of Zeus, by a Persian astronomer of the sixteenth century. He is shown holding the head of Medusa, whom he had been sent to kill.

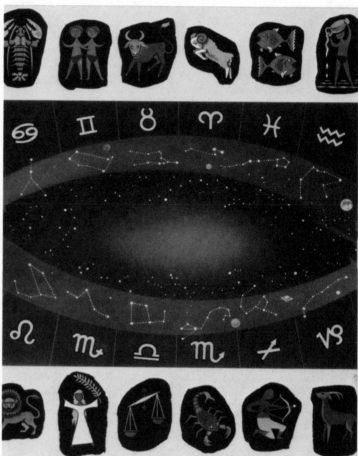

A drawing of the 12 constellations in a band or circle of animals forming the Zodiac, together with their astronomical symbols and pictures. The 12 signs of the Zodiac are Aries, the Ram; Taurus, the Bull; Gemini, the Twins; Cancer, the Crab; Leo, the Lion; Virgo, the Virgin; Libra, the Scales; Scorpio, the Scorpion; Sagittarius, the Archer; Capricorn, the Mountain Goat; Aquarius, the Water bearer; and Pisces, the Fishes.

Of particular interest among the constellations are those that constitute the Zodiac (literally "circle of animals"). The Zodiac consists of a group of 12 prominent constellations that lie in the yearly path of the sun through the sky. Here too the impact of particular cultures made itself felt. The signs of the Zodiac soon acquired a meaning all their own. The Scorpion came to be considered evil and the time it rose in the sky unfavorable. The Lion, it was thought, would have an influence in accordance with its character. Since the sun (and moon and planets) pass through the 12 Zodiacal signs in succession in the course of a year, it seemed reasonable to assume that the influence of a particular sign would be particularly strong when the sun was in that area of the sky. It was no coincidence that the rainy season was at hand when the sun was in Pisces (fishes) or in Aquarius (water carrier, *aqua* means "water").

The signs of the Zodiac were found in amulets, which were used to ward off bad spirits, in several mosaics, and even in the motifs of postage stamps. It was only a small step to connect the Zodiac with human character and fortune. For example, a person born when the sun was in the Lion would be strong. The correspondence even went so far as to associate facial features with the particular Zodiacal sign. Thus, the foundations for astrology were laid.

THE 88 RECOGNIZED CONSTELLATIONS

Abbreviation	Name
And	Andromeda (Princess of Ethiopia)
* Ant	Antlia (Air pump)
* Aps	Apus (Bird of Paradise)
Aqr	*Aquarius* (Water carrier)
Aql	Aquila (Eagle)
Ara	Ara (Altar)
Ari	*Aries* (Ram)
Aur	Auriga (Charioteer)
Boo	Boötes (Herdsman)
* Cae	Caelum (Chisel)
* Cam	Camelopardalis (Giraffe)
Cnc	*Cancer* (Crab)
* CVn	Canes Venatici (Hunting dogs)
CMa	Canis Major (Big Dog)
CMi	Canis Minor (Lesser dog)
Cap	*Capricornus* (Goat)
* Car	Carina (Keel)
Cas	Cassiopeia (Queen of Ethiopia)
Cen	Centaurus (Centaur)
Cep	Cepheus (King of Ethiopia)
Cet	Cetus (Whale)
* Cha	Chamaeleon (Chameleon)
* Cir	Circinus (Compasses)
* Col	Columba (Dove)
* Com	Coma Berenices (Berenice's hair)
CrA	Corona Australis (Southern crown)
CrB	Corona Borealis (Northern crown)
Crv	Corvus (Crow)
Crt	Crater (Cup)
* Cru	Crux (Southern Cross)
Cyg	Cygnus (Swan)
Del	Delphinus (Dolphin)
* Dor	Dorado (Swordfish)
Dra	Draco (Dragon)
Equ	Equuleus (Little horse)
Eri	Eridanus (River Eridanus)
* For	Fornax (Furnace)
Gem	*Gemini* (Twins)
* Gru	Grus (Crane)
Her	Hercules (Hercules)
* Hor	Horologium (Pendulum clock)
Hya	Hydra (Water snake)
* Hyi	Hydrus (Lesser water snake)
* Ind	Indus (Indian)
* Lac	Lacerta (Lizard)
Leo	*Leo* (Lion)
* LMi	Leo Minor (Little lion)
Lep	Lepus (Hare)

Abbreviation	Name
Lib	*Libra* (Scales)
Lup	Lupus (Wolf)
* Lyn	Lynx (Lynx)
Lyr	Lyra (Lyre)
* Men	Mensa (Table Mountain)
* Mic	Microscopium (Microscope)
* Mon	Monoceros (Unicorn)
* Mus	Musca (Fly)
* Nor	Norma (Level)
* Oct	Octans (Octant)
Oph	Ophiuchus (Serpent holder)
Ori	Orion (Orion)
* Pav	Pavo (Peacock)
Peg	Pegasus (Pegasus)
Per	Perseus (Perseus)
* Phe	Phoenix (Phoenix)
* Pic	Pictor (Easel)
Psc	*Pisces* (Fishes)
PsA	Piscis Austrinus (Southern fish)
* Pup	Puppis (Stern)
Pyx	Pyxis (Compass)
* Ret	Reticulum (Net)
Sge	Sagitta (Arrow)
Sgr	*Sagittarius* (Archer)
Sco	*Scorpius* (Scorpion)
* Scl	Sculptor (Sculptor)
* Sct	Scutum (Shield)
† Ser	Serpens (Serpent)
* Sex	Sextans (Sextant)
Tau	*Taurus* (Bull)
* Tel	Telescopium (Telescope)
Tri	Triangulum (Triangle)
* TrA	Triangulum Australe (Southern triangle)
* Tuc	Tucana (Toucan)
UMa	Ursa Major (Great bear)
UMi	Ursa Minor (Little bear)
* Vel	Vela (Sail)
Vir	*Virgo* (Virgin)
‡ * Vol	Volans (Flying fish)
Vul	Vulpecula (Fox)

* Constellations that have been identified within the last century. Twenty-eight constellations are found above (northerly) and the 48 below (southerly) the Zodiac (the twelve constellations that constitute the Zodiac are italicized).

† This constellation is sometimes referred to by its two parts, Serpens Caput (Serpent's head) and Serpens Cauda (Serpent's tail).

‡ This constellation is also called Piscis Volans (Flying fish).

2. Religion and Astronomy

To make these predictions, extensive records had to be kept. The Babylonians, for example, maintained detailed records of the sun; thus they were able to predict celestial events, such as an eclipse, fairly accurately. Moreover, they were astonishingly honest in recording their observations. Failure to observe an eclipse of the sun or moon was recorded as:

The month of Addaru [Adar] will have thirty days. On the thirteenth, and during the night from the thirteenth to the fourteenth we made an observation. On the fifteenth, Sun and Moon were seen together, but no eclipse took place. Seven times I arose, but no eclipse took place. I will send later the final decisive report. [signed] Tabu-sil-Marduk, nephew of Inlil-nasir.

Not everyone was capable of performing the intricate measurements and calculations necessary to make these predictions. It was the priests who were the astronomers of ancient times, and they used their knowledge to exert their rule. Divine worship became equivalent to astronomy, and astronomy equivalent to determining the will of the gods. These gods, in turn, became identified with heavenly bodies—the city-god of Babylon, Marduk, became the planet Jupiter; Ninurta, the god of war, became Saturn; and so on. It is no wonder, then, that the priests could speak with authority about the will of the gods, since they were, so to speak, in daily contact with them and saw their actual "faces."

Undoubtedly, many temples and monuments also were simple observatories used by the priests in their work. The Tower of Babel was an example of such a structure. It was also called the Temple of the Seven Transmitters of Commands from Heaven to Earth. Even more interesting are the temples of ancient Egypt. A temple was built in such a manner that at certain times light from the outside could pass freely along its axis in a straight line toward the sanctuary. The solar temple of Amon-Ra, the sun-god, at Karnak (Thebes) is a case in point. There is a stone avenue at the center, five hundred yards in length, situated so that the central axis is completely free. The structures at the sides were so arranged as to limit the amount of light that could pass through, like the diaphragm of a camera. Most of the year the temple would be shrouded in darkness, but once a year—and then even only for a short time—the sanctuary would be flooded with light passing through the whole temple. This dramatic event, which heralded the beginning of the new year, occurred at the time of the summer solstice, when the sun had reached its highest point. The significance of that event went even further, since its occurrence coincided with the time the river Nile rose and gave the land the water it so sorely needed. Clearly, an event of such magnitude deserved to be commemorated annually by an equally impressive spectacle.

Stonehenge, the famous stone circle in Salisbury Plain, England, is another ancient monument with astronomical connections. It was built by the Beaker People some time between ca. 1800 and 1400 B.C. The exact use of Stonehenge is unknown, but it seems that the stones were so arranged that the shadows of the sun (and also of the full moon) cast by certain stones would point exactly toward the center at certain times, namely those times

Part of a Babylonian clay tablet, written in cuneiform script, the wedge-shaped writing of the ancient Babylonians. It lists from left to right the intervals from new moon to new moon and lunar velocities during the 25-month period for the years 103 to 101 B.C.

The Tower of Babel as visualized in an old drawing. The tower served as both an observatory and a temple, as might be inferred from the particular arrangement of steps and floors.

A replica of the Tower of Babel on this sixteenth-century Italian dish shows the actual building process, as described in the Bible (Gen. 11).

Plan of the Temple of Amon-Ra and some of its surroundings, including the sacred lake, at the upper right.

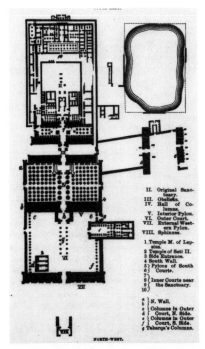

corresponding to the shortest and longest days of the year.

Another old monument that might have served as an observatory is the Caracol Tower of Chichén Itzá in Yucatán, Mexico. Its lack of aesthetic appeal—it looks like "a two-decker wedding cake on the square carton in which it came"—suggests a strictly functional motivation for its design. In addition to being a kind of watchtower, surveying the flat Yucatecan landscape and charting the course of sun, moon, and stars, the peculiarities and orientation of the structures can best be explained as those of a repository of directions having astronomical significance. In particular, the window at the top of the tower could have been used for precise astronomical observations.

It is not difficult to see how natural phenomena were endowed with supernatural powers and how early astronomy and religion were interwoven. Most prominent among the ancient gods were the sun-gods and moon-gods who regulated man's daily life. The sun-god of the Egyptians, for example, had many names and forms, depending on the season and the time of day. The morning sun was Hor (or Horus), a child with his characteristic side lock of hair. The god Ra, according to tradition, symbolizes the sun at noon. It is often compounded with other names, such as Amon-Ra, Min-Ra, or Sebek-Ra, referring to different seasons. Amon-Ra with his golden headgear probably refers to the sun at the summer solstice (the longest day in the year). The evening sun was Tum (or Atum), and the setting sun was Osiris, often shown as a mummy and typifying old age.

The ancient Egyptians were also familiar with the powers of darkness. The chief gods opposed to the sun were Set (Seth, Sutekh, called Typhon by the Greeks) and

The remains of Stonehenge, the circle of stones in England. It points (Heel stone at the far background) nearly to the sun rising at the summer solstice, longest day of the year. The trilithons (arches) at the center are believed to be part of a later structure, Stonehenge III (soon after 1600 B.C.).

The Caracol Tower of Chichén Itzá (foreground) and Castillo (in the rear) viewed from the south. The orientation of the lower platform seems to be significant; the southwest-northeast diagonal points toward the sunrise positions at summer solstice and the sunset positions at winter solstice. Similarly, the diagonal in the upper platform is a precise indicator of the same events.

Top:
The Orkney Islands are rich in archaeological sites of many kinds and periods, but perhaps the most impressive is the Ring of Brogar, standing in a commanding position on the peninsula that separates the Loch of Harray from the Loch of Stenness, so that the stones can be seen from far and near. The stones, flat slabs up to 15 feet in height, form a perfect circle with a diameter of 125 yards. The ground on which the ring stands is by no means flat, and a more level site could easily have been found. However, the particular alignments of the ring—especially its center—and several cairns close by form a lunar observatory from which the moon was observed on 3 foresights.

Above:
Callanish I, an ancient site that may once have been used for astronomical observations, at the head of Loch Roag on Lewis in Scotland's Outer Hebrides. Although not as famous as Stonehenge, Callanish is the more spectacular. The view is toward the northeast, across part of the central flattened circle and along two stone avenues. These may be aligned on the rising Capella (a double star in the constellation Auriga), which gives a date of 1800 B.C.: an independent reliable date is not available for the site. The view back down the avenues to the southwest may be on the setting summer moon at major standstill.

The stone Medicine Wheel in the Big Horn Mountain of northern Wyoming is a well-known archaeological structure, commonly attributed to early Plains Indians. The "wheel" is a pattern on the surface of the ground, made up of an imperfect circle of stones, about 25 meters in diameter (roughly 39 inches to the meter), with a central cairn about 4 meters in diameter. From this hub, 28 unevenly spaced stone spokes radiate outward, connecting to the rim. At regular intervals along the periphery there are 5 smaller cairns, each an open circle 1 to 1.5 meters in diameter, with a sixth cairn about 4 meters beyond the rim. The Medicine Wheel is usually associated with religious or magic uses, the word *medicine* having been used by the Indians to mean "magic" or "supernatural," but there is good reason to believe that the Medicine Wheel also served astronomical purposes.

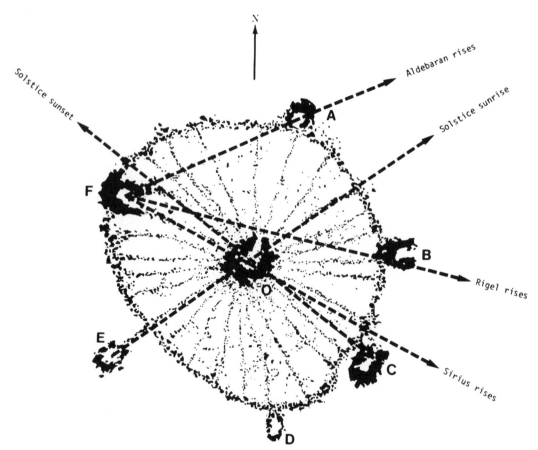

The diagram shows the plan of the Medicine Wheel, with O being the central cairn and A, B, C, D, and F the periphery cairns; E is the outlying one. A pole placed in the central cairn would serve as foresight, together with one of the others as backsight, to define the rising or setting of some important celestial object. This view is strengthened by the fact that even during snowstorms (which occur also during the summer) the cairns are swept free by winds and would provide the rudiments of an observatory, while the wheel itself (spokes and rim) only served as a day counter or as decoration. Of the different possible alignments, the most important ones are E–O and C–O, which define sunrise and sunset at the solstice. F–O gives the rising of Sirius, which announces the coming solstice. Of the other cairns, none defines an event when used with O, but F–A and F–B give the time of rising of Aldebaran and Rigel, two other bright stars that are closely connected with the rising of the sun at solstice and the onset of warm, and dangerous, weather. This leaves only D unaccounted for, which may have been a crude attempt to define the celestial pole N. It may be imagined that the Medicine Wheel was used by the "medicine man" or priest of the tribe to mark the day of the summer solstice for an ensuing Sun Dance ceremony. Only he and a few others, knowledgeable in the secrets of the cairns, would climb atop the inhospitable mountain to make their observations and return with the message from the sun to start the ceremony.

An aerial view of what might have been a prehistoric observatory at Rujun-el-Hiri on the Golan Heights in northern Israel. It consists of several rings of stones with large markers aligned along the summer solstice and other important directions.

Mosaic depicting the sun as shown in the eighteenth-century Golden Temple in Amritsar, India.

A diagram of Stonehenge as it might have looked. It consists of a series of stones arranged in concentric circles, the inner ones acting as some kind of diaphragm to keep the light out, the outer ones to align the light rays. In front of the Heel stone (black dot at top) are a series of 4 post holes used for sighting. On the outside, there is a circle consisting of 56 equally spaced holes, the Aubrey Holes (named after their discoverer John Aubrey in the seventeenth century), which played an important role in the use of Stonehenge.

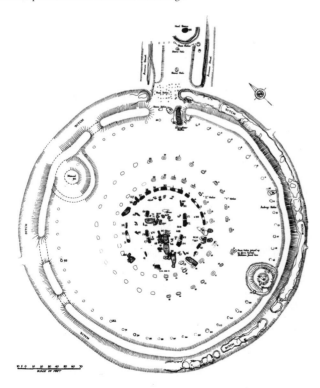

Anubis. Two forms are associated with the moon: Khons-Lunus and Thoth-Lunus. The relationship between them is not obvious, the only connection being their headgear. Thoth is also connected to the year with various forms, but all are based on the bird figure Ibis.

However, the planets also—unique among the stars since they are seen to wander among them—were supposed to influence human destiny. They bear the names of gods of ancient mythology:

Mercury, also known as Hermes, who presided over commerce;

Venus, the goddess of love and beauty;

Mars, the god of war;

Jupiter, or Zeus, ruler of the heavens and judge of men; and

Saturn, a son of heaven and earth, the last of the five planets known to the ancients.

They (and the sun and the moon) were believed to rule not only the months but also the days of the week, which take their names from the sun, moon, and planets. Some of these names derived from Teutonic equivalents. The Teutons were a number of European tribes, with chosen chiefs or kings (frequently including gods in their genealogical trees), who had their period of greatest expansion during the fourth to sixth century, when they spread over Europe in hordes. Other names they gave to the days were borrowed from the Romans, such as Sunday and Monday, honoring the sun and moon, respectively, and Saturday, which commemorates Saturn. (In other languages, of course, there are slight changes. For example, the French equivalent of Wednesday is *mercredi,* which derives from Mercury.)

Ra, the sun at noon in its full strength, together with its variations, Min-Ra and Amon-Ra, referring to different seasons.

Sirius (left) and Orion, dating from the eighteenth dynasty (ca. 1700 B.C.). Sirius was worshiped under the name of Sothis (or Sept) and was personified as Isis or Hathor, two Egyptian deities.

Modern astronomy has come a long way from these ancient beliefs and superstitions, but it has to thank the priests and astrologers for starting man on a search of the unknown and arousing his curiosity—the necessary ingredient of research and understanding, without which modern science would be impossible. By continuing along the path set by our forefathers, we have come a bit closer to an understanding of the world we live in, and perhaps also to an appreciation of the orderliness and beauty underlying it. As the psalmist put it so aptly:

> The heavens declare the glory of God;
> And the firmament showeth His handiwork.
>
> (Psalms 19:1)

3. Early Progress

The Babylonian clay tablets constitute the earliest known astronomical records. These tablets date back at least twenty centuries. We find, for example, Hammurabi, king of Babylon, writing to his minister: "Since the year is not good, the next month must be noted as a second Ululu." (By so doing, an extra month was inserted to synchronize the lunar and solar year.) He then continues: "Instead of delivering the tithes to Babylon on the 25th of Tishritu [the normal date], have them delivered on the 25th of Ululu II." Even Babylonian kings would not wait for their taxes.

The Sumerians, who inhabited the southern region between the Euphrates and the Tigris, were the inventors of the cuneiform wedge typescript, in which each sound, consisting of a vowel and one or two consonants, was represented by a special character. The characters were incised by a stylus in a clay tablet that was then hardened by baking it in fire. The Sumerians based their calculation on a sexagenary system of numbers; instead of using a basis of 10 as in our decimal system, they used the basis of 60. This system, although cumbersome, is especially suited for recording observations, since it allows a greater subdivision than is possible with, say, the decimal system of numbers. Our way of dividing a degree into 60 minutes of arc or a minute into 60 seconds is a carryover from the Babylonian sexagenary system. The tablets that have been found consist of rows of numbers without headings, interspersed with Zodiacal signs. It required great ingenuity, in many instances, to decipher them and compare the results with other observations.

The Babylonian astronomers were interested in determining the appearance of the new moon for their calendar, but the Egyptians centered their attention on Sirius, whose appearance was connected with the important flooding of the Nile. It may have been a coincidence at first, when the Egyptian priests noticed that Sirius—that bright star near Orion—appeared just before sunrise when the Nile rose from its banks. That event was particularly noticeable, since for some time before, Sirius had risen after the sun and therefore could not be seen. As a result, the Egyptians concluded that the "rising of Sothis," as Sirius was called by the Egyptians, marked the beginning of the new year and, in fact, was responsible for the flooding of the Nile. The Egyptians were also responsible for conceiving the 365-day year. Originally, they, like the Babylonians, kept to the lunar cycle, but then they began to calculate 12 equal months of 30 days each. Later, to make the new year coincide with the rising of Sirius, five additional days were added. (According to mythology, the sky-goddess Nut had married Geb, her twin brother, secretly and against the will of Ra the sun-god. Ra then ordered that she should bear a child "in no month of no year." However, Thoth took pity on her and won five new days from the moon. Since they were outside the existing calendar, Ra's decree did not apply and Nut was able to give birth. She successively bore five children.) Later, an additional day was added every four years, resulting in the concept of a leap year.

Whereas the Egyptians used Sirius to fix the beginning of the new year, the Mayans of Central America much later checked their calendar against the motions of Venus. This planet played a special role in Mayan religion, for after the sun it was the main deity, having displaced even the moon-god of ancient Babylon. To determine the period of Venus exactly—the time it takes to make a complete revolution—is no simple feat even now, but the Mayans seemed to have achieved it, as can be seen from an ancient manuscript, one of three in existence. Unfortunately, not much else is known about their astronomical activities apart from their calendars, which became the motif for their art and were used to decorate every building. Yet we are fairly certain that they were astronomy-minded. By reconstructing the positions of the heavenly bodies throughout the ages it is noted that Mayan chronology takes its starting point from a singular event, the conjunction or union of Moon, Venus, Mercury, Mars, and Jupiter. Such an event is rare, indeed, but it occurred on May 25, 482, the possible starting point of the Mayan calendar.

Another source of information about astronomy is contained in the *kudurru*. These are stones positioned at the boundaries of fields and placed under the protection of gods to prevent their removal. The pictures or symbols representing the different gods were engraved together with others representing constellations.

In many cases astrological interpretations went hand in hand with the observations. When the earth's shadow covered the moon, eclipsing it, or, more awesome, when the moon blotted out the sun, it was often considered to be the work of demons. At such times it was customary for the king to fast and to avert the evil decrees the gods undoubtedly had imposed. When the eclipse did not take place as predicted—as was the case quite often—it was not the astronomer who was to blame but rather heaven, which, for some reason, behaved irregularly. The more reason to be careful, since one never knew what the gods meant by such inconsistency.

Even more fascinating were the early concepts of the universe as a whole. The ideas were more or less the same: the earth was believed to be flat, or, in some instances, a hemisphere. The ancient astronomers found it difficult to conceive of a spherical earth inhabited on both sides. The idea of a spherical earth came later, when Aristotle was able to marshal convincing arguments for it. Until then

From a Mayan manuscript, dealing with the motion of Venus over a 104-year period. The figures at the top are sky-gods. The middle ones are angry and about to kill the sun or Venus. The two "dead" figures at the bottom represent either the sun during an eclipse or Venus in its invisible phase.

The daily journey of the sun traversing the sky in a boat from east to west. The female figure of the sky, Nut, literally surrounds Geb, the earth; Nut's feet and fingertips span the horizon. Geb is the reclining figure, separated from Nut by Shu, the god of air or sunlight.

Kudurru, or astrological stone of Melishipak II, a Kassite king of Babylon (ca. 1200 B.C.). Note the symbols of the sun, moon, and Venus; on the reverse are figures representing the constellations, a bull, an ear of corn, a dog, a serpent, a scorpion, and a fish-tailed goat (Capricorn).

the earth was considered to be surrounded by a great river or ocean on which it floated, surmounted by a hollow dome forming the heavens.

The Babylonians thought of heaven as a great vault— immobile and solid—whose foundations rested on a vast ocean *(Apsu,* meaning "the deep"). Above the vault was the "dwelling of the gods" from which the sun comes through a door every morning and returns every evening through another door. The earth was supposed to be a mountain, hollow underneath, also supported by *Apsu.* The abode of the dead, *Sheol,* the land of darkness and the shadow of death, was just above the hollow interior but inside the earth's crust. The Egyptians held similar ideas.

Their universe was a box, the earth being the floor— naturally with Egypt at its center. Heaven was the ceiling of that box, thought to be flat by some and vaulted by others. It was supported by four columns at the corners. Later these were superseded by four lofty mountain peaks and connected by a series of mountains.

Nearly at the top of the mountain range flowed a great river, partially hidden from view by the mountains. The sun-god Ra was in a boat carried around the earth on that river. The boat was seen only during the day, while at night it traveled behind the mountains and therefore beyond our view. Later, it was thought to be necessary for the sun to be able also to travel below the earth, which

According to the Chaldean conception of the world, the hollow, semispherical earth is surrounded by masses of water, while the stars are fixed on a dome supported by pillars.

In the Egyptian universe the stars hang like lamps from a ceiling, in part supported by high mountains surrounding the world as it was known at the time. The picture clearly depicts the eastern part of the Mediterranean – Egypt and Mesopotamia.

was supposed to be supported on pillars. For the Hindus, Earth was supported by four elephants standing on a giant tortoise swimming in a river of milk.

As fanciful, and even naïve, as these ideas appear now, they represented the thinking of the day and to some extent appeared again in the Middle Ages. They explained and interpreted natural phenomena, as well as could be done then, and, more important, they satisfied the inclination to interpret mythology in astronomical terms, and, conversely, celestial objects as gods. However, it was left to the Greeks to develop these ideas into a meaningful cosmology, or study of the universe.

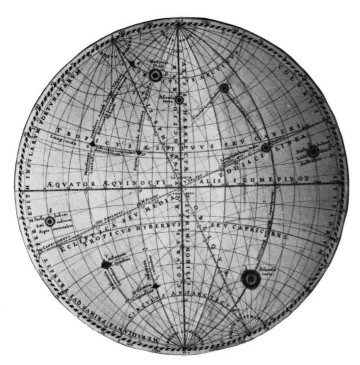

4. Some Facts

The idea of the domed heaven of the Egyptians and Babylonians was extended by the Greeks to that of a giant sphere, the celestial sphere, carrying the stars on its inside and rotating around its vertical (north–south) axis. We still find it convenient to adopt this point of view, although we now know that the apparent rotation of the celestial sphere is due to the actual rotation of the earth

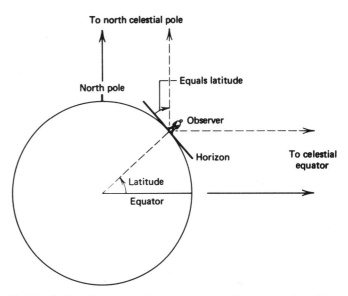

The latitude of an observer on earth is the angle the earth's equator makes with a line from the observer to the center of the earth. From the figure it can be seen that it is equal to the angle made by a line drawn from the polestar (here assumed to be exactly at the northern point of the celestial sphere) and the horizon. In other words, the latitude of an observer is equal to the elevation of the polestar (measured in degrees) above the horizon.

A drawing by Cellarius of the celestial sphere (or, more correctly, hemisphere) showing the equator, the ecliptic, the Tropic of Cancer, the Tropic of Capricorn, and the meridians.

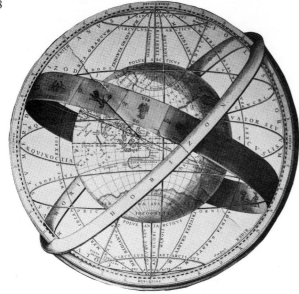

A view of the celestial sphere encircling the central earth, the horizon—corresponding to a latitude of approximately 45 degrees—and the Zodiac belt.

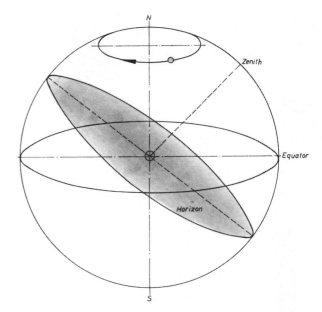

The celestial sphere is a convenient device with which to locate stars in the sky. It was assumed by the Greeks to rotate around a vertical axis, N–S, whose North Pole is at present located about 1 degree away from the North Star, Polaris. Stars are carried during a revolution along a horizontal circle, indicated by the small circle at the top. The point directly over the observer is the zenith, and the shaded circle (at a right angle to the zenith) is the horizon.

around its own axis. However, such simple observations as the apparent motion of the stars in the sky cannot differentiate between these two points of view—stationary Earth and rotating celestial sphere or rotating Earth and stationary celestial sphere—and it required more refined observations to show that it was the earth and not the celestial sphere that, in fact, rotates around its axis.

As the celestial sphere rotates around its axis, certain stars are seen never to rise or set. They are always above the horizon, that plane or line where earth and sky are seen to meet and which is imagined to be parallel to the ground where we are. Other stars will be seen to rise when they come above the horizon and set when they dip below it, while still others will never be visible to us if their paths always lie below the horizon. Of course, the position of the horizon depends on our latitude, that distance above (or below) the earth's equator measured in degrees. For an observer at the earth's North Pole, for example, the horizon coincides with the equator. For him the stars in the Northern Hemisphere are never seen to rise or set, while those in the Southern Hemisphere are always invisible. (At the earth's South Pole the situation is the reverse.)

An observer at the earth's equator, on the other hand, sees all stars rising straight up (in the east) and setting straight down (in the west). His horizon goes through the celestial axis. At intermediate latitudes in, say, the Northern Hemisphere, we find the situation described earlier, some stars never rising or setting, others rising at an oblique angle in the east and setting at an oblique angle in the west, with still others being invisible. The number of stars of its kind as well as their position in the sky, of course, depends on the actual latitude of the observer. Not only is the part of the celestial sphere that

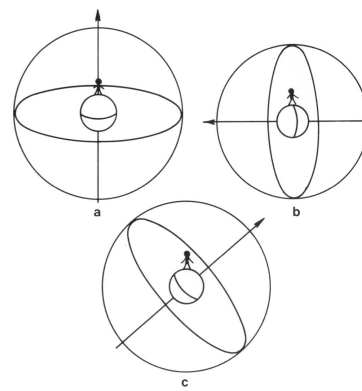

The appearance of the celestial sphere depends on the position (latitude) of the observer. (a) At the North Pole: The horizon coincides with (or is parallel to) the celestial equator. The zenith is along the vertical axis of the celestial sphere (indicated by an arrow). (b) At the equator: The earth's equator is parallel to the equator of the celestial sphere, but the horizon is perpendicular to it and passes through the axis of the celestial sphere (arrow). (c) At a northern latitude: The earth's equator is again parallel to the equator of the celestial sphere and, as in all cases, the earth's axis coincides with the vertical axis of the celestial sphere (here shown as a slanting arrow). However, the horizon is parallel to neither the equator nor the axis, but inclined to them.

The 4 diagrams picture the relative position of the sun at different times of the year but at the same time of day. (The earth is here shown as revolving around the central sun, but the effect would be the same if the opposite were the case.) The 4 directions toward the celestial sphere are represented by arrows A, B, C, and D. Only that part of the celestial sphere can be seen that is away from the sun. Thus in figure 1 that part of the sky defined by BAD can be seen; in figure 2 the earth has moved a quarter of its annual revolution and the area defined by ABC is visible; after another quarter revolution, BCD becomes visible, and finally ADC as shown in figure 4.

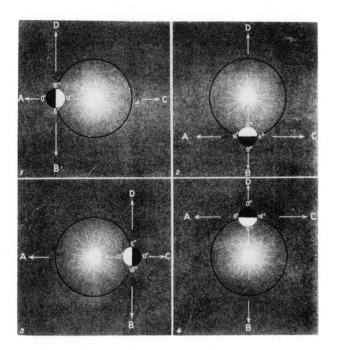

can be seen different for various positions of the observer, but it also depends on the season of the year. This is because stars can be seen only when the sun is not in that part of the sky (except in the rare case of a solar eclipse, when the sunlight is blocked by the moon).

The concept of latitude as used for measurement on the earth can also be applied to the celestial sphere. Distances on a sphere are not measured in miles or kilometers but in degrees, minutes, and seconds of arc. For this purpose the surface of the sphere is covered with a network of intersecting circles. Those passing through the vertical axis are called meridians, while those intersecting them at right angles are circles of equal latitude. In particular, the great circle, a circle whose center is the center of the sphere as well, halfway between the poles, is the equator. A position on a sphere, such as the earth or the celestial sphere, is then determined by two angles: the latitude, which gives the elevation above (or below) the equator, and the longitude, which is the position, east or west, from a given meridian. (On Earth, longitudes are measured east (E) or west (W) from the meridian that passes through Greenwich, England, the site of the Royal Observatory.)

In the case of the celestial sphere, two different but related systems are used, depending on whether the equatorial plane or the horizon is employed, and on the meridian from which longitudes are measured. The simpler one is that in which angles are measured from the horizon. The altitude or elevation of a star is then simply

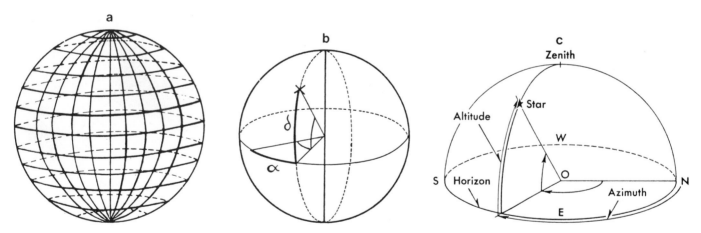

Angular measurements. (a) Meridians: Taking the vertical axis of the sphere (celestial sphere or Earth's globe), as defined by its rotation axis, a number of circles are drawn passing through the end points of that axis. These are the meridians. Cutting the meridians at right angles are the circles of equal latitude, the equator being halfway between the poles. A position on the sphere is then determined by its latitude circle and meridian (measured from a fixed meridian).
(b) Latitude and longitude: The angle measuring the position of a place (or star) above (or below) the equator is the latitude (δ). On the earth's sphere it is sometimes called elevation, and on the celestial sphere it is the declination. The angle α, giving the location of the particular meridian from a fixed one, is the longitude. On the celestial sphere it is called right ascension.
(c) Altitude and azimuth: A great circle is imagined drawn through the position of the star and passing through the zenith of the observer. The altitude of the star is the angle along this circle measured from the horizon; it is the "elevation" of the star. The angle along the horizon from that circle (the meridian of the star) to a line passing through the North Pole is the azimuth. Again, altitude and azimuth together determine the position of the star with respect to the observer.

the angle between a line from the observer to the star and a line parallel to the horizon. The corresponding longitude, which is called the azimuth, is measured from a meridian passing through the north point, an extension of the earth's North Pole on the celestial sphere. This system is simple but suffers from the obvious disadvantage that measurements depend on the position of the observer.

We have seen that the location of the horizon, and hence measurements based on it, will differ for various latitudes. Astronomers therefore use a system fixed to the celestial sphere itself, in which latitude or declination measures the star's position above (or below) the celestial equator, while right ascension determines the longitude from a fixed meridian.

The concept of the celestial sphere also gave rise to the idea of a spherical earth. Apart from aesthetic considerations, which suggested the same perfect form for the earth as for the universe, there were more concrete considerations already advanced by the Greeks, and taught in particular by Aristotle (384–322 B.C.). The heavenly bodies were known to rise and set at different times for different parts of the earth, which would not be the case if the earth were flat. Moreover, when traveling on the sea the tips of mountains appear first, while the remainder is hidden by the curvature of the earth.

To describe the sun's motion in this picture required

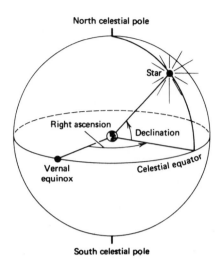

Declination and right ascension: The declination of a star is its elevation above the celestial equator, while its *right ascension* (R.A.) is the angle its meridian makes with the vernal equinox.

some modifications. In the first place, a solar day is somewhat longer than a sidereal, or star, day. In other words, it takes 24 hours for the sun to revolve once around the earth, but the stars on the celestial sphere complete their circuit in only 23 hours and 56 minutes

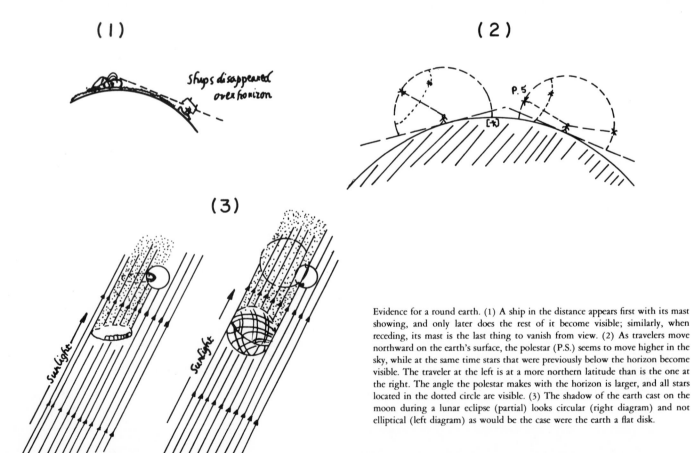

Evidence for a round earth. (1) A ship in the distance appears first with its mast showing, and only later does the rest of it become visible; similarly, when receding, its mast is the last thing to vanish from view. (2) As travelers move northward on the earth's surface, the polestar (P.S.) seems to move higher in the sky, while at the same time stars that were previously below the horizon become visible. The traveler at the left is at a more northern latitude than is the one at the right. The angle the polestar makes with the horizon is larger, and all stars located in the dotted circle are visible. (3) The shadow of the earth cast on the moon during a lunar eclipse (partial) looks circular (right diagram) and not elliptical (left diagram) as would be the case were the earth a flat disk.

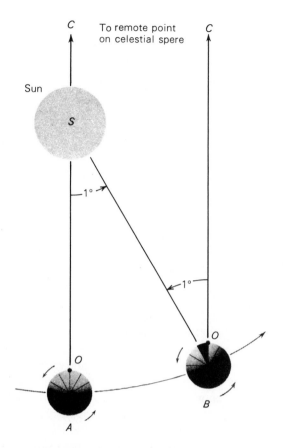

C To remote point on celestial spere C

Sun

S

—1°—

—1°—

O

O

B

A

Sidereal and solar day. After a complete rotation of the earth (or celestial sphere) an observer at O will again see the stars in the direction OC. However, in that time the earth relative to the sun has moved from A to B and the sun has not yet returned to O (it is slightly to the east), the difference being 1 degree of arc.

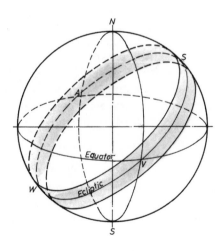

The path of the apparent motion of the sun on the celestial sphere is the ecliptic. It is inclined to the celestial equator by an angle of about 23½ degrees of arc, called the obliquity. The points where the ecliptic intersects the equator are V (vernal equinox) and A (autumnal equinox). The intersections with the meridian are W (winter solstice) and S (summer solstice) respectively. N and S denote the North and South celestial poles respectively. The shaded area straddling the ecliptic is the band of the Zodiac.

(and 4.09 seconds). Since a complete revolution corresponds to 360 degrees of arc, which takes 24 hours–and therefore 15 degrees per hour–the difference of 4 minutes is just 1 degree per day. During a year, then, the stars complete just over 1 extra revolution. On the other hand, we could equally take the constant motion of the stars as our norm and say that the sun loses 1 degree during each revolution of the celestial sphere. If we then place the sun, as well as the stars, on the inside of the celestial sphere, it will be carried by the swift motion of the sphere but it will also move slowly backward (more like a tortoise than Apollo's fiery chariot), making a complete revolution during the course of a year.

It had already been noticed by early astronomers–in particular, the Greeks–that the annual path of the sun took place along a great circle that intersected the celestial equator at an angle. This is the ecliptic, so called because eclipses (of the sun or moon) can occur only if the moon is on this circle or close to it. The angle that the ecliptic makes with the celestial equator is called the obliquity of the ecliptic and is, at present, 23½ degrees of arc. (It changes slightly during the course of centuries.) Actually, it is not the sun's orbit that is inclined to the celestial equator, but the plane of the earth's orbit around the sun. This, however, was not known to the ancient Greeks, and for the present discussion it is immaterial whether the sun revolves around the earth or vice versa.

It is this slant of the sun's path that is responsible for the different seasons. Because of the tilt the top half of the earth's globe leans toward the sun in summer, making the period of daylight longer. In winter the top half of the globe leans away from the sun, resulting in shorter periods of daylight. The points at which the ecliptic cuts the celestial equator are the spring and autumn equinoxes, so called because day and night are equal in length when the sun is there (and sunrise and sunset are exactly east and west respectively). As the sun moves eastward from the vernal, or spring, equinox (March 21) toward the autumnal equinox (September 23), it spends more time above the celestial equator and the days grow longer (for points in the Northern Hemisphere), while during its motion from the autumnal to the vernal equinox the opposite holds true. (In the Southern Hemisphere, of course, the situation is exactly the reverse.)

Not until the later Greeks, notably Hipparchus (fl. 146–127 B.C.), did the moon's motion get the attention it deserves. Its apparent motion is similar to that of the sun, except that its path is inclined to the ecliptic by about 5 degrees of arc (and thus inclined to the celestial equator by 28½ degrees of arc). It also moves faster than the sun and completes a circuit of the celestial sphere in about a month (27⅓ days with respect to the stars or 29½ days with respect to the solar day). Its proper motion, i.e.,

THE SEASONS ON EARTH

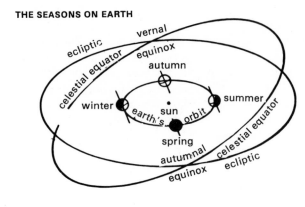

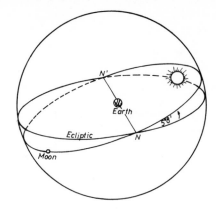

The moon describes a path that is inclined to the ecliptic by about 5 degrees. It interesects the ecliptic at 2 points, N and N¹, known as the ascending and descending nodes respectively.

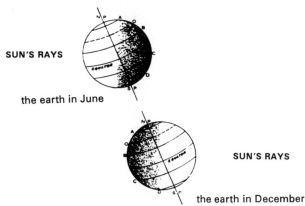

SUN'S RAYS

the earth in June

SUN'S RAYS

the earth in December

Seasons. The earth's axis is inclined to the ecliptic, and, as a result, one hemisphere leans toward the sun while the other leans away, producing a difference of temperature (summer for one hemisphere, winter for the other). Half a year later, the earth has circled to the other side of the sun and the situation is reversed. The top diagram shows the four seasonal positions of the earth (December 21, March 21, June 21, and September 23) as well as the earth's relation to the ecliptic and the celestial equator. The lower two diagrams depict the situations in June and December. The shaded area, which receives no sunlight, represents nighttime at any given moment.

angular change, is about 13 degrees per day compared with the 1 degree of the sun. It is this race with the sun that is responsible for the various phases of the moon. Whenever the moon passes the sun, it is generally not visible (unless it eclipses the sun), resulting in a new moon. As it gains, more and more of the moon becomes visible until we reach full moon—when the moon is exactly opposite the sun on the celestial sphere. As it continues to gain, it wanes, more and more, until it again becomes hidden and a new cycle begins. Aristotle was quite familiar with the moon's phases, and only their actual *mechanism* was unknown to him.

The Egyptian and Babylonian astronomers were, as was noted, very much concerned with eclipses of the moon and, in particular, of the sun. However, not until the relative motion of the sun and the moon was better understood, at first by the Greeks, was it possible to arrive at a satisfactory explanation, as seen below.

The path of the moon crosses the ecliptic, the track of the sun, only at two points, known as the ascending and descending nodes. Actually, of course, the two paths only seem to cross; both sun and moon are in the same (or opposite) line of sight when viewed from the earth. A lunar eclipse will occur when the sun and the moon are simultaneously at those opposite nodes, i.e., in opposition. On the other hand, for a solar eclipse to occur the sun and moon must appear to be both at the same node, i.e.,

in conjunction. This alone does not guarantee the occurrence of an eclipse. In addition, the position of the earth must be between the sun and the moon so that its shadow hides the moon, for a lunar eclipse; the moon must be between the sun and the earth so that the shadow cast by the moon reaches the earth's surface, for a solar eclipse.

If the sun were a point source of light, like a candle, the shadow cast by an object, such as the earth, would be well defined. On a screen it would cast a uniformly dark shadow. However, for a broad source of light, as is the case in actuality, two kinds of shadows will be observed. The black part in the middle, from which all light is excluded, is called the umbra (or, simply, shadow) and the part that receives some light is the penumbra (or partial shadow); thus we have partial and complete lunar and solar eclipses. A complete lunar eclipse occurs when the moon—it will be a full moon, since it is in opposition to the sun—is within the umbra cast by the earth; it will be a partial eclipse, if only part of the moon is in the umbra and the rest in the penumbra.

Anyone who has ever been privileged to observe a total solar eclipse—indeed a rare event—will have been impressed by the spectacle. As the moon covers more and more of the sun's surface, the part of the sun visible to us gets smaller and smaller, more like the moon in its phases, until finally the sun is completely hidden by the moon. Not quite—because the sun's corona, the sun's outer atmosphere, comes suddenly into view. The eclipse does not last long, and soon the sequence is reversed and the sun is visible once more. A complete solar eclipse will take place when the moon—this time the new moon, since it is in conjunction with the sun—is just so close to the earth

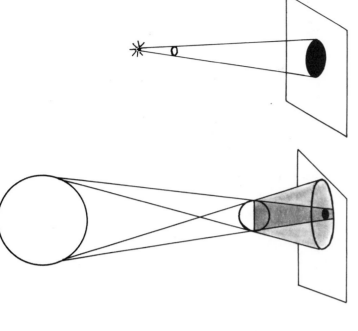

Shadows. Depending on the size of the source, different types of shadows are possible. *Point source:* A uniformly dark shadow is formed by an object placed between a small light source (point source) and a screen. *Extended source:* Each point of the source emits light, only part of which is completely blocked off by the intervening object. The central black region is the umbra, defined by lines from the extremities of the source to the extreme ends of the object; this region does not receive any light. The gray region is the penumbra, from which only part of the light is excluded; it is defined by the intersecting lines.

A lunar eclipse occurs if the moon passes through the shadow cast by the earth. A total lunar eclipse takes place when the moon passes completely into the umbra (path A); a partial eclipse occurs when only part of the moon passes through the umbra (path B). Astronomers also speak of a penumbral eclipse, when the moon passes through the penumbra only (paths C and D). However, such eclipses are usually not noticed, even by astronomers.

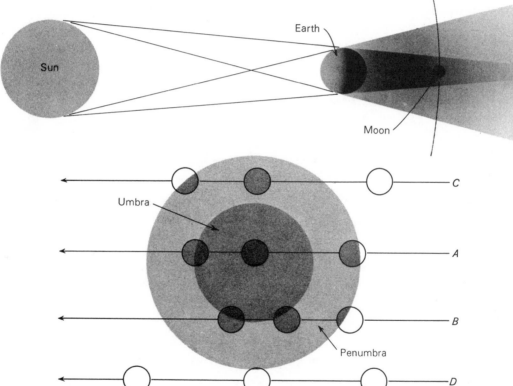

that the observer is in its umbra. Only a small part of the earth's inhabitants can observe a complete solar eclipse, since, at best, the moon's shadow (umbra) just reaches the earth's surface. Many more observers will have seen a partial eclipse of the sun, since the penumbra covers more area.

The motion of the five planets known to the Greeks (Mercury, Venus, Mars, Jupiter, and Saturn) posed additional problems. Compared to the sun and the moon,

they appear only as pinpoints or small disks that could be distinguished from the stars only by observing their motion at many regular intervals. The planets appear to move along the Zodiac—that band of the celestial sphere that straddles the ecliptic—and complete their circuits in periods ranging from a quarter of a year (for Mercury) to 29 years (for Saturn). However, their motion is not regular; they seem to slow down, stop, and reverse their paths along the Zodiac for a while, stop again, and

Photo of the sun during the total solar eclipse of September 22, 1911, taken at Wallal, Australia. Note the bright white halo; it is the sun's corona.

In addition, Mercury and Venus are always found in the vicinity of the sun, sometimes overtaking it, sometimes lagging behind. It was for this reason that early observers thought that Venus was two stars, the morning star when it rose in the sky before the sun was east of it, and the evening star when it set after being west of the sun.

One cannot but marvel at the ingenuity and patience of the early astronomers who, practically unaided by instruments, were able to chart the course of the heavenly bodies, fix positions of stars, and predict the occurrence of eclipses; they were content to make observations and to relate them to their day-to-day experience.

But it was left to the Greek philosophers to try to explain these phenomena through various theories. As we shall see, many of their intricate and fanciful geometrical models were constructed to account for the greatest puzzle of all—the retrograde motion of the planets; during their course in the sky the planets were seen occasionally to trace out loops and move with a backward (retrograde) motion before proceeding in their forward paths. In early astronomy, then, we find a perfect illustration of how theories should work: to explain existing phenomena and observations and to make predictions that can be checked by observation.

continue in their eastward motion. That this retrograde motion was known to the ancient astronomers appears from records made by the Babylonians. For example, we find a certain Mar-Istar reporting to the king:

As to Marduk [Jupiter], I recently reported. My prediction was based on his position in the Anu path [belt of the Zodiac]. I now report that he has been delayed. He has truly run backward; therefore my interpretation was mistaken. But it would not have been mistaken if Marduk has remained on the Anu path. May my Lord King understand this.

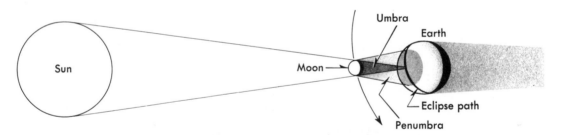

The section of the earth within the umbra experiences a total solar eclipse, while in the penumbra is observed a partial eclipse. (If the umbra does not reach the earth's surface, an annular, or ring-shaped, eclipse is observed.)

APPROXIMATE PLANETARY FIGURES (Major Planets)						
	Mercury	Venus	Earth	Mars	Jupiter	Saturn
Distance from the sun (in terms of Earth-Sun distance)	0.4	0.7	1	1.5	5.2	9.5
Time taken for one orbit (in years)	0.24	0.6	1	1.9	11.9	29.5
Diameter (in terms of Earth's diameter)	0.4	1.0	1	0.5	11.0	9.0
Number of moons (satellites)	—	—	1	2	13*	10

* Possibly 14.

II·GREEK ASTRONOMY

1. Flat Earth Universe

At the beginning battle of a long war between the Lydians, who lived in Asia Minor, and the Persians in 585 B.C., day suddenly changed into night. Stranger yet, this solar eclipse had been predicted by Thales (ca. 640?–546 B.C.), probably the best known of the Ionian philosophers. Thales was a resident of Miletus, the most southern and dynamic of the twelve cities that constituted Ionia (now the western part of Turkey). He had visited Egypt and Babylonia, where he may have gained his knowledge of eclipses. Yet he was not satisfied with mere prediction–he wanted to know *why* eclipses took place. He discovered that solar eclipses occurred when the moon passed in front of the sun, which also proved that the moon received its light from the sun.

Thales was the founder of the "art" of geometry, which became the main pursuit of Greek mathematics and, indeed, was the preferred branch of mathematics until the time of Isaac Newton in the seventeenth century. Several theorems found in Euclid's *Elements of Geometry,* the standard work on elementary geometry, can be attributed to Thales. He is also credited with the original idea that water was the primary matter–when rarefied, it would become air, when condensed, earth, and when incandescent, fire.

Thales was considered a prodigy, who not only could predict eclipses but also could correct weather forecasts–a rare feat even today. According to Diogenes Laertes, a Greek philosopher, he foretold the storm that saved the life of King Croesus of Lydia (known for his incredible wealth). Thales was known to have predicted–in winter–a good harvest of olives during the coming year. He put this knowledge to practical use. Having a little money, he placed deposits on all the olive presses in Miletus and later hired them out for a considerable profit.

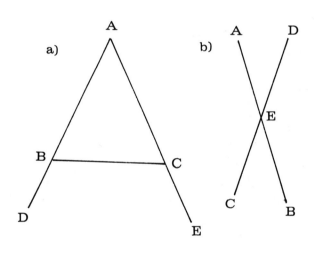

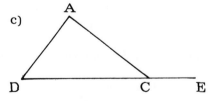

Theorems from Euclid's *Elements,* without the proofs: (a) Book I, Proposition 5: In isosceles triangles the angles at the base are equal to one another, and if the equal straight lines be produced further, the angles under the base will be equal to one another. In other words, if sides AB = AC, then angle ABC = ACB and angle DBC = ECB. (b) Book I, Proposition 15: If two straight lines cut one another, they make the vertical angles equal to one another. The straight lines AB and CD cut each other at E. Angle AED = CEB. (c) Book I, Proposition 32: In any triangle, if one of the sides is extended, the exterior angle is equal to the sum of the two interior opposite angles, and the sum of the three interior angles of the triangle is equal to two right angles. In the triangle ADC, the exterior angle ACE is equal to the sum of the two interior angles ADC and DAC. Also the sum of the three interior angles ADC + DCA + CAD is equal to two right angles, i.e., 180 degrees.

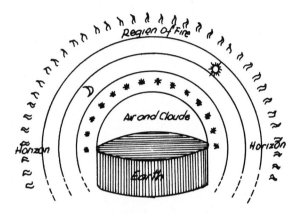

Anaximander's universe was divided into a number of heavens, the lowest for air and clouds, another for all the stars, a higher heaven for the moon, a still higher one for the sun, and, a region of fire, the lightest, on top. The successive heavens were in layers, like the shells of an onion, transparent and invisible. Instead of ending at the horizon these layers were continued a little below to allow for the passage of the heavenly bodies between setting and rising. (It was perhaps for this reason that Anaximander stipulated an earth in the shape of a cylinder, populated only on top. The heavenly bodies could then disappear from view but would still not be below the earth.)

His concept of the universe, on the other hand, was as primitive as the concepts believed in by the Babylonians. Thales imagined the earth to be a circular disk floating "like a piece of wood or something of that kind" on water, the primary substance. It was surmounted by vapor, the rarefied form of water, while the incandescent forms, such as the sun and the stars, moved around within it. In view of Thales' other accomplishments, it might seem odd that the concept of a round earth eluded him. But much of his work and predictions—such as the prediction of the solar eclipse that is credited to him—were based on Egyptian and Babylonian observations, and it is quite natural that he would have carried over their cosmic ideas as well. The significant difference between his concept and the concepts of his "masters" is that no god or gods intervened, and matter just followed its natural course. This view alone must be considered an important advance.

Not much further progress was made by Anaximander, a younger contemporary of Thales (ca. 611-547 B.C.). However, Anaximander rejected the idea of water as the primary substance and, instead, postulated that the material cause and first element of things was the infinite, i.e., matter without any determinate property. He imagined the earth to be flat, not a disk as postulated by

Thales but rather more like a cylinder, its height one third of its width. (No reasons were given for these particular dimensions.) According to Anaximander, the sun, moon, and stars moved in separate "shells" enclosing the earth and its surrounding air, all surmounted by a region of fire. Here, for the first time, we find the heavenly bodies to be at different distances, although it is strange that Anaximander placed the stars closer to Earth than he did the moon. He should have noticed the occultations of the stars by the moon, which are only possible if the moon is closer to the observer than the eclipsed star.

Since the moon seemed to be nearer to the earth than the sun and since both appeared to be the same size, it was assumed that the moon had to be smaller. Anaximander asserted—quite boldly and apparently without observational evidence, which could not have been available to him—that both the moon and sun were larger than the earth. He calculated that the sun was 27 times the size of the earth and the moon 19 times.

Other members of the Ionian school did not come much closer to creating a rational model of the universe. The earth remained the floor of the universe and heaven a vaulted dome. They only speculated on possible mechanisms for the motion of the heavenly bodies. According to Anaximenes, also of Miletus (ca. 545 B.C.), and the third-ranking Ionian philosopher, the stars were fixed to the celestial vault "like nails," while the sun, moon, and planets were flat disks supported by air, floating in it "like a leaf." The heat of the sun was caused by the rapidity of its motion, but the heat of the stars went unnoticed because of their distance. Anaxagoras (ca. 500?-428 B.C.), another member of the Ionian school, suggested that the heavenly bodies were prevented from "falling down" by a whirlwind sweeping around the earth. He also suggested that the stars were part of the earth torn off by the whirlwind, and he attributed their brightness to heat caused by the friction when they separated from Earth.

At the end of the sixth century B.C. there arose another school—at the opposite end of the Greek empire, in the south of Italy—where more rational ideas of the nature of the world were developed. The school was founded by Pythagoras (ca. 580-500 B.C.) and occupied so central a place in early Greek astronomy that it deserves special consideration, which we will give it in the next section.

Soon afterward another philosophical school sprang up

in Elea on the southern coast of Italy, not far from Crotona on the instep of the Italian boot where the Pythagoreans flourished. Its most prominent exponent was Parmenides, who lived in the early part of the fifth century. He is credited with asserting that the earth is round; he was the only one who thought so besides Pythagoras before the time of Plato and Aristotle. Parmenides also extended Anaximander's idea and conceived of spherical concentric shells surrounding a central (and stationary) earth. The outermost of these layers was a solid vault, "Olympos," followed by a layer formed by a subtle element, the Ether. Under this—but still floating in the Ether—comes the morning and evening star (of whose identity he was aware), then the sun and then the moon, both of equal size. The other stars were placed in a fiery place he called the Heavens and were closer to the earth.

This was a considerable advance in thought, since it dispensed with the idea of a sun hidden by mountains, or stars being lit and extinguished. All simply disappeared below the horizon as the celestial sphere rotated.

According to Leucippus, who had come to Elea at about 435 B.C. to study under Zeno—successor to Parmenides and famous for his paradoxes—the earth resembles a tambourine, flat on top and round at the bottom, surmounted by a hemisphere of air. The whole is surrounded by a sphere containing the moon, followed by another sphere with the planets, a sphere with the sun, and finally a sphere with the stars. Here we have a combination of the concentric spheres of Parmenides, but a flat (or at least flat-top) earth in accordance with accepted belief. Only the top of the earth was inhabited.

Leucippus and his famous disciple Democritus were the originators of the atomic theory of matter. They taught that matter consists of an infinite number of small, finite, indivisible bodies—atoms—moving in the void. Democritus's ideas on the constitution of matter were amazingly correct and foreshadowed modern developments. His universe, on the other hand, still suffered from the prejudices of his time. His earth was a flat disk, somewhat higher at the circumference and lower at the middle—probably to prevent its contents from spilling over the side. It fit on a hemisphere of air "like a lid" (as Aristotle put it) and was surmounted by another hemisphere of air, dividing the whole sphere into two equal halves. The heavenly bodies are again placed inside a series of spheres surrounding the central sphere. But while Leucippus placed the sphere carrying the sun outside that carrying the planets, Democritus reverses the order and brings the sun closer to the earth. It is interesting to note that both models permit occultations of stars by the moon, which was impossible in the universes of Anaximander and Parmenides.

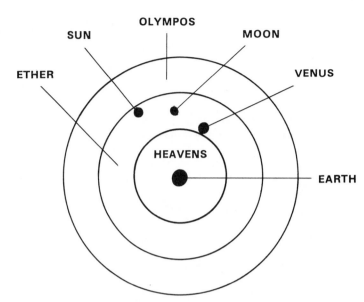

The universe according to Parmenides. For the first time, the sun and moon were seen as moving in concentric circles. The universe is divided into three regions, Olympos, Ether, and the Heavens. Sun, Moon, and Venus (the morning and evening star) float in the ether but describe circular paths of their own.

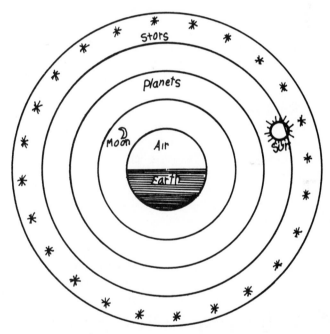

The universe according to Leucippus. The earth was thought to be a hemisphere on which another hemisphere of air was fitted, the whole surrounded by the supporting crystal sphere, which held the moon. Above this came the spheres for the planets, then the sun, and probably the stars were outside this.

Democritus's scheme was pleasing to the Greek sense of symmetry, but one puzzle remained. If, indeed, the earth was flat and at the center of the universe, then the celestial North Pole should be directly overhead at the zenith and the celestial equator should coincide with Earth's horizon. (This, of course, is actually the situation if the observer is at the North Pole of the earth, as we have seen in Chapter I. Therefore, to account for the observed slant of the celestial sphere, Democritus (and

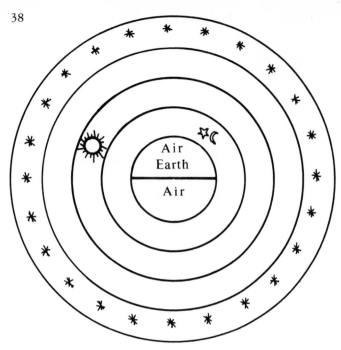

Democritus's Earth, a flat disk dividing a surrounding sphere of air into two equal parts. Only the top of the disk is inhabited. The air sphere is surrounded by a crystal sphere containing both the moon and the morning star, followed by a sphere containing the sun, another for the planets, and finally the stars.

also Leucippus) suggested that the earth had tilted from its original horizontal position owing to the weight of the fruit growing on its southern side. Alternatively, it was suggested that it was the celestial sphere's axis that may have shifted from its vertical position.

As crude as this picture of the universe may have been, it satisfied the Greek curiosity and imagination. But it also provided a real advance in that it depicted the apparent daily path of the heavenly bodies as a circle, although only a part of the path could be seen. Furthermore, the sun, moon, and stars, although they were all projected onto a single celestial sphere, were placed at varying distances.

2. Harmony of the Spheres

The first real advance in astronomy was made by Pythagoras of Samos and the school that he founded at the age of fifty. It was more like a brotherhood or religious sect than a philosophical school, since the students were bound by a series of strict regulations governing their dress, diet, and general everyday life. They had taken vows of secrecy regarding their beliefs, which is probably the reason why so little is known about their activities. The word of the "master" was absolute, and it was even believed that he was a semigod, the son of Apollo and a mortal woman.

As a philosophical school, the Pythagoreans were devoted to science and, in particular, the study of numbers. According to their philosophy, number is everything. It was even the cause of natural phenomena. They delighted in numbers and classified them according to their "shapes": triangular, square, and oblong. These, in turn, could be built up by simple addition. For example, triangular numbers are simple sums of successive integers, or whole numbers. The perfect number was $1 + 2 + 3 + 4 = 10$, the divine tetraktys (the holy fourfoldness). Square numbers were formed by the addition of successive odd numbers, while oblong numbers were sums of successive even numbers. In similar fashion, more complicated arrays such as "cubic numbers" or "pyramidal numbers" could be constructed.

Another remarkable example of the interrelation of numbers and geometry is the well-known Theorem of Pythagoras taught to schoolchildren in elementary geometry classes. It asserts that if we construct a square over each side of a right-angled triangle (i.e., a triangle, one of whose angles is 90 degrees), then the sum of the squares of the two sides adjacent to the right angle is equal to the square of the hypotenuse, the side opposite the right angle. Pythagoras was supposed to have been so pleased by his discovery that he sacrificed one hundred oxen to the gods in thanksgiving.

The main contribution of Pythagoras to our understanding of the universe, undoubtedly, is the conception of a spherical earth. How he arrived at this remarkable—for his time—conclusion is not certain. (Parmenides was also credited with perceiving a spherical earth, but his influence was minor and his successors reverted to belief in a flat earth.) One suggestion is that he was among those who observed the round shadow cast by the earth during a lunar eclipse. More important, Pythagoras was a philosopher who believed in perfection. The universe is perfect and thus its constituents are perfect and must move along perfect orbits. Since the circle is the perfect curve and the sphere the perfect solid, it follows naturally that the heavenly bodies, including the earth, are spheres.

The universe of Pythagoras featured a fixed, spherical earth at its center. The stars were on the inside of a giant crystal celestial sphere that rotated about an axis passing through the center of the earth. The planets were carried along but had a motion of their own, opposite to the rotation of the celestial sphere. At first, at least, no assertion was made about the relative motion of the planets and their order except the belief that they were five in number. Aristotle tells us that the Pythagoreans divided the universe into three regions: Ouranos, or sky; Cosmos, the region of sun, moon, and planets; and Olympos, the place of pure elements.

Pythagoras, having once heard the musical intervals

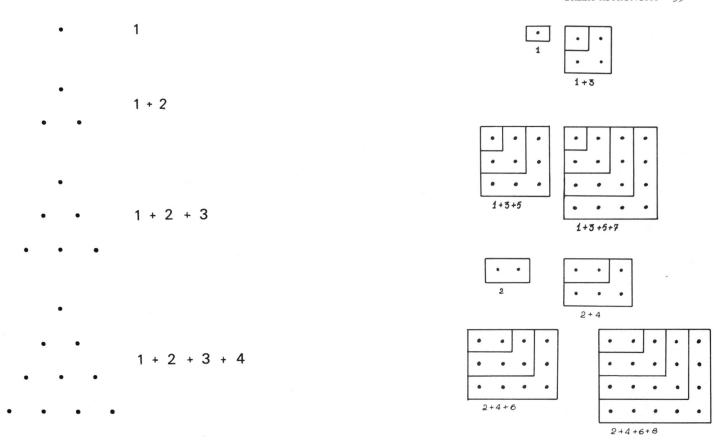

• 1

•
 1 + 2
•   •

•
•   •   1 + 2 + 3
•   •   •

•
•   •
•   •   •   1 + 2 + 3 + 4
•   •   •   •

Triangular numbers: The sum of any series of consecutive whole numbers starting with 1, such as 1+2, 1+2+3, 1+2+3+4, etc. could be arranged in the form of a regular triangle. The number 10, being the sum of the first four integers, is the tetraktys (the holy fourfoldness).

Square numbers: The sum of a series of consecutive odd numbers starting with 1 could be arranged in the form of squares with sides equal to 2, 3, 4, etc., units.

Oblong numbers: The sum of consecutive even numbers could be arranged in the form of rectangles with increasing sides (2×3, 3×4, 4×5, etc.).

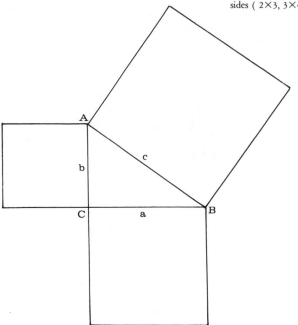

Probably one of the best-known results of Pythagoras is the theorem that in a right-angled triangle the square of the hypotenuse (side opposite the right angle ACB) is equal to the sum of the squares of the other two sides. Thus, in the right angle triangle ABC, the square surmounting side ABC = c, is equal to the sum of the squares surmounting the other two sides, AC = b, and CB = a. This can be written as an equation, $a^2 + b^2 = c^2$

According to Pythagoras (and perhaps also Parmenides) a spherical earth was placed at the center of the universe. The daily motion of stars, sun, moon, and planets was accounted for by the rotation of the celestial sphere. In addition, the heavenly bodies moved slowly backward through the star pattern in the course of a year.

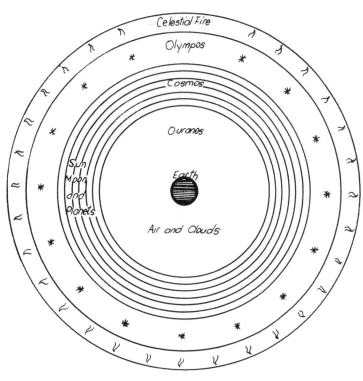

According to Aristotle, the Pythagoreans divided the universe in three: the Ouranos, or sky, within which exists all that is changing and corruptible (Air and Clouds); the Cosmos, the place of ordered movements or the region of sun, moon, and planets; and the Olympos, the place of pure elements, which held the stars. The region of Celestial Fire came beyond this, and finally Apeiron, the Infinite Space or Infinite Air, from which the world draws its breath.

Musical chords. In these panels from Franchino Gafurio's *Theorica Musice* (1492), musical chords and proportions are illustrated. At the upper left Jubal, the father of music, in the Bible, is shown perceiving the consonances (4, 6, 8, 9, 12, 16) by means of hammers of various weights (usually attributed to Pythagoras). At the upper right Pythagoras and his follower Philolaus are shown demonstrating tones with bells of different sizes, again showing the various ratios (e.g., 16:8), and with glasses filled to different levels. At the lower left Pythagoras uses strings stretched by different weights; and at the lower right both use pipes of different lengths. The important fact that follows from all these examples is that the different concordant intervals of the musical scale can be expressed as simple ratios depending on the length of cords, pipes, etc.

produced by a series of hammers in a blacksmith's shop, rushed home and investigated the musical qualities of strings and pipes. He observed, upon subdividing a fixed vibrating string, that the pitches of the vibrating segments were dependent on the different lengths. In other words, the harmonious intervals of the musical scale could be expressed as simple ratios of integral numbers depending on the length of the strings of a monochord. Once the fundamental concept of musical harmony had been established, it seemed logical (at least to Pythagoras) to extend it to the universe itself: sun, moon, and planets traveling along their orbits in such a way as to create celestial harmony, just as the lengths of the strings of a

harp create musical harmony. Air was thought to pervade all space, which when disturbed by the motion of the heavenly bodies produced musical tones. It is as if the universe were an immense lyre with circular chords, producing a celestial concert, the Harmony of the Spheres.

The actual assignment of musical intervals differed for various authors, but all agreed that the lowest note was produced by the moon (which is closest to the earth) and the highest by the circle of stars (which are farthest). This harmony could be heard only by a few select people, and it was said that only Pythagoras himself could actually hear the music of the spheres

Since the musical tones depend on the lengths of the

Raphael's fresco *School of Athens* in the apartments of Pope Julius II in the Vatican. Seated in the left foreground, with a large book in his hands, is Pythagoras; the turbaned Spanish-Arab philosopher-physician Averroës appears to be leaning over him. In the background (center), Plato and Aristotle are entering the hall.

HARMONY OF THE SPHERES

	Left scale (Pliny)		Right scale (Censorinus)	
Earth				
	1 tone		1 tone	
Moon				
	½ tone	3 ½ tones (a fifth)	½ tone	3 ½ tones (a fifth)
Mercury				
	½ tone		½ tone	
Venus				
	1 ½ tones		1 ½ tones	
Sun				
	1 tone		1 tone	
Mars				
	½ tone	2 ½ tones (a fourth)	½ tone	3 ½ tones (a fifth)
Jupiter				
	½ tone		½ tone	
Saturn				
	½ tone		1 ½ tones	
Stars				
	6 tones		7 tones	

NOTE: The scale on the right is from *De Die Natali,* an essay on astrology and chronology by Censorinus (ca. 238). It corresponds to C, D, E ♭, E, G, A, B ♭, B, D. In the scale on the left by Pliny the distance from Saturn to the fixed stars is ½ tone. The fixed stars then correspond to a C instead of a D and the whole forms an octave (C to C). The terms *octave, fourth,* and *fifth* represent ratios of lengths of string (at equal tension) in the ratios 1:2, 3:4, and 2:3 respectively.

chords producing them, this provided an indication of the size of the universe. For example, Pliny in his *Natural History* reports that Pythagoras made the distance from the earth to the moon—which was one note—equal to 126,000 stadia (one stadium is about one-tenth of a mile). Therefore, according to the table, the distance from the earth to the sun would be three and a half times that distance. It doesn't matter that these distances are unrealistic; what is important is that they resulted in a "shell" universe. Nothing much was said about the mechanism that turned the spheres, except that it was some kind of "celestial machinery"—the primum mobile.

In the Pythagorean version the outer sphere carrying the fixed stars rotated once in a twenty-four-hour day, while the others moved slightly slower to indicate the lagging course of the sun, the moon, and the planets. It was soon realized that the common twenty-four-hour rotation against the slower-moving objects could be justified by assuming that the outer sphere carried all the others with it. The inner ones would simply be spinning slowly *backward* with an appropriate rate of rotation, once a year for the sun, once a month for the moon, etc.

Much later it was realized—probably by Heraclides of Pontus (388–338 B.C.), a student of Plato, although sometimes it is attributed to Ecphantus, a little known spokesman of the Pythagoreans—that a spinning earth

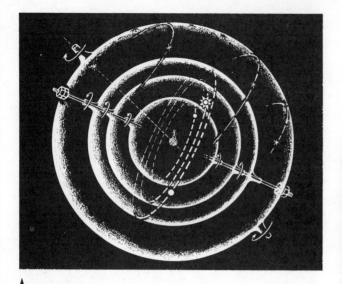

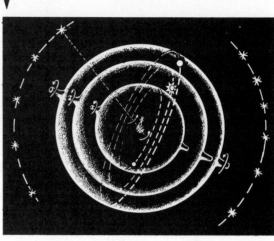

In the later system of crystal spheres, instead of the celestial sphere rotating about its axis, a spinning earth accounted for the daily motion of the stars and heavenly bodies. This left the yearly motions of the sun, moon, and planets to be accounted for by the rotation of their respective spheres in the *same* direction as the spinning earth.

▼

▲
Part of the early system of crystal spheres. The outer sphere represents the celestial sphere, which carries the inner spheres of the heavenly bodies and spins about its axis daily. In addition, the inner spheres, carrying the sun, moon, and planets, spin about their axes in accordance with their yearly motion.

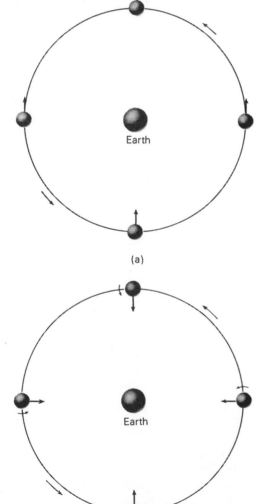

(a)

(b)

It was erroneously believed that while the moon revolved around the earth, it did not rotate about its axis. In this example (a) it would turn all its sides to our view. It was not realized that only if the moon rotates about its axis with the same period as it revolves around the earth (b) will the same side always be visible on earth.

could account for the daily motions of the sun, moon, planets, and stars, leaving to the rotations of the inner spheres the task of their periodic or yearly motions.

Philolaus, a follower of Pythagoras, who was believed to have lived at the end of the fifth century B.C., proposed a rather remarkable scheme. Instead of having the celestial sphere rotate in one direction for a complete revolution every twenty-four hours, with the sun, the moon, and the five planets moving in the opposite direction but at different speeds, he suggested that the stars were at rest and that the heavenly objects as well as the earth revolved around a fixed center. If the earth were to revolve around that center once every twenty-four hours, always keeping its same side facing that center, this would account for the apparent daily motions of the stars and heavenly bodies, and it would explain night and day on the earth.

It is not clear why Philolaus did not adopt the simpler scheme of having the earth stationary but rotating, or spinning, around its own axis. He may have been guided by the erroneous example of the moon, which was thought to revolve but not rotate; if the moon had an orbital motion and always kept the same side toward its center, couldn't this be so for the earth also? One would prefer to think that Philolaus may have realized that the earth did not occupy a privileged position in the universe.

At the center he placed the hearth of the universe, the

42

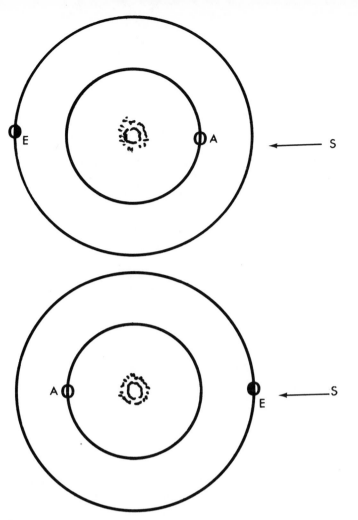

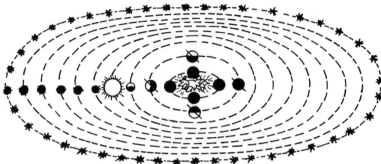

Philolaus's system. The central fire is at the center of the universe, followed by antichthon—the counterearth—and finally Earth. Because the inhabited side of Earth is always turned away from the center, both the central fire and antichthon are hidden from Earth's view. The top view is of Earth at night, and the bottom—in which Earth and antichthon have completed half a revolution—depicts the daytime. S indicates the sun.

Philolaus's central fire and 10 spheres, 1 each for the earth and antichthon (each shown in 4 positions), the moon, the sun, and the 5 planets, indicated by dark circles, and finally the stars.

"central fire." It was hidden from view, since the inhabited part of the earth is the side farthest from the center. Also invisible to our view was another "earth," antichthon, the counterearth, placed on an orbit between the earth and the central fire. The counterearth apparently was introduced to preserve the harmony of the spheres; inclusion of the earth as a moving body spoiled the sacred number of seven (sun, moon, and five planets), but, adding antichthon and counting the sphere of the stars brings the total to ten, the divine tetraktys. More likely, however, it served to explain eclipses of the moon.

The sun played only a secondary role. Philolaus held it to be transparent like glass, receiving the reflection of the central fire and transmitting it. In this sense the sun was confused with the central fire, and Philolaus was credited with originating a heliocentric, i.e., sun-centered theory.

Philolaus's system did not win any adherents except among the Pythagoreans, partly because it was difficult for the Greeks to believe in an unseen central body whose existence seemed in doubt. Travelers returning from the Pillars of Hercules (modern Strait of Gibraltar), the farthest part of the inhabited earth, who might have glimpsed antichthon and the central fire or at least heard rumors of their existence, failed to bring back reports of its (antichthon's) existence. The earth again was returned to its central position, the central fire transferred into the

earth's core, and the counterearth identified with the moon.

3. Plato's Problem

While the Pythagoreans tried to reconcile their ideas with reality, Plato (ca. 427?–347 B.C.) was concerned only with the world of ideas. For him the stars, however beautiful, were only a part of the visible world, no more than a shadow of the real world of ideas. To understand astronomy one would have to concentrate on abstract problems, as in geometry. Over the entrance of Plato's Academy—so called after the Greek hero Academus—were the words "Let no one enter here who knows no geometry." And geometry, indeed, became the main scientific endeavor of the Academy. Euclid (fl. ca. 300 B.C.), a follower of Plato, and Theaetetus (ca. 414–369 B.C.), another disciple, showed that there were only five Platonic solids—regular solid figures that can be built from equilateral triangles, squares, or regular polygons. Plato used them for his theory of matter, while Kepler based his earlier model of the universe on them.

Plato's system of the universe was another example of

The regular or perfect solids are sometimes called Platonic solids, since they were used by Plato for his theory of matter. Each of the four elements is represented by one of the solids: fire by tetrahedron, air by octahedron, earth by cube, water by icosahedron. In addition, the universe itself is represented by the dodecahedron.

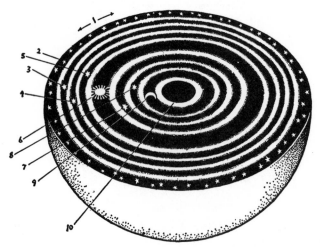

Plato's cosmos. The rims of the set of hemispheres are the whorls that carry the stars and planets: (1) propelling sphere—invisible and immovable; (2) star sphere, carrying the other spheres with it (period of revolution: 1 day); (3) Saturn sphere (period of revolution, apart from the motion imparted from (1) above: 29 years); (4) Jupiter sphere (period of revolution: 12 years); (5) Mars sphere (period of revolution: 2 years); (6) sphere carrying the sun (period of revolution: 1 year); (7) Venus sphere (period of revolution: 6 months); (8) Mercury sphere (period of revolution: 3 months); (9) sphere carrying the moon (period of revolution: 1 month); (10) stationary Earth at the center.

geometrical perfection. He accepted the Pythagorean concept of spheres and circles for the perfect cosmos but ridiculed the idea of celestial harmony. His universe consisted of a series of "tops" fitting into one another like a nest of bowls. The rims of these hemispheres were the "whorls" that carried the stars, planets, sun, and moon.

The whole system revolved around an axle, the "axle of Necessity," while the inner circles again revolved in the opposite direction, pushed by the three Fates—Lachesis, Clotho, and Atropos—who were the daughters of Necessity, on whose knees the axle turned.

As a geometrical model, it gives a good description of the overall motion of the heavenly bodies, although it requires some imagination to understand it—exactly what Plato intended. Presumably, the whorls are pure mechanisms to provide plane circular orbits for the sun, the moon, and the five planets. Plato takes the widths of the whorls, i.e., the differences between the outer and inner rims as a measure of each planet's relative distance from the earth, and he indicates each planet by the color of the whorl.

One question still had to be answered: how to explain the retrograde motion of the planets. Plato formulated the problem—sometimes referred to as Plato's Problem—as follows: "What are the uniform and ordered movements by the assumption of which the apparent movements of the planets can be accounted for?" In other words, the actual motion of the planets must remain ordered and circular, but some combination of such movements should account for the retrograde motions. According to one story, Plato found one of his students, Eudoxus (ca. 400–350 B.C.) engaged in using geometry to devise machines for practical use. This was against the teachings of the Academy. Geometry was to be used only as a pure intellectual pursuit, and so Plato assigned to Eudoxus the solution of his problem. Eudoxus was a mathematician in his own right and hardly needed an incentive to work out complicated problems. He was the author of the *Fifth Book of Euclid* and the first to suggest a 4-year solar cycle—3 years of 365 days each and 1 year (the leap year) having 366 days—300 years before it was introduced by Julius Caesar.

Eudoxus's system is ingenious and elegant, and it deserves more consideration than it has received. It consists of several sets of concentric spheres, fitting inside one another and diminishing in size. Each set simulated the various motions of a particular planet, the sun, or the moon, and moved quite independently of all other sets. At the common center of all spheres was a small sphere—the earth—while the outermost sphere was the celestial sphere. Since all the heavenly bodies possess a daily motion similar to that of the stars, each set contained a sphere that moved exactly like the celestial sphere. For the sun (and the moon) a second sphere was contained within the first, its axis inclined to the first and its poles resting on it. The outer sphere gave the daily motion, while the inner one—revolving around its axis once a year in an opposite direction—described the yearly motion. A third sphere was added to account for the fact that the sun does not rise at the same point on the horizon throughout the year. In the case of the planets, Eudoxus found that four spheres for each planet could simulate their daily and yearly behavior, including the retrograde motion. The combined

PLATO'S WHORLS				
Whorl	Heavenly Body	Order in Breadth	Order in Speed	Colors
1	Propelling sphere	–	–	–
2	Fixed stars	1	–	Spangled
3	Saturn	8	5	Yellower than sun and moon
4	Jupiter	7	4	Whitest
5	Mars	3	3	Rather red
8	Mercury	6	2	Like Saturn in color
7	Venus	2	2	Second in whiteness
6	Sun	5	2	Brightest
9	Moon	4	1	Light borrowed from sun
10	Stationary Earth	–	–	–

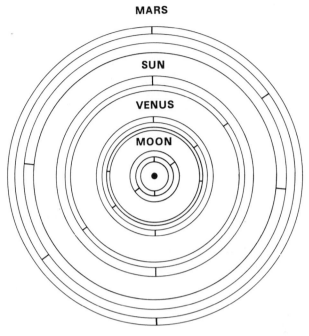

Several sets of concentric spheres of Eudoxus's scheme. The sets of four spheres each belong to planets (here Mars and Venus), while the set of three spheres are for the motion of Moon and Sun respectively. The circle at the center is the earth, about whose center all spheres revolve.

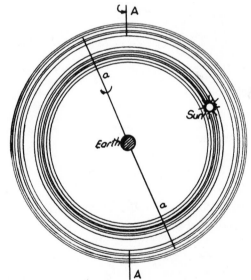

The spheres of the sun. The outer sphere revolves around its axis AA once in 24 hours, while the inner one turns about its axis aa in the opposite direction—but carried forward by outer space—once in a year. The axes of the 2 spheres are inclined to each other by an angle corresponding to the obliquity, or the 23½ degrees of the ecliptic. The sun itself is embedded in the inner sphere and thus experiences the motion of both spheres, traveling through the sky with the daily and yearly motions, as seen from the earth.

◄

Stellar magnitudes corresponding to the six magnitudes are compared with multiples of the earth's diameter (measured on the vertical axis). Between stars of first and second magnitude is the orbit of Jupiter, drawn for comparison.

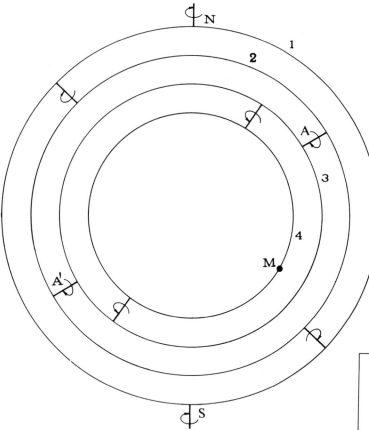

The planetary 4 spheres. Each planet (M) was embedded in the innermost of a system of 4 spheres, each rotating about its own axis and at a different speed. The outer sphere (1) rotating once a day about its NS axis accounts for the daily rising and setting of the planet. The axis of the next sphere (2) is inclined at an angle— equal to the obliquity—to that of the outer sphere in which it is embedded. It gives the yearly motion of the planet. To account for the retrograde, or looping, motion of the planets, spheres (3) and (4) are introduced. Although they rotate uniformly, as is proper for celestial spheres, their axes are inclined to each other and they rotate in opposite directions—producing an irregular oscillation.

Callippus (ca. 370–300 B.C.) tried to improve the scheme by adding another sphere to the set of spheres of Mars, Venus, and Mercury. He also noted that the seasons were of unequal length (i.e., apparently it took the sun a longer time to pass from the vernal to the autumnal equinox than the other way around). He found that he could account for these discrepancies by adding two extra spheres to the sun's set. Similarly, he added two additional spheres to the moon's set, bringing the total to thirty-four (five each for sun, moon, Mercury, Venus, and Mars; four each for Jupiter and Saturn, and one for the star-sphere). Although Eudoxus's and Callippus's systems did not stand up to the test of time, they were the first serious attempts to bring theory into agreement with observation, and thus they mark the beginning of "observational astronomy."

EUDOXUS'S PERIODS				
	Synodic Period *		**Zodiacal Period †**	
	Eudoxus	*Modern Value*	*Eudoxus*	*Modern Value*
Saturn	390 days	378 days	30 years	29 years 166 days
Jupiter	390 days	399 days	12 years	11 years 315 days
Mars	260 days	780 days	2 years	1 year 322 days
Mercury	110 days	116 days	1 year	1 year
Venus	570 days	584 days	1 year	1 year

* A synodic period is the interval between two successive occurrences of the same configuration of a planet, e.g., between the times when the earth lies on a straight line between the sun and a particular planet.

† A Zodiacal period is the time taken by a planet to traverse the ecliptic, the angular path of the sun, along which the Zodiac lies.

motion of the latter two spheres, whose relative speeds had to be adjusted carefully, causes the planet to describe a figure "eight" bearing a fair resemblance to the actual looping motions of the planets.

This construction described the behavior of the sun, moon, Saturn, and Jupiter quite well but failed in the difficult case of Mars. It was not too satisfactory for Venus and Mercury either. As a solution to a mathematical problem, it was quite a feat, but it lacked any physical features. Eudoxus gave no indication of the mechanism producing the rotation of the spheres (which would have to be transparent) or their thickness and mutual distances. However, the periods of the planets as given by Eudoxus agree fairly well with modern results, again with the exception of the period of Mars.

4. A Premature Hypothesis

Aristotle (384–322 B.C.) accepted Eudoxus's scheme, to which he added a number of further spheres. These were interspersed between the various sets of the individual planets and were to provide the mechanism that drove them. The motion of the celestial sphere was transmitted to the outer sphere of Jupiter; and between the inner sphere of Jupiter and the outer sphere of Saturn three additional spheres were interposed; this cancelled the effect of Jupiter's motion on Saturn and restored the original motion of the celestial sphere. Another three spheres between the inner sphere of Saturn and the outer sphere

A drawing from Andreas Cellarius's *Atlas* (1660) illustrating the Egyptian, or Heraclidean, universe, with Mercury and Venus revolving around the sun, and the remaining planets as well as the sun turning about a central earth.

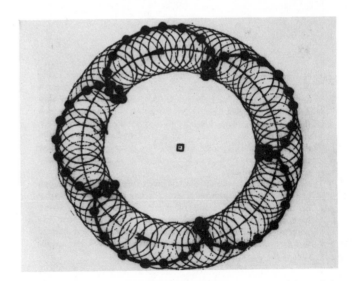

of Mars neutralized the effect of Saturn's motion on Mars. Continuing this process, Aristotle arrived at a system of fifty-six spheres, all driven from one "divine sphere." It was the only self-moving sphere; all other fifty-five spheres depended for their motion on the various linkages between them.

Aristotle's scheme was respectable and it made mechanical sense, i.e., it was more than a geometrical abstraction; it provided a mechanism, albeit a complicated one. In contrast to later adherents of Earth-centered cosmology, Aristotle permitted criticism. In his *Physical Problems,* he admitted that Mercury and Venus change in brightness, indicating that they alternately approach and recede from the earth. Clearly, this would not have been the case if they revolved unchanged around us, which would have been necessary for an Earth-centered universe. Moreover, both seemed to be close to the sun during their wanderings, sometimes in front, overtaking it, and sometimes falling behind. For this reason, Venus at times appeared as the morning star (Phosphorus), greeting the sun, and as the evening star (Hesperos), bidding her farewell.

Heraclides suggested that Mercury and Venus revolve around the sun, which together with the other planets revolve around the earth. This masterly conception at the same time solved the problem of the "changing" inner planets and was the first step toward a truly sun-centered system. As seen from the central earth the paths of these two inner planets (Mercury and Venus) will appear to form "loops," moving forward and backward relative to the sun. Simplicius, writing in the sixth century, reports that Heraclides tried to explain the retrograde motion of the other planets by assuming that these planets also

The loops of Mercury and Venus. Mercury and Venus travel around the earth in orbits that are the combination of two separate circular movements, that of the sun and their own motion around the sun. The resulting track appears to form loops (across the central path of the sun).

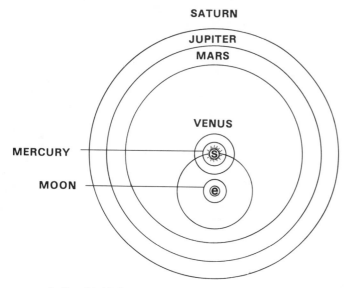

In Heraclides' heliocentric system, the moon and sun revolve around a central earth, but all five planets revolve around the sun.

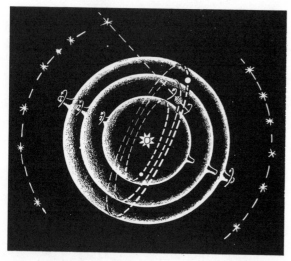

Aristarchus's scheme included a complete heliocentric system with a central sun and spinning earth. The stars are on a fixed sphere, while the planets (and Earth) revolve around the sun. Only two planets are shown: one of the outer planets Mars, Jupiter, or Saturn and either of the inner planets Venus or Mercury.

describe loops moving toward and away from the earth during their regular circular motion. Such an explanation would require some knowledge of the theory of epicycles, circles whose centers move on the circumference of other circles (covered later in this chapter). But as far as is known, these were proposed by Hipparchus much later than Heraclides.

From the idea that some of the planets revolve around the sun while others revolve around the earth, it is only a small step to assume that *all* planets revolve around the sun, which in turn revolves around the earth. Again we find that Heraclides is often credited with the idea for this type of model. It was actually proposed later by Tycho Brahe, the sixteenth-century astronomer we will discuss in a later chapter. It is not surprising that Heraclides was considered the originator of ideas developed centuries later. His two great discoveries, the rotation of the earth around its axis and the fact that Venus and Mercury revolve around the sun, have earned him such an outstanding reputation that it seemed natural to suppose that he was also responsible for their extensions. However, neither of the two systems found favor with the official Greek school of thought, nor did they satisfy the Greeks' sense of beauty. It was unthinkable to have a combination of motion—around the sun *and* around the earth.

Aristarchus of Samos (fl. ca. 270 B.C.) took the next step and proposed that the earth, the moon, and the five planets revolve around a motionless sun. Also, his earth spun around its axis, which did away with the necessity of a rotating sphere of fixed stars. The work in which Aristarchus puts forward this remarkable idea unfortunately is lost, but it is reported by such authorities as Archimedes and Plutarch. There can be no doubt that Aristarchus, indeed, was the first to propose a truly and complete sun-centered universe.

One can only guess what led Aristarchus to these remarkable hypotheses. He was a great mathematician and a well-known observer, and he may have been guided by the fact, observed by himself, that the size of the sun is several times that of the earth, and that its distance from the earth is at least 18 times the distance of the moon from the earth. It might thus be reasonable to consider the heavier body to be at the center of the universe. And he may have been impressed by Heraclides' scheme or by Philolaus's central fire.

Aristarchus's contemporaries thought otherwise. They nearly ignored his idea about the universe and thought it a foolish notion held by an otherwise great man. For example, to account for the daily motion of the stars, Aristarchus assumed—as Heraclides had—that the earth spins around its axis. Nevertheless, that idea seemed to contradict common sense, and so it was inconceivable to persons unfamiliar with the laws of gravitation. What would prevent us from flying off a spinning earth? Moreover, without the knowledge of gravitational attraction, why assume that bodies rotate around the sun? It is just as natural to say that the sun moves around the earth as to claim the opposite; only observation and the laws of motion could differentiate between the two.

This drawing, originating in the Middle Ages, shows some of the early schemes of planetary motion, as well as those of Tycho Brahe and Copernicus. In the Ptolemaic system the stationary earth is orbited by the Moon, Mercury, Venus, Sun, Mars, Jupiter, Saturn, and the sphere of the fixed stars. In the earlier, Platonic, system the sun's orbit follows that of the moon with the five planets and the sphere of the fixed stars next in order. Moon, Sun, Mars, Jupiter, Saturn, and the sphere of the fixed stars orbit around the earth, while Mercury and Venus circle the sun. This is Heraclides' innovation, but it is called the Egyptian system because some authors think that Heraclides "imported" this scheme from Egypt. In Tycho's system the earth is orbited by the moon, the sun, and the fixed stars, while all the planets revolve around the sun. This system credited to Heraclides and Tycho Brahe, has Jupiter and Saturn, as well as the moon, sun, and stars, orbiting around the earth, with the remaining planets revolving around the sun. Fig VI: all the planets, including the earth, revolve around the sun, as do the fixed stars. The moon alone, being Earth's satellite, revolves around the earth. This system had also been proposed by Aristarchus of Samos but did not find favor with the Greeks or, for that matter, with medieval thinkers.

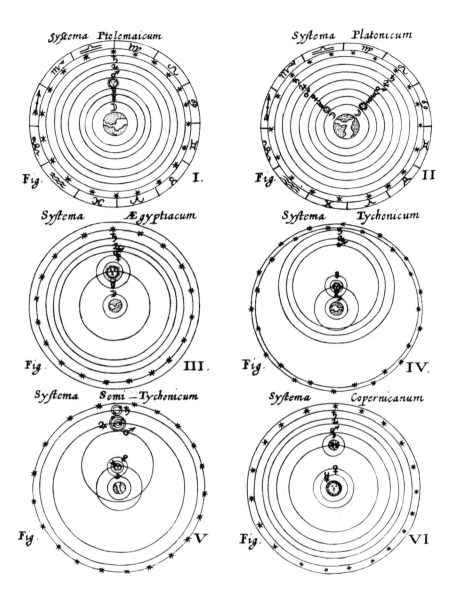

However, even more difficult to understand was the absence of an apparent shift in the position of the fixed stars in the course of the earth's orbit around the sun. If the earth indeed revolves around the sun, then at different points in its orbit a parallax—an apparent displacement of an object owing to a motion of the observer, in this case, the motion of the earth—should be observed (this phenomenon is discussed in the next few pages). That none was found is not surprising. The distances involved are so immense that the crude instruments of the Greeks could not detect any parallax. Aristarchus had guessed the reason and pointed out that the orbit of the earth was so small compared to the size of the celestial sphere that it was like the center of a sphere of infinite radius. But not even Archimedes, who is so well known to us for his keen understanding of the behavior of fluids and mechanics, and who was rather influential, could accept Aristarchus's explanation. The Greek mind could not grasp such concepts as infinity, which they abhorred as "nature abhors a vacuum."

Aristarchus's scheme was laid aside to be forgotten until Copernicus resurrected it eighteen centuries later, after a long and tortuous journey into cycles and epicycles, as well as a confrontation with religious prejudice.

5. Observations and Measurements

It would be wrong to assume that the Greek philosophers only speculated on the nature of the universe without making any observations. In fact, some of the results the Greeks obtained using primitive instruments came quite close to modern observations.

As we have seen, a round earth, postulated by Pythagoras, was confirmed by Aristotle when he pointed out that it cast a circular shadow on the moon during an eclipse; if it were a disk, there would be some occasions when the sunlight striking it edgewise would produce at best an ellipse. Furthermore, northbound travelers observed stars hitherto not visible, while other stars disappeared behind the southern horizon (those going southward observed the opposite effect).

The first fairly accurate determination of the earth's circumference was carried out by Eratosthenes (ca. 276–194 B.C.), librarian of the Alexandrian Museum. The museum was a collection of buildings, whose residents carried out research in astronomy, mathematics, medicine, and the liberal arts. It was thus similar to a modern institute for advanced studies. Eratosthenes, a native of Cyrene–the noted intellectual and cultural center–had already acquired a reputation as a geographer and a man of learning when he was called to Alexandria, where he spent the rest of his life. His method of determining the size of the earth consisted in observing the sun at noon at the summer solstice at two sites: Syene (in the vicinity of modern Aswan) and Alexandria. While the sunlight was directly reflected from a well at Syene, indicating that it was directly overhead, at Alexandria it made an angle with the vertical (as determined by a tower there). Assuming that the rays of the sun at both places were more or less parallel, Eratosthenes then concluded that the angle subtended by the distance between Syene and Alexandria was 7 1/5 degrees, or 1/50 of 360 degrees. Thus, the distance between Syene and Alexandria must also be 1/50 of the earth's circumference (assuming that both places lie on the same meridian). In ancient times it was not simple to measure such large distances, and special "pacers" were employed to go from town to town, counting their steps as they walked along. The royal pacers had found that Syene was about 5,000 stadia from Alexandria, so that the earth's circumference would be 50 times 5,000, or 250,000 stadia. The figure quoted, however, is 252,000 stadia (the extra 2,000 seem to have been added so that 1 degree would equal exactly 700 stadia). Also, it is not certain which of the different stadia

were used. The length of a Greek stadium as used for games would give too large a value, but the stadium that equaled 1/10 mile would give us the nearly perfect value of 25,000 miles, only 100 miles longer than the actual value of 24,900 miles around the equator. In any case, the method employed was ingenious, and the result highly credible.

The relative distances of the moon and the sun, and their sizes, in terms of that of the earth were first estimated by Aristarchus. Although he was known as a mathematician, he was listed by Vitruvius as among the few great men who possessed an equally good knowledge of the various branches of science. (His reputation as a mathematician was so great that he was "forgiven" when he proposed that the sun and not the earth was at the center of the universe.) The results of his astronomical calculations are contained in a scholarly work, translated as *On the Sizes and Distances of the Sun and Moon,* which is an example of painstaking calculations and excellent geometry. He derives 18 propositions starting from the following hypotheses:

1. That the moon receives its light from the sun.

2. That the earth is in the relation of a point and center to the sphere in which the moon moves.

3. That, when the moon appears to us halved, the great circle that divides the dark and the bright portions of the moon is the direction of our eye.

4. That, when the moon appears to us halved, its distance from the sun is then less than a quadrant by 1/30 of a quadrant.

5. That the breadth of the (earth's) shadow is (that) of two moons.

6. That the moon subtends 1/15 part of a sign of the Zodiac.

Some of his hypotheses were not true, and his results were only approximately correct. The first, third, and fourth hypotheses were confirmed by later observers, such as Hipparchus and Ptolemy. As for the second, according to them the earth has the relation of a point and center not to the sphere in which the moon moves but to the sphere of the fixed stars. In the fifth, the breadth of the (earth's) shadow is 2½ moons as in the illustration that describes the distance to and size of the moon, and in the sixth hypothesis the moon subtends 1/16 part of a sign of the Zodiac.

However, his methods were resourceful and used rather often by later researchers.

To find the distance between the sun and the earth,

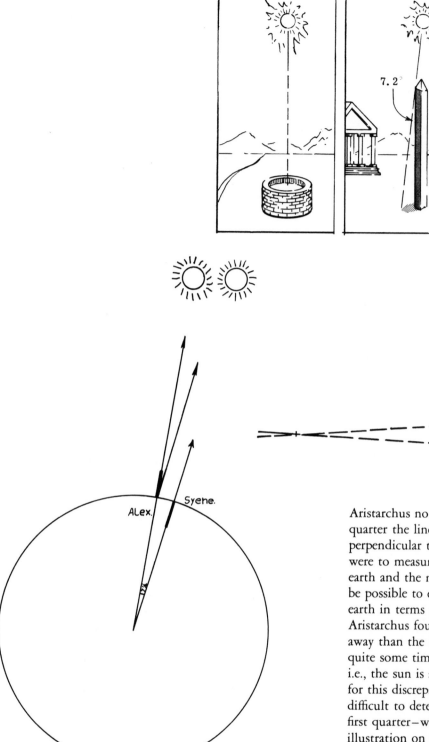

7 1/5° = 1/50th of 360°

Measurement of Earth's size. *A tower and a well:* At noon on June 21 (summer solstice) the sun was directly overhead at Syene (Aswan), but at Alexandria it cast a shadow from a tower.

A difference in angle: Since the sun's rays are parallel to each other (at Syene and Alexandria), the difference of angle is due to the earth's curvature. The distance between Syene and Alexandria forms an angle at the earth's center equal to that formed by the zenith and sun at Alexandria.

A difference in distance: The angle observed was 7⅕ degrees, or 1/50 of 360 degrees. Consequently, the distance between Alexandria and Aswan is also 1/50 of the earth's circumference. (The circumference of a circle is $2\pi r$, where r is the radius and $\pi = 3.14$; hence, if the circumference is known, the radius r can be determined.)

Aristarchus noted that during the moon's first and third quarter the line from the earth to the moon should be perpendicular to a line from the sun to the moon. If one were to measure at that instant the angles between the earth and the moon and the earth and the sun, it would be possible to express the distance of the sun from the earth in terms of the distance of the moon from the earth. Aristarchus found that the sun was about 20 times farther away than the moon. This figure, although accepted for quite some time afterward, is too small by a factor of 20, i.e., the sun is about 400 times farther away. The reason for this discrepancy is twofold. First, it is extremely difficult to determine the exact time the moon is in its first quarter—when EMS (Earth, moon, sun in the illustration on page 52) forms a right angle. Aristarchus had also assumed that the earth was at the center of a circular orbit of the moon (Hypothesis 2). This is not quite correct, since the moon describes a somewhat elliptical orbit. More important, however, Aristarchus found that the sun subtends an angle of 3 degrees at the Earth-moon distance, while, in fact, the angle is only about 1/6 degree. In other words, the lines from the sun to the moon and the earth are practically parallel.

In his treatise Aristarchus mentions that the moon subtends 1/15 part of a sign of the Zodiac (Hypothesis 6). Since each sign of the Zodiac occupies 30 degrees of the

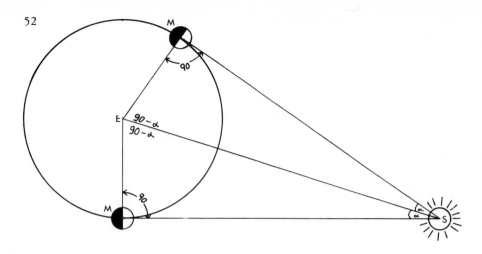

Measurement of distance to the sun. *The method:* The moon appears to be exactly half full (first or third quarter) when the line dividing the light and dark halves is a straight line as viewed from the earth. However, the moon is spherical, and hence the dividing line (lying on a spherical surface) must be curved. It can appear as a straight line only when at the same time the line of sight from the earth to the moon makes a right angle with the line from the moon to the sun, which is assumed not to be infinitely far away. To make the measurement: The angle α at the sun can be determined from the two positions M and M'. When that angle is known, it then becomes possible to express the sun's distance—in terms of the moon's distance from the earth.

DISTANCES AND DIAMETERS OF SUN AND MOON *

	Aristarchus	Hipparchus	Posidonius †	Ptolemy	Actual
Mean distance of moon from Earth	9½	33⅔	26 1/5	29½	30.2
Diameter of moon	0.36	0.33	0.157	0.29	0.27
Mean distance of sun from Earth	180	1,245	6,545	605	11,726
Diameter of sun	6.75	12.3	39.25	5.5	108.9

* All figures are based on the earth's mean diameter, 1,716 geographic miles, e.g., the diameter of the moon (actual) is 0.27 × 1,716 = 463.32 miles.

† Posidonius (ca. 135-51 B.C.) was a successor of Hipparchus and a member of the Stoics, a philosophical school. Among other measurements, he made a fresh determination of the earth's circumference, basing his calculations not on the sun but on the star Canopus. His results were essentially the same as those of Eratosthenes.

celestial sphere (12 signs equal 360 degrees), this would give 2 degrees (1/15 of 30 degrees) for the angular diameter of the moon, which is too large. In his treatise *The Sand-Reckoner* Archimedes mentions, however, that Aristarchus discovered that the sun appeared to be about 1/720 of the Zodiac. Since he also maintains that the sun and the moon subtend the same angle, this would make the angular diameter of the sun (and the moon) ½ degree, which is in fair agreement with present data. Taking this figure and assuming that the moon's orbit is a perfect circle, it then follows that the moon's distance from the earth (by dividing 30.2 by 0.27) is about 112 moon diameters.

It still was necessary to find the moon's radius in relation to the earth's diameter. The earth's diameter was worked out when the distance between Aswan and Alexandria was determined. Aristarchus measured the breadth of the earth's shadow during a lunar eclipse and found it to be twice the moon's diameter (Hypothesis 5), but the figure was revised by Hipparchus to 2½ moon diameters. It takes the moon approximately 28 days, or

672 hours, to make a trip around the earth; 672 hours to travel a distance of 360 degrees, which is equal to 720 moon diameters. It thus takes the moon roughly 1 hour to travel ½ degree, which is its angular diameter. By timing, Hipparchus found that it took the moon 2½ hours to traverse the earth's shadow, which is therefore roughly 2½ moon diameters wide. Furthermore, the earth's shadow is not equal to its diameter but tapers. The shadow cast by the earth narrows exactly by 1 moon's diameter so that the diameter of the earth is not equal to 2½ moon diameters, but greater by 1 moon diameter, viz., equal to 3½ moon diameters.

The advent of trigonometry, a branch of mathematics developed by Hipparchus, made it possible to deal with the relations between the sides and angles of triangles. Distances, both on earth and in space, can be determined by the method of triangulation. A base line is fixed and the object sighted from its end points. The length of the base line and the two angles the object makes with the base line determines the object's distance. A modification of this approach was used by Ptolemy (A.D. 126–161) to

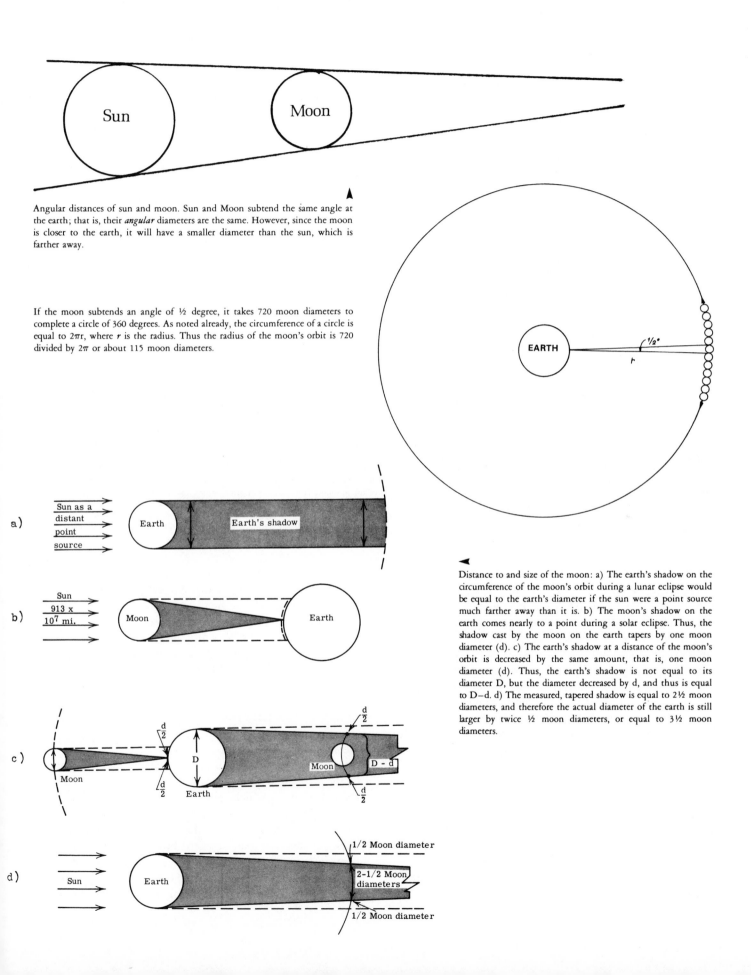

Angular distances of sun and moon. Sun and Moon subtend the same angle at the earth; that is, their *angular* diameters are the same. However, since the moon is closer to the earth, it will have a smaller diameter than the sun, which is farther away.

If the moon subtends an angle of ½ degree, it takes 720 moon diameters to complete a circle of 360 degrees. As noted already, the circumference of a circle is equal to $2\pi r$, where r is the radius. Thus the radius of the moon's orbit is 720 divided by 2π or about 115 moon diameters.

Distance to and size of the moon: a) The earth's shadow on the circumference of the moon's orbit during a lunar eclipse would be equal to the earth's diameter if the sun were a point source much farther away than it is. b) The moon's shadow on the earth comes nearly to a point during a solar eclipse. Thus, the shadow cast by the moon on the earth tapers by one moon diameter (d). c) The earth's shadow at a distance of the moon's orbit is decreased by the same amount, that is, one moon diameter (d). Thus, the earth's shadow is not equal to its diameter D, but the diameter decreased by d, and thus is equal to D–d. d) The measured, tapered shadow is equal to 2½ moon diameters, and therefore the actual diameter of the earth is still larger by twice ½ moon diameters, or equal to 3½ moon diameters.

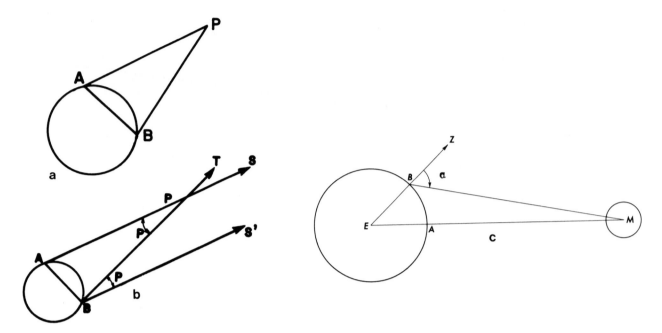

(a) Triangulation. By fixing a base line AB and measuring the angles PAB and PBA, the triangle ABP is completely determined, and hence the unknown distances AP and BP can be found (as well as the angle APB). If the object P is a heavenly body, such as the moon or a planet, then points A and B must be taken as two distant points on the surface of the earth. For objects still farther away, A and B may have to be regarded as positions on the earth's yearly orbital path.

(b) Distant objects. If the object P is far away, the angle P (with the arrows) can be measured directly. From A, P appears in the direction AS, where S is a very remote star. From B, the same star appears along the direction BS', parallel to AS, since it is so far away. On the other hand, P now appears in the direction BT. The angle TBS' = angle APB = angle P, since AS and BS' are parallel. (This method is similar to the method of parallax.)

(c) Ptolemy's method of measuring distance to the moon. An observer at A sees the moon directly above him, while at the same time an observer at B notices that the line BM makes an angle α with the line to the zenith Z. (In practice it is not necessary to have another observer at B, since the rotation of the earth carries us there and we can observe the angle α then. However, one has to correct for the motion of the moon in its orbit during the interval between the two observations.) Knowing the angle α one can then find the angle EBM, since the sum of the two angles is 180 degrees. Also knowing the distance AB, the angle BEA is found (as in the example of Aswan–Alexandria). Furthermore, if BE, the radius of the earth, is known, the triangle EBM is completely determined and hence EM can be found. From this, Ptolemy determined the moon's distance to be 59 times the earth's radius (modern results give about 60 times the earth's radius for the moon's distance). Note that here the base line EB has not been measured directly, but the result has been given in terms of it.

determine the distance to the moon; it is essentially identical to the method used at present. For distant objects, the angle subtending the base line can be measured directly, under the assumption that the object appears to be in the same direction from the two end points. Another way to determine distance is by apparent size. If the size of an object is known and if one can measure the angle it subtends at the position of the observer, the object's distance is simply the ratio of these two quantities. Conversely, if one knows the distance and can measure the angle, the size of the object can be found.

Of great importance in determining large distances is the method of *parallax*. It is known that the direction of an object seems to change as the result of the motion of the observer. Also, the amount of the apparent shift is a direct measure of the distance of the object, the shift being smaller for more distant objects. Because for celestial objects the shift is extremely small and impossible to see with their crude instruments, the Greek philosophers, such as Aristotle, were convinced that the earth did not move.

Next to Aristarchus, it was Hipparchus who furthered the cause of Greek astronomy. Although he belonged to the Alexandrian school, he did most of his work in his native Rhodes, where he set up an observatory of his own. There, surrounded by his simple instruments, he set about making observations at night and carrying out calculations during the day. He was, indeed, "a lover of toil and truth," as Ptolemy describes him, since he set out to compile a star catalogue comprising the 1,080 stars he could see. This catalogue was copied by Ptolemy in his *Almagest* (also known as the *Megiste Syntaxis),* a monumental work on astronomy, in thirteen volumes; it became the basis for all future star catalogues. The places of the stars are described not only according to the constellations in which they are found, but also according to their altitude and azimuth (the equivalent of earthly longitude), as is done today. Hipparchus also classified the stars according to their apparent brightness, dividing them into six categories or magnitudes. These categories remain in use today, although they have been refined with an additional decimal point, and further magnitudes have

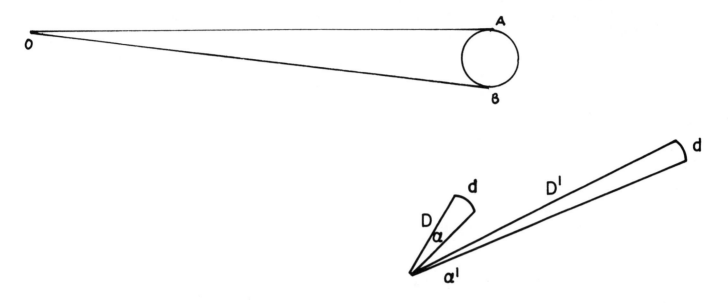

been added for the fainter stars visible only with the help of modern telescopes.

Hipparchus's greatest contribution was his discovery of the precession of the equinoxes. Upon comparing his observations with those of Timocharis, who preceded him by about 150 years, he found that the bright star Spica (Ear of Corn) in the constellation Virgo seemed to have shifted or moved forward by about 2 degrees. Both he and Timocharis apparently measured the position of Spica indirectly by comparing it with the position of the moon, which was eclipsed at the time—and therefore known to be opposite the sun and on the ecliptic, or the circle. To find the distance of the sun from the equinox was an easy matter, since its yearly course had been carefully studied. Thus, from the known position of the sun, that of the moon was found, and so that of Spica deduced. Satisfied that Spica did not move by itself, Hipparchus concluded that its motion was part of an apparent movement of the whole celestial sphere. A similar motion was observed in other stars, whose longitude, measured with respect to the ecliptic, changed slowly during the centuries. Hipparchus

and his successors concluded that at that rate of movement, or precession, the celestial sphere revolved around an axis—at right angles to the ecliptic—once in 26,000 years. (The figure is correct.) It is a small movement, less than 1 degree per century, but it has some far-reaching consequences. In the first place, the star we now call the polestar (i.e., the star pointing due north) was not always the North Star. During the ages, the earth's axis has pointed toward different stars. (The polestar 5,000 years ago was Thuban; 14,000 years from now it will be Vega.) More important, the band of the Zodiac, which lies along the ecliptic, will have shifted about one constellation every 2,000 years. The beginning of spring, the new year of the ancients, is marked by the vernal equinox, where the ecliptic intersects the celestial equator. It is also called the "first point of Aries," since it coincided with the constellation Aries (Ram). At present, the vernal equinox is found in the constellation Pisces (Fish), while at the time of the more ancient civilizations (4300–2100 B.C.), it was in the constellation Taurus (Bull). Astrologers still use the old Zodiacal signs, starting

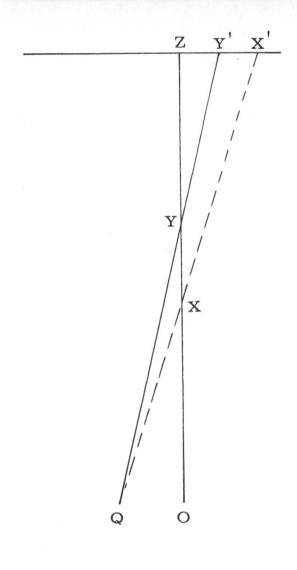
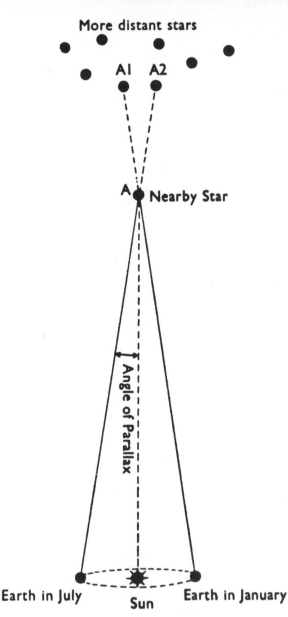

Top

Method of parallax. *As motion of observer:* The two photographs were taken at the same time by two cameras 10 feet apart. Because of parallax the boat is seen in a slightly different position relative to the cliffs in the background. The two cameras represent two positions of a moving observer and the boat the star whose parallax is observed with respect to the fixed stars (here the cliff) in the background.

Above left

Relative size of shift: The shift observed (at position O) depends on the distance of the object. For the nearer star X the shift (at Q) is ZX′ while for the more distant star Y the shift is only ZY′. The farther away the star, the more difficult it is to detect the parallax.

Above right

Parallax of star: As the earth moves around the sun, a nearby star (A) appears to change its position with respect to the more distant stars. In January (at one extreme of the earth's orbit) the star appears to be at A1, while in July (at the opposite point of the orbit), the same star appears to be at A2. The angle between the sun and the earth is the angle of parallax. (If that angle is 1 second of arc—the figure shows an exaggerated situation—the distance from the sun to the star is 1 parsec, derived from *parallax* and *second,* or about 3 light-years.)

Opposite

Stellar magnitudes. As the telescope aperture and the exposure time are increased, smaller and smaller stars appear on the photographic plate. *Top left:* stars of the 12th magnitude (14-inch telescope, 1-minute exposure). *Top right:* stars of the 15th magnitude (60-inch telescope, 1-minute exposure). *Lower left:* stars of the 18th magnitude (60-inch telescope, 27-minute exposure). *Lower right:* stars of the 20th magnitude (60-inch telescope, 4-hour exposure). Note how the apparent size of the star at the bottom of each frame increases with increasing aperture and exposure.

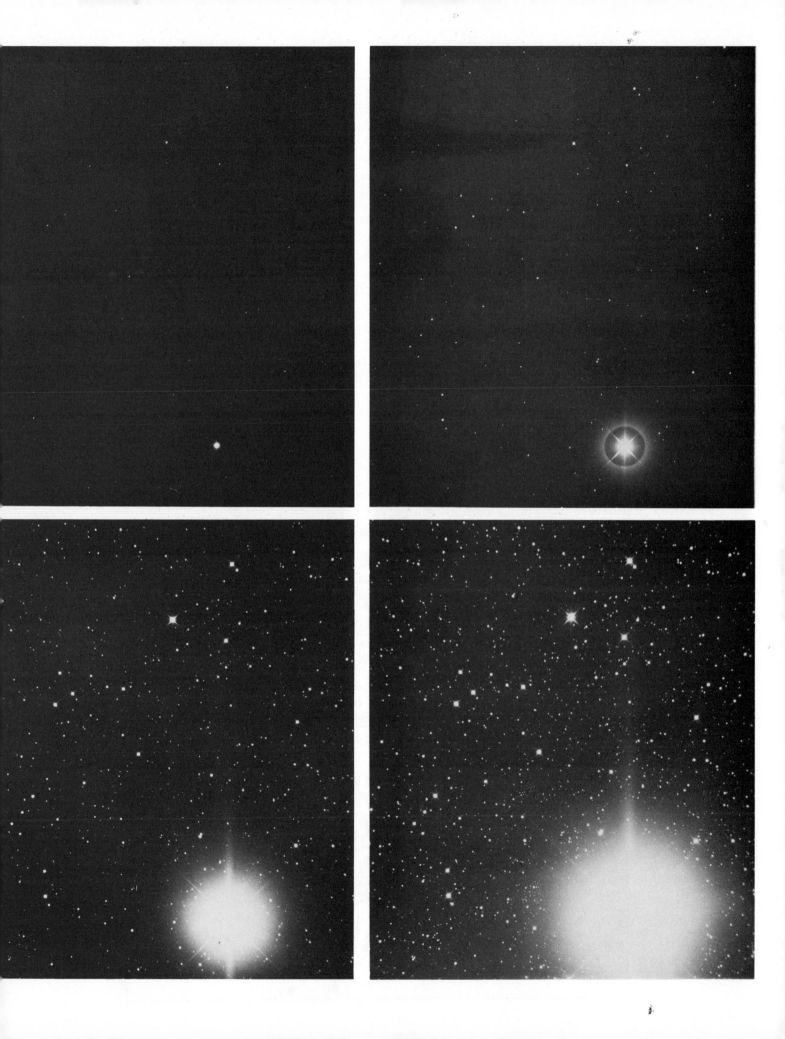

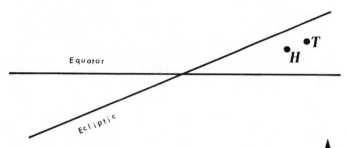

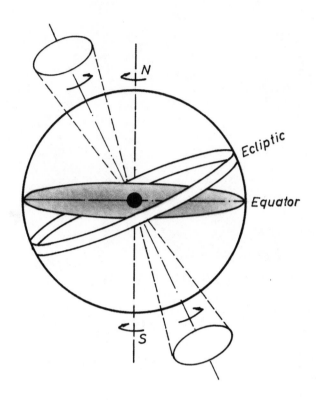

The movement of Spica. T denotes the position of Spica as measured by Timocharis. H denotes the position of Spica as measured by Hipparchus. In the 150 years that elapsed between the two measurements, Spica seems to have moved about 2 degrees along the ecliptic. Hipparchus satisfied himself that both his and Timocharis's measurements were reliable, and that Spica did not really move among the stars, but that its motion is part of a slow apparent movement of the whole heavens—a precession of the equinoxes. The line of the ecliptic crosses the celestial equator at the autumnal equinox.

Precession of the equinoxes. In addition to the daily rotation of the celestial sphere about its axis (NS) perpendicular to the equator, there exists a slow rotation about an axis perpendicular to the ecliptic. However, it is not a simple rotation, but rather like the motion of a top, with the rotation axis moving or precessing along a conical surface (dotted lines). ►

The motion of the polestar during the ages. Owing to the precessional movement of the earth's axis, the point where the earth's axis cuts the star pattern (what we call the North Star, or polestar) moves slowly around a circular path making one revolution in 23,667 years. Radii from the true center of that circle mark off the positions of the polestar during the centuries. For example, in 2170 B.C. it was at α-Draconis in the constellation Draco; in 1900 (and today) it is at α-Ursae Minorii in Ursa Minor. In 3000 it will be still farther along the circle toward Cepheus. It is located by extending a line (shown dotted in the diagram) from the Big Dipper (Ursa Major). Other northern constellations are also drawn in the figure to help fix the position of the precessional circle and polestar.

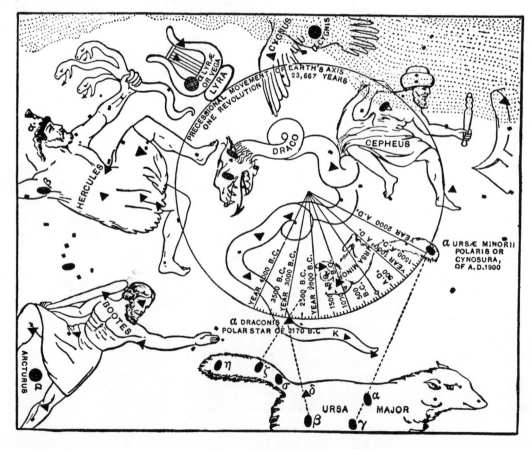

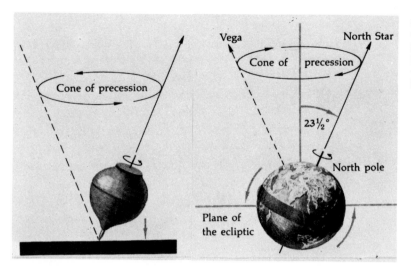

Left: A spinning top that is acted upon by forces such as its own weight, though it tends to topple over, will precess. Its axis describes a conical path. *Right:* Similarly, the pulls of the sun and the moon on the earth produce forces tending to topple the earth's equator toward the ecliptic. As a result, the earth's axis of rotation also sweeps out a cone of precession (whose vertex angle is 23½ degrees).

from Aries at the vernal equinox, and arbitrarily divide the Zodiac belt into twelve signs. These, however, are no longer identical with the constellations they originally represented.

We know that it is not the celestial sphere that rotates or precesses, and that the apparent precession of the equinoxes (or rather the Zodiac) must be due to the motion of the earth itself. Under the different forces acting on the earth (as we will see in Chapter V), it behaves like a top, which is rotating and precessing. It is this precessional motion that is responsible for the precession of the equinoxes, the changing polestar, and the motion of stars like Spica.

6. Epicycles and Eccentrics

Apart from Aristarchus's short-lived heliocentric system, the prevailing point of view held by the Greek astronomers and philosophers was a geocentric (Earth-centered) cosmology. Supported by such authorities as Plato, and especially Aristotle, it became the only accepted view. Nevertheless, Aristotle's many spheres had become cumbersome, and different explanations were sought for the retrograde motion of the planets (Plato's Problem).

It was probably Hipparchus who introduced the notion of epicycles. According to that picture, a planet moves uniformly on a small circle, the epicycle, whose center moves on the circumference of a larger circle at whose center is the earth. The combination of the motion of both these circles then produces a cycloidal pattern of the planet's motion. It looks very much like the loops of Heraclides, described earlier in this chapter, which is the reason why Heraclides is often credited with the invention of epicycles. In his model, Venus and Mercury describe epicycles, if one considers the path of the sun as their deferent. However, in a true epicycle picture the sun's motion is completely independent of that of the planets. Epicycles afforded a far simpler and more accurate representation of the movements of the planets than the homocentric spheres of Eudoxus.

An alternate picture, the movable eccentric, had been proposed by Apollonius (ca. 272–190 B.C.). Here, the planet moves uniformly on the circumference of a circle whose center itself revolves around a fixed earth. This scheme could also account for the retrograde motion of the planets if one adjusted the radius and speed of the inner circle. But this was distasteful to the Greek's sense of symmetry, since it displaced the earth from the exact center of the universe. Only later was it realized that, in fact, the two schemes are completely equivalent. The same type of motion (cycloidal) will be produced for the planets, whether one uses epicycles or an eccentric earth. Of course, a combination for a planet of an epicycle motion and an eccentric motion will produce an even more involved motion that can be made to simulate the actual movement of the planets. As more and more data on the planetary orbits were obtained, it became necessary to add more epicycles and to place the center of the

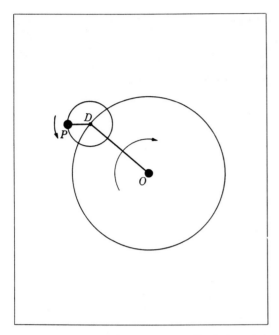

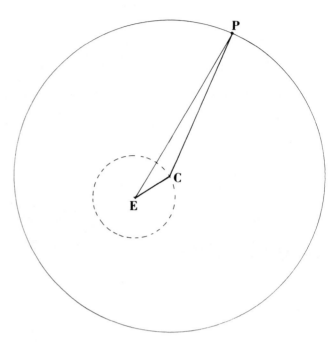

Epicycle motion. The planet P moves uniformly in a circle about D, which itself moves uniformly about the earth (O). The large circle, with its center at O, is called the deferent, while the small circle, with its center at D, is the epicycle. The planets move on epicycles, whereas the sun travels along the deferent.

Eccentric motion of planet. The planet P moves with constant speed along a circle whose center (C) revolves around the earth (E). Adjusting the speeds of the two circles will produce the desired retrograde motion of the planet.

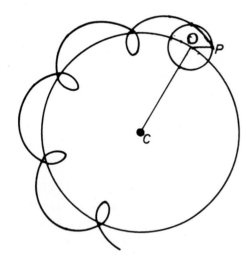

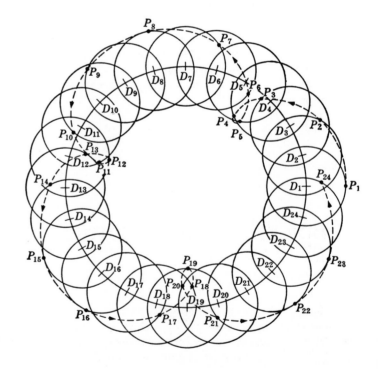

Left: The circular motions of the epicycle and the deferent combine to produce an epicycloid pattern. *Right:* Detailed view of the epicycle motion of a planet. D_1, D_2, D_3, and so on denote the positions of the epicycle's center on the deferent. P_1, P_2, P_3, and so on are the corresponding positions of the planet on the epicycle (a displacement of 15 degrees on D corresponds to a displacement of 50 degrees by the planet on the epicyle), with the dotted curve tracing the epicycloid pattern of the planet. Note the reversals of direction of motion at P_4, P_{11}, and P_{18}.

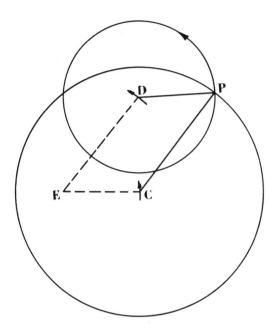

In the eccentric scheme the planet P moves in a circle whose center (C) revolves around the earth (E). In the epicycle scheme the planet (P) moves on an epicycle whose center (D) (the deferent) moves around the earth (E). As long as EC = DP and ED = CP (as seen in the diagram) the two schemes are equivalent.

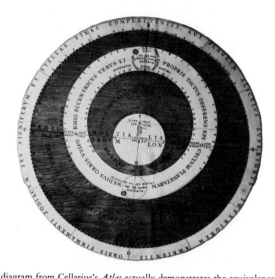

This diagram from Cellarius's *Atlas* actually demonstrates the equivalence of the eccentric and epicycle schemes. The planet is seen to move along an epicycle that touches the eccentric orbit equivalent to it.

►

Claudius Ptolemaeus (126–61), known as Ptolemy, a Greco-Egyptian astronomer who worked in Alexandria. In the Ptolemaic universe, the earth is near the center, and the sun, moon, planets, and stars revolve around it in a pattern of epicycles. This system, embodied in Ptolemy's great work the *Almagest* (the name given it by its Arabic translators) formed the basis of western astronomy throughout the Middle Ages.

planetary orbit itself on the circumference of an epicycle.

The crowning touch was provided by Ptolemy of Alexandria. As mentioned earlier, he is the author of the *Almagest,* which contained a full description of all astronomical knowledge of his time, as well as his own contributions. It provides us with an insight into the thinking of the Greeks and is the source from which most of our knowledge of Greek astronomy is derived. It became the astronomical bible of the Middle Ages. Of particular interest are the introductory chapters dealing with what may be termed the postulates of Ptolemaean astronomy. There, Ptolemy gives very convincing arguments why the earth must be spherical. (It is strange, however, that he omits the eclipse argument of Aristotle—possibly because it seemed too difficult.) He dismisses the idea of a spinning earth as absurd but, instead, assumes the earth to be immovable at the center of the universe, "a point compared with the surrounding star-sphere."

In the Ptolemaic system, each planet is still provided with an epicycle and a deferent, but the center of the great circle, the deferent, is not at the earth's center. Instead, it is situated a short distance from it, at a different point for each planet. The whole system was then assumed to rotate slowly around its common axis to account for the known precession of the equinoxes. In this way it was possible to account for the irregular motions of the planets fairly

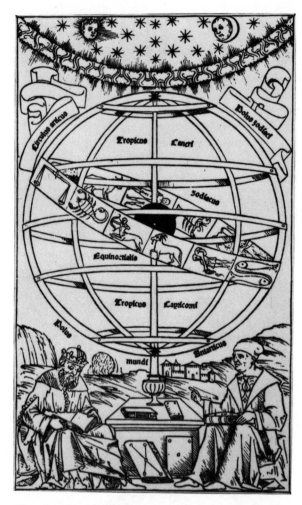

Illustration for the 1496 translation of Ptolemy's *Almagest*. The translator is to the right, Ptolemy to the left. In the center is a replica of an astrolabe, an instrument first introduced by Ptolemy to determine the altitude of the sun or other celestial bodies. It consists of graduated circles and indicates the signs of the Zodiac.

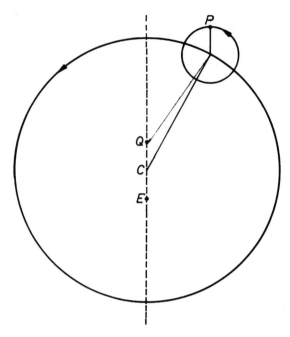

Ptolemy introduced two modifications of the epicycle system. The center of the deferent (C) is no longer the earth's center (E), which is a small distance away. Furthermore, the motion of the deferent is not uniform with respect to its center but with respect to another point (Q), the equant, situated along the line EC and at the same distance from C as C is from E (i.e., EC = CQ).

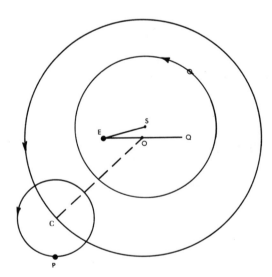

Planetary motion in the Ptolemaic system. Each planet P (only one shown here) moves along an epicycle whose center (C) lies on the deferent. The center of the deferent (O) is halfway between the earth (E) and its corresponding quadrant (Q). The distances QE as well as the radii of the deferent and epicycle are different for each planet, as are the speeds. The sun has no epicycle motion but revolves around S, some distance away from the earth.

accurately and yet to preserve the basic idea of motion along circles with *constant* radii and *constant* speed. For example, Ptolemy was able to explain the irregular motions of Mars more satisfactorily than had been done by Apollonius.

We have already discussed how Ptolemy determined the distance of the moon. Now he discovered that its speed when it was full and when it was new was different from its speed at other times. This effect is known as evection, which means perturbation of the moon's orbital motion due to the attraction of the sun.

Ptolemy accounted for the varying speeds of the moon by placing it, too, on an epicycle. However, while the epicycles of the planets moved in the same direction as the main circles, the epicycle of the moon revolved in the opposite direction. Mercury and Venus, too, had to be treated differently from the other planets. These planets

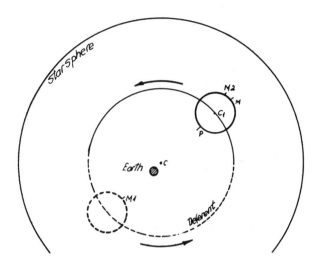

A simplified representation of the Ptolemaic planetary system. The orbit of the sun (D) as well as the deferents of the planets and the moon (A) are assumed to be centered at the earth. Mercury (B) and Venus (C) are on circles closer than the sun, while Mars (E), Jupiter (F), and Saturn (G) are outside. Each planet moves in a small epicycle (X) whose center (Y) lies on the main circle or deferent.

According to Ptolemy, the moon travels on an epicycle (centered at C_1) whose direction is opposite to that of the main circle (centered at C). Their periods are nearly the same, and the moon never reverses direction but only speeds up or slows down. During half a revolution of the epicycle, the moon also has nearly made half a turn on its axis and has reached M_1 where the motion seems to be faster (than at M), as seen from the eccentric earth. Upon completing its epicycle revolution, the moon will not be at M again, but at M^2. Thus, its apogee, the point where it is farthest from the earth, is seen to travel from Taurus toward Gemini. It will be in Taurus again after nine years.

The orbit of Mars, according to Apollonius and Ptolemy. According to Apollonius (top diagram), Mars describes an eccentric orbit with respect to the earth, but it traverses equal distances when measured from its own center. Ptolemy drew an overlapping circle (bottom diagram) near Apollonius's circle, the distance of its center from the earth being twice that of Apollonius. This is, of course, the equant, describing a uniformly moving planet. As seen from the earth, however, the planet describes an extremely eccentric orbit, in fair agreement with observation.

Epicycles of Mercury and Venus in the Ptolemaic system. Both Mercury and Venus travel on their respective epicycles, whose centers always keep in step with the sun's motion. At the top position, Mercury has reached its farthest point from the direct line of the sun and appears as a morning star, while Venus is nearly in the line of the sun and becomes invisible. At the second position, Mercury has reached its farthest point east and is an evening star, while Venus now is a morning star, which is nearly at its farthest position to the right of the sun.

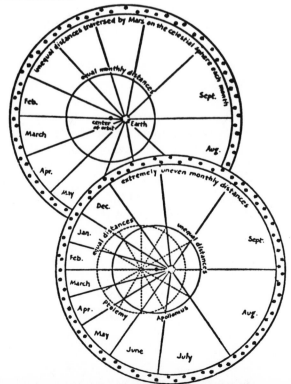

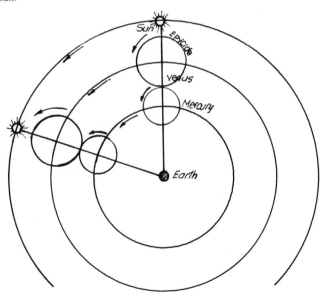

were always close to the sun. For this reason the centers of their epicycles had to remain on the same line with that of the sun from the earth, and their periods on the deferents had to be the same as that of the sun, namely one year. In this way Ptolemy built up his system, adding further epicycles whenever the data warranted it, until he arrived at 40 cycles and epicycles, including the celestial sphere. He seemed to be aware of its complication, for in the last book of the *Almagest,* he proffers some kind of justification. One must remember, he says, that we are not dealing with man-made machines that suffer wear and tear, but with celestial bodies that have no weight, cause no friction, and are eternally unchangeable.

If we are inclined to smile condescendingly at the Greeks and their immediate successors, we must remember that such a model corresponded to the tenor of the time—

as well as the belief, unchallenged for centuries, that the earth was at the center of the universe. Many modern theories were "discovered" when they filled the need for a change in outlook, and not only because they could explain natural phenomena. As a scientific model, the Ptolemaic system worked, since it could account for observed data in much the same way as, say, the atomic theory of Niels Bohr explained the hydrogen spectra. Finally, if we object to the use of an increasing number of cycles and epicycles, we must bear in mind that these simply represent the geometrical way of decomposing a complicated motion into its constituent parts just as modern mathematicians analyze a curve in terms of sines and cosines. Later representations of the Ptolemaic system ignored these "complications" and were content with a simple geocentric picture of the universe.

III · MEDIEVAL ASTRONOMY: AN INTERLUDE

1. Medieval Cosmology

We now come to the "dark ages" in the development of cosmology. From Aristotle and Ptolemy until Copernicus thirteen centuries later, no apparent advance had been made. It even took until A.D. 1000 for the West to accept a round earth and Ptolemy's system. However, to understand the background of the Copernican revolution that was to follow, we should know the important factors of those intervening nonproductive years, which included political and religious considerations affecting the study of cosmology.

Greek science was an intellectual activity restricted to the leisure class of the philosopher and had no relation to the everyday needs of a society supported largely by slave

labor. The decline of the Greco-Roman empire and its mode of life witnessed an equal slide in intellectual endeavor. At the same time the rise of Christianity discouraged any original thinking not in conformity with the official church dogma. But at first, there was no real conflict between the sciences and the early followers of the Apostles, who were content to interpret Scripture symbolically, and even in harmony with pagan teachings. According to Clement of Alexandria (ca. A.D. 200), the Tabernacle and its accoutrements represented the whole world, a view that would in the sixth century dominate the church's thinking. A seven-armed candelabrum, with three branches on either side, corresponded to the motion of the sun among the planets; two golden cherubs were the two hemispheres; and the Ark itself was the realm of thought.

However, in its desire to stamp out any pagan influence, the church soon adopted a rigid interpretation of Scriptures and rejected anything that might even remotely challenge her influence. Lactantius (ca. A.D. 240– ca. 320), writing on the false wisdom of the philosophers, ridiculed the belief in a spherical earth. His arguments were the ancient ones about the impossibility of walking upside down, and places where rain and snow fall upward. Biblical, poetic descriptions of the heavens, which was likened to a tent, were taken literally:

It is He that sitteth upon the circle of the earth, and the inhabitants thereof are as grasshoppers; that stretcheth out the heavens as a curtain, and spreadeth them out as a tent to dwell in.

(Isa. 40:22)

The idea of a spherical earth was abandoned in favor of that of a disk surmounted by a dome-shaped heaven.

In his *Six Orations on the Creation of the World*, Severianus, the Bishop of Gabala (fl. late fourth century–d. after A.D. 408), would brook no world system other than that of Genesis. Nevertheless, he adds his own interpretation, according to which on the first day of Creation the heaven was created–not the one we see but one above it. The whole forms a building with two stories, with a roof in the middle and the waters above it. The lower heaven, the one we see, was created on the second day; it is full of congealed water able to resist the flame of the sun, moon, and stars. This water will also be used to put out their fires on the last day. It is difficult to see how a simple passage–"And God said, Let there be a firmament in the midst of the waters, and let it divide the water from the waters" (Gen. 1:6)–could give rise to such an elaborate scheme. The conception of the motion of the sun is again deduced from verses taken from the Scriptures:

The sun was risen upon the earth when Lot entered into Zoar.
(Gen. 19: 23)

The sun also ariseth, and the sun goeth down, and hasteth to his place where he arose.

(Eccles. 1:5)

Even more dogmatic was the teaching of Cosmas (fl. sixth century), also called Indicopleustus, the Indian navigator. He lived up to his name and traveled widely–in the Mediterranean, the Red Sea, and the Persian Gulf.

A dome-shaped heaven with a flat earth is depicted nineteenth century art nouveau, probably by Camille Flammarion. A traveler putting his head through the vault of the sky sees the machinery that moves the stars.

Although one might think that his journeys should have convinced him that the earth was spherical (he must have reached places near the equator), the opposite is the case. In his twelve-volume work *Topographia Christiana (Christian Topography)*, written in a monastery in Sinai that he had joined as a monk, he endeavored to present a cosmology free of pagan influence. It is again the Tabernacle that forms its basis. A veil separating the inner from the outer part represents the firmament, dividing the universe in two, upper and lower. The table of the shewbread (the twelve loaves of blessed, unleavened bread) placed east to west signifies the earth; the earth is a rectangular plane twice as long as broad–in accordance with the dimensions of the table–and also extends from east to west. The earth is surrounded by the ocean–as is the table by its wave border; a second border signifies a second earth, formerly the seat of man but now uninhabited. From the edges of that second earth four planes are constructed–like the walls of the Tabernacle– which are the walls of the universe. Its roof is a half cylinder resting on the north and south walls, making the whole structure look something like a traveling trunk with a curved lid. The earth, placed at the bottom as the footstool of the Lord, is at a slant in a northwest to southeast direction since the "sun goeth down" (again quoting Eccles. 1:5). As a result, rivers such as the Tigris and Euphrates, flowing south, are much faster than the Nile, flowing north or uphill. (One may wonder why it was permissible for a river to flow uphill while it was absurdly believed that rain could not fall or "flow uphill," at the antipode.)

At the north Cosmas placed a huge conical mountain that hid the sun at night. If the sun passed near the top

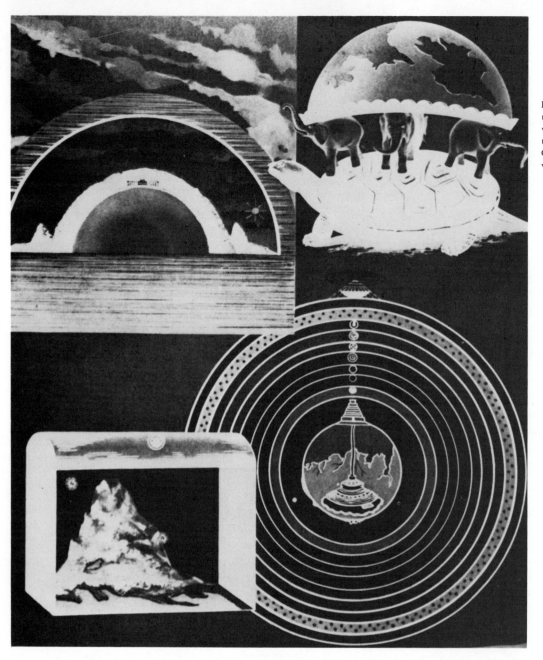

Four different versions of the universe. At the top left is the Babylonian universe with its great vault resting on the oceans. At the top right is the Hindu earth. The rectangular cosmos of Cosmas is at the bottom left, and Dante's universe appears at the bottom right.

of the mountain, it became summer; near the base where it was obscured longer, the days were shorter and it was winter. Naturally, the sun had to be much smaller than the earth to be hidden by it. Cosmas devoted an entire book to prove that this is so, using irrational arguments about the size of shadows at varying places. As for the stars and other heavenly bodies, they were carried around in their orbits by "angles," and also passed behind the mountain, which hid them during the day. His books bristle with passages from the Bible—taken out of context—that were supposed to support his thesis. Numerous quotations from the church fathers, especially Severianus, are included to provide authority. In its frantic endeavor to remove pagan influences, the church revived ideas that had been abandoned eight hundred years earlier. The result was a stagnation of scientific thought that would last for centuries.

Fortunately, not all medieval clergymen, successors to the Greek philosophers, took such an extreme view. Foremost of the enlightened thinkers was Bede (ca. A.D. 673-735), an English monk who was known as the Venerable Bede. In his treatise *De natura rerum (Of Natural Things),* based on Pliny's writings, he states clearly that the earth is spherical. His sun is much larger than the earth, and the planets move around it. The essential features of the Greek cosmos were reinstated, except that Bede still held to the notion of water surrounding the heavens and denied the possibility of habitation in the Southern Hemisphere because it would be inaccessible through the vast ocean.

Although the church did not approve of "heretical" teachings—such as the existence of life on the Southern Hemisphere of the earth—it did not go so far as to threaten proponents of such teachings with bodily harm, as was the case later under the Inquisition. In 748 an Irish ecclesiastic by the name of Fergil, better known as Virgilius of Salzburg, taught the existence "of another world and other people under the earth," i.e., on the other or lower side of the earth. The incident was reported to Pope Zacharias who proposed that a council be set up and Fergil expelled from the church, if indeed he had taught such heresy. Apparently, nothing drastic happened, since Virgil, or Virgilius, became Bishop of Salzburg in 767, a position he held until his death in 784. He was later canonized in 1223 by Pope Gregory XI on account of the miracles wrought by his bones after they had been discovered in 1171. The incident is interesting because it illustrates the philosophical climate of the time. A round earth was frowned upon, but as long as it was at the center of the universe and *fixed,* some kind of compromise could be worked out.

When the eminent scholar, mathematician, and astronomer Gerbert became Pope Sylvester II in 999, the idea of the rotundity of the earth was reinstated. Gerbert had been familiar with the scientific works of Plato, Eratosthenes, and others, and he used celestial and terrestrial globes in his earlier days for his astronomy lectures. He died in 1003, but in those four years he undid the damage done by his predecessors. By 1000 the crest of the Dark Ages had passed, and slowly Greek science was rediscovered. However, while the Greek sphere rotated, the Middle Ages sphere had to remain fixed and stationary.

The records of that period bear witness to the ambiguity of the times. Greek astronomy had been rediscovered, notably the works of Aristotle, but it had to conform to theology. To make the best of two worlds—the present world and the promise of a hereafter—scholars combined fact with fantasy. For example, in 1245 Omons, in an encyclopedic work *Image du monde,* tells of the existence of two heavens, one crystalline and another empyrean. The latter is inhabited by angels whose bodies are formed from the ether, the air of the heavens. The celestial music, undoubtedly that of Pythagoras's spheres, can be heard by children only, since they alone possess the necessary innocence. Omons' source of information is Ptolemy's *Almagest,* although he referred to him as the King of Egypt, apparently confusing him with the kings of the Ptolemy Dynasty centuries earlier.

At first, Aristotle's works were banned, especially when, in the guise of Aristotelian treatises, translations of Arabic speculations reached the West. In 1209 a provincial council in Paris decreed that neither the books on natural philosophy by Aristotle nor commentaries on them could be read there publicly or privately. Gradually, however, the church came to regard Aristotle's teachings as an acceptable discipline and even prescribed the number of

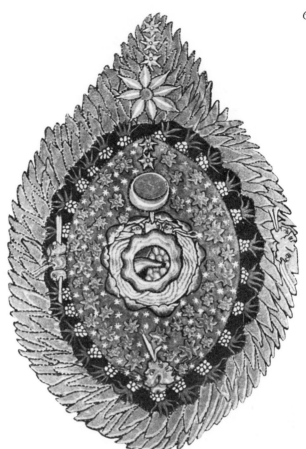

A pear-shaped picture of the universe made by St. Hildegard (1098?–1179). At the center is the earth, surrounded by stars, with the moon above. Beyond the moon are the inner planets (Mercury and Venus), the sun, and finally the outer planets (Mars, Jupiter, and Saturn).

A medieval concept of the universe. The earth (Terra) with its seas (Aqua) is surrounded by spheres of air (Aer) and fire (Putat Ignis). The sun, moon, and stars are in another concentric sphere (Coelum Sydereu), itself surrounded by the outer waters (Aquae Super Coelestes) and a sphere of fire (Empyreum).

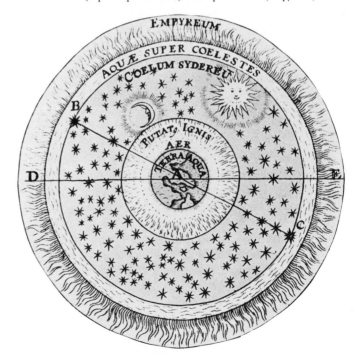

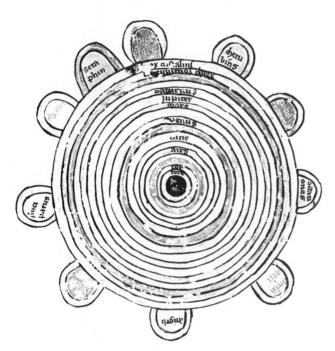

During the fourteenth century several encyclopedic works on the universe became popular. Shown here is a drawing from the *Imago Mundi* of Gautier de Metz (fl. thirteenth century). The earth is at the center surrounded by various concentric spheres of the planets, while the outer pockets are the locations of the angels, archangels, and other celestial inhabitants.

hours that should be devoted to expounding his works. In this, they were greatly aided by the excellent translations of Albertus Magnus (1193–1280) and, especially, his disciple Thomas Aquinas (1225?–74). Aquinas, in particular, contributed greatly to the spread of Greek science, bridging the gap between it and theology, a gap that for some still exists. Revelation, Aquinas firmly believed, was the important source of human knowledge. Nevertheless, for him human reasoning was another way of finding truth, and both were ultimately derived from the same source. Therefore, his thinking resolved contradictions between science and theological doctrine or, at least, made such contradictions less important. Aristotelian philosophy became firmly established, and as happens frequently in cases where a formerly unacceptable theory becomes dogma, any criticism of it was considered heresy. Nevertheless, a heretic did appear in the person of the Franciscan monk Roger Bacon (1214?–94).

Bacon was not satisfied with accepting authority blindly and advocated independent investigation, both by experiments and mathematical methods. (In one story, no doubt apocryphal, scholastics wrote learned papers on the number of teeth in a horse's mouth without bothering to look and count them.) In his *Opus Majus* Bacon exhibits a thorough understanding of the works of Ptolemy, whom he follows, though not verbatim. For Bacon the earth is only an insignificant speck in the vast expanse of the universe, albeit at its center. He admonished the church fathers to make a thorough study of science and to give up a literal interpretation of the Bible, from which he quoted several passages in obvious contradiction to known facts. No wonder his words were not taken kindly by the clergy; he was accused of witchcraft and thrown into jail for ten years, and his work lay forgotten. It took four hundred years before it was finally printed.

Apart from Bacon, and to some extent Thomas Aquinas, the prevalent ideas of the day were those of Aristotle, freely interspersed with theological reasoning. This is best illustrated by the cosmology of Dante Alighieri (1265–1321), given in his magnificent *Divine Comedy*. In that work, and others, Dante demonstrated his familiarity with Aristotle, Aquinas, and Pliny.

And this is where matters stood at the end of the thirteenth century. The learned doctors had not added one iota to the sum total of knowledge of the universe. They had talked and argued but discovered no new facts. All they had achieved—and this may not be such a small feat considering the early opposition of the church—was the spreading of the works and commentaries of Aristotle. It would be left to the Oriental astronomers to make further advances and to bring additional ideas to the West to prepare it for the great revolution that was to follow.

2. Astrology

While the study of astronomy was frowned upon, astrology flourished. In ancient Babylon the two were interconnected, and it was the task of the priests to interpret celestial events, such as eclipses, in relation to the state and the king. This aspect of astrology is commonly referred to as mundane astrology and is practiced even today, such as the foretelling of natural disasters.

The early Greeks had no time for astrology; they were mainly concerned with observations and cosmology. However, there were exceptions. In 250 B.C. the Babylonian astrologer Berosus established a school of astrology in the Greek island of Cos. (The particular topography of Greece with its many islands was ideal for the establishment of different schools, none of which had to have any relation with another.) Popular manuals began to appear and astrology became the vogue. It was not the mundane astrology of the Babylonians but genethliacal astrology, which concerns itself with the fate of individuals. It is not surprising that this form of astrology caught on immediately, for who does not want to know what the future has in store for him. Ptolemy asserted that foreknowledge can reconcile one to one's fate, as well as equip one to avoid dangers. Man could take precautions against his temperament just as he could against the weather.

The Romans, who by nature were superstitious and held strong beliefs in various omens, took to astrology like fish to water. The new form of forecasting, supposedly based on "scientific" rules and close observation, was more appealing to them than their more traditional ways of fortune-telling. The emperor Augustus (63 B.C.– A.D. 14), for example, was so impressed by fortune-telling that he had a coin minted depicting Capricorn, the Zodiac sign of his birth.

About this time a strange new cult, that of Hermes Trismegistus (Thrice-Greatest Hermes) came from Egypt, which had become part of the Roman Empire in 30 B.C. Hermes, the Greek name for Mercury, was the fictitious name of the author of a lengthy treatise (it is said that Hermes wrote twenty thousand books) combining astrology with witchcraft. Hermes talks about "correspondences" between celestial and earthly objects and events. The sun and the moon correspond to man's eyes (the right being related to the sun and the left to the moon), and each of the twelve signs of the Zodiac govern a part of his body, from the Ram at the head to the Fishes at his feet. This is the origin of the *Zodiacal Man,* which is still in use today.

Of course, the church took a dim view of astrology, including natural astrology, now known as astronomy. One of the fiercest and most powerful opponents of the astrologers was St. Augustine (354–430). In his *City of God* he demands that all those who "hold that the stars manage our actions or passions for good or evil have to be silenced, since this opinion flatly excludes the deity."

However, the opposition of the church was not motivated by the irrationality of astrology. Astrology was held to be immoral, as science was immoral. Yet the clerics could not stem the tide for long. Astrology with its various ramifications of fortune-telling and magic again became respectable and was even finally employed by the church itself. Chairs of astrology were established at the University of Rome by Pope Leo X (1475–1521) and the then-new University of Oxford. Oxford's first chancellor, Robert Grosseteste (ca. 1175–1253), is said to have noted that no human activity, whether it be the planting of vegetables or the practicing of alchemy, could dispense with the advice of the astrologer.

Astrology soon pervaded nearly all human endeavors. Medicine was practiced according to the stars, and medicinal herbs could be gathered and administered only at certain propitious times. The Dominican Albertus Magnus was a great believer in the magical powers of herbs. In his *Naturalia* he relates the magical and

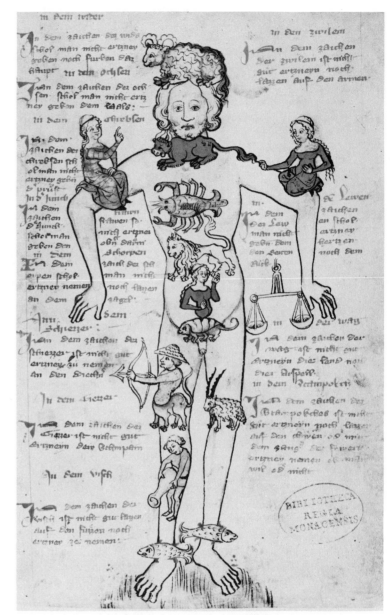

According to astrological belief, each sign of the Zodiac governs a particular part of the human body. In this illustration from a fourteenth-century German astrological manuscript, the human body is shown together with the figures of the Zodiac situated at the parts of the body they govern. They are Aries: head and face; Taurus: neck and throat; Gemini: arms and shoulders; Cancer: breast, stomach, and lungs; Leo: heart and back; Virgo: belly and guts; Libra: hips; Scorpio: bladder and sexual organs; Sagittarius: thighs; Capricorn: knees; Aquarius: legs; Pisces: feet.

medicinal properties of herbs to planetary and Zodiacal influences. The astrologer replaced the priest of old to advise kings and subjects alike. Even political treaties could be signed only at times determined by astrologers. Guido Bonatti, one of the most famous astrologers of the thirteenth century, is said to have climbed a high church tower at the beginning of a battle. When he gave the

Two pages from the *Naturalia* by Albertus Magnus. On the left is the martagon lily "in sympathy" with Saturn; at the right chicory is connected with the sun.

signal, bells were rung and only then could the battle start. He also held that astrologers could predict such trivial matters as the menu at a forthcoming dinner, affording a guest the possibility of either accepting or declining, according to his taste.

One might think that with the onset of the period of enlightenment, the Renaissance, astrology became discredited. The opposite was the case. True, strong opposing voices were raised, such as that of the Italian humanist Pico della Mirandola (1463–94), who prepared a scathing attack on astrology. He cited examples from his own experience, where astrologers predicted a good life, while one disaster after another had struck his family. He even went so far as to check the weather against astrological predictions and found that out of one hundred thirty days, the predictions were correct for no more than six. This created quite a sensation, since nobody had cared or bothered to carry out any tests before. However, he died suddenly at the age of thirty-one at the precise moment when Mars entered the House of Death.

Over and over Mirandola had maintained that the two branches of astrology, natural and genethliacal, must be kept separate. He accepted the former as a respectable branch of philosophy but maintained that the astronomer could not believe in wild speculations not based on evidence or reason. This distinction was certainly not observed by such astronomers as Regiomontanus, Johann Müller (1436–76), or by his famous successors Copernicus (1473–1543), Tycho Brahe (1546–1601), or even Johannes Kepler (1571–1630). It is not clear whether they actually believed in their own predictions or made them only to please their patrons and to earn a living. However, we will see in the following chapter that Kepler combined a rare genius for the analytical with mystic superstitions.

During this time in 1493 a work was published in Paris that brought "practical" astrology to the general literate public. It was *The Kalendar and Compost of Shepherds.* There, in the words of shepherds, considered by tradition the guardians of wisdom, were expressed all the astrological lore and traditions known at that time. The shepherds, in their infinite wisdom, gave advice on matters close to their experience, not only when to plow, to reap, or to sow, but also when to conduct business in general. In addition, the *Kalendar* contained medical advice and the relation of the planets and Zodiac to the human body. However, it was Paracelsus, a Swiss physician whose real name was Theophrastus Bombastus von Hohenheim (1493?–1541), who introduced astrological symbolism into medicine. Not only were the different parts of the body controlled by the stars, but the various sections of the brain came under the influence of the planets. Palmistry, the art of hand reading, also had its origin in the alleged influence of the planets.

Another famous astrologer of the Middle Ages was Nostradamus (Michel de Notredame, 1503–66), who used

Among the best-known astrological works of the Middle Ages was *The Kalendar and Compost of Shepherds*. This woodcut from a 1527 edition of the *Kalendar* shows the shearing of sheep under the influence of the month's Zodiac signs Gemini and Cancer.

anagrams and other mystic devices to confuse his readers and render his predictions as ambiguous as possible. In his *Complete Prophecies* he predicts a world revolution to be preceded by a world war in the "year 1999 and 7 months." It is said that he predicted the French Revolution, but few of his other predictions came true, and we shall have to see about "1999 and 7 months."

Undoubtedly, one of the reasons why astrology was held in such high esteem during the fifteenth and sixteenth centuries was the fact that it was endorsed and practiced by men of high repute, such as Dr. John Dee (1527–1608), who was no less than the private astrologer of Queen Elizabeth. The invention of the telescope and, in particular, the discovery of planets beyond Saturn seriously jeopardized the "ancient art." Despite serious efforts to adjust to the new discoveries and incorporate them into the astrological systems, many people realized the arbitrariness of the alleged connections between stars and man. As a result, astrology lost its previous status but not its appeal.

Unscrupulous proponents of astrology continued to take advantage of the public's desire to know its future, and even today there are many popular publications that include a horoscope *(hora* meaning "hour" and *skopos* meaning "observer"). On the other hand, serious astrologers–banded into various societies such as the American Federation of Astrologers–have been looking for a scientific basis for astrology. Statistical studies, such as those carried out by C. G. Jung, proved inconclusive as one might expect, although Jung cautiously suggested that it might just be conceivable that there is a causal connection between the planetary aspects and the psychophysiological disposition. It is easy to blame the stars for one's fault or fate, but as Shakespeare's Cassius so eloquently noted:

> Men at some time are masters of their fates.
> The fault, dear Brutus, is not in our stars,
> But in ourselves, that we are underlings.
>
> *(Julius Caesar*, 1.2, 139–41)

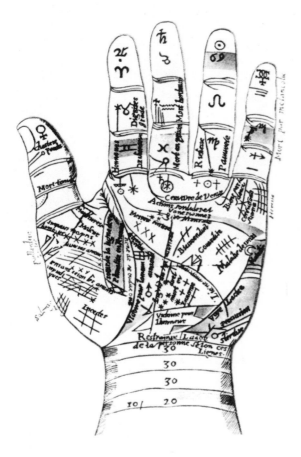

An astrological chart showing the symbols of the planets and signs of the Zodiac, as well as the various lines–such as the Lifeline and the Heart line–in the hand. Palmistry, or hand reading, is still practiced today.

An illustration from a fifteenth-century French text shows the relationship of sun, moon, and planets to the signs of the Zodiac. A personification of the planet is shown linked to the sign (or signs) it rules: Saturn–Capricorn and Aquarius; Jupiter–Sagittarius and Pisces; Mars–Aries and Scorpio; Venus–Taurus and Libra; Mercury–Gemini and Virgo. Not shown linked are sun–Leo; moon–Cancer; Uranus–Aquarius; Neptune–Pisces; Pluto–Scorpio. With the discovery of the outer planets Uranus, Neptune, and Pluto, astrologers were hard-pressed to include them in their schemes and arbitrarily associated them with existing signs.

An illustration from an Italian manuscript depicting Jupiter's influence on man. Jupiter is seen as a young man with his signs Pisces and Sagittarius. At the bottom, an apothecary serves a customer, an alchemist sieves precious metals, and a mathematician does his calculations–occupations thought to be under the influence of Jupiter; anyone born under these signs would be considered particularly well suited to these activities.

A fifteenth-century allegorical picture of Saturn and some of the people associated with the planet. Saturn, depicted as a horseman, rides in the sky above his two signs, Capricorn and Aquarius. His influence is considered to be malignant, causing misfortune, disease, and death–indicated by the various figures. The occupations shown are a farmer (plowing), a gardener (digging), and a tanner (skinning a horse), all considered inferior.

THE SIGNS OF THE ZODIAC				THE PLANETS AND THEIR SYMBOLS			
Aries	♈	Libra	♎	Sun	☉	Jupiter	♃
Taurus	♉	Scorpio	♏	Earth	●	Saturn	♄
Gemini	♊	Sagittarius	♐	Moon	☽	Uranus	♅
Cancer	♋	Capricorn	♑	Mercury	☿	Neptune	♆
Leo	♌	Aquarius	♒	Venus	♀	Pluto	♇
Virgo	♍	Pisces	♓	Mars	♂		

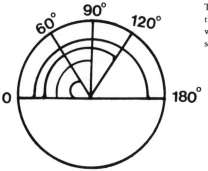

The positions of the planets relative to each other, or aspects, are defined according to the angles they make with each other. Conjunction equals zero degrees (or small angle); at sextile two planets would be 60 degrees apart; square, 90 degrees; trine, 120 degrees; opposition, 180 degrees. Trine and sextile are favorable aspects, opposition and square are "difficult," and conjunction is neutral.

A drawing from Cellarius's *Atlas,* showing an Earth-centered universe and the band of the Zodiac. The lines connecting the various signs indicate some of the major aspects—square, sextile, and trine.

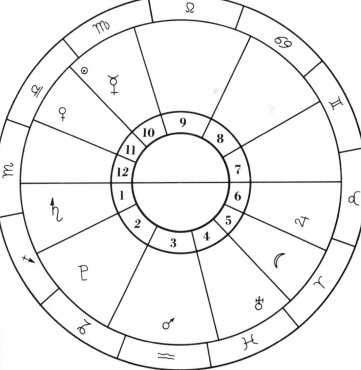

A sample horoscope for a person born under the sign of Virgo. The outer ring gives the signs of the Zodiac, which are so arranged that the ascendant, the degree of the ecliptic rising above the eastern horizon, is opposite the first house. The houses from one to twelve, are indicated by the inner circle. The positions of the planets (as well as the sun and moon), here indicated by their symbols, are then found from known tables, or are calculated, and entered in the horoscope. Predictions are then based on the assumed characteristics of the Zodiac signs, the planets, and their relative positions.

3. Arab Astronomy

While the study of astronomy was for all practical purposes nonexistent in Europe, it flourished in the East under the comparative tolerance of early Islam. In the middle of the seventh century an immense Arabian empire arose, spreading eastward as far as India and westward to Spain. It was ruled by a series of caliphs, successors to Muhammad (ca. 570–632), theoretically divine vice-regents, spiritual and temporal. It is told that one day a scholar from India appeared at the court of Caliph al-Mansūr (754–75), laying before him a book that dealt with the stars and the foretelling of eclipses. Al-Mansūr was so impressed with it that he had it translated into Arabic, and it became the standard treatise of astronomy for half a century. However, it was probably a copy of the *Brahma-sphuta-siddhānta (The Opening of the Universe)* that the Indian astronomer presented to al-Mansūr. After the conquests of Alexander the Great (356–323 B.C.) and later Macedonian rulers of Bactria, Greek science had spread also to India. In particular, under the Gupta Dynasty in Hindustan (ca. A.D. 300–600), there arose a literature of mathematical and astronomical writings known as siddhāntas. Among these was the *Brahma-sphuta-siddhānta,* which contained a fair representation of the Greek view of the universe with its cycles and epicycles.

Al-Mansūr's son, Hārūn ar-Rasīd (765–809), the famous hero of *The Thousand and One Nights (The Arabian Nights Entertainment),* continued the collection and translation of Greek manuscripts. It was he who ordered the translation of Ptolemy's great work, the *Megiste Syntaxis (Great System),* which then became known as the *Almagest (Al-magest* in Arabic).

However, it was his son and successor, al-Ma'mūn (786–833) who promoted the study of astronomy and the work of the Baghdad Observatory, the first observatory of its kind. This encouragement of astronomy was a welcome contrast to the oppression and theological dogmas of the Western world at that time. The caliphs were interested in promoting astronomy for several reasons, an important one being the lunar calendar, for which they needed exact determinations of the new moon, lunar eclipses, and other celestial events. The study of astrology, too, although not actually encouraged, was not neglected. The caliphs, like their Western counterparts, were not insensitive to predictions of good fortune, and they paid well for the service.

Islamic astronomy was not fettered by the restrictions that a rigid—and erroneous—interpretation of the Bible imposed upon Western astronomers. Conversely, the *Quran,* the sacred book of Islam that was supposedly revealed to Muhammad by Allah, seemed to encourage a study of astronomy:

Verily, in the creation of the heavens and of the earth, and in the succession of the night and of the day, are marvels and signs for men of understanding heart.

(III:187)

It is He who has appointed the sun for brightness, and the moon for light, and has ordained her stations that you may learn the number of years and the reckoning of time.

(X:5)

Al-Ma'mūn himself was well versed in astronomy and was not merely content with collecting and translating its works. He had his astronomers repeat Ptolemy's measurements and, in particular, the length of a degree of latitude. It is said that observers went as far north and south from a given point until they found that the latitude had changed by 1 degree. This they calculated at 56⅔ Arabic miles (each equal to 4,000 black ells). (Assuming that a black ell corresponds to a Babylonian one, this would make the circumference of the earth 26,500 miles instead of the accepted value of roughly 25,000 miles.) Disregarding their accuracy, the nature of their measurements conclusively demonstrates that they did not question that the earth was spherical.

One of the most famous astronomers of the Baghdad Observatory was Abû'l Abbas Ahmad ibn Muhammad ibn Kathir al Farghânî, better known as Alfraganus (ca. 840). His *Elements of Astronomy* became the earliest work in its specialty known in the West. But for practical purposes, it was no more than a popular and abridged edition of Ptolemy's *Almagest.* Unfortunately, its only original contribution—an estimate of planetary distances—was wrong. Alfraganus argued that there was just sufficient space between the various planetary spheres to allow their epicycles to pass one another. He was led to that conclusion by the fact that Ptolemy's least distance of the sun was 1,160 Earth radii, a completely wrong figure, while the greatest distance of Venus (i.e., the sum of the radii of the deferent *and* the epicycle) was 1,150 Earth radii calculated by this method. Proceeding in this manner, he then arrived at the planetary distances that, of course, are much too small. Although the measuring instruments of the Arabs were far superior to those of the Greeks, their results did not differ much from Ptolemy's erroneous estimates. Nevertheless, that observations were carried out shows the advanced thinking, for its time, of Islamic astronomy.

At about the same time Ibn Yûnis (d. 1009), working in Cairo, published a set of astronomical tables, the *Hakemite Tables,* which he named in honor of his patron, Caliph al Hâkim, the customary—and rewarding—thing to do; often such a tribute became the only remaining

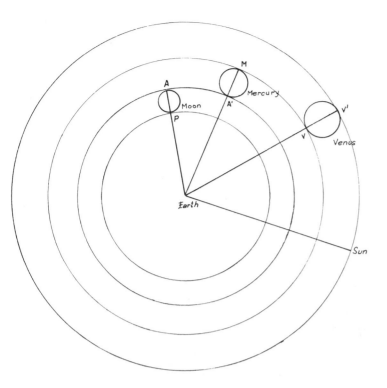

Alfraganus estimated the planetary distances by assuming that the epicycles of the planets just fit between the respective deferents. If the greatest distance of the moon from the earth EA (sum of AP and PE) is equal to the least distance of Mercury EA', one can find its largest distance EM, since the ratio EA' to A'M is known. This distance is then assumed to be equal to the smallest distance of Venus EV. Adding to it VV' (known from the ratio VV' to EV) gives ES, the distance of the sun. It was the coincidence of these distances that led Alfraganus to his results, and in this fashion he obtained the remaining planetary distances.

contribution of the reigning monarch. In 1252 on the day of his ascension to the throne of Spain, King Alfonso X (1221–1284) had published the *Alphonsine Tables,* which were a bigger and better edition of previously published tables in Toledo known as the *Toledan Tables.* Alfonso had followed the example of the caliphs and collected at his court a number of prominent Christian and Jewish astronomers, whom he had set to work preparing the tables. He did not seem to have been too impressed by the system of Ptolemy, since he has been quoted as saying that he would have given God some good advice had He consulted him upon creating the world. Nevertheless, he did not come up with anything better, as is evidenced by the *Libros del Saber de Astronomia del Rey D. Alfonso X de Castella,* an encyclopedic work on astronomy. The planetary theory follows Ptolemy, except that the center of the equant is placed midway between the earth and the center of the deferent, while Ptolemy places the center of the deferent midway between the earth and the equant. This difference results in a curious figure: the deferent of Mercury takes the form of an ellipse, the curve described by the center of the epicycle of Mercury in Ptolemy's picture. A dot at the center, representing Ptolemy's small circle, has often been identified with the sun, crediting Alfonso's astronomers with having anticipated Copernicus's great discovery (which is covered in the next chapter).

When Hulagu Khan (1217–65), a grandson of the Mongol conqueror Genghis Khan, captured Baghdad in 1258, the caliphate of Baghdad had grown weak and was finally destroyed. With it went the Baghdad school. However, the khan took the advice of his vizier, Nasîr al Dîn al Tûsî (1201–74), an outstanding astronomer he had taken into his service as political adviser a few years

Nasîr al Dîn al Tûsî (1201–74) was one of the best-known astronomers in Islam. He was responsible for directing the work at the Maragheh Observatory, one of the largest and best equipped. Hulagu Khan was at first skeptical of spending the money necessary for its construction. However, Nasîr al Dîn pointed out to him that it would be necessary in order to make valid astrological predictions. Suppose, he said, the khan ordered someone to drop a large object from a high place. It would produce a very loud noise and frighten all people standing nearby who were not aware that the object was to be dropped. Only you and the person carrying out the order would remain calm, for you both knew what was going to happen. Similarly, only someone familiar with the motion of the stars could predict what would happen.

previously, and founded a magnificent observatory at Maragheh in the northwest of Persia (Iran). Here, a number of astronomers worked under the supervision of Nasîr al Dîn with instruments carefully constructed and of remarkable size—probably better than any in Europe— which would be surpassed only by those constructed by Tycho Brahe in the sixteenth century.

Arab astronomers taking down data and compiling astronomical tables such as the *Hakemite Tables* and later editions.

Nasîr al Dîn himself developed a remarkable planetary system, which he believed to be more acceptable than eccentrics and epicycles. It consisted of a system of "guiding spheres" prescribing the orbit of the planet.

A somewhat similar system was introduced by al Jagmini, who probably lived during the thirteenth or fourteenth century. The sun (or planet) is constrained to move between two eccentric spheres that themselves are forced to move along other eccentric spheres. Neither of these and other valiant efforts to replace Ptolemy's system were successful for the simple reason that his was the best of the earth-centered universes. As long as his hypothesis remained unshaken, any attempt to improve on his mathematical models, which were perfect, was doomed to fail. What was needed was a radical change of the fundamental idea. Although Arab astronomers were aware of the rotation of the earth, as evidenced by their familiarity with Greek writings, it obviously did not occur to them that the earth itself might be revolving; if it did, it does not appear in their writings.

The observatory at Maragheh was short-lived and came to an end with the death of its founder, Nasîr al Dîn, and its patron, the khan. It took nearly one hundred fifty years for another great astronomical institution to rise in Islam.

An armillary sphere, one of the most important astronomical instruments, first introduced by the Greeks (Hipparchus) and later vastly improved by the Arabs. It consisted of six circles, the largest representing the meridian, placed on a stand. On the meridian's inner rim, pivoted at two points (the North and South Poles), moved another slightly smaller circle representing the ecliptic. Two further circles, similarly pivoted, gave the latitude and longitude, and finally the last circle was furnished with two sights at opposite ends. By aligning the rings with various celestial bodies one could measure the tilt of the earth's axis and the position of the sun and calculate the time of day and year.

About 1420 Ulūgh Beg (1394–1449), the ruler and grandson of the Tartar Tamerlane—the savage and terrible conqueror—founded an observatory at Samarkand (the present Russian Turkestan). Ulūgh Beg must have been a remarkable person. It was said of him that he knew the Quran by heart and at suitable occasions cited elegant passages. He was well versed in jurisprudence and acquainted with logic. His mastery of mathematics and astronomy was so great that he could carry out intricate

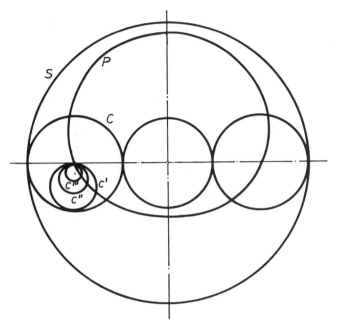

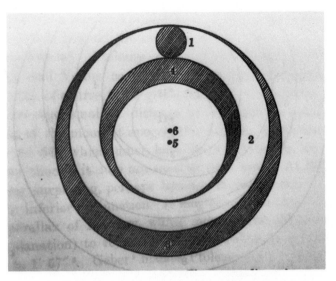

Astronomy of al Jagmini. *Spheres of the sun:* The sun is a solid spherical body (1) fitting between two eccentric spherical surfaces (3 and 4), which touch two other surfaces (2 and 6), in the common center of which the earth (5) is situated, and which between them enclose an "intersphere," named by al Jagmini al-mumattal, or the equably turning sphere, which has the same motion from west to east as the fixed stars.

Guiding spheres of Nasîr al Dîn. He discovered that a point of contact of two circles, one touching the other internally, will move along the diameter of the larger circle, provided that the diameter of the larger circle is twice that of the inner smaller circle and that the speed of the inner circle is twice that of the outer one, both moving in opposite directions. Using this result, he constructed a system of spheres (or circles) prescribing the orbit of the planet. A circle C is constrained to move along the inside of a rotating sphere S concentric with the world. Another circle C′ (of half the diameter of C) moves with opposite velocity within C. Contained in C′ are two further circles C″ and C‴ (each half the diameter of the previous one but moving at twice its speed). As a result, the planet carried on the circumference of the smallest circle C‴ (corresponding to the epicycle of Ptolemy) will describe an orbit resembling an eccentric circle P. (The remaining two circles are introduced to keep the system steady.)

calculations in his head while riding horseback. He had a genuine interest in science, and one may wonder how a person of his stature—he was king and must have had many administrative duties—found the time and devotion to carry out scientific work. Like most astronomers of his time, he was also interested in astrology, and it is said that he read in the stars that he would die by the hand of his son. (Although the father was a good-natured and modest person, to avoid this fate he had his son exiled; this act offended the son so much that he had his father murdered. And although there were other factors that contributed to their strained relations, there may be some truth to the story that astrology was a factor in their initial distrust of each other.)

The Samarkand Observatory was one of the most if not *the* most important in Islam. Its dominant feature was a central section that housed the giant quadrant. In this

The Qibla is a kind of compass or guide showing the way to Mecca. It is fairly recent, dating from the nineteenth century. The compass at the top is a later addition.

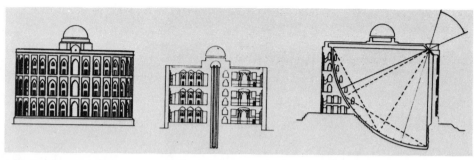

Observatory at Samarkand. At the left is a general view of the observatory with its central dome. The central diagram shows the size and position of the great meridian arc. It is said that it was more than 30 meters above ground level and several meters below ground. At the right is a full view of the meridian arc, or quadrant, on which the longitudes of stars could be read with considerable accuracy.

◄

Next to Nasîr al Dîn, Ulûgh Beg (1394–1449) was the most prominent astronomer of Islam and an outstanding patron of science. He is shown at the right in this reproduction from a Persian manuscript of the seventeenth century.

Taqî al Dîn, director of the Istanbul Observatory in the sixteenth century, and some members of his staff in front of the main building of the observatory.

respect it resembled modern observatories where one giant instrument—the telescope—occupies a commanding position and overshadows other instruments. The most important work carried out by Ulûgh Beg at his observatory was the preparation of a star catalogue, the first since Ptolemy and probably the first independent one after Hipparchus. The positions of the stars were noted with unusual precision, their latitudes and longitudes being recorded in minutes as well as degrees of arc. But like the observatory at Maragheh, it fell into disuse with the sudden death of its founder. Apparently both Nasîr al Dîn and Ulûgh Beg were unable—or unwilling—to train

The small observatory at Istanbul, with astronomers at work in the single room. The roof is tiled, on the wall are recessed bookshelves, and at the center of the room is a large desk or table with various instruments. Altogether there are sixteen persons engaged in various activities, such as drawing, calculating, and measuring. In the foreground is a large terrestrial globe showing Africa, Asia, and Europe. The dimensions of Africa along the equator are exaggerated.

build an observatory in Istanbul in order to carry out the necessary measurements required in the revision of the available astronomical tables, which had grown outdated. The observatory was built and Taqî al Dîn was named its director. He was a controversial figure, and it is said that he secretly received instruction in astronomy from the Jewish astronomer David the Mathematician, who was on his staff between 1577 and 1578. However, he was quite convincing because the observatory was credited as being one of the largest in Islam, comparable to those in Maraghah and Samarkand. It was an elaborate building, which probably contained living quarters and offices for its personnel, as well as a small observatory that housed about ten different instruments.

The Istanbul Observatory was completed in 1577; in November of that year the 1577 comet appeared. Taqî al Dîn used the occasion to predict success of the Turkish Army against Persia and other good fortune for the sultan. Although the Turks did defeat the Persians that year, they also suffered great losses; in addition, there was an outbreak of the plague, and the deaths of several important people occurred in quick succession. These factors as well as a general animosity against the vizier, who supported the building of the observatory, created a negative attitude toward it. The religious leaders of Islam urged the sultan to destroy the observatory, claiming that it brought bad luck because it was used to pry into the secrets of nature, which should remain hidden. A wrecking crew demolished the observatory in 1580. Depending on which report one accepts, the astronomers working there were taken by surprise or Taqî al Dîn had given his consent. In either case, it was the death knell for Arab astronomy.

No original ideas can be credited to the Islamic astronomers, but they performed several important functions. They had the remarkable ability to absorb the ideas of others, such as the Greeks, to carry them forward, and to preserve them for posterity. Most of the Greek works were transmitted to the West via translations from the Arabic; many astronomical terms, such as *nadir* (the point on the celestial sphere opposite the zenith), and some of the names of stars (Rigel, Betelgeuse, Vega, and so on) have Arabic roots. It was probably also the first time that special buildings were erected and equipped to serve as astronomical observatories. Temples and other structures may have served the purpose, but not until al-

qualified successors, and the astronomers working under their direction were either incapable of or unwilling to assume the responsibility of directing the work at the observatories. Furthermore, in both cases the assistance of a powerful ruler was needed, and when he died there was no continued support. With the cessation of work at Samarkand, the influence of Arabian astronomy also began to decline until it became practically nonexistent. Fortunately, by that time, interest in it had begun to rise in the West, as we shall see in the next section.

Before that decline one other important observatory was founded in Islam, this time by the Ottomans, in Istanbul (Turkey). It had a curious short history, which may illustrate some of the problems facing astronomy at that time. Taqî al Dîn, who had been a judge in Egypt, had come to Istanbul, the capital of the Ottoman Empire, and accepted the position of head astronomer in 1573. He convinced Sultan Murad III (1546–95) of the need to

The title page of *Zurrat Ha-aretz (The Shape of the Earth),* by the medieval Jewish astronomer Abraham bar Hiyya Hanasi, as printed in Hebrew in 1720. The drawing on top shows the Ptolemaic universe with the earth at the center; the figures at the sides are the high priest Aaron (left) and Moses with the two Tablets.

A nineteenth-century Persian miniature representing the seven stages of heaven, with the earth below. Scholars prepare themselves in their little cubicles for eventual entrance via the ladder.

A sample page from *The Shape of the Earth,* showing a Greek version of the cosmos with the labels written in Hebrew. The top two diagrams show a sphere rotating about its diameter and give relations for its area. The lower figure shows a geocentered universe with spheres for Water, Fire, Moon, Mercury, Venus, Sun, Mars, Jupiter, Saturn, the fixed stars, and the primum mobile.

Ma'mūn built the observatory in Baghdad was there a special building just for astronomy.

Yet the important and necessary feature of an observatory, secured existence and continuity, did not materialize in Islam. More important contributions are our present number system, taken over from India, and the calculus of trigonometry that treats these functions as algebraic quantities in terms of formulae rather than only as geometrical constructions. This was a powerful tool and contributed greatly to the advancement of modern astronomy.

Mention was made earlier of the Jewish astronomer David, who worked for Taqî al Dîn. It was mainly under the influence of the Arabs and in their service that there were Jewish astronomers. There had been no real development of Jewish astronomy because, in the first place, there was no real need for an astronomer to fix the Jewish calendar and determine exactly the rising of the sun, moon, and stars. The Jewish calendar is based on the moon, with the exception that it was somewhat synchronized to the solar year by the addition of an extra month. The new moons—and thus the beginning of the new month—were not calculated but actually observed each time. This information was then conveyed by means of fire signals on hills and messengers from place to place. To this day, observant Jews (outside of Israel) observe each Jewish festival for two days on account of the ambiguity in the dates of the new moons. More important, however, was the prohibition against idol worship and the making of images. Astrology was frowned upon and even considered idolatrous. Although the signs of the Zodiac are found in Jewish life, this was for decorative purposes only. The Talmud, a collection of works containing explanations of Biblical laws, commentaries, and parables—says that Israel does not put its "luck" into the *mazeloth* (the twelve signs of the Zodiac) but only in God. (This is an interesting play on words, since luck in Hebrew is *mazel.*) Judaism, with its belief in one Creator without visible shape, had no need for deities represented by planets, sun, or moon.

One of the most distinguished Jewish astronomers of his time was Abraham bar-Hiyya Hanasi, known also as Savasorda, who lived in Spain and southern France at the end of the eleventh and beginning of the twelfth century. He had published one of the earliest tables (before 1136), called the *Tables of the Prince,* or *Al Battani Tables,* named after the Arabian astronomer of that name who had been active in the Baghdad school. Many of bar-Hiyya's writings are lost, but one important one, *Zurrat Ha-aretz (The Shape of the Earth),* is accessible. It is a geographical and cosmological exposition, showing that the author was quite familiar with Greek cosmology, including Eudoxus's spheres.

Possibly the most important Jewish astronomer of the Middle Ages was Levi ben Gershon, also known as Gersonides, who lived during the early part of the fourteenth century in southern France. He invented a device for astronomical observations, later called Jacob's staff, which facilitated the measurement of the angular distance between two stars. His immaculate, scientific approach is exemplified by his having calculated—and verified by experiments—the exact location of the eye's center of sight for proper use of the instrument. Gersonides was also the first to employ the camera obscura (a pinpoint camera without film) for astronomical observations. He was a careful observer and warned against error in observations owing to the refraction of light by the earth's atmosphere. His great philosophical work, *The Wars of the Lord,* contains several chapters on astronomy, including tables of eclipses and solar and lunar positions. It was hailed by Pope Clement VI of Avignon (1291–1352) as an outstanding contribution, although scribes and printers wanted to omit these chapters, contending that they were not relevant to the main theme of his work.

The fate of Jewish scholars in the Middle Ages is illustrated by the life of Abraham Zacuto, who was born in the middle of the fifteenth century in Salamanca, Spain, to a family of refugees from France. He studied astronomy and mathematics at the Christian university in Salamanca. Zacuto's works were considered of such importance that they were immediately translated into Latin and Spanish (from the Hebrew original). His biggest achievement was the revision and correction of the *Alphonsine Tables,* which may have saved Columbus's life. Columbus had used the tables to calculate an eclipse, thereby amazing, and subduing, the Indians when he seemingly carried out his threat to extinguish the moon. Ironically, in 1492, the year of Columbus's first voyage, the Jews were expelled from Spain and Zacuto fled to Portugal, where he was appointed royal astronomer. There he encouraged Vasco da Gama to undertake his great voyage, partly based on astrological readings. In 1497, when Vasco da Gama sailed, the Jews were expelled from Portugal. Refusing to change his religion, Zacuto fled once more, this time to Africa. On the way, he was twice taken prisoner by pirates, but he finally reached Tunisia. However, he did not find the rest he sought there, and he spent his remaining years in Asia.

The spiritual atmosphere of post-Renaissance Europe was hardly conducive to Jewish participation in science in general or astronomy in particular, although a number of Jews did manage against great odds to study and contribute to the field. Only after the Emancipation did Jews again succeed in taking an active part in scientific endeavors and become prominent among researchers.

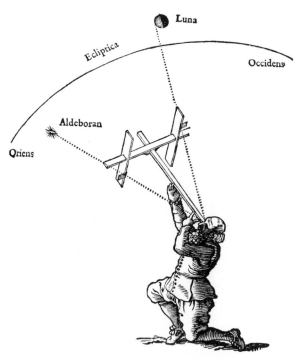

The Jacob's staff had many uses, as shown in this medieval drawing. At the left it is used to measure the angular distance between a star and the moon. At the center it is used to find the height and distance of a building by sighting from two ends of a measuring line (of known length). At the right is found the distance of an inaccessible building, whose height is known.

Jacob's staff. The cross-staff, or Jacob's staff, consists of a graduated lath (the long piece against the viewer's eye) and a crossbar, which is moved down the lath until its two edges are aligned with two stars (here the moon and Aldebaran) or one star and the horizon. From the fixed diameter of the crossbar and the graduated length of the lath, the angle that the two stars make (or a single star makes with the horizon) can be obtained.

4. Revival in Europe

While astronomy in Islam declined, a remarkable renaissance was taking place in the West. The Arabs were unable to improve upon Greek cosmology, which had reached its peak with Ptolemy. But astronomers in Europe made it their starting point. Yet it was along a tortuous road that progress was made, and then only as the result of the revolutionary ideas of such men as Copernicus, Kepler, and Newton.

As mentioned earlier, one of the main contributions of Islam to astronomy was the preservation of Greek ideas and literature. These were brought to the West, at first surreptitiously, later openly in the form of translations, to a large extent by Christian and Jewish astronomers who had been working in Spain (e.g., at the court of Alfonso X). At first, scholars were satisfied with studying the works of the ancients—notably those of Ptolemy—in translation, but, not being satisfied with the sometimes corrupted results, they went directly to the sources. Later, they made their own observations, mainly with simple instruments inherited from the Arabs.

France led the way until it was ravaged by the Hundred Years' War with England (1337–1453). Until his death in 1256 John Halifax of Holywood, better known as Sacrobosco, which is Holywood Latinized (fl. 1230), had taught mathematics in Paris. He produced an elementary text on astronomy, *Sphaera Mundi,* on the results of the daily rotation of the celestial sphere. It was so popular that by the end of the sixteenth century it had appeared in over more than sixty editions. At the University of Paris, as early as 1300, a group of philosophers, Jean Buridan, Albert of Saxony, and Nicholas Oresme, challenged Aristotle's physics.

After Paris lost its leading role, several schools sprang up in Germany and Austria. Nicholas of Cusa (1401–64) wrote a remarkable book, *De docta ignorantia (On Learned Ignorance),* in which he pointed out that the human mind could not conceive the absolute, which he meant as infinity. To him, the universe was infinite and therefore could not have a center, and hence the earth could not be at the center of the universe. It was simply an illusion to think that we could be at the center of the world, for if a person stood at the North Pole of the earth and another at the celestial North Pole, each would think that he was

The frontispiece of a book of psalms from a thirteenth-century French miniature. Three monks are shown carrying out astronomical observations. The man in the middle is using an astrolabe, an instrument introduced by the Arabs, to obtain the altitude of a star. The assistant at the right reads from astronomical tables, while the one at the left enters the observations.

his own handwriting and appearing after his book had been published in which he again returns to the notion of a revolving earth:

The earth cannot be fixed but moves like the stars, only half as fast. The earth revolves around the poles of the world once in a day and night, while the eighth sphere [carrying the stars] revolves twice in a day and night. The effect to an observer on the earth is the same as if the earth were stationary and the stars were revolving once in a day and night [i.e., 24 hours].

It would be wrong to conclude from this unpublished fragment that Cusa anticipated Copernicus, especially since his notions are quite vague and are not substantiated by calculations or observations. However, the fact that here we find speculations unfettered by Aristotle's dogma is quite refreshing.

At about this same time Georg von Peurbach (1423–61) had grown up in the small town of Purbach at the Austrian-German border, and at the age of twenty-seven he became professor of astronomy and mathematics at the University of Vienna, where he had studied. Peurbach wrote an excellent textbook, *Theoricae novae planetarum (New Planetary Theories),* which, though it did not go beyond Ptolemy, concisely explained the various constructions. He did, however, adopt the notion introduced by the Arabs of solid crystalline spheres and touching epicycles. But not being satisfied with translations from the Greek, which in many cases were translations from the Arabic, he decided to study Greek literature in Italy. However, before he and his student, Regiomontanus, could set out on their trip, Peurbach suddenly died.

Regiomontanus, whose real name was Johann Müller, also known as Johannes de Monte Regio, was the son of a miller. Attracted by Peurbach's fame, at the age of sixteen he went to Vienna to study under his direction. He worked with him for several years, carrying out measurements in order to improve the *Alphonsine Tables.* After Peurbach's sudden death, Regiomontanus proceeded alone to Italy, where he spent several years studying the Greek manuscripts. Upon his return, he settled in Nürnberg where he published profusely, using the printing presses that had recently come to that German town. Most famous among his works were the *Astronomical Ephemerides (Astronomical Tables),* which became invaluable to the Portuguese and Spanish

at the center. Also, Cusa assumed that everything was in motion, and therefore the earth too was in motion, but we couldn't conceive it in our ignorance since we perceive motion only with respect to fixed objects. How would one in the middle of the ocean, far from any land, know that his ship was really moving?

Although none of the above was based on any observation and was quite speculative, it is indeed remarkable that in a crude form he anticipated the principle of relativity, according to which all motion is relative.

In a later passage, Cusa states that God put the earth in the middle of the universe and decided that it should be heavy so that it would always remain in the center, an obvious contradiction to his earlier assertion that the universe has no center. Of particular interest is a note in

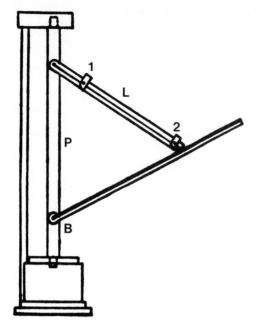

Regiomontanus's three staff–the dreistab, or triquetrum. It consists of a lath (L) about 9 feet long, with two sights (1) and (2) directed toward a star. It is hinged at the upper end to a vertical pole (P) and at the lower end pressed against another graduated lath (AB) also hinged to the pole. The lath is moved until the star is sighted through both (1) and (2), and the distance AB measured, which is an indication of the inclination of the star.

sneered at people who imagined the earth like meat on a spit with the sun being the fire. Not counting the Greeks, among the pre-Copernican writers only Celio Calcagnini (1479–1541) suggested that the earth might be spinning, but not revolving, in a short essay published in 1544, after his death. He was not taken very seriously, and contemporary writers took no notice of his ideas. Petrus Apianus (1495–1552), a voluminous writer on astronomy, accepted Regiomontanus in his *Cosmographia*. He and Fracastoro made interesting observations on comets and observed correctly that the comet's tail always points away from the sun, a fact that is of great interest in modern work.

So the sixteenth century finds astronomy not much further advanced than was Ptolemy many centuries earlier. Yet artists and astronomers alike drew inspiration from the medieval drawings in the classical writings, and an interest in astronomy had been reawakened, setting the stage for the great discoveries to come.

explorers. He also improved on Ptolemy's instruments and designed some simple ones himself. He also completed and republished an edition of Peurbach's book on planetary theory, which became quite popular and was reprinted several times. It brought out the discrepancy between Aristotle's view, according to which the sphere carrying the stars was responsible for the daily motion of stars, and Ptolemy's, which adds an additional sphere to account for the precession. According to Peurbach's scheme–probably influenced by the writers of the Baghdad school–the fixed stars are on a sphere called the firmament, while outside is another sphere, known as the primum mobile, which moves all the others.

Later writers added further spheres to account for the changes in the obliquity of the ecliptic. Girolomo Fracastoro (1483–1553), who wanted to avoid the complications introduced by Ptolemy's epicycles, revived Eudoxus's scheme of homocentric spheres. In his work *Homocentrica* he proposed a system that had no fewer than the following spheres: 8 carrying stars and planets, 6 for the daily rotation and precession, 10 for Saturn, 11 for Jupiter, 9 for Mars, 6 for the sun, 11 for Venus, 11 for Mercury, and 6 for the moon and a sublunary sphere. Indeed, a poor substitute for Ptolemy's system of cycles and epicycles.

Several writers have credited Regiomontanus, albeit wrongly, with discovering the rotation of the earth and thus being a forerunner of Copernicus. He did valuable work and undoubtedly his fame is responsible for some of this undeserved posthumous recognition. Not only did he not subscribe to the idea of a rotating earth, but he

A picture of the universe taken from Peter Apian's *Cosmographia* (1539). The terrestrial region at the center (composed of the four elements Earth, Water, Air, and Fire), is separated from the firmament, carrying the stars, by spheres of the moon, Mercury, Venus, the sun, Mars, Jupiter, and Saturn. Beyond this are the "ninth" and "tenth heavens," or crystal sphere and primum mobile. Surrounding all is the Empyrium, the dwelling place of God.

IV · BIRTH OF MODERN ASTRONOMY

1. The Copernican Revolution

No revolution, political or scientific, was more peaceful and no revolutionary was less suited for his role in it, less convinced of his ideas than Nicolaus Copernicus (1473–1543). Yet it was this quiet, pious, lackluster man who changed the course of astronomy with one book, which for thirty-six years he hesitated to publish.

Niklas Koppernigk (or Copernicus, as he is called by his Latin name) was born on February 19, 1473, in the little town of Toruń on the Vistula. Toruń, situated in West Prussia, had changed allegiance several times, and in 1466, seven years before Copernicus's birth, it had again become a Polish town. Not very much is known about Copernicus's early life, except that his father, a merchant who also owned several vineyards, died when Nicolaus was ten. His education was taken over by his uncle (on his mother's side), the Bishop Waczenrode of Ermland, who also became the boy's guardian, protector, and, later, employer. The bishop, a good friend of the Polish king, was a politician by inclination and loved an intrigue.

At the age of eighteen, Nicolaus entered the University of Cracow, the capital of Poland. It was an obvious choice, since his father's family came from Cracow, and Uncle Lucas Waczenrode had started his studies there also. Moreover, the university had a good reputation for mathematics and astronomy. His first teacher in astronomy was Albert of Brudzew (Brudzewski) who had written a commentary on Georg von Peurbach's *Theoricae Novae Planetarum (New Planetary Theories)* as a student's guide. Brudzewski was a follower of Ptolemy and Aristotle, like nearly everyone else.

Copernicus took no final examination at Cracow, nor did he finish his studies. Uncle Waczenrode had nominated his nephew for a canonry at Varmia, a position that had become vacant through the death of its

A copper cut made in the second half of the sixteenth century shows Nicolaus Copernicus (1473–1543) at prayer.

incumbent. This could be a lucrative, lifelong position, with fixed income and usually no duties, or only light ones. No theological education or even interest was required. Any new canon without an academic degree was obliged after a year's residence at the cathedral to take a leave of absence with pay and to study at a university. But unfortunately for Copernicus, the position became vacant in September, an odd and not an even month; it appears that the successor of a canon dying in an even month was named by the bishop, but if the canon died in an odd month, the pope had that privilege. Copernicus did not get his canonicate and he complained bitterly. He was luckier the following year because a canon at Frauenburg obligingly died in August. Thus, Copernicus became a canon at the age of twenty-four, a position he was to hold until his death.

Immediately after becoming a canon, he set out for Italy where he studied under the well-known astronomer Domenico Maria da Novara (1454–1504) at the University of Bologna. Teacher and student soon became good friends and observed the sky together. It was in Bologna that Novara and Copernicus watched as Aldebaran,* that "brilliant star in the Hyades," was eclipsed by the moon on March 9, 1497. This was the first astronomical observation that Copernicus was to use later to demonstrate his theory of the lunar parallax. Maria da Novara was an excellent practical astronomer and had redetermined the positions of all the stars in Ptolemy's *Almagest.* He is credited with two important contemporary findings: the systematic decrease of the obliquity of the ecliptic (the value quoted by Copernicus being 23° 28.4′) and the (erroneous) shifting of the North Pole with which he had hoped to disprove Ptolemy's theory. Although he was something of a revolutionary, he was an ardent astrologer, and as the "astrologer of Bologna" he became famous.

Copernicus did not get a degree at Bologna—he had set out to study jurisprudence, in which he did not excel—and after a year at Rome he returned to his canonicate in Frauenburg. However, he stayed only long enough to get another study leave and returned to Italy, this time to study medicine at Padua. He seemed to have succeeded, for later he was "revered like a new Aesculapius," the Greek god of the art of healing. Nevertheless, he took a doctor's degree in canon law at Ferrara, where the great mathematician Bianchi lived and Maria da Novara had studied. Finally, in 1506, Dr. Copernicus returned home, having spent about nine years at various Italian universities. He had acquired a well-rounded education; he had studied under great teachers, and had become proficient in astronomy, jurisprudence, and medicine, but as yet there was no indication of what he was to become— the greatest revolutionary of his time, and honored ever since.

* Aldebaran (or Tauri α) is the brightest star in the constellation Taurus. It is a slightly reddish giant, whose color is described as orange. It has a diameter of 22.5 million miles, about 25 times that of the sun. Aldebaran is found at one tip of a V-shaped cluster called the Hyades, which contains about 200 stars. Although Aldebaran is often identified through the Hyades, it is not part of that cluster but is located at a different distance.

Back in Ermland (now Eastern Prussia), Copernicus did not return immediately to Frauenburg but stayed with his uncle at the episcopal castle of Heilsberg for six years. There he acquired his knowledge of statesmanship, which served him so well later. He became the bishop's companion, secretary, and private physician, but had enough time left to read, write, and study.

After the sudden death of Bishop Waczenrode—it was rumored he was poisoned—Copernicus became what he had been in name only, a canon of the church.

Life in Frauenburg was quite different from the gay times in Italy or even the interesting times in Heilsberg. It was a sleepy town, dominated by its cathedral, which was entirely unsuited for astronomical observations. Copernicus took an active part in the administration of the diocese and his own flock. He suggested a uniform coinage to the King of Poland and managed, with arms he had previously been accused of purchasing unnecessarily, to defend Allenstein Castle in Ermland against the attacks of the Knights of the Teutonic Order. In spite of all these activities, he found ample time to carry on his own scientific work in his little study, which was said to be in the tower of the cathedral.

His colleagues and friends had the first inkling of a coming revolution in astronomy. Obviously hoping for their comments, Copernicus sent a short manuscript, *Commentariolus,* to a few of them, summing up his ideas in seven propositions, or assumptions, which deserve to be listed in full:

1. There is no one center of all the celestial circles or spheres.

2. The center of the earth is not the center of the universe, but only of gravity and of the lunar sphere.

3. All the spheres revolve about the sun as their midpoint, and therefore the sun is the center of the universe.

4. The ratio of the earth's distance from the sun to the height of the firmament is so much smaller than the ratio of the earth's radius to its distance from the sun that the distance from the earth to the sun, in comparison with the height of the firmament, is imperceptible.

5. Whatever motion appears in the firmament arises not from any motion of the firmament but from the earth's motion. The earth together with its circumjacent elements performs a complete rotation on its fixed poles in a daily motion, while the firmament and highest heaven abide unchanged.

6. What appear to us as motions of the sun arise not from its motion but from the motion of the earth and our sphere, with which we revolve about the sun like any other planet. The earth has, then, more than one motion.

7. The apparent retrograde and direct motion of the

Frauenburg (Frombork), where Copernicus spent most of his life. It is seen here from the west in an engraving by F. von Quast (1807–77). The Cathedral of Frauenburg is shown in the center, and the so-called Copernicus tower is the small square tower slightly to the right. It is there that—according to tradition—Copernicus worked and carried out his observations. (Recently, doubt has been cast on this theory because of the small size of the windows and comparative inaccessibility of the tower. It is probable that Copernicus had a small observatory in his house located outside the city.)

planets arise not from their motion but from the earth's. The motion of the earth alone, therefore, suffices to explain so many apparent inequalities in the heavens.

The two fundamental innovations—or rather resurrections, if one remembers that Aristarchus had already proposed similar ideas—are, of course, that the sun and not the earth is at the center of the universe and that it is the motion of the earth that accounts for the apparent daily rotation of the celestial sphere, as well as for the other "apparent inequalities in the heavens."

Copernicus considered the rotation of the earth about its axis as a natural consequence of its spherical form, and countered the objections that it would fly apart by the argument that it is a "natural" as opposed to a "violent" motion and that a rotating universe (and stationary earth) would encounter the same difficulties. It is not known whether he was aware of similar arguments by Nicholas of Cusa who, we have seen, was concerned with the same question.

Copernicus was well aware that as far as observation was concerned, it did not matter whether the earth was in motion and the sun and the fixed stars at rest, or vice versa. This idea, already stated by Aristotle, is known commonly as the principle of relative motion and is beautifully expressed by Virgil in *The Aeneid* (III: 72): "Leaving the port the land and cities are receding."

To apply these ideas to an apparent rotation about the observer is slightly more difficult, since the eye cannot determine whether an object has moved but only that it has moved with respect to some fixed position. This applies both to the daily rotation of the earth and its yearly motion around the sun. These two are quite

A page from Copernicus's *De Revolutionibus,* demonstrating his heliocentric hypothesis. Because Venus and Mercury were never seen far from the sun, it followed that their paths were nearer to the sun than that of the earth (5); Mercury (7) was closer to the sun than Venus (6), since it was never seen as far from the sun in the sky as Venus. The other three planets must move in orbits larger than that of the earth, as they were seen at times in a direction opposite the sun. The order of their distances from the sun could be inferred from the disturbing effects produced on their apparent motion by the earth. Saturn (2), being least affected, must be farthest from the sun, preceded by Mars (4) and Jupiter (3). Beyond them all is the sphere of the fixed stars (1).

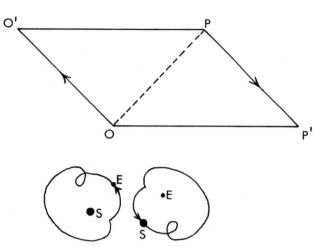

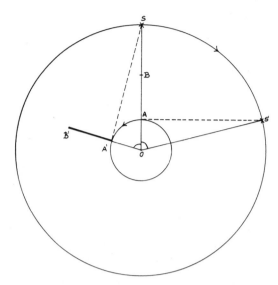

Relative motion. Suppose an observer is at O and an object at P. Then whether the object moves from P to P', the observer remaining at O, or the observer moving an equal distance in the opposite direction from O to O', the object remaining at P, the effect to the eye is exactly the same. In either case the distance between object and observer and their relative direction, OP' or O'P, are the same. The same applies also to motion along a closed curve. The effect, to the eye, is the same, whether E is moving and S is at rest, or E is at rest and S is in motion.

Earth's rotation. Let S be the position of a star on the celestial sphere directly over an observer (A) on the earth (the direction determined through the line AB), and O the common center of earth and the celestial sphere. Now, suppose first that the celestial sphere turns clockwise until S comes to S' and A sees the star on his horizon. Next assume that the star S and the celestial sphere remain at rest, but that the earth turns counterclockwise until AB comes to A'B' and the observer (now at A') again sees the star on his horizon. In both cases, the observer will see exactly the same motion in the sky. It can be seen from the diagram that the angle SOS' through which the celestial sphere was assumed to turn is equal to the angle AOA' through which the earth turns in the second case, but that the two rotations are in opposite directions.

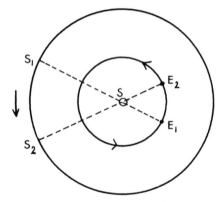

Sun's apparent motion. As the earth moves in its orbit from E_1 to E_2, the apparent position of the central sun (S) as seen against the background of the fixed stars is from S_1 to S_2. Again, while the earth moves counterclockwise, the sun appears to move clockwise. Actually, according to Copernicus, the sun is not at the center of the earth's circular orbit, but 1/25 off center. Hence, the apparent motion of the sun is not uniform but has a maximum deviation of 2 1/6 degrees.

independent and distinct, and it might be possible to accept one without the other. As a matter of fact, since Copernicus—like his contemporaries—assumed that a rotating body revolved as if it were rigidly attached to a central fixture, a third motion was added that kept the earth's axis fixed in space. (Of course, it is this fixed axis that explains the seasons.) The real advantage of the Copernican system, however, lies in the fact that the apparent retrograde motion of the planets appears as a consequence of the earth's motion.

This is the essence of the Copernican system as it appears today. However, in order to explain the varying velocities of the planets in their orbits, Copernicus had no

choice but to revert to the use of epicycles, since circular motion (or a combination of circular motions) was the only permissible one. He rejected the notion of the equant, considering it foreign and inconsistent with the principle of uniformly described circles. He avoided the equant rather ingeniously, by placing the sun off-center and introducing a small epicycle for each planet. As far as the yearly motion of the earth was concerned, he had nothing to add to the corresponding construction Ptolemy had used for the motion of the sun around the earth. Three motions were sufficient. In the case of the moon, he replaced Ptolemy's eccentric deferent by a second epicycle and accounted for its motion by four circular motions. The outer planets and Venus each needed five, while Mercury required an additional two to account for its oscillation. He was aware of the fact—as we have seen used by Nasîr al Dîn—that the combination of two circular motions could produce a straight line motion. Interestingly, in Copernicus's final manuscript there is a sentence struck out in which he observes that two unequal circles may combine to describe a conic section, which mathematicians call an ellipse. This remark has often been taken as an indication that Copernicus somehow anticipated Kepler, whose life and work we will discuss later, but it is completely irrelevant to his construction. As a matter of fact, the combination of two circles results only in a hypocycloid looking like an ellipse,

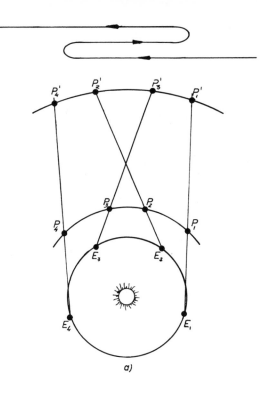

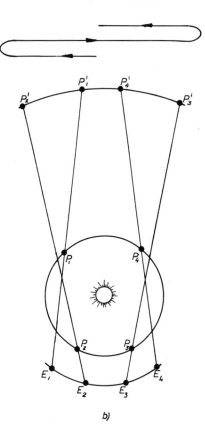

Retrograde motion. Let E_1, E_2, E_3, and E_4 in diagram (a) be four consecutive positions of the earth in its orbit, and P_1, P_2, P_3, and P_4 the corresponding positions of a planet. As the earth moves steadily in its orbit from E_1 to E_4 and the planet from P_1 to P_4, the planet's apparent position with respect to the fixed stars will move along P'_1, P'_2, P'_3, and P'_4. Diagram (a) shows the situation for an outer planet: from P_1 to P_2 it will appear to move forward ($P'_1 P'_2$), but from P_2 to P_3 it will appear to move backward, and finally from P_3 to P_4 it will again move forward. For an inner planet (b) the situation is similar, except that now the planet seems to oscillate between the two limits P'_2 and P'_3–moving first forward, from P'_1 to P'_2, then backward and again forward to P_4. The points at which the planets seem to change direction are called "stationary" points.

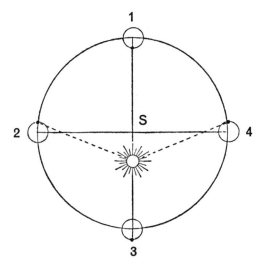

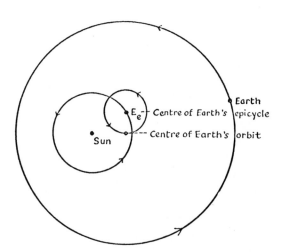

Copernicus used an ingenious mechanism to replace the equant, which had been necessary to account for the variable speeds of the planets and their deviation from circular motion. He solved his problem by making the distance of the sun from the center (S) equal to three-halves the eccentricity, and having a planet describe a small epicycle whose radius was one-half the eccentricity. At aphelion (1) and perihelion (3) the net difference between the two effects of eccentricity and epicycle accounted for the greater (1) and smaller (3) distances of a planet from the sun. At positions (2) and (4) the two effects combine doubling the radius of the eccentricity.

Although Copernicus's system also needed cycles and epicycles to account for the irregular motion of the earth and the planets, the roles of the main circle and the epicycle were often interchanged. Start with the sun: the center of the earth's epicycle revolves around the sun. The center of the earth's orbit lies on that epicycle, which the earth itself revolves around. Those three motions were necessary to account for the daily and yearly motion of the earth.

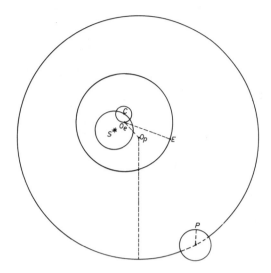

The three circles for the earth's motion and the motion of a planet (P) moving on an epicycle: The earth (E) revolves around a circle whose center (O_e) rotates about point C—which lies on another circle with the sun (S) at its center. Note that the main circle (the deferent) does not revolve around the sun but around the center O_p at a distance (exaggerated) from S. In *Commentariolus,* Copernicus lists 34 epicycles and circles, 3 for the earth, 7 for Mercury, 4 for the moon, and 5 for each of the other planets.

and that is probably the reason why Copernicus struck out that particular remark.

"Altogether, therefore, thirty-four circles suffice to explain the entire structure of the universe and the entire ballet of the planets." This is the final sentence of *Commentariolus.* Unfortunately it is not correct; left out are the precession—the toplike motion that accounted for the changing equinoxes over the centuries—the motion at aphelion, and the lunar nodes (the opposing intersecting points on the ecliptic), which bring the total to thirty-eight. However, even this figure seems to be an underestimate. In any case one might be hard pressed to choose between Copernicus and Ptolemy in this regard—both requiring epicycles and giving the same results.

At first there was no reaction to the new theory expounded in *Commentariolus.* However, the word slowly spread, lectures on the Copernican system were given, and Copernicus acquired some fame—or notoriety—although as yet he had published nothing.

He was invited to participate in a Lateran Council on the reform of the calendar but refused on the grounds that no reform of the calendar was possible until the motions of the sun and the moon were known more accurately. Martin Luther described Copernicus as a fool for holding an opinion in obvious contradiction to the Bible, and other reformers even suggested that such an opinion should not be tolerated. On the other hand, Cardinal Nicolaus von Schonberg, Archbishop of Capua, a very liberal-minded scholar and councillor to Pope Paul III, asked for copies, at the cardinal's expense, of whatever Copernicus had written.

Copernicus realized that he had to refine his calculations and get more data if his theory was to be shown to be the correct one. He was not much of an observer and had been satisfied to use the known observations of the ancients, not just Ptolemy's. He now set out to check his calculations and to improve them if he must. A new star catalogue was prepared and planetary distances obtained. It is interesting to note that these data were already available to Ptolemy had Ptolemy taken planetary distances from the sun. From Copernicus's own observation of Venus—during an occultation, or eclipse, by the moon in 1529—together with Ptolemy's, he was able to deduce its period. For Mercury, he had to rely on observations by Bernard Walther (1430–1504), the benefactor of Regiomontanus, and Johannes Schoner, a well-known astronomer who in 1533 had published a memoir containing, among other items, a dissertation by Regiomontanus against a rotating earth; the reason given was that Mercury is rarely seen on account of the "vapours" of the Vistula River.

The result of all that work was Copernicus's book, in six volumes (patterned after the *Almagest), De Revolutionibus (On the Revolutions,* meaning here "rotation"). (The book was later published under the more specific title *De Revolutionibus Orbium Coelestium,* or *On the Revolutions of the Celestial Spheres.)* The first volume contains an outline of his theory, the first eleven chapters describing its entirety step by step, starting with the idea of a spherical world and ending with the three motions of the earth; the remaining two chapters are an exposition of spherical trigonometry. The second book is devoted to

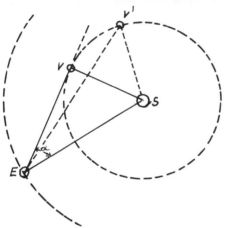

Orbit of Venus. Let (V) and (V') be two positions of Venus in its orbit around the sun (S). When Venus appears to be farthest from the sun, the angle α, made between the sights from the earth (E) to Venus (V) and the sun (S) respectively, will be a maximum (i.e., largest). At that time, the line of sight from Earth to Venus (V) is tangent or at right angles to the orbit. Knowing the sun-earth distance and that angle α, it is then a simple matter to deduce the sun-Venus distance. To find the period of revolution, Copernicus obtained two successive observations of Venus at nearly the same position (relative to the sun and the stars) and found that Venus completes a revolution in 225 days.

mathematical astronomy and the armillary sphere, an instrument for observation. It also contains a star catalogue, on the whole reproducing Ptolemy's but with some corrections. The third book covers the orbit of the earth, the second part devoted to an explanation of tables in a way that makes no difference whether the earth or the sun is in motion. The motions of the moon and eclipses are described in the fourth book, while the remaining two books concern themselves with the planetary motions. The main part of *De Revolutionibus* was completed by 1533 and the remainder a few years afterward, but Copernicus had refused to publish it, except for the tables, probably because he dreaded the repercussions his revolutionary theory might have. He was already an old man of sixty-six and wanted his peace, but fate willed otherwise.

Georg Joachim von Lauchen (1514–76), who called himself Rheticus, the man of Rhaetia, was a professor of mathematics at the University of Wittenberg. He had heard of Copernicus's work from his teacher Johannes Schoner and in 1539 set forth to Frauenburg to learn the truth from the old master himself. He intended to spend only a few weeks with Copernicus, who welcomed him very cordially, but he became a devoted disciple and stayed for two years. When he thought that he had grasped the main idea, he got permission to write a short treatise, *Narratio Prima de Libris Revolutionum (First Account of the Books on Revolutions)*. It was in the form of a letter addressed to his teacher Schoner but was obviously written for publication.

PLANETARY DISTANCES		
Planet	Copernicus	Modern Value
Mercury	0.3763	0.3871
Venus	0.7193	0.7233
Earth	1.0000 *	1.0000 *
Mars	1.5198	1.5237
Jupiter	5.2192	5.2028
Saturn	9.1743	9.5388

* All values are given in terms of Earth-Sun distance.

In contrast to the poor reception *Commentariolus* had received, *Narratio Prima* created a sensation. It was well written, stressing the main parts of the Copernican system, and contained many quotations. It was dedicated to Schoner and full of praises for the "teacher," whom Rheticus never referred to by name but only as the Canon of Toruń. A good friend of Copernicus, Bishop Tiedemann Giese, the Bishop of Kulm, saw to it that it received as many readers as possible, including Duke Albrecht of Prussia. Both Rheticus and Giese urged Copernicus to have his *De Revolutionibus* published. Spurred on by the enthusiasm of his disciple, he finally agreed, despite his continued concern for the consequences. Rheticus copied the manuscript, all 424 pages of it, and induced Duke Albrecht to recommend him to the Elector of Saxony and the University of Wittenberg as the editor of *De Revolutionibus*. Rheticus's plan was to get the book printed in Nuremberg by Petreius, who printed Rheticus's *Narratio Prima* and who specialized in astronomical works. But Nuremberg was the stronghold of Luther, who was opposed to the Copernican system, and some protection would be helpful. The duke obliged, and Rheticus was appointed editor and took his copy, together with Copernicus's original manuscript, to Petreius who began to set up the type in the spring of 1542.

The printing proceeded satisfactorily, but two incidents marred what would otherwise have been the perfect culmination of a man's lifework. Rheticus left Nuremberg and the University of Wittenberg—it is said for personal reasons—to take up the coveted Chair of Mathematics at the University of Leipzig, leaving the supervision of the printing in the hands of Andreas Osiander (1498–1552), who had in the past already shown a great interest in Copernicus's work. Not only did Rheticus turn over the editorship of the most important work in his life—which he had, so to speak, fathered—to someone else, but he suddenly lost interest in Copernicus and his theory. A biography on which he had worked was never finished, nor was a pamphlet in which he wanted to demonstrate that the heliocentric theory was not in contradiction to the Bible. There may be several reasons for this sudden loss of interest, such as preoccupation with other matters, but a possible explanation is found in *De Revolutionibus* itself. While Rheticus was still in Nuremberg, Copernicus had sent him a dedication for the book. It was dedicated to Pope Paul III. This was obviously done to assure the most powerful church that no sacrilege was intended. The dedication mentions how Copernicus's misgivings about publishing were overcome by his good friends Nicolaus von Schonberg and Tiedemann Giese, as well as many other eminent and learned men. Rheticus is not

mentioned anywhere in the book. It may have been an oversight, owing to Copernicus's advanced age, as pointed out later in a letter Giese wrote to Rheticus, but it certainly came as a shock to the devoted Rheticus.

The second incident is even more scandalous. There is a preface to *De Revolutionibus* that, in fact, negates everything the book stands for. It is not signed and for a long time it was thought that Copernicus was its author, although it duplicates in some way the dedication and refers to the author in the third person in laudatory terms. It was Kepler who discovered in his copy of *De Revolutionibus* a note that named the author—Andreas Osiander, the trusted editor. Although Kepler made it known, it took several editions before the world accepted the true author of the preface. Osiander was a leader of the reform movement then sweeping the church and may have added the preface to protect himself, or he may have wanted to protect Copernicus against possible persecution—this time from the Lutherans—but the result was the same. Copernicus did believe in the truth of this system, but the preface said he did not. The first galley proofs, probably including the preface, reached Copernicus when he was already weak and plagued by fever. He suffered a stroke and became partially paralyzed. If he read the preface, he was certainly too weak to react to it; it may even have caused the stroke in the first place. He died a few months later, on May 24, 1543, a few hours after he had received one of the first copies of *De Revolutionibus Orbium Coelestium*. Osiander had even changed the title.

Copernicus was dead, and it seemed that his theory would die with him. *De Revolutionibus* was written in Latin and therefore accessible to only a select few—and they were not interested. Osiander's preface had made it seem that the author himself did not believe in his work and considered it only a mathematical device to calculate the planetary orbits. In fact, for a long time only the tables were popular. Erasmus Reinhold (1511–53), professor and later dean and rector at the University of Wittenberg, used the tables to cast a horoscope for Martin Luther! Unfortunately these tables were not too accurate, and Reinhold, who was an expert mathematician, applied Copernicus's trigonometry to redo the calculations. These became the *Prussian Tables,* in honor of Duke Albrecht of Prussia (one still needed a sponsor for scientific work). In England some recognition was given to Copernicus, and in 1576 Thomas Digges (1546–95) published *A Perfit Description of the Caelestiall Orbes* in which he adopted Copernicus's system.

At best Copernicus was hailed as a great astronomer; but his theory was ignored, even ridiculed. All the classical arguments against a moving earth were resuscitated and passages from the Scriptures were cited to refute him.

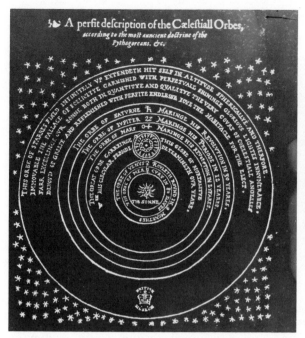

Thomas Digges's diagram of the Infinite Copernican Universe, from *A Perfit Description of the Caelestiall Orbes,* 1576. Note that here the stars are depicted outside the celestial sphere, indicating the infinity of the universe.

Portrait of Giordano Bruno, the frontispiece from *Opere di Giordano Bruno,* 1830.

Only one man believed in the Copernican system. He taught it, defended it courageously, and died for it. Giordano Bruno (1458–1600) entered a Dominican monastery in Naples at the age of fourteen and was consecrated a priest at the age of twenty-four. There, he first read *De Revolutionibus* and became imbued with its spirit.

He hated the authoritarian view of Aristotle and replaced it with that of the gentler Lucretius. The strict monastery life was not for a man of his independent outlook, and he left it and the priesthood to become a humanist. For the next sixteen years he roamed through Europe to preach his poetic cosmopolitan faith, only to be ridiculed and persecuted.

He acquired a doctor's degree from the University of Toulouse and in 1581 became an assistant professor at the College de France. Two years later Bruno went to England as the guest of the French ambassador Michel de Castelnau, and there he spent the happiest years of his life. Within two years he published seven important works, all extolling truth and attacking blind faith. He was regarded as a heretic. In *De Innumerabilibus sive de Immenso* he refuted Aristotle and extolled Copernicus. Bruno was not bound by observations and went further than Copernicus. In *De Monade* he visualized the fixed stars as suns freely suspended in limitless space, all of them surrounded by planets but inhabited. He saw the sun only as a star among many, rotating, and not at the center of the universe. The center of the universe, according to Bruno,

was wherever the observer was. God was the nature of nature, the monad of monads. His divine soul permeated the universe. He was the supreme cause. What better way of worshiping Him than by studying His laws, the laws of nature?

Bruno was like the founder of a universal religion. But he was not interested in accepted authorities. He wanted to reach the true elite, and he thundered against the "learned asses." Only an ass, he said, could have written the preface to *De Revolutionibus*—for the benefit of other asses. From England he returned to France and then to Germany.

To the consternation and astonishment of learned Europe, he then accepted, in 1591, an invitation by Giovanni Mocenigo, an agent provocateur of the Inquisition, to come to Venice as his teacher. It has been speculated that he probably was homesick for his native Italy. A few months later he was handed over to the Inquisition, charged not only with heresy but with having praised Queen Elizabeth and other heretic rulers. The Roman Inquisition demanded his extradition from Venice, and in February of 1593 Bruno disappeared into its torture dungeons—to reappear in 1600 for his trial. The outcome of that trial—prosecutor and judge were the same—was obvious. He was condemned, defrocked, and turned over to the secular arm, as was the custom. Nine days after sentence Giordano Bruno, the extoller of truth, was burned alive at the stake.

Of course, it was not only for teaching the Copernican

The world system of Ptolemy, as shown by Andreas Cellarius in his *Star Atlas*, 1661. The outer ring gives the four points of the compass and meridian (equal day and night). The horizontal circles, in order, are the North Pole, north polar circle, Tropic of Cancer, the Zodiac band, orbits of Saturn, Jupiter, Mars, Sun, Venus, Mercury, and Moon; celestial equator, Tropic of Capricorn, south polar circle, and the South Pole. The vertical circles are the meridians with the solstices especially marked. At the center is the earth with its axis.

The world system of Copernicus, as shown by Andreas Cellarius in his *Star Atlas,* 1661. The various circles (from outside to center) denote the Zodiac and circle of fixed stars and the orbits of Saturn revolving in 30 years, Jupiter in 12 years, Mars in 2 years, Earth in 1 year, Venus in 9 months, and Mercury in 89 days. The four positions of the earth are shown at vernal equinox, summer solstice, autumnal equinox, and winter solstice; the sun is at the center.

system that Bruno paid the supreme price, but rather for his free and independent religious views, which the church could not suffer. Bruno's fate discouraged others from accepting Copernicus and his theory, and it took some time until another champion arose, in the person of Galileo Galilei (1564–1642), who, by recanting, narrowly avoided a similar fate. Even much later, when the truth of the Copernican system seemed well established, one could still see the two systems side by side, as in the *Star Atlas* of Andreas Cellarius published in 1661.

But the real significance of the heliocentric system lies in the greatness of its conception rather than in the discovery itself. By his concept of a moving earth, Copernicus laid the cornerstone for modern astronomy.

2. The Celestial Palace

A portrait of the nobleman Tycho Brahe (1564–1601) with the decoration of the Order of the Elephant.

Tycho (or Tyge, as he was called originally) Brahe (1546–1601) was born on December 14, 1546, the first child of Otto Brahe, a privy councillor and member of the ancient Danish nobility. Otto had promised his younger brother Jørgen, who was childless and wealthy, that he could bring up his first son as his own, but he reneged; Tycho was a twin, but his brother had been stillborn. Nevertheless, the uncle was not put off so easily and within a year kidnapped his nephew, as soon as Otto Brahe was blessed with another son. The parents objected at first but gave in, knowing that the boy was in good

hands and would receive an education they were unable and perhaps unwilling to give him. At least it would have been difficult since within ten years Otto Brahe would become the father of five sons and five daughters (not counting the stillborn son).

Jørgen Brahe was a man of his word and hired a special tutor for his nephew. At the age of seven Tyge began to study Latin and even wrote some fairly good poetry in that language. In those days it was not unusual for students to enter the university at a very early age even for the rudiments of an education. And so at thirteen he was sent to the University of Copenhagen to study law and philosophy in preparation for the career as statesman his uncle had picked for him. Tycho's first contact with astronomy was on August 21, 1560, when he witnessed a partial solar eclipse predicted to occur on that day. (The eclipse was a total one in Portugal, as reported by Clavius, but only a partial one in Copenhagen, Denmark.) It struck him "as something divine that men could know the motions of the celestial bodies so accurately that they could long before foretell their places and relative positions." For the sum of two thalers, he purchased a copy of the works of Ptolemy (published in Basle in 1551) and spent the next three years studying it diligently.

Partly to remove him from the influence of his scientifically minded friends in Copenhagen, and partly because it was the custom, Jørgen Brahe sent his nephew—at the age of sixteen—to the University of Leipzig together with his mentor, Anders Sörensen Vedel, a young man of great promise, only four years Tycho's senior. (Vedel later became Royal Historiographer and is known for his works on early Danish history.) They both entered the university, Tycho to study law and Vedel to listen to lectures on history, but there is no record to show that Tycho finished his law courses, or even took any examinations. On the contrary, he continued his astronomical studies surreptitiously, while his mentor was out or sleeping. There was no doubt that stargazing was to be his true avocation and not the more sensible occupations suitable for a man of his noble background. In August 1563 Tycho made his first astronomical observation—the occasion of a conjunction (having the same celestial longitude) between Saturn and Jupiter. The observation was considered important for its astrological implication. The instrument used was the crudest imaginable—a pair of ordinary compasses with each leg aligned to a star and the angle read from a circle drawn on paper and divided into degrees—but it was sufficient to show that the *Alphonsine Tables* were wrong by a month and the later *Prussian Tables* by a few days. It was then that Tycho Brahe realized that only through a steady course of observations would it be possible to obtain a better insight into the motions of the planets.

In May of 1565 Vedel and Tycho returned to Denmark; war had broken out between his country and Sweden, and Uncle Jørgen, who was a vice admiral, probably thought that his nephew's place was at home. Tycho did not remain there long.* Tycho went first to Wittenberg, but the plague broke out and he continued on to Rostock near the Baltic Sea. The university did not have anyone

specializing in astronomy, as few did, but lectures were given in astrology, alchemy, and medicine. The connection between these studies and astronomy was an inherent ingredient of Aristotelian teaching. Tycho seemed to have benefited by these lectures, and he applied his knowledge to practical matters. He wrote prescriptions against the fever for his friend Vedel, and he later experimented with several metals, probably endeavoring to make gold. But his knowledge of metals had other practical ends. In Rostock he lost part of his nose in a duel with another Danish nobleman over an argument about who was the better mathematician. To conceal his disfigurement, he constructed a covering of silver and gold and always carried a salve to keep it stuck on. About that time he had his first experience with astrology. During a lunar eclipse he predicted—in verse form—the imminent death of Sultan Soliman, who in the previous year had attacked Malta. The news of his death—he was about eighty—reached Rostock a few weeks later. Tycho was praised as a great astrologer until it appeared that the sultan had died before the time of the eclipse. Tycho tried—unsuccessfully—to explain that he had predicted the sultan's death from his horoscope.

From Rostock, Tycho returned to Denmark, but the budding astronomer seemed not to have been too happy with his reception, although King Frederick granted him a formal promise for the first vacant canonicate. He returned to Rostock to observe another lunar eclipse but soon left for Wittenberg and the University of Basle, from which he was graduated early in 1569. Immediately thereafter he went to Augsburg, the capital of Suabia (Swabia), now part of Bavaria. On the way he paid a visit to Cyprianus Leovitius (Livowsky), a well-known astronomer who had published an edition of Regiomontanus's trigonometric tables and had written books on astrology; he thought that the end of the world would occur in 1584, after the next conjunction. Leovitius was more astrologer than astronomer—as were most of his colleagues—and Tycho must have been disappointed when Leovitius admitted that he had no instruments and only occasionally, with the help of clocks, observed solar and lunar eclipses. He would compare the result with the *Alphonsine Tables* and the *Prussian Tables*.

Apparently Tycho felt at home in Augsburg, where he associated freely with men of culture and wealth. In particular, he struck up a close friendship with two brothers, both amateur astronomers who were interested in having a good instrument at their country seat, a village close to Augsburg. Upon Tycho's instructions, a huge quadrant, about 19 feet in diameter, was built. This differed from most of the others that Tycho later built in that it was suspended by the center and was movable around it. While in Augsburg, Tycho also designed a new

---

* His uncle died following a cold he had caught when rescuing King Frederick II who had fallen into the water while making his way into the castle of Copenhagen.

QVADRANS MAXIMVS QVALEM OLIM
PROPE AVGVSTAM VINDELICORVM
EXSTRVXIMVS.

This quadrant, on Tycho's instruction, was built by Johann Baptist Hainzel and Paul Hainzel and situated at their countryseat in Göggingen. A planet or star is sighted through E and D; the plumb line keeps the instrument aligned. The altitude is read from the graduated scale (BC, accurate to 1 minute of arc). The instrument can be rotated by handles in the fixed stand.

instrument, the sextant, which he presented to his two friends. His stay in Augsburg was cut short by the death of his father in 1571 at the age of fifty-three. Tycho inherited one-half of the estate at Knudstrup but apparently found the life there not to his liking. Instead, he joined his mother's brother at Heridsvad Abbey, near Helsingør, where he continued his chemical experiments. Alchemy, the mother of chemistry, was then considered a part of astrology, every planet being associated with a metal (Moon, silver; Mercury, quicksilver; Sun, gold; Mars, iron; Jupiter, tin or gold; Saturn, lead). It was, therefore, not unusual for an astronomer-astrologer to pursue that branch of his science. However, he was soon to return to his observations and become the greatest observer of his time.

On November 11, 1572, Tycho—as he was wont to do—looked up at the sky while on a walk and noticed a very bright star, where until then, as he was well aware, no star had been seen previously. In disbelief, he asked passersby, who confirmed his observation. The "new star" was as bright as Venus at its brightest. It appeared in the constellation Cassiopeia, north of the three stars forming the first part of the well-known W of that constellation, and formed a parallelogram with them. Tycho immediately set out to measure the position of the new star with respect to the nine principal stars of Cassiopeia and continued with his measurements whenever there was a clear night. In time, the star grew fainter: by December it was as bright as Jupiter; by February as bright as a star of the first magnitude; April, of the second magnitude;

June, of the third, like the other principal stars in Cassiopeia; and so on. At the end of March 1574, sixteen months after its first appearance, the star was no longer visible. Tycho not only had measured its position but had attempted to find its distance by parallax measurements. He concluded that the new star was neither "in the region of the Elements, below the moon, nor among the orbits of the wandering stars [the planets], but in the eighth sphere among the other fixed stars."

Tycho collected his results in a small book, *De Nova Stella (On the New Star)*, which he hesitated to publish, partly on account of the prevailing prejudice that it was not proper for a nobleman to write books. However, pressed by his friends, who at first did not believe in the appearance of the star, and because of the emergence of nonsensical accounts of the star, he agreed to publication. Two things puzzled Tycho and other astronomers: the nature of the star and the meaning of its appearance. Their imaginations ranged and the wildest speculations were made. The only other known celestial objects to appear from time to time were comets, but these came much closer than *Nova Stella*. It now appears very likely that this was a nova, or supernova, a star that has exploded; we will cover this in a later chapter. Indeed, a very small star of the tenth magnitude discovered in 1865 very close to the position determined by Tycho could have suffered that sudden outburst. Tycho spent considerable time and effort tracing the history of the new star, going as far back as 125 B.C. to the time of Hipparchus—when a new star was supposed to have appeared. He devoted more than 300 pages in his later work, *Astronomiae Instauratae Progymnasmata (Introduction to the New Astronomy)*, to its meaning. His final prediction is interesting because it seemed to announce the reign of King Gustavus Adolphus (1594–1632), although one has to stretch a few points to accommodate the prediction. However, the real mission of the star was to start Tycho on his career and, as Kepler later wrote, "If that star did nothing else, at least it announced and produced a great astronomer."

After finishing *De Nova Stella,* Tycho planned to go abroad; he even thought of settling outside Denmark. He wanted to found an institute for the regular observation of stars—in short, an observatory. In Cassel (in West Germany), Landgrave (or Count) Wilhelm IV of Hesse had installed various instruments under a movable roof in his castle and had made several observations. Tycho visited him on several occasions, and they had struck up a friendship. But whatever plans Tycho had at the time, they were changed, partly on account of an illness and partly because he formed an attachment with a young woman. There is no record of a church wedding, but under Danish law she definitely was considered his wife,

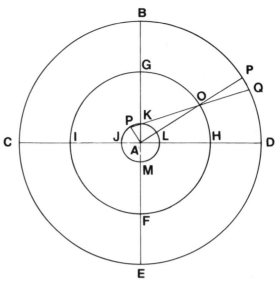

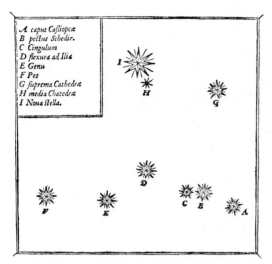

The new star (I) discovered by Tycho Brahe as it appears in his book *Nova Stella*. Tycho measured its position against the other principal stars in the constellation Cassiopeia. In modern terminology these stars are now designated by Greek letters; the stars A, G, and D in the diagram correspond to Cassiopeia beta, alpha, and gamma.

Tycho carried out very careful measurements to see whether *nova stella* showed any parallax, or shifting, which would place it within the lunar sphere. In this diagram taken from his book, the circle CBDE represents the meridian of the Primum Mobile, JKLM the earth, and GHFI the lowest circle of the lunar sphere. If G corresponds to the moon's highest position (which is practically at the zenith) and O its lowest position (which lies on the horizon as seen from R), then PQ would be the parallax as seen from R (or K) and A (at the center). Now, knowing AO and determining the angle BKO, PQ would have to be 58.5' of arc, if *nova stella* lies on (or near) the lunar sphere. However, no such shift was found by Tycho, from which he concluded—correctly—that the star is not on the lunar sphere but must be much farther.

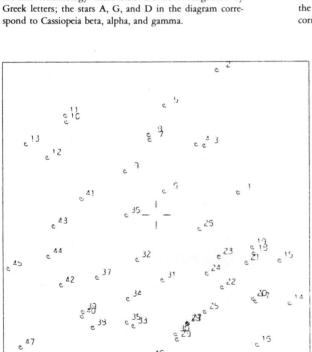

Throughout the ages *nova stella* has decreased in size and shifted its position. At present it is identified with a star of the fourteenth magnitude (the higher the magnitude the lower the brightness), Cassiopeia β. Its coordinates are right ascension: $0^h\ 19^m\ 14^s$; declination: $63°\ 35.6'$. The diagram represents the computer search carried out by Mrs. Kupo of Tel Aviv University.

and the marriage, which lasted twenty-six years, seemed to be quite happy. However, Tycho's family had objected, since she was not a gentlewoman and was considered below his noble standing. But by then Tycho had shed most of his former prejudices.

In the meantime, his growing reputation had attracted considerable attention and he was persuaded by the king—as he made certain to point out—to give a series of lectures at the University in Copenhagen. These lectures took the form of an oration on astrology and the origin of astronomy, which he traced to Seth, son of Adam and Eve, and to Abraham who had concluded, by observing the motion of the sun, moon, and stars, that there was only one God. Tycho then proceeded to trace the influence of the sun and moon on the seasons and weather, and hence on all human endeavors. He was definitely a practicing astrologer, but he differed from his contemporaries in that he considered man's fate not absolutely settled by the stars but alterable by God's will.

Having finished his lectures early in 1575, Tycho finally set out on his rather extended trip, which took him to many places, including Cassel, Basle, and Venice. At all these places he tried to meet prominent astronomers and exchange with them ideas and experiences, just as is the custom of astronomers nowadays when they attend professional meetings. Returning home, Tycho definitely seemed to have made up his mind to settle in Basle. Although he had not made his plans public, he received a summons to appear before the king. The landgrave had written to King Frederick II urging him to provide proper

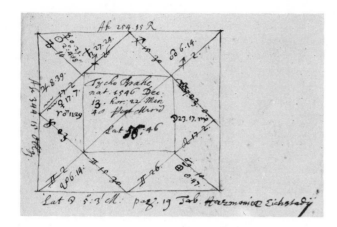

A horoscope cast by Tycho Brahe indicating the year, month, day, hour, and minute of his birth. Like Copernicus, Tycho also had to occupy himself with astrology. Part of his services to the king, for example, consisted of supplying him with a yearly almanac showing the events for the coming year.

The Landgrave Wilhelm IV of Hesse was known for his active interest in astronomy, his observatory, and the instruments he had built for himself. In 1964 this portrait of him was discovered in Cassel; it had been painted in 1577 by an unknown artist. Of particular interest is the globe *(left)*, the sextant *(right)*, and the two figures *(right bottom)*. One figure, shown only partially, is the Landgrave's technical assistant, and the second is undoubtedly Tycho Brahe, who is depicted probably in commemoration of his stay at the observatory in 1575. In the right background is a view of the Lusthaus, part of the Landgrave's residence.

In 1579 Jost Bürgi was called to the court of Cassel as a clockmaker; he built several astronomical clocks. One of the most famous is the Globus Coelestis (Bürgi globe), seen here, which was begun in 1585 and completed in 1693. The construction and diameter of the globe (roughly 28 inches) indicates that it may have been patterned after the instrument shown in the earlier painting of the Landgrave.

Etched on the Bürgi globe are not only the stars making up the various constellations but the constellations themselves. Shown in this detail are Perseus, Auriga, Taurus, and Orion.

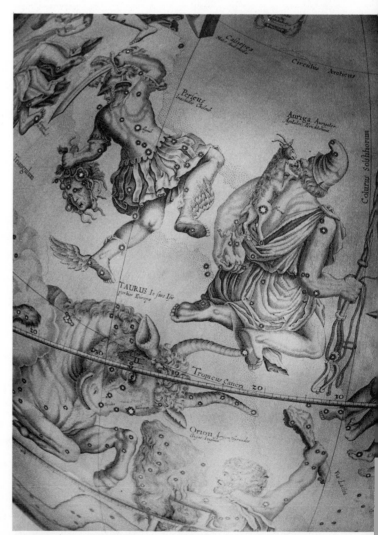

A companion portrait depicts Sabine, wife of Landgrave Wilhelm IV of Hesse and the former Princess of Württemberg. Two additional instruments, partly overlapping, appear at the lower left, apparently a torquetum and a quadrant.

facilities for Tycho to devote himself to his astronomical studies, which would be of great value for the advancement of science, and a credit to his king and country. The king had always been fond of learning and was a benefactor of science. He offered Tycho the island of Hven, enough money to build a house there, and an annual allowance of "five hundred good old dalers" (the equivalent of 400 pounds, at the time a considerable sum). Tycho was urged by his friends to accept this very generous offer, and soon there arose on Hven a magnificent building equipped with the best instruments.

Hven was well suited to be the home and workplace for a man who wanted to be undisturbed by the hustle and bustle of everyday life. Halfway between Helsingør and Copenhagen, the island afforded a beautiful view. Steep cliffs with narrow glens sheltered it from curiosity seekers, with only Bäkvik, an area on the southeast coast, that could serve as a port. Hven's inhabitants lived in a village near the north coast and tilled the farms, of which there were about forty. Most of the southern half of the land was used for grazing, and Tycho built several fishponds

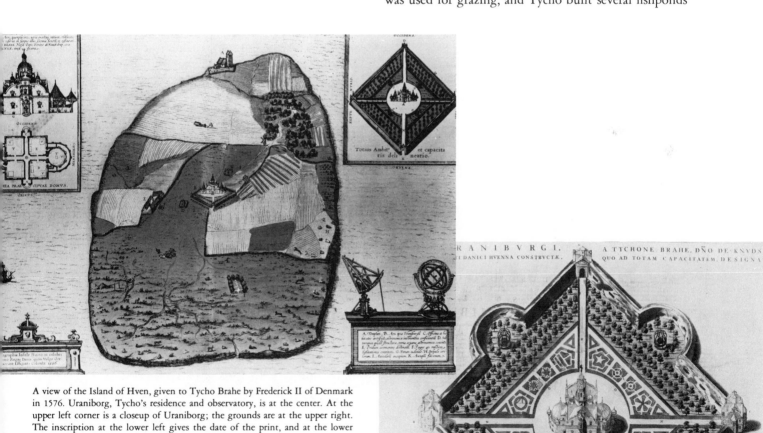

A view of the Island of Hven, given to Tycho Brahe by Frederick II of Denmark in 1576. Uraniborg, Tycho's residence and observatory, is at the center. At the upper left corner is a closeup of Uraniborg; the grounds are at the upper right. The inscription at the lower left gives the date of the print, and at the lower right are replicas of Tycho's sextant and armillary sphere.

Uraniborg. The enclosure was formed by earthen walls, 16 feet thick, and 248 feet from corner to corner. Small buildings at the corners, in the style of the main building, housed the printing press and rooms for servants. There was also an underground prison for refractory tenants. Inside the walls were orchards, consisting of about 300 trees, and gardens. The main building, reached from the gates, was guarded by dogs.

A cutaway view of the main building at Uraniborg, showing the location of the various instruments. The main two observatories, the higher-domed north and south towers, are 18 feet high. The southern one contained a vertical semicircle for measuring azimuths, a sextant, a triquetrum, and a quadrant. In the northern observatory was another triquetrum and a sextant. The triquetrum is an instrument used to find the elevation of a star. (It differs from the quadrant in that angles are not measured directly; the lengths of variable sighting rods are measured, and from these the angles are then deduced.) Connected to each of the main observatories was a smaller one, standing on a single pillar and containing an armillary sphere. All four observatories were covered with conical roofs made of triangular boards, which could be removed. Around the observatories were galleries for observation with smaller instruments.

there. At the center of the island, which was slightly higher than the rest of the rather flat land, Tycho built Uraniborg (Castle of the Heavens). The buildings he put up were as remarkable for their magnificence—suitable to his noble rank—as for their scientific utility. The spacious grounds were in the form of a square with the four corners pointing toward the points of the compass. The main building, at the center of a circular space and on a level slightly higher than its surroundings, was in the

Gothic style. It became famous in the history of Scandinavian architecture.

Tycho attracted a large number of students and assistants, and at times he had as many as forty people working for him on scientific work, which included chemistry as well as astronomy. The best known of his students was Longomontanus (Christen Sörensen Longberg, 1562–1647), the son of a poor farmer. Longomontanus had tired of helping out on the farm after his father's death and at the age of fifteen went to a grammar school. He stayed eleven years and then went to the University of Copenhagen, and the following year he became an assistant at Uraniborg. He stayed with Tycho until 1597, when they both left.

A painting by Heinrich Hansen depicts the observatory at night, aboveground, with Tycho's assistants at work.

Clearly, such a large establishment needed a lot of manual labor, which was supplied by Tycho's tenants in Hven. With the grounds, he had also acquired control of the farms and, in addition to his annual grant, collected rent money. Tycho was an exacting master and the tenants who did not work to his satisfaction—everyone had to give him two days per week—were put in a jail he had built on the grounds. He could be kind but had a very short temper, which made him many enemies and antagonized some of his friends.

To provide for his assistants and the increasing number of instruments, Tycho built another observatory, Stjerneborg (Castle of the Stars). It was situated on a small hill some hundred feet southeast of Uraniborg. To protect his instruments from the weather, he placed them in subterranean rooms, leaving only the movable roofs aboveground. Uraniborg and Stjerneborg were undoubtedly the most advanced and best equipped of the pretelescope observatories. This fact, together with Tycho's ingenuity in designing and constructing his instruments

The Jantar Mantar (House of Instruments) in Delhi was built by Raja Sawai Jai Singh II in 1724, at a time when the telescope had already been in use for a hundred years. But these buildings relied on naked-eye observations; they became permanent monuments to Jai Singh not only as the observer but as the inventor and architect. Seen here are *(top left)* the *Samrat Yantra* (Emperor of Instruments), which is a large stone triangle oriented along the local meridian. Its hypotenuse, or gnomon, is inclined to the horizontal at an angle equal to the latitude, and thus parallel to the earth's axis. Two large graduated quadrants are attached to its base, forming a semicircle centered upon the hypotenuse. The shadow of the gnomon as it sweeps along the quadrants indicates solar time; thus the Samrat Yantra is a giant sundial. However, by graduating the hypotenuse it was possible to read off solar altitude as well; *(bottom left) Jai Prakash* (Light of Jai), perhaps the most ingenious and original of Jai Singh's inventions. It is a concave hemisphere inscribed with the celestial coordinates and oriented so that the positions of all heavenly bodies can be mapped directly onto it. Two

horizontal wires north-south and east-west were attached to it, and an observer moved about the bottom of the concave bowl until he could sight a particular star or planet through the intersection of the two wires; *(right) Ram Yantra* (Ram's Instrument), consists of a pair of large, complementary structures with vertical columns at the centers. In the photograph one of these structures is shown (with part of the central column at the extreme right). Both the inside wall and floors are graduated to permit measurements of altitudes and azimuths. During the day, measurements were made by noting the shadow cast by the sun, while at night a string was tied to the top of the central column and the star sighted along it. To facilitate these operations a number of radial sectors were cut out of the floor so that the observer could stand with his eyes on the same level as the graduations. Likewise, apertures were cut into the walls so that he might climb with facility. Thus, as in the case of Jai Prakash, each Ram Yantra consisted of two complementary structures with the access area of one corresponding to the graduated areas of the other.

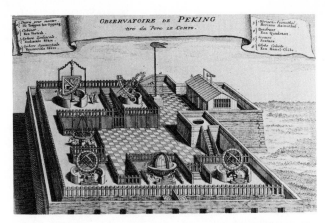

The Jesuit Observatory at Peking, from a copper cut from *Histoire des Voyages*, 1747. The letters and numbers indicate: a. entrance steps; b. observatory containing a study; 1. armillary (Zodiac) sphere; 2. Equatorial Armillary sphere; 3. azimuthal horizon; 4. quadrant; 5. sextant; 6. celestial globe. The steps at the right center lead to a sundial of sorts.

and his outstanding ability as an observer, to a large extent made it possible for man to resolve the riddle of the planetary motions.

In 1577 there appeared a very bright comet, which Tycho observed with his usual care. Although, at the time, he did not possess all the instruments used for subsequent observations, he convinced himself, and others, that the comet was at least three times as far from the earth as the moon and revolved around the sun at a distance from it greater than that of Venus. He thereby shattered the belief that comets were generated in the earth's atmosphere. At the same time, his discovery seriously challenged the concept of crystalline spheres, since these ought hardly be penetrated by a comet.

He was so impressed by these and other results that he decided to write a monumental work on astronomy. The first volume, *Progymnasmata,* although it was begun in 1588, was completed and published by Kepler only after Tycho's death. The second volume, *De Mundi Aetherei Recentioribus Phaenomenis Liber Secundus (Second Book about Recent Appearances in the Celestial World),* dealt with the comet and was printed in Tycho's printing shop in Uraniborg in 1588. A third volume dealing with later comets was never written, although extensive notes exist. The second volume is of particular interest, since there Tycho expounds his own planetary theory. According to his concept, which, as he says, came to him as if by inspiration, the five planets move around the sun, which revolves around a stationary earth, with the whole celestial sphere also turning around the earth once a day. He was led to this model because of two objections to the Copernican system: the motion of "the sluggish and heavy earth" being contrary to "physical principles" and the need for a large distance between the stars and the planets, required by Copernicus.

In addition to the usual arguments against a moving earth, which were taken from the Scriptures, Tycho cited other, more "physical," reasons:

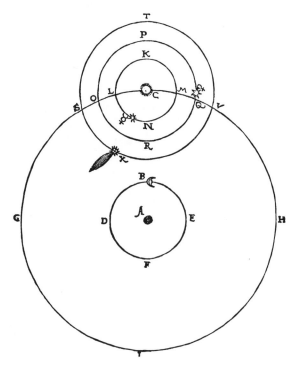

Tycho was aware of the periodic recurrence of comets. Tycho's Earth (A) is at the center surrounded by the lunar sphere (BEFD) and the circuit of the sun (C). Mercury moves around the sun in orbit (NLKM), followed by Venus (QROP). The comet (X) also has a circular orbit around the sun (described by STVX). Note that the tail of the comet is shown drawn diametrically away from Venus (rather than away from the sun as is actually the case). Tycho pointed out that this illustration is an approximation, as is the circular orbit. It appeared in his book *De Mundi Aetherei recentioribus Phaehomenis,* which dealt with the 1577 comet.

1. The motion of the earth is unfelt and difficult to imagine.

2. If the earth is moving, then the relative positions of the stars should change, but the constellations always preserve the same aspect.

3. If the earth revolves, or even rotates around its axis, then a stone or other objects that are dropped to the ground should be left far behind.

4. If the earth revolves around the sun, then Mercury and Venus should show phases similar to those of the revolving moon.

Some of these objections are based on fallacious arguments, while others pose real problems, and it might be worthwhile to examine them more closely.

1. It may, indeed, be difficult to imagine that the earth does move, but that is no reason by itself against a moving earth. It is not felt because we move with it.

2. Tycho was right. The relative positions of the stars should change, i.e., there should be parallax. But if the stars are very far (practically at infinity), parallax would not be observed. This was not established at Brahe's time, although Copernicus himself pointed it out.

3. That a stone should be left behind is fallacious and based on an ignorance of the laws of mechanics. We now

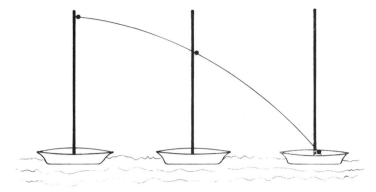

The velocity of the dropped ball has two components, one horizontal and equal to that of the moving ship, and one vertical due to gravity. An observer *not* moving with the ship will see the combined effect; for him the ball describes a parabola, as in the illustration. On the other hand, an observer on the ship can notice only the motion relative to his own. This relative motion is the vertical one due to gravity. Thus, he sees the ball reaching the bottom of the mast irrespective of the ship's motion. The same situation, of course, pertains also to the moving earth. We can only notice that motion of dropped stones, flying birds, etc., that is relative to the motion of the earth.

know, thanks to Galileo, that an object dropped from a moving ship or carriage, etc., will share its motion. The only effect is that of gravity and it will land on the deck of the moving ship on the same spot whether the ship is moving or not.

4. Any planet or moon closer to the sun than we are *should* exhibit phases, if the earth is moving, since we see varying amounts of the illuminated part. Both Venus and Mercury do exhibit phases, but it took the invention of the telescope to demonstrate this. Again, Copernicus understood this and ventured to guess that the phases would be seen if our powers of vision were improved.

Tycho felt more secure with his system, especially since the retrograde motion of the planets could be explained by both the Copernican and Tychonic systems. Moreover, they are equivalent geometrically. Contrary to the common belief that the Tychonic system constitutes a regression, it was more like a bridge between the Ptolemaic and latter-day Copernican systems by ridding the former of its crystalline spheres and paving the way for further investigations. Again we find accounts of both systems in later treatises. Tycho was not a mathematician,

Equivalence of Tychonic and Copernican systems. In the Tychonic system *(left)* the sun (S) is carried eastward (counterclockwise) about the stationary earth (E) by the rigid arm ES. At the same time the planet M (here shown as an outer planet, such as Mars) rotates about S westward (clockwise). As ES rotates faster than SM, the net motion of M is eastward (toward M'), except for periods when SM crosses over ES. In the Copernican system *(right)* both arms SM and SE are shown revolving around the fixed sun (S). The relative positions of E, S, and M in both diagrams will remain the same.

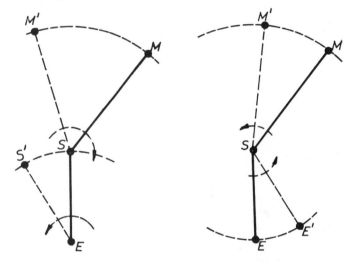

A representation of the Tychonic system, with the earth and belt of the Zodiac prominently displayed at the center. Tycho is shown at the left foreground with a diagram of his system in the background. His celestial globe is in the right foreground in front of the Round Tower in Copenhagen (built later); the relative sizes of the sun and planets appear in the background.

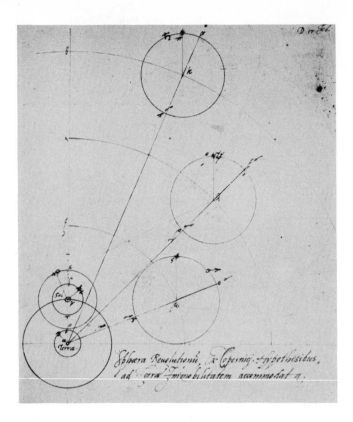

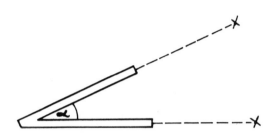

This system was drawn by Tycho on February 17, 1578. Venus and Mercury are shown circling the sun, which revolves around the earth. The deferents of the outer planets Mars, Jupiter, and Saturn are centered about the earth. The epicycle of each planet is of the same size as the sun's orbit. The final form of the Tychonic system is then simply obtained by connecting the positions of the planets (drawn vertically above the centers of the epicycles) to the sun. This construction, incidentally, also demonstrates the equivalence of the Ptolemaic system with the Tychonic system. The diagram was discovered by Professor Owen Gingerich in the unpublished pages bound into Tycho's personal copy of *De revolutionibus orbium coelestium*, at present in the Vatican library in Rome. In the meantime it has been established that the diagram is not due to Tycho Brahe, as suggested by Gingerich, but by Paul Wittich, an astronomer who was associated briefly with Tycho.

The simplest sextant was just a compass, with one of the legs pointed at a celestial object and the other at a point on the horizon. The angle α between the two legs is the altitude. By pointing each leg at a celestial object, one obtains the angular distance between them.

and in his book one finds only the bare outline of his ideas. However, a copy of *De Revolutionibus Orbium Coelestium* recently discovered in the Vatican Library contains about thirty pages of notes in his handwriting. There, one sees not only diagrams describing his construction but also an earlier version of the system in which only Mercury and Venus revolve around the sun. This also raises the question to what extent Tycho was influenced by earlier work, and whether others founded his system. He carried on a long feud with Nicolai Reymers Bär who claimed to have shown the system to the landgrave *before* Tycho published his results. Tycho countered that claim by stating that Bär, who had been a student, had visited him in Uraniborg and stolen or copied the diagrams. Whether this is true or not, it is known that Tycho had "discovered" his system long before he published it but that he kept it secret for fear that it might be plagiarized. It is common enough that certain results are independently discovered by several investigators at the same time, and it is therefore possible that Bär had arrived independently at a similar conclusion, which is sometimes even credited to Heraclides.

3. Instruments

Tycho Brahe was supposed to have shaken his head in astonishment when he received a simple instrument used by Copernicus; he could not imagine how Copernicus had succeeded in making accurate measurements with it for his

theory. Tycho's were precision instruments, most of them made in his own workshop in Uraniborg.

The purpose of these instruments—as is the case with modern ones today—was to measure angles in order to fix the position of a star on the celestial sphere or find its relative position with respect to another star. The type of instrument used depends on the kind of measurement to be made; in general, one would use separate instruments to measure a star's longitude (right ascension) and latitude (or altitude).

Tycho's favorite instrument was the sextant; in its simplest form it consists of two sticks joined together at one end with sights at the other. Tycho improved it by attaching an arc to one end and moving the other by means of a screw. It was this instrument—the first he actually built—which he presented to his friends and benefactors Johann Baptist and Paul Hainzel in Augsburg. In a more refined version, a stick with a movable crossbar was used, making the instrument a Jacob's staff. But the instrument designed by Tycho, the triangular sextant, very ingeniously used a known principle: angles made by two intersecting lines are equal. By aligning the plane of the instrument along the vertical, it becomes an astronomical sextant used to measure altitudes. The modern sextant with its telescopic sight, although a far cry from Tycho's simple instrument, uses the same principle.

Another important instrument was the quadrant, mentioned in an earlier chapter. It is so called because its

In the astronomical sextant the fixed leg is kept horizontal by means of a plumb line (K), while the movable arm (M) is sighted toward the star. The angle between the two arms then gives the star's altitude. Tycho's instrument had a radius of 5½ feet.

In the modern sextant, light from two stars (S and S′) enters the telescope (at L). While light from star S′ travels directly – through the partially silvered mirror M′ – the light from star S′ is reflected by mirrors (M and M′). Mirror M can be rotated until both images coincide, and the angle between S and S′ is then read on the scale (V).

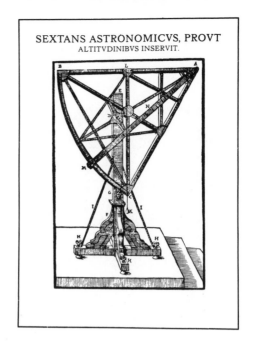

SEXTANS ASTRONOMICVS, PROVT
ALTITVDINIBVS INSERVIT.

The great steel quadrant in Uraniborg was one of Tycho's favorite instruments. Supported by columns (X), the frame could rotate about a central axis (KN). It was kept vertical by a system of plumb lines (V, W), while the arm was balanced by counterweights (H). Readings could be taken both from the horizontal (QRPS) and vertical (O) scales, giving altitude and azimuth.

main constituent is the quadrant of a circle. It can be used to measure the altitude of a star or, by rotating it about the vertical axis, the azimuth of a star. An important use to which quadrants were put at Uraniborg was the measurement of time, for example by noting the position of the sun or its altitude at certain intervals. At Stjerneborg Tycho had his great steel quadrant measuring 7 feet. However, most famous was his mural quadrant in Uraniborg, fastened to the wall, featuring a brass arc, 5 inches wide, and 2 inches thick, with a radius of 6¾ feet. The space within the arc contained a mural of himself.

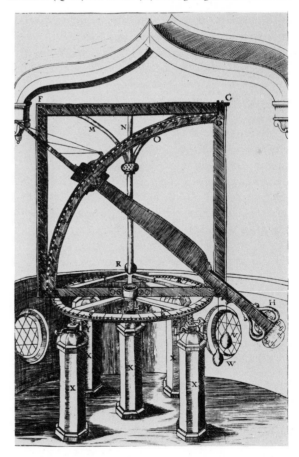

One of Tycho's showpieces was the mural quadrant in the southwest room in Uraniborg. In the mural Tycho points toward an opening in the wall through which the star was sighted by means of a movable sight attached to the brass arc. At his feet lies a dog to whom he referred as "an emblem of sagacity and fidelity." In the background are views of his laboratory, library, and observatory. Small oval pictures of King Frederick II and Queen Sophia on the wall behind him flank a miniature globe, which was an automaton showing the daily motions of the sun and moon, as well as the moon's phases. In the foreground, not part of the mural, several assistants take readings and record them.

Tycho's quadrants became standard equipment in early observatories; today one uses transit circles instead.

The declination and right ascension of a celestial object could be found directly by means of an armillary. Spheres, or armillae zodiacales (Zodiacal armillaries), as Tycho called them, were, as we have seen in the previous chapters, already known to the Greek astronomers and were widely used by the Arabian astronomers, through whom they came to Europe. In their original form they consisted of six circles and were rather cumbersome. A simple hand model was constructed by Gemma Frisius, and we also find table models.

Tycho is credited with inventing the far simpler equatorial armillary, although Alhazen, known for his work on the refraction of light, credited himself with their invention; two of Tycho's instruments were in the small observatories in Uraniborg, while a third and by far the largest, the great armillary, was in the large crypt at Stjerneborg. It was used extensively by Tycho, who considered it one of his most accurate instruments.

One of Tycho's problems—and that of other instrument builders as well—was size. Clearly, the larger the instrument, the more cumbersome and the more difficult it would be to adjust. The same problem, of course, exists with modern telescopes, which must be capable of easy and accurate adjustment. However, Tycho prided himself on the accuracy of his instruments and the ease with which they could be moved. To get an accurate reading the various arcs have to be large enough so that even minutes of arc can be read easily. In his *Progymnasmata* Tycho described at length how he endeavored to find out how large an instrument would have to be to readily distinguish single minutes and estimate fractions. The result of that calculation was the construction of his first quadrant discussed earlier. Later, by introducing transversals he was able to reduce the size of his instruments and still obtain the same accuracy.

A 6-inch transit circle, in 1899, essentially like Tycho's quadrant but equipped with telescopic sights and more refined recording equipment. A Clark chronograph (to record time intervals) is toward the left on the table against the wall, while the north collimator (to adjust the sight line) is at the extreme left of the photograph. Note the marble piers and the sunshade.

◄

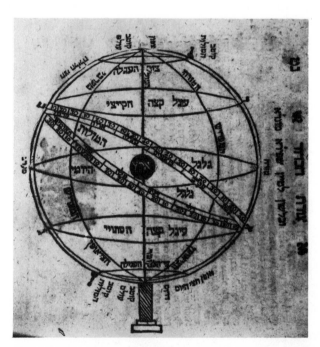

Gemma's astronomical ring is held by means of a loop (at S), the vertical circle being the observer's meridian. If P is aligned toward the celestial pole, the inner two circles represent the celestial equator and meridian. The observer's latitude as well as the star's position can be read off the graduated circles.

A Hebrew armillary sphere. At the center is a small sphere representing the earth, while the ecliptic is the inclined, graduated band. Not indicated are the graduations of the meridian and equator.

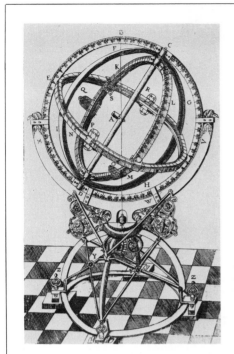

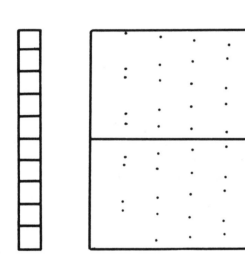

Above left

Another favorite instrument of Tycho was the Equatorial Armillary, of which he had several, both at Uraniborg and at Stjerneborg. Its main part is a rod (CD) around which a number of graduated circles can rotate. The rod is aligned along the earth's axis, with the circle ENMR being along the equator. Another circle (KLM) represents a great circle (meridian) and can rotate about the central rod. Sighting is done through sights P and R for the equatorial plane and O and Q for the meridian, thus enabling the observer to read off declination and right ascension directly.

Above right

The great armillary. The huge declination circle (9½ feet in diameter) was fitted with two movable sights on pointers turning around a small cylinder at the center. This permitted the taking of double observations of the declination, first with one pointer and then with the other, reversing the circle. Its axis could be adjusted by means of screws. This largest of Tycho's instruments was supported by 8 stone pillars, with steps leading to the bottom of the crypt.

Left

Instead of dividing a scale directly with equally spaced lines *(at the left),* the method of transversal points permits finer divisions, which are indicated by vertical rows of 10 points at constant distances. The same method can also be used for an angular scale.

Transversals are simply a series of ten equally spaced points, already used by Bartholomaeus Scultetus, a mathematician at Leipzig University. But Tycho first applied the method to a graduated circle.

Ordinarily, to find the position of a celestial object accurately, the aperture should be as small as possible, about the size of a pinhole. But it is extremely difficult to locate and sight through a pinhole. On the other hand, if the hole is sufficiently large, there is no problem, except that if the sighting is not centered within the hole the position could be off by a fraction of a degree. Tycho was surprised that previous astronomers did not deal with the problem, but this is exactly where he differed from others. He was concerned about accuracy and took steps to obtain

it, while others were content to manage as best they could. An ingenious innovation was his sighting method, and he also introduced parallel sighting whereby an image could be seen simultaneously along parallel slits. These were only two examples of the various improvements Tycho introduced to get the best results possible, and his measurements bear this out.

When Tycho was in Augsburg (1570), he arranged for the construction of a celestial globe, 5 feet in diameter, made of wood and covered with brass plates on which the position of the stars could be marked. It was completed after he had settled in Hven. But he decided to make a precision instrument out of it. He had cracks repaired and restored it to a spherical shape with layers of parchment.

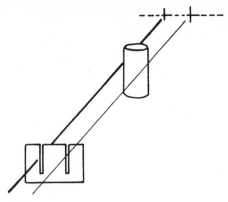

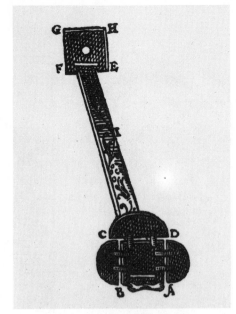

Tycho devised a cylindrical sighting method, in which a cylinder is used as a front sight and two slits, with a spacing equal to the diameter of the cylinder, as a rear sight. The sights are so arranged that the star appears equally bright on both sides of the cylinder when the eye is moved—from one slit to the other—up and down (for altitude measurements) or left and right (for azimuth measurements).

Parallel sighting. For altitude measurements, an alidade was pointed correctly if the image could be seen along both BC-FG and AD-EH. For azimuth measurements the alignment was along AB-EF and CD-GH. For an object like the sun, the image had to pass through a hole in plate EFGH onto a circle drawn on the inner side of plate ABCD.

Finally, two great circles, representing the equator and the Zodiac (divided into degrees and minutes) were engraved on the brass plates. But instead of marking approximate positions of the stars—as would be expected with a model—he entered the positions based on his own accurate observations. After twenty-five years to complete his great brass globe, he commented: "If it has been done well enough, it has been done quickly enough." It was mounted in the library at Uraniborg, where it became another showpiece and a valuable aid.

Unfortunately, none of his instruments survived the stress of time. Critics surveying his two dozen or so instruments in *Astronomiae Instauratae Mechanica* suspected that the instruments were made primarily to keep his craftsmen busy. Nothing could be further from the truth; Tycho selected his instruments carefully and built only those from which he could get maximum use. Of course, he rejected instruments too. He thought little of the

Great brass globe. According to Tycho, the positions of 1,000 stars were recorded accurately on it. It was mounted on a stand and equipped with a movable quadrant and with graduated circles for the horizon and meridian. A hemispherical silk cover could be lowered to protect it from dust. Tycho was extremely proud of this globe and wrote, "A globe of this size so solidly and finely worked and correct in every respect has never I think been constructed up to now anywhere in the world. May I be forgiven if I boast."

As an observational instrument, the astrolabe was used to measure altitudes (when held vertically), such as the sun's position above the horizon, or azimuths (when held horizontally) of celestial bodies, using a graduated circle and a sighting device (alidade). It served also as a computational device for reading off a star's declination and right ascension and finding the observer's geographical latitude. The fretted network, known as rete, is a reproduction of the heavens, the tiny pointers indicating star positions. The eccentric circle, at the bottom, is the ecliptic, while the circles and arcs are lines of equal latitude and longitude.

COMPARISON OF POSITIONS OF STANDARD STARS

Star *	Right Ascension						Declination					
	Tycho's Observations			Computed ‡			Tycho's Observations			Computed		
α Arietis	26°	0′	30″	26°	0′	44.7″	+21°	28′	30″	+21°	27′	33.0″
α Tauri	63	3	45	63	4	11.2	+15	36	15	+15	35	35.6
μ Geminorum	89	29	10	90	28	41.0	+22	38	30	+22	37	48.5
β Geminorum	109	58	0	109	57	47.9	+28	57	45	+28	56	19.1
α Leonis	146	32	45	146	33	19.7	+13	57	45	+13	56	56.9
α Virginis	195	52	10	195	52	36.4	− 8	56	20	− 8	58	22.0
δ Ophiuchi	238	11	20	238	11	9.8	− 2	33	15	− 2	33	21.5
α Aquilae	292	37	20	292	38	36.2	+ 7	51	20	+ 7	50	35.8
α Pegasi	341	2	30	341	3	1.3	+13	0	40	+12	59	47.1

* The identification of the various stars follows modern usage, first introduced by Johann Bayer (1572–1625).
† For 1586 and listed in his *Progymnasmata*.
‡ As obtained by James Bradley, third Astronomer Royal, in 1755 and corrected for their proper motion.
The differences between Tycho's observations and the calculated values appear larger than they really are, since Tycho failed to correct for refraction, or the deflection of light, which he thought to be negligible at Uraniborg's northern position.

astrolabe, which was very popular in the Middle Ages and could be quite useful, since it was portable and not too expensive to make. Tycho's horizontal circles, for example, were built on the same principle, although without the astrolabe's intricate mechanism. Another rejected instrument (it was "too clumsy") was the torquetum.

Although it too seems useful, Tycho pointed out that since the poles of the ecliptic occupy different positions with respect to the meridian at different times, the necessary adjustment would affect the accuracy of the measurement. It was designed by Regiomontanus and Nicholas of Cusa but apparently has not been used much.

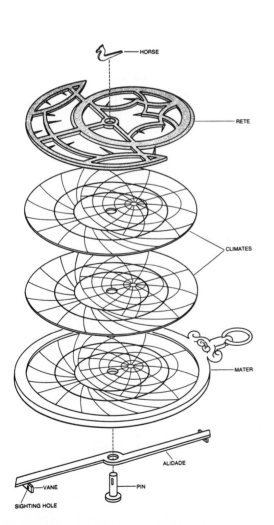

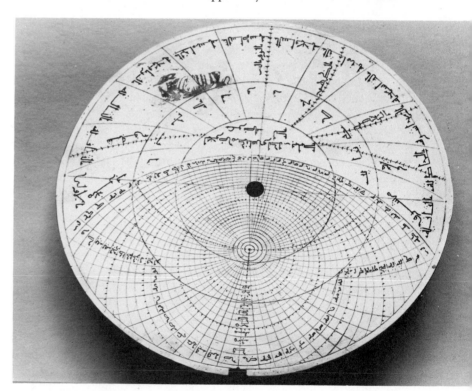

A Moroccan astrolabe dating from the first half of the eighteenth century.

Parts of the astrolabe and their relationship to one another. The main part is the mater (mother), with an engraved circle showing coordinate lines for a particular latitude. The climate circles were different for various latitudes; a standard astrolabe had as many as four. When not in use, they were stacked on top of one another, as shown. Some astrolabes had no extra climates; in those instruments the mater was the only climate and contained coordinate lines for different latitudes, making it quite difficult for anyone but the expert to use. Over the climate fits the rete, which can rotate about its center, representing the celestial pole. The alidade at the bottom is a straight rule, equipped with two vanes containing sighting holes. The alidade could also rotate about its center hole. The astrolabe was held together by the pin and secured by the horse, a wedge usually in the shape of a horse's head.

The oldest European torquetum in existence, said to have been bought by Nicholas of Cusa in 1444. The instrument is shown from the front, indicating the ecliptic (at the base, inclined to the stand), the graduated semicircle with plumb line, and the full disk behind it. Also shown is an astrolabe in the center foreground, flanked by a celestial sphere and a globe.

Tycho hardly left his island, where he lived very comfortably, surrounded by his family, his assistants, and his instruments. No astronomer—or other scientist—ever lived in such splendor. He had many visitors, including dukes, counts, and even Queen Sophia, but for some reason never King Frederick. Tycho provided lavish banquets, organized hunts and games, and entertained his guests with alchemic experiments and demonstrations of his automata. He even kept a dwarf, called Jeppe, who sat at his feet and was supposed to be gifted with telepathic powers.

When King Frederick II died, in 1588, the crown prince, Christian, was only eleven years of age, and the privy council elected four protectors to rule until Christian's twentieth birthday. Among the protectors were Tycho's friends, notably the Chancellor Niels Kaas, and his benefits continued. But Tycho seems to have eroded his still excellent situation. He picked a quarrel with one of his tenants, Rasmus Pedersen, and the case went before the High Court of Justice. Tycho had gone so far as to put Pedersen into irons and to evict him from his farm. But when the court ruled against Tycho, it annoyed him even more and he continued to harass the poor man, which did not improve Tycho's standing with the young king, who prided himself on his fairness to all, irrespective of social standing. Another matter involved the upkeep of a chapel in one of his holdings. Tycho was quite willing to enjoy the income, but he neglected to look after the chapel, despite several reminders. These and other matters undermined a position that was already the envy of his

fellow noblemen. When Niels Kaas died in 1594, Tycho lost a powerful supporter and he started to make overtures to others in high places. The final blow came when Christian IV—he had come to full accession to the throne—stopped several sources of Tycho's income, including the yearly grant of 500 dalers. Obviously the young king was not as interested in astronomy as his father, and he regarded the large expenditures at Hven as an unnecessary expense. He was probably also annoyed by the treatment of his tenants, and perhaps he wanted to show Tycho who was the master. Nevertheless, he must have been aware of the world fame Tycho had won through his work, both for himself and his country, and did not cut off his income completely.

Tycho, in disgust, left Hven and for a while lived in Copenhagen, after which he left the country for Rostock, Germany, where he had friends. He must have had second thoughts about his rash action, for he wrote a letter to the king offering to return if his endowments were reinstated and his services appreciated. However, his overtures came too late. The king, annoyed by Tycho's sudden departure from Denmark, in his reply enumerated his various complaints but suggested that Tycho first return. Instead, Tycho, who had brought his printing press with him, set out to publish a description of his instruments. The result was a handsome small volume, *Astronomiae Instauratae Mechanica,* which he sent to all his friends, a quite common procedure even today when scientists send reprints of their publications to colleagues. It had the desired effect. A copy reached Emperor Rudolph II (1552–1612), King of Bohemia and Hungary, who was a known benefactor of the sciences and who must have been pleased with the dedication to him.

Notwithstanding the stern treatment he had received from King Christian, Tycho sent him a copy of the *Star Catalog* he had recently completed, with a letter congratulating the king on his marriage. In the meantime, he was in communication with Emperor Rudolph and the Prince of Orange, and after a time in Wandsbek, near Hamburg, and Wittenberg, Tycho finally arrived at Prague, the Bohemian capital, in June 1599.

The emperor promised Tycho 3,000 florins (about 900 pounds) a year, and he left all matters in the hands of his chamberlain. It was a handsome salary and, as Tycho wrote his friend Vedel, it was larger than anyone at court received. In addition, he was given the choice of a castle "for the exercise of his studies." Tycho selected Benatek, about 20 miles north of Prague. He moved his family and what instruments he had brought with him; the others were shipped from Denmark, via the Elbe, and arrived a year later. Tycho also wrote to his former assistants and associates asking them to join him. Only a few did, including Longomontanus, who arrived in 1600 with

Tycho's son. During this time Johannes Kepler (1571–1630) who had gained fame with the publication of his first work, *Mysterium Cosmographicum (Cosmic Mystery)*, was advised by his teacher and friend Michael Mästlin to contact Tycho. Kepler, who was then provincial mathematician at Graz and not too secure in his position, took the advice. Correspondence between the two resulted in Kepler's visiting Tycho and, after some initial difficulty, Kepler settled down to work with him; Kepler had resented being treated as a mere "assistant" and without the respect due his scientific standing, which turned out to be superior to his master's. However, Kepler was a kind and humble person, and an agreement was drawn up that provided for him and his family.

As it turned out later, it was a most fortunate arrangement. In the beginning, Kepler was set to work to refute the book by Nicolai Reymers Bär, an occupation he could not have liked, especially since he did not even believe in Tycho's world system but was a supporter of Copernicus. Tycho had even started libel proceedings against his alleged plagiarist, but these came to an abrupt end with the latter's death. And Longomontanus, having finished the lunar theory and tables, returned to Denmark (where in due course he became professor at the University of Copenhagen). This left Kepler with Tycho's prized possession—the detailed observations on planetary orbits, in particular those of Mars. He set to work trying to untangle Mars's motion, convinced that it would solve the whole planetary motion problem, as indeed it did. One may wonder what would have happened had Tycho not left Denmark or had Longomontanus not returned. It is very unlikely that Kepler would have made the long trip to Hven; certainly he would not have obtained the important tables. As it was, before everything else was grabbed by Tycho's son-in-law, Kepler took the tables without permission after Tycho's death, which occurred following a visit to the house of the Baron of Rosenberg in October 1601. Tycho's health already deteriorating, he was seized by a sudden illness during supper. He lingered on for a few days, most of the time delirious; he died on October 24. He was buried with great pomp in Prague, and later a huge monument was erected at his tomb. However, nothing remains of Uraniborg and Stjerneborg, except a few ruins.

Tycho's tomb at the church of Teynkirche (Týnskýkostel) in Prague. It shows a full figure of Tycho in relief, clad in armor, with the left hand on the hilt of his sword and the right on a globe. Underneath is a shield with the arms of Brahe and Bille (his mother's side) and Ulfstand and Rud (the families of his grandmothers). Around the tablet is inscribed his name, date of death, and highlights of his life.

Title page of *Machina Coelestis* by Johannes Hevelius, 1673. The two figures sitting near the celestial globe represent Hipparchus and Ptolemy, while Copernicus and Tycho Brahe, standing, discuss a point. The figure in the carriage is Astronomia; Immortality and Time, at the upper corners of the page, indicate the greatness of the four astronomers.

Very little is left of the once-illustrious Uraniborg and Stjerneborg. At the upper right are the concentric steps leading to the base of the Great Steel Quadrant. The base of the equatorial armillary can be seen partially at the lower left, with the subterranean entrance in the center foreground.

A close-up of the remains of the Great Steel Quadrant at Stjerneborg. The concentric steps and column on which it was fastened are clearly visible.

During his delirium he had expressed over and over his hope that he will not have lived in vain. In few instances can the answer be more affirmative: his fame lives on, to no small extent in the work of his successor Johannes Kepler.

4. The Cosmic Mystery

Johannes Kepler (or Keppler, as he sometimes referred to himself) was born on December 27, 1571, at Weil der Stadt (Weil the Town) in Württemberg, the wine country of southern Germany. Kepler's father, Heinrich, was a mercenary whose only pleasures seem to have been wine and running off to one of the many wars being fought at the time. His mother, Katherine, was an innkeeper's daughter, and according to Kepler's own family horoscope, she too was not a very steady person. The family's only claim to stature was grandfather Sebaldus, the mayor of Weil, in whose house the whole family, including uncles and aunts, lived.

Shortly after Johannes's brother was born, Father went off to fight in the Netherlands under the Duke of Alba. Thereafter he leased an inn, called At the Sun, in nearby Elmendingen. Johannes and his two brothers had to help out in the beer hall, and so Kepler started his life as a bar boy—quite a different life from the easy and pleasant boyhoods of his predecessors Copernicus and Brahe. Even this did not last long, for Heinrich Kepler became restless and left his family to fend for itself.

Johannes was a sickly child, suffering from boils and rashes as well as stomach and gallbladder troubles. All this and more he described in detail in a horoscope he set for himself. He attended elementary school irregularly, partly on account of various sicknesses and partly because he had to help out at home. Both Copernicus and Tycho Brahe had benefactors who saw to it that their protégés received a good education, but nobody seemed to care whether

Johannes Kepler received an education at all. Fortunately, the Dukes of Württemberg had instituted a system of scholarships for the children of the poor and faithful who were diligent and God fearing. (They needed brilliant men who could hold their own in the controversies with the Catholics, and the Protestant universities of Wittenberg and Tübingen were to provide them.) Kepler, who was a brilliant student despite his various handicaps, was sent first to the seminary in Maulbronn, where he learned Latin and Greek, and then, after mastering these subjects, to the University of Tübingen. Since he was deeply religious and interested in philosophy and theology, a clerical profession suggested itself, and Kepler, at the age of eighteen, enrolled in the Faculty of Theology. At the university he met Michael Mästlin, an excellent astronomer, a former village pastor, and then professor of mathematics at Tübingen. Mästlin became Kepler's close friend and adviser and taught him the principles of the Copernican world system, privately, since the university administration frowned upon such heretic studies.

Kepler saw in the Copernican system not only a theory but a vindication of God's harmony, and he tried to impart his vision—unsuccessfully—to his fellow students. He was graduated in 1591, second in a class of fourteen, and then devoted himself mainly to a study of theology. Master Kepler was not too popular among his colleagues. They couldn't accept his unorthodox views on the universe or his attempts to bring "harmony" to his coreligionists as he urged them to patch up their quarrels with the reformists. When the dual position of mathematician to the Province of Styria (Austria) and teacher at the Evangelical Seminar, a Protestant lower school, in Graz fell vacant at the death of its incumbent Georg Stadius, the senate of the Protestant university at Tübingen recommended Kepler for the post. (Styria was under Catholic Habsburg dominance, but Graz was predominantly a Protestant town and therefore had both a Catholic university and an Evangelical school.) Kepler, bent on a career as a clergyman, professed no interest in

Johannes Kepler as the imperial mathematician, by Jakob von Heyden (1620/21). Kepler suffered from multiple vision as well as myopia, or nearsightedness, which made it impossible for him to carry out any astronomical observations.

The marketplace in Weil der Stadt (near Stuttgart), Kepler's birthplace. Grandfather Sebaldus's house faces the marketplace. Note the foreground fountain. One of the more vulgar stone faces serving as spouts is supposedly that of the mayor. In the background is a statue of Kepler (seated).

Michael Mästlin is shown with the young Kepler at his side during a lecture on the Copernican system. From a frieze of the Kepler Monument in Weil der Stadt by A. V. Kreling (built 1869/70).

either mathematics or astronomy and hesitated at first. But he finally accepted the appointment since it afforded a certain amount of financial independence—150 guldens (about $75) per year plus free lodging and heating—and appealed to his inborn love of adventure. So in 1594 Johannes Kepler became "Mathematicus of the Province of Styria" and a glorified high-school teacher. The demand for mathematics at Graz did not seem to have been very high, since he had only two students in his class—the same number Einstein had when he became an instructor. The school authorities felt that he should earn his keep, and so Kepler also taught Latin and several other humanities. One additional duty was the preparation of annual astrological calendars, for which he received a further 20 gulden. In his first calendar he predicted—to his own

surprise—an extremely cold winter and an invasion by the Turks. Both events occurred, and he gained a reputation as an astrologer quite surpassing what he had as a mathematician and teacher. Kepler became a lifetime dabbler in astrology, casting and interpreting horoscopes for fun and money. But he does not seem to have taken the art too seriously. Although he accepted the influence of the stars, he rejected contemporary astrological practice.

While teaching and casting horoscopes in Graz, Kepler continued the cosmic speculations he had started in Tübingen, except that now he applied to them his knowledge of mathematics. What fascinated him was the relationship between planetary distances and their velocities. He wanted to find a single law of geometrical construction that would explain the observed orbital

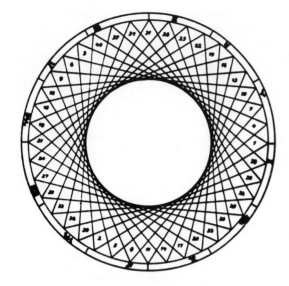

arrangement of the planets. This helped single out Kepler from others who attempted to solve the "cosmic mystery," and it put him on the dividing line between mere speculation and scientific investigation.

His first idea came to him, as he tells it, when he wanted to show his students how the great conjunctions jump through eight signs of the Zodiac and pass from one trigon, that is, at distances of 120 degrees, to another. For the purpose, he had drawn a large number of triangles within a circle in such a way that the end of one always formed the beginning of the next. Remarkably, the points at which the triangles cut each other formed a circle and the difference between the radius of the inner circle and that of the outer circle corresponded to the difference in distance between Saturn and Jupiter. A coincidence, but Kepler felt that he had stumbled upon the key to a secret. "The delight that I took in my discovery," he wrote, "I shall never be able to describe in words." He expanded the idea by inscribing a square for Mars, a pentagon for the earth, and so on, but the idea did not work. The Divine Geometer had not followed such a simple scheme.

Kepler, however, undaunted, tried again. If plane figures did not work, perhaps solid ones would. He tried a system of spheres and cubes, but this procedure did not work either. He now hit upon a really remarkable device.

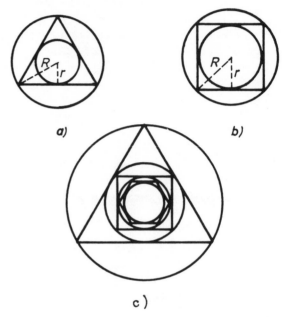

Kepler's first guess. A number of regular plane figures, circumscribed and inscribed by circles, provide a series of circles that might correspond to planetary orbits. The ratio of their radii has one value for triangles and another for squares, with still other values for pentagons. For example, in figure (a), upon inscribing a circle (radius r) in an equilateral triangle (in which all sides are equal) and then circumscribing a circle (radius R), it will be found that the ratio of the two radii $r/R = \frac{1}{2} = 0.5$ In the square (b), if a circle (radius r) is inscribed in a square, and another circle (radius R) circumscribes the square, the ratio of the two radii $r/R = 1/\sqrt{2} = 0.707$.

Kepler's second guess, in which he tried spheres circumscribing cubes (passing through the eight corners) and spheres inscribed in cubes (touching the six faces). For a cube of length L, the radius of the inscribed sphere is L/2, while the radius of the circumscribed sphere is $\sqrt{3}$ L/2; thus, the ratio of the two radii is the square root of 3, or roughly 1.73.

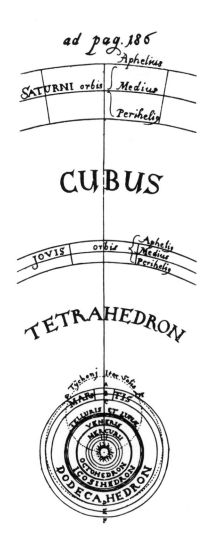

ad pag. 186

Aphelius

SATURNI orbis { Medius { Perihelis

CUBUS

JOVIS orbis { Aphelis { Medius { Perihelis

TETRAHEDRON

Diagram for Kepler's planetary orbits. For each orbit there are three circles corresponding to the outer, middle, and inner radii of the spheres that circumscribe and enclose the perfect solids. (The names of the solids appear between the different systems of circles.) The radii of the different circles correspond to the distance of the planet at the aphelion and perihelion; the central one is the average of the two distances. The question why the planets are found at these particular distances still has not been satisfactorily answered.

The *anima motrix* of the sun, which is responsible for driving the planets around in their orbits. The rays are restricted to the plane of the ecliptic. Therefore, at twice the distance from the sun, only half the rays fall on a planet; thus the planet's orbital velocity will be only one-half that at the original distance.

He knew that there are exactly five perfect solids in nature out of the many regular ones. The number itself appeared to be remarkable, since it corresponds exactly to the number of gaps between the six planets: Mercury-Venus-Earth-Mars-Jupiter-Saturn. Kepler was convinced he was on the right track. Each planet has its own sphere circumscribing and being circumscribed by one of the five solids. The sphere of Saturn contains a cube in which the sphere of Jupiter is inscribed; Jupiter is circumscribed by the tetrahedron, followed by the sphere of Mars. This circumscribes the dodecahedron and the sphere of the earth (and the moon). The icosahedron is inscribed within that sphere; next is the sphere of Venus followed by the octahedron, and finally the sphere of Mercury. The orbits of the planets are not perfect circles but are eccentric, and each sphere is given a thickness to allow for the difference between distance at aphelion and perihelion.

Although Kepler felt he was divinely inspired, he had to test his theory by comparing it with observations. Apart from some minor adjustments, agreement with the values given by Copernicus was fairly satisfactory, but he was still not satisfied. Knowing that Copernicus referred his distances not to the central sun but to the center of the earth's orbit, Kepler proceeded to correct them (with the help of Mästlin, whose knowledge of mathematics was

superior to his), and thereby made his first important contribution—a truly sun-centered universe. He also endeavored to find the "driving forces," or *animae motrices,* that make the planets go round in their orbits. In his later life he nearly discovered the universal law of gravitation, but at this stage he talked about it only in general terms. Nevertheless, this was the first time that physical arguments were used to explain geometrical relationships; thus Kepler may be said to be a true forerunner of modern astronomy.

Finally, he endeavored to find the "proportions of the motions to the orbits." Since the periods of revolutions are not proportional to the distances from the sun, it must be assumed that either the *animae motrices* of the farther planets is weaker, or that there is one *anima motrix* associated with the sun, which decreases with distance. He adopted the possibility, and assumed that the influence is inversely proportional to the radius of the circle over which it is spread, i.e., decreased linearly with distance. At the same time, the period of revolution would increase with the length of the circumference. Starting with Saturn, he then obtained the ratios of distances of the other planets. The agreement with observation was quite good. Moreover, apart from his misconception of the driving force—an assumption he held at all times—Kepler recognized the central, solar nature of that force.

The result of this work is contained in *Mysterium Cosmographicum (Cosmic Mystery),* published in 1596 when Kepler was twenty-five years old. It is a strange mixture of geometry, physics, and metaphysics, written in Kepler's characteristic style, rambling and taking the reader along the tortuous road he himself followed. Although the basic idea of the *Mysterium Cosmographicum* was wrong—that the universe is built around the perfect solids—it laid the foundation for his further investigations and brought the

In 1604 Kepler discovered a nova (actually a supernova) whose magnitude reached –2.2. The optical remnant seen here, now identified as SN Ophiuchi 1604, consists of a fan-shaped region containing a number of bright knots. It is remarkable that the similar supernova of 1572 (Tycho's, seen earlier in this chapter) produced quite different optical remnants. In particular, Tycho's remnant did not contain any nebulosity resembling the slowly expanding fan of flocculi associated with Kepler's supernova.

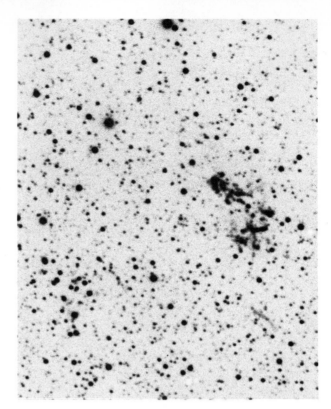

Kepler profited greatly from his association with Tycho Brahe, from whom he received the observational data for his computation. From J. G. Doppelmaier's *Atlas Coelestis* (Nuremberg, 1742).

young mathematicus to the attention of Tycho Brahe.

Kepler knew that Tycho was the only person who could supply him with the observational data he needed to "erect his edifice," but Tycho refused to publish his observations until he had finished his own theory. Fortunately—for Kepler and the cause of astronomy—Tycho, then in Prague, was in need of assistants. A letter Kepler wrote asking whether he might come to examine Tycho's observations was answered very cordially: "Come, not as a stranger, but as a very welcome friend; come and share in my observations with such instruments as I have with me and as a dearly beloved associate." Kepler arrived in Prague on January 1, 1600.

The two men were opposites in everything, except in their devotion to their lifework, and there was much friction. Tycho was middle-aged, at the peak of his career,

rich and respected, a nobleman; Kepler was young, at the beginning of his work, poor, misunderstood, and a commoner. He spent several months at Benatek, mostly working on Tycho's problems but becoming acquainted with his painstaking way of making observations.

Tycho offered him the assistantship rather than the partnership he had expected. And he couldn't guarantee Kepler's salary requirements, since the emperor was reluctant to employ another mathematician. Their negotiations went on for some time, in the course of which Kepler stated his conditions. He would carry out every astronomical task, insofar as it was compatible with his health (because his eyes were too weak, he could not carry out any observation and had no skill for mechanical work). He would share his day with Tycho (work in the mornings or afternoons and pursue his own ideas the other half of the day) and reserve as much free time as necessary to attend religious services and to take care of his own affairs. Tycho accepted Kepler's conditions good-naturedly, obviously realizing that he needed a competent mathematician to complete his work.

In the meantime, Kepler had returned to Graz but had found the situation there unbearable. Archduke Ferdinand (later Emperor Ferdinand II) of Habsburg was bent on ridding the provinces of heretics and had closed all Protestant schools; earlier, only Kepler had been permitted to return. Now all Lutheran citizens of Graz had to appear before a commission and either declare their willingness to return to Catholicism or be expelled. Kepler absolutely refused to change his religion. In vain he asked Mästlin to get him a position at a Protestant university, "even a small one." It was then that Tycho's agreement to his conditions arrived, and Kepler set out again for

Prague, this time with his wife, a young widow he had married while he was still at the school in Graz. When Tycho died a few months later, Kepler officially became the imperial mathematician.

5. The New Astronomy

Kepler arrived at Benatek to find Longomontanus occupied with Mars, a fact Kepler later described as an act of Divine Providence, since Mars alone could provide the solution to the puzzles of astronomy. Mars's orbit is more eccentric than all the outer planets—and this was the reason Tycho and Longomontanus could not reconcile its observed motion with their contrived circular ones, even in combinations. Kepler took over the problem and Longomontanus turned to lunar theory, which he completed before his departure.

Six years and thousands of pages of calculations later, Kepler succeeded in wresting from Mars the secret of the *New Astronomy,* the title of his second book, a monumental work published as *Astronomia Nova.* He had not been given a free hand. Tycho had asked him to treat the motions of Mars according to his Tychonic system, and he repeated the request at his death. Kepler tried to fulfill the request, and this partly explains the unusual form of *New Astronomy* in which all astronomical problems are treated according to the methods of Ptolemy, Copernicus, Tycho—and finally Kepler. Moreover, as in his earlier *Mysterium Cosmographicum,* or *Cosmic Mystery,* he takes the reader along his journey, so to speak, and shares with him all his successes, failures, and tribulations; this is a quite different method from the less revealing style of some of our modern authors so accustomed to "it can be shown that" or "after some computations we obtained. . . ." As a result, *New Astronomy* is one of the most pertinent works of science, though difficult to read because of the need to separate the wheat from the chaff.

Quite early in his battle with Mars (in his dedication to *New Astronomy* Kepler describes his work as such), Kepler scored a victory when he showed that the plane of Mars's orbit did not oscillate but remained constant, that it was inclined to the ecliptic by a constant angle of 1 degree 50 minutes and passed *through* the position of the sun. This confirmed Kepler's thesis—already stated in his first book, *Cosmic Mystery,* that the entire planetary system should be referred to the sun's true position, not off-centered. Another innovation introduced by Kepler concerned the speed of a planet in its orbit. It will be recalled that

Ptolemy introduced the equant, with respect to which motion was uniform, while Copernicus replaced it with an off-centered sun and additional epicycles but still kept to uniform motion. Kepler, on the other hand, argued that the velocity of a planet should be related to its distance from the sun, since it is the sun that provides the driving force. This, indeed, was quite a departure from traditional cosmology, as far as geometry and physical principles are concerned. He also reintroduced the notion of the equant but only as a mathematical device.

Encouraged by his success, Kepler embarked on the ambitious and tedious task of determining Mars's orbit, using Tycho's observational data. If the orbit was indeed circular, this would be a fairly simple process. Using some of Tycho's observations (three would be enough for a circle) for calculations and still others to check his results, he found to his chagrin that the orbit was not a circle. The next step was to construct the orbit of Mars without any assumptions and then to find the curve that would fit it. However, before he could do this he had to be sure that he had the correct motion of the earth itself, since all measurements were carried out relative to the earth, and any error in its motion would naturally affect all others. To find the earth's true motion, Kepler designed an ingenious yet simple method. It consisted in plotting the earth's position at successive Martian years, that is, at times when Mars had returned to its original position. As one might have expected, the motion of the earth was not uniform. Moreover, at its two extremes (aphelion and perihelion) the speed was exactly inversely proportional to its distance (larger speed for smaller distances and vice versa). The question remained, If the speed is not uniform, what is? Kepler tried many ideas and finally, by equating an area with the sum of an infinite number of adjacent lines (a hitherto mathematically inadmissible procedure), found that the areas swept out in equal times were equal. This result, a foundation in modern astronomy, is the original formulation of what is now referred to as Kepler's second law. (It was a stroke of luck that he first examined the earth's motion, since the earth's orbit differs only slightly from a circle.)

Confident that he now had a basis on which to work, Kepler computed the orbit of Mars. Although he was able to fit a circular orbit for 10 observations within an error of less than 2 minutes of arc, when he added 2 more points he found a discrepancy of 8 minutes of arc. Admittedly, 8 minutes of arc is not large—Copernicus said he would be satisfied with observations within an error of 10 minutes—but it would have been large to Tycho. His observations were accurate to within 2 minutes of arc, and anything larger was not admissible. The theory did not fit the observations, and therefore the theory had to be wrong,

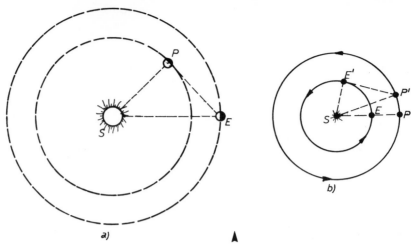

a)   b)

Under the assumption that the orbit is circular, it is a simple matter to determine that orbit. For an inferior planet (a), such as Venus, it is sufficient to measure the angle SEP when Venus (P) seems farthest from the sun (when SPE is as seen here, a right angle). Knowing the angle, one can then determine Venus's distance from the sun (relative to the earth-sun distance of approximately 93 million miles). For a superior planet (b), such as Mars, the situation is somehwat more difficult. Let P be the position of Mars and E that of the earth when they are aligned with the sun at S. Since the earth travels faster than a superior planet (but slower than an inferior one), there will be two other positions, E' and P', for which the angle SE'P' is a right angle. The time it takes the earth to travel from E to E' equals the time it takes Mars to go from P to P' (although, of course, the angles traversed are not the same). During one period the earth (and Mars) make a complete revolution—that is, they go through 360 degrees and describe angles ESE' and PSP' respectively. Thus, these angles (that is, their fraction of 360 degrees) are proportional both to the time it took to traverse these distances and to the planets' respective periods. Therefore, knowing the time and the periods, these angles can be determined. Further, the angle E'SP' is just the difference of the angles E'SE and P'SP, and we have the same situation as that pertaining to the inferior planet above: knowing that angle, we can determine the distance of Mars from the sun (that is, SP'), again relative to the earth-sun distance.

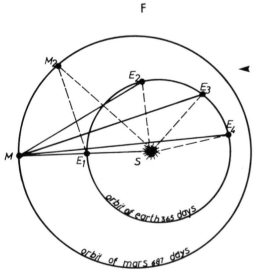

Nonuniform motion. As seen from the center (B), the planet (D) moves faster when nearer E than F. If those changes obey a simple law, then it is possible to find an observational point (A) from which the planet *seems* to move at uniform speed. Since, therefore, the planet seems to move faster the closer it is to the observer, this point (A), or *punctum equans*, must lie somewhere between B and F; the angle EAD is called the true anomaly. There are two other anomalies, the eccentric anomaly given by the angle EBD, and the mean anomaly determined by the angle EGD, which is proportional to the time—the point G is closer to E, the planet moves there faster, and hence the time taken would be shorter. Kepler pointed out that any two of the three anomalies could be calculated if the third was known.

Plotting the orbit of Mars and the earth. Kepler determined the orbit of the earth as it might appear to an observer on Mars, and then used the data to find the orbit of Mars. The initial positions are taken when Mars (M), the earth (E_1), and the sun are in a straight line. After 687 days—a Martian year—Mars has returned to its original position, but the earth is still short of its initial position, shown at E_2. Similarly, after two more revolutions the earth will be at E_3 and E_4 respectively. This determines the angles E_2SM, E_3SM, and E_4SM. On the other hand, the angles SME_2, SME_3, and SME_4 were given from Tycho's observations. Since a triangle is completely determined by one side and two adjacent angles, this is sufficient to determine the sun-earth distances SE_1, SE_2, SE_3, and SE_4 (in terms of the basis SM) and hence the earth's orbit. Similarly, using consecutive earth years when the earth is at E_1 and Mars at M, M_2, etc., Tycho determined the orbit of Mars.

The formulation for Kepler's second law—the time taken for a planet to move from a position P to P'—depends on the area of the orbit enclosed within these points. SP, in both instances here, sweeps out *equal* areas in equal times; that is, the shaded areas are equal. In formulating this law, Kepler took the orbit to be circular, with the sun (S) off-center (C). He realized, however, that he made two doubtful assumptions: one, that the sum of an infinite number of lines can be equated to an area, and two, that the orbit was circular.

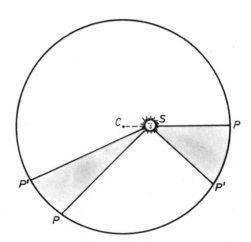

ET QVIA cap. XXXIV obiter in motus LVNÆ mentionem incidi;lubet totum negocium delineare paulo clarius,nefcrupulus aliquis a LVNA injectus lectorem in toto hoc tractatu torquear, quo minus expedite mihi fuum præbeat affenfum:quin potius ut mirifice confirmetur, evidentifsima motus LVNARIS contemplatione:denique ut Aftronomiæ pars Phyfica hoc libro fit integra. Nam etfi in theoriam LVNÆ paucula quædam differenda funt, feu aliter tradenda, feu particularius explicanda: illa tamen hinc orientur.

Animadvertit TYCHO BRAHEVS per diutinas & creberrimas obfervationes LVNÆ in omni fitu cum SOLE,quod in LVNA præter anomaliam epicycli,& præter illam anomaliam menftruam,quæ etiam PTOLEMÆO notafuit,ipfe etiam medius motus(refpectu harum duarum inæqualitatum fic dictus) nondum fit plane medius, fed intendatur fub conjunctiones & oppofitiones cum SOLE,remittatur in quadraturis; ut etiamfi nullis turbaretur epicyclis, tamen LVNA ipfa,etiam in concentrico TERRAM circumiens,inæqualiter circumiret.

Sit s

not the other way around. The answer was obvious, at least to Kepler: the orbit was not circular.

Now began a long and frustrating search for the true orbit, leading from one cul-de-sac to another. That the orbit was not circular was in itself not surprising; this had been realized by Ptolemy and Copernicus. However, since for them a circular motion was the only one permissible, they had to introduce a system of deferents and epicycles. Kepler cut that Gordian knot by giving up the idea of circular motion—as he already had done away with the idea of uniform motion—and he looked for *the* curve that

This page from Kepler's *Astronomia Nova* illustrates the triangulations used in determining the orbits of Earth and Mars. In order, going away from the center, are the orbits of Mercury, Venus, Earth, and Mars. The text discusses the motion of the moon.

would describe the orbit without a system of epicycles. However, he could not shake completely the prejudices of his time and he used a circular motion as the basis for his calculations—which cost him months of unrewarding work. By autumn, 1602, the conclusion was unmistakable:

The planet's [Mars] orbit is not a circle; but [starting at aphelion] it curves inward little by little and then [returns] to the amplitude of the circle at perigee [perihelion]. An orbit [line] of this kind is called an oval.

(New Astronomy)

This might have been the end of the story, but Kepler was not satisfied. Having rid astronomy of epicycles, he was left with "only a single cartful of dung," he wrote to Longomontanus. Circles and spheres possessed the aesthetic beauty that made them so attractive to Pythagoras and everyone thereafter, but an oval—even a perfect one and not the "planetary egg" that he found—did not. "If only the orbit were an ellipse," he wrote to his friend Fabricius, a theologian in Ostela, East Friesland, "then the problem would have been solved already by Archimedes and Apollonius."

Kepler discarded his previous work and started all over, and then—after another unsuccessful battle with his egg—a curious accident happened. His new calculations again indicated that the orbit of Mars was not a circle but was flattened at opposite sides. However, the difference between this (at the maximum flattening) and a circumscribed circle gave a value of 0.00429 (half of the original 0.00858). Also, the ratio of Mars's distance from the center of its orbit to Mars's distance from the sun

PLANETARY ELLIPSES					
Planet	Semimajor * axis	Period †	Speed km/sec	Eccentricity ‡	Inclination to ecliptic
Mercury	0.3871	0.2408	47.8	0.2056	7.00°
Venus	0.7233	0.6152	35.0	0.0068	3.39°
Earth	1.0000	1.0000	29.8	0.0167	0.00°
Mars	1.5237	1.8809	24.2	0.0934	1.85°
Jupiter	5.2028	11.8622	13.1	0.0484	1.31°
Saturn	9.5388	29.4577	9.7	0.0557	2.49°
Uranus §	19.1820	84.0130	6.8	0.0472	0.77°
Neptune §	30.0580	164.7930	5.4	0.0086	1.77°
Pluto §	39.4390	247.6860	4.7	0.2502	17.17°

* In terms of the Sun-Earth distance (called astronomical units) equal to roughly 93 million miles. In other words, Mercury, at .3871, compared with Earth, at 1.0000, is only roughly one-third of Earth's distance to the sun.

† In terms of tropical years, i.e., the time it takes the earth to revolve around the sun starting at the vernal equinox.

‡ The eccentricity of circles is zero; planetary ellipses differ very little from them.

§ The outer planets, not known at Kepler's time.

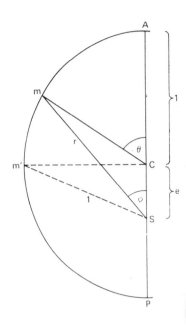

After discarding the idea of a circular orbit, Kepler found that the orbit of Mars resembled an oval: In a sudden flash of inspiration he had noticed that at quadratures (i.e., when m is at m' and the angle θ is a right angle) Mars is exactly at its mean distance from the sun (i.e., AC = m'S). This suggested to him a simple law – the radius (Sm) varies with the angle θ, which depended on only the distance or eccentricity of CS. (Later corrections also included the angle ϕ).

◄

Orbit of Mars. As Mars (M) moves along its orbit, the angle SMC (called the optical equation) changes; but Kepler noticed that it reached a maximum value when MC was at right angles to the axis PP'. Also at that point the two distances MC and MS showed a simple relationship; that is, with the addition of the maximum width of the shaded area (the "lune" between the orbit and the surrounding circle) they were equal. Kepler realized that this was more than just a coincidence, that it indicated the existence of a general relationship among three elements: the Mars-Sun distance (SM) (at any given time); the angle PCM; and the two given constants, the radius CP and the fixed distance of the sun from the center (CS). He had discovered the equation of the elliptic orbit described by Mars (and the other planets).

▼

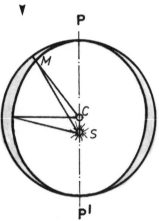

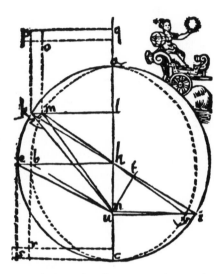

Kepler's triumphant diagram taken from *Astronomia Nova* showing the true orbit of Mars (dotted lines) and the auxiliary circle. The diagram also illustrates the proof of the second law of equal areas, which holds for the ellipse exactly. To show his pleasure, Kepler added a drawing of Victorious Astronomy at the top of the diagram.

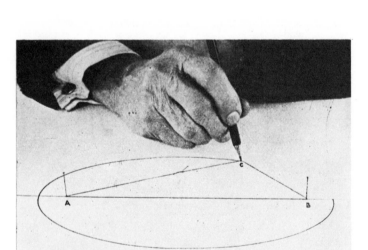

Mechanical construction of an ellipse: The ellipse is a plane curve, the path of a point C that moves so that the sum of its distances from two fixed points A and B (called the foci) remains the same. In other words, AC+BC is constant (the value of that constant, of course, depends on the fixed distance AB). This provides us with a simple method of drawing an ellipse. A loop of string of fixed length is placed around two pins at A and B and kept taut with a pencil, as shown. As the pencil moves around the paper (always keeping the string taut), the curve described will be an ellipse. Kepler also found a mathematical equation, defining an ellipse, which can also be constructed by geometrical methods.

showed an interesting maximum value: 1.00429. Kepler realized that this "coincidence" must be due to some relation between these distances (and angles they make with each other).

In fact, he found the equation of the ellipse without realizing that he had done so. By that time, however, he felt that the orbit must be close to an ellipse and he used ellipses to describe it. He used geometrical methods to construct elliptical orbits and then finally noticed that these and the equations gave the same result. Now, everything fell into place. The first law of Kepler (referred to as Kepler's First Law) could then be formulated rigorously in regard to an elliptical orbit with the sun at a focus.

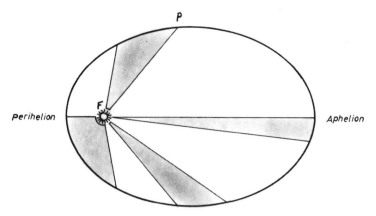

Perihelion

P

F

Aphelion

Kepler generalized his results for Mars to all planetary orbits. These laws may be summarized as follows (the first law): (1) The sun is at the focus F of an ellipse described by the planet P; (2) equal areas are swept out by the radius vector FP in equal times. In the diagram this is indicated by the shaded areas, which are equal; thus a planet travels faster when near the perihelion and slower when near the aphelion. (The figure is exaggerated, since planetary orbits are nearly circular.)

Kepler succeeded where others before had failed. Not only did he do away with epicycles and bulges, but in their stead he formulated the laws governing planetary orbits in a simple and natural way. He laid the foundations of the new astronomy, although this was not recognized at the time. Galileo, for example, ignored Kepler's work completely, and even Newton, much later, paid scant attention to it, although without it Newton's famous law of universal gravitation would be more difficult to understand. In part, this rejection may have been owing to the difficulty of reading *New Astronomy* and the inherent prejudice against any sun-centered theory. But to a large extent it was due to the nature of the laws themselves. Theoretically, there is no reason why planets should move along ellipses or ovals or even circles. Only when the underlying physical mechanism is understood does it become clear why certain forms are preferred over others. But in Kepler's time such a mechanism did not exist. This was the reason why Kepler, even before he "discovered" the laws of planetary motion, was concerned with the physical nature of the driving force.

Kepler's outlook is best illustrated by his letters. To Fabricius he wrote, "The difference consists only in this, that you use circles, I use bodily forces." He is even more explicit in a letter to Herwart von Hohenburg, a Bavarian statesman, "My aim is to show that the heavenly machine is not a kind of divine, live being, but a kind of clockwork. . . ." In the introduction to *New Astronomy* he describes gravity in terms that seem to anticipate Newton: "Gravity is the mutual bodily tendency between material bodies toward contact; two stones for example [outside the reach of a third force and placed anywhere in space] would come together, after the manner of magnetic bodies, each approaching the other in proportion to the other's mass." This was the seed of universal gravitation, but the next step was wrong—Kepler's Aristotelian conception of the law of inertia, wherein inertia is identified with a tendency to come to rest. In that concept the moon and earth, for example, are kept in their respective orbits by a spiritual or equivalent force.

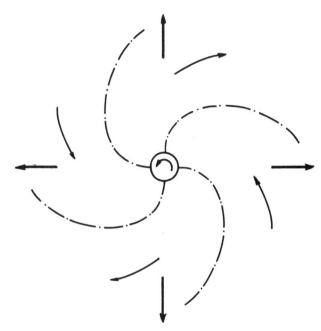

Solar wind. Although Kepler's idea of an *anima motrix* was erroneous, the sun does emit radiation that includes part of the corona, which the sun's attractive, gravitational force cannot hold. This gas, called plasma, pervades the solar system as an interplanetary medium and interacts strongly with the sun's magnetic field. In fact, the plasma becomes "frozen" into it. In the diagram, thin arrows show the direction of the magnetic field, and broad arrows the motion of the solar wind.

However, Kepler correctly explained the tides as a result of the combined gravitational forces of the moon and the sun.

And yet, later, in his *Epitome Astronomiae Copernicanae (Epitome of Copernican Astronomy),* he adopted quite a different mechanism. The book, published in 1612, contained a detailed defense of the Copernican system. Therefore it was immediately placed on the *Index Librorum Prohibitorum,* the list of books forbidden by the church to good Christians. It also contained a discussion of the planetary motions and mechanism and the statement that the sun rotated (a fact later established by the motion of sunspots) and carried the planets along through its *anima motrix.* Kepler, who had read with care *De Magnete, Magneticisque Corporibus, et de Magnu Magnete Tellure (Concerning Magnetism, Magnetic Bodies, and the Great*

Magnet Earth), an extensive treatise investigating magnetism, published in 1600 by William Gilbert (1540-1603), suggested that the planets were huge magnets carried around by the sun's action. Kepler reasoned that these planetary magnets were inclined to remain parallel to each other, with one pole attracted by the sun *(soli amica,* friendly to the sun) and the other *(discors,* hostile) repelled. As a result, planets will describe their orbits, first being attracted and then repelled.

Kepler's explanation of planetary motions was the first serious attempt to interpret the mechanics of the solar system. It is a strange mixture of neo-Platonism and modern physics. While gravitational interaction between two bodies is introduced, it is not considered to be the prime cause of planetary motion—Kepler thought the sun's rotation was responsible. And the idea of planetary magnets could have been extended to magnetic fields in general, with some stretching of the imagination even to the gravitational field of the sun, so ingeniously proposed by Einstein years later. Despite his remarkable analogies between gravity and magnetism or motive force and magnetism, it would be incorrect to consider Kepler a forerunner of Newton or Einstein. But the ingredients were there; only the connections were missing. This is not surprising, since Kepler was reared in Aristotelian thinking. One wonders not why he missed finding the law of universal gravitation, but how he managed to proceed as far as he did.

6. Harmony of the Universe

The years Kepler spent in Prague were probably the happiest and most fertile of his life, but they came to an abrupt end. Emperor Rudolph, who at best had been an apathetic ruler, was declared insane and forced to abdicate in 1611 in favor of his brother Matthias. Rudolph died the following year, and Kepler, who lost his wife and a son during the epidemics that raged in Prague, moved to Linz in Upper Austria. His position there was similar to the one he had held in Graz, and although he retained his title as imperial mathematician to the emperor—occasionally receiving some of the money owed him by his former employer—it was a letdown after the fashionable life in Prague. He no longer had his wife, who had been homesick for Austria and for whose sake he had decided to go to Linz, and he missed his former friends. And his difficulties over his religious beliefs were renewed. Pastor Hitzler, a former schoolmate, refused to grant him communion, and labeled him a heretic. Kepler rejected overtures by Paul Guldin, Jesuit father and professor of

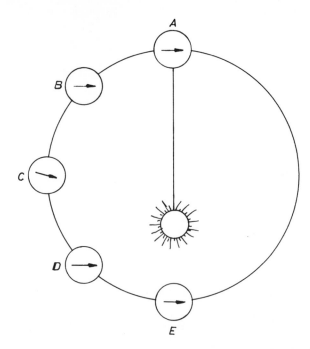

Magnetic attraction and repulsion, according to Kepler. Starting from a neutral position A, where both magnetic poles are equidistant from the sun, neither will be attracted or repelled and the sun will just move it through its *anima motrix.* As the planet moves through the positions B, C, and D, the *soli amica* will be turned toward the sun, while *discors* is turned away from it. At E, both attraction and repulsion balance each other again, but now the *discors* pole will face the sun and the planet will be repelled (and the distance will increase) until it again reaches the neutral position A. By this ingenious, although incorrect, scheme Kepler tried to explain the noncircular nature of the planetary orbits.

mathematics in Vienna, to embrace Catholicism and thus obtain imperial favor. He wisely rejected an offer to go to Bologna, ostensibly because he preferred to live among Germans, but really because he was wary of sharing Bruno's or even Galileo's fate (although he did not live to witness the worst of Galileo's troubles). "I have enjoyed since early youth a freedom in manners of speech whose use, if I went to Bologna, might easily involve me in discredit if not in danger, cause suspicion, and expose me to the denunciations of injudicious people," he wrote.

Kepler's deep religiosity and nonconformist convictions caused him untold hardships. He admitted of no contradiction between science and the Holy Bible, which, he wrote in his introduction to *New Astronomy,* never intended to inform men concerning natural things. Yet his God was not only the God of Luther, as revealed in the Bible, but also the God of Pythagoras "whom in the contemplation of the universe I can grasp, as it were, with my very hands." Kepler saw the universe as a physical entity governed by forces, as a mathematical harmony, and as a central theological order. This point of view is probably best exemplified by his monumental work *Harmonice Mundi (Harmony of the World)*—a continuation and culmination of his *Cosmic Mystery*—which contains the famous relation between orbits and periods, known as Kepler's third law.

Kepler's *New Astronomy* had answered some of the

questions of planetary motions; it had described the shape of the orbit and shown why planets move faster when closer to the sun and slower when farther away. But he had treated each orbit separately, generalizing the results for the earth and Mars. The relationship among the various orbits, discussed in *Cosmic Mystery,* still had to be found. The distances derived from the five perfect solids did not agree with the more exact values of Tycho any more than they had agreed with the ones given by Copernicus. The five perfect solids had identified the then known planets, but they were only approximations of celestial geometry. The Divine Architect was certainly capable of taking into account more complicated shapes, such as star-pointed polyhedra or variations of the five perfect solids. Although the geometric picture of the universe is attractive, it is more suited for a static universe than for one of continuous motion, nonuniform at that. Now if one speaks of motion, one needs velocities, and velocities convey the notion of time in addition to distance. These are contained in musical harmonies, thus God the Creator is also a musician—as Pythagoras had already understood in his Harmony of the Spheres.

While Pythagoras tried to explain the musical ratios (1:2 for an octave, 2:3 for a fifth, 3:4 for a fourth, etc.) by number, Kepler felt that the answer key to the relationship among the various orbits lay in geometry (which also had mystic meaning). The sphere, being perfect, represents the Holy Trinity (center, surface, and radius constituting the three components); the plane symbolizes the world. The circle, the intersection of the sphere and the plane, represents man's dual nature. In his characteristic thoroughness Kepler discussed harmony, or the geometrical proportions, in the first two volumes of *Harmonice Mundi (Harmony of the World)* and devoted the remaining three volumes to its application in music, astrology, and astronomy.

Star polyhedra. Kepler is the "inventor" of two types of star polyhedra shown here. They differ mainly in that in one, the sides of the pentagon, located at the center, form the basis, whereas in the second, the center itself is prominent.

Kepler believed that a celestial harmony must exist within the greatest and smallest distances of the planets from the sun. When no harmonic ratios could be found for the distances, he turned to the velocities and again drew a blank—at first. Only after he took the angular velocities (that is, the angle through which the planet turns in unit time)—seen "from the common fountain of motion, the sun"—did his hunch work. According to

OCTAVES OF THE PLANETS

Velocity of	at	divided by	is	Octave
Saturn	aphelion	$2^0(=1)$	1′ 46″	Lowest
	perihelion	$2^0(=1)$	2′ 15″	Lowest
Jupiter	aphelion	$2^1(=2)$	2′ 15″	First
	perihelion	$2^1(=2)$	2′ 45″	First
Mars	aphelion	$2^3(=8)$	3′ 17″	Third
	perihelion	$2^4(=16)$	2′ 23″	Fourth
Earth	aphelion	$2^5(=32)$	1′ 47″	Fifth
	perihelion	$2^5(=32)$	1′ 55″	Fifth
Venus	aphelion	$2^5(=32)$	2′ 58″	Fifth
	perihelion	$2^5(=32)$	3′ 3″	Fifth
Mercury	aphelion	$2^6(=64)$	2′ 34″	Sixth
	perihelion	$2^7(=128)$	3′ 0″	Seventh

MUSICAL INTERVALS *

	Aphelion	Perihelion	Ratio	Musical Interval	Divergent	Convergent
Saturn	1′ 46″	2′ 15″	4/5	Major third		
					⅓	½
Jupiter	4′ 30″	5′ 30″	5/6	Minor third		
					⅛	5/24
Mars	26′ 14″	38′ 1″	⅔	Fifth		
					5/12	⅔
Earth	57′ 3″	61′ 18″	15/16	Major semitone		
					⅗	⅝
Venus	94′ 50″	97′ 37″	24/35	Minor semitone		
					¼	⅗
Mercury	164′ 0″	384′ 0″	5/12	Octave plus minor third	—	—

* The first column gives the angular speed of the planet (in minutes and seconds) at aphelion (slowest motion and lowest note); the second column gives it at perihelion (fastest motion and highest note). The third column gives the ratio between the two (with some minor adjustment) and the next the name of the corresponding musical interval. The divergent (interval) is the ratio of speed at aphelion to perihelion of the next planet, while the convergent (interval) is the ratio of speed at perihelion to aphelion of the next planet. For example, using Saturn and Jupiter as our start, 1′ 46″ / 5′ 30″ = ⅓ and 2′ 15″ / 4′ 30″ = ½.

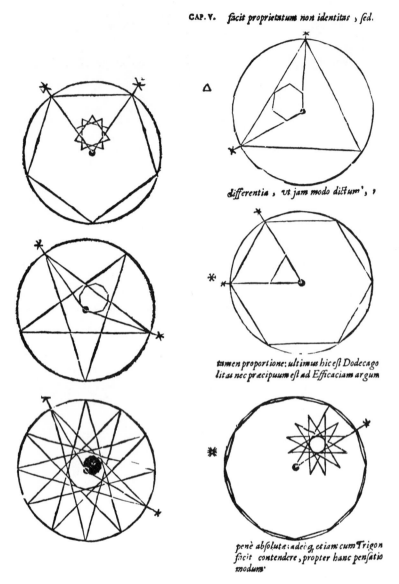

differentia , vt jam modo dictum', ,

*tamen proportione: ultimus hic est Dodecago
litas nec præcipuum est ad Efficaciam argum*

*penè absoluta: adeoq, etiam cum Trigon
facit contendere, propter hanc pensatio
modum.*

Kepler, the frequency, that is, the number of vibrations per second, of a "note" corresponded to the angular velocity of the planet. Since the angular velocity changes during the orbit—from aphelion to perihelion—the frequency of the note will do likewise. The ratios of the angular velocities—at aphelion and perihelion—are then equal to the ratios of the frequencies and form the musical harmonies. To complete the picture, it is also necessary to find the octave to which a particular tone belongs. For this purpose Kepler divided his angular velocities by powers of 2, so that the ratio will lie within an octave (that is, have a ratio smaller than 1:2); the power of 2 then indicate the octave to which the note belongs (thus, 2^0 equals 1, lowest octave; 2^1 equals 2, the next octave; 2^2 equals 4; and so on). The result then gives tunes of the celestial orchestra. It should be stressed, however, that Kepler did not imagine the existence of any astral music. For him the harmony was only a mathematical conception that he used to test his laws and geometrical constructions.

Harmonic configurations consist of a central figure and a circumscribed figure constructed in such a manner that the angle between two sides of the inner figure is equal to the angle between two radii of neighboring points. The reciprocal character also appears in the figures themselves. For example, in the diagram at the upper right, the central figure is a hexagon and the outer one an equilateral triangle, while at the right center the situation is the reverse. A different kind of reciprocity is illustrated at the left. In the upper diagram the outer figure is a pentagon and the inner figure a 10-pointed (regular) star, while in the central diagram the outer figure is a 5-pointed star and the inner one a regular decagon (10-sided polygon). Note that the outer circle connects to the central point (and vice versa) in all diagrams, and that with each configuration Kepler associates two light rays (the aspect), which determine man's fate (according to the Zodiac).

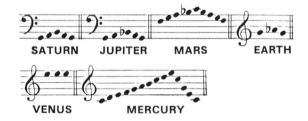

SATURN   JUPITER   MARS   EARTH

VENUS   MERCURY

Musical notation based on Kepler's *Harmonice Mundi,* showing the individual tunes played by the planets, the pitch of a note being proportional to the speed of the planet. Note that Venus has an almost circular orbit, which results in an almost constant note, while Mercury possesses a considerable variation because of its large eccentricity.

Then came the most remarkable discovery of all. By themselves the harmonic ratios are not too startling—they confirmed that the planets moved faster when closer to the sun and slower when farther away. But if an exact relationship between distance and velocity (or period of revolution) were known, then the mean distances could be computed from the celestial harmony. Kepler was convinced that the Divine Musician used such a relationship in ordering the motion of the planets—and he found that relationship: "The periodic times of any two planets are in the sesquialteral ratio to their mean distances," that is, their mean distances from the sun. In other words, the period (or the time it takes to make a complete revolution) is proportional to the three-half (3/2) power of the mean distance. For example, the mean distance of the earth from the sun is 92.9 million miles, which makes the three-half power equal to 895.4 billion

miles. The mean distance of Mars from the sun is 141.5 million miles, giving 1,683 billion miles for its three-half power. The ratio of these two numbers is 1.88, which is equal to the ratio of their periods—the earth's being 365.25 days (one year) and that of Mars being 686.96 days (or 1.88 years). Similar results are obtained by taking the mean distances and periods of the other planets. All of this is Kepler's third law, which later was shown by Newton to be a consequence of his law of universal gravitation.

Contrary to his usual explicitness, Kepler did not describe the process that led him to this striking discovery, except that he had come back to it after it had not worked (probably because of a mistake in his original calculations). Whether it was by trial and error, as some believe, or an inspired guess, the result is the same—a fundamental discovery in planetary physics.

PERFECT SOLIDS

The radius of the sphere inscribed in the		Distances calculated from harmony	
Cube (Jupiter)	5.194	Mean	5.206
Tetrahedron (Mars)	1.649	Aphelion	1.661
Dodecahedron (Earth)	1.100	Aphelion	1.018
Icosahedron (Venus)	0.781	Aphelion	0.726
Octahedron (Mercury)	0.413	Mean	0.392

KEPLER'S THIRD LAW

	Mean distance from sun: D *	Length of year: T †	Cube of distance: D^3	Square of time: T^2
Mercury	0.3871	0.24084	0.05801	0.05801
Venus	0.7233	0.61519	0.37845	0.37846
Earth	1.0000	1.0000	1.0000	1.0000
Mars	1.5237	1.8808	3.5375	3.5375
Jupiter	5.2028	11.862	140.83	140.70
Saturn	9.5388	29.457	867.92	867.70

    * Relative to Sun-Earth distance.
    † In Earth year time.
    When the last two columns are compared, it is seen that D^3 equals T^2 or D^3/T^2 equals 1. Had we not expressed both D and T in terms of Sun-Earth distance and Earth year, the constant obviously would not be 1 as in the table. In general, Kepler's third law can be stated as follows:

(Mean distance from sun)^3: (period of revolution)^2 equals a constant, the constant being the *same* for all planets.

MEAN DISTANCES *

	Distance of orbits calculated by Kepler at		Distance taken from observations of Tycho Brahe at	
	Aphelion	Perihelion	Aphelion	Perihelion
Saturn	10.118	8.994	10.052	8.968
Jupiter	5.464	4.948	5.451	4.949
Mars	1.661	1.384	1.665	1.382
Earth	1.017	0.983	1.018	0.982
Venus	0.726	0.716	0.729	0.719
Mercury	0.476	0.308	0.570	0.307

    * The mean distance of Earth from the sun is taken as 1.000, and all other distances are multiples or fractions of it. This figure is calculated by dividing by two the sum of the distance at aphelion and perihelion.

Now that he had found the missing link, he calculated the ratios of smallest to largest velocities, the eccentricities, and, finally, the maximum and minimum distances of the orbits, including the radii of the spheres inscribed in the perfect solids. The agreement with observations was quite good and the harmonic theory held up. Kepler was thankful but wistful because his results were too modern and radical to be accepted immediately. But he was willing to wait a hundred years. "Did not God wait six thousand years for one to contemplate His works?" he asked.

Even while engaged in solving the mysteries of the universe, Kepler had to take time out to fight the growing persecutions by the Counter-Reformation. He was attacked and his library was locked and sealed. Witch-hunting had become popular; his mother was accused and barely escaped burning. At the time, she was old, quarrelsome, and meddling, and she enjoyed preparing all kinds of herbal remedies. It seems that she had given a drink to the town glazier's wife, who had later become ill and now accused his mother of poisoning her. (As it turned out later, the illness was due to an abortion, but this fact was conveniently forgotten.) Another incident that aroused suspicion involved a young girl who, while carrying bricks past Mrs. Kepler's house, felt a stabbing pain, which resulted in a temporary paralysis. (Kepler was later able to show that the pains were due to the heavy load the girl was carrying and that they ceased soon after.) Matters were not helped by *Somnium*, an allegory that Kepler had written and privately circulated to colleagues. It was about a dream involving a journey to the moon in which the hero, a boy Duracotus, lived with his mother, Fiolxhilde, who sold herbs and conversed with demons. Fiolxhilde conjures a friendly demon from Levania (Levana in Hebrew means "moon"), who agrees to take them to the moon during an eclipse (the only time they cannot be hurt by the sun's radiation). Once they are there, conditions are described in realistic fashion. The moon itself is inhabited by two peoples, the Subvolvans and the Privolvans, and the earth is called Volva by them. Subvolva is the half of the moon always turned toward Volva, and Privolva is the dark side of the moon.* It is a beautiful story, and Kepler was shocked when people took its personalized aspects literally. Obviously, he was identified with Duracotus and his mother with Fiolxhilde. He set out immediately to add explanatory footnotes to his manuscript, which turned out to be longer than the original text: Duracotus represented science and Fiolxhilde ignorance, while the father, who had died, was reason.

Volva, of course, means "to roll" (from the Latin volvere) or "to turn," and the purpose of the whole dream is to underline the idea of the rotation of the earth. The *Dream* was unfortunately not finished in Kepler's lifetime and was published four years after his death by his son Ludwig, a candidate for a doctorate in medicine.

With great effort and Kepler's several personal interventions—after a delay of several years during which his mother was kept incarcerated most of the time—a trial took place. Despite Kepler's painstaking evidence to refute the charges, she was sentenced to the torture chamber to confess, but she remained steadfast, although she was not put to actual torture. A new court was then summoned, which finally acquitted her, with a warning not to return. But the persecutions continued, and six months later she died, poor but unbroken.

In the meantime *Harmonice Mundi* had been published, followed by *Epitome Astronomiae Copernicanae; De cometis,* on comets; and *Nova Stella,* or *A New Star.* He also had not forgotten Tycho's wish and had worked for many years on the planetary tables, which finally were published as the *Rudolphine Tables* in 1627. Since this work was in memory of Emperor Rudolph, it would be proper, Kepler thought, if the Crown would pay for it, especially since the Crown still owed him some 6,000 florins. He therefore traveled to Vienna to collect his money. After a lengthy runaround, he finally managed to get about a third of the money, enough for the paper, and decided to pay the rest from his own pocket, although he had to use a trust fund that had been set up for his children.

Linz had been occupied by the troops (the Thirty Years' War was in progress), and he was forced to go to Ulm, in 1626, where the work was printed under his personal supervision. The tables contained positions of 1,005 stars (enlarged from the original catalogue of 777 found by Tycho), as well as tables and rules for predicting planetary positions. The *Rudolphine Tables* were so accurate that they remained an invaluable tool for astronomers for more than a century.

Kepler now found it hard to take care of his growing family. Within a year after his arrival in Linz, in 1612, he had remarried. His bride, Susanna Reuttinger, was seventeen years his junior and, as he tells in his letters, one of eleven candidates for his hand. If he was surprised that he was so sought after despite his poor financial standing, he still went about choosing a bride as though he were computing the orbit of Mars. However, the marriage was a happy one, and Susanna bore him seven children, of whom four survived (in addition to the two surviving children of his first marriage). Because he could not return to Linz, where conditions had grown hopeless, he tried to get a position in Strassburg, offering to instruct students in the use of the *Rudolphine Tables,*

---

* *See* Lear, John, *Kepler's Dream* (Berkeley and Los Angeles: University of California Press, 1965).

Frontispiece of the *Rudolphine Tables,* showing a Greek temple in which astronomers—a Babylonian, Hipparchus, Ptolemy, Copernicus, and Tycho Brahe—are engaged in conversation. Kepler is depicted sitting in a small niche busily writing. The central scene at the base is a replica of the island of Hven. Inside the temple are several instruments, such as a quadrant and sextant. The eagle on the roof is a symbol of the Austrian Empire. It is dropping gold coins from its beak, two of which have landed on Kepler's working table, with three more in the air—an obvious hint.

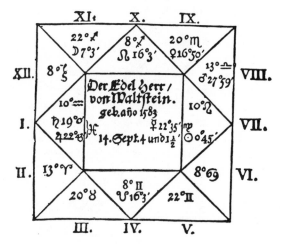

A horoscope of the Count of Wallenstein cast by Kepler in 1608. At the time it was cast, Kepler did not know to whom it belonged, but he was able to guess the identity and he wrote a glowing analysis of the future leader. When he was in Wallenstein's employ in 1624, he revised the horoscope, predicting that March 1634 would bring dreadful disorders. Wallenstein was assassinated in February 1634.

But his laws remained:

1. All planets move in elliptical paths, with the sun at one focus.

2. A line drawn from the sun to a planet sweeps out equal areas in equal times.

3. The squares of the periods of revolution of the several planets about the sun are proportional to the cubes of their mean distances from the sun. The figures are as follows:

The ratio

$$\frac{93 \times 93 \times 93 \times 10^{18}}{365 \times 365} \frac{(miles)^3}{(days)^2} = 6.04 \times 10^{18} \ (miles)^3/(days)^2$$

calculated for the earth is the *same* for all planets.

The man who gave us these laws was persecuted and misunderstood, as were so many other scientists in his day and later, and only many years after his death did the world realize how important was his contribution, hidden, as it was, among much that was, to say the least, of questionable value. Perhaps his work can best be summed up in the requirements he himself had formulated at the age of thirty:

He who predicts as completely as possible the motions and positions of the heavenly bodies, fulfills his duty as an astronomer; but he who in addition advances true theorems about the form of the world achieves even more and deserves even greater praise. For the former reveals the truth insofar as it can be perceived by the senses; the latter satisfied not only the senses by his deductions, but also reveals the innermost essence of nature.

(Cosmic Mystery)

which had just been published, and even to cast horoscopes. The Strassburg Council refused a position to Germany's most famous astronomer but offered him residence.

Kepler then went back to Prague, where he joined General Wallenstein, who served Emperor Ferdinand, King of Bohemia and Hungary. Kepler was informed that Wallenstein would also take care of the debt owed him by the Crown. So Kepler became Wallenstein's court astrologer, a position he despised. When Wallenstein was dismissed, Kepler's promissory notes became valueless, and he went to Regensburg, one of the oldest of German cities, where the Imperial Diet met, in the hope of settling his financial affairs. There he contracted a fever from which he did not recover; he died November 15, 1630, at the age of fifty-nine. He was buried in the Evangelical Cemetery, which was soon after destroyed in the war. Only the epitaph, which he wrote himself, remained: "I measured the skies, now the shadows I measure/Sky-bound was the mind, earth-bound the body rests."

Only after his death was Kepler's genius appreciated. The photograph shows the Kepler Monument at Regensburg, built in 1808.

"the wrangler," which pointed up a characteristic inherent in all his later work.

One day, while attending Mass at the cathedral in Pisa, he idly observed a swinging lamp. He noticed that, while the lengths of the swings, the amplitudes, got smaller, the time of each complete swing, or period, remained the same—timing it with his own pulse, the only watch he possessed. When alone, he immediately proceeded to repeat the experiment with a simple pendulum consisting of a string and bob, which led him to discover the laws for the simple pendulum.

Galileo was never satisfied with qualitative results—he also wanted to know "how much." At the same time, he was quite practical and used the principle he discovered to design a "pulsilogium," a device with which doctors could compare a patient's pulse rate with the swing of a pendulum.

In 1585 he was forced to leave the university, since his father could not afford the high fees (he had another son and three daughters to look after besides Galileo) and he did not get a scholarship, although there were forty available for poor students. Whether this was owing to the unpopularity of his views or of his personality is not clear; the fact remains that he did not get one, despite the unmistakable proof of his brilliance. Galileo returned home to Florence, an academic dropout; he never received a university degree. When Ostilio Ricci, the distinguished mathematician and friend of the family, came to Pisa, Galileo asked him to teach him the elements of Euclid, to

7. Message from the Stars

On February 15, 1564, Galileo Galilei (1564–1642) was born at Pisa, at that time part of the Grand Duchy of Tuscany, when Cosimo de' Medici was Duke of Florence. Galileo's life overlapped that of Tycho Brahe, and he was a contemporary of Kepler, whom he outlived.

Galileo's father, Vincenzo, was an impoverished member of a good Florentine family; he was of independent outlook and was well versed in music, mathematics, and the classics. Although Galileo was at first meant to become a merchant, his father recognized his mechanical and academic talents.

After attending the monastery school of Santa Maria di Vallombrosa near Florence, in 1581 he was sent to study at the University of Pisa. It was intended that he study medicine, which he did briefly, as a more lucrative profession than the natural philosophy to which his interest pointed.

At this early age he already exhibited that independence of outlook and refusal to accept beliefs unsupported by experimental evidence, and it earned him the nickname

This copper cut shows Galileo at the height of his career, as chief mathematician to the Grand Duke Cosimo II of Florence and principal professor of mathematics at the University of Pisa.

The swinging lamp in the Cathedral of Pisa that supposedly led the young Galileo to study and formulate the laws of the pendulum. Fresco by L. Sabatelli in the Tribuna Galileiana in Florence.

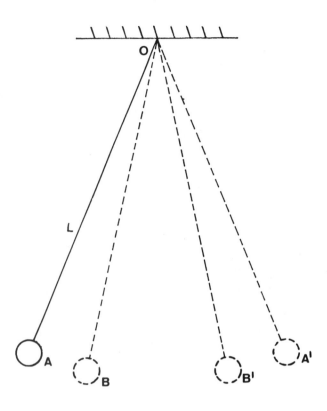

Galileo observed that the period of a simple pendulum—the time it takes to complete a swing (going from A to A′ and back to A)—is independent of the length of the swing (distance AO). In other words, the time it takes to go from A to A′ (and back to A) is the same as that of another pendulum that swings only from B to B′ (and back to B). On the other hand, the period does vary with the length (L) of the string.

which the old man consented. After that came Archimedes, and little by little Galileo mastered the basics of mathematics and physics as known at the time.

He perfected a hydrostatic balance, which brought him to the attention of Guidobaldo, Marquis del Monte (1545-1607), upon whose recommendation he was appointed professor of mathematics at the University of Pisa—at the age of twenty-six. The position carried a stipend of 60 scudi a year (less than $100), a sum Galileo augmented by giving private lessons. In this city he was supposed to have performed his celebrated experiment of dropping two different weights from the campanile, the Leaning Tower of Pisa. (Few scholars today believe that he actually did drop the balls from the Leaning Tower. Almost certainly, he did not.) Galileo's experiments—instead of bringing him fame and recognition—made him unpopular with the adherents of Aristotle, whose teaching he was now questioning. Matters came to a head when he was consulted about a dredging machine designed by Giovanni de' Medici for the Leghorn harbor. Galileo minced no words and told the inventor that it was useless—as it turned out to be. This made his position

even less attractive, and Galileo resigned even before his three-year appointment had come up for renewal. Also, at this time, his father died, and it fell upon him to care for his brother and sisters.

Fortunately, the Chair of Mathematics at the University of Padua had been vacant, and Galileo was offered the position by the Senate of Venice (which had jurisdiction over it). The appointment was for six years, but he was so successful that it was renewed for another six years and then given for life. Altogether, Galileo spent eighteen years in Padua; they were his most brilliant and successful years.

He was an eloquent speaker and an excellent teacher. Students began to gather around him, and soon his fame spread. When he lectured on the Nova Stella of 1604, the great hall seating more than 1,000 persons was not sufficient and the lecture had to be held out-of-doors. Galileo used the opportunity to exhort his listeners to pay attention to the more important truths about permanent stars—his first reference to the Copernican system. When Kepler sent him a copy of *Cosmic Mystery,* he acknowledged the gift, stating, "I have been for many

The distance traversed by a ball rolling down a plank is proportional to the square of the time it takes. In this fresco by Giuseppe Pezzuoli in the Tribuna Galileiana in Florence, Galileo, seated at the left, is dressed in the robes of a professor of the University of Pisa. Iacopo Mazzoni di Cesena performs the experiment, and various Aristotelians look on, rather skeptically. At the center, Don Giovanni de' Medici, son of Cosimo I, argues with the Aristotelians. Through the open window can be seen the Cathedral and the Leaning Tower of Pisa.

years an adherent of the Copernican system." Galileo continued to say that he had collected many arguments but did not venture to make them public for fear of sharing the fate of Copernicus, who had become an object of ridicule and scorn. If there were more like Kepler, he wrote, he would publish his speculations, but since this was not the case, he would refrain from such an undertaking.

Kepler continued to urge Galileo to publish his arguments in favor of the Copernican theory, but for the time being Galileo remained silent.

In April 1609 a report reached Venice that a Dutchman had presented Count Maurice of Nassau with a certain optical instrument by which distant objects appeared as if they were near, but no further details were known. According to later reports, the credit for that remarkable invention belongs to one of two spectacle makers, Zacharias Janssen and Hans Lippersheim, both of Middelburg. According to one legend the son of Janssen had put some lenses together and by chance had hit upon the telescopic combination. Janssen, experimenting with the lenses, enclosed them in a tube and presented the tube to Count Maurice, who ordered it to be kept a secret (he found it a great aid in his wars). Nevertheless, the secret

leaked out, and twenty years after the first telescope had been built, news reached Venice. Galileo, hearing about the telescope, rushed back to Padua and, after a few trials, succeeded in arranging two lenses—one convex and one concave—so that they magnified the apparent size of an object. (A detailed description of the action of lenses and telescopes will be found in Chapter VI.)

Galileo's first telescope had a magnification of three (about that of a simple toy telescope sold today). He later improved his design and finally was able to achieve a magnification of thirty-three times. Galileo demonstrated his instrument to the nòbiles of Venice, and he presented one to the Signoria (Senate), which on the following day confirmed his professorship for life and gave him an additional bonus of 1,000 scudi. A few years later Galileo's instruments could be bought in shops for much less.

Galileo's contribution did not lie in the construction of the telescope but in the use he made of it. He directed it toward the sky and saw things no man had seen before. The result, in 1610, was the publication of a little book, *Sidereus Nuncius,* popularly known as *Message from the Stars,* or *The Starry Messenger.* Its first object of interest was the moon and Galileo demonstrated conclusively the existence of lunar mountains—to the chagrin of the

Fresco by L. Sabatelli in the Tribuna Galileiana, Florence. Galileo is demonstrating his just-completed telescope before members of the Council of Ten and the Doge of Venice (Leonardo Donato), seated at the left.

The title page of Galileo's *Sidereus Nuncius,* published in 1610, reads like a modern advertisement: "THE STARRY MESSENGER, Revealing great, unusual, and remarkable spectacles, opening these to the consideration of every man, and especially of philosophers and astronomers; as observed by Galileo Galilei, Gentleman of Florence, Professor of Mathematics at the University of Padua, With the Aid of a Spyglass lately invented by him. The surface of the Moon, innumerable Fixed Stars, Nebulae, and above all Four Planets swiftly revolving about Jupiter at differing distances and periods, and known to no one before the Author recently perceived them and decided that they should be named The Medicean Stars. Venice, 1610."

The first page of *Sidereus Nuncius* in Galileo's handwriting.

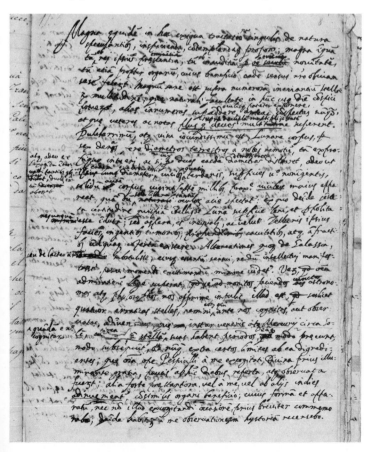

Aristotelians who had assumed it to be a perfect crystalline sphere. Not only did he interpret the moon in earthly terms, but he attributed the visibility of the "old moon" to "earth-shine," the sunlight reflected by the earth. A dark earth had been one of the arguments against the Copernican theory.

Galileo saw a whole new world. The Milky Way, which had been thought to be an atmospheric agglomeration of stellar matter, now was seen to be an endless collection of stars. Tycho, when he had tried to explain the nature of *his* Nova Stella had suggested that it was formed of celestial matter taken from the Milky Way. In fact, Tycho

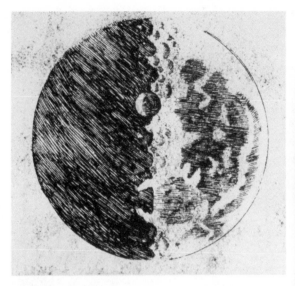

One of Galileo's drawings of the moon taken from *The Starry Messenger*. Galileo correctly identified small markings, both bright and dark, as mountaintops just catching the sunlight and the shadows cast by them. The large dark spots he identified incorrectly as caused by water; they were later named "seas." He also noticed the absence of clouds.

The full moon, showing a slight phase effect around the north pole. In the photograph, the north and south poles are inverted, in accordance with the inverted image normally seen in an astronomical telescope. ➤

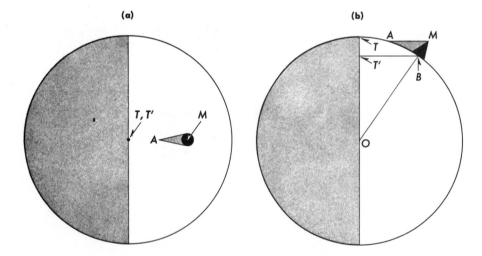

Galileo was able to estimate the height of lunar mountains from the lengths of the shadows cast. The left diagram (a) shows the moon's disk as it appears in the sky. The central line is the terminator, or the line of sunrise or sunset, separating night and day. M denotes a mountain peak and A the vertex of its shadow cone. The right diagram (b) illustrates the geometry, with the moon shown at right angles to the line of sight from the earth. Here AM is the length of the shadow and BM the required height of the mountain. The line AM is perpendicular to OT, and AB is at right angles to the moon's radius OB, from which it follows that the two triangles OT'B and ABM are similar (similar triangles have equal angles and therefore their sides are proportional to each other). Thus, BM/AM = T'B/OB. Now AM and T'B can be measured (OB is the known radius of the moon) and BM calculated. Lunar mountains are known to reach heights as large as 25,000 feet, comparable to the highest peaks of the Himalayas.

erroneously thought that he could see a gap, or hole, where there had been none before. Galileo's discovery was the first step in a long process, which finally resulted in the correct identification of the Milky Way as the "Galaxy." He saw stars that could not have been seen with the naked eye because they were too faint.

His most spectacular discovery, however, was Jupiter's moons. On January 7, 1610, when Galileo noticed three starlets next to Jupiter, he thought they were among the fixed stars. But he was puzzled by the fact that they appeared to lie in a straight line, parallel to the ecliptic. Two were at the left (east) of Jupiter and one to the

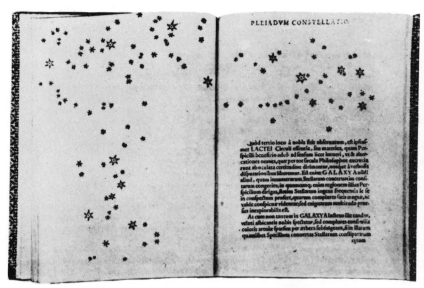

Pages from Galileo's *Starry Messenger* showing many new stars. The page on the left shows Orion, which till then had appeared as a group of only 9 stars. The right-hand page shows the Pleiades; Galileo counted as many as 36 stars, where before only the 7 brightest could be seen.

A large-field photograph of the Pleiades made with the 18-inch Schmidt telescope on Mount Palomar, showing the configuration of the 7 brightest stars as well as the faint, diffuse nebulosity around Merope. The structure of the Pleiades is difficult to discern because of the many outside stars that intrude on it (foreground and background).

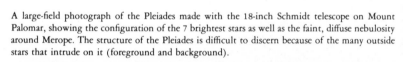

Jupiter and its four principal satellites (from left to right): Callisto, Io, Europa, and Ganymede, photographed September 16, 1915, at Lowell Observatory.

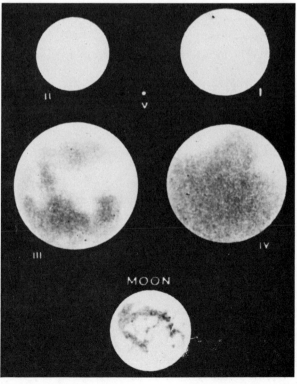

► Sizes of the principal satellites of Jupiter compared with the moon. Galileo observed the four largest satellites, which he called the Medicean planets in honor of the Medicis. In modern terminology they are I: Io; II: Europa; III: Ganymede; IV: Callisto.

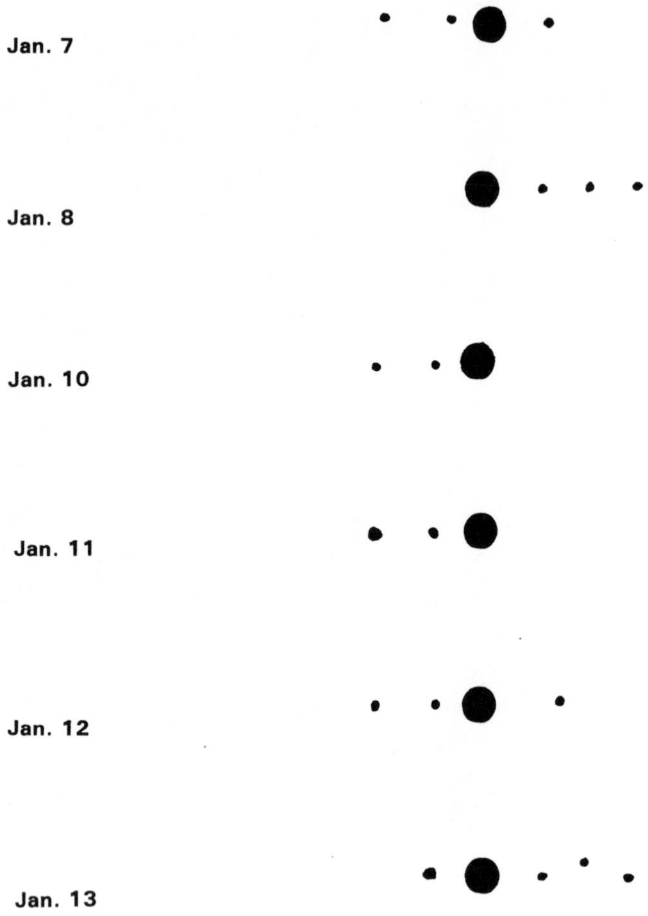

Jan. 7

Jan. 8

Jan. 10

Jan. 11

Jan. 12

Jan. 13

Various stages of the discovery of Jupiter's satellites, after a drawing from *The Starry Messenger*. Only on the sixth day did Galileo see all four satellites.

Galileo's drawing of his observations on Jupiter's satellites from November 28, 1620, to the following January.

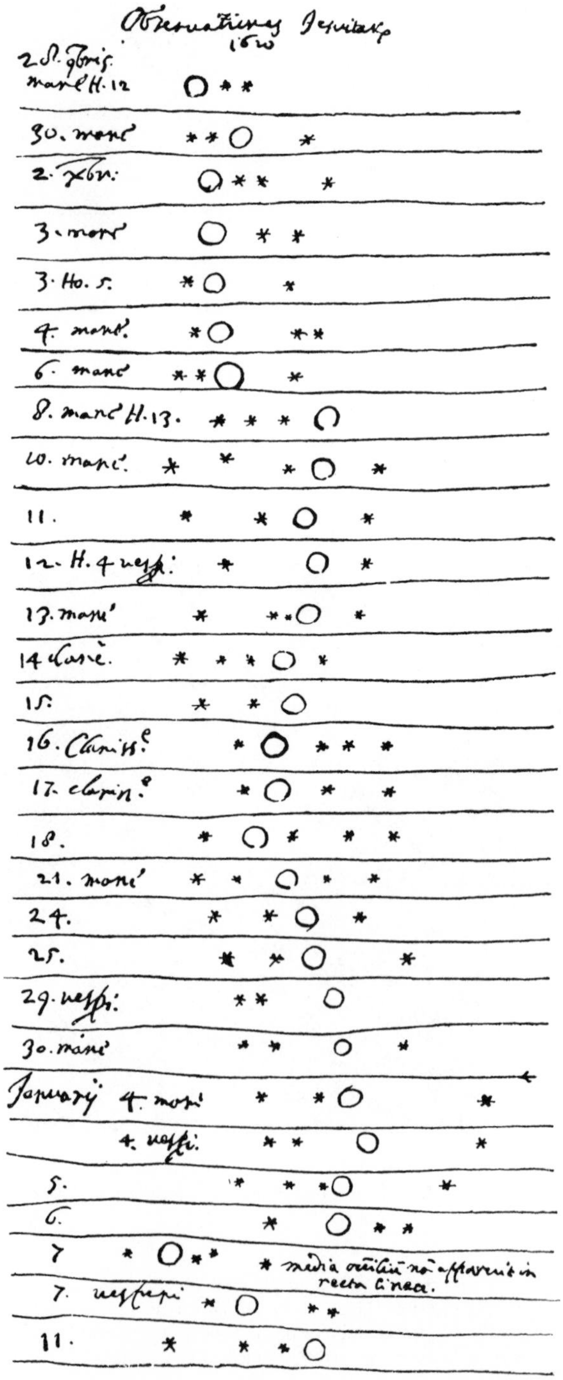

right. The following night all three were to the right of Jupiter, and Galileo wondered how Jupiter had got east of them. The next night was cloudy, but on January 10 only two were seen; this time they were east of Jupiter (the third supposedly was hidden by the planet). Galileo thereafter deduced that there were four satellites. They were always close to Jupiter, sometimes preceding, sometimes following it (and at times hidden by Jupiter), undoubtedly because they revolved around it. The discovery raised a storm. Kepler, for example, upon hearing the news wrote excitedly to Galileo, and he longed for a telescope to see for himself. (However, Kepler suggested that there should be two planets [really moons] around Mars, four or six around Saturn, and one each around Mercury and Venus in order to keep his proportions correct.)

Some colleagues, such as the Florentine astronomer Francesco Sizzi, refused to believe Galileo's discovery. Sizzi maintained that seven was the correct number of "planets," corresponding to the seven days of the week (each governed by a celestial object) and the seven

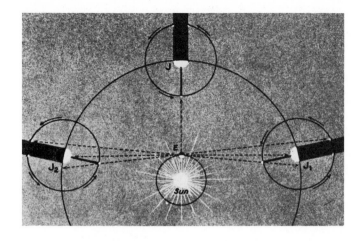

Different ways in which Jupiter and its system appear to the earth. E represents the earth, and J, J₁, J₂, different positions of Jupiter. When the satellite is directly in front of Jupiter (between Earth and Jupiter) it will be visible to the earth only if the line of sight from the earth does not pass through Jupiter (as at J₁ and J₂). In these cases its shadow may also be seen as cast on Jupiter. A satellite passing into Jupiter's shadow may disappear from sight even before it is actually occulted, or eclipsed, by the planet. Obviously, Galileo was unable to see the shadows cast by the satellites, and therefore the satellites were invisible to him whether in front or behind (in the shadow).

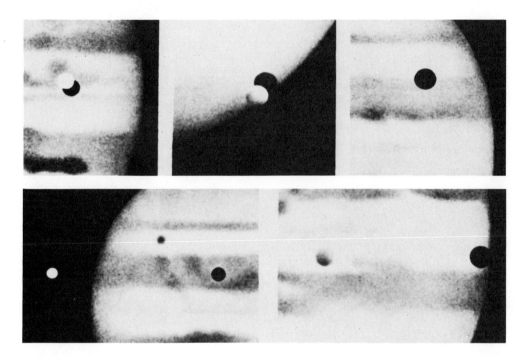

"windows" in the head (nostrils, eyes, ears, and mouth). Others, such as Cremonini of Padua, an important professor of philosophy, refused even to look through the telescope. Giulio Libri (1550–1610), leading philosopher of Pisa also refused to look through the telescope. Various arguments were leveled against the existence of new planets, but to no avail. Even Galileo's enemies finally admitted the truth, trying to outdo him by exploring for still other planets.

The significance of Galileo's discovery was much more than the existence of additional "planets." It gave credence to Copernicus, who had maintained that the earth was not the center of the universe, but a planet with its moon. The inference was obvious. If Jupiter, a planet, had moons, then the earth, with its known moon, might be an equal among equals. Also, Jupiter's moons provided another set of data for Kepler's third law.

Meanwhile, Galileo, still at the University of Padua, had become tired of teaching, which he had to augment with outside work. His income had increased but so had

Upper left and center: Two of Jupiter's satellites and their shadows at the moment of opposition. *Upper right:* Callisto's shadow passing in front of Jupiter. *Lower left:* The shadows of Io and Europa on Jupiter's disk at quadrature. *Lower right:* Transit of Ganymede and its shadow across the face of Jupiter (both the satellite and its shadow are visible).

his expenses. He had two daughters, Virginia and Livia, and a son, Vincenzio, born to his mistress Marina Gamba, for whom he kept separate quarters; he himself lived in a large house with his students, sometimes as many as twenty. In addition, he had to find a dowry for his sister and take care of his brother, Michelangelo, who was musically inclined and made excessive demands on him. Throughout his life Galileo seems to have provided for his brother and sisters much better than he did for his own children. He wanted to devote his time to writing—at which he excelled—and get back to his native Florence, away from the dull life at Padua. He had become world famous, through his telescopes (which were masterworks of precision—he ground the lenses himself), his observations, and his books. He applied to his friend Belisario Vinta, the Florentine secretary of state, and in July 1610 was appointed chief mathematician to Grand Duke Cosimo II de' Medici as well as principal professor of mathematics at the University of Pisa—without teaching duties. His friend Sagredo, a Venetian aristocrat and man of great culture, tried to warn him against exchanging the comparative freedom of an academician for the intrigues of life at court and a place where the authority of the friends of Berlinzone (a nickname for the Jesuits) stood high. However, Galileo had made up his mind. He resigned his position at Padua and returned to Florence with his children.

At first, life at Florence was pleasant enough. Galileo

SATELLITES FOR EACH PLANET *

Mercury	–
Venus	–
Earth	1
Mars	2
Jupiter	13 (possibly 14)
Saturn	10
Uranus	5
Neptune	2
Pluto	–

* Modern data.

JUPITER'S SATELLITES AND KEPLER'S THIRD LAW

Satellite	Period of revolution T in hours	Distance from Jupiter D *	T^2/D^3†
I	42.47	6.049	8.149
II	85.23	9.623	8.152
III	177.72	15.350	8.153
IV	400.53	26.998	8.152

* The distance D is expressed in Jovian radii (the radius of Jupiter being 42,912 miles).

† Note the figures for the ratio (period, or time)^2/(distance)^3 are practically constant, in agreement with Kepler's third law.

SATELLITES OF JUPITER

Satellite [1]		Diameter in miles [2]	Distance 10^3 miles	Revolution period			Discoverer	Year
V	Amalthea [3]	100	113		11h	53m	Barnard	1892
I	Io	2,000	262	1d	18h	28m	Galileo	1610
II	Europa	1,800	417	3d	13h	14m	Galileo	1610
III	Ganymede	3,100	666	7d	3h	43m	Galileo	1610
IV	Callisto	2,800	1,170	16d	16h	32m	Galileo	1610
VI	Himalia	60	7,120	250d	14h		Perrine	1904
VII	Elara	20	7,290	259d	14h		Perrine	1905
X	Lysithea	10	7,300	260d	12h		Nicholson	1938
XIII	Leda [4]	10	7,700	282d			Kowal	1974
XII	Ananke	10	13,000	625d			Nicholson	1951
XI	Carme	10	14,000	700d			Nicholson	1938
VIII	Pasiphae	10	14,600	739d			Melotte	1908
IX	Sinope	10	14,700	758d			Nicholson	1914

1. The satellites, although numbered according to the year of their discovery, are arranged by distances (which are further related to their orbital periods in accordance with Kepler's third law).

2. The diameters of the outer satellites (VI-XIII) are in considerable doubt and represent only estimates obtained from the reflected sunlight.

3. The names for satellites V–XIII have been approved by the XVIth General Assembly of the International Astronomical Union, 1976; Amalthea, suggested by C. Flammarion, has been in unofficial use for many decades; Leda was proposed by its discoverer, Charles Kowal. For satellites VI–XIII, those with direct orbits have names ending in "a," those with retrograde orbits end in "e."

4. At approximately this distance on September 30, 1975, Kowal discovered another faint object (magnitude 21), which may be satellite XIV.

FIVE PHASES OF VENUS

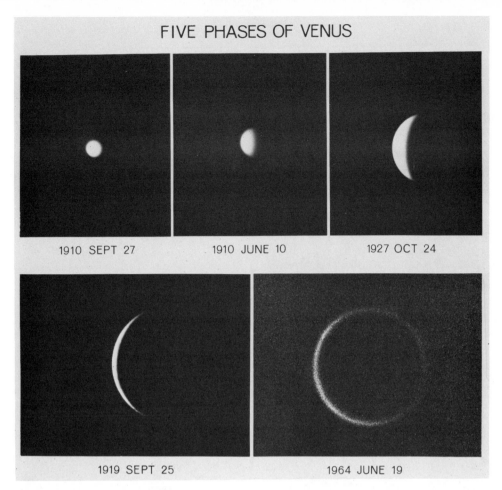

| 1910 SEPT 27 | 1910 JUNE 10 | 1927 OCT 24 |
| 1919 SEPT 25 | | 1964 JUNE 19 |

Five phases of Venus taken at different times but with constant magnification. The planet appears larger in the crescent phase (September 25, 1919), when it is closer to Earth.

was feted as the brilliant philosopher and he participated at many festive banquets. It was during one of these that he became involved in a discussion of the factors governing floating bodies in water. According to the prevailing Aristotelian view, shape was important and was considered to account for the floating of a piece of ice, which, being frozen water, was supposed to be denser and should therefore ordinarily sink. Galileo, on the other hand, pointed out that ice of any shape would float. This later led him to experiment with floating bodies; his studies resulted in *Discourse on Bodies in Water,* his first publication on experimental physics. Always his great contribution lay in his experiments and observations—"my own complete ignorance compelling me to seek information directly from nature itself," a view directly opposed to that of the Aristotelians.

In a short period Galileo made three more important astronomical discoveries, which would further confirm the Copernican theory. And to guard against plagiarism he framed the first of these as an anagram. Only when Emperor Rudolph's curiosity was aroused did Galileo disclose the solution: "I have observed the highest planet [Saturn] in triplet form." Galileo's telescope was not powerful enough to observe Saturn's rings; he thought he had discovered two of Saturn's moons, one on each side.

Kepler beseeched Galileo to disclose the meaning of another anagram ("You must see that you are dealing with honest Germans," he wrote). Finally Galileo

condescended and revealed it—not to Kepler but to de' Medici: "The mother of love [Venus] emulates the shapes of Cynthia [moon]." Galileo had discovered that Venus, like the moon, exhibited phases. It will be recalled that one of the main objections to the Copernican system was the apparent absence of phases for Venus and Mercury. Now that the existence of their phases was established (Mercury was later shown to exhibit phases), so too were their revolutions around the sun. (This was still not a complete vindication of the Copernican system, since in the Tychonic system Venus and Mercury also revolve around the sun, but it definitely ruled out the Ptolemaic system.)

An even greater setback to the Aristotelians was Galileo's discovery of sunspots. The perfect sun was covered with spots that slowly formed and changed, and by their movement indicated that the sun was rotating approximately once a month about its axis.

These discoveries "must convince the most obstinate," wrote Father Benedetto Castelli, a monk of Montecassino and Galileo's favorite pupil. However, Galileo was more realistic. "It would not be enough even if the stars came down to earth to bring witness about themselves," he answered, and he decided to make his findings public. He

Since Mercury is much smaller than Venus (and farther from Earth) its phases were detected later. Again, its apparent diameter changes according to its phase, largest at the crescent and smallest at full phase. At the extreme right, Mercury is shown as it would appear when closest to the earth in its "new," or invisible, phase.

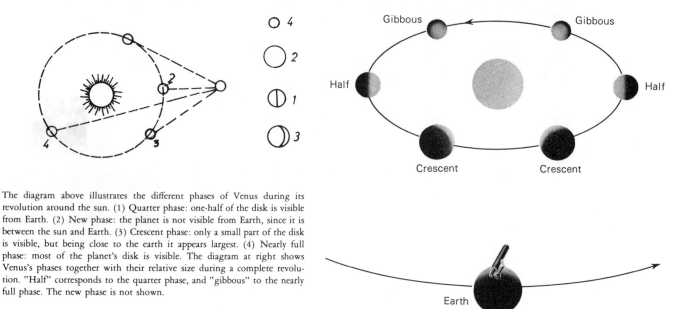

The diagram above illustrates the different phases of Venus during its revolution around the sun. (1) Quarter phase: one-half of the disk is visible from Earth. (2) New phase: the planet is not visible from Earth, since it is between the sun and Earth. (3) Crescent phase: only a small part of the disk is visible, but being close to the earth it appears largest. (4) Nearly full phase: most of the planet's disk is visible. The diagram at right shows Venus's phases together with their relative size during a complete revolution. "Half" corresponds to the quarter phase, and "gibbous" to the nearly full phase. The new phase is not shown.

bypassed the universities with their ingrown prejudices and wrote in Italian instead of Latin. He spent the next few years issuing tracts, pamphlets, letters, dialogues, and comments. In Rome he hoped to obtain from the Jesuit astronomers an endorsement of his discoveries, which would put an end to his enemies' attempt to drag religion into the controversy. He reported to his friend Filippo Salviati that he was well received by the cardinals and prelates, who seemed pleased. Even the pope himself, Paul V, had granted him an audience and showed great benevolence.

When he returned to Florence he published *Letters on Sunspots* under the sponsorship of the Accademia dei Lincei—to which he was elected—showing that only the Copernican theory could explain these telescopic discoveries. It didn't help that the Jesuit Father Christopher Scheiner, professor of mathematics at Ingolstadt, had also announced the discovery of sunspots in 1612. Because he interpreted them as stars revolving around the sun, another controversy started and set the powerful Jesuit against Galileo.

The Aristotelian philosophers now felt threatened; they had begun to realize that their life's work was endangered by this newfangled device of a telescope. As long as the Copernican system was just a mathematical theory, as Osiander had maintained, everything could be forgiven,

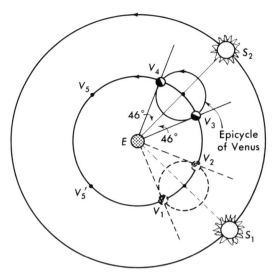

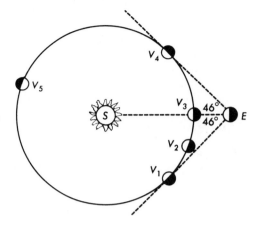

Right: Venus, Earth, and Sun according to Copernicus (or Tycho). The maximum angle between the lines from Earth (E) to Sun (S) and from Earth to Venus (V_1 or V_4, both quarter phases) is known to be 46 degrees. *Left:* Venus, Earth, and Sun according to Ptolemy. Venus moves on an epicycle, with V_1 to V'_5 as the various positions; Earth is at the center, and S_1 and S_2 are two positions of the sun. If Venus circles Earth within the sun's orbit—as required by Ptolemy—it can never get into a position for a full phase, V'_5, without exceeding the 46-degree maximum angle. But when it circles the sun within Earth's orbit, as in the diagram at right, it has no difficulty getting into full-phase positions within the 46-degree optimum range. This, then, ruled out the Ptolemaic system but still permitted the Copernican or Tychonic systems, since in both these cases Venus revolves around the sun.

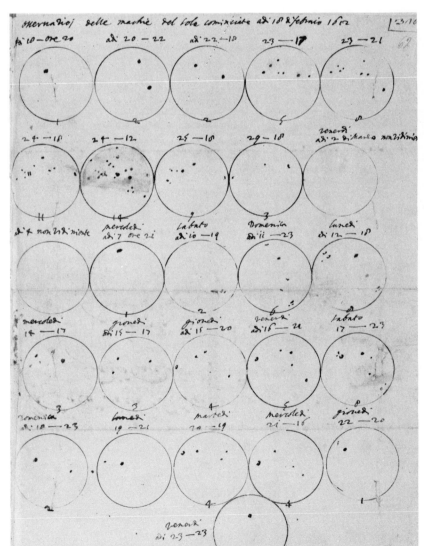

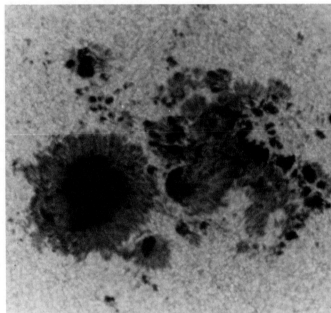

A photograph of a sunspot group, about 100,000 miles long. A sunspot consists of a very dark area, the umbra, surrounded by an extensive lighter zone, the penumbra. The penumbra appears to consist of numerous filaments converging on the center, giving the impression of a gigantic whirlpool of gases. The umbra, which consists of hot gases, appears dark only in contrast with the surrounding surface, the photosphere. In fact, it is more brilliant than an electric arc but at a lower temperature than the four-to-five-times more intense photosphere.

A series of Galileo's observations of sunspots from *Letters on Sunspots,* written to his friend Weiser in 1612 and published the following year. Galileo claims to have seen the spots in 1610, but he made a formal announcement of his discovery only in May 1612. Sunspots had been observed also by the English mathematician Thomas Harriot, the Dutchman Johannes Fabricius (who in 1611 was the first to publish), and the Jesuit Christopher Scheiner. Dark spots on the sun had been observed even earlier by the naked eye, but it was assumed that they were a result of the transit of Mercury across the face of the sun. However, it was Galileo who described their change in form and position, which he correctly ascribed to the rotation of the sun.

The corona, the outer atmosphere of the sun, beyond the chromosphere. It has a temperature of over 2 million degrees Fahrenheit. The loop structures seen here are due to, and thus outline, the magnetic field.

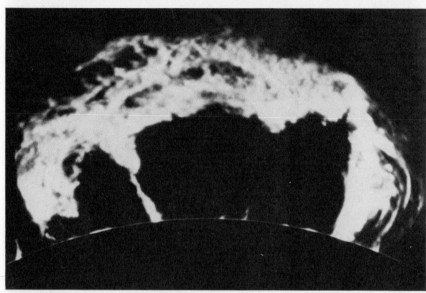

A prominence, or great cloud of gas, erupts from the surface of the sun, sending atomic particles out into space (although it appears so, the clouds are not aflame but are luminous). The mass of gas is carried outward by its supporting magnetic field. These particular prominences form loops at the rim of the sun (referred to as the limb) and demonstrate the turbulence of the sun's atmosphere.

A small limb prominence about 30,000 miles high, showing the characteristic vertical structure. These types of prominences are termed hedgerow prominences because of their hedgerowlike appearance.

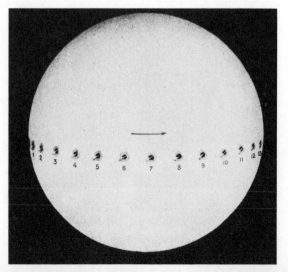

Motion of sunspot. All early observers had noticed that the sunspots appeared to move across the sun, from east to west. Galileo noticed that while it took a spot approximately 14 days to cross the sun's disk regardless of whether it was near the center or at some distance from it, its speed along the path was not uniform. It took a longer time near the edges than at the center, as illustrated by the bunched positions 1, 2, and 11, 12, 13. He recognized this as an effect of foreshortening; the effect would be visible only if the spot were very near the sun. On the other hand, if the spots were some stars circling the sun (and consequently some distance from it), this irregular motion could occur only if their motion was irregular—slower when near the edge and faster when near the center, as seen from the earth, no matter where it was. Since Galileo saw no reason for such behavior, the obvious conclusion he reached was that the spots were indeed on the sun and that the sun itself rotated.

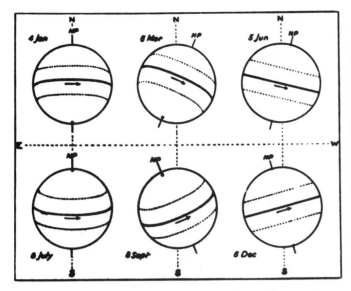

Yearly motion. The apparent motion of the sunspots not only reveals the sun's rotation, but shows also that its axis is inclined from the perpendicular to the plane of the ecliptic by a small angle of 7° 15'. As a result, it presents a different view to an observer on Earth at different times of the year, as illustrated in the figure.

Sunspot trail. A series of white light photos of the sun showing the transit of an active sunspot region across the disk in March 1966. The numbers at the right indicate the dates.

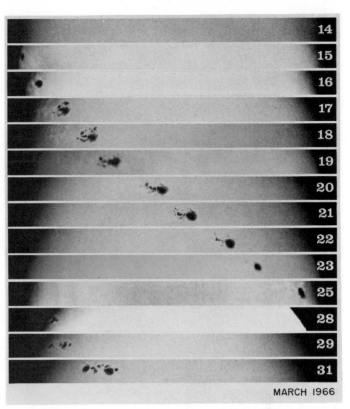

but a physical reality had to be fought. The church, too, had a stake in this, for it could not permit a heterodox point of view—apparently in contradiction to the Holy Scriptures—to be taught openly and undermine its authority. Bound by deep-rooted fears and prejudices, the enemies of the "Galileisti" joined together in what came to be known as the Pigeon League (its leader was Ludovico delle Colombe—colombe is Italian for "dove" or "pigeon"). Unable to defeat Galileo with logical arguments, they shifted the battle to safer grounds.

At a court dinner in Pisa, Father Castelli was challenged by the Grand Duchess Dowager, Madama Cristina of Lorraine, on the orthodoxy of the Copernican system. The incident had been sparked by Cosimo Boscalgia, a philosophy professor at Pisa, who remarked that any double motion of the earth would be contrary to the Holy Scriptures. Castelli, well versed in the Scriptures himself, answered spiritedly and managed to appease the Grand Duchess. Here the incident could have ended, but Galileo felt that he owed it to Castelli and the Grand Duchess— who was very influential at court and known for her piety—to take the responsibility and stop the meddling of philosophers into theology. Galileo was a deeply religious person and believed in the teaching of the Catholic Church, but he felt that the object of the Bible did not include the teaching of astronomy. Nevertheless, in his answer, which took the form of a letter to Castelli, he tried to show how even Joshua's stopping the sun could be reconciled with the Copernican theory. The letter was a didactic masterpiece, but it provided ammunition for his enemies. They were now able to say that Galileo had

meddled in theology and had assailed the authority of the Scriptures. A copy of this letter—circulated privately—fell into the hands of the Dominican Father Lorini, professor of ecclesiastical history of Florence, who promptly forwarded it, with his comments, to the authorities in Rome. (Father Lorini had made a fool of himself earlier when he inveighed against the new theories in a sermon and had to write a letter of apology.)

The next shot was fired by Father Tommaso Caccini, a friar of the Dominican Convent of Santa Maria Novella in Florence, who preached a sermon on the fourth Sunday in Advent (December 20, 1614) on the topic, "Ye men of Galilee [meaning Galilei], why stand ye gazing up into heaven?" in which he maintained that mathematics was of the devil and that mathematicians should be banished. The Dominicans, followers of Thomas Aquinas, naturally declared the Copernican system un-Biblical and close to heresy. Caccini was reprimanded by his superiors, but the damage was done. A small scandal started, with counteraccusations followed by further accusations, and so on—exactly what the Pigeon League intended. Such disturbances, sooner or later, would force the Holy See to act. And act it did. Cardinal Robert Bellarmine (later St. Robert Bellarmine), a masterful scholar who was well versed in mathematics, was ordered to investigate the various charges; witnesses were called, including Caccini who had come to Rome to testify "for the exoneration of his conscience."

Galileo, who had heard that something was amiss, decided—naïvely optimistic—to make another trip to Rome to win friends for the Copernican theory. But he found a

Pope Paul V Borghese in 1614 at the height of his power. He was known to be a literal-minded, rigid martinet, adverse to anything intellectual. Although he granted an audience to Galileo at which he assured him of his esteem, it would have been too much to expect any consideration from him.

Cardinal Robert Bellarmine was the official investigator appointed by Pope Paul V to question Galileo. He was also the author of the famous decree of 1616 enjoining Galileo to abandon the teaching of Copernicus. He is shown here, aged sixty-two, in his study in Rome in 1604. Santa Maria in Via and the Antonine Column (in the background) can be seen through the open window.

deep-rooted opposition both to his arguments and to the teaching of Copernicus. He was received well enough— even flattered in official quarters—but was unable to change prevalent opinions. Finally, on February 23, 1616, the Qualifiers (official experts) of the Holy Office (of the Inquisition) acted on two points submitted for censure:

The Sun is the center of the world and hence immovable and devoid of local motion.

The Earth is not the center of the world, nor immovable, but moves according to the whole of itself, also with diurnal motion.

They declared unanimously that the first proposition is "foolish and absurd philosophically, and formally heretical" in that it contradicts the doctrine of the Holy Scripture in many passages, both in literal meaning and interpretation of the Fathers and Doctors. The second proposition was found "to deserve the same censure in philosophy, and, as regards theological truth, to be at least erroneous in faith."

The action was taken ill-advisedly on testimonials of several witnesses, none of whom was really competent. The wording of the propositions—another unfortunate term—supposedly taken from Galileo's *Letters on Sunspots* was certainly not the way any Copernican would phrase it. They were Caccini's accusations under the name of Galileo's propositions—and nobody bothered to examine them carefully.

The censure was submitted to the General Congregation of the Inquisition and returned, with the direction of His Holiness, to Cardinal Bellarmine. The cardinal was to summon Galileo and admonish him to abandon his opinions. If Galileo refused to obey, he would, before a notary and witnesses, be commanded to abstain altogether from teaching or defending his opinions and doctrines, or even discussing them. Before Bellarmine, Galileo acquiesced and was given a certificate by the cardinal stating that he was not to hold or defend said opinions: "Rome has spoken and the matter is closed."

Galileo returned to Florence in disgust. He continued to work and write, although he suffered from frequent illnesses, partly brought on by his despondency.

In 1623 Maffeo Barberini was elected Pope Urban VIII.

Barberini had been a friend of the arts and an academic himself; only three years before his election he wrote a congratulatory poem to Galileo, when the latter published his *Discourse on the Comets*. Persuaded by the pope's private secretary, Monsignor Giovanni Ciàmpoli, Galileo now defended himself against Father Orazio Grassi who had earlier published *The Astronomical and Philosophical Balance* under the pseudonym of Lothario Sarsi, in which he had vigorously attacked many of Galileo's ideas. Galileo's defense was *Il Saggiatore* (*The Assayer*—who uses not just any balance but only the most accurate one), a masterful polemic. In it, Galileo not only refuted Sarsi but presented strong arguments in favor of firsthand experience, intellectual freedom, and the need for mathematics. It took the form of a letter to Virginio Cesarini, Lord Chamberlain to the Pope, and was well received.

Galileo seemed to have effected a comeback, highlighted by another visit to Rome. During his stay he had six audiences with the pope, which seemed to have gone well—judging from various letters and reports—but the pope would not alter the church's position, although he praised Galileo for "his virtue and piety." A hypothesis was tolerable, but to suggest that an all-powerful God is restricted by a double motion of the earth was not.

As far as Galileo understood, he could present his arguments to the public, as long as the formal requirements of form and submission were met. At long last, he put into final shape what was to be a masterpiece of exposition and scientific erudition: *Dialogue Concerning the Two Chief World Systems—Ptolemaic and Copernican*. As the title implies, it is a discussion among three persons—Sagredo, Salviati, and Simplicio. It is spread over four days, each day's discussion being devoted to a different topic. On the first day, Aristotle's, or Simplicio's, ideas of celestial perfection are contrasted with such imperfections as sunspots. Resemblances between the earth, the moon, and other planets are then discussed, with emphasis on Jupiter's moons and the phases of Venus, which are cited as evidence for the earth's motion. (Galileo completely ignores Tycho's model, which could also account for these effects and was quite popular at the time, being a natural compromise between the two chief systems.) The second day is devoted to a consideration of the arguments for and against the motion of the earth, particularly its daily rotation. While Simplicio cites the usual arguments—birds being left behind and stones falling sternward from the mast of a moving ship—Salviati, or Galileo, emphasizes that the motion of such a body is not affected by the ship's motion. In fact, he goes further and asserts that such a stone would actually fall slightly forward owing to its greater speed at a greater distance from the earth's center.

On the third day the disputants consider the annual revolution of the celestial objects and stellar parallax. The failure to detect any stellar parallax is correctly ascribed to the large distances involved. Finally, on the fourth day, Salviati, or Galileo, presents his main reason for believing in the Copernican theory—the explanation of tides, which, unfortunately, was erroneous since he ascribed tidal phenomena entirely to the combination of the earth's annual and daily motions. The closing argument given by Simplicio, in the words of Urban VIII, again reaffirms the all-powerful Creator and the impossibility of obtaining true knowledge. It is not a very strong argument, and it is out of character. Even so, it would have been wise to have left it at that. Instead, Salviati counters by stating that in searching for God's work we assert His infinite wisdom. How much better an ending—and it was considered at one point in the *Dialogue*—would it have been for Salviati to reveal himself finally as a skeptical mystic, leaving all his science to God.

Even now, when we know so much more, it still seems an informative piece of work, lucidly written. Galileo took great pains to present the Aristotelian arguments as well as possible and then roundly defeated them through Salviati's well-reasoned discourse. Ironically, at no point was any mention made of Kepler's work, although Galileo owned a copy of the *New Astronomy,* or *Astronomia Nova.* One may wonder how differently the *Dialogue* may have fared, even Galileo's own fortunes, had he used the powerful arguments of Kepler's three laws. However, after their initial contacts the two men had drifted apart— Galileo apparently repelled by Kepler's mysticism and Kepler too meek to reproach his former friend for ignoring his discoveries.

Galileo took no chances and submitted the manuscript to Padre Riccardi, who, as Master of the Holy Apostolic Palace, was chief censor. Not too well versed in astronomy, the padre passed the manuscript to others for their "expert" opinion; a few minor changes were made. Riccardi then decided to go over the manuscript himself, page by page, before submitting it to the printer. However, he held on to the preface, which was to be rewritten to conform to the papal wishes to make the work appear to be a hypothetical treatment: "dreams, nullities, paralogisms, and chimeras"—shades of Osiander. The preface was so flimsy that the "discerning reader" to whom it was addressed could easily see through it to discern its true nature—a smokescreen. More delays and further revision followed, but Riccardi could not withhold a license he had already granted. And he dared not approach the pope again. Finally, in February 1632 Galileo presented the first printed copy of the *Dialogue* to the Grand Duke.

Frontispiece for Galileo's *Dialogue Concerning the Two Chief World Systems—Ptolemaic and Copernican.* At the top is the dedication to Ferdinand II, Grand Duke of Tuscany (the Duchy of Florence); the three figures represent Salviati, Sagredo, and Simplicio, the characters of the *Dialogue.* Filippo Salviati is represented as having a light and quick mind, relying more on his sharp logic and scientific instinct than on an academic education; this is Galileo himself. Giovanni Francesco Sagredo at the age of twenty-five has a quick intelligence and good judgment, is a man of the world, a loyal friend of Galileo, and a critical listener. Simplicio, or Simplicius, the pseudonym of the author of the *Commentaries* (an exposition of the Ptolemaic system), represents the average obstinate professor, a believer in Aristotle and an opponent of Galileo; later it was alleged by Galileo's enemies that he was really Pope Urban VIII.

Without stating whether it was correct or not, Cellarius portrayed the Copernican universe as adopted by Galileo. This engraving shows a central sun with the different planets revolving around it; each planet is shown as a small star-shape surrounded by a circle. Note the satellites of Jupiter and the earth-moon system. At the periphery are the twelve Zodiac signs representing the sphere of the fixed stars.

Now if the *Dialogue* had been as difficult to read as *De Revolutionibus* or as obscure as *Astronomia Nova,* that would have been the end of the matter. However, it was in Italian and was very clearly written. As a result, its sales soared. Too late did the authorities realize their mistake in granting permission. The pope was furious. Riccardi was dismissed. The Aristotelians had intimated to His Excellency that he himself was Simplicio—a cheap libel but apparently convincing. In any case, the arguments that Simplicio had put forward were made to look silly by

J. N. Robert-Fleury's 1847 painting of Galileo's trial, *Galileo Before the Holy Office* (Louvre), shows him standing in front of the presiding cardinal, recoiling as if threatened physically. At the long table in the background are the ten judges of the Tribunal: Cardinal Gasparo Borgia, Cardinal Felice Centino d'Ascoli, Cardinal Guido Bentivoglio, Cardinal Desiderio Scaglia, Cardinal Antonio Barberini, Cardinal Laudivio Zacchia, Cardinal Berlingero Gessi, Cardinal Fabricio Verospi, Cardinal Francesco Barberini, Cardinal Marzio Ginetti. The final sentence was signed by only seven; Francesco Barberini, Gasparo Borgia, and Laudivio Zacchia refused to sign.

Salviati's last remarks, and this Urban VIII could not suffer. He blamed his subordinates for misleading him and for showing a lack of confidence in his own superior judgment. He obviously realized that the very foundation of his authority was endangered, not to speak of the whole educational system.

The book could not be recalled, but its sale was stopped and Galileo was summoned to Rome—to appear before the Inquisition, in chains, if necessary, despite his age (he was now seventy years old and suffering from various illnesses). On February 13, 1633, Galileo arrived in Rome and was permitted to stay at the home of the Florentine ambassador, instead of being thrown into the dungeons of the Inquisition. After several preliminary examinations, he appeared before the Holy Office, where he was confronted with an injunction, dated February 26, 1616, stating that he was neither "to hold the opinion [that the sun is the center of the world and that the earth moves] nor to hold, teach, or defend it in any way whatsoever, verbally or in writing."

Now one of the crucial questions of this whole sad affair—still unsolved—is where did this injunction come from? The certificate given to him by Cardinal Bellarmine stated only that he was not to hold or defend said opinion, while the order of Paul V stated that such an injunction was to be given only in case of Galileo's refusal to abandon the opinion and if invoked, it had to be properly notarized and witnessed. But Galileo did not refuse to abandon such opinion, nor was the document that was produced at the interrogation authenticated or

Statue of Galileo by Costoli in the Tribuna Galileiana (Shrine of Galileo) in Florence. This recognition came to Galileo two hundred years after his death.

Galileo's tomb in the Church of Santa Croce in Florence. Only in 1737 were Galileo's remains transferred to the tomb, having previously been deposited in a side niche.

properly witnessed. It appears to be a copy, forged in 1632, as some suggest, or added to the files in 1616 as an afterthought, just in case. Only Cardinal Bellarmine could have solved the puzzle, but he had long since died.

Galileo, when asked about the alleged command contained in that injunction, said that he did not remember having received it—an obvious answer given under stress. It seems very unlikely that he would have forgotten such an obvious command, or failed to obey it, being the pious Catholic he was. Throughout the whole examination Galileo steadfastly maintained that he had never received any injunction, except Bellarmine's certificate—which he produced—thus foiling the Inquisition. When asked why he did not tell Riccardi about the certificate when he had asked him for permission to print the *Dialogue,* Galileo explained that he did not think that he was acting against any command. Where Galileo really made a mistake was in stating that he had shown that Copernicus's arguments were weak and

not conclusive, and therefore there was no reason to mention the certificate. However, Simplicio's closing argument certainly did not support that contention and Galileo's emphasis on the tides, discussed on the fourth day, were strong arguments for the Copernican theory. In fact, it now seemed to the judges that he was trying to deceive them. After three hearings and lengthy deliberations, Galileo was found guilty of having disobeyed the injunction and of believing in the physical basis (tides) of the Copernican system.

Galileo was persuaded to admit his guilt and to throw himself on the mercy of the court, in return for which he was to be let off with a reprimand and a new injunction. However, the Inquisitors were not assuaged that easily and a formal sentence was passed, including recantation, imprisonment for life, and the recitation of the seven penitential psalms every week. It is perhaps a small sign of contrition that out of the ten cardinals who were the judges, three refused to sign the decree.

Owing to Galileo's advanced age and poor state of health, he was allowed to go to Arcetri, where he was able to meet his daughter, a nun, only a few days before her untimely death. He spent the last years of his life here under house arrest; he was refused permission to return to Florence.

The news spread quickly, and copies of his renunciation were sent to all the universities. Whether Galileo pronounced the words *"E pur si muove"* ("and yet it does move") attributed to him after his official recantation is not important; we know that these were his true sentiments, as evidenced in the *Dialogue*.

His mind thereafter was not idle, and he produced his second great work, *Dialogue Concerning Two New Sciences*. It again took the form of a discussion, lasting four days, between the former disputants, and it contains Galileo's laws of motion and projectiles, as well as practical matters related to the strength of structures.

Galileo's eyesight had begun to fail, and he had to dictate part of his second *Dialogue* as well as his many letters, in which—somewhat disguised—he continued to defend the Copernican system; he had sworn not to commit any heresy, but he did not consider himself obligated to recognize the arbitrary and unconstitutional decisions of his enemies. The forbidden *Dialogue* was smuggled out of Italy and published in Leyden, Holland.

Galileo, now completely blind, was attended by his faithful disciples Torricelli, Castelli, and Viviani. On January 8, 1642, he died after a lengthy illness. A public funeral proposed by Florence was denied and he was buried in a small chapel in the church of Santa Croce. The Grand Duke, who wanted to erect a monument over his grave, was warned by the pope that he would consider it a slight to his authority. Nearly a hundred years after his death, Galileo's remains were transferred to a more accessible part of town, and still later a memorial was erected.

Galileo's contributions to science were twofold. His telescopic discoveries opened the heavens to further investigations, replacing the crude, albeit careful, measurements of Tycho; and his experiments, notably those on motion, form the basis of the laws of mechanics. Galileo at heart was an experimental physicist; he observed and made quantitative measurements.

V · GRAVITATION

1. Universal Gravitation

Galileo had been silenced, and with him—so it seemed—all those who taught that the earth was not at the center of the universe. Notwithstanding the telescopic evidence, there was no "proof" why the earth—if it moved—should move the way it did. The crystal spheres of the Greeks had been shattered and pierced, but so far nothing had taken their place. Kepler had shown that the planets move in elliptic orbits. Galileo had described the motion of falling objects as well as those of projectiles, but he had not related this finding to the motion of the heavenly bodies. According to him, their inertia (or laziness) would make them go around in circles, not ellipses. No wonder then that the opponents of the Copernican system could be complacent; their "primum mobile" did all their work and even spared them the need to think.

It would be wrong, however, to assume that no advances were made or that new theories were lacking. Quite the contrary. Galileo's *Dialogue* had found its way to countries outside Italy and was slowly being assimilated by the intelligent citizen. England, especially, was on the threshold of its literary and scientific rebirth, and men like William Gilbert of Colchester (1540-1603) had left an indelible imprint on science. In France, also, discussions were to be held in the Académie Française (French Academy) under the patronage of Cardinal Richelieu, but this was to come later, in 1637. The outstanding personality of that period was René Descartes (1596-1650), a man of genius and imagination, who did for mathematics what Galileo had done for physics. Born into an old French noble family at La Haye, near Tours, Descartes was destined for a career as a gentleman in the service of France. He was a sickly child, and his father (his mother had died a few days after René's birth) took great pains to look after the "young philosopher." He was sent to the excellent Jesuit college at La Flèche, whose rector, taking cognizance of the boy's delicate health, told him to stay in bed as long as he liked and to join his classmates only when he felt up to it. This rather novel therapy not

Postage stamp issued in 1937 by France to commemorate the third century of the publication of *Discours de la Méthode (Discourse on the Method)* by René Descartes (1637).

only improved his health but became a habit he adopted also in later life. Descartes asserted that those long quiet mornings in bed were the times when he did his best thinking in philosophy and mathematics. Even before he left the college at the age of seventeen armed with a thorough knowledge of Latin, Greek, and rhetoric, he began to question what he had been taught. He found the dogmas of philosophy and ethics mere superstitions and the humanities empty of real values. Accepting nothing on authority, he began to lay down a system of rules—a "scientific method" of controlled experiments and rigorous mathematical reasoning. This he published later as *Régles pour les directions de l'ésprit (Rules for the Direction of the Mind).* The main thing was to think for oneself: *"Cogito ergo sum,"* his famous dictum, "I think, therefore I am."

Disappointed by the futility of the studies he had so ardently pursued, Descartes took advantage of his youth—and his financial independence—and, with a number of like-minded companions, took up a life of pleasure in gay Paris. This life did not satisfy him either, and to escape his rowdy friends, he joined the military. Learning the profession of war under Prince Maurice, the first beneficiary of the telescope, Descartes became disgusted with the dreary camp life and transformed his allegiance to the Elector of Bavaria, who at the time was waging war against Bohemia.

At this point in his life, Descartes said that he had a vision, a series of three dreams, revealing to him the real truth underlying all science. Although there is no explicit reference to the nature of that revelation, it is generally assumed to have been the application of algebra to geometry and, more generally, the investigation of natural phenomena by mathematics. Descartes is the "inventor" of that branch of mathematics known as analytical geometry, a cornerstone of modern mathematics. Its basic idea is extremely simple, as are all really great innovations, and consists in describing the position of a point (on a line, on a surface, or in space) by a set of numbers, its coordinates, called Cartesian coordinates in his honor. From a series of such points an equation of a curve may be deduced, or, conversely, starting with an equation, its algebraic and analytic properties may be interpreted geometrically. The possibilities are unlimited; for example, the geometrization of physics is now possible (it will be

discussed later in this chapter). In his *Discours de la Méthode (Discourse on Method),* he applied these ideas to philosophy as a whole and, starting from some a priori statements, or axioms, arrived in a logical way at the desired—or unexpected—conclusions.

After further soldiering, interpersed with a few years of meditation and social activities in Paris, Descartes, now thirty-two years old, traveled to Holland where he spent the next twenty years wandering from place to place. He occupied his time not only with mathematics and philosophy but also with optics, chemistry, medicine, and astronomy. It was in astronomy that he made an

Cartesian coordinates. Any point in a plane can be specified uniquely by two numbers, its coordinates. Two intersecting lines are laid down on the plane (at right angles to each other), the horizontal one being the x-axis (or abscissa) and the vertical one the y-axis (or ordinate). Starting from the point of intersection—the origin—intercepts are then measured (in specified units) along these axes; usually positive if they are to the right or up, and negative if measured to the left or down. The pair of numbers (x, y) then are the coordinates of the point with respect to these axes. In space a third axis, the z-axis has to be introduced, which is at right angles to both the x- and y-axes; measurements along it give the "height." Thus, three numbers are now necessary to specify the coordinates with respect to these axes.

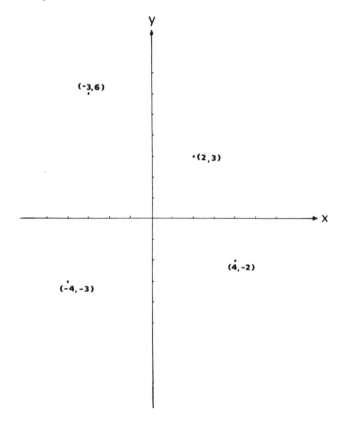

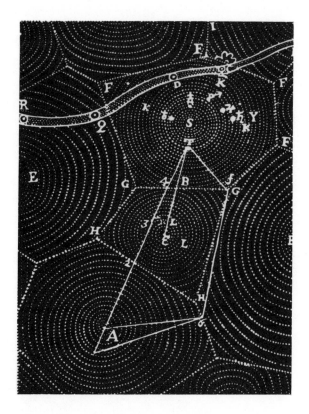

The system of vortices with which Descartes sought to account for the motion of celestial bodies are considered to be "whirlpools" in a space filled with a pervading fluid. For the planetary system the vortex carried the planets around the sun (S). A comet, shown by the irregular path at the top, is carried briefly into the solar system (interacting with the vortex) and then moves away.

important but often misunderstood contribution. Descartes postulated that all space was pervaded by some kind of fluid. If there was no interaction, a planet would move in a straight line, but owing to local movements in the fluid, the vortex, it would describe its particular orbit.

Descartes's system of vortices was accepted during the seventeenth century, but later it was completely discredited.

Descartes had collected his various investigations and was in the process of having it published—the imposing treatise was called *Le Monde (The World)*—when news reached him of Galileo's trial and subsequent recantation. He was thunderstruck; if Galileo could be persecuted for what ostensibly was a hypothetical treatment of the Copernican system, what would happen to someone who had *shown* that it was the only one possible? Descartes was not only a realist—he had too much respect for the authority of the church and the inevitability of the pope's opposition. So he withdrew the publication of *Le Monde,* requesting that it be published only after his death, at which time the contradiction in the two points of view might be resolved. Nevertheless, he did publish his theory of vortices some ten years later in the *Principia Philosophiae* under the encouragement of Cardinal Richelieu himself. To be on the safe side, he formally denied that the earth moved and said it was only carried along in one of the motions of the fluid that produce the daily and yearly revolutions of the solar system. This did not help, and the

book was placed on the *Index,* but at least he saved himself from any repercussions.

While living in a small village near The Hague, and minding his own business, Descartes was approached by the exiled Princess Elizabeth, daughter of Frederick, King of Bohemia. Elizabeth seemed to have quite a desire for learning, having mastered six languages and an extensive literature. She was now turning to mathematics. Descartes, being the gentleman he was and being in awe of royalty, agreed to be her tutor. A friendship developed that continued even after Elizabeth left Holland—as evidenced by the mountainous correspondence between them. But being unable, or unwilling, to withstand the whims of royalty proved to be his undoing. Queen Christina of Sweden, a young and energetic woman, decided that Descartes must teach *her* mathematics also. He held out for some time, but finally in 1649, when she sent Admiral Fleming to fetch him, he agreed to come. Everything would have been fine, except for the caprice of the young woman, who decided that five o'clock in the morning was the time to study mathematics—an ungodly hour for anyone but especially for a philosopher who was used to remaining in bed until at least eleven A.M. This mode of life, coupled with the cold climate of Sweden, undermined his health and Descartes fell ill with inflammation of the lungs. He grew weaker, was bled—which did not improve matters—and received the last sacraments of the church. He died on February 11, 1650, at the age of fifty-four. Seventeen years later he was reburied in the Panthéon in Paris, *sans* the right hand that the French Treasurer General kept as a souvenir. A public oration was cancelled, since his doctrines were still too controversial.

In addition to laying one of the foundations for modern mathematics, without which advance in scientific work would have been impossible, Descartes is responsible for introducing a mathematical method of reasoning out of which, starting from a few given premises, can be built a whole structure of the universe. This method (together with experiments to test the theory) has become the backbone of modern science and was used effectively by men such as Isaac Newton and Albert Einstein.

Isaac Newton (1642-1727) was born on Christmas day in the year of Galileo Galilei's death. A star had set and another was rising. The infant was puny owing to a premature birth, and though he was not expected to live,

A drawing by Newton of the Manor House at Woolsthorpe in Lincolnshire, where he was born and carried out some of his most important work.

A portrait of Sir Isaac Newton (1642–1727) at the height of his career.

he grew into a robust little boy. His father, also named Isaac, had died at the age of thirty-seven, before his son was born, and his mother was persuaded to marry the Reverend Barnabas Smith, an old bachelor looking for "a good woman." Young Newton spent his early years on the farm on which he was born and attended the local village schools. He was by no means an outstanding pupil, nor was he attracted by Latin grammar; he preferred to spend his time making kites—on which he strung lanterns to make the village folk think they saw comets—and mechanical toys, which worked remarkably well. At this early age he showed the mechanical aptitude that would be useful later, but it was hardly appreciated by his young peers. His mother in particular felt that he should help on the farm, but he preferred to sit behind a hedge and read. He read everything he could lay his hands on, and he kept notebooks in which he recorded recipes of his own invention, solutions to geometrical problems, astronomical tables, and so on, all arranged according to subject matter. There was even an entry recording how far he could jump with and against the wind, thus measuring its force, in the great storm of 1658.

Fortunately, his uncle, the Reverend William Ayscough realized that those were not just the ordinary pursuits of a boy, and he prevailed upon his sister to send Isaac back to school and prepare him for college. One must also thank Mr. Stokes, the Master of Grantham School, for his part

in this decision—he even remitted his forty shillings a year salary usually received from out-of-town students.

While in Grantham, Newton lodged with a Mr. Clarke, the village apothecary, who had two great attractions: a parcel of old books (in his attic) and an attractive stepdaughter. Newton devoured the books and fell in love with Miss Storey. Although he became engaged to her, his subsequent departure for Cambridge pushed the romance into the background. Newton never married, although he seemed to have been quite fond of his erstwhile sweetheart and carried on a long correspondence with her.

Newton entered Trinity College in Cambridge in 1661 as a subsizar, a student who had to do menial work to earn his fees and upkeep. His background was passable in the classics but not in mathematics. However, he soon made up his deficiencies studying Euclid, which he found easy, and Descartes's analytical geometry, which baffled him for some time. He seemed to have led a lonely life at Cambridge. Since he was not the athletic type, sports meant little to him and his strict religious training did not endear him to his fellow students. Nor did he appeal to the scholarly type, for he was neither witty nor talkative; and being a subsizar excluded him from associating with the "gentlemen." Instead he became absorbed in his work and soon made some remarkable discoveries in mathematics, which were carefully written out but which he kept to himself. Nevertheless, his aptitude was recognized by Dr. Isaac Barrow (1630–77), an eminent mathematician in his own right and the first occupant of the Lucasian Professorship at Trinity College. He was an excellent teacher and befriended the budding scientist, whom he took under his wing. Newton was homesick, and when the Great Plague (bubonic) struck Cambridge as well as London in 1665, it was an ideal opportunity for him to return to his home in Woolsthorpe.

The next two years were probably among his most fruitful. In the quiet and pleasant surroundings of his home he invented the method of fluxions—from the idea of finding the "flow" or growth of variable, or "flowing," quantities. (This branch of mathematics is now known as calculus and is an essential tool for any mathematician or physicist.) He also showed that sunlight was composed of light of all colors (this was the basis of that branch of physics known as spectroscopy, which will be discussed in the next chapter). But most important of all, he discovered the law of universal gravitation. The story is often told that he was led to its discovery when he was hit by an apple falling from a tree. The incident surprisingly has some truth to it. Upon seeing the fall of an apple, he concluded that the force that made the apple fall should also be responsible for the attraction between the earth and the moon, or the earth and the sun. It is an inverse square law, which means that the force decreases with the square of the distance—not with the distance alone, as Kepler had thought. Newton also made some rough calculations to see whether his law would account for Kepler's three laws on the motion of the moon, but he found that the result did not agree and, consequently, put his calculations away. It is now assumed that the reason for the discrepancy lay in the fact that the mass (or weight) that he took for the earth was incorrect, and this resulted in a twenty-year delay in the publication of his law of gravitation. Another explanation, more prosaic but perhaps more credible, is that he had not yet solved the preliminary problem of the total attraction of a solid sphere on any particle outside that sphere. Such a problem now can be solved fairly quickly, but Newton had to develop exactly those mathematical methods that made it amenable to a solution.

Newton had also published a couple of mathematical papers, and upon his return to Cambridge in 1667 he was elected a fellow of the college. This provided him with free room and board as well as a small salary. Two years later, Dr. Barrow, who wanted to devote himself to theology and was impressed by his former student's erudition, resigned his professorship and recommended Newton as his successor. Thus at the age of twenty-seven, Newton became Lucasian Professor at Trinity College. His duties were light and consisted of giving one lecture—on a subject of his choice—and two conferences a week (should any students want to consult him). The rest of the time he could devote to his own work. Newton could have chosen chemistry (alchemy), astronomy, mechanics, or optics—all close to his field of interest. He chose the last. In his lectures on light, later published as *Opticks*, Newton discussed in great detail the reflection and refraction (bending) of light, lenses, and colors. And he described experiments and observations supporting his propositions. Mention has already been made of his work on the spectrum (the decomposition of light into its constituent colors); this work he now extended to the effects of light on thin plates of glass. Equally important was his invention of the reflecting telescope, in which he replaced the telescope lens with a spherical mirror; telescopes will be covered in some detail in the following chapter. His work created quite a stir among the fellows of the Royal Society of London, the august scientific and literary body of England; they promptly elected him a fellow. However, he became embroiled in lengthy and bitter arguments with some of its members, notably Robert Hooke (1635–1703). Like Newton, Hooke showed great mechanical ability at an early age and claimed to have invented the air pump and several clocks and watches. In 1662 he was appointed curator to the Royal Society, and he agreed to "furnish the Society every day they meet with three or four considerable experiments, expecting no recompense." He possessed a keen mind, but partly because of his poor health and partly because of his executive duties, he did not complete his works, works that he suggested to others. As a result, his ideas were developed by others and he received no credit. His only major publication, the *Micrographia,* contained a great deal of his work on light; Newton's work on thin films and diffraction shows conclusively that Newton was influenced by it. Hooke was notorious for his hot temper, for his criticism of the work of others, and for his insinuations that others had plagiarized his work. Both he and Newton were suspicious, jealous, and sensitive to criticism; but while Newton countered opposition by refusing to publish, Hooke exploded into bitter recriminations and accusations to the effect that his ideas had been stolen.

The first of several controversies between the two arose when Newton sent the Society the results of his investigation on the nature of light. He suggested that the various properties of light, so clearly demonstrated by his observations, could best be explained by a corpuscular theory (light consisting of particles), but not excluding the alternate wave theory (light being a wave motion). This latter point of view was held by Christian Huygens (1629–95) and was supported by Hooke. Newton at first accepted Hooke's criticism in good spirit but later became annoyed at the petty arguments deduced from pure

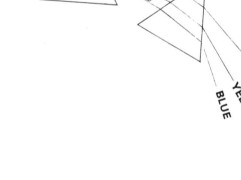

"In the Year 1666 I procured me a Triangular Glass-Prism to try therewith the celebrated Phaenomena of Colours. And in order thereto, having darkened my Chamber, and made a small Hole in my window-shuts, to let in a convenient Quantity of the Sun's Light, I placed my Prism at its Entrance, that it might be thereby refracted to the opposite Wall." Newton was surprised when the resulting spectrum was oblong or rectangular rather than semicircular as he expected. This led him later to his crucial experiment, in which he demonstrated that white light, traveling in straight lines, is dispersed by the prism into its constituent parts—the basic colors found in the rainbow.

Above right
When white light (such as sunlight) passes through a prism, it is resolved or dispersed into its constituent colors. A second prism placed alongside the first will refract, or bend, the light further, but no additional dispersion takes place. Newton thereby proved that the dispersion is not a property of the prism but of the light itself.

Right
If the second prism is placed opposite the first, as shown, the different colors will recombine into one ray of white light. Colors, therefore, are properties of the light; the prism acts as some kind of sorting device, separating the various colors by refracting them differently, red light being bent the least and blue light being bent the most. (An object will appear red—or blue—because it absorbs part of the light while reflecting the red—or blue—part. Similarly a red piece of glass absorbs all but the red part of the light.)

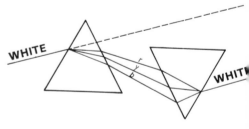

The universal law of gravitation is an example of an inverse square law. Another instance of the inverse square law pertains to the decrease of light intensity. If at a distance r the light covers the area ABCD, at a distance 2r the same amount of light covers the area A'B'C'D', which is four times the area ABCD; while at a distance 3r the area A''B''C''D'' covered is nine times that of ABCD. However, with the increased distances, the intensity has been reduced to one-quarter and one-ninth respectively, indicating that the intensity of light varies inversely as the square of the distance.

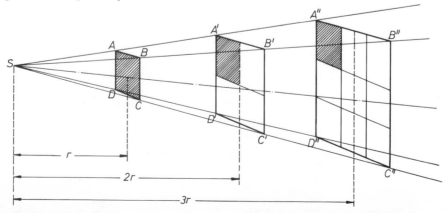

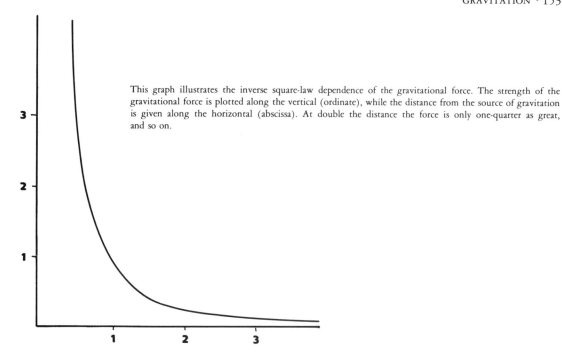

This graph illustrates the inverse square-law dependence of the gravitational force. The strength of the gravitational force is plotted along the vertical (ordinate), while the distance from the source of gravitation is given along the horizontal (abscissa). At double the distance the force is only one-quarter as great, and so on.

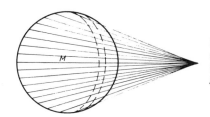

Every point on and in the sphere of mass M acts as a center of attraction, as shown in the top figure. Newton showed that the combined effect of all these attractions is equivalent to the attraction of a particle of mass M (bottom figure) situated at the center of the sphere. This considerably simplified the calculations of the gravitational attraction between two masses.

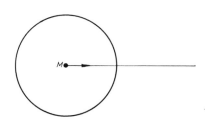

hypothesis and without any reference to the experimental results. The dispute was further sharpened by Henry Oldenburg (1626–78), the secretary of the Royal Society, who disliked Hooke personally and urged Newton to reply to the criticism. After a while Newton tired of the whole business and stopped sending letters and generally communicating with the Society, but he continued with his experiments. Although the wave theory was later vindicated, mainly owing to the work of Thomas Young (1773–1829), we now accept a dual nature of light—it behaves sometimes like particles and sometimes like waves, depending on the kind of experiment performed. Thus Newton was not so wrong after all.

Newton continued to give his weekly lecture; sometimes there was no audience, but he is said to have delivered his lecture nevertheless. Many are the anecdotes told about the absentminded professor. Two in particular

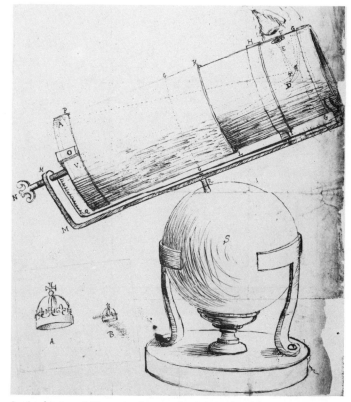

In the drawing of Newton's telescope, after being reflected by mirror V, light is focused on the smaller mirror T and enters the eyepiece F. Screw N is used to move the mirror and thereby focus the telescope. The two crowns A and B show the result of the magnification.

bear retelling, since they shed some light on his character. It is known that Newton did not have much contact with the opposite sex after his early engagement to Miss Storey had been broken off. However, one day—so it is told by Cruickshank—he was persuaded to propose to a young lady. While holding her hand, he raised it—not to his lips, but absentmindedly used the little finger to tamp his pipe. When she cried out in pain, Newton apologized, "Ah, my dear madam, I beg your pardon! I see that it will not do. I see that I am doomed to remain a bachelor." The veracity of that story which was widely spread during Newton's time cannot be vouched for, although he did remain a bachelor. The second episode, recounted in the *Esquire*-like London *Gentleman's Magazine,* concerns his inexperience in worldly affairs. From friends abroad he received a curious glass prism—at that time a scarce item. When he went to the Customs House to claim it, he was asked by the officer to state its value so that a duty could be put on it. Newton, who was more concerned with the value the prism had for his work than with the price of the glass, replied that "the value was so great that he could not ascertain it." When pressed to estimate its price, he persisted, saying that "its value was inestimable." The officer, taking him at his word, consequently fixed the duty several times higher than the price the prism warranted.

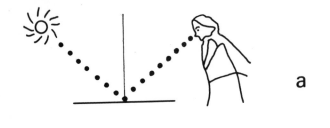

a

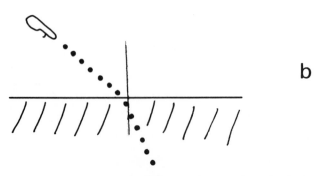

b

According to the corpuscular, or particle, theory, light consists of corpuscles, or particles, that are ejected from the source. Upon impinging upon a reflecting surface, they are bounced off like billiard balls so that the two directions make equal angles with the normal surface (a). If they enter from one substance to another (b), say, from air to glass, the angle in the denser glass will be smaller than that in the rarefied air. The advantage of this theory was that light could travel in empty space and no medium would be required.

When Oldenburg died, Hooke became secretary of the Royal Society. Apparently, in order to show that there were no ill feelings, he wrote to Newton asking him "to continue your former favours to the Society by communicating what shall occur to you that is philosophical." The letter also contained news of several scientific activities that might be of interest to Newton and the admission that in the past there had been misunderstandings between them. Newton did not want to get involved in another controversy and replied that he was "taken with other business" and was determined to abandon philosophy (science) permanently. However, in order to "sweeten" the refusal, he added the description of an experiment that could show the earth's diurnal motion. Hooke got quite excited about it and presented the letter to the Society, which shared his enthusiasm. At this point his vanity and jealousy again overcame his better nature, and he bluntly pointed out some errors in what obviously was a hastily written letter: the path of the falling object was not a spiral as Newton suggested but an "excentrical elliptoid"—whatever that might mean. He was additionally tactless in communicating his answer to the Society before informing Newton of it. Newton admitted the error but, peeved by the criticism, did not reply to further communications from Hooke, in which Hooke described the successful completion of Newton's experiment. The results must have been purely accidental, since the expected deviation of an object falling from a height of twenty-seven feet—an experiment carried out by Hooke—was less than one-fiftieth of an inch and could not have been observed by means of the crude arrangement used. The incident had the unfortunate effect of estranging the two men even further, but at the same time it made Newton return to the problem he had abandoned earlier.

From these letters it also became apparent that Hooke, as well as others, had "guessed" that the force of attraction between the sun and the planets was proportional to the inverse square of the distance and that it apparently changed for different positions within the body of the earth. However, the vague term "excentrical elliptoid" indicated that he was ignorant of the true orbit. One day, early in 1684, Robert Hooke, Edmund Halley (1656–1742), a young astronomer of whom we shall hear more in the next chapter, and Sir Christopher Wren (1632–1723), the noted astronomer and supreme architect of his time, met for discussion in a coffeehouse, a favorite meeting place for philosophers then and now. The discussion turned to Kepler's laws and the force of gravitation, in particular to the idea that gravitation would produce an elliptic orbit. Hooke claimed that he had the answer—that is, the proof that it was so—but hesitated in producing it for fear that someone might make a prior claim to it. His fears were partly justified,

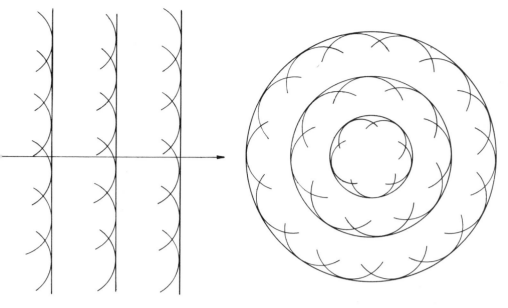

Instead of thinking of light as particles, light can be considered as wave motion, similar to the waves and ripples generated by dropping a stone into a pool of water. Christian Huygens assumed that each particle or portion of the matter through which the wave is propagated not only communicates its motion to the next particle, along a straight line, but that it also necessarily gives a motion to all the other particles that touch it. The result is that around each particle there arises a wavelet of which this particle is the center. (The surface that envelops all these wavelets at a given time is called the wavefront.) At the left is shown a plane wave—that is, one traveling along a straight line—while at center is a spherical wave. Since it was thought that light waves required a carrier—like waves in water or air—a medium, the "luminous ether" (or ether, for short), was postulated. It had some rather strange properties, such as being rigid and yet elastic, weightless, invisible, and exerting no pressure.

Christian Huygens. At the age of twenty-two he was an astronomer and two years later the author of several treatises on geometry. In physics he is known for his work on light while in astronomy he is credited with the discovery of Titan, the brightest and largest of Saturn's satellites. He might have discovered some of Saturn's other satellites, for his telescopes were powerful enough, but he reasoned that there should be only six, since there were only six planets known at the time. He disguised his explanation of Saturn's rings in the form of an anagram that, when deciphered, read: The planet is surrounded by a thin flat ring, nowhere touching it, and inclined to the ecliptic. In his *Cosmotheoros*, published after his death, he touched upon the infiniteness of the universe and the multitude of worlds.

Motion of a falling body. Suppose that BDG represents the globe of the earth, carried around once a day about its center (C) from west to east according to the order of the letters B,D,G. Let A be a heavy body suspended in the air and moving around with the earth so that it hangs perpetually over the point B. Then imagine this body to fall, and its gravity will give it a new motion toward the center of the earth, without diminishing the old one from west to east. Since it was more distant from the earth when it began to fall than when it arrived on the earth, it will not descend along the perpendicular AC but will outrun the earth and will shoot forward to the east side, describing in its fall a spiral line ADEC, "contrary to the opinion of the vulgar who think that, if the earth moved, heavy bodies would be outrun and fall on the west"—i.e., behind the perpendicular. In fact, the object does not fall along the spiral as thought by Newton but along an ellipse.

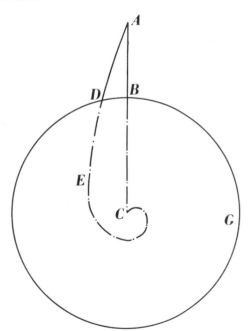

since they were dealing with an actual reality, and others, notably Huygens, had part of the answer. Wren thereupon offered a price in the form of "a book worth forty shillings" to anyone who would bring him proof within two months that the path of a planet subject to the inverse square law was an ellipse. Moreover, he guaranteed that the results would be published immediately so that there would be no fear of anyone else claiming priority. Time passed and no proof was forthcoming, either from Hooke or from anyone else. Finally, in August, Halley decided to visit Newton in Cambridge, for if anyone would know the answer it would be Newton. Upon arrival he immediately went to the heart of the matter and asked Newton point-blank what would be the path described by a body attracted by a force varying as the inverse square of the distance. Newton's answer was just

as straightforward: "An ellipse with the center of force at one focus." How did he know, Halley inquired. "I have calculated it" was the simple answer. Newton could not produce the calculations at the time—it had been quite some time since he had performed them—but he subsequently sent Halley what appeared to be a complete treatise on motion. This was the beginning of Newton's most famous work *Philosophiae Naturalis Principia Mathematica (Mathematical Principles of Natural Philosophy)*, referred to simply as the *Principia*. It took Halley's constant prodding and encouragement to get Newton to complete what was to be a three-volume work. When the first volume reached the Royal Society in 1685, another controversy broke out. Hooke immediately claimed that he was the discoverer of the inverse square law and that he expected proper acknowledgment. Halley immediately informed Newton, as tactfully as he could; of course, Newton was furious and refused to mention Hooke's name in the preface or anywhere else. It was one thing to guess or even predict a result but quite another matter to prove it, and "there is not one proposition to which he can pretend." In the meantime the Society decided to publish the *Principia,* but it was short of funds; Halley, who was by no means well-to-do, agreed to pay the expenses out of his own pocket. Although it turned out later that he did not lose by this decision and even profited from the sales of the work, it was that act of generosity that ended the dispute with Hooke. At first Newton wanted to withhold the publication of the third volume, but realizing that this would seriously undermine the salability of the work and thus harm his young friend who was underwriting it, he finally agreed to publish all three volumes. Being appeased, he even agreed to acknowledge that Hooke and others had deduced the inverse square law. The *Principia* was published in the summer of 1687 and it established Newton's fame. Halley, who had made important contributions of his own, as we shall see later, freely admitted that *his* most important contribution to natural philosophy was his part in the publication of the *Principia*.

2. Orbits

The *Principia* set forth the laws of motions, thus establishing the science of mechanics. It also showed that these laws were universal, and, moreover, it contained, albeit distributed over many pages, the law of universal gravitation with all its ramifications. Of it Newton said, "I frame no hypotheses." This approach was quite different from the usual one relying on observation and deduction, and the *Principia* did not win immediate acceptance.

A number of definitions and axioms were followed by the three "laws of motion"–crediting the first two laws to Galileo and the last to Wren and Huygens:

Law I
Every body perseveres in its state of rest, or of uniform motion in a straight line, unless it is compelled to change that state by forces impressed thereon.

Law II
The alteration of motion is proportional to the motive force impressed, and is made in the direction of the straight line in which that force is impressed.

Law III
To every action there is always opposed an equal reaction; or the mutual actions of two bodies upon each other are always equal, and directed in opposite direction.

The first book deals mostly with orbital motion. It is shown that if a body moves along an ellipse (or in general, a conic section), with a stationary point as its focus, the force producing that motion will be one that varies inversely as the square of the distance (i.e., the inverse square law), and that it is an attractive force. This is the content of Kepler's first law and could also be stated conversely: if the force of attraction varies inversely as the square of the distance, the orbit is one of the conic sections. And if it were not for the force of attraction, the body would move along a straight line–in accordance with Newton's first law; due to that force, the actual path will deviate from the straight line. Whether it describes an ellipse, parabola, or hyperbola depends on its initial velocity. This will be the situation for comets that enter the solar system or for spaceships trying to escape the pull of the earth.

Kepler's laws may be considered to be consequences either of the law of universal gravitation or–what is historically more natural–of the known facts upon which the law is based. Thus, one can say either that equal areas are swept out in equal times by the radius vector drawn along the direction of the force or that the fact that equal areas are covered in equal times shows that the force responsible for that is a central force varying inversely as the square of the distance. Similar arguments can be used for Kepler's third law (the fact that *one* attracting body acts on *all* the planets with a force inversely proportional to the distance causes the cubes of their mean distances to be proportional to the squares of their periodic times): the fact that the cubes of the mean distances of planets are proportional to the squares of their periods shows that they are all acted upon by the same force, obeying the inverse square law. But while Kepler was able to show only the proportionality, Newton could actually calculate the constant and show that it depended on, among other things, the mass of the sun. Therefore, knowing the mean distance and period of revolution of any planet, it is possible to find the mass of the sun (in terms of that of

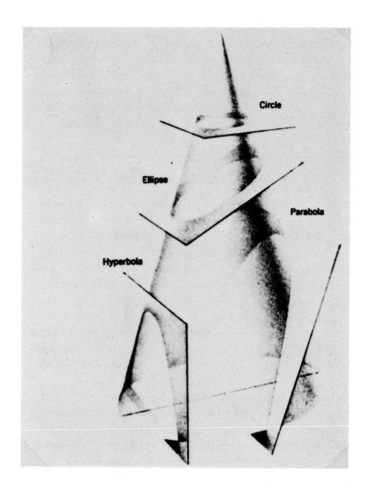

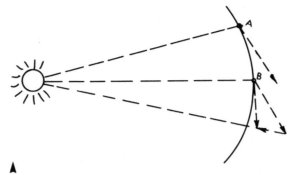

▲

Gravitation as an attractive force. Without gravitation the planet would proceed along a straight line. Gravitation is responsible for the change from A to B, with a corresponding alteration in velocity (suggested by the outside dashed lines). The change in velocity, and thus the attractive, or centripetal, force, keeps the planet in orbit around the sun.

Take a cone and through it pass a plane making various angles with the horizontal plane. The cross sections will be bounded by curves, the conic sections. If the cutting plane is parallel to the horizontal, the cross section will be a circle. As the angle the plane makes with the horizontal increases, the corresponding cross section will be an ellipse. If the cutting plane is parallel to one edge of the cone, the resulting conic section is a parabola. If the angle between the plane and the horizontal is increased still further, we get a hyperbola.

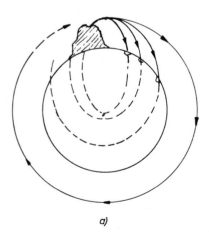

a)

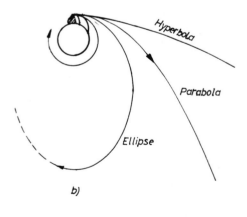

b)

(a) A projectile or rocket fired from a high mountain will describe paths that are part of an elliptic orbit, with the earth's center at the farther focus. (For practical purposes they can be taken as parabolae, which they resemble.) As the horizontal velocity is increased, these orbits more and more approach a circular trajectory, and the projectile will be in orbit. (b) When the velocity is increased even further, the satellite orbits will be ellipses, with the earth at the nearer focus. When the escape velocity is attained, the projectile (or spaceship) will describe a parabola and escape. For velocities larger than the escape velocity the orbit will be part of a hyperbola.

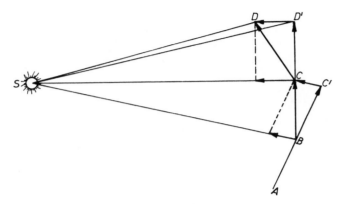

A derivation of Kepler's law of areas. In the absence of any attractive force, the planet moves along AB. A force at B along BS changes its direction so that it now moves toward C (instead of C'). Similarly, another pull at C produces a motion along the new direction CD (instead of CD'). Now the triangles SBC and SCD' are of equal area since they have the same height SC and their bases are of the same length: BC = CD'. Similarly, the areas of the triangles SCD and SCD' are the same, having the same base SC and equal heights. From the two equalities it then follows that the areas of the triangles SBC and SCD are the same, which are the areas swept out by the planet in equal times (going from B to C and C to D). It has been here assumed that the force acts only intermittently at points B and C (and again at D).

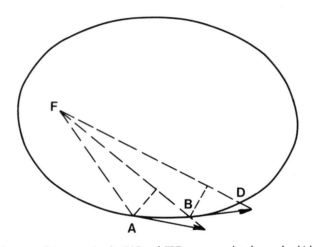

The areas of the two triangles FAB and FBD are assumed to be equal, which implies that their heights (short dashed lines) are also equal, since they have the same base FB. As the planet moves along its orbit, it receives a pull at A, changing its direction and velocity; this is followed by another pull at B, with a corresponding change, and again at D, and so on. As long as the pull acts toward F, this does not affect the height of the triangle swept out in unit time, which thus remains constant. One can then conclude that equal areas imply a central force, that is, one directed toward F.

the earth). Kepler's law applies equally well to moons or satellites revolving around a planet, such as Jupiter. Thus one can calculate the planet's mass knowing the mean distance of the satellite (its period can be observed readily), or, conversely, the mean distance of the satellite can be calculated if the mass of the planet is known.

Newton made the inverse square a truly universal law of gravitation in assuming gravity to be the universal cause of motion. In this he had to depend on his

experience of celestial motion, since the experimental verification of the universal law was found only much later by Henry Cavendish (1731-1810).

The second book of the *Principia* is devoted mainly to a discussion of the motion of fluids. And if one wonders why such a large part of this work should be devoted to this subject, the reason becomes immediately clear if one remembers that Descartes's vortex theory was *the* predominant explanation of planetary orbits at that time.

Newton showed conclusively that vortices could not account for Kepler's laws: the periodic times of a fluid swished around by a rotating sphere vary as the square of the distance from the center of the sphere and not as the three-half power as required. If the medium was a frictional fluid, which would decrease the attraction, the orbit would not be stable at all but would spiral into the central body. Newton, who took the vortices as "material" (i.e., having a definite mass), then concluded: "the hypothesis of vortices is utterly irreconcilable with astronomical phenomena, and rather serves to perplex than explain the heavenly motions." A harsh criticism and not quite justified, if one bears in mind that Descartes did not have material vortices in mind. But it was sufficient to destroy the theory of vortices.

In its place came the universal law of gravitation, which could explain the motions of celestial bodies. But, as Newton freely admits, he assigned "no cause to the power of gravity" but acknowledged that there may be "an elastic and electric Spirit which pervades and lies hid in all gross bodies. However, these things cannot be explained in a few words, nor are we furnished with experiments which could demonstrate the laws by which this Spirit operates." This was Newton's way of acknowledging the existence of a Divine Creator.

The third book dealt with various applications, the most important being various laws of planetary motion, the planetary theory of comets, precession of the equinoxes, tides, and the lunar theory. Newton argues that a spinning body, originally spherical, tends to bulge at its circumference (or equator) and shrink along its axis. If it is made of some plastic (or elastic) material, subject to a given force and rotating at a given (constant) speed, it would take the form of an oblate spheroid, whose shape can be calculated. For a sphere the size of the earth, rotating about its axis once a day (twenty-four hours) and held together by its own gravity, the two diameters would differ by twenty-eight miles, the equatorial diameter being 8,028 miles and the polar diameter being 8,000 miles. However, if the body is extremely rigid, as the earth is now, it would not yield. Now Newton argued that even if the earth is rigid, the water on it, forming the oceans, is not and would flow toward the equator, forming an ocean 14 miles deep (on either side) and leaving the land near

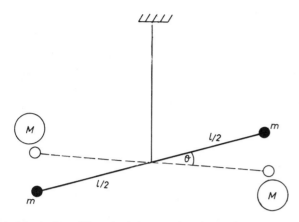

In principle, the Cavendish torsion balance consists of a thin beam suspended by a fine wire and an optical device (not shown) with which the deflection θ can be measured. The attraction between the two masses M and m produces a torque, causing rotation. If the masses, the length L of the beam, and the angle θ are known, the torque and hence the force of attraction can be determined.

Right

Oblate spheroid. If an ellipse is rotated about its minor (smaller) axis (b), one obtains a doorknoblike figure—the oblate spheroid. Its cross sections parallel to the major axis (a) of the ellipse (which caused the figure) are circles, and it can be thought of as a sphere pushed in from two opposite sides. (The shape of the earth resembles an oblate spheroid with its two axes nearly equal.)

Far Right

Prolate spheroid. When an ellipse is rotated about its major (larger) axis, a cigar-shaped figure, the prolate spheroid, results. Its cross sections parallel to the minor axis of the ellipse, causing the figure, are circles, and it can be thought of as a sphere pulled out from two opposite ends.

the poles completely dry. This is not the case, and therefore sometime in the past the earth must have been plastic enough to have adjusted itself to its present shape.

Since the other planets also rotate about their axes, it follows that they too are oblate in form, the oblateness depending, of course, on the speed of rotation. From the shape, the speed of rotation—and hence length of day—can be calculated, and vice versa. The oblate effect is especially marked for Jupiter, since Jupiter rotates rather quickly about its axis, namely once in roughly ten hours.

Two important results follow from the spheroidal shape of the earth and its rotation. First of all, the weight of a body will be different when weighed at the poles and at the equator (at the equator we have the combined effect of the rotation and the greater distance from the center); a mass of 194 pounds at the poles weighs 195 pounds at the equator. More important, the pull of gravity of the sun does not pass through the earth's center, resulting in a small force that in effect changes the direction of the earth's axis. Since the earth is rotating about that axis, this will result in a precession, which is responsible for the earlier observed precession of the equinoxes or the earlier occurrence of the equinoxes in each successive sidereal year. It takes about 26,000 years for a complete revolution of the equinoxes. The precession of the equinoxes had already been noted by Hipparchus, who thought that it was the celestial sphere whose axis of rotation was precessing. Copernicus, and later Galileo, realized that the inclination of the earth's axis was responsible for the precession, and he tried to explain it by additional motions of the earth. It was Newton, however, who realized that the nonspherical shape of the earth *and* its rotation were the cause.

ROTATION OF THE PLANETS

Planet	Mean Diameter *	Oblateness	Rotation period	
Mercury	0.38	0	59	days
Venus	0.95	0	243	days
Earth	1.00	0.0033	24	hours †
Mars	0.53	0.0052	24½	hours
Jupiter	11.19	0.067	10	hours
Saturn	9.47	0.105	10	hours
Uranus	3.69	0.071	10¾	hours
Neptune	3.50	0.025	16	hours ‡
Pluto	0.47 §	0	6	days

* In terms of the earth diameter (12,742 kilometers).

† These and the following figures are approximate; the actual rotation period of the earth, for example, is 23 hours 56 minutes 4 seconds.

‡ This figure is in doubt.

§ This is an upper limit only; the actual diameter could very well be less.

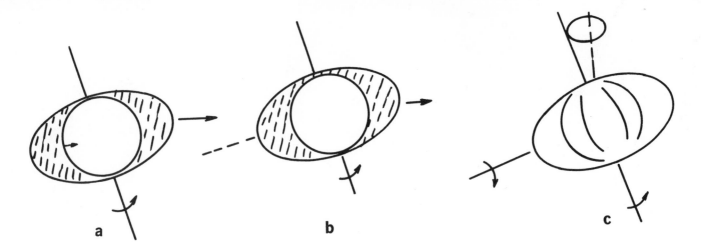

Precession. (a) Because of the earth's bulges (shown here exaggerated) the sun's pull is unequal, larger at the nearer part and smaller at the far part. (b) These pulls are equivalent to a force along the centers (central force) as well as a small force (indicated by the straight arrow) that produces a torque trying to change the direction of the earth's axis. (c) Since the earth is rotating about its axis, this torque will not topple it over but gives rise to a precession of the rotation axis, just as in a top.

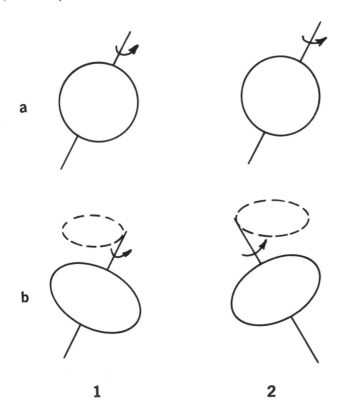

Spinning bodies and precession. (a) A spherical earth is pulled by the sun with a central force and therefore there is no torque. As a result, it would not precess even if it were spinning. (b) An oblate earth is pulled by the sun with a central force *and* a force giving rise to a torque. As a result, an oblate earth (here shown exaggeratedly oblated) is precessing, the spin axis slowly describing a cone. The positions in figures 1 and 2 are some time apart.

The successful explanation of the precession of the equinoxes was the first real evidence of a rotating earth. An actual demonstration of the earth's rotation was provided only much later by Jean Foucault (1819–68) who showed that the oscillating plane of a pendulum in the Panthéon in Paris rotated.

Another striking vindication of the law of gravitation as well as of Newton's mathematical genius was his explanation of the tides. Kepler had likened the earth to an animal whose breathing, affected by the moon, produced the tides. This view was ridiculed by Galileo, who credited the rotation of the earth with the production of tides, forgetting that this would at best account for one tide every twenty-four hours. The subject remained a mystery until Newton calculated the perturbing effect of the sun and moon on the water masses forming the oceans. The moon's attraction is different for various parts of the earth, larger for nearer areas and smaller for those farther away. This difference produces the perturbing effect, which varies directly with the mass and inversely with the cube of the distance (the inverse square law applies only to the main attraction between the centers, while the perturbation is due to the differences). As a result, the water masses closer to the moon will experience a larger force than the surrounding earth and will be pushed up. At the same time the water masses away from the moon will experience a smaller force than its surrounding earth and thus "lag behind." The result will be two gigantic water humps (and, of course, two low marks) traveling around the earth once during a lunar day (24 hours and 50 minutes). Also the sun's attraction produces a perturbation, but due to the much larger distance (and even though the sun's attractive force is much greater than that of the moon) it is smaller, and consequently so are the humps. However, twice a month—at full moon and new moon, when the sun and moon are in line with the earth—the two effects reinforce each other and give rise to the spring tides (the large rise and fall), while at times between—at the first quarter and the third

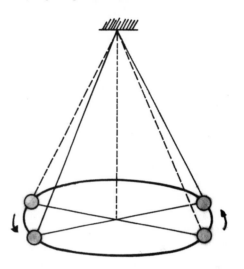

In 1851 Jean Foucault suspended a 200-foot pendulum weighing 60 pounds from the ceiling of the Panthéon in Paris and set it swinging. A stylus attached to the pendulum cut a path into a layer of sand placed on a table under the pendulum. It was found that the pendulum's oscillating plane seemed to rotate. Since the force of gravity was the only force acting on the pendulum, in a downward direction, the rotation demonstrated that the earth itself must be rotating.

Foucault's pendulum. Since the earth is rotating, the plane of oscillation appears to rotate in an opposite direction. The time for a complete rotation of the plane depends on the latitude of the observer. For example, at the North Pole it takes 24 hours (or more exactly 23 hours and 56 minutes) corresponding to a complete rotation of the earth, while at the equator (zero latitude) no rotation is observed, the time being infinite. At intermediate latitudes the time required for a complete rotation through 360 degrees would have a value between 24 hours and infinity, depending on the latitude.

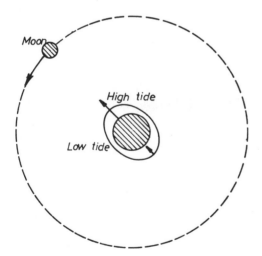

The moon's attraction on Earth varies at different points on Earth. In this simple picture, tides are caused by the differential forces, that is, perturbations caused by the moon's attraction on different parts of the earth's surface. The water masses closer to the moon experience a larger force than the rest of the continent and are pushed up; so are the oceans farther away from the moon, which experience a smaller force than the ground beneath them.

quarter of the moon—the two effects oppose each other, giving rise to the neap tides.

These are the main effects, but Newton did not stop there. He also considered geographical details of the coastline—as compared with islands in midocean—and the effects due to the inclination of the equator and varying distances. From the sun's mass he was able to calculate the height of the solar tides, and hence from the height of the spring and neap tides the effect of the lunar tide alone, from which he estimated the mass of the moon. The subject of tides is important and difficult, but Newton satisfactorily explained the main features and many complex details.

Another area to which Newton gave much of his attention was the lunar problem, i.e., the orbit of the moon as a result of the attraction of the earth and the sun, including other perturbing effects. Even if the moon and the earth were the only bodies in space, the problem would not be simple. The earth's spheroidal shape, tidal effects, and precession all affect the moon's motion. Also, the sun's gravitation turned a "two-body problem" (Earth-Moon) into a three-body problem; a solution to which has

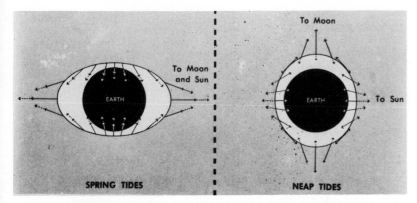

The sun also causes tides on the earth, but they are less pronounced (owing to the much larger distance of the sun from the earth). Spring tides–those with the greatest rise and fall–are produced by the combined gravitational pull of the sun and the moon. This will occur either at new moon, when sun and moon are aligned on the same side of the earth *(left)* or at full moon when they are aligned on opposite sides *(not shown)*. At both times spring tides are approximately the same size, since tidal bulges occur on both sides of the earth. Neap tides, with the least rise and fall, occur *(right)* when the moon is at quadrature (first or last quarter, when the sun, the earth, and the moon form a right angle). At those times the tides produced by the sun partially cancel those caused by the moon.

been found only recently—and then only framed in modern mechanics.

The first real attack on the lunar problem was made by the brilliant English clergyman-astronomer Jeremiah Horrocks (1617?–41) at the age of nineteen, three years before his premature death. The most spectacular contribution of his short life was his observation in 1639 of the transit of Venus across the sun's disk.

Newton improved and extended Horrocks's lunar theory and was able to explain several of Horrocks's previous observations—such as "variation" and "annual equation"—and to predict others. The variation refers to the fact that full (and new) moon occur a little bit before the time one would expect them to occur, while the quadratures (first and last quarter) are a little late. This is caused by the varying pull of the sun during the moon's revolution around the earth; half the time the moon is closer to the sun than the earth is, and thus experiences a larger pull, while during the other half the earth is closer to the sun and thus is pulled more. In other words, just before new moon (from decreasing half to new moon), the moon moves toward the sun and is pulled more, thus arriving at new moon sooner; from new moon to first quarter it is moving against that pull, so that half-moon is late—at that instant it is farther from the sun than the earth, which gets pulled more, thus making the full moon appear earlier. Following this progression, the decreasing half-moon occurs late. The "annual equation," or angle giving the annual deviation, is simply due to the varying

distance of the sun at various seasons and depends on the eccentricity of the earth's orbit.

In order to develop his lunar theory, Newton was completely dependent on accurate observations of the moon's position. It is often stated that Newton could not complete his work on the lunar motion, because John Flamsteed (1646–1719), the Astronomer Royal at the Greenwich Observatory, withheld his observations of the moon from Newton (based on a letter from Leibnitz to the Danish astronomer Ole Romer). Even if this accusation was true, the fact that Newton did not complete his theory when his good friend Halley succeeded Flamsteed as Astronomer Royal in 1720 seems to indicate that the real reason must lie somewhere else. Newton, as we have seen, was reluctant to publish and had to be pushed into it, as was the case in the publication of the *Principia* itself. He was more interested in satisfying his own curiosity than in convincing others. For example, unpublished papers recently found in the Portsmouth Collection (the Earl of Portsmouth inherited Newton's papers from his grandmother, Catherine Barton, Newton's niece) show that Newton had solved the problem of the rotation of the moon's apsides (the two points in the moon's orbit closest and farthest from the earth) fifty years before the eminent mathematician Alexis Claude Clairaut (1713–65) published his results.

The relation between Newton and Flamsteed is one of the unpleasant chapters in both their lives. Flamsteed was a man of great integrity, and he carried out his work at the observatory against great odds. He was poorly paid and had to give private lessons and to spend much of his time on purely mechanical work for the lack of proper assistants. He was often incapacitated by headaches, which made him irritable. Contrary to what has been said earlier, Flamsteed did not withhold his observations from Newton. He is known to have given him immediately one hundred fifty pieces of data and later another thirteen, which were all he had. Apparently, Newton was impatient to receive them immediately, as raw data without calculations, and offered to pay Flamsteed. This hurt the astronomer deeply, since it affected his pride; although poor, he was after all the Astronomer Royal and thought of himself more as a collaborator than just an assistant taking data. He had also stipulated that Newton should not communicate the data to anyone else or impart the theoretical results to others without his consent. This request was directed specifically against Halley whom Flamsteed hated and feared; although Newton did not say so explicitly, he resented the slurs against his protégé. Newton did honor the first part of the agreement scrupulously but apparently forgot the second part—or felt that he was no longer bound by it—since the *Astronomiae*

The Octagon Room at the Greenwich Observatory at the time of John Flamsteed (1646-1719), the First Astronomer Royal. There he carried out his painstaking observations on the lunar positions that were necessary for Newton's work on the moon.

Elementa (Elements of Astronomy) published in 1702 by Gregory, a student of Newton's, mentions that the lunar theory was given to him verbatim by its originator, Newton.

Such incidents—magnified out of proportion—contributed to the bad relationship between the two men, who were incompatible from the beginning. Strangely, the final breach occurred after Newton urged Flamsteed to publish his *Historia Coelestis Britannica,* even offering to find a sponsor—George of Denmark, the Prince Consort. Flamsteed refused, since he was afraid to put himself "wholly into Newton's power." However, a prospectus reached the Royal Society, which was immensely impressed by the scope of the work and instructed a committee, headed by the president—at the time Newton—to approach the prince, who approved of the work and granted the money. An editorial committee was appointed without the approval of Flamsteed, and an Article of Agreement was drawn up. It was not very favorable to Flamsteed, but he signed it nevertheless. After three years of bickering, the first volume was published, but the more important second volume, which was to contain the catalogue of stars, had not yet been begun. The committee had wanted to include the catalogue in the first volume, but Flamsteed had refused since he wanted to recheck the positions. This seemed a reasonable request, but it apparently angered Newton, and the committee of referees

proceeded to edit the catalogue nevertheless. In the meantime the prince had died, and everything came to a standstill until a new sponsor could be found. Newton managed to obtain another royal grant for completion of the *Historia* and to effect the appointment of a Board of Visitors of the Greenwich Observatory—both under the auspices of the Royal Society, with himself as chairman. Very likely the appointment of the Board of Visitors, a sort of watchdog, was beneficial to the observatory, but its appointment at that time was unwise; it angered Flamsteed, who at any rate was close to retirement. It would have been far better to let him finish his years in peace and publish the *Historia* as he wished. Instead, the new committee, which in fact was identical with the old one, took complete charge of the publication of the second volume, without giving Flamsteed the opportunity to include any new observations. When finally the mutilated volume was presented to him, he burned all copies "that none might remain to show the ingratitude of two of his countrymen, who had used him worse than ever the noble Tycho was used in Denmark." If this sounds like self-pity, it probably is, but it should be remembered that a man's lifework was at stake. The *Historia Coelestis Britannica* was his only major work and its star catalogue, containing the positions of 2,935 stars, was a very valuable part of it.

Flamsteed recopied his enlarged catalogue and

observations—the original was in the hands of Newton who refused to return it—and the work was finally published by his assistants Joseph Crosthwaite and Abraham Sharp in 1726, six years after his death.

The publication of *Principia* brought fame and recognition to Newton. It is gratifying to note that England recognized her great son while he was still alive and that he did not suffer the fates of his predecessors Copernicus, Kepler, and Galileo. Upon the recommendation of Charles Montague (later Lord Halifax) he was appointed Warden of the Mint in 1695 and four years later Master of the Mint at a considerable increase in income. His position there during the first few years was a difficult one, since he had to supervise the recoinage of the currency. Clipping of the handmade silver coins had become so widespread that a shilling was worth only sixpence in its actual silver content; this caused many arguments between buyers and sellers.

Under Newton all the old coins were collected and melted down, while a new coinage with marked edges had to be prepared quickly. This put a great strain on the Mint and its Warden.

In 1703 Newton had been elected President of the Royal Society, and he was reelected annually until his death. During his presidency the Society moved to new quarters and gained considerably in reputation. Despite his work at the Mint he presided at the Society's meetings. He also took time to prepare the *Principia* for a second edition and spent his "spare time" solving mathematical problems. One incident, in particular, is of interest because it sheds some light on another unfortunate controversy that marred Newton's later life. The problem was set by John Bernouilli in June 1696 and concerned the curve connecting two fixed points (one higher than the other but both on the same vertical line) that a body would describe if acted upon only by its own weight. The curve is known as a brachystochrone (meaning "shortest time") and required for its solution the use of calculus—which was well known to Bernouilli. To this and an accompanying problem only four solutions were offered: one each by Bernouilli, Leibnitz, Guillaume L'Hôpital, and an anonymous source in England—when Bernouilli saw the solution by the anonymous source he is said to have exclaimed, "Thus the paw of the lion is recognized." It was, indeed, Newton who had sent in the anonymous solution, and one may wonder why he bothered to take the time when he was at his busiest at the Mint and even told Flamsteed that he could not "trifle away" his time (supposedly with the lunar problem). The answer becomes fairly obvious, if that problem is considered as a test case in the ongoing controversy between Newton and Leibnitz. Gottfried Wilhelm Leibnitz (1646–1716) was a veritable Jack-of-all-trades. Mathematics was only one of the many

Gottfried Wilhelm Leibnitz (1646–1716). At an early age he taught himself Latin and Greek and studied history from the books in his deceased father's library. At the age of fifteen he entered the University of Leipzig, which refused to grant him a doctor's degree at the age of twenty, supposedly on account of his youth but more likely because he outshone his mentors. He received his degree from Nuremberg in 1666, the same year Newton had plunged into his work on gravitation and calculus. Leibnitz died in 1716 from an overdose of medicine, but his fame as a mathematician and historian survives.

fields in which he showed considerable aptitude, even genius. He made contributions as well in law, religion, logic, metaphysics, and speculative philosophy, each of which would have gained him well-deserved recognition. However, it was diplomacy that attracted him most, and he spent most of his life in the service of well-paying royalty, which in the end rewarded his loyal services by abandoning him.

It will be recalled that Newton developed his method of fluxions at an early age, but he did not publish it. An announcement of his discovery was contained in the form of an anagram, which was too difficult to decipher, let alone to understand. In the meantime, Leibnitz had developed his method of calculus and published it. In the *Principia* Newton acknowledged that "this illustrious man" had discovered a method that he communicated to Newton and that differed only slightly from his method of fluxions. A short account of the fluxions was finally published in the *Collected Works* (*Opera,* Vol. II) by John Wallis (1616–1703), the foremost English mathematician of his time, and only then could the two methods be compared; they were found to be quite similar (the purpose of Bernouilli's problem was to test Newton to see whether his method was as powerful as he claimed it was). Leibnitz was the first to publish and therefore was the rightful "inventor" of calculus, but Newton always felt that the credit belonged to him, since he was the first to have thought of it (the credit usually goes to the person who publishes first, which is the reason why modern scientific articles often bear the legend "received on . . . ," since the actual publication date may be some time later). The matter could have stopped there, were it not for the obstinacy of both men and their respective supporters. Accusations of plagiarism began to fly back and forth, Leibnitz accusing Newton in an anonymous book review of having based his method of fluxions on the calculus. A counterattack was launched by one of Newton's disciples. A committee was set up by the Royal Society, which found that "the method of fluxions was known seven years before Leibnitz had published anything on it, and further that he could have seen a report from it in the house of Mr. Collins." (Newton had sent a draft of his early paper on fluxions to Collins via his former teacher Barrow.) This was hardly an unbiased review, especially in view of the political tension between England and Germany at the time. The controversy raged on and became national in character, with English mathematicians on one side and German and French on the other. It fianlly waned when Newton, sick and weary, refused to be involved any further, and Leibnitz died suddenly on November 14, 1716, from an overdose of medicine. The whole affair offended the British mentality and seriously hindered the advance of mathematics in England–it was Leibnitz's calculus that was developed, becoming the basis for further investigations by Adrien Marie Legendre, Joseph Louis Lagrange, and others, while the British wanted nothing to do with it.

In April 1705 Newton had been knighted by Queen Anne at a ceremony in Cambridge. This was the first time that a scientist had been thus honored for distinguished work in his field and it reflects the esteem in which he was held by his country. During his later years he occupied himself a great deal with chemistry, his old love, and chronology and theology.

Newton has sometimes been criticized for being heterodox and even heretic in his religious beliefs. To the contrary, he was a deeply religious man and, like many scientists, did not let his philosophy interfere with his religion. Leibnitz's criticism of the *Principia* as being materialistic and subversive of Christianity–an accusation that must be attributed to a large extent to personal animosity–upset Newton even more than the controversy over the invention of the calculus. Leibnitz claimed that Newton's God was merely a super-mechanic who could not even create a satisfactory universe but had to repair its worn parts in order to keep it going. (This resulted in a spirited exchange of letters between Dr. Samuel Clarke [1675-1729], a prominent philosopher and theologian, and Leibnitz.) As far as can be ascertained from Newton's writing on the subject, he considered the universe–at least that part that can be explored–a vast and complicated machine created by a spiritual God who also fixed laws for its operation. These laws He set aside, temporarily, in order to show His power to the ancients with whom He had intimate relations, as revealed in the Old Testament. For Newton, the time was now past, and the Divine purpose was manifested in modern science, which thus becomes an essential tool of religion. God had created the world machine. Now He limits Himself to its correct functioning.

Newton lived very comfortably in his old age. He began preparations for the publication of a third edition of the *Principia,* but since he was eighty years old, the task was too much for him alone. Fortunately, he found an able assistant (John Pemberton) and the new edition was finally completed in 1726; the previous reference to Leibnitz's discovery of the calculus did not appear (Flamsteed had been deleted in the second edition). How much of this was due to Newton's initiative and how much to the advice of others is difficult to say. (Newton resented opposition and was easily influenced by flattery.)

Newton's health deteriorated as the result of frequent attacks of gout and bladder trouble. After an ill-fated trip to London to attend a meeting of the Royal Society (he had moved to Kensington on account of its better air) he became violently ill (the diagnosis was a stone in the bladder), without hope of recovery. He died a few weeks later on March 20, 1727, and was buried in Westminster Abbey with all honors of the Empire. The journal of the Royal Society bore the simple entry: "The chair being vacant by the death of Sir Isaac Newton, there was no meeting this day."

When one tries to evaluate Newton's contribution to science and, in particular, to astronomy, one is faced by the difficulty of measuring genius by standard methods. Newton said that if he saw further than other men, it was because he stood upon the shoulders of giants. Yet he was himself a giant, dwarfing even men like Kepler and Galileo. While they were able to show how the celestial bodies moved, he explained the motions in terms of simple laws. Gravity is still a riddle, but it was Newton who pointed the way–if not to its complete explanation, then at least to a better understanding of the problem. Only a short while before his death Newton said: "I do not know what I may appear to the world; but to myself I seem to have been only like a boy, playing on the sea-shore, and diverting myself, in now and then finding a smoother pebble or a prettier shell than ordinary, whilst the great ocean of truth lay all undiscovered before me." The veneration of his contemporaries and their feeling that nothing remained to be discovered is probably best expressed by Alexander Pope:

Nature and Nature's laws lay hid in night:
God said, Let Newton be! and all was light.

to which was added a modern sequel (credited to Sir John Collings Squire):

It did not last; the Devil howling Ho!
Let Einstein be, restored the status quo.

Before leaving the subject of universal gravitation, mention must be made of at least two other men who have contributed to our understanding of gravity and planetary orbits. (In fact, many more should be listed, but space does not permit it.) Joseph Louis Lagrange (1736–1813) is said to have become professor of mathematics at the Royal Artillery School in Turin at the age of sixteen, lecturing to students much older than himself. He organized the most able of his students into a society that later became the Turin Academy of Sciences. Its first volume of *Transactions,* published in 1759, contained several articles by the brilliant young professor, which won him admission to the illustrious Berlin Academy. A few years later he won the prize offered by the Paris Academy of Sciences for an essay on the libration of the moon. In this essay he not only gave a satisfactory (although yet incomplete) account of the libration based on the nonspherical forms of both the moon and the earth, but he also developed a general method for the treatment of dynamical problems. In 1766 he won yet another prize for tackling Jupiter and its satellites. Considering the sun and Jupiter with its (then known) four satellites, this is a six-body problem for which even now no exact solution exists, but using approximate methods he made several notable advances in explaining the observed orbits. That same year he accepted an invitation by Frederick the Great to head the physics-mathematics section of the Berlin Academy. During his stay in Berlin, which lasted 21 years until Frederick's death, Lagrange wrote several important papers on mathematics and astronomy for which he repeatedly captured the Paris prize. In Berlin he also wrote his masterpiece, the *Mécanique Analytique (Analytical Mechanics),* which was an elaboration of Newton's laws of motion, but dressed in very elegant mathematical form. It was already conceived when Lagrange was a boy of nineteen, but it was published only in 1788 since no publisher could be found. In it he derives his famous "equations of motion," which result from making certain mathematical functions a "maximum" (largest value) or "minimum" (smallest value). Lagrange was a pure analyst, who did not make use of geometry. "No diagrams will be found in the work," he says in the preface to the *Mécanique Analytique,* but somehow as an afterthought he adds that mechanics may be considered as the geometry of a space of four dimensions, three Cartesian space coordinates and a time coordinate, which is sufficient to locate a point (particle) *both* in space and time, a view that later became important in the hands of Einstein.

After Frederick's death in 1786 the climate in Berlin had become unpleasant for foreigners, and Lagrange was glad to accept an invitation by Louis XVI to join the French Academy. He was welcomed with open arms and assigned comfortable quarters at the Louvre, but he felt that his career as a mathematician was finished. It was clearly a case of nervous exhaustion owing to his long and excessive overwork. He became melancholy and, like Newton, turned to metaphysics. The French Revolution shook him out of his stupor, and he renewed his interest in mathematics. He became professor of mathematics at the Ecole Normale and later at the Ecole Polytechnique (1797), a position he held until his death. There he taught Napoleon's young engineers the rudiments of algebra. Lagrange was undoubtedly the greatest and yet most modest mathematician of his time—"the lofty pyramid of the mathematical sciences," as Napoleon Bonaparte called him.

The Marquis Pierre Simon de Laplace (1749–1827) has often been called the Newton of France. His rise as a mathematician was rapid and brilliant; he submitted paper after paper to the French Academy of Sciences, each demonstrating his formidable capabilities. Laplace's main concern was the application of Newton's law to the solar system as a whole. It had been known, for example, that Saturn and Jupiter over the years alternate, advancing or lagging behind their expected positions. If these "perturbations" were cumulative, it might happen, as Newton feared, that the whole solar system would be disjointed. Laplace showed that the perturbations were periodic and therefore that, after some time, equilibrium conditions would again prevail. However, his solution of the problem of stability is only valid in idealized situations, when forces such as tidal friction are ignored. These effects, though small, always act in the same direction, somewhat like a brake on the diurnal motion of the planets. Consequently, one cannot conclude, as Laplace did, that nature arranged the operations of the celestial machine "for an eternal duration." The results of these and other investigations appeared in Laplace's magnum opus *Mécanique Céleste (Celestial Mechanics),* which was published in five volumes over a period of twenty-six years. The first two volumes dealing with the motions of planets appeared in 1799; the investigations were continued in two other volumes published in 1802 and 1805; and the final volume was printed in 1825. The books are as voluminous as they are difficult to understand, and it is probably here where the famous phrase *"Il est aisé à voir"* ("It is easy to see")—so often found in the most difficult and unclear reasoning—had its origin. It is also characteristic of Laplace that no references

A portrait of Joseph Louis Lagrange (1736–1813) wearing the Grand Cross of the Legion of Honor. Lagrange was the outstanding mathematician of his time, and he was honored as such by the French.

A portrait of the Marquis Pierre Simon de Laplace (1749–1827) at the height of his career. In addition to the Grand Cross *(shown),* he also held the Order of the Reunion. He was made a count by Napoleon and a marquis by Louis XVIII. An outstanding mathematician and astronomer, Laplace later entered politics and managed to hold outstanding positions during the Revolution and the periods of Napoleon and the Bourbons. ►

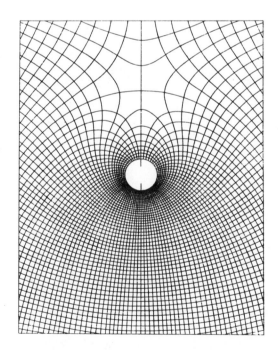

The potential describes the interaction of various charges or masses and has the great mathematical advantage of providing the several components of a force or intensity from the solution of only a single equation. In the diagram, the lines of equal (electric) potential are represented by the closed curves, and the lines of force by lines drawn at right angles to them. The electrical force or intensity will be largest in regions where the equal potential curves are closest to each other since there the gradient is at its maximum or steepest. The intensity can then be read off from the diagram simply by noting the rate of increase (or decrease) of the equipotentials.

to other authors, except Newton, are found, although he "borrowed" heavily from the works of Legendre and, in particular, Lagrange.

Probably Laplace's greatest single contribution was the Laplace equation, which governs the behavior of the potential in empty space. The concept of the potential, originally proposed by Lagrange, is not only of greatest importance in gravitational theory but of equal significance in electromagnetism and the mechanics of fluids. In particular, it made it possible to formulate Newton's universal gravitation as a field theory, where the behavior of one function, the potential, throughout space determines the resultant interaction with other particles (masses). (It was this concept that Einstein successfully generalized in his general theory of relativity.)

3. The Relativity of Space and Time

It looked as if at last the key to the mysteries in the universe had been found. Kepler's laws were successfully explained by the law of universal gravitation and the motion of the planets was determined. Jean d'Alembert, Lagrange, Laplace, and their successors refined the calculations. Perturbations, which could not be accounted for readily, pointed to the existence of other planets, which were subsequently discovered (see Chapter VI). True, there were several questions that remained unanswered, such as how forces act at a distance or how the earth moves relative to the ether. Either the ether moves together with the moving earth—somewhat like the earth's atmosphere—or it is stationary (like the fixed stars) and only the earth moves relative to it. If the ether moves with the earth, then light from a fixed star should enter a telescope at a point on the moving earth at the same angle—as if that point were stationary. Yet it is necessary to tilt the telescope in the direction of the earth's motion; the angle through which the telescope must be tilted measures the aberration discovered by James Bradley (1693–1762). The situation is similar to that of a person walking in vertically falling rain and holding an umbrella. If he stands still, he will hold the umbrella vertically, but if he walks, he will tilt it slightly forward, the angle being larger if he walks faster. This is due to the fact that, relative to him the resulting motion of the raindrops is the sum of the actual motion and the motion of the walker relative to it. If the sheet of rain represents rays of light and their motion through the ether and the person walking represents the moving earth, the fact that the umbrella (read: telescope) has to be tilted—i.e., that aberration is present—means that the earth moves relative to the ether. (The discovery of stellar aberration, incidentally, was another indication that the earth is moving.)

Now if the earth moves through the ether, then the time taken by light to travel a certain distance in a direction parallel to the motion in the ether should not be equal to the time taken by light to travel the same distance perpendicular to the motion in the ether. We can, again, illustrate this by a simple example—a stream moving with velocity v and a boat moving with speed c (in still water). If the boat moves downstream a distance s and then returns to its starting point, it can be shown that the return trip will take *longer* than the time taken to cross the stream, also width s, and return to the shore. Again, if the motion of the boat represents rays of light and the stream the motion of the earth, then one would expect that there should be a difference in time light takes to travel a certain distance along (and against) the earth's motion and the time taken to travel the same distance perpendicular (and back) to it. To find this difference was the purpose of a series of very careful experiments carried out by Albert A. Michelson and Edward W. Morley in 1887. From this difference it would then be possible to find the velocity of the earth with respect to the ether or, equally well, the relative velocity of the ether with respect to the earth. However, no such difference was observed; the speed of light was the same whether it was measured along or perpendicular to the earth's motion, or, as it was stated at the time, the relative speed of the ether could not be measured. Several explanations were put forward, the most interesting that of G. F. FitzGerald and H. A.

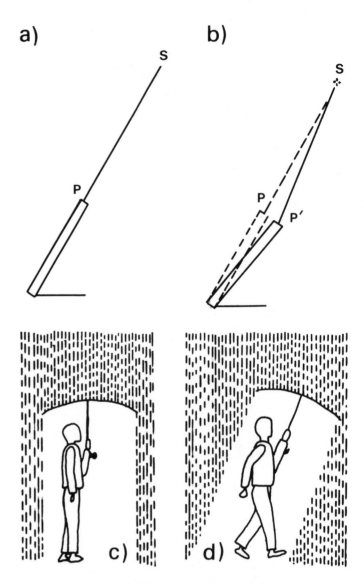

Aberration. (a) *Directed telescope:* Light from star S enters the telescope at point P. Both the telescope and the ray of light are in a straight line. (b) *Tilted telescope:* The telescope has to be tilted forward to catch the light from star S at an angle we call the aberration. Light now enters the telescope at P′. (c) *Standing person:* A standing person will hold his umbrella vertically in the direction of the rain. (d) *Walking person:* A person walking in the rain will tilt his umbrella forward, in the direction in which he is moving.

Lorentz, suggesting that with respect to the ether measuring rods seem to shrink along the motion of the earth (or other objects). This contraction, called the FitzGerald-Lorentz contraction, would be sufficient to offset the negative result of the Michelson-Morley experiment. However, it was only when Albert Einstein put forward his special theory of relativity that the puzzle of the "vanishing ether" was solved.

Among scientists Albert Einstein was unique; he possessed insight into physical problems comparable to those faced by Newton, whom he revered, but he did not have the latter's jealous and petty temperament. He was a

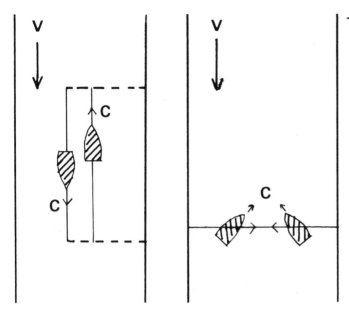

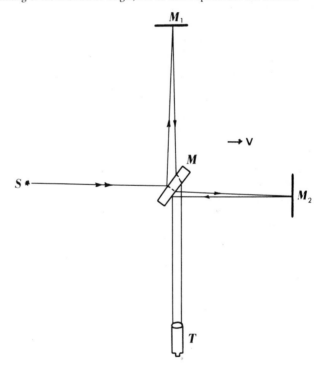

A boat moving with a certain speed c is traveling in a stream moving with velocity v. *Left:* It moves downstream a certain distance and then returns to its starting point. Downstream its effective velocity will be c+v, while upstream it is c−v (we assume here that c is larger than v). *Right:* It moves across the stream an equal distance and returns to its starting point (note that for both trips the boat has to be faced into the direction of the stream in order to move directly across), giving us the square of its effective velocity: c²−v² in both cases. Intuition to the contrary, the time taken for the boat to move downstream and upstream will be longer than that for the trip across the stream and back.

Michelson-Morley experiment. Light from a source (S) is partially reflected and partially transmitted by a half-silvered mirror (M) and continues in two directions at right angles to each other. After further reflections by two plane mirrors (M₁ and M₂), both rays arrive at the observer (T). (A glass plate, not shown, is interposed so that the paths of the two light rays are exactly equal.) The whole apparatus moves with the earth's orbital motion relative to the ether. Upon entering the telescope T there will be an interference between the two light rays. Now, if owing to the earth's motion there was a difference of time between the two different paths of light there should also be a relative displacement or shifting of the interference fringes, but no such displacement was observed.

Albert A. Michelson. Following his graduation from the U.S. Naval Academy, this son of a Polish immigrant became an instructor there. While he was preparing a lecture in optics, a modification of Foucault's method for the measurement of the velocity of light "suggested itself" to him. It consisted simply in replacing the concave mirror of Foucault with a lens and a plane mirror, increasing the optical path, and thus the accuracy, by a factor of twenty. In 1880 while on a leave of absence at Potsdam he set out to measure the motion of the earth with respect to the "ether" by means of a special interferometer that he had designed, which was to become one of the precision instruments of modern optics. The result was negative but could not be taken as evidence against the ether theory owing to uncertainties in the results caused by external perturbations. After returning to the United States, he became first professor of physics at the Case Institute of Technology in Cleveland where he became close friends with Edward W. Morley, professor of chemistry at the adjoining Western Reserve College. It was then that the Michelson-Morley experiment was carried out and definitely showed the absence of any ether-drift. In 1889 Michelson became the head of the physics department at the University of Chicago. In 1923 Michelson, at the age of seventy and past retirement age, was asked by George E. Hale, his former associate and then director of the Mount Wilson Observatory to come to Pasadena to repeat his velocity of light measurements. However, before the work could be completed, Michelson suffered a stroke. He died in 1931.

visionary like Kepler but managed to keep his ideas firmly rooted in reality. When fame came to him, it did not change his simple way of life. There was no trace of vanity or self-importance in his soul: "I do not care for money, decorations or titles. I do not crave praise. The thing I value above all else is the understanding and appreciation of my fellow workers."

Einstein was not only a brilliant physicist but also a warm and generous person, who took the time and effort to help others and to speak out openly for his beliefs and principles. "Concern for man himself and his fate must always form the chief interest of all technical endeavors. Never forget this in the midst of your diagrams and equations," he said.

Albert Einstein was born on March 14, 1879, in the little town of Ulm in Germany, the son of Hermann Einstein, a proprietor of a small electrotechnical business. There is nothing in Einstein's early childhood to indicate his future greatness. In fact, he was considered backward—suffering from learning disabilities. Business did not go well for Hermann Einstein, partly on account of his easygoing manner, and he moved soon after Albert's birth to Munich, where he and his brother Jakob, an engineer, set up another small electrotechnical factory. There the young boy attended the local elementary school; it was a Catholic school, but Einstein's Jewish education was not neglected. He received private lessons and thus at an early age became acquainted with the teachings of both Moses and Jesus. The young boy was rather shy and loved to play by himself or take walks into the fields and woods alone, pondering the marvels of nature. He made his first contact with science at the age of four or five, when his father bought him a small magnetic compass to amuse him while he was sick in bed. Here was an object, the magnetic needle, which seemed to have a life and will of its own, always pointing toward one direction no matter how it was placed. It was a mystery that defied ordinary everyday experience. As Einstein himself recalled in his *Autobiographical Notes,* the experience made a deep and abiding impression on him. In his later quests for understanding, he found an able and willing instructor in his uncle Jakob, who introduced him to algebra: ". . . when the animal we are hunting cannot be caught, we call it x temporarily and continue to hunt it until it is bagged," his uncle had said. Making use of this rule, the boy was able to solve algebraic equations and prove for himself, at the age of eleven, among other things, Pythagoras's theorem.

In addition to Uncle Jakob, there was Max Talmey, a medical student who in the hospitable tradition of Jewish homes shared the Einstein table one day a week. He gave young Albert a copy of Spieker's *Lehrbuch der ebenen Geometrie,* a popular text on geometry. At his weekly meal, Talmey was shown the problems Einstein had solved the previous week. However, Einstein did not stop there, and when he began to teach himself advanced mathematics, his "tutor" turned to philosophy where he could still keep abreast of his pupil. School, on the other hand, did not provide much challenge or inspiration. Albert, of course, excelled in mathematics and physics, but he did not take to the rote memory work of the school curriculum. He had a hatred of the military discipline that reigned, and still reigns, in German schools. His instructors impressed him as militaristic martinets, who would have made excellent sergeants but were poor pedagogues. They, on the other hand, regarded the boy who could not cope with their rote memory work and disciplinary manner as

somewhat stupid. There was only one teacher, by the name of Reuss, who was able to inspire in the boy the love for art and the literature of the Greek and Latin language.

In the meantime, the financial situation of his parents had gone from bad to worse. The elder Einstein, who had always had an open hand for anyone who asked for help, now had to appeal for assistance himself. Cousins in Milan offered help, and so the family, with the exception of Albert who still had three years before his matura (matriculation), left for the sunny south of Italy. Albert, in the meantime, deprived of the warm sympathy of his parents, found it rather difficult to live in hostile surroundings. So he decided to leave school and, armed with a medical certificate, left to join his family in Italy. It is told that before he could even present his certificate he was expelled from the school "on grounds that his presence in the class is disruptive and affects the other students." Albert Einstein had become a dropout.

In Italy, for the first time, he was free. With no militaristic disciplinarians to guide every step of his daily routine, he ambled through the countryside, visited museums and art galleries, and read; his thirst for knowledge was insatiable. The electrical engineering business his father had started so enthusiastically had received one setback after another, and the young searcher was told to forget his "philosophical nonsense" and settle down to a "practical" trade, such as electrical engineering. That he had not been graduated from the Luitpold Gymnasium (the secondary school in Munich) barred his entry into a German university. However, in Zurich there was the famous Swiss Federal Institute of Technology (FIT), also known as the ETH (Eidgenössische Technische Hochschule), which required only the passing of an entrance examination. In 1895 Einstein, sixteen years old and two years below the age of entrance, was permitted to sit for the examination. He failed. Not in mathematics and physics, as is often said—in those subjects he excelled—but in botany and languages. Einstein later admitted that the failure was entirely his own fault. He was advised to complete his secondary education at the cantonal high school in Aarau. There, amid pleasant surroundings and friends—Professor Jost Winteler, at whose home he stayed, became his close friend and adviser—he finished his studies and obtained the matriculation certificate that opened the doors of the ETH. Here he enthusiastically continued his studies in mathematics and physics under the guidance of such men as the physicist Heinrich Weber and the mathematicians Gayser and Hermann Minkowski (Minkowski made an important contribution to his student's later researches). But even the famous teachers at the Institute were not sufficient for him; he often cut classes to study on his own the works of Heinrich Hertz,

Hermann von Helmholtz, and other physicists.

Einstein's financial position was not a very good one. Apart from 100 francs ($20), which well-meaning relatives sent him every month, he had to rely on tutoring to get himself through college. Out of this small income, every month he put 20 francs toward the cost needed to obtain Swiss citizenship. (When Einstein left Munich, he asked his father on his behalf to renounce his German citizenship, and so he had become stateless.)

Many a day the young Einstein had to go without a square meal. However, that did not deter him from his goal to study and find out things for himself. In addition, he was interested in music—he played the violin extremely well—art, and literature, and spent his spare time at concerts, that is, when he could afford it. He had many friends. One, in particular, was a brilliant girl from Serbia, named Mileva Maric, who shared his enthusiasm for mathematics and whose companionship grew into a romance and, later, marriage. Another was Marcel Grossmann, whose well-kept notes Albert frequently copied when he had cut classes and examinations were near. Grossmann later became a close collaborator of Einstein when he developed his general theory of relativity.

Einstein graduated from the ETH at the age of twenty-one a full-fledged scientist. He knew that a "practical profession" was simply unbearable to him. He loved to teach, and several of his professors had indicated that the position of assistant lecturer would be available for him after graduation. However, when he approached his former professors after commencement, he met with refusals. (In the European university system a junior instructor works directly under the direction and guidance of a senior professor.) By his forthrightness and opposition to authority he had alienated many of his former professors and, in particular, Professor Weber, who resented Einstein's addressing him as only Herr Weber. Einstein was considered a difficult person who wouldn't let anyone tell him anything. After graduation, his monthly allowance stopped, and 1901 was a hard year for the struggling scientist, brightened only by his becoming a Swiss citizen.

Marcel Grossmann had heard of Einstein's plight, and he induced his father to intervene on his behalf with Director Friedrich Haller of the Swiss Patent Office at Berne. The director took a liking to the shy scientist, whose wide knowledge in scientific problems he discerned immediately, and promised him a provisional job when a vacancy occurred. In the meantime Einstein continued to tutor and held odd jobs while waiting for the promised vacancy. In Berne, together with two other like-minded friends, he "founded" the Olympia Academy, an informal debating society; the three would meet usually in

Einstein's apartment, partake of a simple dinner, and discuss whatever struck their fancy. Finally, the long-awaited vacancy occurred and Einstein became Technical Expert, Third Class, at an annual salary of 3,500 francs. It was not much, but it was sufficient to start a family, and he married his former colleague, Mileva Maric, who bore him two sons, Hans Albert and Eduard.

The position at the Patent Office required no great intellectual exertion and left Einstein time to perform his own calculations, which he used to hide surreptitiously in his desk when he heard someone approaching. It was, as he called it, a "shoemaker's job" and he later advised young students to get similar shoemaker's jobs, where they were not paid for research but for a different service and could still do their original thinking. Einstein spent the next few years of his life dividing his time between family, office work, and scientific investigations.

In one year, 1905, he published four research papers, each of which would have made anyone a name in scientific circles. If one also remembers that this work was carried out not in the congenial atmosphere of a university, among colleagues with whom ideas can be discussed, but in the comparative isolation of the Patent Office, with its meager library facilities, the result is the more astonishing. But then Einstein had an independent outlook and clear understanding of the basic principle of physics, which needed no outside influence.

The first of these papers was so revolutionary that it took physicists more than ten years until they finally accepted it, and then only with great reluctance. In 1900 Max Planck had suggested that the energy of heat radiation emitted by a hot body is not emitted continuously but in "jumps," called quanta (quantum meaning "how much"). Planck himself was not very happy with this idea, which he used to explain the observed energy distribution of such a hot body. For five years nobody took Planck's quantum hypothesis seriously, with the exception of Einstein. There seemed to be a fundamental difference in the way in which matter and light were treated: matter was assumed to consist of particles, while light was treated as a wave motion. When matter and light interact—as for example in shining light on certain metals, with the resultant emission of electrons—a conflict between the two concepts must arise. Einstein cut the Gordian knot by assuming that light, too, under certain conditions behaves like particles. Here we have Newton's corpuscular theory of light (discussed earlier in this chapter) but now with a new twist: the energy of these light particles divided by the frequency is a constant—the same constant that Planck used to specify the size of his quanta. (For this reason, this constant, usually denoted by the letter h, is called Planck's constant.)

The young Albert Einstein *(right)* with two friends of the Olympia Academy, Konrad Habicht and Maurice Solovine, around 1902.

Max Planck (1858–1947). Born in the seaport of Kiel, he moved with his family to Munich where he received his early education. Interested in the sciences, he decided to study theoretical physics—a rather obscure field at the time—first at Munich and later at Berlin. It was quite natural that in his study of energy Planck should turn to the problem of black-body radiation. It was known that the energy distribution depended on the wavelength and temperature of the radiation, but it had been impossible to find one expression that fitted both the ultraviolet (short) and the infrared (long) part of the spectrum. In what appeared first as a mathematical exercise Planck was able to fit the experimental curves to one single formula. However, in order to justify his result, he made the unusual assumption that a body does not radiate continuously but emits energy discontinuously in "quanta." Naturally, when Planck presented his theory at the close of 1900, it did not find many followers. In 1905 Einstein was able to explain the photoelectric effect by assuming that light consists of photons, carrying discrete quanta of energy. In 1913 Niels Bohr used the quantum concept to explain radiation from atoms, and finally Planck's quantum theory became established as one of the pillars of the new physics.

By assuming that light can act like particles, now called photons, Einstein was able to explain several effects formerly not understood, the most notable being the photoelectric effect. When light hits certain metals, electrons are emitted. These electrons can be used to close an electric circuit. Such an arrangement is called a photoelectric cell and it finds many practical uses, such as in the automatic opening of doors, burglar alarms, etc. It is found that the number of electrons emitted per second is directly proportional to the energy of the radiation falling upon the surface per second (i.e., its intensity), but that the velocities with which the electrons are ejected are independent of this energy. Furthermore, no electrons at all are ejected unless the frequency of the impinging light exceeds a certain critical frequency, the threshold frequency. Neither of these results could be explained by the conventional theory, according to which light is a form of electromagnetic radiation and is propagated like waves; but the explanation becomes simple if one considers light to consist of particles, photons.

Einstein's second paper of 1905 dealt with the properties of molecules in solutions, such as might occur if sugar is dissolved in water. Considering the sugar molecules as little spheres, Einstein worked out their rate of diffusion in the water or fluid increasing its viscosity (that is, the internal resistance or friction of the fluid). He submitted that paper to the University of Zurich as a possible doctoral dissertation.

As long ago as 1827, the botanist Robert Brown had noticed minute particles of pollen in liquid in a state of quick and irregular motion when observed under a microscope. Those particles were barely visible and darted in all directions, as if they were alive. He later repeated the experiment with inert matter, such as dried dust of mosses, but the same agitation was observed. Different explanations were advanced, such as electrical charge, heat,

Photoelectric effect. (a) *Photoelectric cell:* In this circuit containing a photoelectric cell, when light falls on the light-sensitive plate (P), electrons are emitted (the broken lines) that cause an electric current to flow, closing the circuit. (b) *Emission:* Einstein explained the photoelectric effect by assuming that light consists of particles—photons—that are bombarding the plate. If their energy, or frequency *(right)*, exceeded a certain limit, electrons (photoelectrons) would be emitted (left). This critical energy, or frequency, was needed in order to "free" the electrons from their atoms and let them escape. Increasing the intensity of the radiation increases the number of photons arriving per second and therefore increases the number of electrons ejected per second, but it in no way affects the energy given to an electron when it "absorbs" a single photon. On the other hand, the velocity of the ejected electron depends on the energy of a single photon, which in turn depends only on the frequency.

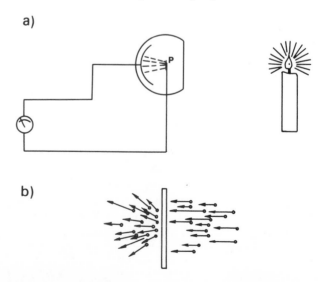

a)

b)

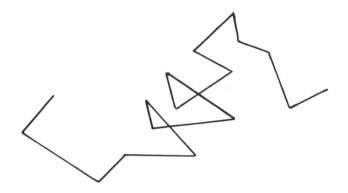

Brownian motion. The irregular zigzag motion of pollen particles is due to their collisions with the particles (atoms or molecules) of the fluid in which they are found.

convection currents, or vibrations, but none could account fully and quantitatively for the random motion of the particles. By considering the molecules of the fluid as small spheres in constant motion due to their thermal energy, the Brownian motion is then simply the result of collisions of the small molecules of the fluid (which cannot be seen) with the larger particles (which can be seen). What was important was not just the explanation of the random zigzag motion of the pollen but the demonstration of the existence of molecules having a definite, albeit small, size, which convinced the skeptics, who were quite numerous at the time.

However, the paper that made Einstein famous was the fourth—"On the Electrodynamics of Moving Bodies"—usually referred to as the paper on the special theory of relativity. Even as a boy of sixteen Einstein was wondering what he could see if he could follow a beam of light at its own speed through space. The answer, as simple as it is puzzling, is an electromagnetic field, which was oscillating but otherwise not moving. This, however, was a contradiction since it would mean that the laws of electromagnetism were different for an observer at rest, who sees the light rushing by, and for an observer in motion. Newton had stated in his fifth deduction following his laws of motion that "the motions of bodies included in a given [vehicle] are the same among themselves whether that [vehicle] is at rest or in uniform motion," and it could be argued that this should also apply to electrodynamics. Alternately, for an observer it would prevent travel at the speed of light. As an example of uniform motion, passengers traveling in an enclosed railway car at constant speed on a stationary earth could imagine themselves at rest and the outside moving (in the opposite direction). Absolute motion cannot be detected, only relative motion of the railway car with respect to the embankment, or vice versa.

It was then that Einstein made two postulates so far-reaching that they would upset the prevalent notions of time and space:

(i) All observers who move relative to each other with *constant* speed are equivalent as far as physical laws are concerned.

This is the principle of relativity, which excludes the notions of absolute time and space (as separate entities). "The same laws of electrodynamics and optics are now also valid for those frames of reference [coordinate systems] for which the laws of mechanics hold good."

(ii) The speed of light [in vacuum] is the *same* for all observers, viz. 186,000 miles per second, and is *independent* both of their motion and the motion of the source of light.

This would then explain the failure to discover the motion of the earth through the ether (recall the Michelson-Morley experiment to determine parallel and perpendicular time-light differences), and it would answer the question that bothered Einstein as a boy. It is often stated that the special theory of relativity is "based" on the Michelson-Morley experiment. In the first place, it is not clear that Einstein, at the time he wrote his paper, was aware of the experiment; certainly there is no mention of it in his paper. However, in his paper he discusses a very basic result of Michael Faraday's experiment concerning the relative motion of a magnet and a loop of wire. Faraday discovered that the same current will be generated in the wire whether the loop is moving and the magnet is at rest or vice versa, although "the customary point of view" draws a clear distinction between the two cases, a distinction that was removed only by the application of the principle of relativity. If Einstein had thought that the Michelson-Morley experiment was a "crucial experiment," like that of Faraday, this would have been the place to mention it. More important, however, Einstein seldom developed his theories to "explain" experiments; he derived them from a set of assumptions in a logical and self-consistent manner, which was sufficient to convince him of their validity; experiments, at best, were only the means to test the theories.

While the constancy of the speed of light and its independence of the velocity of the source or the observer might be understandable in the case of light, which is just a form of electromagnetic radiation, it is difficult to conceive of this in mechanics, where one is used to the fact that velocities add up in a simple way. Try the following as a thought experiment. Both a bus and taxi travel at their respective velocities, as seen by a boy on the street. The bus will have a relative speed, as seen from the taxi, which is the difference between the two velocities. A passenger walking forward in the bus will have a combined velocity (his own and the bus's). However, these simple laws of addition of velocities have to be modified, if the speeds are large and approach those of

Hendrik Antoon Lorentz (1853–1928). Lorentz was born in Arnhem and attended Leiden University, from which he obtained his doctor's degree summa cum laude in 1875 to return there only three years later as professor of theoretical physics, a position he held until his death. It was Lorentz who suggested that atoms of matter consist of charged particles, and that it was their oscillation that produced visible light. If this was indeed the case, then placing a light in a strong magnetic field ought to affect the nature of the oscillations and therefore the wavelength of the light emitted. This was confirmed experimentally by Pieter Zeeman, a student of Lorentz. When J. J. Thomson discovered the electron, there could be no more doubt of the truth of Lorentz's theory, and Lorentz was awarded the Nobel Prize in 1902, jointly with Zeeman. Lorentz also explained the negative results of the Michelson-Morley experiment (there would be a contraction of length with motion). In addition, he showed that the mass of a particle must depend on its velocity, a result that was verified experimentally and that was shown to be a consequence of Einstein's special theory of relativity.

Henri Poincaré (1854–1912). Poincaré has often been called the last universalist, for there was no field of mathematics, applied or pure, in which he was not at home. At the age of twenty-seven he became professor at the University of Paris, where he remained the rest of his life. Between 1878, when he wrote his thesis, and his death in 1912 he wrote more than 500 papers on new mathematics, not to mention treatises on mathematical astronomy, such as his periodic orbits, which started a whole new branch in this field.

light, but in no instance may they exceed the speed of light. For example, a beam from a headlight will always travel at the speed of light, whether the car is moving or not.

Taking postulates (i) and (ii) together seems to lead to irreconcilable difficulties, and a person of lesser stature than Einstein might have felt the need to give up one of them. As a matter of fact, Henri Poincaré (1854–1912) at about the same time, and quite unknown to Einstein, submitted two papers that contain the gist and most of the mathematics of the special theory of relativity but not its far-reaching consequences. Poincaré and Lorentz were trying to find a mathematical apparatus, the Lorentz transformations linking observers in relative motion, while Einstein developed a theory in which they were "concerned with the nature of space and time in general." Later developments by Einstein and Minkowski, Einstein's former teacher, make even space-time appear as a natural consequence.

A price had to be paid for the reconciliation of the two postulates, and that price was the abandonment of some of our ideas of space and time and, in particular, their

independence. Consider, for example, our idea of simultaneity. We say that two events occur simultaneously, that is, at the same time, if they are observed at the same time by an observer located at equal distance from the positions where the events take place—but the same time with respect to what? Suppose lightning strikes two places A and B at the same time with respect to an observer standing exactly between them—light from A and B will reach him at the same time. However, an observer in a rapidly moving car traveling toward B will say that the lightning at B struck first. As Einstein put it, "we cannot attach any absolute significance to the concept of simultaneity"—an event that was simultaneous with respect to one observer will no longer be simultaneous with respect to another one moving relative to the first one. The same reasoning applies to our measuring of distances. We measure something when we apply both ends of a foot rule at both ends of an object at the same time. There is no difficulty involved when the measured object is at rest relative to us. However, what happens when we want to measure the length of, say, a moving railway car? A person in the railway car will have no difficulty at all, since he is at rest with respect to the car. Owing to the difference of simultaneity, our results—even if we are lucky enough to obtain them—will differ from his. We will get values that are smaller than his; to our eyes the moving car seems to have shrunk in the direction of motion, undergone a FitzGerald contraction. There is no way of saying who is right, since in his own system each observer applies his own measuring rods and clocks. It is here that the constancy of the speed of light and the principle of relativity come into the picture. All observers agree on the constancy of the speed of light. And since all observers moving relative to each other with constant velocity are equivalent, both the stationary (with respect to the earth) observer and the one in the moving railway car are right. And all that is needed to get from one set of observations to the second—the connecting link—are exactly the transformations introduced by Lorentz to explain the Michelson-Morley experiments, which are usually referred to as Lorentz transformations.

Transformations from one coordinate system to another do occur in Newtonian mechanics. If one system moves relative to another that has a definite velocity v, the change of the coordinates is determined by a simple transformation, involving the space coordinates; but the time t remains unchanged. Such a transformation is referred to as a Galilean transformation. The essential difference between the Galilean and the Lorentz transformations consists—apart from a factor involving the ratio of v to c, the velocity of light—in the fact that now also the time undergoes a transformation, thereby connecting space and time into one unified description. That time enters into the picture is not new—only the manner in which it does so is new. To describe an event, one needs in addition to the three space coordinates a time coordinate also. For example, it is not sufficient to say that you are waiting for your friend at the corner of Park Avenue and Thirty-fourth Street (in New York), you must also specify the time, say, six o'clock on such and such a day. Graphic descriptions of a series of events—one following the other continuously—are provided, for example, by "graphic timetables." A line or curve in such a graph is the world line of the event in question. Hermann Minkowski made use of this comparatively simple idea; his great contribution lay in translating Einstein's physics into a geometry. After his stint as a teacher at ETH, Minkowski, who was of Russian origin, went to Göttingen in 1902—the Mecca of theoretical physics and mathematics. He immediately became interested in the theory of relativity and was one of its staunchest supporters. His work on the geometrization of relativity was published in 1908 shortly before his untimely death. For Minkowski the world lines were not

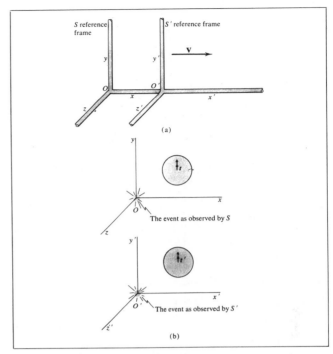

Galilean transformation. Consider two frames of reference (S and S') moving relative to each other with constant velocity (v) (taken, for simplicity, along the x-direction). During a given time (this can't be shown, but we'll call it t), system S' has moved a distance vt (distance = velocity × time), so that a point (P) that originally was a distance x from O will now be a distance x' to the right of O', where x' = x − vt, that is, closer to O' by the distance it has moved during time t. However, two clocks (one is S and one is S') will show the same time, that is, t = t'.

just a convenient way to represent motion graphically but were actually realized in the physical world, where time is an additional dimension. On account of the constancy of the speed of light, which is also the upper limit of any attainable speed, not all the world lines are permitted, but only those that lie within the "light cone." The light cone is that section in space-time that is obtained by rotating the world line of light around the vertical time-axis. Just as in ordinary three-dimensional space the distance between two points remains invariant, that is, it does not change under a Galilean transformation, so in the four-dimensional space the space-time "distance" between two events is invariant under a Lorentz transformation. Suppose we have two similar spaceships in uniform motion and moving relative to each other with constant speed, say, 10,000 miles per second. At two different times the captain of one of the spaceships performs a measurement, such as measuring the length of a table in the ship. (This, in fact, involves two distinct operations—first placing the measuring stick at one end of the table and then noting the reading at the other end—carried out at two different times, although the time interval may be small.) The second spaceship happens to pass by and its captain observes the operation. If they compare notes

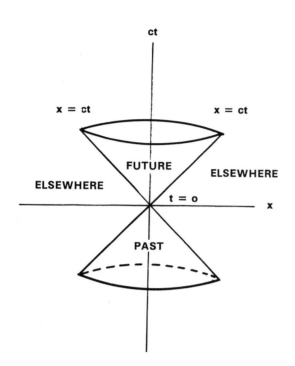

Light cone. Since no velocities larger than c, that of light, are allowed, the permissible world-lines are restricted to lie within a "cone," the light cone, bounded by the world-lines of light. Only a cross section of the cone is shown, determined by the x-axis and ct- or time-axis. The two intersecting lines (x = ct) define the cone, which is obtained by rotating the figure about the vertical axis. (Actually, the light cone is a four-dimensional figure impossible to imagine.) The upper cone, for which t is positive–that is, larger than zero–represents the future, while the lower cone, for which t is negative–smaller than zero–represents the past; the central point, t = 0, is the present. The two outer regions, marked "elsewhere," cannot be reached by a light signal since they lie outside the cone as defined above.

When an atomic nucleus of uranium is bombarded with neutrons, the uranium nucleus splits into two smaller particles, with a resultant loss of mass. If at the same time additional neutrons are produced, as is actually the case, they will produce further splittings (fission), resulting in a chain reaction. But the lost masses of all the particles and fission products convert into the enormous energy that makes up an atomic explosion. That energy would be equal to the lost mass multiplied by the square of the velocity of light (c^2 in the equation). The velocity of light squared is over 34 billion. Even if the mass is a minute amount, one can begin to imagine the enormity of the result. (The amount of matter changed into energy in the bomb dropped on Nagasaki was one gram.) Einstein at first was not aware of the possibility of producing nuclear weapons based on his formula, for when a young man approached him in 1921 in Prague with exactly that idea, he told him: "You haven't lost anything if I don't discuss your work with you in detail. Its foolishness is evident at first glance. You cannot learn anything more from a longer discussion."

afterward, they will find that they do not agree either on the length of the table or on the time that has passed between the two measurements. (The same, of course, applies also to the situation where the captain of the second spaceship performed the measurement in *his* ship and was observed by the one in the first one.) However, if each one calculates the *time-distance* between the two events (i.e., the time multiplied by the speed of light), squares it, and subtracts from it the square of the *space-distance* (i.e., the spatial distance), both will obtain the same result.

It took some time before physicists, and the world at large, could get accustomed to the new ideas. The first to see in Einstein's theory a more complete and truer picture of the universe was not Poincaré, who never referred to it in print, nor Lorentz, who found it difficult to give up the idea of an ether, but Max Planck, the originator of the

quantum theory, who wrote to Einstein congratulating him on having given a new understanding of nature's way, "which affected the very roots of our physical thought." Einstein's fame reached Switzerland, and the University of Geneva tendered an invitation for the conferment of an honorary degree on the occasion of its 350th anniversary (it had been founded by Calvin in 1559). Einstein, thinking that the invitation was just an announcement, ignored it, but when the university inquired about why no reply was forthcoming, he duly accepted it. At the same time he also delivered his first major "invited" lecture at the annual conference of the Naturforscher, an important organization similar to the American Association for the Advancement of Science. It was there that he first mentioned in public the famous relationship between energy and mass: $E = mc^2$. What it means is that energy (E) and mass (m) are closely interrelated and, in principle, one could be converted into the other. Moreover, it showed that radiation, such as light, which by its nature is massless, has associated with it a mass equal to its energy divided by the square of the velocity of light ($m = E/c^2$). Conversely, if a body emits radiation, it will lose some of its mass in the form of energy. The stupendous result is that mass is energy and energy is mass—the two are just different forms of the same fundamental quantity.

Einstein had been feeling the strain of his duties at the Patent Office combined with the pursuit of his own scientific work—in this period he published paper after paper—and was looking for a position that would give him more time for research. Professor Alfred Kleiner held out the possibility of a position at Zurich University, but first Einstein had to become a privatdozent. The position of privatdozent is unique to European universities; it carries no salary, but the holder receives a fee for lecturing, the amount depending on the number of listeners. Since the well-attended lecture courses were given by the professors, who thereby augmented their regular teaching salaries, it was the specialized and poorly attended course that went to the privatdozent; it was the lowest rung of the academic ladder. Einstein became a privatdozent at Berne University and had to give lectures in addition to his regular work at the Patent Office. He had only two listeners, his good friend Michelangelo Besso, who worked with him at the Patent Office and whose help and suggestions he generously acknowledged in the paper on relativity, and Lucien Chavan, an electrical engineer in the Federal Post and Telegraph Administration. Finally, an appointment at Zurich University came through, but not until Friedrich Adler, the other candidate—his father was the founder of the Austrian Social Democratic Party and had considerable influence—generously withdrew his candidacy. "If it is possible to obtain a man like Einstein for our university, it would be absurd to appoint me," he wrote to the board. Later, when Einstein left Zurich for Prague, he wanted Adler to succeed him, but by that time Adler had left physics for politics.

Although Einstein now had more time to devote to his research, there was no improvement in his financial position. The salary was the same as that at the Patent Office, but the living expenses of a professor in Zurich were quite a bit higher; to make ends meet, his wife had to take in a boarder. As a result, when he was offered the position of professor ordinarius (full professor) at the German university in Prague, he accepted. Even so, there were difficulties associated with it. He was preferred over his competitor Gustav Jaumann, a staunch follower of Ernst Mach, the former rector at the university and the man whose teaching had a fundamental influence on Einstein, mainly because of Planck's prophetic statement that "if Einstein's theory should prove correct, as I suspect it will, he will be considered the Copernicus of the twentieth century." However, there was the question of religion; Einstein had declared himself unaffiliated, which did not go over well with the Austrian officials, who wanted their professors to have a religious affiliation, especially if they were "foreigners." However, Einstein convinced them that he now considered himself to be of the "Mosaic [Jewish] faith." This was not just an idle statement to get by a cumbersome government regulation but was the start of Einstein's identification with his heritage. In Prague he came into contact with Jews who lived and thought as Jews, and he began to understand the particular problems that beset them. He was deeply religious, but his God was the God of Spinoza who reveals Himself in the orderly harmony of what exists, but yet Einstein also believed in a more personal God.

Einstein was happy in Prague—he was part of a fine institute with a magnificent library and people to talk to. Yet he could not fail to notice the political strife and quarrels between the Czechs and their overlord, the Austrian Empire, which troubled him greatly. In the meantime, he had become known in the scientific world, and offers came from Utrecht, Vienna, which proferred a princely salary, and ETH in Zurich. Marcel Grossmann had been trying to get him to return to Zurich, and both Madame Curie and Poincaré had written glowing letters of recommendation. Einstein could not resist them—moreover Mileva wanted to leave Prague—and so he returned in 1912 to the Institute to which he had come as a poor student sixteen years earlier and which had denied him an assistantship. Now he was a famous professor and students rushed to his lectures, but nothing had changed—he was still the easygoing and even untidy dreamer. He had already started to try to generalize the theory of relativity, and now he continued his work with his old friend and colleague Marcel Grossmann, prying deeper and deeper into the mysteries of the universe.

Einstein probably would have been content to remain in Switzerland, but others thought differently. Max Planck tried to get for his friend one of the coveted positions at the Prussian Academy of Sciences in Berlin and in 1914, after the death of the physicist Jacobus Hendrikus van't Hoff, succeeded. Einstein had misgivings about leaving neutral Switzerland for a militaristic Germany, but the offer was too tempting. The Academy was the center of theoretical physics and the gathering place of the most famous physicists. In addition, he could now devote all his time to fruitful research, undisturbed by lecturing, which he described as a "performance on the trapeze." So in the spring of 1914 the Einsteins moved to Berlin. In his inaugural address to the Academy he thanked them for making it possible for him to devote himself entirely to

The Solvay Congress, 1911, the first of a series of scientific conferences sponsored by the Belgian industrialist Ernest Solvay, to which only the top physicists in the world were invited. Einstein's presence was a recognition of his work and fame. Seated, from left to right, are Nernst, Brillouin, Solvay, Lorentz, Warburg, Perrin, Wien, Mme. Curie, and Poincaré. Standing, from left to right, Goldschmidt, Planck, Rubens, Sommerfeld, Lindemann, de Broglie, Knudsen, Hasenöhrl, Hostelet, Herzen, Jeans, Rutherford, Kamerlingh Onnes, Einstein, and Langevin.

scientific studies. He then outlined the directions his efforts would take him—the generalization of the special theory of relativity and the need to test it. But even Einstein could not have dreamed of the world-shaking developments he had quietly hatched in his head and written on scraps of paper over the years.

4. Gravitational Fields

The problem Einstein was trying to solve was the generalization of the principle of relativity to *all* observers, whether they were moving with constant velocity or not. At first sight this seems an impossible task. We might be inclined to concede that uniform motion is relative, i.e., a person traveling in a railway car at constant speed could imagine that he is at rest and that the embankment, with its many telegraph poles, houses, etc., is moving in the opposite direction. But acceleration, or a change in velocity, is a different matter—so it seems. Suppose, for example, that the railway car is stopped (or at least slowed down) by an application of the brakes. The occupants of the railway car will then experience, in accordance with Newton's first law of motion, a corresponding jerk forward. It would thus appear impossible to assume that the *same* physical laws apply to the nonuniform motion of both the slowed car and the embankment and the car in uniform motion. Yet, Einstein argued, if velocity is relative, what is there so unique about acceleration that makes it seem to be nonrelative, or absolute?

In Newton's second law of motion, the force is proportional to the acceleration for a given (constant) mass. However, the mass enters in two different ways. Objects dropped from a tower—or thrown in the air—will fall, owing to gravity, with the same acceleration (if we discount air resistance). This is the acceleration of gravity,

which determines the "weight" of a body and, through it, the gravitational mass of the object. On the other hand, in the absence of gravity—say, in interstellar space—one can produce the same acceleration by an equal force, such as from a spring; the mass in this case is the inertial mass, a characteristic constant of the accelerated body. For example, if a body is under the action of a centripetal force, it will experience an acceleration and fly off a turntable.

Newton, and his successors, tacitly assumed that the two kinds of mass are equal, as indeed they are, and used the concept of mass both as a measure of the object's inertia and to account for its gravitational effect. The equality of the two types of mass was first demonstrated experimentally by Count Roland von Eötvös (1848-1919), a Hungarian physicist; recently more refined experiments were carried out in Princeton. Einstein, with his infallible intuition, realized that this was no mere numerical coincidence but that it provided the key to a deeper understanding of inertia and gravitation. Thus, there is complete equivalence between gravitation and accelerated systems. This can best be demonstrated by a simple thought experiment, which we have presented here, using an elevator removed from gravity but pulled up by a rope attached to its roof with an acceleration g. Any objects dropped in this elevator seem to reach its floor with a constant acceleration g, although, in fact. it is the *floor* of the elevator that meets them at that rate. Relying on his knowledge of gravity, the observer in the elevator will thus come to the conclusion that he, the object, and the elevator are simply acted upon by gravity. Thus, owing to the equivalence of inertia and gravitational mass, the two processes—(1) no gravity, but tension in the rope and inertial mass; and (2) no external forces, but gravity and gravitational mass—are equivalent. This, in essence, is what Einstein later called the principle of equivalence.

Returning for a moment to our traveler in the railway carriage, one might, perhaps somewhat unrealistically but

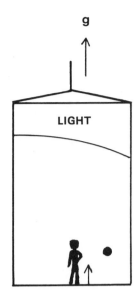

Einstein's elevator. *Left:* Accelerated: An elevator, removed from gravity, is pulled upward with an acceleration g. An object dropped remains suspended in the air but (to an observer in the accelerated elevator) appears to be falling toward the floor of the elevator, which, in fact, is rising toward it. Similarly, because of the elevator's upward acceleration, a ray of light entering at one side seems (to an observer in the accelerated elevator) to curve downward. *Right:* Acted upon by gravity: The elevator is at rest but is acted upon by gravity. Objects fall to the ground because they are attracted by the gravitational force of the earth. A beam of light will be bent by the gravitational attraction.

correctly physically—attribute the application of the brakes and consequent stopping of the train to the presence of gravity, which is directed forward and which changes with time. Under its influence, the embankment and the earth move, nonuniformly, in such a manner that their original velocity—in a backward direction (remember, the earth is moving and not the train)—is continuously reduced until it is zero. The train, or rather the earth, is now at rest. It was thus possible to apply the same principle of relativity to bodies in nonuniform motion and to those moving with constant speed.

Einstein had formulated the principle of equivalence as early as 1911 and was now looking for some experimental tests—not that he needed them, for he was convinced of the power of his arguments. "The sense of the thing is too evident," he wrote to his old friend Besso. Light is known to travel in straight lines, but what happens if the whole laboratory, like the elevator, is pulled up? As the floor of the laboratory rises to meet the ray of light, the distance between them will decrease and the ray of light will appear to be bent. According to the principle of equivalence, this means that light should be bent if it passes close to massive objects, such as the sun. On the basis of his as yet incomplete theory, Einstein calculated that a ray of starlight passing close to the limb of the sun should be deflected by about 0.87 seconds of arc. (This amount is exactly one-half the amount he predicted later, which actually was observed.) Photographs of stars close to the sun would have to be compared with others taken when the sun was in another part of the heavens—not a simple procedure under any circumstances. Moreover, they would have to be taken during a total eclipse of the sun,

since under normal conditions the light from the sun outshines that from any star in its vicinity.

The next total eclipse of the sun was to occur in the fall of 1914, in the Crimea, in Russia. Erwin Finlay-Freundlich, a young astronomer at the Berlin Observatory, was anxious to make the observations and organized an expedition, at his own expense, but nothing came of it, since World War I had broken out by that time and Finlay-Freundlich and his staff had been taken prisoners of war. (He was later released under an exchange of prisoners and continued to work at the observatory.)

The war, of course, also affected Einstein's private life. Enthroned at the Kaiser Wilhelm Institute for Physics, he had to watch as a whole nation enthusiastically plunged into a war they themselves had initiated. He was shocked when ninety-three of his scientific colleagues signed a "Manifesto to the Civilized World" (known later simply as "The Manifesto of the 93") disclaiming Germany's guilt and justifying the brutal invasion of Belgium. Einstein, being a Swiss citizen, was not expected to sign, but it is quite certain that he would have refused to sign it. The best proof of this is the "Manifesto to Europeans," a reaction to "The Manifesto of the 93." According to Georg Nicolai, professor of physiology at the University of Berlin and a prominent pacifist, Einstein coauthored the work with him. It certainly disclosed Einstein's belief that scientists and scholars of the warring nations should cooperate with one another, and it called for the establishment of a League of Europeans. In addition to Nicolai and Einstein, only two others signed it. Einstein could not stand by idly and, for the first time, joined a political party, the Bund Neues Vaterland, which tried to bring about an early peace and called for the creation of an international body that would make future wars impossible; the Bund was later outlawed. Einstein was quite active; he made speeches and wrote letters, but he must have been conscious of being a lone voice in a world bent on war.

Mileva and the children had gone to Switzerland during the summer of 1914, and when war broke out, it was decided that they would remain there, at least for the time being. The marriage had not been a happy one; Einstein complained that his wife was jealous of his friends, and

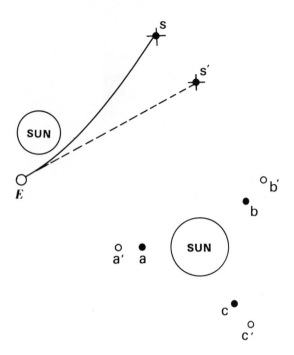

Deflection of light. Light from star s in the vicinity of the sun is bent by the sun's gravitational attraction and appears to come from s'—since it is assumed that light travels in straight lines. (The actual amount of bending of light is 1.73 seconds of arc and thus the diagram is highly exaggerated.) Stars that really are at a, b, and c will appear to be at a', b', and c' respectively.

The chart, adapted from Lick Observatory Bulletin 346, shows displacements of stars during the solar eclipse of September 21, 1922. The inner and outer omeletlike areas (near the sun's disk) represent the sun's coronas. Each star is plotted in its true position; the short lines indicate the star's displacement in accordance with the scale at the right. Only displacements of the more reliable observed stars are given. The scale at the left determines the positions of the stars relative to that of the sun. The results are completely in agreement with Einstein's final prediction.

Mileva felt left out of her husband's work, which, being a mathematician herself, she might have shared or at least understood. The marriage was dissolved by mutual consent, but Einstein and Mileva remained friends. One of the problems that bothered Einstein was how to take care of his wife and sons. It was finally solved by Mileva herself, who suggested that she receive the interest accrued from the Nobel prize—so sure was she that her husband would receive it. Einstein later married Elsa Einstein, his cousin and former childhood companion. Elsa, a charming person, was able, until her death in 1936, to become the professor's closest companion and friend. Taking care of his home, she provided all the comforts he could wish for. She also guaranteed him peace from an increasingly curious public that made excessive demands on his time.

Einstein's daily routine was simple. Living in a simple but pleasant apartment in Haberlandstrasse, he led the life of an average citizen. Early in the morning he retired to his study in a little corner turret fifteen feet square, separated from the rest of the apartment by a staircase, two doors, and a passageway. The room was furnished

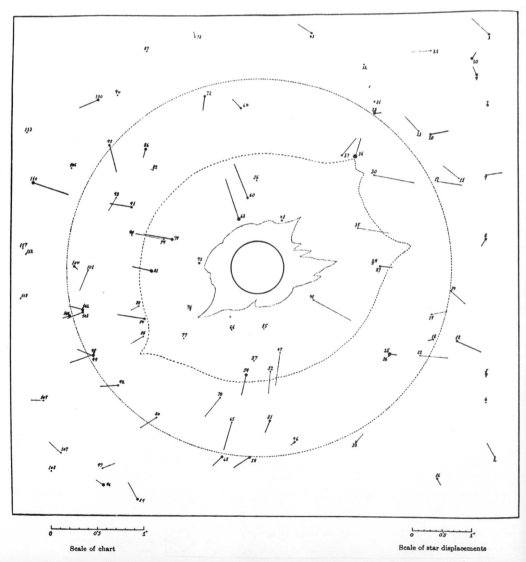

Scale of chart

Scale of star displacements

with a table, littered with papers and pamphlets, two ladderback chairs, a couch, shelves filled with scientific books and magazines, two fat Bibles, and a desk, which held a picture of Newton. There he spent all his time when he was not ambling through the woods or lecturing at the University of Berlin. From that room, while the whole world was filled with the early victories and defeats of a war that was to bring desolation to the whole of Europe, came a message that will stand when the world has forgotten there ever was a World War I: the general theory of relativity.

The principle of equivalence was an important cornerstone in the building of the theory of general relativity, but it was not sufficient; Einstein still had to find *the* equation (or equations) that were to replace Newton's law of universal gravitation. Newton's law was an action-at-a-distance law determining the force (or interaction) between two masses separated by a certain distance. It could be, and was, also formulated in terms of fields. The attracting mass, e.g., the sun, "creates" a gravitational field, which in turn interacts with the mass that is being attracted, e.g., a planet. Fields were known to exist in nature and, in the case of magnetic fields, for example, their effects can be made visible. (Scatter iron filings on a sheet of paper and place a magnet under it. The iron filings will arrange themselves along the lines of force of the magnet's magnetic field.)

Observers use coordinate systems to describe an event or to fix the position of a point in space; the question was how to construct a field theory that would be valid for all

This chance picture of Einstein was taken by a passerby, Charles Holdt, on December 1, 1932, just a few days before Einstein left Berlin, never to return.

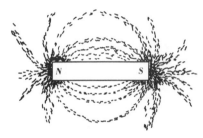

A magnetic field made "visible" by the scattering of iron filings onto a sheet of paper placed directly over a magnet. The filings orient themselves along the lines of force of the magnetic field, and the potentials—at right angles or perpendicular to them—can then be drawn.

Georg Friedrich Bernhard Riemann (1826–1866). Riemann's contributions to mathematics are many, but probably his best-known publication is his inaugural lecture. He managed to present the subject of his space-curvature hypotheses in terms that were understandable even to colleagues who were unfamiliar with higher mathematics. It was, of course, his space-curvature hypothesis that later was used so brilliantly by Einstein in his theory of relativity. Riemann worked until the day before his death; his last unfinished work was concerned with the theory of sound transference based on hydraulic principles.

Gravitational field. The circles represent the equipotentials, or the lines of equal potential, of the earth-moon system (assuming the moon to be stationary and neglecting the effect of the sun). The numbers on the circles are the values of the potential. The lines drawn perpendicular to the equipotentials are the gravitational field's lines of force. P is the equilibrium point, or the position of zero gravitational field intensity. The numbers along the horizontal axis give the distances in miles from the earth's center.

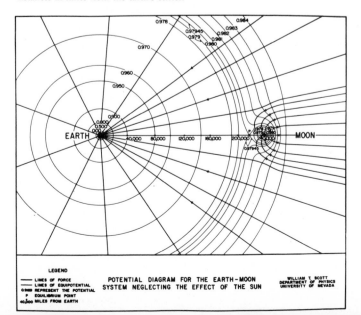

kinds of coordinate systems, rectangular (like the Cartesian system) or curved ones. The equations of physics, and in particular those describing the gravitational field, would have to be expressed in such a way that they would apply to all kinds of coordinate systems. This principle, which Einstein later called the principle of covariance, together with the principle of equivalence discussed earlier, would ensure the validity of physical laws for all kinds of observers, no matter whether they were at rest or moving with constant velocity, and, most important, for observers moving with a variable velocity.

Georg Friedrich Bernhard Riemann (1826–66) in a magnificent paper had developed a geometry for curved space. In ordinary experience one is accustomed to Euclidean geometry–parallel lines do not meet and the angles of a triangle add up to 180 degrees–but in the Riemannian geometry this is no longer the case.

Karl Friedrich Gauss (1777–1855), the child prodigy and prince of mathematics, had studied the properties of curved space in two dimensions and had shown that its properties could be described by a set of quantities–three for a space of two dimensions.

These quantities are the components of what was later to be known as the metric tensor. The branch of mathematics that concerns itself with tensors and their transformation properties under general coordinate transformations is known as tensor calculus and was mainly developed by the Italian mathematician Gregorio Ricci. Since equations written in tensor notation hold for any kind of coordinate systems, this was exactly the tool Einstein needed to guarantee that the principle of covariance would be observed. The principle of equivalence would provide the necessary transition from accelerated systems to gravitational fields, and Riemannian geometry the framework.

But it was the metric tensor, properly generalized to four dimensions, that would describe the gravitational field. This was a revolutionary idea–space itself as a manifestation of the gravitational field. The metric tensor plays a dual role: it determines the structure of the Riemannian geometry and at the same time is the potential of the gravitational field. However, instead of the Newtonian single potential, Einstein now had ten, corresponding to the components of the metric tensor in four dimensions. This was a tremendous step, which Einstein took boldly, and he had to find the proper field

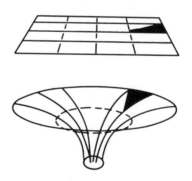

The flat and empty space (upper diagram) is curved in the presence of matter (lower diagram). The amount of curvature will depend on the space's proximity to a large mass (not shown), eventually becoming flat space at large distances. The situation can be simulated by dropping a heavy object on a stretched rubber sheet and noting the resulting shape.

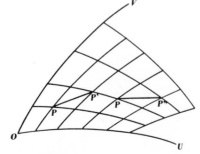

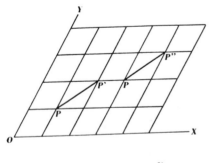

Curved space. The upper diagram shows "flat" space, for which the distance between two points (even when measured in different units along the two axes) is always the same, that is PP' equals PP''. Note that the two axes (X and Y) are not at right angles to each other and the distance PP' (or PP'') depends also on the angle between the axes. In the lower diagram, "curved" space is shown (in two dimensions). Although the coordinate lines still divide the plane into an infinity of little parallelograms, for which the lengths along the two axes (here denoted by U and V respectively) are the same, the distance between two points is no longer the same; that is, PP' does not equal PP''. The distance between any two points is determined from the components of the metric tensor. For a two-dimensional surface, as shown here, it has three components (roughly defined by the two directions and the angle between them) and–being a function of the coordinates U and V–will change from point to point.

equations, generalizations of Newton's single equation, whose solutions would give the gravitational potentials and describe the space.

The presence of large masses, such as the sun, is responsible for the gravitational field, which "warps" the otherwise empty and flat space. Particles, such as planets, are influenced by the warping of the space and move along geodesics, the analogues of "shortest" distance. Bertrand Russell in his book *The ABC of Relativity* has given a beautiful illustration of this idea. Imagine that we are in an airplane in a very hilly region and where there is a high mountain with a strong beacon of light at its summit. A number of cars are traveling on the roads around the mountain. Owing to the difficulty of the terrain, they cannot travel in straight lines (up and down the mountain) but have to go around it. It is night, and we in our plane see only the headlights of the cars; it looks to us, for one reason or another, as if the headlights are reluctant to come too close to the beacon, and so they revolve around it in circles or ellipses as if attracted by a central force. With daylight the picture becomes clear. The mountain represents the attracting gravitational mass and the cars represent the planets that revolve around it, not because they are attracted by some force but because they follow the easiest possible path. It took Einstein some time to clear up attendant problems, and finally in 1916 he produced "The Foundation of the General Theory of Relativity."

It was a beautiful theory, but there seemed to be no immediate way to test it experimentally. True, proof would be provided in that light would be deflected by the gravitating mass of the sun, but the next solar eclipse was several years away and World War I seemed to make an expedition unfeasible. Einstein was convinced of the correctness of his intuition, and he confirmed it by solving a puzzle that had bothered astronomers for years. The planet Mercury revolves around the sun in an ellipse that seems to shift or, in other words, it does not return to its original position until after 220,000 years. The shift is not large—only 43 seconds of arc in 100 years (after all other perturbing effects, such as that of Venus, have been taken into account). To account for the discrepancy, several explanations had been advanced. Asaph Hall, the discoverer of Mars's satellites, suggested that Newton's inverse square law might not hold and adjusted Newton's exponent 2 to 2.0000001612. Another hypothesis first advanced by Urbain Jean Joseph Leverrier—who actually discovered the above discrepancy and predicted the existence of Neptune—was the presence of another planet between the sun and Mercury, which would perturb the orbit of Mercury sufficiently to account for the 43 seconds. That unknown planet had even been named (Vulcan), but nobody could demonstrate its existence. Now Einstein

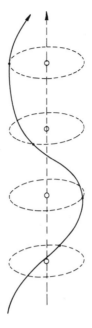

The motion of a particle is represented by the geodesic (solid curve) of the earth moving around the sun in this two-dimensional time-space diagram. Each plane represents the situation at a particular time, with the sun's position being that of the circle at the center of the orbits and the earth's position that of the dots.

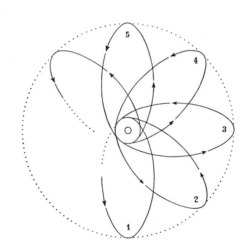

In its motion around the sun the planet Mercury (as well as the other planets) describes an ellipse whose perihelion—the point nearest to the sun—advances slightly but continuously during successive revolutions, making a complete cycle in 220,000 years. In the diagram, which is highly exaggerated, the motion of the planet is indicated by the unbroken lines, with successive ellipses numbered.

showed that the shift in Mercury's perihelion, the missing 43 seconds, could be explained by his theory (it "causes me great joy," he wrote).

There was another result, whose definite confirmation, however, came much later in a beautiful experiment carried out by R. V. Pound, G. A. Rebka, Jr., and J. L. Snider at Harvard University. When an atom (or nucleus) emits radiation, this radiation will be absorbed by another atom in the same energy state. This resonance is similar to the tuning of a radio receiver (absorber) to the exact frequency of the transmitter (emitter). Now when such

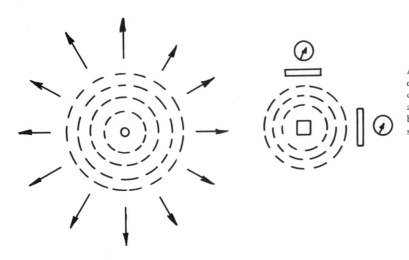

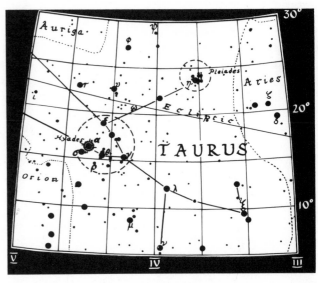

A beam of gamma rays–electromagnetic radiation at very short wavelength–emitted from a nucleus (left) reaches a target nucleus (right). Detectors (indicated by the two rectangles) measure the radiation received (aligned and at right angles to each other); the meters note the amount of radiation. At resonance, both meters show similar readings; this indicates that the target nucleus is in the same state as the emitting one.

radiation falls through a gravitational field, even one as weak as that of the earth, there is no resonance and the receiver has to be "retuned." Similarly, if the emitting atom is in a gravitational field, the frequency of the emitted radiation will be lower than that of an atom in free space. Since this effect would show up in the shifting of spectral lines toward the red end of the spectrum, it is usually referred to as gravitational red shift. A red shift does occur in the sun, where it is very small, and in large stellar masses. It is difficult to distinguish from another type of red shift (usually referred to as Doppler shift, which we shall consider in detail later on) connected with the motion of these masses. However, the Harvard University experiment was able to detect even the minutest shifts and did not have to contend with competing effects.

Arthur Stanley Eddington (1882–1944), Plumian Professor of Astronomy at Cambridge, had become very much interested in the theory of general relativity; he was later to make important contributions to it. He had received a copy of Einstein's paper from Willem de Sitter in neutral Holland and was immediately impressed with its importance. He and Frank Dyson, the Astronomer Royal, decided to push ahead with an eclipse observation that would occur on May 29, 1919, when the sun would be near some very bright stars, part of the Hyades group, which would prove an excellent opportunity to observe the bending of their light, if indeed it should occur.

The Hyades, a group of stars called an open star cluster in the constellation Taurus (the Bull). Their brightness made them particularly noticeable during the solar eclipse that occurred in that part of the sky in May 1919.

Arthur Stanley Eddington (1882–1944), who may easily be considered one of the most outstanding British astronomers. Except for some time at the Greenwich Observatory (1906–13), where he concerned himself with practical astronomy, he remained at Cambridge all his life. His major contribution to theoretical astronomy was a mathematical description of processes within stars, combining the forces of gravitation with radiation pressure; it was published in his work *The Internal Constitution of the Stars*. He spent his later years attempting to combine gravitation with the then new quantum theory, attempts that, on the whole, were too speculative and unorthodox to be accepted or even understood by his contemporaries. The photograph is from a drawing by Augustus John in Trinity College, Cambridge.

27. IX. 19

Liebe Mutter!

[handwritten postcard text in German]

A postcard sent by Einstein to his mother September 27, 1919, in which he mentions the light deflection observed by the English expedition. "Dearest Mother, Today, pleasant news. H. A. Lorentz has wired me that the English expeditions actually proved the light deflection near the sun...." Although Einstein was known not to have been overly excited by the result, which he expected, he apparently thought it would give pleasure to his mother.

Einstein and Chaim Weizmann upon their arrival in New York in 1921 on a fund-raising tour. Weizmann later said, "All throughout the transatlantic trip he [Einstein] explained to me his theory, and on my arrival I was fully convinced that he understood it."

While the war was still at its fiercest, with German U-boats tightening their blockade of Britain, the English astronomers prepared to send two expeditions, one to Sobral in Brazil and the other to Principe Island off the coast of Africa. At those places the solar eclipse would be total. Despite clouds and rain on May 29, 1919, the expedition obtained results: preliminary measurements of the observed deflection agreed with Einstein's prediction.

Newspapers carried the story on the front page for weeks, and Einstein's picture appeared all over the world. At social gatherings or on the street, people who had never heard of Newton's law of gravitation talked about Einstein's theory. Books and magazine and newspaper articles tried to make the theory understandable to the layman. Einstein remained unperturbed by the general acclamation. He continued to live the simple life he had led before, despite the large sums of money offered to him for articles, pictures, and advertisements.

Only in Germany did Einstein encounter opposition, even hostility. A so-called Study Group of German

Natural Philosophers had banded together to "disprove" Einstein's theories, which they branded as Jewish, Communist, and non-German (later they would call them non-Aryan). The "Antirelativity Company," as Einstein called it, spent huge amounts of money to attack Einstein and his theory in the press and in public meetings. And they had gained some respectability from the support of Philipp Lenard, a Nobel Prize winner and discoverer of the photoelectric effect. This was the same Lenard who had previously referred to Einstein as a "deep and far-reaching thinker." Of course, more level-headed men, such as Max Laue and Walter Hermann Nernst, both prominent physicists and Nobel Prize laureates, tried to check the attack and spoke up for Einstein, but the avalanche that would find its culmination when Hitler came to power in 1933 was unstoppable.

Einstein was aware that his fame carried some responsibility toward his people, and when he was approached to join Chaim Weizmann on a fund-raising tour to America for the Hebrew University to be founded in Jerusalem, he felt it his duty to agree to go. Weizmann, a biochemist, had discovered a method of synthesizing acetone, essential for the manufacture of explosives. His main interest was to work toward a Jewish homeland, and he later became the first president of the State of Israel. Einstein and Weizmann became good friends and respected each other's views, which were often opposite–Einstein regarded Weizmann as too much of a "realpolitiker" (politician), whereas Weizmann regarded Einstein as an impractical idealist. When it became known that Einstein was to travel to America, he was inundated with invitations and honorary degrees. What was to be a simple fund-raising campaign, with Einstein being the showpiece, turned out to be a major lecture tour. The tour was a huge success, and although not as much money was raised as was hoped, the future of the medical faculty of the university was ensured.

Einstein's travels were not over; in fact, they had just begun. The following year he and his wife visited Japan and Palestine. (Elsa Einstein always accompanied her husband to protect him from the many curiosity seekers.) In Japan where he was not given the time to wander around, honors and presents were showered on him, and he was received by the empress, an unusual honor. The visit to Palestine was an emotional experience both to him and to the enthusiastic crowds.

That year he also received the Nobel Prize in physics for 1921 "for his services to theoretical physics and in particular for the discovery of the law of the photoelectric effect." The committee was certainly justified in awarding the prize for the explanation of the photoelectric effect, an outstanding achievement in itself, but by not mentioning relativity specifically the committee had wanted to avoid any complications. The subject was still politically too controversial, although another solar expedition (September 2, 1922) had again verified Einstein's prediction.

When Einstein finally returned to his modest home in Berlin, he was appalled by the resurgent nationalism and the postwar inflation that had brought chaos and hunger. He continued to work for peace, remained active in the International Committee on Intellectual Cooperation, referring to it later as "the most ineffectual enterprise with which I have been associated." He must have seen the writing on the wall, but despite the rise of anti-Semitism and attacks against himself, he decided to remain at the Kaiser Wilhelm Institute, thus showing his support of the Weimar Republic. In 1930 he again went to America, this time strictly for research, as visiting professor at the California Institute of Technology at Pasadena. His most memorable experience was a visit to the Mount Wilson Observatory to see for himself the wonders of the universe he had so well described. It is told that he became excited when he saw the apparent rotation of the mountain. Director Walter Adams assured him that it was the dome and not the mountain that was to blame: "You know, relativity."

In the meantime, the situation in Germany worsened. At Pasadena he received the news of the Reichstag fire and the subsequent rise of Hitler in 1933; he refused to return to Germany but instead went to Le Coq-sur-Mer in Belgium, where he was guarded day and night because of rumors of attempts on his life. He gave up his German citizenship and membership in the Prussian Academy of Sciences, as he was "unable to serve the Prussian State under the present government." The Academy, which had been glad to receive him in 1913, now denounced him as an atrocity monger and betrayer of his people. Einstein, in his reply, denied any atrocity propaganda and pointed out that any defense of the German dictatorship would be a repudiation of justice and liberty, for which he had stood all his life; moreover it would help the cause of those who were undermining those ideas and principles that had given Germany a place of honor in the civilized world.

He received offers from the University of Madrid; the Collège de France, which wanted to create a special chair of physics and mathematics for him; England, which offered him British citizenship; and America, where he joined the Institute for Advanced Study (Princeton).

Early in 1939 news reached the scientific community in America that the German chemists Otto Hahn and Fritz Strassmann had succeeded in splitting the uranium nucleus–experiments that were confirmed by Lise Meitner, their former collaborator, who had taken refuge in Sweden. (In 1934 Leo Szilard had already realized the possibility of a chain reaction–if the fission products contained more than one neutron.) There was the awesome possibility that the Germans might be able to produce an atomic bomb, since the occupation of Czechoslovakia had supplied them with sufficient uranium ore. Szilard induced Einstein–who had been completely unaware of the nuclear work that was going on–to write to President Roosevelt, recommending that atomic bombs be made. This was the extent of Einstein's involvement in the Manhattan Project (the code name for the subsequent American nuclear war effort). However, Einstein wrote again, later, urging that the bomb not be used in the war against Japan, but it arrived too late: on August 6, 1945, an atomic bomb was exploded over Hiroshima. From then on Einstein, as well as other leading scientists, spearheaded a drive to inform the public–as well as the politicians–of the bomb's full impact. (He also took up the cudgels for civil liberties during the difficult McCarthy period. In 1954 he wrote to his old friend, the Queen Dowager of

Belgium, "I have become an enfant terrible in my new homeland because of my inability to keep silent and to swallow everything that happens here.")

5. New Horizons

The Institute for Advanced Study in Princeton had been planned as a haven for outstanding scientists, well paid and with no duties to detract them from their work. Its director, Abraham Flexner, had tried for some time to get Einstein to accept at least a part-time position, similar to what he had in Pasadena. Einstein accepted partly because the Institute had agreed also to make a place for his assistant, Walther Mayer. They had started to collaborate on a unified field theory and Einstein wanted the collaboration to continue and also wanted to take care of his assistant; this was especially important now since Mayer was Jewish also. Einstein's concern for young and promising but unknown scientists was quite characteristic. When the Hebrew University offered him a position, he refused, partly because he did not agree with its chancellor, Judah Magnes, on matters of policy but also because he felt that the university should provide a haven for the promising young scholars who might not be able to get positions as easily as the well-known ones. So what was to be a part-time position now became full-time and Einstein arrived in Princeton accompanied by his wife, his secretary, Helen Dukas—who was to watch over him after Elsa's death and even now helps look after his estate—and Dr. Mayer. He soon came to like America, which made him forget the tribulations of the exile; and America liked the scientist who was so amiable and unconventional. Passersby in Princeton could see strolling through the streets an elderly gentleman with long white hair, without an overcoat, in bedroom slippers, completely oblivious of his surroundings, engrossed in thought.

For some time, Einstein had tried to link gravitation and electromagnetism in one unified picture, a unified field theory. Notable attempts had been made by Hermann Weyl, then professor at ETH in Zurich, later at Princeton; Theodor Kaluza in Germany, who introduced a "fifth" dimension; and Eddington. Einstein worked ceaselessly on the problem with a number of collaborators and produced several different theories. But as beautiful as his theories were, he had to discard them for one flaw or another. Yet he did not give up. "I need more mathematics," he said, and he continued his work until his death on April 18, 1955. The idea of a "unified field theory" is aesthetically pleasing, and one should expect its existence. However, even if Einstein had succeeded in combining gravitation with electromagnetism, that would have been only the first step in uniting it with other interactions, such as those found in the atomic nucleus. There are four different kinds of forces or interactions, of which gravitation is the weakest, and it would be a Herculean task to unify them, all being of different strengths.

Einstein's unfaltering quest for the unified field theory made him the maverick among theoretical physicists, a position aggravated even more by his opposition to quantum mechanics, the offshoot and culmination of Planck's quantum theory discussed earlier. Whereas Einstein had shown that light could behave not only as waves but also as particles, Louis de Broglie showed that particles, such as electrons, could behave as waves. His hypothesis was confirmed experimentally by C. J. Davisson and L. H. Germer in 1927 and now forms the basis of the electron microscope. But Niels Bohr (1885–1962) had received world fame after he proposed his theory of the atom, according to which electrons move around the atomic nucleus in orbits without radiating energy—in defiance of electromagnetic theory. Only when they "jump" from one orbit to another will they radiate or absorb energy, that is, light, and then only in well-defined quanta, the same quanta that had been stipulated already by Planck and applied to the photoelectric effect by Einstein. A bizarre picture—it was no wonder it appealed at first to only a few, including Einstein who called it "one of the greatest discoveries"—but it worked, at least in the case of hydrogen. Bohr's theory was a crude makeshift one, and it was doomed when Einstein publicized de Broglie's idea in a paper dealing with photons as particles. Now things began to happen fast and furiously. Guided in part by de Broglie's idea of matter as waves, the Austrian physicist Erwin Schrödinger proposed an atomic theory treating matter as waves. In Germany Werner Heisenberg, who was later to head Germany's scientific war effort, went even further. He showed that it was impossible to accurately determine both the position and the momentum of a particle, such as an electron. This is the principle of indeterminacy, which was to play an important role in the development of quantum mechanics. It is not as strange as it may seem at first sight, if one remembers that in order to "see" an object one has to shine light on it. Light, as Einstein told us, consists of photons acting like bullets; nothing much happens if the object is of ordinary size, that is, much larger than a photon, but the situation is quite different if the object is an electron or other particle whose wavelength is comparable to that of the photon. In a movement similar to Brownian motion, the incoming photon will jolt the electron or particle, and as a result we cannot be sure anymore of its position (prior to the collision) or the way

In recognition of his accomplishments, Einstein received the Planck medal from Max Planck in 1929. He promptly put it in his pocket without even looking at it.

The electron microscope operates on the same principle as an ordinary microscope, except that electrons take the place of light rays (thereby making it possible to magnify an image whose dimensions are smaller than the wavelengths of visible light); also, either electrostatic or magnetic lenses substitute for glass lenses. Electrons enter the instrument at the top and are accelerated downward by an "electron gun," operating like an ordinary radio tube. The electrons then proceed through a condenser and a magnetic lens that brings the electrons to a focal point. The electrons then pass through still another lens and the specimen, and are projected on to a viewing screen (for visual observation) or a photographic plate (for picture taking.) ▼

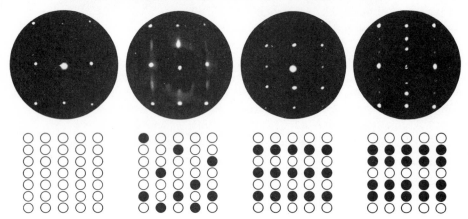

C. J. Davisson and L. H. Germer had shown that electrons could be diffracted by small obstacles, such as the atoms in a crystal. This is beautifully illustrated by the electron diffraction patterns shown here, which were produced by the adsorption of oxygen on crystalline nickel surfaces. The upper figures are actual photographs of the diffraction patterns, while the lower diagrams show the underlying crystal structures producing them. The white circles indicate the nickel crystal, while the black circles represent the adsorbed oxygen. Beginning at the left is the pure crystalline nickel, followed by the pattern produced by the adsorption of oxygen. In the second figure the oxygen occupies random locations, while in the third and fourth diagrams it follows a regular pattern, alternate rows either singly or doubly occupied. Since diffraction is a wave phenomenon, this indicates that particles, such as electrons, can also exhibit characteristics of wave motion.

it was going (before being hit). All one can predict is the "probability" of its being at a certain place. Schrödinger's matter waves became "probability waves" describing the probable path of the electron. So far so good, but more was to follow. Not only is it impossible to observe the position and momentum of the electron, but there was no way to predict its actual course, but only the probability given by waves of "probability amplitudes." This was too much for Einstein; "God does not play dice with the world" has become a famous line and sums up Einstein's view of quantum mechanics. "Quantum mechanics is certainly imposing," he wrote to Max Born, another pioneer in its development. "But an inner voice tells me that it is not yet the real thing. The theory says a lot, but does not really bring us any closer to the secret of the Old One." It would lead us too far afield even to sketch the

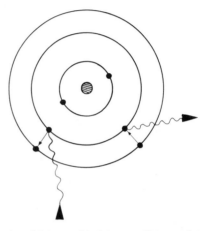

A schematic drawing of Bohr's model of the atom. The central circle represents the atomic nucleus, with electrons moving in their respective orbits. If an electron "jumps" from an outer to an inner orbit, energy is released in the form of radiation (wavy line). On the other hand, the absorption of a sufficient amount of energy permits an electron to transfer from an inner to an outer orbit.

Niels Bohr (1885-1962). Bohr received his doctorate from the University of Copenhagen in 1911 for his work on the electron theory of metals, which became a classic in its field. After a brief stay at Cambridge, he went to Manchester where, under the guidance of Rutherford, his ideas on the atom gradually took shape, culminating in his paper of 1913. In 1916 he returned to Copenhagen; in 1920 he assumed the directorship of the Institute of Theoretical Physics, which became a mecca for theoretical physicists; and in 1922 he was awarded a Nobel Prize. At the Institute he worked on the quantum theory and laid the foundations of the new quantum mechanics. In 1955 Bohr was instrumental in founding the Danish Atomic Energy Commission and soon afterward the Nordic Institute for Theoretical Atomic Physics, a joint research institute of the five Nordic countries. The direction of both institutions took a heavy toll of his time and health, and he died suddenly on November 18, 1962.

further development of quantum mechanics, as the new mechanics became known, except to mention Einstein's fight against the rigid interpretation, known as the Copenhagen doctrine. This was not like Newton's squabbles with Hooke over light, or with Leibnitz over who invented calculus; it was a matter of principle—and belief. However, Einstein and Bohr, who was then Director of the Institute of Theoretical Physics in Copenhagen, continued their warm friendship despite their disagreement.

Einstein produced powerful arguments and thought experiments to circumvent the indeterminacy principle, arguments that had Bohr nearly beaten. At last Bohr found a way out: Einstein's thought experiment had not taken into account the principle of equivalence—a rather ironic twist. The arguments continued until most physicists were convinced of the validity of quantum mechanics and the Copenhagen doctrine, with the exception of Einstein, Schrödinger, and, in a way, de Broglie, and Max Planck, the originator of the quantum theory. The question is not completely resolved even now; according to the strict interpretation of the Copenhagen school we can only get answers in terms of probabilities, even to questions with a definite yes or no answer. In a classical example proposed by Schrödinger, a cat is placed in a closed room next to a vial of cyanide. A radioactive atom is placed in a detector which—if the atom undergoes radioactive decay—will trigger a mechanism breaking the vial and thus killing the cat. If the atom has a 50-50

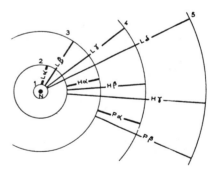

The diagram illustrates a hydrogenlike atom (N being the nucleus) and possible electron transitions (between the various electron orbits from level 1 to 5). For an ordinary (not excited) hydrogen atom the electron will be found in the lowest level. In the case of heavier atoms—having several electrons—successive orbits, or levels, will be occupied. (The number of electrons that are permitted are two for the lowest, eight for the next, eighteen for the third, and so on.) Whenever an electron "jumps" from a higher to a lower (unoccupied) level, it will radiate energy; conversely, transition from a lower to a higher level will absorb energy. The transitions, which will produce the lines of the spectrum, are indicated by the various lines in the diagram. These lines can be grouped into various series depending on the level at which the transition takes place.

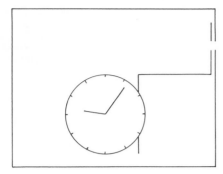

Einstein's thought experiment in answer to Bohr consisted of a box with a small hole in the side that could be closed with a shutter controlled by a clockwork in the box. The box contained a fixed amount of radiation. The clock was set to open the shutter for a minute interval when a single photon could be released at a moment known with as great an accuracy as desired. The box could be weighed before and after the event. Given the equation $E = mc^2$, one could then calculate the escaped energy with any accuracy wanted. Thus, both the time and energy could be determined, in contradiction to the principle of indeterminacy.

Candid photograph of Einstein and Bohr taken by Paul Ehrenfest.

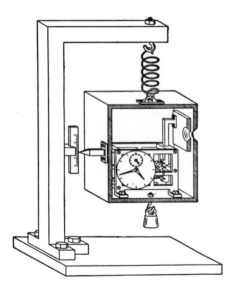

Bohr's reply used the same type of apparatus (although the method of weighing is illustrated in detail). The box is suspended by a spring and furnished with a pointer to read its position on a fixed scale. The weighing—to any desired accuracy—is then performed by adjusting the balance to its zero position by means of suitable loads. The essential point is that to determine the zero position with any accuracy requires some leeway in controlling the box's momentum. (The more accurate the position is to be, the greater will be the uncertainty of the momentum; this uncertainty, of course, must be smaller than the total momentum or impulse, the weight, or loads, times the time involved in making the measurement). And the greater the accuracy of the reading of the pointer, the longer must be the balancing interval in the weighing of the box. Now, according to the theory of general relativity, a clock when displaced by a gravitational force will slow or speed up by an amount depending on the gravitational field strength and the amount of displacement. Since the flexibility in the displacement of the clock involves an uncertainty of the momentum, and consequently of the mass, it follows that the uncertainty in the time measurement involves an uncertainty in the mass—or the energy (since the energy is proportional to the mass). Thus, the uncertainty in the time measurement is connected to an indeterminacy of the energy. Hence, both the time and the energy cannot be determined accurately; a use of the apparatus as a means of accurately measuring the energy of the photon will prevent us from controlling the moment of its escape.

chance of undergoing radioactive decay in an hour, the question is whether or not the cat will be alive or dead at the end of the period. One would expect a definite answer, which could be ascertained by opening the door of the room and taking a look. However, according to the strict interpretation of the Copenhagen doctrine, our taking a look—which should not change the result— actually causes a drastic change in the mathematical description of the state of the cat, changing the 50 percent probability of its being alive or dead to one of certainty in which the cat is definitely alive or dead. Einstein, on the other hand, believed that it is only our ignorance and the incompleteness of the theory that deny us an answer. Only the future will tell whether Einstein was mistaken in his intuition and too far from the mainstream of physics or a lone voice in the wilderness.

It has been said that only twelve persons in the world understood the theory of general relativity; this might have been true in the beginning, but now every student familiar with the geometry of Riemann and Gauss and the mathematics of Tullio Levi-Civita and C. G. Ricci can master it. For many years only Einstein and a small circle of workers occupied themselves with the theory, which seemed to have only a limited connection with experiments. Since then general relativity has made an impact also in astrophysics and given rise to some very exciting developments, which we will cover in later chapters. We mention here only a few of the more recent and spectacular results.

It had already been noted by J. Lense and Thirring that the gravitational field of a rotating body should be different from that of a nonrotating mass. Their solution to the appropriate equations was an approximate one, valid only for slow rotations—such as one might expect in celestial objects—but even so the effect is too small to be observed. (Recently, an exact solution to the problem has been given by Roy Kerr, but the exact nature of the rotating mass still poses some questions.) An experimental

test based on the Lense-Thirring work has been suggested by Leonard I. Schiff involving the precession of a gyroscope revolving around the earth, say, in a satellite. It should undergo two relativistic precession effects, one due to the satellite's orbiting motion and yielding a predicted precession of approximately 7 seconds of arc per year and one due to the rotation of the earth of 0.05 second of arc per year. Experiments to measure these effects are under development by the U.S. Navy and at Stanford University.

Ever since Einstein showed that in the weak field approximation (an approximation in which the gravitational field is assumed to differ from its flat space value by small quantities only) his equations take the form of "wave equations," there has been considerable discussion on the existence of gravitational radiation. The situation is similar to that of electromagnetic theory, where accelerated or oscillating charges produce currents that change periodically and are propagated through space in the form of electromagnetic waves. If two masses are made to oscillate, one might expect the generation of gravitational waves, except that these require "quadruple moments" (equivalent to four electric charges in the electromagnetic case) and are extremely difficult to detect. Solutions of the weak field equations may be an indication of the possibility of gravitational waves, but one would

Above left

Enrico Fermi (1901–54). Although he excelled in theoretical physics and had even published several papers, his doctoral thesis was on X-ray diffraction, partly because, at the time, theoretical physics was not recognized as a respectable discipline in Italy and partly because he enjoyed experimental work. From 1924 to 1926 Fermi held a temporary position as professor at the University of Florence, where he made his first major contribution to physics—the Fermi statistics for particles of half-integral spin, such as the electron and proton. (The neutron had not yet been discovered, but it also obeys the Fermi statistics.) When a new chair of theoretical physics was established at the University of Rome, the committee unanimously chose him for it, though he was only twenty-six years old. In Rome, Fermi became the undisputed leader of a group of young and brilliant Italian physicists who tried to bring the "new physics"—quantum mechanics had just been developed—into Italy. In 1934, when Irène and Frédéric Joliot-Curie succeeded in producing artificial radioactive elements by bombarding boron or aluminum with alpha particles, Fermi suggested using neutrons as bullets. Also, either by chance or by intuition, he found that the radiation would be enhanced rather than weakened by placing a layer of paraffin between source and target. A large program was initiated in which all kinds of elements would be bombarded, from the lightest to the heaviest. In the process two new elements, neptunium and plutonium, were discovered; Fermi, in fact, had produced fission without realizing it. When the political situation in Italy deteriorated and free discussions became impossible under the dictatorship, Fermi reluctantly decided to leave Italy. (Also, his wife, Laura, was Jewish and in danger, while he personally was attacked by the Fascist press.) Awarded the Nobel Prize for his neutron work, he took the opportunity to go to America via Sweden. In America, shortly after he started to work at Columbia University, he heard of the fission work by Otto Hahn, Fritz Strassman, and Lise Meitner and realized the implication of a sustained chain reaction. Eventually, the Manhattan Project was established and Fermi built a pile, an arrangement of layers of graphite and chunks of uranium, which produced a chain reaction. After the war he went to the University of Chicago, where he continued his work, pressing to unravel the secrets of the nucleus.

Above right

Lise Meitner (1878–1968). Born in Vienna, she went to Berlin to study physics under the great Max Planck. Together with her colleague Otto Hahn she began experimental work on the natural radioactivity of atoms, which resulted in the discovery of a radioactive element. She became professor of physics at the University of Berlin, one of the first women to hold that rank in the history of the university. From 1917 until 1937 she was the head of the physics department of the Kaiser Wilhelm Institute for Chemistry. In 1938, when Austria became part of Germany, she left for Stockholm. While there, she heard of the pioneering work of Hahn and Fritz Strassman in splitting the atomic nucleus. Meitner repeated the experiment and confirmed their result; the nucleus of uranium was split into barium and krypton, releasing a tremendous amount of energy. The implications were realized by Bohr, who informed American scientists of the dangerous possibilities of a nuclear weapon being used against them. After the war Lise Meitner spent several years in America, teaching at American University; after her retirement she returned to Sweden, the second woman to be honored by a foreign membership in the Swedish Academy of Science (the first was Marie Curie).

Left

The last photograph of Einstein, taken on his seventy-sixth birthday (March 14, 1955), only a month before his death. His health had been deteriorating, and he knew his time was limited—he suffered from stomach troubles, and an operation in 1948 had shown an aneurysm in the main artery—yet he continued to be as active as before, taking occasional naps. His last official act was the signing of a public statement drafted by Bertrand Russell bluntly asking to renounce war. Einstein never finished a speech he was preparing, to be broadcast on the occasion of Israel's seventh anniversary of its independence; he had to be moved to a hospital. The pain decreased and he continued to work on the speech, but after a restful day he died in his sleep in the early hours of April 18, 1955. He had asked that his brain be given to science and his body cremated. There was to be no special ceremony. He had lived without seeking honor and recognition, and he persisted to the end.

Earth-rotation effect

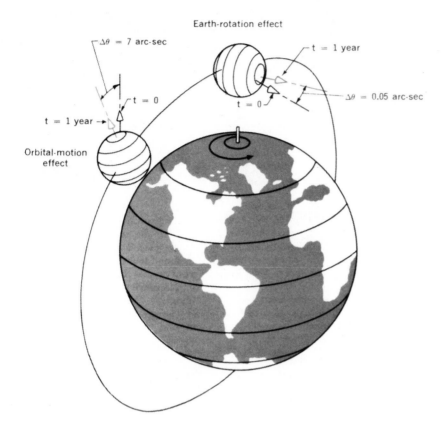

$-\Delta\theta = 7$ arc-sec

$t = 1$ year

$t = 0$

$t = 0$

$\Delta\theta = 0.05$ arc-sec

$t = 1$ year →

Orbital-motion
effect

The spinning gyroscope (the small sphere) will experience two relativistic precession effects, one produced by its orbital motion and one by the rotation of the earth. The gyroscope, in a satellite, will be aligned with a fixed star. For a satellite moving in a polar orbit the two effects above are at right angles to each other.

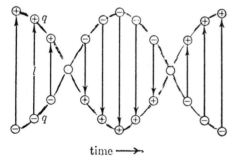

time ⟶

Electromagnetic waves. The positions of two oscillating charges, one positive (+) and one negative (−), are shown as functions of time (the displacement along the vertical, and the time along the horizontal). It is seen from the diagram that each performs a periodic motion (alternately reaching a highest and lowest point, then repeating the process) but that the system as a whole has zero absolute displacement (one charge is as much above the equilibrium position as the other is below it). A system of two opposite but equal charges moving in such a manner is called an oscillating electric dipole, and it emits electric radiation. In the case of gravitation, there is only one kind of mass, namely positive, which here plays the role of the charge. However, two masses coupled by a spring could be made to oscillate and would emit gravitational radiation as predicted by Einstein and Eddington.

J. Weber adjusting sensors on an aluminum cylinder used in the detection of gravitational waves. As the cylinder vibrates, the vibrations are converted into electric impulses at a receiver, which is then converted into mechanical vibrations for a generator.

like exact solutions—especially those representing waves originating from a point and proceeding out radially. Even so, those solutions could be spurious ones, resulting from a coordinate transformation, rather than being physically meaningful. The required criteria are that energy is transmitted by the waves and that at least some components of the curvature tensor do not vanish. (This latter requirement ensures that space is not flat and that at least some of the components of the Riemann curvature tensor are different from zero.) Recent theoretical work has produced solutions satisfying these requirements, and it now seems fairly certain that, at least theoretically, gravitational radiation may exist. Until now there has been no conclusive experimental observation showing the existence—generation and receiving—of gravitational waves. However, for some time now, Joe Weber at the University of Maryland has performed painstaking and elaborate experiments claiming to have detected gravitational radiation. But his results have not been confirmed by any other group carrying out similar work.

Another facet of Einstein's relativity is that within the last few years there has been a proliferation of rival theories of relativity—in some cases based on a different (and, as it turned out later, incorrect) interpretation of existing tests but in other cases also giving the correct experimental result. The reason for this is that at present known observations (viz., the bending of light, precession of the perihelion, gravitational red-shift) can be accounted for by weak gravitational fields; hence a theory that reduces to this limit—and satisfies the mathematical and physical principles of equivalence and covariance—is a possible candidate. However, of all these theories only Einstein's is aesthetically satisfying in that it represents gravitation as a manifestation of the curvature of the space-time continuum in terms of one set of variables only. Unless serious discrepancies with observation, based on exact solutions and strong fields, should be found, there seems to be no point at the present in looking for other theories (unless, of course, they provide a more unified picture of nature).

VI · THE DISCOVERIES

1. The Telescope

Because the great discoveries of the last two hundred years were largely due to the invention of the telescope, it would be useful to review its development, as well as the types in use today. However, in this chapter we shall limit ourselves to optical telescopes, that is, those using visible light; the important radio telescopes will be discussed in Chapter VII.

Even in ancient times it was known that light will bend, refract, at the interface of two media, such as glass and air. The separating surface need not be sharp; it can be graduated, as occurs when layers of air are of different densities, as in mirages. Also, it had been known quite early that glass of varying thicknesses can produce images

and, in particular, focus parallel light rays. From this knowledge the construction of an actual lens was inevitable. Depending on whether the central portion is thicker than the edges or vice versa, one then speaks of convex or concave lenses. The two types of lenses of particular importance (for telescopes and for other optical instruments) are convex and concave lenses, for which both surfaces are similar. The type and size of image obtained depends both on the lens and on the object's distance from it.

During our childhood most of us have held a convex, or converging, lens against the sun so that we could cast a bright beam onto a sheet of paper, which would burn a

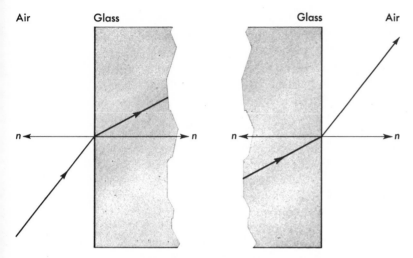

Air   Glass   Glass   Air

Refraction of light. Left: When light passes from air to glass (here at an angle), it is bent toward the normal (n—the line drawn at right angles to the surface separating them). *Right:* Similarly, when a ray of light passes from glass to air it is bent away from the normal. In general, light will be bent toward the normal if passing from a rarer to a denser medium, and away from the normal in the opposite case.

In a mirage, light passing through layers of expanded or rarer air to more dense layers will be bent: In the desert the air is rarer near the surface being heated, while upper layers are more dense. Light passing from an object, such as a palm tree, will be bent until it reaches a point (in the dense air) where it is completely reflected—or thrown back into the expanded air instead of passing outward as would be expected. As a result, the image of the tree will appear inverted as if mirrored in a body of water.

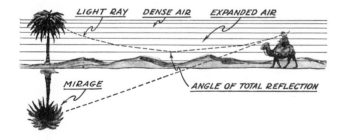

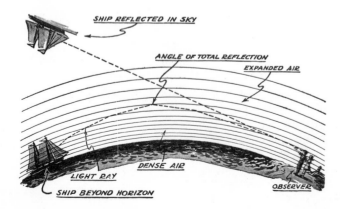

hole in the paper. The spot through which that beam passes is called the focus of the lens, and all rays parallel to the axis of the lens pass through it. The distance from the focus to the center of the lens is the focal length and depends on the radii of the two spherical surfaces making up the lens. It also determines the scale of the image, which is a measure of its size. For this reason it is advantageous to use lenses of as large a focal length as possible. The brightness of the image, of course, depends on the amount of light gathered, and for that reason lenses having a large diameter are preferable. When we speak of a 40-inch telescope, for example, we are referring to a telescope that has an objective, or a lens, of 40 inches in diameter. However, there are practical limitations on the size of the lens imposed by problems of construction— the surfaces must be ground smooth—and there are inherent problems owing to aberrations or imperfections. Since a lens, especially a converging one, is in some respects similar to a prism, white light falling on it will be dispersed. Since the lens bends different colors by different amounts, the colors in the spectrum cannot be brought together to form an image at the same focus, and this gives rise to chromatic aberration. This effect is not too serious in lenses of large focal lengths; more important is the spherical aberration caused by light striking different points on the lens and focusing at different points. It is, of course, not necessary that the object be far from the lens, but if it is closer to the lens than the focus—its distance being smaller than the focal length—as in a magnifying glass, it is impossible to catch the image on a screen. The light in effect appears to come from it, and for this reason the image is called a virtual image rather than a real image, which can be caught on a screen.

In the case of a concave, or diverging, lens, all images are virtual no matter where the object is placed. As the name implies, light diverges from the lens but appears to come from the focus. Thus an object far away (at infinity) will produce an image at the focus, but it cannot be seen on a screen placed at the focus.

A refracting telescope (because it refracts, or bends, the light rays) is a combination of two lenses: one a convex lens, called the objective, at the lightgathering end; and either a convex or concave lens, called the eyepiece, at the other end. Light from a distant star, for example, enters the telescope at the objective and comes to a focus. The eyepiece, at the other end, acts as a magnifying glass, which can be moved forward or backward, that is, focused, to produce a clear, enlarged image.

The air near the surface of an expanse of water is denser than the layer above it. The image of a ship below the horizon is thrown upward, toward the sky. It is then reflected at the boundary between the expanded and the dense air which acts like a mirror for rays of light coming in at a reflecting angle.

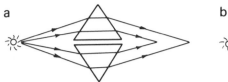
a

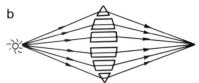
b

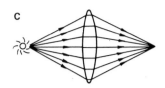
c

Focusing of light.
(a) Light entering and leaving a glass prism is bent twice, once upon entering and once upon leaving. Rays passing through two prisms placed base to base will reach the same point and be focused. However, rays passing through points near the bases will come to a focus closer than those passing near the two apexes. (b) The focusing can be improved by cutting the prisms into sections and changing the angle of the prismatic sections—larger angles in the middle and smaller angles as one proceeds to the two outer sections. (c) A continuous surface will result if the number of prismatic sections is increased and the edges rounded off—the result being a convergent "lens."

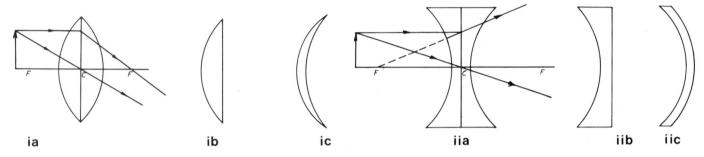

ia   ib   ic   iia   iib   iic

Lenses. *Convex, or converging:* ia) Both surfaces are convex (parts of spheres centered at opposite sides of the lens). ib) One surface is convex and one is plane. This is a plano-convex lens. ic) One surface is convex and one is concave (both are parts of spheres centered at the same side of the lens). This is a convex-concave lens. Two typical rays are shown in diagram ia. One passes through the center (C) of the lens and leaves the lens practically unchanged in direction. The other is a parallel ray (i.e., parallel to the axis) and after refraction passes through the focus (F). *Concave, or diverging, lenses:* iia) Both surfaces are concave (parts of spheres centered at opposite sides of the lens). This is usually referred to as a concave lens. iib) One surface is concave and one is plane. This is a plano-concave lens. iic) One surface is concave and one is convex. This is a concave-convex lens. Two typical rays are shown in diagram iia. One passes through the center (C) of the lens and leaves it unchanged in direction. The other is a parallel ray; it is refracted (diverges) and *appears* to come from the focus (F).

Chromatic aberration. Light of different wavelengths will be focused at different points, closer for violet and farther for red *(left)*. To compensate, two lenses of different material (such as crown and flint glass) are placed in contact *(right)*. The deviations will now balance each other, resulting in one image for all colors.

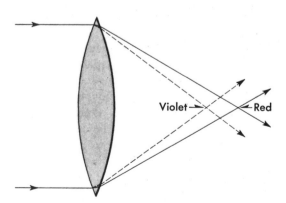

Violet → ← Red

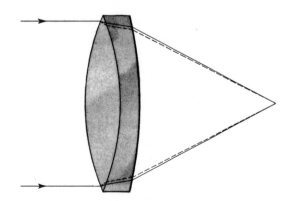

e   o

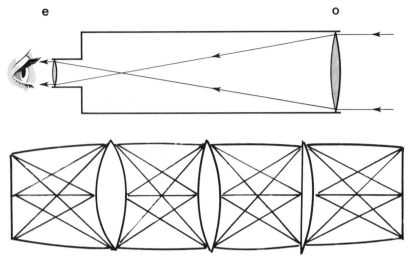

Refracting telescope. Light from a distant source, such as a star, enters the telescope and is brought to a focus by the objective lens (o). The image is then viewed through another lens, the eyepiece (e), placed so that the image (which now acts as the object) lies just within the focal length of the eyepiece. The result is an enlarged but inverted image. This inversion does not matter for astronomical objects, but when the telescope is used in viewing terrestrial objects a diverging lens is used for the eyepiece, which changes the orientation so that the final image is again right side up.

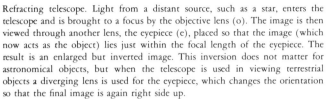

A schematic drawing of the first telescope constructed by Hans Lippersheim and Zacharias Janssen, after an illustration from Peter Borelli's *De Vero Telescopic Inventore* published in 1655. The telescope consists of a system of three converging lenses, the middle one acting as a kind of separator. The various lines are supposed to represent the different light rays, but since at the time the laws of refraction were unknown they are hardly more than a crude attempt to indicate what is going on. Nevertheless, Galileo was able to construct his own telescope based on a crude drawing like the one shown here.

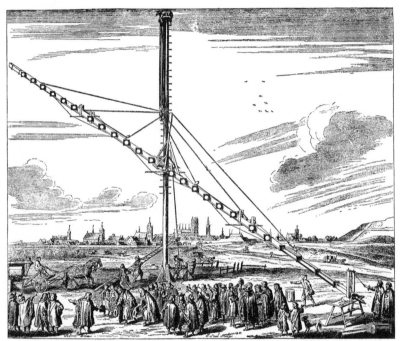

Hevelius's mammoth astronomical telescope, from an engraving from *Machina Coelestis* by Johannes Hevelius, ca. 1670. The large size was intended to reduce chromatic aberration and to produce as large a scale of image as possible.

We have seen that the first telescope was constructed by two Dutch lens makers, Hans Lippersheim and Zacharias Janssen; it consisted of a system of three convex lenses. Galileo's telescope followed theirs. Both the number and sizes of telescopes kept increasing. Johann Hevel of Danzig (1611–87), better known as Hevelius, used a telescope 150 feet long to get an image with as little achromatic aberration as possible. But his star

catalogue, comprising about 1,500 stars, with positions somewhat better than those given by Tycho, was compiled without the aid of a telescope.

By the time the problem of achromatic aberration was solved by Chester Hall and John Dolland, who used a combination of two lenses of different materials, which cancelled their respective aberrations, Newton had already invented the reflecting telescope, using mirrors.

It was, of course, well known that mirrors, silvered pieces of glass, reflect light. If a combination of plane mirrors is properly arranged–forming part of a semicircle–they could be used to converge or diverge light from a distant source. Better yet are spherical mirrors. Just as there are two kinds of spherical lenses, there are two kinds of spherical mirrors, concave and convex, both parts of a spherical surface but with the opposite sides being the reflectors. (It is the concave mirror that converges light, whereas the convex mirror has a diverging action; the opposite is the case with lenses.) In addition to spherical mirrors, one finds parabolic ones, the mirror surface being part of a paraboloid, such as in the headlights of an automobile. The size and type, real or virtual, of the image depends on the kind of mirror and the distance of the object.

Basically, the reflecting telescope consists of a concave mirror, which acts as the objective gathering the light, and some device bringing the image to the observer. Newton used a small plane mirror, placed near the focus and at an angle of 45 degrees with the axis of the telescope, but different focus arrangements can be used.

At first, mirrors were made of highly polished metal surfaces, but as their size increased, it became more difficult to achieve the necessary curvatures. Joseph

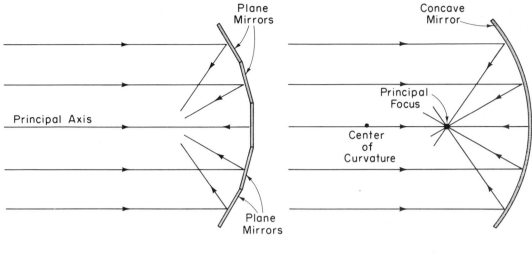

Plane Mirrors

Principal Axis

Plane Mirrors

Concave Mirror

Principal Focus

Center of Curvature

Light that impinges on a plane mirror is reflected at the same angle at which it strikes the mirror. *Left: Converging action:* When a number of plane mirrors are arranged as part of a circle, parallel light will converge at or near a point *(left)*. If the number of mirrors is increased indefinitely (while at the same time their width is decreased), a concave mirror will result, its focus being midway between it and the center of curvature *(right)*. *Below: Diverging action:* The mirrors are again arranged as part of a circle, except that its center is now on the other side. Parallel light striking them will diverge *(below left)*. If the number of mirrors is increased indefinitely (at the same time that their width is decreased), a convex mirror will result; the light will appear to diverge from a virtual focus halfway between the mirror and its center of curvature *(below right)*.

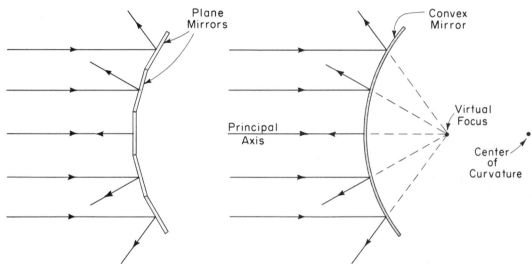

Plane Mirrors

Convex Mirror

Principal Axis

Virtual Focus

Center of Curvature

The four main focusing arrangements. *Prime focus:* The observer (in most cases just a photographic camera) is placed at the focus of the mirror. *Newtonian focus:* Light entering the telescope is reflected by the objective mirror, which is concave. Just before the light reaches the focus it is reflected out of the telescope into the eyepiece–a simple converging lens–by means of a small plane mirror placed at an angle of 45 degrees to the axis of the telescope. *Cassegrain focus:* A small convex mirror is placed just before the focus of the main mirror. This convex mirror reflects the light, which passes through a small opening out of the telescope. *Coudé focus:* Instead of passing out behind the telescope the light is reflected by an additional plane mirror placed at an angle of 45 degrees with the axis. Thus, the Coudé focus uses both the convex mirror of the Cassegrain focus and the plane mirror of the Newtonian focus.

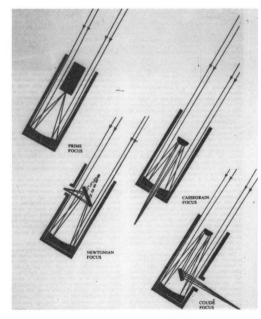

Fraunhofer (1787–1826) had solved the problem of how to construct refracting telescopes free from any aberration, a process that had been begun by Dolland. Fraunhofer's 9½-inch refractor was of such excellent quality that, as a reward for its construction, he was exempted from paying city taxes to Munich.

Just when it seemed that the refracting telescope had won, Jean Foucault discovered how to silver glass mirrors. It then became possible to construct mirrors of any desired

On the grounds of his estate at Datchet, near Windsor, William Herschel (1738–1822) erected a 20-foot telescope with which he and his sister Caroline observed the sky. It was a rather risky business, since the observer had to sit near the top of the tube, which could be raised and lowered or rotated in a horizontal plane.

The Leviathan of Parsonstown, the gigantic telescope built in 1845 by the Third Earl of Rosse. The lowest part of the large tube was held by a universal joint, and the telescope could be driven by a long screw turned by hand. The earl, a talented engineer, constructed the 72-inch mirror as well as the rest of the machinery and building. Because of its structure—supported between two huge stone walls—the telescope could be used only to observe near the meridian. Its most significant use was in the discovery of the spiral form of a number of galaxies and the measurement of thermal radiation from the moon.

The 26-inch refractor soon after it was mounted in Washington at the Naval Observatory in 1873. Simon Newcomb is at the eyepiece and Admiral Benjamin F. Sands, Superintendent of the Observatory, is seated in the background.

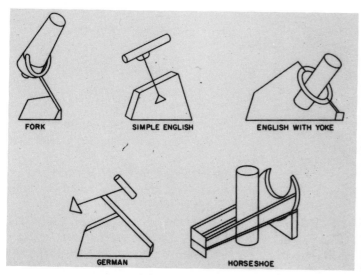

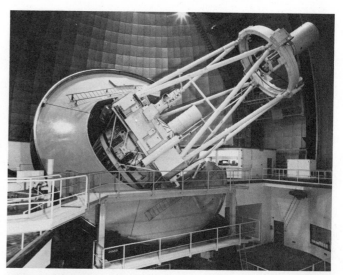

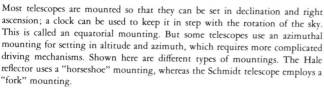

Most telescopes are mounted so that they can be set in declination and right ascension; a clock can be used to keep it in step with the rotation of the sky. This is called an equatorial mounting. But some telescopes use an azimuthal mounting for setting in altitude and azimuth, which requires more complicated driving mechanisms. Shown here are different types of mountings. The Hale reflector uses a "horseshoe" mounting, whereas the Schmidt telescope employs a "fork" mounting.

Above right

The region of the sky around the southern celestial pole is not observable from the major observatories in the Northern Hemisphere, where until recently all large powerful telescopes have been located. The Anglo-Australian Observatory at Siding Spring Mountain in New South Wales, a joint venture by the Australian and British governments and the Australian National University, is trying to fill that need with its new telescope. The heart of the telescope is a 150-inch-diameter circular mirror—a block of glasslike material coated with a thin layer of aluminum. The instrument rests on a horseshoe mounting and can be adjusted precisely with the help of computer-controlled driving mechanisms.

Right

George Ellery Hale's dream was the building of the 200-inch reflector at Mount Palomar, California, but although he was responsible for its plans and execution, he did not live to see it completed. The Hale telescope with its prime, Cassegrain and Coudé focus was dedicated in 1948 to his memory. It was until recently the world's largest telescope (the USSR is constructing a 236-inch reflector) and has uncovered many of nature's secrets. The central skeleton tube contains the primary mirror at the bottom; the observer's cage is at the top. The large horseshoe mounting is aligned along the declination axis, permitting the telescope to swing along it; two other positions are indicated faintly in the diagram. The telescope is housed in a huge dome, 137 feet in diameter, provided with a movable shutter.

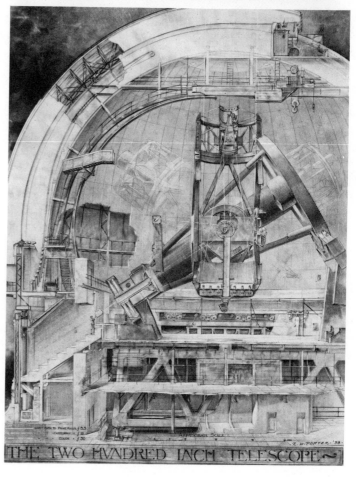

The 200-inch mirror of the Hale telescope. Through its transparent body can be seen the honeycomb pattern cut out of the back. This was done to lighten it, but even so the mirror weighs 15 tons.

size simply by constructing a glass surface and spraying it with aluminum. The glass had to withstand expansion, owing to heat, and it had to be rigid, but it did not have to be as perfect as the glass used in lenses. It could be of poorer quality and might even contain air bubbles, as long as its surface was smooth enough.

To complete the survey of telescopes, mention should also be made of the Schmidt optical system, invented by the German optician Bernhard Schmidt. It uses a concave mirror together with a correcting lens placed at the plane passing through the center of the mirror's curvature. In its simple form it can only provide photographs taken by a camera placed at the focus of the mirror. The concept of replacing visible images with photographic ones had become important; modern telescopes, such as the one developed by the American astronomer I. Bowen, formerly director of the Mount Wilson and Palomar Observatories, combine the desirable properties of a regular telescope with those of a camera. Various auxiliary equipment, such as photometers measuring the light intensity and spectrometers to study the spectra, is often found at the end of the telescope.

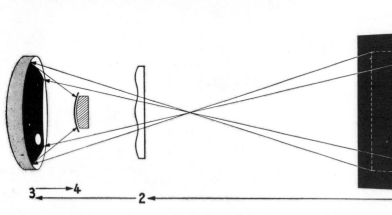

The Schmidt optical system. A wide area of the sky (1) is reflected by a concave mirror (3) and projected onto a curved film (4). At the plane passing through the mirror's center of curvature a correcting lens (2) is inserted, which eliminates the spherical aberration of the mirror. The main difficulty with the Schmidt optical system is that the correcting lens is not spherical and is difficult to manufacture.

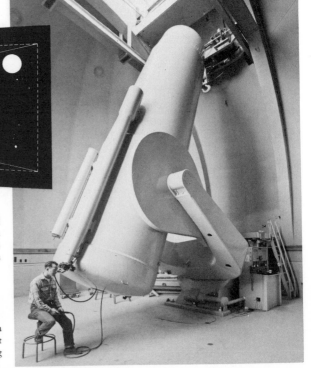

The 48-inch Schmidt telescope at Mount Palomar. In addition to the reflecting mirror, it has a correcting lens. Its main use is for wide-angle photography; the photographic plate is inserted at the focus of the mirror. Exposure is started and ended by uncovering and covering the correcting lens.

The Florence and George Wise Observatory, named for the principal donors, is located on Mount Zin, nearly 3,000 feet high and about an hour's drive from Tel Aviv University, with which it is associated. The location is particularly suitable because of the comparatively large number of clear nights and good viewing conditions, brightness of sky, low humidity, and steady temperature. It gives astronomers even more observation time than at Mount Palomar. The small cylindrical extension in front of the dome houses the Coudé spectrometer. The single-story building contains workshops, darkroom, sleeping quarters, kitchen, and library along its periphery, with the central section giving access to the 40-inch telescope.

The 40-inch Bowen Cassegrain telescope used in the Florence and George Wise Observatory in Israel. It has a 7-meter focal length and two Cassegrain secondary mirrors of different focal lengths. The short one is used for photography; the longer one serves mainly for observation of the light intensity or spectrum of a single star.

Scale model of the Multiple Mirror Telescope (MMT), perhaps one of the world's most unusual optical instruments. It clusters six 72-inch mirrors symmetrically around a central core, which contains a 30-inch guiding reflector, to create light-gathering capability equivalent to a single telescope with an aperture of 175 inches. It will be contained in a rectangular, four-story structure that will rotate with the instrument. Offices, control rooms, laboratories, and other facilities will be housed in the same structure, and thus partake of its rotation. This permits placement of the control and service rooms adjacent to the telescope, not possible in conventional domes. A joint project by the Smithsonian Astrophysical Observatory and the University of Arizona, the telescope will be located on Mount Hopkins in the Santa Rita Range near Tucson, Arizona.

202

Observatories are usually associated with and situated near universities, but as cities grew and their lights and smoke hindered observation, the newer observatories were located at remote areas. Probably best known are the Mount Wilson and Palomar Observatories, now known as the Hale Observatories, near Los Angeles, which houses the 200-inch reflector.

To observe the sun, special solar telescopes have to be used. Atop a 100-foot tower, the McMath Solar Telescope at the Kitt Peak National Observatory in Arizona, the largest of its kind, has a heliostat (reflecting mirror) that reflects sunlight down a 500-foot shaft, part of which is underground; at the bottom another mirror (concave) reflects the light, which finally enters a spectroheliograph at ground level.

Above
Sir William Huggins was the first to make systematic and detailed analyses of star spectra and of nebulae. Shown here is an 8-inch reflector with an attached spectroscope, the instrument used by Huggins.

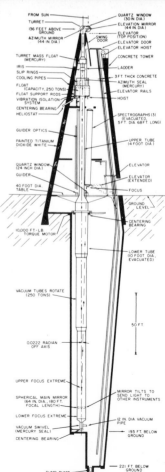

The solar tower (the part that is aboveground) at the Sacramento Peak Observatory. The mirror is at the top, and the tower houses the spectrograph.

Far right
A cross-sectional view of Sacramento Peak's solar tower, the larger part (221 feet) being below ground. The path of the sunlight is indicated by the arrows.

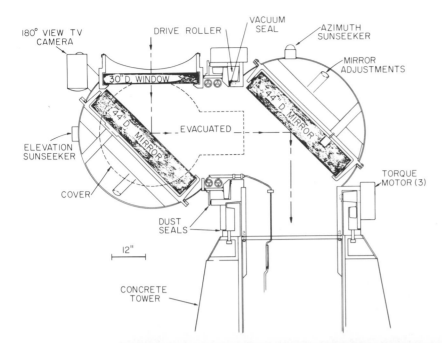

The mirror arrangement at the top of the Sacramento Peak tower. The 44-inch-diameter mirror can be adjusted to collect the sunlight entering through the window.

Mount Wilson Observatory, one of George Ellery Hale's projects, houses a 100-inch and a 60-inch telescope. Originally the Mount Wilson Solar Observatory, it expanded under Hale's leadership and joined forces with Mount Palomar Observatory; together they are now called the Hale Observatories.

2. Comets and Meteors

In the Middle Ages comets were regarded as harbingers of bad tidings, plagues, and other catastrophes. Indeed, the spectacle presented by the "blazing" head followed by the fiery tail streaking through the sky is an unusual and even awe-inspiring sight. The motion of the planets—more or less regular—could be understood, eclipses of the moon and even the sun predicted, but the occurrence of comets was random and unpredictable.

At first it was believed that comets originated in the higher regions of our own atmosphere; even Tycho Brahe believed it until he made careful observations on the comet of 1577. In his book on the comet he refuted the common ideas and showed conclusively that comets must be farther than the earth-moon or sun-Venus distance. He even suggested that comets revolve around the sun, thus explaining their periodic appearance. On the other hand, Kepler thought that they were "merely etherical projectiles which clearly move almost uniformly in straight lines." Hevelius set out to write a comprehensive work on comets, *Cometographia,* comprising twelve volumes in which he collected all known historical records of cometary appearances. After the ninth volume, the appearance of the comet of 1664 sparked a strange controversy. His observations, which later turned out to be correct, failed to get the approval of the rest of the

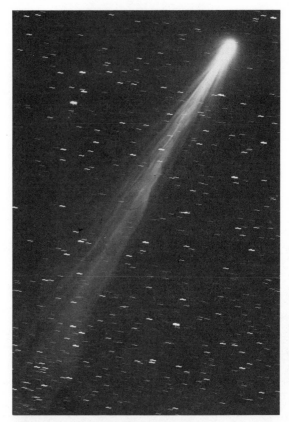

Comets (from the Greek *kométés,* meaning "long-haired") have been observed since ancient times. For example, Chinese records show 372 observations between 611 B.C and A.D. 1621. To the naked eye a comet appears as a diffuse spot of light, about the size of the moon but less bright, and often accompanied by a long nebulous tail. The picture shows the 1908 Morehouse Comet.

The "horrible appearance in the air" seen on August 15, 1670, in the French province of Touraine. Flaming pieces of wood are seen falling, and there are armies in the sky.

The great comet of 1528, from a contemporary engraving. "So horrible was it, so terrible, so great a fright did it engender in the populace, that some died of fear, others fell sick. This comet was the color of blood; at its extremity we saw the shape of an arm holding a great sword as if about to strike us down. At the end of the blade there were three stars. On either side of the rays of the comet were seen a great number of axes, knives, bloody swords, among which were a great number of hideous human faces with beard and hair all awry."

scientific community, including the Royal Society; for three years he tried in vain to have his views accepted, and he finally completed his work in 1668. Like Kepler, he believed that comets are formed from some kind of waste matter and that they try to follow a straight path but can be deflected by any planet. The correct path of comets, ellipses, parabolae, or hyperbolae was calculated only when Newton proposed his laws of gravitation. According to the law, any body acted upon by an inverse-square central force would describe a conic section. In 1682 Edmund Halley observed the great comet, which has subsequently borne his name, identified it as one that had appeared in 1305, 1456, 1531, and 1607, and predicted its return some 76 years later. It was then that the periodic appearance of comets along elliptic orbits was established. Halley's work in astronomy ranged over wide fields, but he is best known for his work on comets and his devotion to

Edmund Halley (1656–1742). At the age of seventeen he entered Queen's College in Oxford; he left at the age of twenty, having decided to engage in practical astronomy. With the aid of his father he made a trip to St. Helena, where he was able to catalogue 341 southern stars. Upon his return, he was hailed as the "southern Tycho," awarded a fellowship by the Royal Society, and given a Master of Arts degree by Oxford without examination. Halley noted that bright comets similar to the one of 1682 had appeared at intervals of 75 or 76 years. He then predicted that the 1682 comet would reappear in 1758. It was indeed observed on Christmas Day by an amateur and made other appearances in 1835 and 1910. Halley also discovered proper motions of stars and drew attention to the presence of star clusters. In 1720 he became Astronomer Royal, a position he held until his death at the age of eighty-six.

According to Hevelius, comets are generated in spirals, they proceed in straight lines, but are deformed dynamically into conic sections, such as ellipses or parabolae. The head is in the form of a small disk (shown by the small lines) oriented at right angles to the sun (at the center).

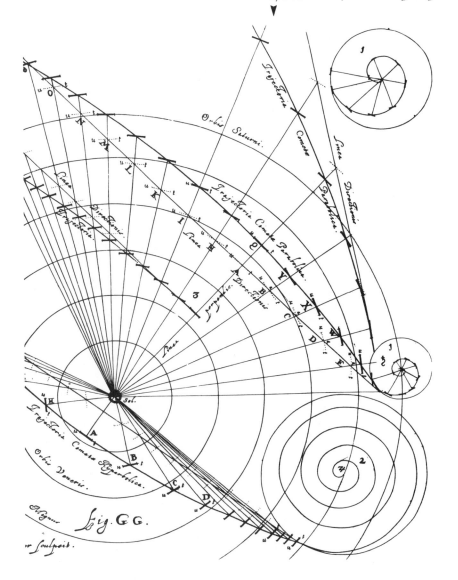

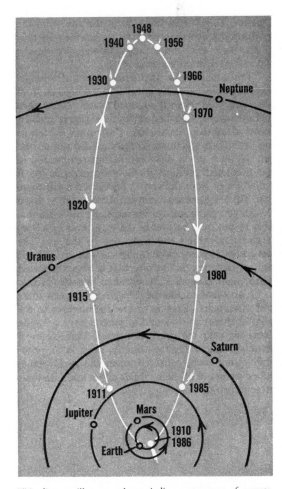

This diagram illustrates the periodic reappearance of comets. Shown here schematically is the orbit of Halley's comet, an elongated ellipse. The comet made its last appearance in 1910 and is expected to return again in 1986.

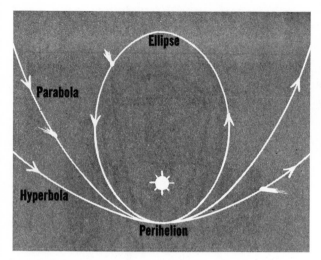

Because of their large eccentricities, it is difficult to distinguish among the different types of cometary orbits when they are at or near perihelion. Moreover, a comet may change its orbit owing to perturbations by planets. Three types of cometary orbits are shown here.

A scene from the Bayeux Tapestry depicts the consternation of King Harold I and his subjects at the appearance of a comet. That was in 1040, and it was the same comet seen again in 1682 by Halley and named for him.

Halley's comet. The bright spot to the right is the planet Venus; a streak, hardly visible, crossing the tail about an inch from the comet's head is a meteor.

Newton, which resulted in the successful publication of Newton's *Principia*. Calculating the orbit of a comet is not a simple matter, since close to the perihelion, where measurements can be made, the orbit does not differ greatly from a parabola or hyperbola. It was after calculating 24 orbits of Halley's and other comets and noting their resemblances and the approximately equal intervals between appearances that Halley was able to establish the periodicity of his comet. Later it became customary to name comets after their discoverers—for example, Halley's Comet, Encke's Comet, etc.

As the power of the telescope increased, so did the number of comets that could be observed, and by now there are hundreds known, not all recurring. How many comets there are nobody knows. Kepler used to say that there are as many comets in the universe as there are fish in the sea. It has been suggested that there exists a "cometary zone" at the edge of the solar system from which comets are brought from time to time by planetary perturbations although they may originally follow a parabolic, or even hyperbolic, path, they may be "captured" by the attraction of an outer planet and then follow very elongated elliptical paths within the solar system. At any rate, perturbations by planets could alter both the trajectory and the period of revolution. As a rule, comets can be observed only if they are less than twice the earth-sun distance away; whether they can be seen from the earth depends on their position in the sky.

It is easy to imagine a comet as a giant ball of blazing gas followed by a tail, like a gown billowing in the wind. This is true only when the comet is approaching the sun;

Photographs from the Hale Observatories of Halley's comet in 1910, April 26 to June 11.

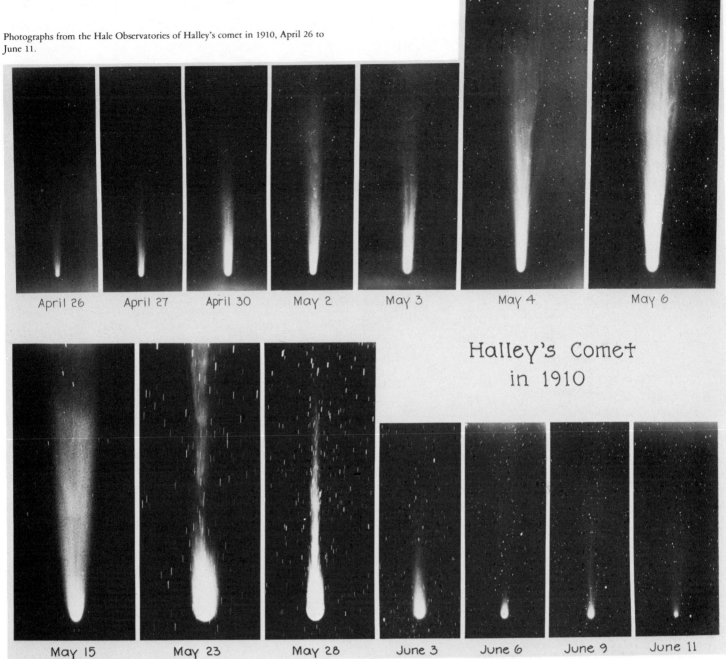

April 26   April 27   April 30   May 2   May 3   May 4   May 6

Halley's Comet in 1910

May 15   May 23   May 28   June 3   June 6   June 9   June 11

when it recedes, the tail precedes the head. Apian, Petrus Apianus (1495–1552), a copious writer on astronomical subjects, is usually credited with noting, as the Chinese had already discovered, that a comet's tail is pointed away from the sun, in apparent contradiction to the law of gravitational attraction. But it is the head that obeys Kepler's laws and moves along an ellipse; the tail, composed of a very tenuous gas, is acted upon by solar radiation pressure or solar wind. This is a repulsive force that predominates if the mass is very small, and it explains the strange behavior of the tail.

An observer at the Harvard College Observatory adjusting the controls of the Super-Schmidt Meteor Camera used to observe and follow the courses of comets.

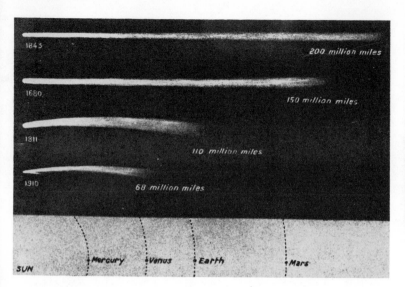

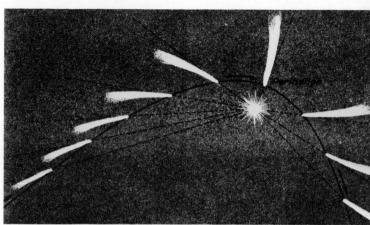

The tail of a comet is always pointed away from the sun. Upon approaching the sun, the tail will follow the head; when receding, the tail will precede the head.

The lengths of comets' tails have been known to vary from negligible to enormous lengths. Shown here are the lengths of four comets compared with the orbital radii of the planets Mercury, Venus, Earth, and Mars.

SOME PERIODIC COMETS

Name	Last observed perihelion *	Observed returns	Period (years) †	Perihelion distance	Semi-major axis (A.U.)	Eccentri-city
Encke	1967	48	3.30	0.339	2.21	0.85
Temple II	1967	14	5.26	1.369	3.0	0.55
Schwassmann-Wachmann II	1968	7	6.52	2.157	3.50	0.38
Wirtanen	1967	4	6.65	1.618	3.55	0.54
Reinmuth II	1967	4	6.72	1.933	3.6	0.46
Finlay	1967	8	6.88	1.077	3.6	0.70
Borrelly	1967	8	7.00	1.452	3.67	0.60
Whipple	1963	5	7.44	2.450	3.80	0.35
Wolf I	1967	11	8.42	2.507	4.15	0.40
Comas Sola	1961	5	8.58	1.777	4.19	0.58
Väisälä	1960	3	10.5	1.741	4.79	0.64
Neujmin I	1966	4	17.9	1.547	6.8	0.77
Crommelin	1956	6	27.9	0.743	9.2	0.92
Olbers	1956	3	69	1.179	16.8	0.93
Pons-Brooks	1954	3	71	0.774	17.2	0.96
Halley	1910	29	76.1	0.587	17.8	0.97

* Only those returns occuring before 1970 have been listed.

† Comets with the largest period (and therefore with longest orbits) also have the greatest eccentricity and semi-major axis.

Heinrich Wilhelm Matthäus Olbers (1758–1840), a German astronomer, developed the first satisfactory method for the determination of cometary orbits, using a system of triangulations. Also, he recognized the formation of the tails as an outflow of very rarefied matter from the head due to some form of solar electrical repulsion. Today it is fairly well established, thanks to space probes, that the sun ejects a million tons of gas per second moving radially at 250 miles per second.

This solar wind, at a temperature of a million degrees, drags with it a magnetic field carried by electrons. There are, essentially, two processes that are responsible for the presence of cometary tails. In one, dust particles are pushed out of the coma, the brilliant nebulosity surrounding the head, by the radiation pressure of the sunlight. These particles scatter the sunlight and become visible, like ordinary dust illuminated by rays of sunlight. The second process is more involved. The high-energy electrons in the solar wind ionize the molecules in the coma, that is, they strip the molecules of some of their electrons. The magnetic field carried along with the solar wind carries these ionized molecules with it, giving them velocities of millions of miles per second. These ions become visible through the absorption and consequent emission of sunlight. The result may be likened to the interaction of a rising column of smoke and the atmosphere—a gracefully billowing stream.

The study of comets is not only interesting in itself but affords us the opportunity of finding out more about the nature of extraterrestrial matter in the solar system; comets may be relics of the "dust cloud" from which the sun and the planets were formed. Let us backtrack for a moment to Newton's experiments with light passing through a prism and the resulting color spectrum. That was in 1672. In 1802 an English chemist, William Wollaston, using a narrower slit to admit the light, discovered not a continuous color strip but a spectrum broken by seven narrow dark spaces or lines. He simply believed that the five strongest lines corresponded to divisions of the colors. A few years later Joseph Fraunhofer, a German optician, in studying the sun's spectrum, discovered about 500 such lines. These Fraunhofer lines, as they are now called, coincide with the *bright* lines produced by glowing chemicals in laboratory spectra. In the sun itself, today, 67 of the 103 known terrestrial elements have been identified.

So with the aid of a spectroscope attached to a telescope, it is now fairly well established that comets consist of molecules composed of carbon, nitrogen, oxygen, and hydrogen in such combinations as methane, ammonia, and perhaps hydrogen cyanide, and others. Recently, it has been found that common water is a constituent of at least some comets. Comet Kohoutek is of particular interest here. Its appearance, late in 1973,

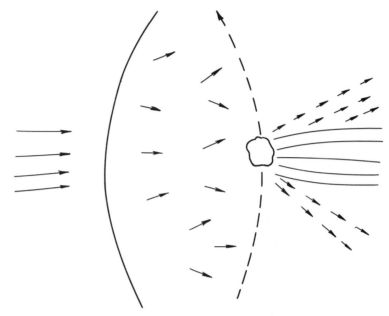

The solar wind (indicated by the arrows at left) produces a bow wave (curved line) around the coma of the comet, while chaotic magnetic fields within the solar wind (arrows at center) act like a "magnetic rake" and carry ions—produced by the high-energy electrons within the solar wind—away from the comet at high speed (stream of arrows at right). Dust tails are formed by the pressure of the sunlight pushing the dust particles out of the comet (curved lines at the right). Note that they are curved and follow the law of motion of orbiting bodies.

Comet Kohoutek—a newcomer to the solar system—approached the earth in the autumn of 1973. It was a disappointment to the ordinary observer: in January 1974, when it attained maximum brightness, it was barely discernible in the evening sky. Astronomers pronounced it a dusty comet, with dust and other particles congealing on the surface (like toffee), thus preventing the vaporization necessary for the formation of a visually spectacular tail. This photograph was taken at the Wise Observatory on November 28, 1973, with the 40-inch reflector during a 30-second exposure.

Although it was a visual disappointment, Comet Kohoutek resulted in an important discovery. Its spectrum, seen here as a heavily blurred line, indicated the existence of ionized water molecules (shown here as H_2O+). This spectrogram was taken on January 10, 1974, at the Wise Observatory.

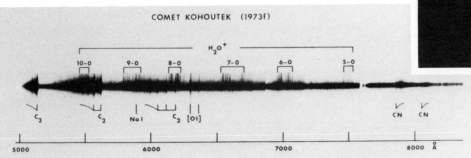

COMET KOHOUTEK (1973f)

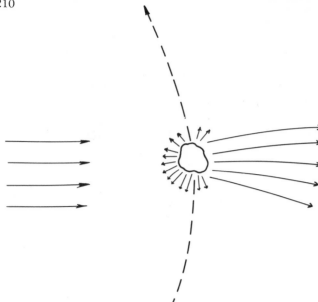

Comets seem to defy the law of gravity by speeding up or slowing down in their orbits. The radiation from the sun (parallel arrows at left) causes the "ice" to evaporate on the side of the comet facing the sun. Molecules are ejected at great speed and, as in a jet engine, push the comet away from the sun.

The especially large meteor shower of October 9, 1933. To the observer, the meteors seem to be coming from a central point—the radiant. But this is only an effect of perspective, as occurs when one looks down a straight line of railroad tracks.

seems to have been its first, and it may be a sample of the primordial material from which the solar system was formed. It also gave further evidence to the "dirty snowball" model proposed by Fred L. Whipple, a leading American astronomer. According to this model, the nucleus—the unseen center of the coma, or the inner part of the comet's head—is composed of frozen matter: ice. Since the comet spends most of its time in regions away from the sun, it will persist in this frozen state. When it comes near the sun, the radiation from the sun causes the ice to evaporate and send out molecules at speeds of several hundred feet per second, forming the coma. According to Whipple, these molecules are ejected from the side facing the sun, causing a "jet" that pushes the comet away from the sun. Indeed, small deviations from the expected elliptic trajectory have been observed. It is also known that comets lose a considerable amount of gas during each passage. If they were composed only of solid material, this would mean that a single passage would remove a considerable fraction of the absorbed gas and the comet would diminish drastically in brightness on its subsequent return, being unable to replenish itself. On the other hand, only a fraction of one percent of the icy substance would be needed to supply the expanded gas. Comets, such as Halley's comet, have continually returned without appreciable loss in brilliance; this fact favors the existence of an icy—but dirty—core.

Meteors (from the Greek *meteōron:* "phenomenon in the sky"), or shooting stars as they are commonly called, are another form of extraterrestrial probe. Originally believed to be caused by the ignition of vapors in the lower atmosphere of the earth, they are solid particles entering the earth's atmosphere from interplanetary space. Moving at high speeds, they are burned up by the friction encountered in the atmosphere and appear briefly as luminous streaks of light. It was the physicist E. F. Chladni (1756–1827), known for his work on sound, who

first suggested that they are small bodies circulating through space, becoming visible through incandescence upon entering the earth's atmosphere. Large meteor showers, like a giant fireworks display, have been observed from time to time, a famous one occurring November 12, 1833. To the observer, this "thick as snow" shower appeared to originate or radiate from a single point called the radiant, located in the Constellation Leo and for that reason called the Leonid meteors. These showers were found to recur periodically, around November, about every thirty-three years. The last Leonid shower occurred on November 17, 1966; the earliest, traced to 902, occurred in October of that year. A less extravagant display occurs in August of every year, when the earth passes through the orbit of the Perseid shower originating from the direction of Perseus. Comparing the orbits of these showers with those of known comets, Giovanni Schiaparelli found that they were nearly identical with the comets of 1866 I (the first comet to pass perihelion in 1866) and 1862 III respectively. This suggested, as borne out in other examples, that meteor swarms are debris left

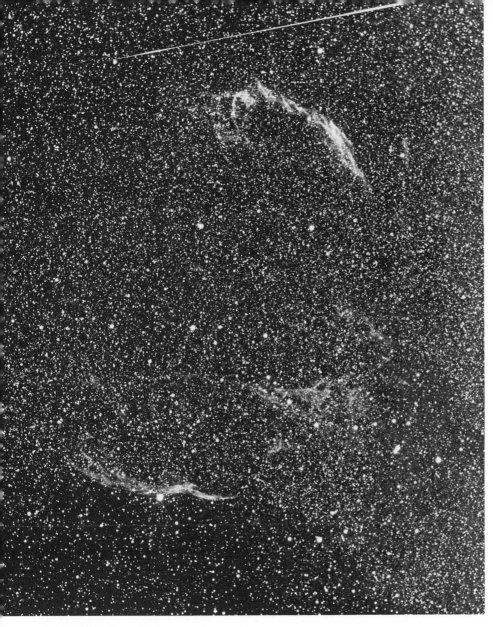

William Herschel, born in Hanover on November 15, 1738, the son of Isaac Herschel, a bandsman in the Hanoverian Guards. He was knighted by King George III for his discovery of Uranus.

"Meteor" refers only to the luminous trail or streak; "meteoroid" is the body itself, and "meteorite" is what survives as we see it on earth. Here, a bright meteor (top) is seen crossing the field of view of the Yerkes telescope at the moment the Veil nebula (seen at right) was being photographed.

The Cape of Good Hope telescope at John Herschel's house at Feldhausen. Devil's Peak is in the background, at right. With his eighteen-inch reflector Herschel was able to catalogue nebulae, clusters, and double stars in the Southern Hemisphere.

along the trail of comets and continuing their solitary journey around the sun.

Although meteorites are fairly rare for any given locality, more than a thousand fall each year over the earth's entire surface. The most common form consists of stones (or aerolites), although irons (or siderites), which are alloys of metals, are also found. Most spectacular are the few craters on the earth formed by the falls of large meteorites, such as the Barringer Meteor Crater. The large size of this crater (4,200 feet in diameter) and the amount of material found (over 30 tons of iron meteorite) seems to indicate, as suggested by F. L. Whipple, that meteoroids may also be the debris of a disintegrated planet or asteroid. Much still needs to be done to identify the origin of our interplanetary visitors, and all that can be said now is that some meteoroids are associated with comets, while others come from the larger asteroids.

3. The Planets

Among his contemporaries William Herschel (1738–1822) was an exception. The son of a musician, he was expected to follow in his father's footsteps. He had no scientific background, only a desire to learn and to see. His early youth was spent as an oboist in the Hanoverian Guards, the exact position his father had had. When the regiment went to England, he moved with them but deserted–for this he later received an official pardon. After a few years of wandering and performing in England, he was invited to become the organist of the Octagon Chapel in Bath, then a fashionable place and one full of cultural activities. But at night he retired to his room to study mathematics, optics, and astronomy. His father became paralyzed in 1763 and died two years later. William then suggested that his brother, Alexander–gifted in music and an excellent mechanic–join him. His sister, Caroline, later joined him too. An unusual partnership evolved. Music was still their strongest bond, but astronomy had become a close second. Not satisfied with available instruments, William decided to build his own. To Caroline's dismay, the house was converted into a giant workshop with tools, lenses, and mirrors strewn about, but she was so devoted to her brother that she did not object and even assisted him. At first it was a 7-foot telescope, then a 10-foot one, and finally a 20-foot telescope with which Herschel systematically surveyed the sky. All were made in his own workshop, and he was assisted by Alexander and Caroline, who read to him while he turned the lathe or polished mirrors. The Herschels led a grueling life, polishing mirrors during the day, giving concerts in the evening, and observing the sky at night. Herschel's observations were not those of an amateur, which he was, but followed a systematic plan. Slowly the telescope was moved across the sky, each area was scrutinized and analyzed in detail, with not only the objects being noted but also their type (double stars, variable stars, or nebulae). Four times Herschel "swept" the heavens, each sweep taking several years, and during the second of his surveys it happened.

On March 13, 1781, Herschel, observing small stars in the neighborhood of H Geminorum, noticed one that appeared visibly larger than the rest. "Struck with its uncommon appearance," he suspected that it was a comet. It seemed indeed to be a comet because four days later it had moved; Herschel communicated his findings to the Greenwich and Oxford Observatories, which confirmed the discovery. But it turned out not to be a comet. When its orbit was calculated, it was more a circular than an elongated ellipse. He had discovered a planet, more than a hundred times as large as the earth and twice as distant

from the sun as Saturn. Herschel, being its discoverer, proposed the name Georgium Sidus in honor of George III; others tried to designate it Herschel, but finally the new planet was christened Uranus, the personification of heaven in Greek mythology. Uranus had been seen several times before, but none of the observers, including Flamsteed (1690) and Bradley (1753), had noticed anything unusual, or moving about it, and it was left to the amateur to make one of the biggest astronomical discoveries of the eighteenth century.

It was a most unusual discovery and aroused great interest in all of Europe. Satellites of existing planets, such as those seen by Galileo, could be readily accepted, but a brand-new planet was a different matter. Since ancient times man had known and become used to the existence of just five planets (not counting the earth or the sun in the Ptolemaean system), and now all his preconceptions had to be thrown overboard. Herschel was made a fellow of the Royal Society, Oxford University gave him a doctor's degree, and King George III asked him to show his telescope at Court. Overnight, the musician of Bath had become a respected and admired astronomer.

Herschel wanted to return to his family at Bath and to continue his observations, but he was prevailed upon by the king to become the king's private telescope maker. So the Herschels moved to Datchet, where he continued to observe and to make his telescopes.

Uranus and its five satellites, named at the right; "Vth" is Miranda, whose apparent magnitude is 17 (the lower the number the brighter the object). Uranus, the third largest planet, is barely visible to the naked eye because of its great distance (more than 1,600 million miles) from Earth; through a telescope it appears as a greenish blur, the surface details obscured by its atmosphere. In this view, south is at the right.

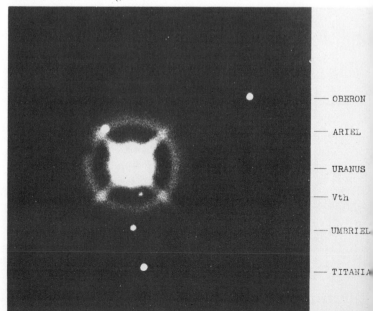

— OBERON

— ARIEL

— URANUS

— Vth

— UMBRIEL

— TITANIA

Recent evidence indicates that Uranus is encircled by five rings, according to observers who studied the passage of Uranus between the earth and a bright star (SAO 158687). Such passages, or occultations, are important because timing of the star's disappearance and emergence from behind the planet can provide extremely precise measurements of the length of the star's track across the planetary disk; measurements from several locations can be combined to yield the planet's size and shape. (Instead of taking photographs, astronomers use their telescopes simply to chart the brightness of the star, noting the times it blinks off and on at the beginning and end of the occultation.)

The five brief occultations were observed over the southern Indian Ocean on March 10, 1977, aboard the Kuiper Airborne Observatory (a NASA jet equipped with a telescope and other instruments) before and after the main blockage of the star by Uranus itself. Similar observations at Australia's Perth Observatory confirmed the signs of five narrow rings around Uranus.

Since none of the rings cause a total occultation (that is, only percentage drops in the light intensity were observed), it is believed that the rings are composed of numerous bodies or moons less than 4 miles in diameter. The five rings occupy a band or belt about 4,200 miles wide (the largest ring of Saturn is over 15,000 miles wide); each of the four inner rings appears to be about 6 miles wide, while the outer ring may be as wide as 60 miles and also either denser or thicker than the others since it occulted about 90 percent of the light from the star, compared with about 50 percent for each of the others. Further explanation of the structure of the rings may be forthcoming from Voyager 1 and 2 (see Chapter IX).

It was with his new 40-foot telescope that Herschel discovered Oberon and Titania—two satellites of Uranus—which were not seen for another forty years until they were rediscovered by his son, John; two other satellites, Ariel and Umbriel, were found in 1851 by William Lassell, another amateur astronomer, working at his house near Liverpool. Not until 1948 was Miranda, the fifth and last satellite, found by Gerard P. Kuiper with his powerful instruments.

In 1783 William Herschel married. This was somewhat of a blow to his devoted sister who now lived by herself but continued to assist her brother, even making some discoveries of her own. As the only daughter of a rich man, Herschel's wife was sympathetic to her husband's pursuits. She could afford to move the family to comfortable quarters at Slough. There Herschel devoted all his time to telescopic observation. His son, Sir John Herschel (1792–1871), followed in his father's footsteps, becoming his assistant and, later, his successor.

William Herschel's great contribution to astronomy was not only the discovery of Uranus, which was important in itself, but also the founding of sidereal astronomy, the systematic and detailed study of the stars and nebulae. Stars had been considered bright dots at large distances, unmoving, and perhaps even embedded in Ptolemy's crystal sphere. Herschel showed that they were moving, at various distances and in worlds of their own, and that our own sun was just one star (and not even an

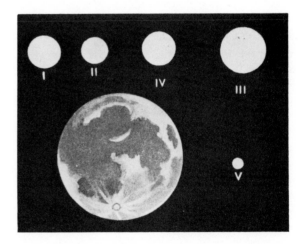

Uranus's satellites compared in size with Earth's moon: (I) Ariel; (II) Umbriel; (III) Titania; (IV) Oberon; (V) Miranda. All five revolve around Uranus's equatorial plane.

important one) within the eternal motion in the universe. Herschel had introduced system into chaos and life and activity into what was thought to be inert.

After Herschel discovered Uranus in 1781, old records were examined to see whether the planet had been seen before and to get more data to fix its orbit. Since the planet had not been known as such, it would appear as a star in those old catalogues, but because it had moved since then, this would have been considered a "wrong

John Herschel, the son of William Herschel, was a well-known astronomer in his own right. After his father's death in 1822, he carried out a vast amount of work with a 20-foot telescope he built. He discovered no fewer than 3,347 double stars, rediscovered the two satellites of Uranus, and carried out sweeps of the sky that resulted in a catalogue of 2,307 nebulae (525 of which were new discoveries), for which he received a knighthood at the age of thirty-nine. The biggest enterprise of his life was the exploration of the sky in the Southern Hemisphere. Accompanied by his family, he set out for South Africa and set up his reflector at Feldhausen, some five miles from Cape Town. During the four years he spent in South Africa John Herschel discovered 1,202 double stars and 1,708 clusters and nebulae, but his most important work was his program of star-gauging, which netted 70,000 stars. When Herschel returned from the Cape he was only forty-six. He spent the rest of his life analyzing the vast amount of data he had gathered and published his results–the monumental *Results of Astronomical Obervations, Made During the Years 1834–38 at the Cape of Good Hope; Outlines of Astronomy;* and, in 1864, the *General Catalogue of Nebulae,* which remained the standard work for many years. Unfortunately, the collection of his father's papers was delayed and still awaits completion.

entry." The thing to do was to look for these wrong entries and to see whether they might correspond to the position of the planet at that time, since the entry could also have referred to a comet–a rather time-consuming procedure in an age when computers were unknown. That is how it was discovered that the planet had been seen but not identified twenty times between 1690 and 1781, when it was discovered by Herschel. (In addition to sightings by Flamsteed and Bradley, Lemonnier of Paris had seen it eight times within a month and each time had catalogued it as a different star. Had he compared his data, he would have preceded Herschel by twelve years.)

Uranus behaved well for several years, but by 1820 its actual position differed considerably from the predicted one. At first, it was thought that the earlier data might have been erroneous, so a new orbit was calculated based only on data after 1781. Ten years later it was evident that even the revised data were not compatible with later positions. True enough, the discrepancy was not large by our standards, but astronomers used to working within minutes of arc were concerned. Even when the perturbations due to Jupiter and Saturn were taken into account, residual discrepancies remained.

In 1845, two years after he had begun to work on the capricious planet, John Couch Adams sent a letter to Professor G. B. Airy, Astronomer Royal at Greenwich, pointing out that the perturbations of Uranus could be accounted for by the existence of another planet–at a distance of about twice that of Uranus from the sun, whose present latitude and longitude he gave. Now John Adams was unknown to Professor Airy, who did not feel that he should disrupt the busy schedule of the Greenwich

Observatory for some possible harebrained scheme; dozens were received every month. Also, the prediction of a new planet based on perturbations was not only unusual but extremely difficult; the usual procedure was to calculate the perturbations from *known* planets, and greater men than Adams had tried and failed. Yet Airy followed up the suggestion and wrote to Adams, asking for further explanations. But Adams failed to reply and there the matter stood.

In the meantime Dominique François Arago (1786–1853), the famous French scientist, had suggested to Urbain Jean Joseph Leverrier, the brilliant young mathematician and professor of astronomy at the Ecole Polytechnique, the study of the perturbations of Uranus as a worthwhile research project. Leverrier set out in a very systematic manner: first he examined all the old data and found them to be correct; then he considered all possible perturbations due to Saturn and Jupiter; next he considered all possible alternatives, such as some deviation from Newton's law of gravitation, a collision with a comet, etc. Only when he was satisfied that none of these could explain the perturbations did he consider the possibility of the existence of an unknown planet. It had to be a planet outside the orbit of Uranus, since otherwise it would also affect the orbits of Saturn and Jupiter, which were satisfactory. Guided in part by an empirical law of Johann Titius and Johann Bode (discussed in the next section) predicting a further planet, Leverrier thought that the unknown planet would be more than twice the distance of Uranus from the sun. Leverrier then carried out the rather complicated calculation that Adams had made about a year earlier. But since he was more experienced in academic matters, he published his results (he also published some of his preliminary conclusions). When Airy saw a copy of the paper, he was astonished to see that the predicted position agreed quite well with the one Adams had given. Slowly the wheels began to spin. Both Adams (who had continued his work) and Leverrier improved their theories, Herschel paid public tribute to them, and Professor Challis at Cambridge began to look for the planet by carrying out a systematic, unhurried sweep of the whole region.

No maps of the sky were available that would show the positions of stars of the tenth magnitude, the apparent magnitude of the suspected planet. Therefore the sensible thing to do was to catalogue all stars and then to compare the observations to see whether a star had moved. If it had, it would be the planet. It is strange that nobody in England or France thought of doing the obvious, namely, pointing the telescope at the position where, according to Leverrier and Adams's predictions, a planet existed. If they had, the planet would have appeared as a disk of some apparent size, albeit small, or as a point if it were a distant star. In 1846 Dr. J. G. Galle, head of the Berlin Observatory, did exactly that and found Neptune the same night that he received Leverrier's letter telling him where to look. He was also more fortunate than his colleagues in England because he had a star chart of the area with which to compare his observations. When Challis received the news, he realized that he had already seen the new planet after four days of observation and that he had neglected to "examine or map the observation," which would have given him the credit for the discovery. Only weeks later, Lassell—the future discoverer of Uranus's Ariel and Umbriel—found Triton, one of Neptune's two satellites. The discovery of Nereid, the second one, had to wait more than a hundred years until Kuiper found it in 1949.

Lassell might even have discovered Neptune, for he had received notification of Adams's work from William R. Dawes, a noted observer, two weeks prior to Galle's discovery. Unfortunately he had sprained an ankle and could not make his observations. (It is perhaps strange that Dawes did not bother to look for the planet himself.)

Just as in the case of Uranus, Neptune had been seen previously by several observers. In particular, J. J. Lalande had seen Neptune on two successive nights in 1795, but he considered the first observation erroneous and did not report it; of course such a discovery would have been only an accidental reward and not the great achievement it was.

A Lick Observatory photograph taken with the 120-inch telescope showing Neptune and the larger of its two satellites, Triton, indicated by the arrow. Because it takes Neptune nearly 165 years to complete a revolution, the planet has not yet been observed through one complete round trip and will not return to the place where it was discovered until 2011.

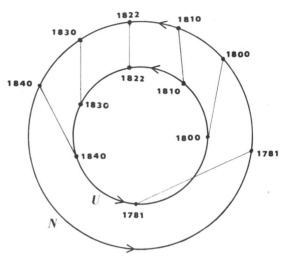

Relative positions of Uranus (U) and Neptune (N) during the period 1781 to 1840. Before 1822 Neptune was ahead of Uranus, tending to pull it; in 1822 they were in conjunction, and while the perturbing force would affect Uranus's distance from the sun, it would not affect its place in the orbit. After 1822 Neptune was behind Uranus, drawing it back.

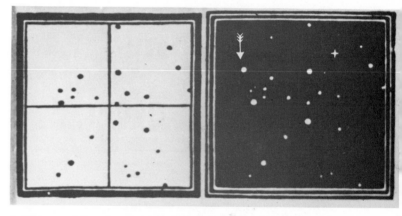

At left is part of the stellar map used by J. G. Galle and his colleague Heinrich d'Arrest. At right is the corresponding part of the sky with Neptune, the planet they discovered in 1846, indicated by an arrow. It clearly does not appear in the star map on the left. The position predicted by Leverrier is indicated on the right side by a small cross.

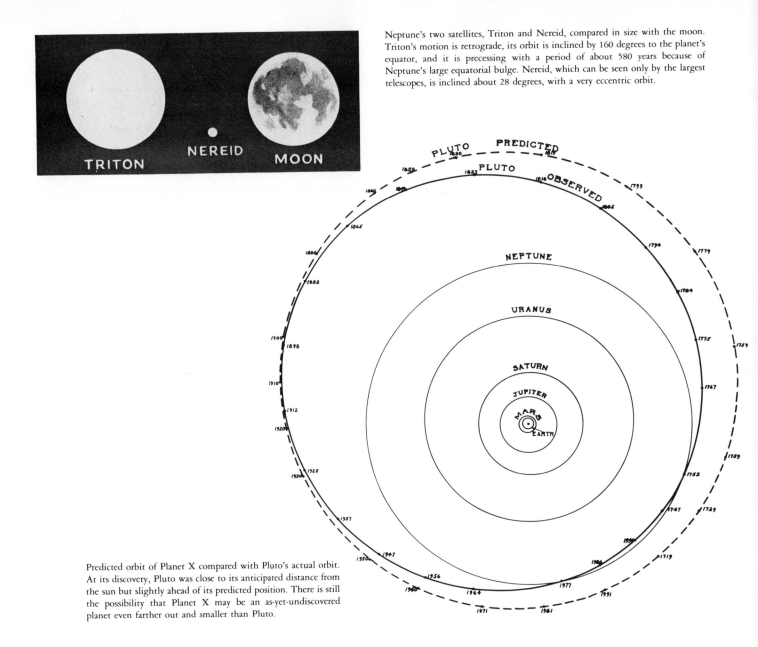

Neptune's two satellites, Triton and Nereid, compared in size with the moon. Triton's motion is retrograde, its orbit is inclined by 160 degrees to the planet's equator, and it is precessing with a period of about 580 years because of Neptune's large equatorial bulge. Nereid, which can be seen only by the largest telescopes, is inclined about 28 degrees, with a very eccentric orbit.

Predicted orbit of Planet X compared with Pluto's actual orbit. At its discovery, Pluto was close to its anticipated distance from the sun but slightly ahead of its predicted position. There is still the possibility that Planet X may be an as-yet-undiscovered planet even farther out and smaller than Pluto.

The discovery of Neptune, or, more precisely, the prediction of its existence and position, was a great achievement; it is only fair that the credit should go to Leverrier and Adams. It was Adams who did the calculation first, although Leverrier—no less brilliant—pushed it through to the ultimate discovery. No unfortunate controversy arose, as was the case with Newton and Leibnitz over the invention of the calculus. On the contrary, in recounting the history of the discovery in the memoirs of the Royal Astronomical Society, Adams is scrupulous in crediting Leverrier: "his researches led to the actual discovery of the planet by Dr. Galle."

The discovery of Neptune spurred astronomers to look for planets even more distant. To discover such a planet, if it existed, became far more difficult. Perturbations on the orbit of Neptune could not be used, since that planet had been seen only over a small range of its 165-year orbit.

Instead, the small remaining discrepancies between the observed and the predicted positions of Uranus had to be used after all perturbations by the known planets (Neptune, Jupiter, and Saturn) had been taken into account.

Such a calculation was carried out by Percival Lowell (1855–1916) who predicted the existence of "Planet X" with a mass seven times that of the earth and forty-three times its distance from the sun. A systematic photographic search initiated by Lowell in 1905 proved unsuccessful. Planet X could not be found.

While Lowell was only a year out of Harvard, Giovanni Schiaparelli in 1877 had carried out extensive observations of Mars and allegedly noted a complicated pattern of straight lines on the face of the planet. These he called *canali* (channels), but a mistranslation rendered them "canals." This fact, combined with their supposedly straight-line character, suggested a manmade structure and

Percival Lowell (1855-1916). One of the best-known astronomers of the late nineteenth century came from a distinguished New England family. Financially independent, he traveled extensively in Japan and Korea after graduating from Harvard College in 1876. Guided in part by Schiaparelli's work on the "canals" of Mars, he set up an observatory especially for the study of planets, in particular, Mars. Lowell Observatory in Flagstaff, Arizona, has become one of the most famous astronomical institutions in the world. In addition to his work on Mars, Lowell must be credited with predicting the existence of Pluto, a prediction that was beautifully borne out at the Lowell Observatory some twenty years after his death. In this rare photograph Lowell is seen at the eyepiece of the 24-inch Clark refractor at Lowell Observatory.

started the belief in life on Mars. Lowell carried this idea much further and with the help of an 18-inch refracting telescope (later with a 24-inch one) took thousands of photographs, many of which were supposed to show the "canals." He was so convinced of there being some kind of life on Mars, which he described vividly, that he found many adherents, especially among laymen. Other observers also observed regular markings but did not ascribe to them the origin Lowell favored. As more observations were made and maps were drawn up, most astronomers began to doubt the existence of life on Mars, at least in a form similar to ours. (If life does exist on Mars, it is likely to be confined to a low form of plant life necessitated by the extreme temperatures and sparse environment.) The red planet is still a mystery and the unraveling of that mystery may result from interplanetary spaceflights. Experiments conducted by Viking 1 and 2 (see Chapter IX) failed to demonstrate conclusively the existence or absence of life on Mars. Early indications had to be discounted, and it is generally believed that unusual chemical processes were responsible for some of the positive results of some of these experiments.

On August 11, 1877, Asaph Hall of the Washington Observatory found a small satellite of Mars and a few days later a second one. They were called Deimos (Fear) and Phobos (Panic); they are extremely small–Phobos is about 10 miles in diameter and Deimos is half that. They are remarkable for their close proximity to Mars and for their rapid motion; the closer one, Phobos, rotates even faster than the planet itself.

The search for Planet X was interrupted by Lowell's death in 1916, but the tradition had been set at the Lowell Observatory that he founded. Clyde Tombaugh, who was too poor to attend college, managed to get a job as an assistant at the observatory in 1929. He knew that to look for the unknown planet was equivalent to looking for the needle in the haystack. The planet would be so faint that to bring it into view in a telescope would require bringing into view a flood of dim stars. True enough, the planet would be distinguishable by its motion, but being so far from the sun (and the earth), the apparent motion would be extremely slight. Tombaugh used an ingenious method; it consisted in looking practically simultaneously at two photographs of the same part of the sky, taken on different nights. If the pictures showed only stars the two views would appear identical, but a planet–owing to its motion–would appear as if it had darted back and forth. Finally, after more than a year of continuous searching, the discovery of a transNeptunian planet was announced on March 13, 1930–the seventy-fifth anniversary of Lowell's birth and the one hundred forty-ninth anniversary of the discovery of Uranus–at approximately the position predicted by Lowell. It was named Pluto, after the god of the underworld, its astronomical symbol being the interlocked letters P and L, which are also the initials of Percival Lowell.

In 1658 Christopher Wren had summed up the perplexing appearance of Saturn.

For Saturn alone stands apart from the pattern of the remaining celestial bodies, and shows so many discrepant phases, that hitherto it has been doubted whether it is a globe connected to two smaller globes or whether it is a spheroid provided with two conspicuous cavities or, if you like, spots, or whether it represents a kind of vessel with handles on both sides, or finally, whether it is some other shape.

It will be remembered that it was Galileo who first saw Saturn through his telescope. As he described it to Belisario Vinta, secretary to the Grand Duke of Tuscany, it appeared as "a composite of three [stars], the middle one being three times larger than the two lateral ones." He discounted other observations–such as those by Scheiner, who had seen the planet in the form of an oval– as being a result of the poor resolving power of the telescope. He was somewhat surprised when, after some time, the two outer bodies disappeared and the planet appeared as a single sphere. Undaunted, he predicted their eventual return, taking them as two moons, similar to the ones he had discovered in the case of Jupiter. It remained

Lowell Observatory.

MARS—1905.

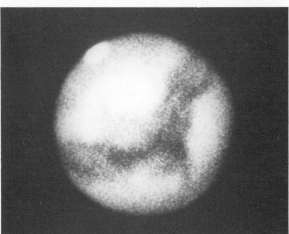

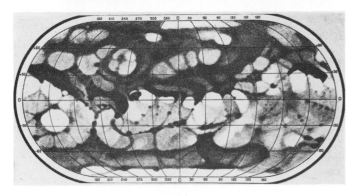

The "canals" first noticed by Schiaparelli in 1877 from the Observatory in Milan have been interpreted as artificial structures by some observers, in particular by Lowell. In this map, drawn in 1901, they appear as more or less straight thin lines cutting the Martian surface in all directions. At the intersections of such "canals," small round spots were noted and were considered to be "oases," which led Lowell to the theory that the canals were the work of Martians irrigating the land.

Mars is about one-half the size of the earth. It also has a smaller mean density, so that an object weighing 10 pounds on Earth would weigh only 3.8 pounds on Mars. Its days and nights are about the same length as those of Earth, but its seasons are about twice as long as ours, because of its longer period of revolution, about twice that of the earth. Its polar caps, which are deposits of ice or frost, change in size with the seasons. Mars has an atmosphere— as evidenced by dark bands near the polar caps during their melting in the spring—and shows that some moisture can remain on the surface, which would not be the case if there were no atmospheric pressure. Cloudlike hazes, obliterating the surface features, have also been observed. Recent findings by Viking I and II indicated the presence of nitrogen and oxygen, but according to latest judgments they do not signify the existence of life.

This chart made by Eugene M. Antoniadi using the 32-inch refractor of the Meudon Observatory in France shows that the canals are composed of small mottlings and dark patches. Only when viewed with an instrument of inferior quality do they appear as a continuous structure, just as a number of closely spaced dots will appear as a single line when seen from a distance. Later observations by Earl Carl Slipher of the Lowell Observatory do show "canals" and "oases," but not as the hairline structures indicated in Lowell's drawings. It is now fairly certain that the canals are not artificial waterways or irrigated land but their true nature remains a mystery.

an open question whether the two outer bodies were satellites or whether Saturn itself consisted of three bodies moving in unison. Johnn Georg Locher, a student of Scheiner, preferred the first possibility since it permitted periods independent of that of Saturn in its epicycle, while if they all moved together the epicycle motion would necessarily fix the periods. In either case, the phenomenon could still be explained satisfactorily by the Ptolemaic system.

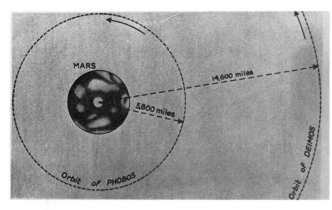

Mars's satellites Phobos and Deimos revolve around the planet (7 hours, 39 minutes and 1 day, 6 hours, 18 minutes respectively) in almost circular orbits, only 1 or 2 degrees inclined to Mars's equatorial plane. A study of their variation in brightness shows that like the moon they always keep the same side turned toward the planet.

The Zeiss blink microscope used by Clyde Tombaugh. The observer is able to look through the eyepiece and see rapidly alternating superimposed views of the same star field on two photographic plates. The succession is so rapid that the eye sees only one picture unless an object on the plates has moved. It then appears to jump back and forth. ▶

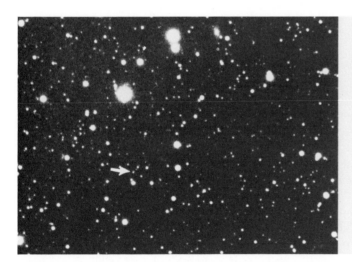

These photographs show the same star field taken on successive nights. The position of Pluto is indicated by an arrow, and it can be seen that it has shifted. When viewed through the blink microscope, it would therefore appear to "jump" backward and forward.

Pluto has an exceptional orbit, which is eccentric and inclined at an angle of 17 degrees to the plane of the other planets. Its orbit even cuts Neptune's, but because of their different inclinations, there is no danger of a collision. In the diagram, Pluto's orbit is the outer one, inclined to the plane defined by the two other planets shown. A is the aphelion; N and N' are nodal points. Pluto is less than half the size of the earth, and there is some speculation that it may have been a Neptune satellite that for some reason moved into an orbit of its own. It is the most puzzling member of the sun's family.

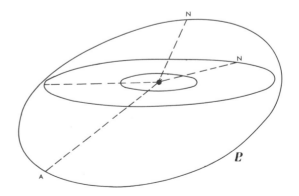

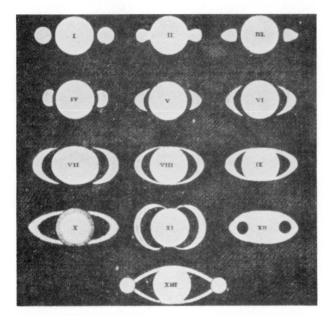

This illustration from Christian Huygens's *Systema Saturnium* shows some early drawings of Saturn. Galileo was the first to announce the apparent existence of two small stars on either side of the main body (I). He later also noticed a form with two "handles" (similar to VIII). Scheiner (1614) suggested II and Riccioli (1641 or 1643) returned to III. Hevelius in his *Selenographia* (1647) speculated on forms IV-VII. Riccioli in 1648-50 seemed to concur (VIII, IX). Divini (1646-1648) has X, while Fontana (1636) suggested XI. Figure XII is one of Gassendi's observations (1638), but had already been postulated by Biancani (1616). Fontana and others in Rome came closest to the actual shape with XIII.

The relative sizes of all but one of Saturn's satellites as compared with the moon. Titan (VI), which is larger than the moon, is the only satellite in the solar system known to have an atmosphere, but since that is composed of methane, a deadly gas, it is hardly conducive to life as we know it. Of the others, only Iapetus (VIII) and Rhea (V) are easily discernible in a telescope. Hyperion (VII) and Phoebe (IX) have an eccentric orbit, and Phoebe is retrograde. It was originally thought that only Mimas (I), Enceladus (II), Tethys (III), and Dione (IV) were responsible for the gaps seen between Saturn's rings. The existence of such a gap led to the discovery of Janus (X) in 1966 (not shown here), which is the same size as Phoebe but the closest to Saturn.

For some time nothing spectacular happened, but when Galileo observed Saturn again in 1616 he must have been shocked, for the planet now seemed to have two handles. Pictures—such as those of Pierre Gassendi, who carried out systematic telescopic observations—with or without handles, alone or with adjoining bodies, spherical or oval, began to appear. As telescopes improved, so did the appearance and reliability of the drawings, but the problem of how to explain the changing appearance of Saturn remained and became even more difficult.

Christian Huygens provided the solution. Building himself a more powerful telescope than had been in use before, he found the first genuine satellite of Saturn in 1656, later called Titan. Its appearance was quite different from the "two neighboring appendages clinging to Saturn." He concealed his hypothesis in the form of an anagram, deciphered as: "It is encircled by a thin, flat ring, nowhere attached, and inclined to the ecliptic."

The phases of this ring, as described in his *Systema Saturnium,* explains the different appearances of the planet. But the nature of the ring itself still posed some unsolved questions.

Jean Dominique Cassini would provide some of the answers. He was a professor of astronomy at Bologna, but upon the invitation of Louis XIV he moved to France in 1668. Five years later, a naturalized citizen, he became director of the Paris Observatory. Cassini discovered four additional satellites of Saturn and, more important, a separation of the rings, which is known as the Cassini division. His son, Jacques, also a noted astronomer, suggested that the rings were composed of small particles. Apparently this suggestion was not taken too seriously at the time because Herschel considered the rings to be made up of solid material—two great halos revolving around the planet. Herschel did notice an inner crepe ring but did not report its existence. It was also found by Galle and reported, but for some reason it remained unnoticed until it was rediscovered by Dawes and others in 1850. Herschel found two more satellites of Saturn, and the eighth was seen by both Lassell and Bond; the ninth, and last, was seen by E. C. Pickering of the Harvard College Observatory in 1898.

James Clerk Maxwell—the creator of the electromagnetic theory of light and an eminent mathematical physicist who received the Adams prize in 1856 for his paper "On the Stability of the Motion of Saturn's Rings"—showed that the rings could not be solid bands because such an unsymmetrical distribution of mass could not be stable for long. He concluded that the only ring system possible was one composed of an indefinite number of unconnected particles (solid or fluid) revolving around the planet at different velocities (in accordance

Huygens suggested that Saturn is surrounded by a thin ring. During the course of a revolution that ring will appear in different positions or phases, which then give rise to the various views of the planet (such as the appearance of handles). Twice in the course of a revolution (B and D) the plane of the ring passes very close to the earth (E) and the sun and therefore it will not be visible. Near these two positions, at Q and R, S and T, the ring appears much foreshortened and will give the appearance of two handles or arms projecting from the main body of Saturn. Still farther, at K and L, O and N, the ring appears wider and the opening between the ring and the planet becomes visible. Finally, at A and C, the ring is seen at its widest.

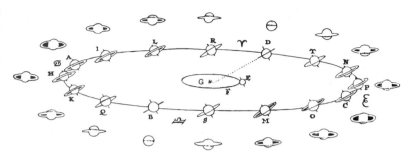

Saturn, the second largest planet of the solar system, is nine times larger in diameter than the earth. Its rotation about its axis (inclined by nearly 27 degrees to the ecliptic) is very fast—10 hours and 17 minutes (similar to that of Jupiter), resulting in a considerable flattening at the poles. Its period of revolution is almost thirty years. Saturn's most spectacular feature, of course, is its rings. There are, in fact, several, each rotating with a different angular velocity (the rate of change of the angular position of a rotating body). The brightest and broadest is the central or bright ring. It is surrounded by the outer ring. The gap, between these two rings, called the Cassini division after its discoverer, is caused by the perturbing influence of Mimas, as well as that of some of the other satellites. A particle between the rings would have an orbital period exactly one-half that of Mimas and therefore would feel its gravitational attraction every second revolution. This gravitational effect, which is cumulative, would eventually force the particle out of that region; this process would produce the gap. This explanation was developed by Daniel Kirkwood, who also explained similar gaps in the distribution of the minor planets. There is a third, fainter, inner ring, the crepe ring. Additional but smaller gaps between parts of the three main rings also exist and are produced by the perturbing influences of the other inner satellites. It was the existence of such a secondary gap that gave rise to the discovery of Janus, the innermost satellite, by Audouin Dollfus in 1966.

James Clerk Maxwell (1831–79), a descendant of the Clerks, a well-known Scottish family. He was graduated from Trinity College in Cambridge in 1854 and plunged into original work, presenting several papers to the Cambridge Philosophical Society. When the chair of Natural Philosophy at Marischal College in Aberdeen fell vacant, he abandoned the life at Trinity for a teaching career, partly to be close to his father. It was during that time that he solved the problem of Saturn's rings. This work led him to the investigation of the kinetic theory of gases, one of his major contributions. Moving to King's College, London, he came into contact with men in his own field of research, notably Faraday and his work on electrical lines of force. Maxwell's dynamical theory of the electromagnetic field was his crowning achievement, combining and unifying the effects of electricity and magnetism in one set of equations for the electromagnetic field.

with their respective distances, obeying Kepler's laws of planetary motion). James Edward Keeler, director of the Allegheny and, later, Lick Observatory, thereafter showed conclusively not only that the rings are composed of particles, but that they exhibited the same composition as meteorites. Even more spectacular was the spectroscopic confirmation of the rings' rotation. Thus, three hundred years after Galileo first noticed something unusual about Saturn, the mystery of the ringed planet was solved.

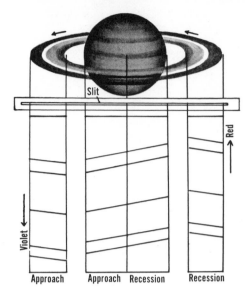

The photograph shows a spectrum of Saturn and its rings, as taken through the slit in the accompanying diagram. To the left and right of the spectrum the spectral lines are displaced from their normal positions, which indicates that the planet and the rings are rotating. This is demonstrated in the diagram: when an object is approaching, it will emit light at a wavelength (as seen by an observer) that appears to be shorter than that of light emitted by a stationary source. On the other hand, if the object is receding, the wavelength of the emitted light seems to be longer. In the first instance there will be a shift toward the violet (short wavelength) part of the spectrum; in the second toward the red (long wavelength). This is known as the Doppler effect, which is important also in determining the speed of an approaching or receding object—in this case to determine the rotational velocity of Saturn and its rings.

SATELLITES OF SATURN				
	Approximate Diameter (miles)	Distance (in thousands of miles)	Revolution Period	Discoverer and Year
Titan	3,000	759	15d 23h 15m	Huygens 1655
Iapetus	700	2,210	79d 22h 4m	Cassini 1671
Rhea	800	327	4d 12h 27m	Cassini 1672
Tethys	600	183	1d 21h 18m	Cassini 1684
Dione	600	234	2d 17h 42m	Cassini 1684
Mimas	300	115	22h 37m	Herschel 1789
Enceladus	400	148	1d 8h 53m	Herschel 1789
Hyperion	300	920	21d 7h 39m	Bond * 1848
Phoebe	100	8,034	523d 13h †	Pickering 1898
Janus	100	100	17h 59m	Dollfus 1966

* Although W. C. Bond is credited with the discovery, the satellite had also been found independently at the same time by Lassell.

† Phoebe has a retrograde motion, included here.

4. A Praiseworthy Relation

In 1772 Johann Daniel Titius, a professor of mathematics at Wittenberg, translated and published a German edition of *Contemplation de la Nature* by the famous natural philosopher Charles Bonnet. This in itself would not be remarkable were it not for the fact that the translator inserted several notes within the text so that only comparison with the French original could identify its source. One addition, in particular, was to be of utmost importance for the future development of astronomy and gave Titius a place in history:

Taking the distance from the sun to Saturn as 100 units:

- Mercury's distance from the sun is 4 of these units
- Venus's distance from the sun is
  4 plus 3 = 7 of these units
- Earth's distance from the sun is
  4 plus 6 = 10 of these units

- Mars's distance from the sun is
      4 plus 12 = 16 of these units.

The distance for the above planets is 4 units *plus* a number that is double the one by which the distance of the previous planet exceeds 4, such as 3, 6, 12, 24, etc. Hence, the next planet should be at a distance of

- 4 plus 24 = 28 of these units

but no known planet was situated at that distance.

Titius remarks that the Heavenly Builder could not have left an empty space and suggests that it is occupied by the then not-yet-discovered satellites of Mars, and continues:

- Jupiter's distance from the sun is
      4 plus 48 = 52 of these units
- Saturn's distance from the sun is
      4 plus 96 = 100 of these units.

Indeed, a praiseworthy relation. The same year, young Johann Elert Bode published his second edition of *Anleitung zur Kenntnis des gestirnten Himmels (Introduction to the Study of the Starry Sky),* in which the above relation—practically in the same words—appears as a footnote. The *Anleitung* became an important and widely read book, and during Bode's lifetime it appeared in nine editions. Only in the later editions, especially the common ninth one, did Bode acknowledge that he had seen Titius's translation before publishing his own second edition. Thus, what is commonly referred to as the Titius-Bode law—and sometimes only as Bode's law of planetary distances—is really the contribution of an otherwise unknown professor of mathematics. Titius seemed to have lost interest in the praiseworthy relation, but Bode, who later became director of the Berlin Observatory and editor of the famous astronomical yearbook *Astronomisches Jahrbuch,* took the law quite seriously. He did not think that the missing place was occupied by a mere satellite of Mars but by a major planet yet to be found. But not much attention had been paid to the Titius-Bode law until Herschel's discovery of Uranus. Uranus's distance (taking the sun-Saturn again as 100) turned out to be 192, only a 2 percent deviation from the predicted 4 plus 192 = 196 units.

Now the search for the missing planet started in earnest. Baron Franz Xaver von Zach, the court astronomer at Gotha, hit upon the scheme of dividing the sky into 24 zones, each to be searched by an astronomer. Before the plan could be put into practice, the Italian astronomer Giuseppe Piazzi independently on January 1, 1801, observed what seemed to be a new star—or possibly

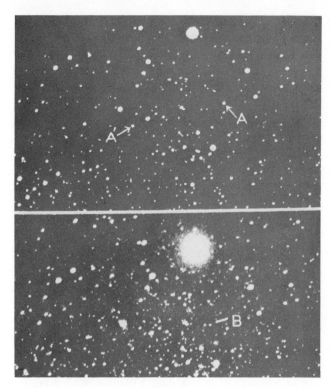

Discovery of a minor planet. The upper photograph shows a star field with an asteroid that has moved from A to A′ from one day to the next. The picture has to be scrutinized carefully to note the motion of the asteroid. The lower photograph is a time exposure, with the minor planet leaving a definite trail, indicated by B. As a result of the increased aperture and exposure time, not only are more fainter stars seen, but stars of smaller magnitudes appear to be brighter, as evidenced by the central top spot in both photographs.

a comet. Excited by his discovery, he communicated it to his colleagues Bode and Von Zach; the new star was to be named Ceres Ferdinandea in honor of King Ferdinand of Sicily, the founder of the observatory at Palermo. When Bode received the communication, he was sure that Ceres was the missing planet between Mars and Jupiter; however, by that time it was too close to the sun and could not be observed. Piazzi had been able to make only a few observations, too close together to determine the orbit with any certainty. It would be several months until the "star" could be seen again, and by that time the search would have to start afresh; Ceres, indeed, was a "missing" planet, a minor planet or, its more common name today, an asteroid, the first to be discovered and the largest known to date.

Johann Karl Friedrich Gauss was undoubtedly the greatest mathematician of his time, and he demonstrated his prowess at an early age. In an arithmetic class he was asked to add a large set of numbers, each number differing by the same amount. Büttner, the schoolmaster, of course knew the formula that would give the result within minutes, but his ten-year-olds did not and would thus be kept busy for a desirably long time. To Büttner's amazement and annoyance, Gauss within seconds handed in his slate, on which was a single number. Gauss later loved to tell that his had been the only correct answer. (Taking the sum of the numbers 1, 2, and up to 100 the first and the last or 1 plus 100, and the second and the next-to-last, or 2 plus 99 and continuing this way, all add up to the same number: 101. Since there are 50 such pairs the result is simply 101 × 50 = 5050.) The method works even if the series does not start with 1, and if the difference is larger than 1 but the same throughout; the method is an arithmetic progression and Gauss at the age of ten had discovered it for himself. It was fortunate for Gauss that Büttner had a young assistant, Johann Martin Bartels, who had a flair for mathematics. The two boys began to help each other and they built a lifetime friendship. Through Bartels, Gauss was brought to the attention of Carl Wilhelm Ferdinand, Duke of Brunswick. The duke, a generous man, was impressed with the modest genius and arranged for his future schooling.

Gauss was a prolific worker to whom ideas came so rapidly that he had time to record only a fraction of them, some appearing in rather cryptic form in his scientific diary. This was a great pity because when the diary was finally published, and understood, it turned out that he had worked out many of the results that were rediscovered by some of his lofty successors.

His first great work was on arithmetical researches, *Disquisitiones Arithmeticae,* published in 1799 as a doctoral thesis and paid for by the duke, to whom it was dedicated. It was a masterpiece but hard reading, even for experts, and has been called the "book of seven seals."

When Ceres was first discovered by Piazzi, Gauss was twenty-four and in the midst of his theory of algebraic numbers, but he became fascinated with finding the now-missing planet. At the age of eighteen he had developed his method of least squares, which made it possible to determine an orbit as long as it is assumed that it is a conic section.

Although mathematicians considered Gauss's occupation with "a couple of clods of dirt" (the planets) a disaster, it was a boon for astronomy. Gauss showed that mathematics and physical science complement each other and can be served by the same man. This practical work also brought Gauss instant recognition as a first-class mathematician and won his independence from the duke.

Gauss predicted the positions of Ceres, which, one year after its original discovery, was found by Heinrich Wilhelm Matthäus Olbers and Von Zach. The mean distance from the sun, as calculated by Gauss, was 27.67 (the Titius-Bode prediction was 28). This was the missing "planet" and apparent proof of the correctness of the Titius-Bode relation. Only a few months before, the German philosopher Hegel had "logically" proved that the number of planets could not exceed seven.

Gauss now devoted most of his time to astronomical calculations. In 1809 he published his second masterpiece, *Theory of the Motion of the Heavenly Bodies Revolving Around the Sun in Conic Sections.*

Carl Friedrich Gauss (1777–1855). This son of a simple laborer not only became the leading mathematician of his time, but made important contributions in astronomy and physics as well. He found a way to calculate the orbits of asteroids, pioneered the theory of electromagnetism, and invented the heliotrope by which signals could be transmitted rapidly by reflected light. As a boy, he had even concerned himself with the difficult task of measuring the curvature of surfaces and conceived of non-Euclidean geometry—concepts that lay dormant until Albert Einstein used them in his theory of gravitation. In 1807 he was appointed the first director of the Göttingen Observatory, which he helped make the most influential scientific center in Europe. He is shown here in a portrait by Professor Bierman (from an original by Christian Jensen).

A few months after Ceres had been rediscovered, Olbers found another asteroid, Pallas, which had a mean distance of 26.70. This hardly fit into the praiseworthy relation, unless these small planets were the fragments of a major planet that had somehow exploded. In that case there should be more minor planets.

When Karl Ludwig Harding found Juno in 1804 and Olbers discovered Vesta in 1807, this explanation seemed to be borne out, and the Titius-Bode relation again was validated. It took some time until a fifth minor planet, Astraea, was found by Karl Hencke in 1845; subsequently many more were discovered, and by 1890 more than 300 were known.

The method of observation had changed, and instead of trying to locate the position from two different observations, one makes a simple time exposure. The image will form a trail and appear as a short line on the photographic emulsion.

By this method thousands of such trails have been seen, some quite accidentally while observers were looking for other objects. A survey in the 1969 edition of the *Minor Planet Ephemeris* lists 1,735 minor planets together with their orbital data. Minor planets are usually named after figures in Greek mythology, but one also finds names such as Washingtonia, Hooveria, and Rockefellia. The 1000th minor planet was named Piazzia, after the discoverer of Ceres and the 1001th is called Gaussia, after the man who calculated Ceres's orbit, making it possible to find it again.

Most asteroids have a nearly circular orbit, but some, such as Adonis and Hidalgo, have quite eccentric orbits. Hidalgo is of special interest because its orbit crosses even

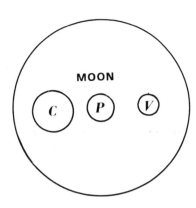

Relative sizes of asteroids Ceres (C), Pallas (P), and Vesta (V), the first three discovered, compared with the moon.

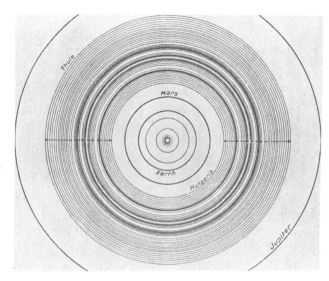

Similar to the Cassini divisions in Saturn rings are the gaps in the almost continuous distribution of the asteroids between Mars and Jupiter. Daniel Kirkwood, the discoverer of these gaps, attributed their existence to the perturbing influence of Jupiter. These gaps occur at distances where the period of an asteroid would be a simple fraction of Jupiter's period. Thus the cumulative effect of Jupiter's gravitational force would eventually draw an asteroid out of that orbit.

that of Jupiter. That planet has a particular influence on the motion of the asteroid, according to two accounts. In 1866 Daniel Kirkwood noted the existence of definite gaps in the distribution of asteroids between Mars and Jupiter. These gaps occurred at distances that are related to that of Jupiter. For example, there is a gap at about five-eighths the distance of Jupiter from the sun. An asteroid at that distance would have a period exactly one-half that of Jupiter, and hence, after two complete revolutions, would be near it. The attraction of Jupiter, always in the same direction, would eventually draw any asteroid out of that area, leaving a gap. Similar "Kirkwood gaps" would occur at distances where the period would be one-third, two-fifths, three-fifths, and so on, of Jupiter's. In 1772 Lagrange found that there exist two points on Jupiter's orbit that are in equilibrium both with Jupiter and the sun. Any asteroid near either of these points could remain there nearly indefinitely and would revolve around the sun in the same orbit as Jupiter and with the same period of revolution. Indeed, fourteen such objects, called the Trojans, have been found so far.

On the other hand, there are asteroids that have extremely small orbits and are known to pass close to the earth. Icarus has the smallest orbit and the largest eccentricity; it passed within about 4 million miles of the earth during its passage in 1968.

On October 18 and 19, 1977 Charles T. Kowal of the Hale Observatories observed a slow-moving object of stellar appearance on exposure with the 148-inch (122cm) Schmidt telescope. A prediscovery image of the same object was identified by Tom Gehrels using plates taken October 11, and the trail was also seen on November 3 and 4. From these observations preliminary calculation showed that the object is about 1.5 billion miles from the earth, which puts it between Saturn and Uranus. Because of the sharpness of its photographic images it was first thought that the new object, named Chiron, might be a mini-planet. The size and brightness of the light (magnitude 18 to 19) indicate that the object has a diameter between 100 and 400 miles. Objects of that size do exist in the solar system and are known as asteroids,

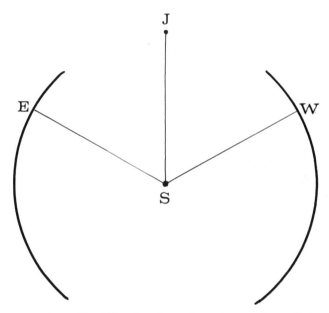

A group of asteroids, orbiting about the sun but at the same time oscillating about two points of equilibrium—E being the eastern point and W the western. Both points are situated on Jupiter's orbit (as are the asteroids themselves) and are nearly as distant from Jupiter (J) as they are from the sun (S). It is probable that they were originally satellites of Jupiter but "escaped" and found their own orbits. The group is known as the Trojans; it has been customary to name those east of Jupiter after the Greek warriors and those west of it for those of Troy, in honor of the famous Homeric epic.

and as a possible asteroid Kowal's object received the preliminary designation 1977 UB from the Minor Planet Center.

The original trail was less than half a degree long, which made it impossible to determine the orbit with any accuracy; efforts to find prediscovery images were

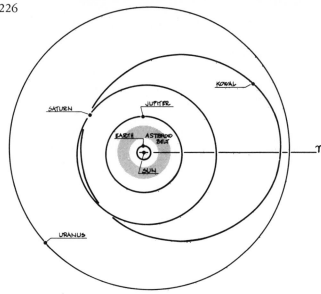

On the nights of October 18 and 19, 1977, thirty-seven-year-old Charles T. Kowal of the Hale Observatories was surveying the sky with the 48-inch Schmidt telescope. When he examined photographic plates made in those observations he discovered a slow-moving object that may turn out to be our tenth planet. A prediscovery image of the same object was identified by Tom Gehrels using plates taken October 11 and 12, and the trail was also seen on November 3 and 4. From these observations preliminary calculations show that the object is about 1.5 billion miles from the earth, which puts it between Saturn and Uranus. It seems to orbit in the same plane as the other planets, but the exact shape of the orbit cannot be determined without further observations. If it were to follow a roughly circular orbit, like most other planets, it would take 70 years to make a complete revolution; if the orbit were more elliptic it would take 115 years. The size and brightness (magnitude 18 to 19) indicate that the object has a diameter between 100 and 400 miles—about one-tenth the size of Mercury, the smallest known planet. Objects of that size do exist in the solar system and are known as asteroids. However, they usually occur in groups and have been seen farther than Jupiter (these asteroids are called Trojans). If the new object is, indeed, an asteroid one would expect to find others in its vicinity. On the other hand, it may be a planet in its own right, albeit a mini-planet. Another question that has to be answered is how the object got into the solar system and, in particular, into its orbit. It is too far from either Saturn or Uranus to have been one of their satellites; more likely it came from outside the solar system and was "captured" by the gravitational field of these planets. At present all this is speculation and we must be content to record the new discovery as "slow moving object—Kowal." The illustration shows the object's position as of December 25, 1977.

successful when Kowal was able to identify his object on plates taken September 10 and 11, 1969. This increased the length of the observed arc to 29°. Based on these observations Kowal's object has an orbital period of 50.7 years (the periods of Saturn and Uranus are 29½ and 84 years respectively). Its distance from the sun ranges between 8.5 a.u. (1.3 billion km) at perihelion to 18.9 a.u. (2.8 billion km) at aphelion. This corresponds to a strongly elliptic orbit with eccentricity 0.38, larger than that of Pluto and most of the known asteroids.

Is 1977 UB a minor planet or a comet? Asteroids usually occur in groups, and the previously known asteroid with the largest orbit is Hidalgo, which at aphelion is just outside the orbit of Saturn. If 1977 UB is an asteroid one would expect to find others in the vicinity, and it might be the first of a group of trans-Saturnian asteroids. On the other hand, comets are known to have large eccentricities and to come from the outer regions of the solar system. At those distances they show little or no nebulosity and are virtually indistinguishable from minor planets on the basis of appearance. In 1996 Chiron alias 1977 UB will be at perihelion (its previous perihelion should have occurred in 1945) and at that time may show signs of cometary activity at present unrecognizable—or it may turn out to be a minor planet after all.

Toro, which was first discovered in 1948 by C. A. Wirtanen at the Lick Observatory, has a period of 1.6 years and a distance from the sun varying from 0.77 to 1.96 A.U.; it too has a large eccentricity. It crosses the orbit of Mars and Earth and comes within 5/100 A.U. of the orbit of Venus. When the orbital periods of Earth, Venus, and Toro are compared, it is found that Toro completes five revolutions around the sun while the earth completes eight and Venus thirteen of their respective circuits. Toro passes close to the earth in January of one year and in August four years later. At those times it is in

The majority of asteroids describe nearly circular orbits, but some are quite eccentric. The orbit of Toro (asteroid 1685) not only crosses the earth's but skims Venus's. The resulting perturbations make it possible to determine Venus's mass. Before the era of space probes, asteroids were useful in determining the astronomical-unit distance of the earth from the sun (one unit is known as A.U. and is roughly equal to 93 million miles). Generally their orbits could be calculated very accurately and hence their distance from the earth—but in A.U. On the other hand, for an asteroid that passed close to the earth, its distance could be found directly by triangulation. Comparing the two results is a way of refining the A.U.

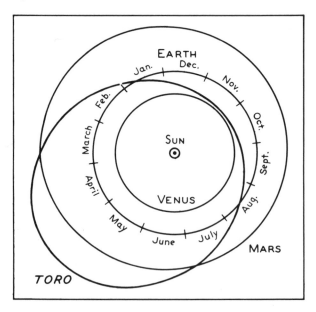

a "capture resonance," which has given rise to headlines in the press describing it as "our second moon" and "a small planetary body that orbits the earth."

The different types and sizes of orbits seriously disrupted the idea of an exploding planet being the cause for the asteroids. Suppose that a shell describing an elliptic orbit suddenly explodes in midair. Its center of mass continues to move exactly along the same orbit traversed

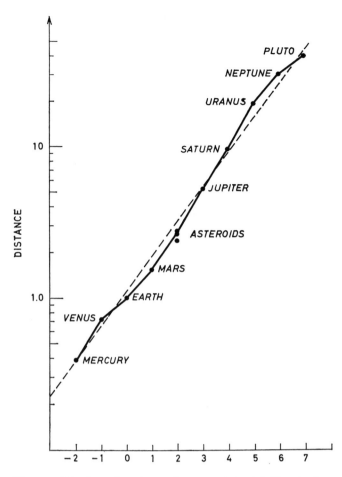

Distances of the planets from the sun (in astronomical units). Note that from their positions we can draw a straight line (shown dashed), indicating the existence of a simple law—based on the inclination of that line. In the original formulation of the Titius-Bode law, the planets were numbered differently, with Venus being 0, the Earth 1, and so on.

Neptune. Both Adams and Leverrier carried out their calculations assuming that the law was valid, using major axes of 37.25 and 36.15 respectively. The predicted value would be $4 + 2 \times 192 = 4 + 384 = 388$ compared with the actual one of 300.7 (taking the sun-Saturn distance as 100). But the law truly broke down with the discovery of Pluto; the predicted distance was almost twice the actual one. As early as 1787 Johann Friedrich Vikarius Wurm (1760–1833) had pointed out that a better fit could be obtained if the two constants in the law were taken to be 3.87 (instead of 4) and 2.93 (instead of 3). This, of course, destroys the simple basis but also introduces some physical features. Wurm was of the opinion that the law should also pertain, perhaps with different constants, for the satellites of the various planets.

In 1913 Mary Blagg used an empirical approach. After much trial and error she found that a good fit could be obtained by using a progression of 1.7275 (instead of 2) multiplied by a periodic function, i.e., one that returns to the same value after some given period. The remarkable fact about her law (and later modifications) is that it not only fits the planets very well but also fits the different satellite systems. Discrepancies still occur, but the question should be asked not why these occur, but why the law holds as well as it does. Only when we understand the origin and evolution of the solar system, will we also know why the planets (and satellites) move in their present orbits.

by the center of the shell before the explosion. Each fragment would describe an orbit of its own, depending on its initial velocity. Since these orbits are ellipses, each fragment would return to its starting point, the place where the explosion occurred. Thus, there should exist some common point through which all asteroids pass sooner or later, if they originated from a planetary breakup. True enough, the different orbits may have been perturbed from their original positions by other planets (Jupiter and Mars) and by their mutual interactions, but the effect would not be very large. Also—this may be a bit of hindsight—the total mass of all the known asteroids is only a fraction of the mass of the earth, hardly the remnants of a major planet. Finally, it is completely unknown where the enormous amount of energy would have come from necessary to break up the unknown planet against its own gravitational field. It seems more likely that the asteroids or minor planets originated together with the other components of the solar system, leaving meteorids to result from their collisions or internal breakup.

Where does all this leave the Titius-Bode law? It received its first major setback with the discovery of

TITIUS-BODE LAW

Planet	n *	Titius Progression		Actual Distance †
Mercury		4	= 4	3.9
Venus	0	4 + 3	= 7	7.2
Earth	1	$4 + 3 \times 2^1$	= 10	10.0
Mars	2	$4 + 3 \times 2^2$	= 16	15.2
Ceres ‡	3	$4 + 3 \times 2^3$	= 28	27.7
Jupiter	4	$4 + 3 \times 2^4$	= 52	52.0
Saturn	5	$4 + 3 \times 2^5$	= 100	95.5
Uranus ‡	6	$4 + 3 \times 2^6$	= 196	192.0
Neptune ‡	7	$4 + 3 \times 2^7$	= 388	300.7
Pluto ‡	8	$4 + 3 \times 2^8$	= 772	395.2

* The successive numbers assigned to the planets (including Ceres). It is the number that determines the power of two in the Titius progression: Distance = $4 + 3 \times (2)^n$. For example, for Mars $n = 2$ so that its distance will be $4 + 3 \times 2 \times 2 = 16$. Agreement is very good up to Uranus but breaks down for Neptune and Pluto.

† All distances for the sake of convenience assume a sun-Earth distance of 10.0. The figure 15.2 for Mars, for example, simply indicates that compared with earth it is roughly one-half farther from the sun, or three-halves the earth-Sun distance.

‡ Not yet discovered when the law was formulated.

BLAGG "LAW" FOR PLANETS			
Planet	n	Calculated Distance in A.U. †	Actual Distance in A.U.
Mercury	−2	0.387	0.387
Venus	−1	0.723	0.723
Earth	0	1.000	1.000
Mars	1	1.524	1.524
Vesta			2.361
Juno	2	2.67	2.670
Pallas			2.767
Ceres			2.767
Jupiter	3	5.200	5.203
Saturn	4	9.550	9.546
Uranus	5	19.23	19.20
Neptune	6	30.13	30.07
Pluto *	7	41.8	39.5

† The distances were calculated based on an empirical law that used 1.7275 instead of the factor 2 in the progression and the number n in the exponent. As seen by comparison with the last column, agreement is quite good.

* Pluto had not yet been discovered when the empirical relation was proposed.

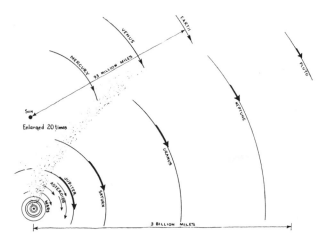

The solar system (with an enlargement of the central portion). Any theory explaining its origin must explain the regularities apparent in the system. The scale of planet sizes is shown in the bottom strip.

5. The Solar System

For thousands of years man has tried to understand the origin of the universe, in particular our own sun and planets—the solar system. Having gone from legends and traditions to scientific explanations, we are still left without a satisfactory theory of our origin.

The arrangement of the planets—revolving around the sun in regular orbits—is convincing evidence that there must have been a definite event behind their origin. Yet their motions themselves pose some interesting questions. With the exception of Pluto, the planets move in orbits that are nearly circular and lie more or less in the same plane. (This gives the picture of a giant carousel, which has been the object of many beautiful models. Those simple constructions soon gave way to elaborate structures faithfully duplicating the motion of planets and stars. The planetarium, whose hemispherical dome serves as a giant screen of the heavens, owes its origin mainly to the pioneering work of Armand N. Spitz, who died in 1971. Spitz, a newspaperman and later director of education at the Franklin Institute in Philadelphia, designed a simple projector using a single light bulb. What started as a hobby became a business venture, and now nearly two out of three planetaria use a Spitz model.)

An eighteenth-century model of the solar system named after the Earl of Orrery. It shows the planets (including the earth) known at the time, together with their satellites. Turning the handle will move the planets around the central sun, giving a visual demonstration of their orbits. Their positions in the sky can be read off an outer dial.

The periods of revolution are by no means uniform but increase steadily from the nearest to the farthest planet in accordance with Kepler's third law. In addition to revolving around the sun, the planets also rotate about their own axes—but with periods that range from hours to days.

Some planets have satellites, ranging from one for Earth to thirteen for Jupiter, whereas others, Mercury and Venus, have none. Some describe eccentric orbits, whereas others are almost circular. They do not all revolve counterclockwise (as seen from the north); one-fifth go in the opposite direction. These irregularities, as well as the origins of meteors, comets, and asteroids, are some of the phenomena that have to be explained by a complete theory of the solar system.

Other aspects also must be explained. Most of the mass of the solar system is concentrated in the sun itself (99.86 percent), with only a tiny fraction contained in the planets (0.135 percent), satellites, and other constituents. The sizes and masses of the planets are irregular but seem to follow some kind of "spindle" distribution, with Jupiter at the center. This particular arrangement led Sir James Jeans (1877–1946) to suppose that a filament of matter had been drawn from the sun, through tidal forces caused by a passing star, and later condensed into the planets. This hypothesis was accepted widely for some time but has now been rejected because of many inconsistencies revealed in mathematical investigations.

On the other hand, most of the solar system's angular momentum, a measure of the rotation, is contained in the planets (as much as 98 percent, although the sun is about 745 times as heavy as all the planets combined). The

The Zeiss Mark VI projector, the heart of the Adler Planetarium in Chicago. It measures 17½ feet in length and weighs 2½ tons. At each end is a metal globe 29 inches in diameter, containing 16 portholes through which the likeness of almost 9,000 stars is cast onto the dome of the theater. One globe depicts the stars of the Northern and the other of the Southern Hemisphere. Additional projectors provide the apparent motion of the sun, the moon, and the five planets visible to the naked eye. The whole instrument may be rotated about three axes to simulate the effect of the earth's daily motion, its precession, and the changes of latitude. Additional projectors depict the Milky Way, variable stars, eclipses, and other effects. A visit to a planetarium gives an inspiring view of the heavens.

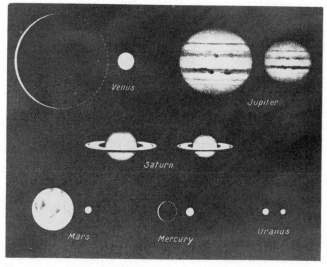

The apparent diameters of the planets change because of variations in their distance from the earth. Shown here are the two extreme positions of six planets (not shown are Neptune and Pluto). Of particular interest are Venus and Mercury, the interior planets, which exhibit phases.

230

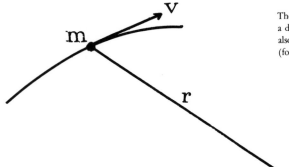

The angular momentum—or the measure of rotation—of a mass (m) rotating about a point (or line) a distance (r) away and moving with a velocity (v) is the product of all of these quantities, but it also depends on the angle between r and v. It will be largest if, unlike here, that angle is 90 degrees (for given values of m, v, and r).

angular momentum of a planet moving in a circular orbit about the sun (which is practically at the mass center of the solar system) is the product of its mass, distance, and speed. The faster-moving inner planets contribute less angular momentum than the outer, more massive ones; Jupiter alone carries about 60 percent of the total angular momentum of the solar system, with the other three giants, Saturn, Uranus, and Neptune, carrying practically all of the balance. And although the sun's mass is a thousand times that of Jupiter, the sun rotates so slowly, once a month, that its angular momentum is only 2 percent of the total.

Kepler's law of equal areas implies that the angular momentum of a planet does not change but remains constant; a planet near the sun will move faster than when it is farther away. No force toward or away from the sun can decrease or increase that angular momentum, and only an external push or drag could provide such a change. The fact that the bulk of the angular momentum is vested in the outer planets, and could have been transferred there from a central core only by some external action, is evidence against the earlier evolutionary theories described below.

The first serious attempt to explain the origin of the solar system was by the eighteenth-century philosopher Immanuel Kant, although Pierre Simon de Laplace in 1796 already presented a similar theory; Laplace's nebular hypothesis was commonly accepted for about a hundred years. According to it, a rotating nebula of gaseous material, flattened because of the rotation, would cool slowly and condense into rings of matter. Further condensation of these rings would form the planets, the center becoming the sun. As attractive as this hypothesis may appear, it is untenable for several reasons. First, there is no mechanism to account for the observed inclined planetary orbits, which would all have to lie in the same plane. More important, however, is that most of the angular momentum would have to be concentrated in (or near) the center to produce the high speed of rotation required to have the rings at distances now occupied by planets. In fact, most of the angular momentum in the solar system at present is not at the center (where the sun

is located) but farther away. Furthermore, Clerk Maxwell showed that a ring of fluid matter, such as that of Saturn, would coalesce into a ring of particles, or planetoids, but not into large planets. At best Kant's proposal could account for the asteroids but not for the rest of the solar system.

Forest Ray Moulton is probably best known for his development about 1900, along with T. C. Chamberlin, a geologist, of the planetesimal hypothesis of the origin of the solar system. This avoided the difficulties over angular momentum encountered by the nebular hypothesis. According to Moulton, the planets owe their existence to a star passing close to the sun, whose gravitational field created tides drawing matter away from the sun. These gases, several times the masses of the planets, were sent spiraling around the passing star. Most of the matter fell back to the sun, but the remainder condensed, with highly elliptic motion, into planetesimals, the larger ones capturing the smaller ones until finally the planets had been formed. The angular momentum of the orbital motion and rotation of the planets and satellites would be provided by the passing star, which consequently transferred some of its angular momentum in the encounter. A modified version of this hypothesis, the tidal theory, by Sir James Jeans (with Sir Harold Jeffreys) has been mentioned above as a spindle arrangement. A long tidal filament is drawn out of the sun by the passing star. The outer part of that spindle escapes into space, while the inner part returns to the sun, with the central portion coalescing into the planets.

Some years later a dispute arose between Jeffreys and Moulton about the authorship of the basic idea, with Jeffreys abandoning the tidal theory and instead suggesting that an actual encounter had taken place between the sun and the passing star; he left the rest of the theory, the formation of the filament and the planets, unchanged.

Henry Norris Russell, the famous American astronomer who later, in 1935, made an important contribution to stellar classification, suggested that the sun had a companion that was struck by the collision and that the planets evolved from the resulting debris. Although both the planetesimal hypothesis and the tidal theory allow for a large part of the angular momentum of the solar system to be vested in the planets themselves, a detailed mathematical analysis failed to give the correct momentum distribution observed. Also, F. Nölke showed that matter drawn out of the sun—a necessary phenomenon in both theories—will dissipate into space

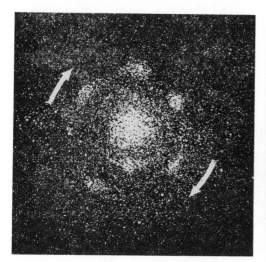
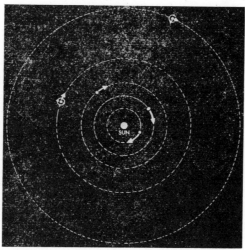

According to Kant (in 1755), the solar system was formed by a condensation or clotting of gas and dust in rotation *(left)*. The clots grew by accretion to form planets and satellites, and the remainder of the nebula contracted to form the sun *(right)*.

long before it can condense into planets. In addition, the low probability of such an "encounter" implies that planetary systems are quite rare and confers on the sun a unique position, which does not seem warranted.

A theory that resembles both Laplace's nebular hypothesis and Descartes's vortex theory mentioned in Chapter V was proposed by Carl Friedrich von Weizsäcker in 1945. He suggested that the planets would be set up within a flattened gaseous envelope rotating about the sun. The material of that rotating disk could derive from the sun by some kind of tidal mechanism as proposed by Moulton and Jeans or as remnants of a cloud that condensed in the sun at an earlier time. The disk would be unstable, some of the material either falling back into the sun or dissipating into space, but part of it would set up internal motion that would be relatively stable. In fact, Weizsäcker was able to show that particles making up the disk would in the course of centuries organize themselves into individual cells rotating about their own individual centers, like whirlpools or eddies, while the whole system would revolve around the sun strung out in concentric rings. Each ring would contain a number of such eddies in increasing number. At the edge of two adjacent rings the eddies belonging to one ring rotate in an opposite direction to those in the neighboring ring; individual eddies would be formed, eventually giving rise to the formation of planetoids and finally planets. These small eddies by a similar process would in turn be responsible for the formation of the satellites. This theory both explains the directional harmony of the revolution and rotation of the planets and predicts distances in good agreement with the Titius-Bode law. But like its predecessors, this theory, too, has serious defects.

The angular momentum acquired by the planets is assumed here to be transferred from the sun by the formation of turbulent vortices. This necessitates that the sun rotate at speeds considerably higher than its present rate of rotation; also, the transfer process would stop if the intrinsic rotation of the sun were equal to its orbital motion, when no more angular momentum could be

transferred—occurring at speeds more than ten times the present rate of rotation. Furthermore, the formation of planets between two giant vortices like so many ball bearings is quite unlikely, especially since no adequate mechanism exists for the necessary condensation of the gaseous matter. Whipple tried to get around this difficulty by assuming that the solar system originated from a rare process in which a condensing cloud of gas and dust happened to carry just the correct amount of angular momentum, which must have been quite small. The dust particles would collide, stick together, and eventually form the planets, and the rapidly collapsing gas in the center would form the sun. The comparative rarity of the occurrence of such a sequence of events makes this dust-cloud hypothesis an improbable candidate for the solar origin.

A similar model was proposed by Andrey Kolmogorov; it formed the basis of Gerard P. Kuiper's theory of protoplanets. Kuiper proposed the existence of a nebula surrounding the sun that contained enough matter to form all the planets. Such a nebula would become unstable under the gravitational action of its various parts on one another and would break up into separate clouds— the protoplanets. Each of these would consist of a solid core surrounded by extensive atmospheres of the lighter elements—hydrogen and helium, as well as ammonia and methane and water vapor. By applying the principles of gravitational stability developed by Edouard Roché (1820–83), Kuiper could show that the planets would form at distances predicted by the Titius-Bode law. What makes the theory untenable is the difficulty of removing the large amount of hydrogen and helium necessary to transform the protoplanets into planets, especially the terrestrial planets (planets that have a composition similar to Earth's, namely Mercury, Venus, and Pluto).

Let us look at the transfer of angular momentum. A hot plasma, a completely ionized gas, which is a good conductor of electric currents, will readily interact with magnetic and induced electric fields that may be present. Mechanical forces resulting from these fields will modify

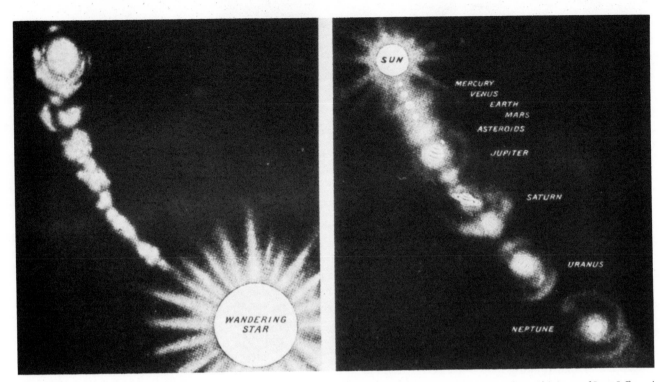

A schematic representation of the encounter theory, including both the planetesimal hypothesis of Chamberlin-Moulton and the tidal theory of Jeans-Jeffreys. A wandering star draws a filament of gas out of the sun *(left),* which eventually condenses into the planets *(right).*

the motion of the gases. Equations governing the behavior of these electric and magnetic fields (electromagnetism) and the motion of the fluids or gases (hydrodynamics) fall into the realm of magnetohydrodynamics (especially important is that the electric and magnetic energy be comparable to that of the gas itself). Its application to cosmic phenomena has been studied and pioneered by Hannes Alfvén who recently received the Nobel Prize in recognition of that work. When the electrical resistance of the gas can be neglected, that is, if the gas is a perfect conductor, the motion of the plasma will follow exactly the lines of force of the magnetic field, or, to put it more picturesquely, the lines of force are "frozen" into the plasma, moving with it. As a result, they add some kind of rigidity to the gas, enabling it to withstand the effect of gravitation and pressure. The lines of force—like elastic threads—wind themselves around a rapidly rotating mass of gas and slow it down. It is this mechanism that was used by Fred Hoyle to account for the transfer of angular momentum from the central sun to the planetary disk.

From recent work on the chemical constitution of the planets a fairly reliable overall picture of their origin seems to emerge. Near the sun one finds planets and asteroids consisting of material that solidifies at comparatively high temperatures, while at larger distances the giant planets are made of substances that vaporize at lower temperatures, indicating that the deciding factor is temperature—determined by the distance from the sun. As the gaseous disk started to condense, the higher temperatures permitted the formation of the heavier terrestrial material while allowing the hydrogen and helium to escape. On the other hand, at distances as far away as Jupiter, and beyond, water could freeze and, farther away, even ammonia and methane, which constitute the bulk of the outer planets Uranus and Neptune. The comets presumably were formed there also in addition containing the available "earthy" material. The satellites may have been formed within their own protoplanets as in Kuiper's theory or, if one follows a theory of accretion, may have been captured as the planets grew from the planetesimals. The origin of the planetary disk itself is still an unsolved problem, as is the material and angular momentum of the planets—the material having come from the sun (before the planets' formation) or from the condensing cloud.

There are two main reasons why it is so difficult to get a detailed and correct picture of the origin and evolution of the solar system. Whatever we know has to be extrapolated to describe conditions that existed millions of years ago. Clearly this permits a large amount of speculation and guesswork, even if it is to some extent based on good observational evidence. Also, although it is fairly certain that there are thousands of stars like our sun, with planets circling them, we are not likely in the near future to learn much about them because of their immense distances. Nevertheless, one can assume that the laws of physics that hold on Earth also are valid in the rest of the universe and have not changed in time. The order that prevails in our solar system is a reflection of the grand design that started it in the beginning from a cloud of gas and dust.

	PHYSICAL DATA FOR THE PLANETS					
Planet	Period of Revolution (years)	Period of Rotation	Inclination of Equator	Surface gravity (cm/per sec)	Escape Velocity (km/sec)	Visual Magnitude
Mercury	0.24085	59 days	28°	363	4.2	−1.9
Venus	0.61521	244.3 days	3°	860	10.3	−4.4
Earth	1.00004	23 hours 56$_m$ 04.1$_s$	23° 27′	982	11.2	
Mars	1.88089	24$_h$ 37$_m$/22.6$_s$	23° 59′	374	5.0	−2.8
Jupiter	11.86223	9$_h$ 50$_m$ 30$_s$	3° 05′	2590	61.0	−2.5
Saturn	29.4577	10$_h$ 14$_m$	26° 44′	1130	37.0	−0.4
Uranus	84.0139	10$_h$ 49$_m$	97° 55′	1040	22.0	+5.6
Neptune	164.793	15$_h$ 48$_m$	28° 48′	1400	25.0	+7.9
Pluto	247.7	6 days 9$_h$				+14.9

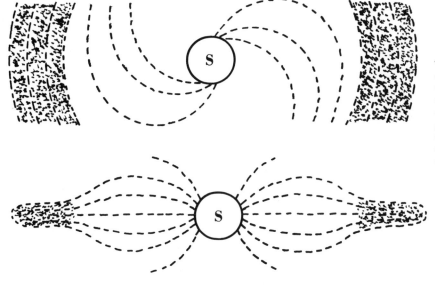

The magnetic lines of force of the sun's magnetic field—which are "frozen" into the gaseous disk of the preplanetary cloud—can wind themselves around the sun. As a result, the sun is slowed down and part of its angular momentum is transferred to the disk, which eventually condenses into planets. The upper diagram shows a cross section of the doughnut-shaped gaseous disk, the sun (S), and the magnetic lines of force, the lower diagram shows a section of the disk viewed from above, with some of the lines of force winding themselves around the sun.

VII·THE UNIVERSE

1. Realm of the Stars

We have seen how in ancient times the stars were believed to be fixed on the celestial sphere, all at the same distance from us. Only with the advent of powerful telescopes, when distance measurements became possible, did it become clear that stars—even those in the same constellation—might be quite distant from one another and at vastly different distances from the earth. Hipparchus classified the stars he could see into six classes—according to their apparent magnitudes. The brightest stars he assigned the number one and those that were just barely visible to the naked eye number six. Originally, that classification was assigned more or less arbitrarily. Today there is a simple relationship between the *apparent magnitude* and the *brightness observed*. A star of magnitude 1 is one hundred times as bright as a star of magnitude 6. As fainter and fainter stars were found, the scale was extended and now reaches 23.5 for the photographic limit of the 200-inch telescope. At the same time stars brighter than magnitude 1 had to be accommodated resulting in extending the scale to −26.5 for the sun.

The difference in the apparent magnitude—and hence brightness observed—of two stars may be due either to the fact that one star is indeed intrinsically brighter than the other or to the fact that they are at different distances, or to both facts.

The observed brightness of a star is proportional to its intrinsic brightness (the actual amount of light emitted). Since the light intensity varies inversely as the square of the distance, the distance of a star can be found from its intrinsic brightness or absolute magnitude. Only in certain cases is it possible to find the absolute magnitude of a star with any degree of certainty and thus determine its distance directly. However, comparing the apparent magnitude of two stars will give the ratios of their respective distances (assuming that their intrinsic brightness is the same).

A more direct way of measuring distances, provided they are not too large, involves the method of stellar parallax, discussed in Chapter II. For celestial objects, which are even closer, direct triangulation may be possible. We thus have a "ladder" of distance measurements. Distance of close-by objects are measured by triangulation, farther ones by parallax, which gives us standards of distances for magnitude-distance measurements—which, in turn, determine stars at larger distances.

Friedrich Wilhelm Bessel devoted all of his life to practical astronomy. His best-known contribution was the measurement of the parallax of a faint fifth-magnitude star in the constellation Cygnus—the Swan. The parallax shift, as measured from the two sides of the earth's orbit, turned out to be one-half second of arc, from which Bessel concluded that the star (numbered 61 in Cygnus) was about 11 light-years away. A light-year is the distance light travels in one year—about sixty thousand times the distance of the earth from the sun, or 6 million million miles. At about the same time, the Scotsman Thomas Henderson, first Astronomer Royal for Scotland, measured the parallax of Alpha Centauri, the bright star in the constellation Centaurus, and found the star to be "only" 4.3 light-years away (our sun is 8 light-minutes away). A more ambitious project was chosen by Friedrich Georg Wilhelm Struve. The star he chose was Vega, in the constellation Lyra, but his measurement was considerably in error (which is not surprising since Vega is 27 light-years away); only 8 stars lie within 10 light-years from us, whereas the great majority are hundreds of light-years away. (Looking at the stars today, one really sees them as they appeared a very long time ago.) At these distances parallax measurements are impossible, and indirect methods such as magnitude-distance relations have to be used.

As long as only comparatively few stars—fewer than a thousand—were known, their grouping according to

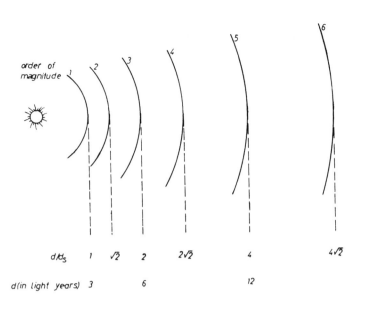

order of magnitude

| d/d_s | 1 | √2 | 2 | 2√2 | 4 | 4√2 |

d(in light years)   3   6   12   24

Magnitude and distance. The consecutively numbered "circles" denote the relative order of magnitude (taking Sirius as a star of magnitude 1). The brightness of a star decreases with increasing order—each order, for example, being half the previous one. Since brightness varies inversely as the square of the distance, the relative distances $(d)/d_s$ (taking d_s here as the "known" distance of Sirius: 3 light-years) increase as 1, $\sqrt{2}$, 2, $2\sqrt{2}$, 4, and so on. Knowing that Sirius (d_s) is 8.7 light-years the absolute distances for each order can be found.

constellations seemed adequate. But even so it is rather awkward to refer to a star as the one in the left forepaw of the bear or by a designation having an Arabic root and being difficult to remember.

Johann Bayer was a German lawyer who lived most of his life in Augsburg; he must have been a person of some consequence, for he served on the Augsburg city council at a salary of 500 silver guldens per annum. In 1603 he published *Uranometria*, a popular guide to the starry heaven. It contained charts for each of the 48 classical constellations, as well as the two hemispheres, and a map of the southern sky showing some of the newer constellations—altogether 51 maps beautifully engraved in copper. In addition to the 1,005 stars classified by Brahe eleven years earlier, *Uranometria* contains 700 stars based on observations of the Dutch navigator P. D. Keyser and others. What is remarkable about this star catalogue is the nomenclature it introduced. Bayer assigned Greek letters to the stars in the constellations. Contrary to common belief, he did not designate stars according to their relative brightness but according to their positions within one of the six main classes.

John Flamsteed in his *Historia Coelestis Britannica* numbered stars in order of increasing right ascension, and he is responsible for such names as 61 Cygni and 32 Orionis, as well as some Latin letter designations.

Today one uses a classification based on Bayer's system. Stars that are bright enough to be seen by the naked eye—and thus appear in the old maps—are designated by Greek and Roman letters, whereas all others are given numbers and are usually preceded by an abbreviation or the name of the compiler. Only the brightest stars are still referred to by their original names. Of course, in the final analysis a star is defined by its coordinates—right ascension and declination.

We have already seen that because of the stars' immense distances their motion cannot be detected by the unaided eye, even during a lifetime. Only if one could compare observations over thousands of years would it be possible to detect appreciable shifts. The small displacements are referred to as the *proper motion* of a star and are expressed in terms of seconds per year. The star with the largest proper motion so far discovered is Barnard's star (a faint star of the tenth magnitude in the constellation Ophiuchus). Its proper motion is 10.3 seconds per year, or to put it more graphically, it will cross the diameter of the moon in 175 years; this comparatively large proper motion has earned it the nickname Barnard's arrow, but its proper motion is mostly due to its proximity. The proper motion has to be taken into account if one determines stellar distances by the

One of the fifty-one star maps showing Cygnus (the Swan). From *Uranometria*, by Johann Bayer (1603).

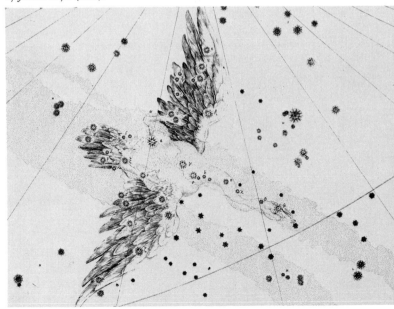

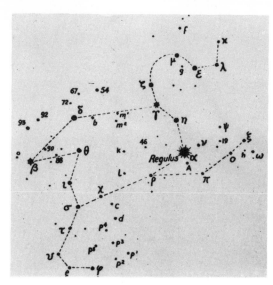

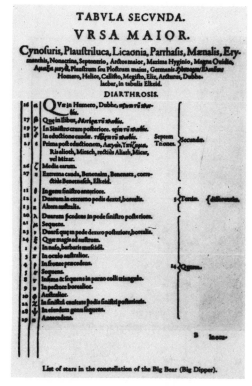

List of stars in the constellation of the Big Bear (Big Dipper).

Stars in the constellation Leo. Within a given constellation stars are designated according to apparent brightness by the Greek letters α, β, etc. to ω followed by the letters a, b, c, etc. After that alphabet was exhausted, numbers were used as an alternative way of designating stars. Also, superscripts appeared for star pairs (or higher multiples)–p^1, p^2, or m^1, m^2, etc.

A typical table taken from *Uranometria* illustrating the system of classification introduced by Bayer. The seven bright stars in Ursa Major that form the Big Dipper are numbered consecutively from α to η; these are followed by the three stars of the third magnitude (θ to κ) and finally the fourteen stars of the fourth magnitude (λ to ω). No distinction is made among stars of the same magnitude.
◄

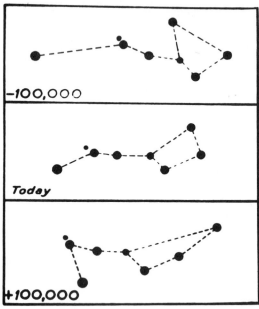

Three views of the Great Bear: as it appeared 100,000 years ago; as it appears now; and as it will look 100,000 years from now. The change is the result of the relative motion of the stars in that constellation.

A typical binary system, Kreuger 60, is shown during a twelve-year period. The bright star in the lower right-hand corner is used as a reference for identification. ▼

parallax method (conversely, the distance has to be known to find the star's velocity). However, the actual motion of a star consists both of its proper motion and its radial motion—the speed with which it approaches or recedes from the sun.

In 1650, only some forty years after Galileo had developed the telescope, John Baptist Riccioli accidentally noted that Mizar (a star along the handle of the Big Dipper) was part of a two-star system. It was thought that such double stars were independent and far from each other—the bright one closer and the fainter farther away but in the same line of sight—William Herschel therefore considered that it provided a good way to measure the parallax of the nearer, or brighter, star with respect to the more distant, fainter one. He published three catalogues listing more than 800 such double stars. To his amazement, it turned out that the majority were members of binary systems revolving around each other. His son, John Herschel, continued the search and established an observatory in Feldhausen near Cape Town (South Africa). John's survey resulted in the discovery of 1,202 double and multiple stars found mostly in the Southern Hemisphere.

In the meantime, another famous father and son team, Friedrich Georg Wilhelm and Otto Struve, at their observatory in Pulkovo, near Leningrad, compiled a catalogue of 3,110 double stars in the Northern Hemisphere.

More and more binaries are being discovered, and it is not unlikely that among the brighter stars (less than magnitude 9.0) at least one in twenty is a visual binary star.

The orbital motion of binaries provides not only another verification of the universal law of gravitation but also a way of determining the relative masses of the two stars, or components, as they are called. If one of the two stars is much more massive than its companion, the latter will describe an ellipse, with the massive star at the focus. Felix Savary was the first to apply gravitational principles to the computation of binary star orbits. In 1827 he derived an orbit for a double star in Ursa Major that turned out to be an eccentric ellipse—completing a revolution in about sixty years.

In some cases the stars of a binary system may be so close to each other—or so far away from the earth—that it is impossible to determine their orbits visually. However, quite often one notices a periodic variation in the amount of light received from such a star system. What happens is that during a complete revolution one of the stars is eclipsed—totally or partially—by the other. In either case the amount of light received will be less during the "eclipses" than during the balance of the revolution. The

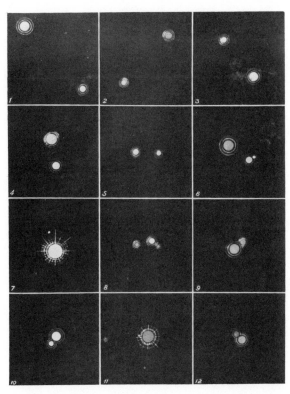

Some binary and multiple stars. Many binary and multiple stars present a beautiful sight through a telescope; some may be bluish or green, like a sapphire or an emerald, with bright yellow, orange, or red companions. The color is an indication of a star's temperature and intrinsic brightness or absolute magnitude.

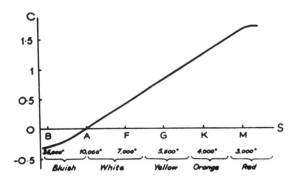

Whereas the eye is most sensitive to yellow-green light, a photographic plate is attuned to shorter wavelengths, the ultraviolet part of the spectrum. Consequently, one speaks of a visual magnitude to denote the brightness of a star estimated by the human eye, and a photographic magnitude that records the brightness of a star on a photographic plate. The difference between these two magnitudes is the color index (C). Because a star's color index depends on its surface temperature, the color provides us with a useful measure of temperature (as long as the passage of starlight through interstellar matter has not absorbed the lower bluish wavelengths). The diagram shows a plot of the color index against the temperature, expressed in thousands of degrees Kelvin (0° Celsius equals 273.2° Kelvin).

238

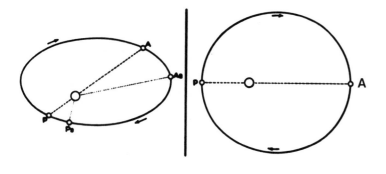

Relation of apparent orbit *(left)* to true orbit *(right)* for a double star. The orbit of a binary appears as an ellipse, but since we may not see it face-on (the orbit not being perpendicular to the line of sight), the primary star may not appear at the focus of the ellipse. In the true orbit, of course, the primary star, if it is more massive than the companion, will be at the focus. The point of closest approach of the secondary star (P) in its orbit is the periastron, the point A being the apastron. (These are analogous to perihelion and aphelion for the planets). In the apparent orbit *(left)* Aa and Pa denote the apparent apastron and periastron respectively, whereas A and P are the true apastron and periastron.

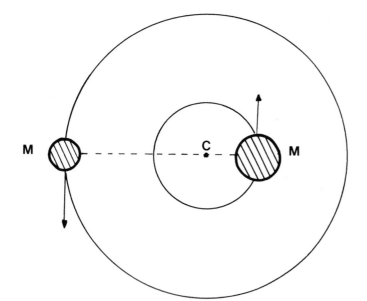

If the masses of the two stars are comparable, their motion takes place about their center of mass, the barycenter (C), in opposite directions, as indicated by the arrows. Furthermore, the heavier star (M) will move in an orbit closer to the barycenter than the lighter star (m), with the product of mass and radius equal in each case. The periods of both stars, or the times of revolution, are the same; consequently, the smaller star will move faster about the barycenter than the heavier companion. For simplicity's sake, circular motion has been assumed in the illustration. However, even in this case the apparent motion will appear to be elliptic if the orbits are inclined to the line of sight.

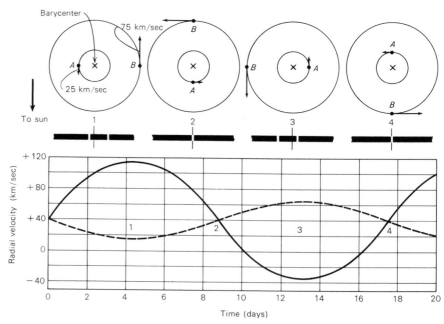

Four positions of a binary system, their spectral lines, and radial-velocity curves. The two components (A and B) moving around their barycenter (center of mass) while the whole system also moves along a straight line. At Figure 1, component A is at its maximum velocity, moving toward the sun, whereas B, at its maximum, is moving away from the sun. These velocities are measured in relation to the barycenter, which moves at 40 kilometers per second (km/sec). At Figure 3 the situation is reversed, while at Figures 2 and 4 both stars are moving across our line of sight, with a radial velocity equal to that of the barycenter—40 km/sec. The dashed line gives the velocity curve of the heavier component (A), and the unbroken line describes the motion of the lighter star (B). The period of the system is seen to be 17.5 days.

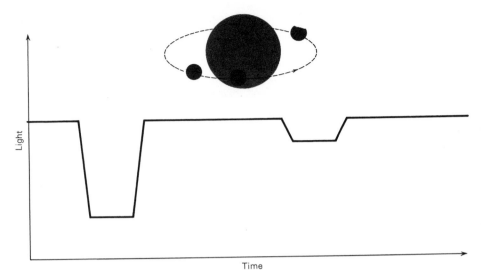

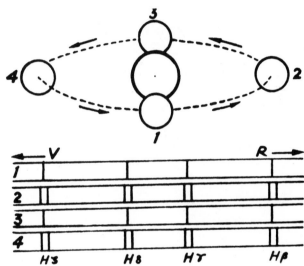

A binary system consisting of a larger and a smaller component revolving around each other in circular orbits. When the smaller star is behind the larger one and completely eclipsed, there will be a definite decrease in the observed light. Another "minimum" occurs when the small star is in front of the larger and partially blocks out its light.

Orbital position and spectrum of spectroscopic binaries. A star in a circular orbit around its companion: at (4) it is approaching, at (2) it is receding, and at (1) and (3) it moves across our line of sight. The observed spectrum would consist of a set of lines (the four belonging to hydrogen (H) are shown here). When the star is receding (2) there will be a shift of its spectral lines toward the red wavelength (R) and a double set of lines will appear, one arising from the shift due to the moving star and one non-shifted due to the other star. (If the masses of the two stars are comparable, both will move and hence there will be a shift of both sets of lines, but of different magnitude, resulting again in a doubling of the lines.) Similarly, when the star is approaching (4), the shift is toward the violet (V), with a corresponding doubling of the lines. At positions (1) and (3) only single lines are observed, since there is no motion toward or away from the observer.

length of time between eclipses—and the velocity curve (determined from the shift in spectral lines)—helps us to determine the orbits.

In 1889 Edward Charles Pickering of Harvard University noticed that the spectral lines of Mizar A—itself part of a binary system—which are usually double, at times became single. He rightly concluded that Mizar A itself is a double star, with the two components revolving around each other once in 104 days. In other words, Mizar is a system of three stars—two revolving around each other that, in turn, revolve around a third. It will be seen in Chapter VIII that whenever a star approaches or recedes, a shift in its spectral lines occurs. Thus, when one component of a binary system approaches us, the other will be receding, and, as a result, each line will appear double. On the other hand, if the stars are moving across the line of sight, their radial velocities are unchanged and only one line will be observed. Binary systems that can only be detected on account of the occasional but regular doubling of their spectral line are called spectroscopic binaries. More than 700 such spectroscopic binaries have been observed and their motion analyzed.

So far we have considered only binary stars whose motion can be observed visually (visual binaries), by light

Velocity curves. The velocity curves of a typical spectroscopic binary system, Capella (α Aurigae). The unbroken curve corresponds to the faster, less massive component, whereas the dotted curve gives the radial speed of the second star. The distance P corresponds to the period of revolution–104 days. While one star appears to recede, the other approaches, and vice versa. The horizontal line describes the motion of the barycenter.

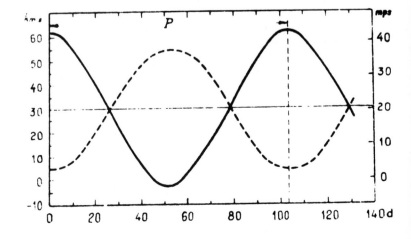

Edward Charles Pickering (1846-1919). Under his direction, the spectra of 10,351 stars were photographed and catalogued as the *Henry Draper Catalogue,* in memory of Henry Draper, a pioneer in stellar spectroscopy (his widow had supplied the necessary funds). He then set to work on a much larger catalogue including the spectra of 225,000 stars. Pickering also became famous—and was sometimes even ridiculed—for his continuous survey of the sky. It has been said that he charted the sky once a month, and brighter stars (less than sixth magnitude) even nightly, so that nothing of interest in the heavens would escape him. Pickering remained active both as director of the Harvard College Observatory and as astronomer until shortly before his death.

Henrietta Leavitt (1868-1921). Assigned as an assistant to Pickering to study the brightness of variable stars, she so excelled in her work that she became head of the department of photometric studies. In the course of her work she classified numerous variable stars and discovered 2,400 new ones and four novae. Her most famous contribution was the discovery that the brightest stars in the Magellanic Clouds also had the longest periods, which led to the period-luminosity law for Cepheid variables.

variations (eclipsing binaries), or by variation in spectral lines (spectroscopic binaries). In addition, there are binaries whose companion cannot be detected by any of these methods. The presence of such stars can be deduced only by noting the perturbations of the primary (similar to the discovery of Neptune by perturbations on the orbit of Uranus). This becomes particularly important, and fascinating, if the companion is an unusual star, such as a neutron star, or even a "black hole," which we will discuss later in this chapter.

The origin of binary stars may be due to a chance encounter of two stars, resulting in their revolution about a common center of gravity—like the encounter theory of the solar system. Another possibility—more probable—may be the existence of independent nucleii in the original dust cloud. Matter would aggregate about the centers—their initial angular momentum sufficient to keep them apart, but their mutual gravitational attraction keeping them revolving about their common mass center. Or a single star may have separated into two components through centrifugal and possibly tidal action influenced by stellar radiation pressure.

In 1924 Sir Arthur S. Eddington showed that there must exist a simple relation between the mass and luminosity of an ordinary star. The result of his work shows that the luminosity increases with the mass according to a simple power law. The more massive the star, the brighter it will be. Without going into a mathematical analysis, it is not difficult to see why this must be so. The gravitational attraction between the various parts of a star produce extremely large forces which tend to contract and collapse it, unless they are balanced by the star's internal pressure, its radiation pushing outward. Stars consist of hot gases whose particles are in rapid motion—the hotter the center of the star the faster their motion, and, consequently, the larger pressure they exert. (The situation is similar to that of a kettle of water being heated; the lid will be pushed up if the temperature is high enough.) Thus, the temperature necessary to offset the effect of gravity will be larger for a star with a larger mass than for one with a smaller mass.

The peculiar galaxy in Centaurus A (NGC 5128) about 12 million light-years away, as photographed with the 200-inch reflector. It appears to be a giant SO galaxy in collision with a spiral, seen edgewise. A strong absorbing band of dust and gas is at the center.

At the same time, the radiation—which depends on the difference between the central temperature and that of the surface—will be larger. Hence, one may expect stars with large masses to be more luminous; they will radiate more energy than stars with smaller masses. The remarkable result of the Eddington relation is that the luminosity depends on the mass, and not on the density or radius of the star.

We now come to stars that exhibit a periodic variation in luminosity but that are not eclipsing binaries. The most important of these are the Cepheid variables, so called because the star δ Cephei (a bright star in the constellation Cepheus) was the first discovered and is the best known of that class. Another Cepheid variable—not quite as spectacular—is the polestar itself. Today there are more than 18,000 known variable stars in our galaxy alone. The variation of the luminosity or magnitude within a given time gives us the light curve of a variable star. For a Cepheid variable the interval between two successive periods of maximum light received (maxima) or two periods of minimum light received (minima) is the same. That interval is called the period. In 1912 Henrietta Leavitt at Harvard was examining photographs of Cepheid variables in the Magellanic Clouds, two small stellar systems that turned out to be galaxies. For practical

purposes it was assumed that all the stars in the Cloud are at the same distance. It then followed that the longer-period stars are actually brighter than those with shorter periods. This work led to the period-luminosity law, which gives a definite relation between the absolute magnitude and the period of a Cepheid variable.

If one knows the period of the star, its intrinsic brightness can then be deduced, and from that and the apparent magnitude one can find its distance. This method has been important in proving that there are large galaxies, such as the Andromeda Spiral, outside the Milky Way.

The exact nature of these pulsating stars is still in doubt, but there exists a definite correlation between their variations in brightness, color, radial velocity, and radius. Harlow Shapley, of whom it can be said that he "broke the barriers of the skies," suggests that the light changes are due to the occurrence of internal or surface pulsations; the hotter gases in the interior rush to the surface and periodically "break through" the outer surface of the star.

One sees regular Cepheid variables with periods of a few days, but there are other variable stars with periods ranging from ten to thirty days. Their light curves are quite similar to those of the Cepheid variables, except that the change from maximum to minimum takes place much

The absolute magnitude and period of a Cepheid follow a definite relation: the brighter the star (in this logarithmic magnitude scale −6 is brighter than −1) the longer its period. A measurement of the period thus enables its absolute magnitude to be deduced; its distance can be inferred from that and the relative or apparent magnitude.

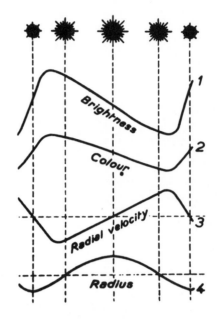

Not only the brightness (1) of a Cepheid variable undergoes a periodic change, but also the color (2), changing from yellow-green to yellow to orange to yellow and back to yellow-green. (The curve here gives the change of wavelength, which corresponds to a change in color.) The radial velocity (3) and radius (4) also undergo periodic changes, the radius being largest midway between maximum and minimum brightness (it is minimum when the light is increasing). Thus, the star expands and contracts periodically with corresponding changes in its radius, temperature, and brightness.

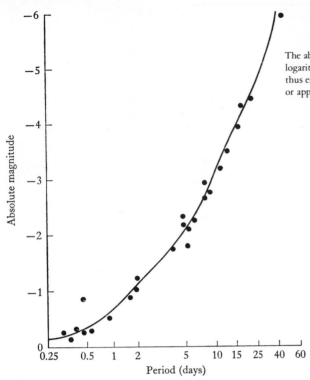

Henry Norris Russell (1877–1957) *(left)* talking to Harlow Shapley (1885–1972) on board ship. Russell began and ended his astronomical career at Princeton University, where he spent sixty-two of his seventy-nine years. Independent of Hertzsprung, he discovered a relationship between a star's brightness, color, and spectral class; this resulted in the Hertzsprung-Russell diagram. At the same time, he published his analysis of the light curves of eclipsing variable stars and devised an ingenious and convenient method of extracting full information from the observation. His method was applied successfully to eighty-seven double stars by Shapley, at that time a young Ph.D. whom "the Lord sent me," as Russell remarked. Russell later became interested in atomic spectra and, together with F. A. Saunders, devised a theory for the coupling of the intrinsic spin and angular momentum. Shapley's years at Mount Wilson Observatory (1913-20) gained him a reputation as one of the most brilliant and original of the young astronomers. In 1921 he succeeded E. C. Pickering as professor of astronomy and director of the Harvard College Observatory. In his study of variable stars in globular star clusters, he used the Cepheids as "standard lamps" and deduced their distances. He then took a bold—and correct—step in assuming that the globular cluster system gives a fair general outline of the Milky Way. He showed that it was much larger than had been assumed and not centered at the sun, as was believed, but at a point in Sagittarius. In a disagreement with Heber D. Curtis, who propounded the idea of a small scale of galactic distances, Shapley based his arguments on the period-luminosity relation and clearly won the argument. But he was proved wrong in a second part of his debate, which concerned itself with the nature of spiral galaxies. Shapley thought them to be truly nebulous objects, whereas Curtis intuitively guessed that they were "island universes"—our present picture of the universe being a blend of both views.

more slowly (because of the longer period). For this reason they are often called Type II Cepheids or W Virginis stars, after their prototype W Virginis, a star in the constellation Virgo.

A period-luminosity relation resembling that for the δ Cepheids is found to hold for these variables too. For this reason it was thought for a long time that they were all one species, and only recently has it been realized that they are different types of pulsating stars.

Another group of variable stars is the RR Lyrae, named after a star in the constellation Lyra, typical of that class. They differ from the Cepheids in that their period is less than one day, ranging from seven to sixteen hours. Most of the RR Lyrae are found in globular clusters. These are conglomerations of stars that, because of their proximity, have a stronger gravitational attraction for one another and form beautiful symmetrical shapes. The most conspicuous of these, such as the one in Hercules, were

M13, the globular cluster in Hercules taken with the 200-inch telescope at Mount Wilson and Palomar Observatories. Containing about 10,000 stars, it has a diameter of approximately 100 light-years and consists mainly of Population II stars, which are at least 7 to 8 billion years old. (Stars in open clusters and related field stars belong to Population I and may be no older than 10 million years or less.)

A typical open cluster, NGC 2682, in Cancer taken with the 200-inch telescope. The study of star clusters is useful for two reasons: because they are roughly at the same distance, the properties of their constituents can be compared, such as luminosity; because the constituents are probably of a common origin, clusters of different age help us understand stellar evolution. Our own galaxy has about 119 globular clusters, more than 800 open clusters, and about 80 associations, which are groupings of very young and luminous stars.

listed in early star catalogues, in particular Sir John Herschel's famous *General Catalogue* of 1864 and Charles Messier's earlier one of 1781. (In fact, the designation M13 of the globular cluster in Hercules refers to Messier.)

However, not all star clusters are globular or spherical, and they may contain only a few stars. One then speaks of open clusters, a typical example being the Pleiades. Since the distances of the members of a particular cluster are approximately the same, these star distances too can be found by applying the period-luminosity law to any variable star in that cluster.

Lesser riddles include the erupting variables, which, from a comparative anonymity, suddenly burst into prominence and then gradually revert to their former state. These include the novae, which may increase in brightness by 160,000 times within a couple of days. As the name indicates, they were thought to be "new" stars but, in fact, are hot subdwarf stars, which we will describe in the next section. In a cryptic communication J. Hartmann (1865–1936) of Potsdam concluded: "Nova problem solved. Stop. Star swells and bursts." This is only part of the story because it does not explain why a particular star becomes a nova; nothing is known about the prenova stage.

Even more spectacular are the supernovae, which flare hundreds of millions of times their former brightness. Tycho's *nova stella* was a supernova reaching a magnitude of −4, but it is hardly visible today. Kepler's nova of 1604 reached a magnitude of −2.5, and the famous supernova of 1054 in Taurus described in the *Chinese Annals* was supposed to have been as bright as Venus, rivaling Tycho's nova. The 1054 remnant today is a faint central star in the

Charles Messier (1730–1817). Born in Badonviller in Lorraine, Messier lost his father when he was eleven years old. He moved to Paris, where in 1751 he was hired by the astronomer Joseph-Nicolas Delisle as a clerk to record observations. At that time he had no knowledge of astronomy and only a good handwriting to recommend him for the position. Under the guidance of the experienced astronomer, he soon became a careful observer, discovering a multitude of comets. In recognition of this work, in 1764 he became a member of the Royal Society. In 1771 he published the first catalogue of 45 nebulae, which he eventually extended in 1784 to 103. This was the first systematic listing of these objects and became known as the Messier Catalogue. It was superseded only when Herschel began a more complete survey. It is remarkable that Messier carried out his observations with a small telescope not larger than 7.5 inches in diameter. He also observed sunspots, occultations, and Uranus—which had been newly discovered—but he is remembered for his catalogue and not for the more spectacular discovery of comets and other objects.

Crab nebula; we shall have occasion to discuss it again.

When the Crab nebula was observed for long periods of time, it was noted that from the central star it continuously expands in all directions. Extrapolating back to the original explosion that gave rise to the nebula, we know it must have occurred between A.D. 1000 and A.D. 1100. Since the crab is 5,000 light-years away—a fact that can be calculated from the rate of expansion—it follows that the eruption took place about 4000 B.C.

RANGE OF MAGNITUDES

Object	Apparent Magnitude
Sun	−26.5
Moon (full)	−12.5
Venus	− 4
Jupiter	− 2
Sirius	− 1.4
Aldebaran	+ 1.0
Polaris	+ 2.0
Eridani	+ 3.74
61 Cygni	+ 5.2
Barnard's star	+ 9.5
Proxima Centauri	+10.7

Limits

Naked eye	6.5
Small telescope	13
200-inch telescope (visual)	20
200-inch telescope (photographic)	23.5

The Crab nebula, the remnant of the supernova explosion observed and recorded by the Chinese in 1054. In addition to visible light, radio energy is emitted (the Crab's progenitor is now a neutron star responsible for pulsar radiation).

NEAREST STARS

Name	Apparent Magnitude	Absolute Magnitude	Parallax (in seconds)	Distance (in light-years)
Proxima Centauri	10.7	15.1	0.765	4.2
α Centauri A	0.0	4.4	0.765	4.2
α Centauri B	1.39	5.9	0.754	4.3
Barnard's star	9.56	13.2	0.545	5.9
Wolf 359	13.66	16.8	0.420	7.6
Lalande 21185	7.5	10.5	0.398	8.1
Sirius A	−1.44	1.5	0.375	8.7
Sirius B	8.67	11.5	0.375	8.7

SOME BRIGHT VISUAL BINARIES

Name	Visual Magnitudes *		Period (in years)
Sirius	−1.4	8.7	50
α Geminorum	2.0	2.9	420
α Piscium	4.3	5.2	720
γ Leonis	2.6	3.8	618
γ Virginis	3.6	3.6	172
ζ Ursa Majoris	4.4	4.8	60
η Cassiopeiae	3.6	7.5	480
ι Cassiopeiae	4.7	7.0	840
ι Leonis	4.1	7.0	204

* The visual magnitudes of the two components, the brighter one first.

244

BRIGHTEST STARS

Name	Designation		Apparent Magnitude	Absolute Magnitude
Sirius	α	Canis Majoris	−1.44	+1.41
Canopus	α	Carinae	−0.73	−5.0
Rigil Kent	α	Centauri	−0.27	+4.1
Arcturus	α	Boötis	+0.06	+0.2
Vega	α	Lyrae	+0.04	+0.6
Capella	α	Aurigae	+0.09	−0.5
Rigel	β	Orionis	+0.15	−6.5
Procyon	α	Canis Minoris	+0.37	+2.7
Achernar	α	Eridani	+0.53	−2.6
Agena	β	Centauri	+0.66	−2.5
Betelgeuse	α	Orionis	+0.7	−4.1
Altair	α	Aquilae	+0.80	+2.4
Aldebaran	α	Tauri	+0.85	−0.6
Acrux	α	Crucis	+0.87	−0.4
Antares	α	Scorpii	+0.98	−4.0
Spica	α	Virginis	+1.00	−3.3

SOME BRIGHT NOVAE AND SUPERNOVAE

Year	Constellation	Magnitude Maximum *	Minimum	Remarks
1572	Cassiopeia	−4	19	Nova Stella
1600	Cygnus	3	4.5–5.5	Variable
1604	Ophiuchus	−2.3		Kepler's star
1670	Vulpecula	3		Not identifiable
1848	Ophiuchus	5	13	
1866	Corona Borealis	2	10.6	Recurrent
1876	Cygnus	3	14.8	
1891	Auriga	4.2	14.8	
1898	Sagittarius	4.9	16.5	
1901	Perseus	0.2	13.5	Now a close binary
1903	Gemini	5.0	16.5	
1910	Lacerta	4.6	14.0	
1912	Gemini	3.5	14.8	
1918	Aquila	−1.1	10.5	Now a close binary
1920	Cygnus	2.0	16.1	
1925	Pictor	1.2	12.7	Slow, close binary
1934	Hercules	1.4	14	Slow, close binary
1936	Lacerta	1.9	15.3	Fast, rapid decline
1939	Monoceros	4.3	16	
1942	Puppis	0.2	17.0	Fast
1950	Lacerta	5.4	13.4	
1963	Hercules	3.9	8 †	
1967	Delphinus	3.7	11.5 ‡	Exceptionally slow
1968	Vulpecula	4.3	12	Fast
1970	Serpens	4.6		
1970	Aquila	6		

* Apparent magnitude; the absolute magnitudes of the novae listed here is about −8.
† A lower limit of the magnitude.
‡ Magnitude prior to the explosion.

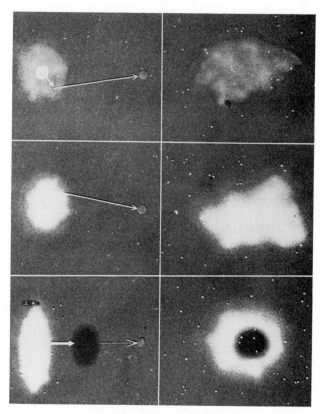

Interstellar matter, which constitutes about 20 percent of the universe, appears in various forms depending on its consistency (gas or dust) and proximity to stars. An interstellar cloud containing a hot star *(upper left)* will radiate its own light and will appear as a predominantly red emission nebula *(upper right)*. If no hot stars are present or the cloud consists of dust, it will reflect starlight *(middle left)* and the cloud will appear as a white reflection nebula *(middle right)*. Finally, if the cloud absorbs starlight *(lower left)*, it appears as a dark nebula *(lower right)*; stars behind it will appear fainter than they really are. The arrows indicate the mechanisms responsible for the appearances above. For example, at the top, the cloud emits light (short arrow), which is then transmitted by the nebula (long arrow).

This photograph from Mount Wilson and Palomar Observatories shows the reflection nebula about Merope (in the open cluster Pleiades). It will appear bluish, since blue light (the shorter wavelength) is scattered more than red light (the longer wavelength). (This is why the sky appears blue.)

The Horsehead nebula in Orion (Mount Wilson and Palomar Observatories) is a typical example of a dark nebula. The "head" of the horse intrudes into the bright nebula in the center of the photograph, obscuring the stars behind it. The stars visible in the lower part of the picture are in front of the dark nebula.

2. Fingerprinting the Stars

A star's fingerprint is its spectrum. From it we obtain not only information about its composition and temperature, but also some insight into its past, present, and future.

Newton, of course, was the first to show that sunlight consists of a series of colors forming a continuous spectrum. This is true not only of sunlight but of light, any incandescent solid, liquid, or gas under high pressure. We have also seen that an atom will radiate energy when an electron "jumps" from an outer to an inner orbit. Each of these transitions produces a specific wavelength, so that a particular atom will be characterized by a series of lines of different wavelength, and consequently of different colors. On the other hand, if our gas consisting of atoms

is an incandescent source, it will absorb light at the exact wavelengths at which it would emit bright lines. As a result, the original continuous spectrum will now contain a series of dark lines characteristic of the absorbing gas. These two kinds of spectra, *emission* and *absorption*, make it possible to identify the atoms constituting the gas.

The instrument used to measure or photograph spectra is called a spectroscope, for direct viewing, and a spectrograph when employed with a camera. It consists essentially of a collimating lens (or tube) that produces parallel light emitted by the source, a prism, and a telescope.

Instead of prisms, modern spectroscopes use diffraction gratings, which consist of thin glass plates (transmission gratings) or a mirror surface (reflection gratings) ruled with many closely spaced parallel lines—thousands per centimeter. Light is transmitted (or reflected) only in the

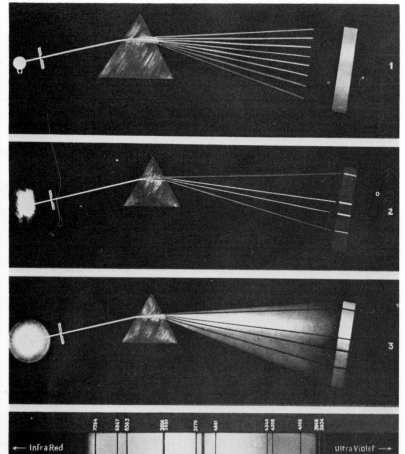

Spectra. 1. Dispersion of white light by a prism—or a continuous spectrum in which all the wavelengths are produced by an incandescent source, such as the filament of an electric light bulb. The dense incandescent gases in the interior of stars produce such spectra. 2. Bright-line spectrum produced by an incandescent gas of low density, such as in a mercury vapor lamp. Only certain wavelengths are present, resulting in a pattern or series of bright lines of different color. 3. Continuous spectrum combined with a spectrum of absorption lines (the dark lines are the absorption lines and are at exactly those wavelengths where the gas would emit bright lines were it heated to incandescence). This spectrum is produced by an incandescent source enveloped by an absorbing gas—e.g., the solar photosphere and the reversing layer. 4. Principal solar absorption lines (Fraunhofer spectrum).

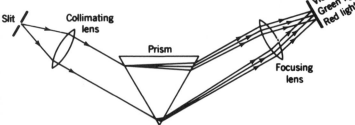

Spectroscope. Light from a source is passed through a collimating lens, which produces a parallel beam that is then dispersed by a prism. Another lens focuses the dispersed light, a different focus for each wavelength. The angle of deviation can be measured by rotating the focusing lens with respect to the prism and the incident beam.

spaces between the lines, and this produces interference patterns. Again, the amount of the deviation is different for different wavelengths of the incident light, and results in a spectrum that can be focused on a screen or photographic plate.

The spectrum of a star, then, is a combination of the continuous spectra, due to its luminous dense gases in the interior, and the line spectra of its more rarefied, outer components. In general, a body will absorb, reflect, and transmit radiation that falls upon it, and eventually it will reach a state of temperature equilibrium in which it re-radiates energy at the same rate at which it absorbs it. Its color, too, will depend on its temperature; for example, a hotter star (7,500 degrees to 11,000 degrees K.) will appear blue, while a cooler one (2,000 degrees to 3,500 degrees K.) will appear reddish.

Of particular interest is a perfect radiator or black body. This is an idealized substance that completely absorbs all radiation falling on it—without reflecting any—until it reaches its critical temperature at which it emits radiation at the same rate at which it receives it and remains in equilibrium at that temperature. It should be noted that a "black body" is black in the sense that it is opaque, or nontransparent, for all wavelengths. For all practical purposes, stars can be considered to radiate energy like black bodies, since they consist of very hot opaque gases that absorb radiation very effectively.

The energy of a star is produced in its interior by thermonuclear reaction—in fact, a hydrogen bomb is like a star in that it produces energy through nuclear reactions at very high temperatures. Energy is transmitted through a star—from atom to atom—until it reaches the outer layer,

the photosphere, from which it escapes in the form of radiation. Although the surface temperature of a star is considerably lower than its central temperature, it can still reach thousands of degrees. The temperature determines the energy emitted per second and per unit area. That quantity multiplied by the surface area of the star gives the star's luminosity, that is, total energy emitted per second.

Depending on the temperature—and hence on the color—stellar spectra have been divided into seven main classes. This classification, first introduced by Angelo Secchi in 1863 and developed further by Annie J. Cannon at Harvard, designates the different types of stellar spectra by the letters O, B, A, F, G, K, and M. A simple mnemonic composed by Henry Russell that includes the later types, R, N, and S, reads: "Oh Be A Fine Girl Kiss Me Right Now, Smack."

Each spectral class is characterized by its color, temperature range, and prominent spectral lines. But just as in the case of stellar magnitudes, a further subdivision was found necessary and the classes are further subdivided, for example, A5 would be halfway between A0 and F0.

Henry Norris Russell (1877-1957) began and ended his career at the Princeton University Observatory where he spent sixty-two years of his life. His research covered many areas, but it is his work on spectra, both in atomic physics and stellar structure, for which he is famous.

If the spectral class is plotted against the luminosity (or absolute magnitude), it is found that the stars are not distributed at random but lie more or less along a diagonal band—from upper left to lower right, with a horizontal line of giant stars near the top. This

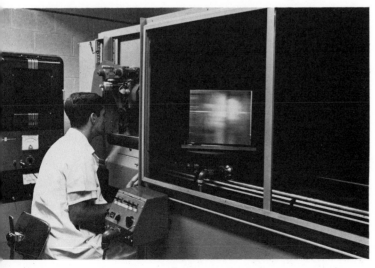

A diffraction grating test bench. On the work table is a 12 x 15-inch grating. It consists of thousands of finely ruled lines that produce interference patterns.

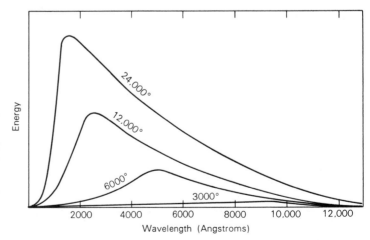

The energy emitted by a black body is plotted as a function of the wavelength (in angstroms) for various temperatures. From the curves it is seen that energy is emitted over practically the whole range of wavelengths but that the distribution is quite asymmetric. The amount of radiation emitted at a given wavelength increases with the temperature, and the hotter the body the more of its energy is emitted at lower wavelengths. Thus, hot stars will appear blue and cooler stars red.

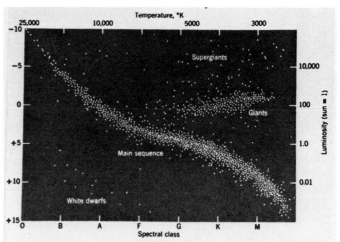

Harlow Shapley *(left)* trying to make a point in a conversation with Ejnar Hertzsprung at the Moscow meeting of the International Astronomical Union in 1958. Hertzsprung pointed out the existence of giant and dwarf stars and laid the foundation of what was later to become the Hertzsprung-Russell diagram. Hertzsprung continued to measure plates for double stars until a few years before his death in 1967. He was an observational astronomer of first rank, in accuracy and devotion comparable to another Dane, Tycho Brahe.

◄

A Hertzsprung-Russell diagram. The left-hand scale is in magnitudes. Most of the stars lie on a band, the main sequence, stretching from high temperatures and brightness (upper left) to low temperatures and brightness (lower right). Shown also, below the main sequence, are white dwarfs; above the main sequence are giants (ten or a hundred times the size of the sun) and supergiants. The great advantage of the H-R diagram is that the magnitude or luminosity of an ordinary star can be determined from its spectral class (including temperature and color); if one knows the magnitude, its spectral class can be found. However, this is workable only for stars that lie along the main sequence. (In general, both luminosity and spectral class of a star must be known in order to place it on the H-R diagram, but from its position general properties can then be deduced—for example, whether it is a dwarf or giant.) ►

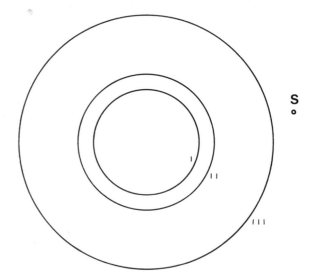

Diameters of three typical giant stars: Capella (I), Arcturus (II), and Aldebaran (III), respectively 17, 29, and 85 times that of the sun.

distribution had been discovered two years earlier, in 1911, by the Danish astronomer Ejnar Hertzsprung who published his findings in a popular photography journal; his results seemed to him like "science fiction." Luminosity plots are known as Hertzsprung-Russell (abbreviated to H-R) diagrams. Note that in the H-R diagram a considerable number of stars lie in the upper-right region of the plot, which contains the cooler and higher luminosity types. These are the giants or supergiants, so called by comparison with main sequence stars.

For these giant stars a classification according to spectral types was not sufficient; for example, Procyon and Mirfak are in the same spectral class, F5, but they differ in luminosity by a factor of several hundred. So W. W. Morgan of the Yerkes Observatory added the luminosity class to the previous classification. (There are five main classes differentiating between giants, supergiants, and main sequence stars.)

The life history of a star can be followed on an H-R diagram. Condensing from a "dust cloud," a star will enter the main sequence, increasing in luminosity and temperature; it then departs, expanding, to become a red giant. A pulsating period may follow, until finally it explodes into a supernova and eventually collapses into a white dwarf. Those are stars that have exhausted their nuclear fuel. Thus gravitational forces have compressed their masses to sizes even smaller than that of the earth,

resulting in densities exceeding many *tons* per cubic inch. In the process, electrons have been stripped from the atomic nuclei, forming a "degenerate gas" (the electrons in this gas are in their lowest state and behave more like a solid, with their large gravitational attraction just balanced by the pressure). As the masses of these burned-out stars increase, their radii decrease—in contrast to main sequence stars—until they reach a critical radius below which they

SPECTRAL SEQUENCE

Spectral Class	Color	Temperature Range in K°	Atoms producing main lines of spectrum	Typical stellar examples
O	Blue	25,000–40,000	Ionized helium and other ionized atoms	λ Cephei
			Neutral hydrogen (w) *	
B	Blue	11,000–25,000	Neutral helium Neutral hydrogen	Rigel
			Ionized silicon, magnesium, oxygen	Spica
A	Blue	7,500–11,000	Neutral hydrogen (s)	Sirius
			Metals (esp. calcium) (w)	Vega
F	Blue-White	6,000–7,500	Hydrogen (m)	Canopus
			Metals (esp. calcium) (s)	Procyon
G	White-Yellow	5,000–6,000	Ionized calcium (s)	Sun
			Neutral metals (m)	
			Hydrogen (w)	Capella
K	Orange	3,500–5,000	Neutral metals (s)	Arcturus
			Hydrogen (vw)	Aldebaran
M	Red	2,000–3,500	Neutral metals (s)	Betelgeuse
			Molecules of titanium oxide (vs)	Antares

* (s) strong, (m) medium, (w) weak, (vs) very strong, (vw) very weak.

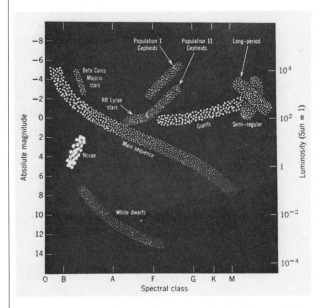

In this schematic view of an H-R diagram, the location of many of the nonstable stars, such as novae and variables, is shown in relation to the main sequence. Of particular interest are the white dwarfs at the lower left. Note that the extreme lower left of the diagram is empty—this indicates that white dwarfs below a critical size and mass cannot exist.

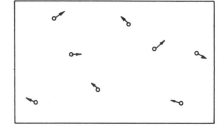

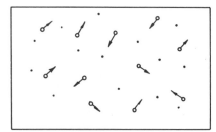

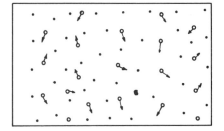

are no longer stable. The exact final state is unknown and also depends on the original mass: a massive star—with a mass about seven and up to fifteen times the mass of the sun—may suffer a supernova explosion and end up as a neutron star (which we will cover later in this chapter), whereas a star with a mass comparable to that of the sun will end up as a white dwarf. In either case, we may expect our sun—now on the main sequence—after several billion years to follow this course and become a red giant; its luminosity having increased by five or more magnitudes, it will burn up its own planets, including all life on earth.

(Top) In a perfect gas the atoms move at random in the comparatively vast expanses available to them. (Center) The gas may be made up of ionized particles—ionized atoms (arrows) and electrons (dots). (Bottom) As the density is increased, more and more electrons are stripped from the atoms, until they form a degenerate electron gas. The motion of the electrons is severely restricted, and only the atomic particles and some electrons move at random.

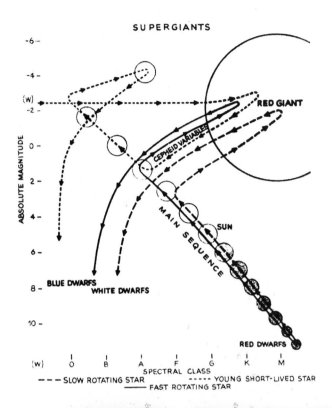

SUPERGIANTS

ABSOLUTE MAGNITUDE

-6 -
-4 -
(W)
-2 -
0 -
2 -
4 -
6 -
8 -
10 -

RED GIANT

CEPHEID VARIABLES

MAIN SEQUENCE

SUN

BLUE DWARFS
WHITE DWARFS

RED DWARFS

(W)   O   B   A   F   G   K   M
SPECTRAL CLASS

- - - SLOW ROTATING STAR   · · · · · YOUNG SHORT-LIVED STAR
————— FAST ROTATING STAR

The life history of a typical star is illustrated on the H-R diagram. Having entered the main sequence, the star will move along it, a process that takes about 150 million years (depending on its mass). It will then move away from the main sequence into the giant region, burning helium first and the heavier elements later. After that period, which lasts about another 100 million years, the star may pulsate (become a Cepheid variable) and finally end up as a white dwarf (or neutron star). The processes differ somewhat if the star is rotating slowly *(dashed line)* or fast *(solid line)*. Also, young, short-lived stars *(dotted line)* enter the giant phase before the main sequence.

The evolutionary sequence of a star will depend on its mass. Shown here are *(top)* the evolutionary sequences of a massive star (about 15 solar masses) and *(bottom)* a star with a mass comparable to that of the sun. Both types of stars will contract from the interstellar material (1) and join the main sequence, the heavy star after about 100,000 years and the lighter one after about 100 million years. They will move up along the main sequence (2), but again the time and positions will differ, the heavy star remaining 150 million years and the lighter one only 100 million years. In both cases they will enter the red giant region (3). The massive star may then undergo a supernova explosion (4) and leave behind a neutron star of very high density and low luminosity (5). The less massive star will become a variable star (4) and after ejecting matter will collapse into a white dwarf (5). ▼

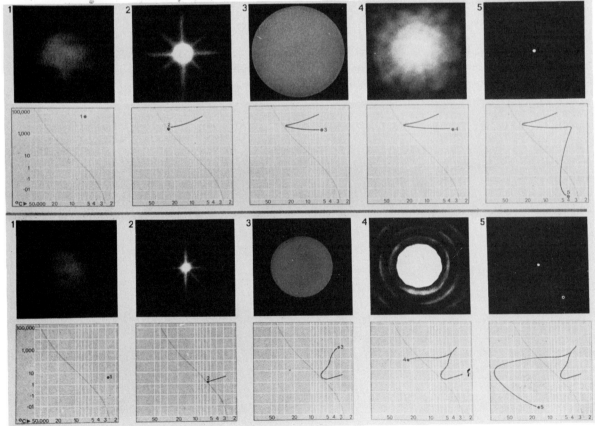

3. The Milky Way

On a clear night a casual observer can see a luminous band that seems to stretch across the sky. This is the Milky Way (or *via lacta),* which passes through the constellations Ophiuchus, Cygnus, Cassiopeia, Perseus, and Orion in the Northern Hemisphere. It is even more spectacular for the observer in the Southern Hemisphere – there it passes through Sagittarius, Scorpius, Lupus, Centaurus, and the Southern Cross, where the band is most brilliant.

Even with simple field glasses it is not difficult to see that the Milky Way is not just a luminous band but rather consists of myriads of stars. It has fascinated observers throughout the ages, but not until recently has its full significance been understood. Galileo in his *Sidereus Nuncius* noted that his telescopic observations of innumerable stars making up the Milky Way "freed us from wordy disputes upon the subject." He undoubtedly referred to the various speculations that began with the ancient Greeks and continued right up to Tycho Brahe who saw the Milky Way as the denser part of a fluid, the ethereal heavens, out of which new stars and comets were formed (he actually thought he saw a "hole" in the Milky Way after the appearance of the comet of 1577). Yet there were others, such as Albertus Magnus, who insinuated that there was a stellar consistency. And Gassendi described the Milky Way as a ring of densely clustered stars that, like a ring of densely clustered trees, appeared as one continuous band. Indeed, the Milky Way does encircle the whole sky, a fact that was taken to support the contention of a finite universe, with the sun and the earth at its center.

Thomas Wright, an amateur astronomer of Durham, in his work *An Original Theory of the Universe* (1750) argued that the Milky Way consisted of an infinite number of small stars embedded between two parallel plane surfaces revolving around a common center. In other words, a huge "grindstone" in form but, of course, not composed of solid material.

William Herschel noted that he could count more stars in certain directions than in others; he arrived at that result by a method he called star gauging. This consisted in counting the stars in selected regions of the celestial sphere. He then argued that those directions in which he saw the largest number of stars extended the farthest. If the distribution of stars were indeed flattened, as Wright suggested, then one would see few stars at right angles to the disk but many more in a direction along it. This would give the illusion of a continuous band.

The Dutch astronomer Jacobus Kapteyn (1851–1922) undertook the monumental task of determining the dimensions of the Galaxy (from the Greek *gala* meaning "milk"). In particular, he wanted to compute the star density, or the number of stars per unit volume, as a function of the distance from the sun and to determine their magnitudes, spectra, and radial velocities. He selected 206 areas distributed over the entire sky. Assuming that the relative number of stars of different luminosity in the sample was indicative of the actual distribution of the stars in the entire Galaxy, he determined by statistical methods the total distribution needed to produce the apparent brightness as seen from the earth. The result was the Kapteyn universe, a circular disk of 27,000 light-years in diameter and 5,400 light-years in thickness, with the sun at its center. Unlike Wright's model, the density of the star distribution was not constant but dropped sharply several hundred light-years from the center.

Quite a different view of the Galaxy was taken by Harlow Shapley. From the directions and distances of 93 globular clusters, he concluded that these are arranged in a roughly spherical system centered not at the sun but at a point in the direction of Sagittarius about 50,000 light-years away. He boldly – and, as it turned out, correctly –

This photograph, in the region of Sagittarius – taken with the 48-inch Schmidt telescope – clearly reflects that our galaxy is composed of countless stars. Each speck in the picture is a star, the sun being only one of thousands of billions. The nearer ones, appearing brighter than the rest, give the illusion of having rings around them. However, the stars can be thought of as points of light.

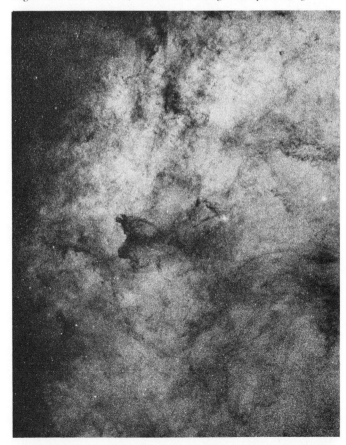

-1 0 +1 2 3 4 5 6 7 8

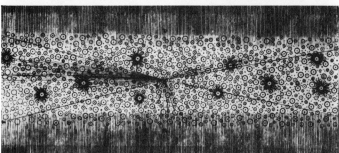

A composite view of the Milky Way made at the Lund Observatory, Sweden, as it would appear along its edge. At the left are the constellations Auriga and Perseus and the bright regions in Cassiopeia and Cygnus. The great dark rift in Cygnus and Aquila appears left of the center, where Sagittarius is situated. To the right are Centaurus, Crux, Carina, Puppis, and Canis Major. The fainter parts on the right are Monoceros and Gemini, and farther right is the continuation of Auriga. At the lower right are the Magellanic Clouds and at the far left, just below the Milky Way, is the Andromeda nebula. Interstellar dust shows in several places as dark clouds, preventing an unobstructed view across the Galaxy. Nevertheless, the faint or distant stars are strongly concentrated along the central line—a single plane in space.

The first definite structure of the Milky Way was proposed by Thomas Wright, an amateur astronomer. He imagined a "vast infinite Gulph or Medium extending like a Plane and enclosed between two surfaces, nearly even on both sides, but of such a depth or thickness as to occupy a space equal to the diameter of the visible Creation and containing all the stars."

Herschel arrived at his rather unsymmetrical model of the Milky Way by selecting 683 areas and "star gauging" them. The sun is indicated by the large dot near the center, while the dots at the edges probably indicate the globular clusters. The large split at the right is caused by interstellar matter, which obstructed Herschel's view of the stars there.

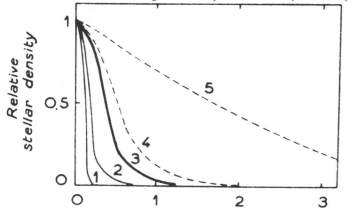

LUND OBSERVATORY

MARTIN KESKÜLA
TATJANA KESKÜLA

Distance from the galactic plane (kiloparsecs)

Relative distribution of several types of objects from the galactic plane: 1) B-type stars; 2) Cepheid variables, open clusters; 3) average of all stars; 4) K-type giants; 5) cluster variables, long-period variables. It can be seen that most are one kiloparsec, or roughly 3,200 light-years, from the galactic plane (in either direction).

concluded that this would also be the center of the Galaxy, whose diameter he estimated at 300,000 light-years. Just as Copernicus removed the earth from its central position within the solar system, so Shapley relegated the sun to a noncentral position, this time in the Galaxy; an ordinary star at the outskirts.

Both Kapteyn and Shapley assumed that there was no absorbing material between the sun and the objects they saw and that the distances measured were actual. But it is now known that there is a large amount of interstellar material, especially in the plane of the Galaxy. As a result, stars appear dimmer and hence farther away than they really are; also, this absorbing material blocks out light from distant stars.

Kapteyn was concerned mainly with stars near the plane of the Galaxy, and consequently he saw only a small part of it. On the other hand, Shapley was concerned with globular clusters away from the plane and also from most of the absorbing material—in fact, he saw no globular clusters in the plane of the Galaxy. Thus, the presence of interstellar absorption completely invalidated Kapteyn's results, whereas it only modified Shapley's conclusions: according to present estimates, the diameter of the Galaxy is 100,000 light-years, and its center is 30,000 light-years from the sun.

That the stars were in motion had already been discovered by Halley. This, of course, implied that the sun, being a star, would be moving in space. In 1787 William Herschel concluded from the proper motions of some thirty stars that the sun is moving in the direction of the constellation Hercules—a fact that was borne out by later investigations. Another remarkable effect had been discovered by Kapteyn in 1905: the motion of the stars is by no means random in direction but consists of *star streaming,* indicating a large-scale systematic motion. In particular, if we plot the radial velocities of all stars in the plane of the Galaxy at a given distance from the sun, we find that they exhibit a simple sinusoidal behavior. This indicates that some stars have a positive radial velocity and are receding from us, while others with negative radial velocity approach us, with still others having no radial velocities with respect to us. This can be explained by assuming that we (i.e., the sun) and the stars are moving in the *same* direction but at different speeds. Those stars that have a positive velocity are moving faster than the sun (either catching up or racing ahead of it); stars with a negative velocity are moving slower than the sun (which is either catching up or moving ahead of them); stars moving in the direction of the galactic center, or away from it, are traveling at the same speed as the sun, and thus they have zero radial velocity (with respect to the sun). From this the Swedish astronomer B. Lindblad (1895-1965) concluded that the Galaxy as a whole was

A schematic view of the Galaxy seen sideways. The blobs outside the actual confines of the Galaxy are the globular clusters. The central dark line indicates the interstellar "fog" belt along which no stars can be seen. This "zone of avoidance," as Shapley called it, is the "dark rift" that divides the Galaxy in two.

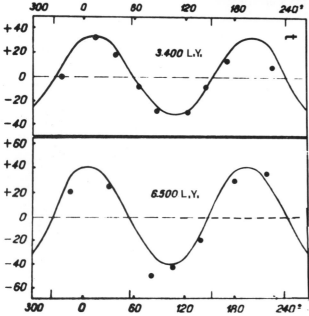

The radial velocities (vertical scale) plotted against their galactic longitudes (horizontal scale) for two groups of Cepheids show a sinusoidal behavior. The dots represent actual measurements, and the two curves are the best fit drawn through them. Although the two curves reach different maximum velocities (+30 and +40 respectively), their shapes are the same. At galactic longitudes 330° (which would be toward the center of the Galaxy), 60°, 150°, and 240°, radial velocities, relative to the sun, are zero, as indicated by the dashed line.

◄

Dutch astronomer J. Oort's measurements of actual rotation speeds bore out this conclusion; moreover, it put the galactic center in the neighborhood of Sagittarius, some 30,000 light-years from the sun—as had already been suggested by Shapley. The sun's orbital speed appears to be about 250 kilometers per second, so that it completes one revolution about the galactic center—clockwise as seen from the North Pole of the Milky Way—in about 200 million years. Thus it has completed about twenty to twenty-five revolutions since its formation nearly 5 billion years ago.

In 1940 when observations of the nebula in Andromeda, a neighboring galaxy similar to our own, indicated a spiral structure, it suggested a similar arrangement for the Milky Way. However, conjecture is one thing, and proof is quite a different matter: only a fraction of our Galaxy is visible from the earth, and even the largest telescopes are unable to penetrate the plane of the Galaxy beyond 20,000 light-years. (In other directions, where absorbing clouds are considerably weaker, galaxies can be seen even millions of light-years away.) In addition to "poor visibility," being situated in the midst of an apparent random distribution of stars, clusters, and nebulae made the task of identifying a spiral structure, if it existed, a near impossibility.

An extensive program of star counting, reminiscent of Herschel's star gauging, was started. Stars were sorted according to their brightness, color, and spectral lines to see whether there might be any "bumps" in the distribution to suggest the presence of spiral arms. The results were negative—until Walter Baade of the Mount

rotating; this also explained its flattened form, as noted by Kapteyn. However, the Galaxy is not rotating like a solid wheel but according to the Keplerian laws. Stars that are farther from the center of rotation move more slowly than those closer to the center; what one observes is the effect of the differential galactic rotation with respect to the sun. The situation can be likened to a three-lane highway. Cars traveling along the left lane will, as a rule, move faster than those in the middle lane, while those in the right lane will be the slowest. Thus, with respect to the cars in the middle lane, those on the left seem to move forward, while those on the right seem to move backward. Analogously stars closer to the center of rotation have a higher speed than those farther out and seem to move forward with respect to the sun. However, stars farther out than the sun have a smaller velocity and seem to move backward.

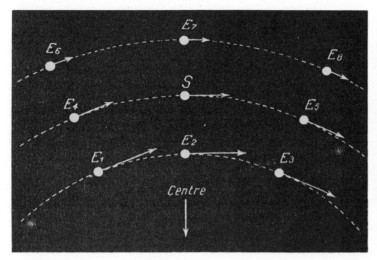

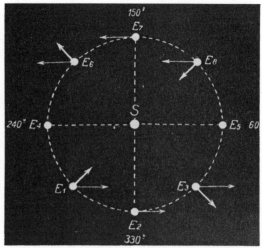

Differential galactic rotation. *(Left)* The absolute velocities of groups of stars (E_1 through E_8) and the sun (S) are indicated by arrows of varying size. For simplicity, it is assumed that the motion takes place in concentric orbits around the galactic center shown here. E_1, E_2, and E_3, which are nearer to the galactic center than is the sun, will be moving more rapidly than the sun; those at the same distance, E_4 and E_5, will have the same velocity as the sun; E_6, E_7, and E_8 at larger distances will move more slowly than the sun. Stars such as E_2 and E_7 have motions only perpendicular to our line of sight, and thus their radial velocities are zero; so too are those of E_4 and E_5, whose orbital velocities are the same as the sun's. *(Right)* Relative and radial velocities of the same stars (the numbers indicate galactic longitudes). As seen from the sun, stars E_1 and E_8 seem to move toward the sun (as indicated by their radial velocities)—E_1 moving faster and catching up, E_8 moving slower and apparently moving backward (note horizontal arrows). Stars E_3 and E_6 seem to move away from the sun, E_3 moving faster and pulling away and E_6 apparently moving backward (the sun is pulling away from it). Stars E_4 and E_5, along the orbit of the sun, appear to be stationary, and E_2 and E_7 have no radial velocities, E_2 seeming to move forward and E_7 backward.

The Great nebula in Andromeda, a galaxy very similar to our own. The disk appears at an angle and the arms are outlined by the dark lanes between them. Also shown are the two small satellite galaxies, M32 (below) and M33 (above), framing the Great nebula. Photograph taken with the 48-inch Schmidt telescope at Mount Palomar.

Wilson and Palomar Observatories examined the spiral of the Great nebula in Andromeda and studied its arms, which, of course, were clearly distinguishable. They were traced by several types of indicators, the most prominent being the bright O and B type stars—like a series of streetlamps marking a street. To map the arms in the Galaxy, then one need only locate those stars near the sun, measure their positions, and plot them on a chart.

Such a program was undertaken by W. W. Morgan and his co-workers at the Yerkes Observatory. To find the distances proved difficult, since the intervening clouds produced a reddening of the light and made the stars appear farther away than they really were—exactly the problem that faced Kapteyn and proved the undoing of his model. However, from the star's spectrum and spectral class its true color can be obtained; comparing this with the apparent color gives an indication of the amount of absorbing material present; and finally, correcting the inverse square law of the distances for the absorption of light yields the actual distances. The result, in 1951, was the first indication of the existence of three distinct spiral arms.

Further confirmation came from radio signals. (Although only a small part of the electromagnetic energy spectrum appears in the visible region, a large amount is transmitted as radio waves.) Such radiation is not only

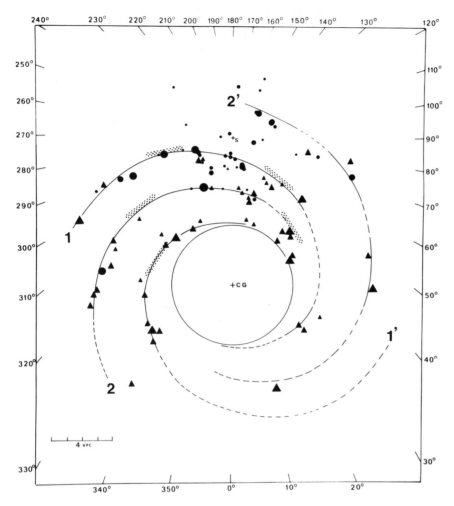

Four-arm spiral model of our galaxy: 1: Major–Sagittarius-Carina arm; 2: Intermediate–Scutum-Crux arm; 1′: Internal–Norma arm; 2′: External–Perseus arm. The identification of the various arms is made mostly by the detection of excited hydrogen lines. The black dots are regions of hydrogen alpha lines, and the triangles are regions with hydrogen 109-alpha wavelengths only. The small-dotted areas are regions of maximum intensity of neutral hydrogen and the continuous long-wavelength part of the spectrum.

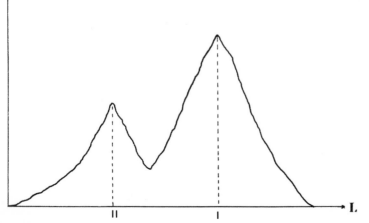

The 21-centimeter line radiation. A plot of the radio signal strength (S) against the wavelength (L) shows two distinct peaks, or sources, at I and II, with the shift in wavelength, of course, indicating a moving source. The relative speeds can then be determined from the difference between wavelengths I (or II) and the standard 21-centimeter wavelength.

more powerful but also less subject to absorption by intervening objects. (We will discuss radio astronomy later in this chapter.)

A characteristic feature of a spiral galaxy is the presence of a large amount of hydrogen, which can be detected by radio signals at a wavelength of 21 centimeters or a frequency of 1,420 megacycles. When a radio telescope was pointed toward areas suspected to be part of a spiral arm, two peaks in the energy distribution were observed at wavelengths slightly less than the magic 21 centimeters. This indicated two sources moving with different radial velocities—which could be determined from the differences in wavelengths. From this and a knowledge of the overall rotation of the Galaxy, the distances of these sources were found. Similar observations along different directions definitely established the existence of spiral arms and gave their distances. Thus, a plot of the spiral structure of the Galaxy was obtained.

Radio signals also indicate the outflow of gas from the galactic center, with strong activity at Sagittarius A. In some way our galaxy is behaving like a Seyfert galaxy. Named after Carl K. Seyfert, Seyfert galaxies are spiral galaxies characterized by small bright nuclei embedded in

A typical example of a (barred) spiral galaxy is NGC 1300 in Eridanus. The arms swirl through space, while the center remains fairly stationary.

rapidly moving masses of gas that are apparently being ejected from the central region. Seyfert nuclei emit extremely large amounts of energy and matter. Whether or not our galaxy is a Seyfert, the outbursts and flow of energy are direct evidence that an explosion of some kind occurred some 10 million years ago.

4. Island Universes

Two hundred years ago the eminent philosopher Immanuel Kant suggested that the hazy nebulous patches of light—commonly referred to as nebulae—were composed of myriads of stars forming galaxies similar to our own. And not only did he anticipate the existence of galaxies—or island universes, as they were later called by Friedrich Wilhelm von Humboldt (1769-1859)—but he also hinted at the infinity of the universe.

But despite his fame as a philosopher, these earlier scientific efforts were forgotten and, not being supported by astronomical evidence, lay dormant for more than a hundred years. The thread was not picked up again until the twentieth century with the work begun by Charles Messier and William and John Herschel in cataloging nebulae. By 1908 more than 15,000 nebulae had been described. Some, such as the Orion nebula, were indeed composed of gaseous matter, whereas others were star clusters.

But the majority defied identification. In the mid-nineteenth century, Lord Rosse had discovered a spiral structure in some of the nebulae—mostly far from the Milky Way—and it was these whose nature was in doubt.

The few spectra available showed absorption lines, such as might be produced by stars, and indicated speeds large enough to remove them from the Galaxy. However, if they were indeed outside the Galaxy, this would lead to linear velocities approaching or even surpassing the speed of light. It later turned out that these measurements were in error, but at the time they provided a convincing argument against the "island universe hypothesis."

The controversy reached its peak in 1920 when the two leading protagonists debated the matter in Washington before the National Academy of Sciences. Harlow Shapley—known for his pioneering work on the Galaxy—recognized that the spirals were outside the Galaxy, but he regarded them as smaller than the Milky Way and as "truly nebulous objects" not very distant. It will be recalled that at that time the size of our galaxy had been overestimated by 30 percent, and the Clouds of Magellan put at a distance of about 75,000 light-years—one-half their actual distance. Heber D. Curtis of the Lick Observatory, however, argued that the spirals were at very large distances, some million light-years, and consisted of star systems like the Milky Way. Although his arguments, based on the wrong concept of a rather small Kapteyn universe, were weak, his intuition turned out to be correct.

The crux of the matter, of course, lies in the distance of these nebulous objects. If they were fairly close—distances comparable to those of observable stars—they would have to be interstellar nebulae, perhaps intermingled with stars. But if they were very far away, as Curtis believed, then they might very well be large systems of stars—galaxies in their own right. The controversy was finally resolved in 1924 when Edwin Powell Hubble realized that the variables he discovered in the great nebula in Andromeda, the Magellanic Clouds, and the nebula in Triangulum were Cepheid variables, those pulsating stars with a periodic variation in brightness due to their corresponding variation in size—like a balloon that is periodically blown up and then deflated again. Although they were supergiants, they appeared as very faint stars of relative magnitude 18. This indicated that they must be very far away. Knowing their luminosities and measuring their brightness, Hubble was able to determine their distance, which turned out to be millions of light-years. In 1924, further study, especially spectroscopic analysis of the nebula in Andromeda, revealed a great similarity with our Galaxy, and the existence of extragalactic nebulae or external galaxies was established. (There has been some confusion in naming galaxies. When first discovered, they were called nebulae because of their faint, ill-defined appearance. Later, to differentiate them from the nebulae found within the Galaxy, "extragalactic" was added; Hubble simply called them nebulae, while for Shapley they

One of the first confirmations of the existence of other galaxies was the discovery of Cepheid variables in NGC 598 (or M33), the Sc-type spiral galaxy in Triangulum seen here.

Host Walter S. Adams (1876–1956), director of the Mount Wilson Observatory (left); Edwin Powell Hubble (1889-1953), smoking his pipe; and distinguished visitor Sir James Hopwood Jeans (1877-1946). Most of Adams's work was in stellar spectroscopy; he was able to measure the radial velocities—as evidenced by shifts in the spectra—of more than 8,000 stars, approximately one-half the total number measured by all observers at the time. His last extensive program concerned the dispersion of lines in stellar spectra produced by the interstellar medium, a study that shed considerable light on the nature of these interstellar gases. Hubble, who had practiced law before turning to astronomy, is probably best known for his classification of the extragalactic nebulae and measurement of their distances and velocities, out of which grew Hubble's law—of fundamental importance in modern cosmology. Jeans applied mathematical analysis to stellar dynamics. He suggested a tidal theory of the origin of planets, wherein they were formed by the gravitational pull of a passing star on the extremely hot solar mass. Similarly, he suggested that binary stars were formed by fission from one mass. He showed that the energy of motion of all stars was the same, small stars moving faster and large ones more slowly. Later, in his books, he popularized relativity, quantum mechanics, and other aspects of cosmogony and their philosophical implications.

were "external galaxies." Today the term nebula is used for the dust cloud, while the extragalactic nebulae are galaxies.)

After demonstrating that the nebulae (at least the "white nebulae" showing absorption lines characteristic of stellar spectra) were in fact "extragalactic objects," Hubble pushed his reconnaissance of extragalactic space to even further distances. In 1929 he discovered that the recession velocities of galaxies increased in proportion to their distances—as estimated from their magnitudes. This "Hubble law of recession" forms the basis of modern cosmology and is taken as evidence for an expanding universe which we will explore in Chapter VIII.

In addition to his renowned study of the red shifts of nebulae, Hubble had undertaken a detailed and comprehensive study of individual galaxies. In 1926 he had set up a classification system, which, with some revisions, is still in general use. It is remarkable that despite the vast number of extragalactic nebulae they can be divided into three definite classes, depending on their shape. First, there are the spiral nebulae, which fall into two distinct classes: the ordinary, or normal, spirals (S) and the barred spirals (SB). Among the spirals, there are three stages—a, b, and c—distinguished either according to the relative size of the central bulge (decreasing from a to c) or to the strength of the arms (increasing from a to c). Then there are the elliptic galaxies, or nebulae, ranging from the globular (E0) to the limiting lenticular form (E7); and finally, the irregulars (I), amounting to only two or three percent of the known galaxies and possessing no rotational symmetry or special shape.

The smooth gradation of forms in the "tuning fork" diagram seen here is suggestive of an evolutionary sequence. It had been proposed that elliptical galaxies gradually flatten, develop spiral arms, and become spiral galaxies. On the other hand, some investigators take the opposite point of view and envision galaxies as irregular forms that gradually develop into spirals and finally ellipses.

There is some doubt, however, whether either of these two interpretations is correct. Galaxies are rotating and possess angular momentum. If a galaxy were to change into a different shape, say, from spiral to elliptic, it would involve a change of angular momentum and, as in the case of the solar system, it is not clear what would happen to the excess of angular momentum (assuming that this is the direction of evolution). It is, thus, very likely that galaxies have been "created" in their *present* shape with their present amounts of angular momentum. Halton C. Arp draws an analogy from the presence of different races existing side by side without necessarily having evolved

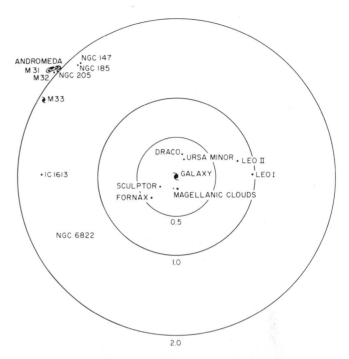

Local group. The positions of the nearest known galaxies are projected on an arbitrary plane, shown roughly to scale. Our Galaxy, or Milky Way, is at the center; the circles indicate distances in millions of light-years. The galaxies include those both numbered and named.

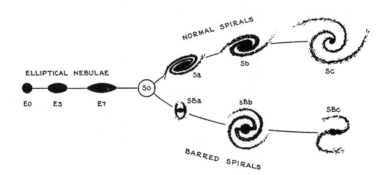

A schematic representation of Hubble's classification of extragalactic nebulae, showing their sequence. It is in the shape of a "Y" or tuning fork, with the elliptic galaxies forming the stem. The junction is represented by the hypothetical class SO. The upper branch represents the normal spirals, and the lower arm shows the barred spirals (a, b, and c provide a further subdivision, from closed to open spirals). The transition between E7 and SB_a is smooth and continuous, but between E7 and S_a, no galaxies are definitely identified.

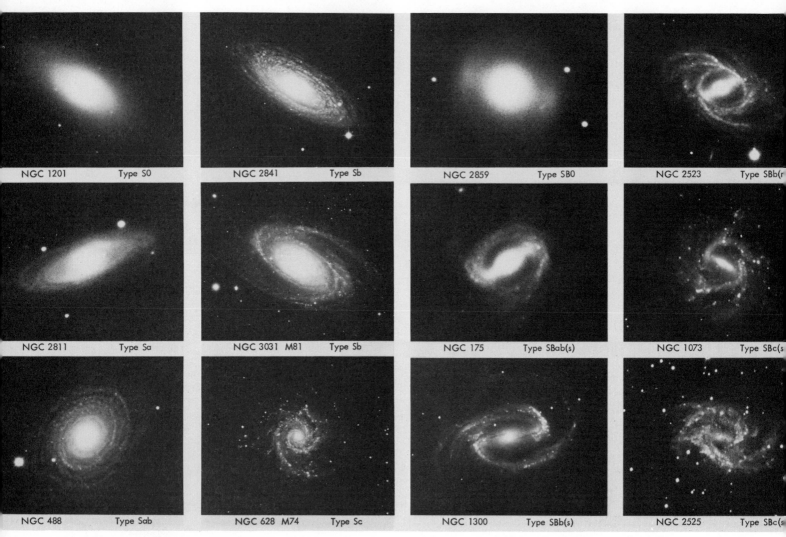

| NGC 1201 | Type S0 | NGC 2841 | Type Sb | NGC 2859 | Type SB0 | NGC 2523 | Type SBb(r |

| NGC 2811 | Type Sa | NGC 3031 M81 | Type Sb | NGC 175 | Type SBab(s) | NGC 1073 | Type SBc(s |

| NGC 488 | Type Sab | NGC 628 M74 | Type Sc | NGC 1300 | Type SBb(s) | NGC 2525 | Type SBc(s |

Typical normal spiral galaxies.   Typical barred spiral galaxies.

A side view of NGC 891 spiral galaxy in Andromeda taken with the 60-inch telescope at Hale Observatories. The central dark line is reminiscent of the dark rift in our own galaxy.

one from another—for example, from light to brown to dark skins. What may have happened is that a protogalaxy may have condensed out of the original expanding gas. After a while several stars may have formed, decreasing the moment of inertia—permitting the matter to rotate faster until finally shedding more material—and the flat galaxy may have evolved, similar to the way planets are formed from protoplanets.

What is difficult to understand is that there are spiral galaxies at all, since under the effect of rotation, after a couple of revolutions they would end up as a ring unless other forces—such as magnetic fields—are present. According to recent calculations on galactic forms, the spirals are not due to the actual motion of matter but are more like density waves, similar to the appearance of a rotating pinwheel with only part being illuminated at a time.

Just as stars occur in groups or clusters, so too do

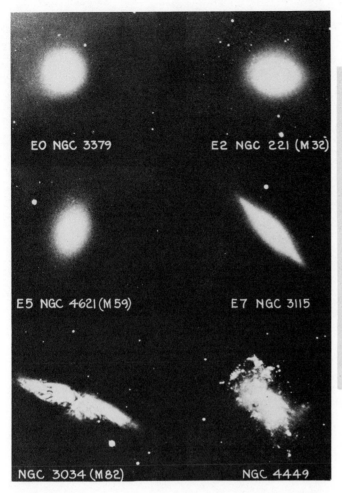

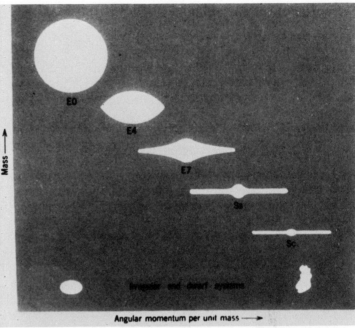

A suggested classification of galaxies based on mass and angular momentum. Presumably the more massive spherical (EO) and elliptical galaxies (E4) possess the smallest amount of angular momentum per unit mass. Increase of angular momentum produces greater flattening, as in the spiral galaxies Sa and Sc. It is difficult to see how angular momentum could be transferred to pass from one form to another. At the bottom are irregular and dwarf systems.

At top and center are views of typical elliptical galaxies, from spherical EO to spindle-shaped E7, taken at Yerkes Observatory. At bottom are two irregular galaxies of the same type as the Clouds of Magellan. *(Left)* NGC 3034(M82) in Sagittarius, a member of the local group. *(Right)* NGC 4449 in Canes Venatici is a more distant galaxy, and save for the most luminous supergiants no resolution into individual stars is shown in this photograph taken with the 60-inch reflector.

galaxies. Double or triple galaxies are quite common—the spiral nebula in Andromeda with its two companions or our own galaxy with the Magellanic Clouds being two typical cases.

Knowing the distance of one galaxy in a cluster is then usually sufficient to provide us with information about the relative distances of the other members in the cluster. Moreover, once these distances are determined, the masses can be obtained from their radial velocities, using methods similar to those employed in binary star systems. The group of galaxies centered about our own galaxy in a region of about 3 million light-years—and containing some seventeen members—is known as the local group. Proceeding farther out to distances of only several times the diameter of the local group, we find other groups and clusters of galaxies—the one in Virgo being the richest in galaxies.

Shortly after Hubble determined the true nature of the

nebulae, he commenced an extensive program to discover their distribution. Since it would be impossible to photograph and count all the galaxies, he employed a method similar to Herschel's star gauging. He selected 1,283 regions of the sky, which he photographed with the 100-inch telescope. His survey indicates that the nearby galaxies are concentrated along a band at right angles to the galactic plane. Fewer and fewer galaxies are seen as one approaches the Milky Way until the "zone of avoidance" is reached, where the light is completely obscured by interstellar matter. Although it is certainly true that the overall distribution of galaxies is more or less uniform, they do not form clusters or associations of galaxies. It has been suggested that our own galaxy may be a member of a supergalaxy, a disk-shaped galaxy whose members are galaxies themselves.

The masses of galaxies can be determined from their rotation. That galaxies are indeed rotating follows from

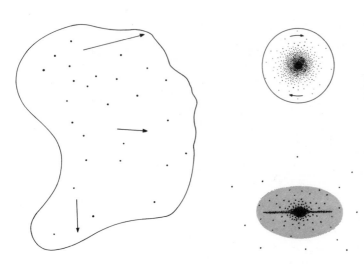

A possible evolutionary process of a galaxy. In the beginning there may have been thin expanding gas *(left)* from which a protogalaxy broke loose. As it began to rotate *(top right)* some stars may have condensed out of it, causing it to rotate faster, finally flattening into a disk *(bottom right)*.

The 100-inch reflector at Hale Observatories shows a group of four galaxies in the constellation Leo. Several types are included–SB_a, SB_c, S_b and E2, with apparent magnitudes ranging from 12 to 13.5. Their distance, calculated from the absolute and apparent magnitudes, is about 7.5 million light-years.

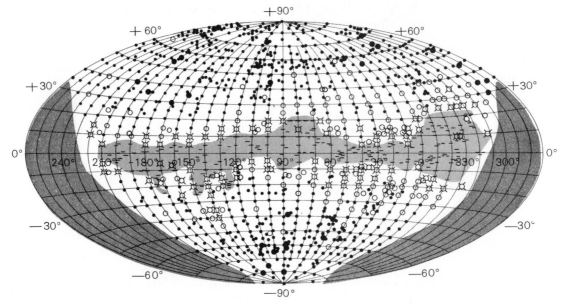

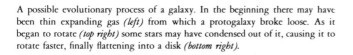

Distribution of galaxies. The bigger the black dot the more galaxies that were counted at that location on a photograph taken with the 100-inch telescope. Dashes and open circles indicate few or no galaxies; the region at the center is the "zone of avoidance"–the part of the Milky Way obscured by interstellar dust.

the fact that they would otherwise collapse under their own gravitation–the gravitational attraction is exactly balanced by the centrifugal force preventing the individual stars from "falling" toward the center and keeping them in their Keplerian orbits. Like stones on a string they whirl around in their nearly circular paths.

The rotation can be measured and the masses calculated from Kepler's laws. In some cases, where there are pairs of galaxies they can be "weighed" like binary stars. The masses that one obtains are by no means uniform, differing by as much as a factor of 100. Of course, one deals also with immense sizes in thousands of light-years.

Obviously Kant in his hypothesis never dreamed of the wealth and complexities within these island universes, whose study, facilitated by the 200-inch telescope, has become an important branch of astronomy. However, it was the radio telescope that really opened new vistas and brought exciting discoveries.

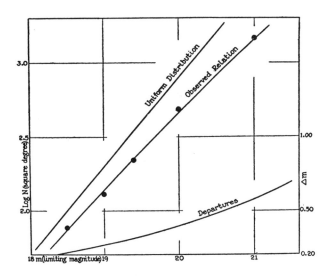

A Hubble diagram shows the apparent distribution of extragalactic nebulae. Each point on the "observed relation" line represents the average number of galaxies per square degree equal to, or brighter than, a particular apparent magnitude. Deviations of the observed distribution from the uniform are plotted in the "departures" curve and are interpreted as effects of red shifts modifying the uniform law of distribution.

The process of clustering. The bottom illustration is of supergalaxies merging into clusters of supergalaxies.

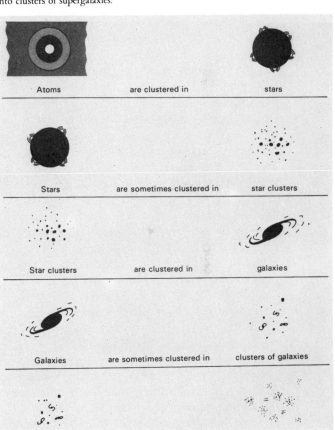

WELL-KNOWN NEBULAE AND STAR CLUSTERS *

Messier Catalogue	New General Catalogue	Apparent Visual Magnitude	Description
1	1952	11.3	Crab nebula in Taurus
4	6121	6.5	Globular cluster in Scorpio
8	6523		Lagoon nebula in Sagittarius
13	6205	5.9	Globular cluster in Hercules
17	6618	7.0	Swan nebula in Sagittarius
27	6853	8.2	Dumbbell nebula in Vulpecula
31	224	3.5	Andromeda galaxy
32	221	8.2	Companion to Andromeda
33	598	5.8	Spiral galaxy in Triangulum
42	1976		Orion nebula
45	–	2.0	The Pleiades
51	5194	8.4	Whirlpool spiral galaxy in Canes Venatici
53	5024	7.8	Globular cluster in Coma Berenices
57	6720	9.0	Ring nebula in Lyra
61	4303	9.6	Spiral galaxy in Virgo
65	3623	9.4	Spiral galaxy in Leo I
66	3627	9.0	Spiral galaxy in Leo II
74	628	9.3	Spiral galaxy in Pisces
81	3031	7.0	Spiral galaxy in Ursa Major
82	3034	8.4	Irregular galaxy in Ursa Major
87	4486	8.7	Elliptical galaxy in Virgo
90	4569	9.6	Spiral galaxy in Virgo
97	3587	11.1	Owl nebula in Ursa Major
100	4321	9.4	Spiral galaxy in Coma Berenices
101	5457	7.9	Spiral galaxy in Ursa Major
105	3379	9.7	Elliptical galaxy in Leo

* The nebulae selected follow the Messier Catalogue.

5. The Unseen Universe

In 1933 Karl Jansky, an engineer at the Bell Telephone Laboratories, was assigned the task of locating sources of interference hampering transatlantic telephone links. He built a radio antenna that could be rotated on wheels and thus pointed at any spot on the horizon. In addition to the usual interference from lightning and other common sources, he picked up a constant "hissing noise"—whose intensity seemed to vary during the day—with a period exactly four minutes shorter than a solar day. Since this is the time it takes the earth to rotate around its axis, relative to the stars, he correctly concluded that the noise had an extraterrestrial origin. Further investigation showed that his receiver was picking up radio waves transmitted by the Milky Way. Since there was nothing that could be done to eliminate this "cosmic" interference, Jansky was taken off the project and the subject was closed.

A few years after Jansky's initial research, a radio ham, Grote Reber of Wheaton, Illinois, read the technical reports describing Jansky's work and decided to find out more about these mysterious radio signals. Although today radio waves are reflected and focused by mirrors just as is light in a telescope, with the difference that the wavelength of radio waves is considerably larger, Reber even then realized its possibilities. Radio telescopes do not "see" or take photographs like ordinary telescopes equipped with a camera but receive a signal that can be amplified and recorded. Believing that such a reflector would be more efficient in collecting the signals than Jansky's simple antenna, he single-handedly built a dish-shaped reflector, 32 feet in diameter, with the antenna at its focus. It caused considerable curiosity when it appeared in his backyard; neighbors mistook it for a rainmaking device, especially since it contained a hole at the bottom to drain rainwater.

Reber not only confirmed Jansky's results but was able to show that certain areas of the Milky Way gave stronger signals than others.* His results were subsequently published in 1940, but did not arouse the interest they deserved.

Not until after World War II, when both cheap radar equipment and research were available, did radio astronomy start in earnest. British radar engineers had discovered a strong interference, which they first attributed to jamming but later found came from the sun. The

Karl Jansky with the world's first radio telescope, which picked up radio signals from the Milky Way. Note the wheels enabling the antenna to rotate.

interference was strongest during a period of visible sunspots. Thus, the spots themselves were responsible for the radio emissions.

For a long time radar antennae, surplus war equipment, were used for astronomical radio research. Some of the most famous centers, such as Dwingeloo in Holland and Jodrell Bank in England, started this way. However, because the wavelength of radio waves is so much larger than that of ordinary light, we have a problem with radio telescopes. The resolving power—or the ability to separate two images or signals—depends on the wavelength *and* the aperture of the telescope (in the case of a radio dish, on the size of the antenna). The larger the wavelength, therefore, the larger should be the size of the telescope—or antenna. The largest radio telescopes are about 250 feet in diameter, which at a wavelength of 20 centimeters can at best resolve two points on the moon about 800 miles apart. One way to improve this performance is to use two or more radio telescopes placed some distance apart. Therefore, the radiation will reach them at slightly different times, and from the "phase difference" the angle the source makes with the baseline (the line between the telescopes) can be obtained fairly accurately. However, there is a compensation in having large wavelengths: the dishes forming the reflectors do not have to be as smooth or as polished as do optical reflectors.

Following Reber's original survey of the Milky Way,

* Jansky's contribution was officially recognized recently when the International Astronomical Union adopted the *jansky* (Jy) as the unit of flux density or radiation.

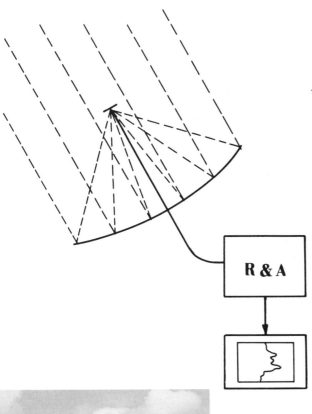

◀ Schematic of a radio telescope: the signal reflected from the dish is picked up by the antenna and is amplified in a receiver (R & A), then fed into a recorder where a pen traces the fluctuations in the strength of the signal onto a moving strip of paper.

Two radio maps of the sun made at a wavelength of 2 centimeters, two days apart (March 6, 1970, and March 8, 1970). The maps clearly indicate the movement of centers of radio activity–associated with sunspots–both as to structure and motion across the disk as a result of the sun's rotation.

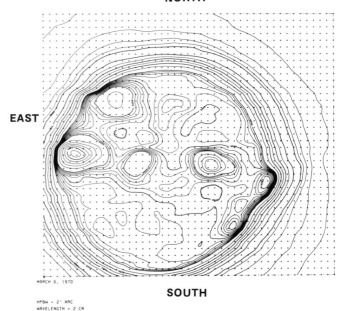

MARCH 6, 1970
HPBW = 2' ARC
WAVELENGTH = 2 CM

Grote Reber's radio telescope, which he built and mounted at his home in Wheaton, Illinois, in 1937. All later "dishes" are based on it. The antenna is at the focus of the 32-foot dish-shaped reflector.

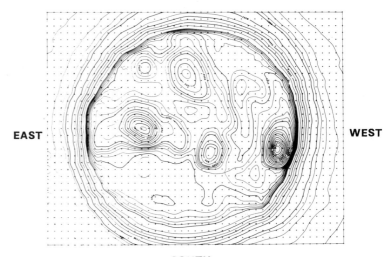

MARCH 8, 1970
HPBW = 2' ARC
WAVELENGTH = 2 CM

A diagram of the first radio map of the Milky Way (1939), obtained by Reber. The coordinates are galactic longitude (horizontal) and galactic latitude (vertical). ▼

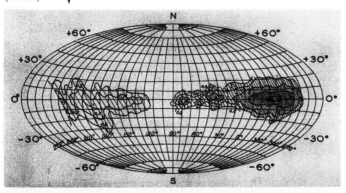

The so-called Würzburg antenna, a German radar dish used in World War II, had been used for making some of the first radio astronomical observations in Holland (Dwingeloo) and England (Mullard Radio Astronomy Observatory, Cambridge).

The giant 600-foot radio telescope of the National Radio Astronomy Observatory (NRAO) at Green Bank, West Virginia. The reflector, consisting of an aluminum network, weighs 20,000 tons, but it can be directed toward any point on the northern celestial hemisphere.

The 250-foot radio telescope of the University of Manchester at Jodrell Bank, Cheshire, England. Until recently it was the largest dish-type radio telescope in the world, designed to follow celestial objects across the sky automatically. Made of steel, it weighs 2,000 tons.

The movements of the Jodrell Bank radio telescope are controlled from this main console. A computer *(left)* gives commands to the guiding mechanism. Sets of dials *(right)* record right ascension, declination, and elevation.

The Arecibo telescope. Most radio telescopes have a steerable dish, which collects the radio signals. At Arecibo, Puerto Rico, the enormous aluminum dish 1,000 feet in diameter is immobile on the earth, while its receiving equipment–600 tons of it–hangs 50 stories in the air and can be steered and pointed by remote-control equipment. The observatory is designed so that one person can operate the entire facility. The Arecibo Observatory is a part of the National Astronomy and Ionosphere Center, a national center operated by Cornell University under contract with the National Science Foundation.

The most remarkable part of the Arecibo telescope, of course, is the giant dish. It consists of 38,778 individual aluminum panels, each about 40 by 80 inches. Specially devised surveying techniques using lasers were employed to align the panels to form the surface. Workers check the dish regularly and make repairs when needed.

more detailed maps were made. From these, several interesting facts became apparent: regions of equal intensity, appearing as contours on the maps, are roughly symmetrical with respect to the galactic plane. The width of the Milky Way, as it appears on the radio charts, becomes increasingly broader as the wavelength is increased, until at very long wavelength (several meters) radiation is received equally from all directions and one can no longer speak of the Milky Way as a discrete source. The different appearance of the Galaxy at varying wavelengths, of course, is due to the different processes that produce the electromagnetic radiation. Most of the radiation produced is due to oscillating currents or high-speed electrons. These are known to spiral along the lines of force of a magnetic field and to radiate continuously along a cone in the direction of its motion. This process is known as synchrotron radiation, since it was first produced in giant accelerators known as synchrotrons. In these, machines particles (such as electrons) are accelerated to extremely large speeds, approaching the speed of light, with the help of strong magnets. The interaction of these fields with the electrons produces a radiation, and it was suggested by the Russian astrophysicist I. S. Shklovsky that similar processes may also occur in space. It turns out that the synchrotron emission produces more emission at longer wavelengths, so that the picture of the Milky Way will appear different for varying wavelengths. At very long wavelengths strong emission will be produced even at a distance of only a few hundred light-years–which will obscure radiation from more distant signals that ordinarily produce a more or less uniform distribution over all of space.

The importance of the 21-centimeter radiation has already been noted as an aid for detecting the arms of the

Radio interferometers—using multiple telescopes coupled to each other. These twin 90-foot radio telescopes of the Owens Valley Radio Observatory of the California Institute of Technology have a baseline equivalent to the diameter of a single-dish antenna of the same resolving power.

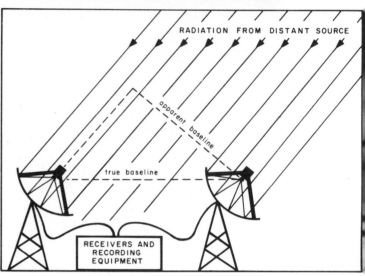

A schematic drawing of the operation of a simple interferometer. Radiation from a distant source hits the two telescopes at slightly different times (the right one first), and from the phase difference the location of the source can be obtained more accurately than would be the case if only one telescope was operating. The "apparent baseline" is the effective diameter of a single dish-antenna producing the same result.

A series of telescopes in Cambridge, England, spaced at equal distances in several rows produces an even better interference pattern. The instrument shown operates on a wavelength of 3.7 meters and covers about an acre. Plans are made to use intercontinental interferometers operating from different locations connected by microwave signals.

An artist's conception shows a possible configuration of the VLA (Very Large Array) of radio telescopes that astronomers at the National Radio Astronomy Observatory have proposed to build in the southwestern part of the United States. Such an array would map regions of the sky in as much detail at radio wavelengths as can presently be obtained by the largest optical telescopes. ▶

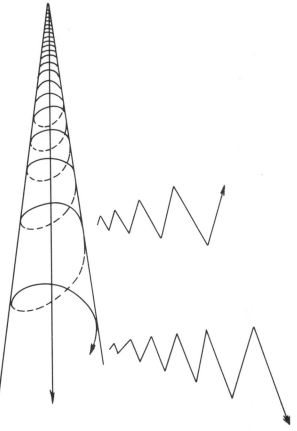

The principle of using several reflectors has been extended in the 5-kilometer radio telescope situation along the line of the former Oxford-Cambridge railway in England. It consists of four fixed and four movable aerials, each 42 feet in diameter. At an observing wavelength of 6 centimeters, the telescope has a resolving power of 2 seconds of arc, comparable with that of the best optical telescope. Shown here are five of the eight dishes with the railway track on which the four most distant can be moved.

Synchrotron radiation. When a high-speed electron spirals around a line of magnetic force (straight arrow), it continuously radiates a cone of energy in the direction of its motion. Under suitable conditions, this radiation is within the radio region of the spectrum and constitutes the main source of radio energy detected by radio telescopes.

A contour map of part of the Milky Way assembled from various radio tracings. The contour lines represent lines of equal intensity, some of which are indicated by numbers 1, 3, 4, and 5. Areas of larger intensity appear as patches, mostly in the vicinity of the Galactic Equator (GE). As a whole, the Milky Way appears as a narrow central band with some sources, such as Cygnus A (A), outside it.

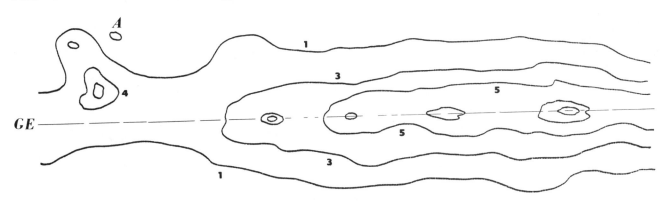

Galaxy. Now radio astronomy made it possible to penetrate into the heart of the Galaxy itself. There explosions and other processes are taking place; this would provide a spectacular view were it not for the gas and dust clouds that obscure these phenomena from the optical telescope and its cameras. Visible light, however, constitutes only a tiny fraction of the electromagnetic spectrum, whereas the major sources of emission have longer or shorter wavelengths. Dust particles, having the dimensions of wavelengths of ordinary light, interfere primarily with it only, while radiation of longer wavelengths, such as infrared or radio waves, moves around dust particles relatively unhindered; X rays and gamma rays, being highly energetic, are able to pass through the intervening gas, although their wavelengths are shorter than the size of the dust particles. Thus, with the help of any of these "windows," it is possible to get a fairly good picture of the galactic center.

In addition to synchrotron radiation and line emission of hydrogen and other molecules, there is also a continuous "thermal" radiation due to the passage of high-speed electrons near nuclei of hydrogen protons.

Most of the synchrotron radiation in the galactic nucleus originates from Sagittarius A, which at first was believed to be a radio source. It is about 36 light-years in diameter and probably the center of explosive events. That gas flows away from the center was demonstrated conclusively in 1960 by J. H. Oort and G. W. Rougoor, two Dutch astronomers. From their careful observations of the 21-centimeter radiation, they deduced not only that the hydrogen rotates with the galaxy but that there exist two "arms" moving away from the center. That these arms are on opposite sides of the center—one moving toward the sun with a speed of 53 kilometers per second and one moving away at a speed of 135 kilometers per second—was shown by the radiation emitted by Sagittarius A. Some of the center's radiation is absorbed at the 21-centimeter line by one arm but not the other; this could only be the case if they are at opposite sides. Another striking feature—discovered only recently from line radiation from molecules—is the existence of an inner molecular ring around the central disk at a distance of about 1,000 light-years and expanding at a rate of 100 kilometers per second. This provides additional evidence that gas is being blown away from the center, perhaps as the result of a recent explosion. The thermal emission, furthermore, is a good indication that new stars are continuously being formed near the nuclear center.

Additional information about the galactic center has been provided more recently by infrared and, at the other side of the spectrum, by X-ray wavelengths. The infrared sky (wavelengths about four times that of yellow light) looks quite different from that presented by visible light.

The gas motions at the galactic center are shown in this contour map. Based on observations made with the 140-foot radio telescope of National Radio Astronomy Observatory, the emission is shown at a wavelength of 21 centimeters, with the various shadings indicating the intensity. The vertical axis indicates radial velocities (in kilometers per second), with negative values denoting motion toward us and positive ones motion away. The hole at the center identifies the central source, known as Sagittarius A. There are two ridges, known respectively as the 3-kiloparsec arm moving toward us and the 135-kilometer expanding arm moving away. The absence of an "absorption hole" at Sagittarius A indicates that this arm is on the far side of the nucleus.

The amount of radiation emitted by a black body depends on the wavelength and temperature. A "cool" star of 2,500 degrees will emit about one percent of its radiation in the visible region, but 10 percent in the infrared. On the other hand, a 10,000-degree K. star will radiate a much larger fraction in the visible region than in the infrared one. Thus, stars that appear bright in the visible region, for example, when photographed by an ordinary camera, will appear faint in the infrared region, and vice versa. The real advantage of infrared photography is that this radiation will not be greatly dispersed by the interstellar dust and one can "see" the galactic center. The picture presented differs from that shown by radio emission, although their positions of the galactic center more or less coincide.

An interesting fact that emerges from all this is that the distribution of flux intensity is very similar to that of the Andromeda galaxy; this indicates again the close

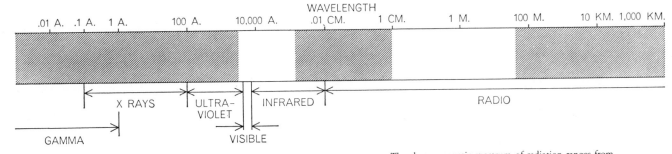

WAVELENGTH

X RAYS — ULTRA-VIOLET — INFRARED — RADIO

GAMMA — VISIBLE

The electromagnetic spectrum of radiation ranges from very short wavelength (or high-frequency) gamma rays to long wavelength (low-frequency) radio waves. In all cases the velocity is that of light, but the production of the particular electromagnetic radiation is different. For example, gamma rays are emitted from the nucleus, whereas X rays originate in the inner shells of atoms. The visible region occupies a comparatively narrow range from 4,000 angstroms to 8,000 angstroms (1 angstrom equals a hundred-millionth of a centimeter). The earth's atmosphere absorbs a great amount of incoming radiation, except at the two regions (visible infrared and radio waves up to 100 meters) indicated by unhatched areas.

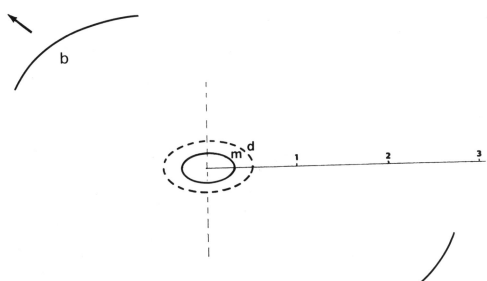

From current observations of the motions of neutral hydrogen and other molecules it appears that the galactic center consists of four parts: a rotating disk of gas (d) extending about .5 kiloparsecs (or 1,500 light-years). The disk is not expanding; its speed of rotation is decreasing slowly, from the edge inward. Inside the disk at about .3 kiloparsecs from the center is an expanding ring of molecular clouds (m) rotating too slowly to balance the gravitational attraction—from which one can conclude that the ring has been ejected from points closer to the center. Finally, there are the two rotating arms of gas: (a) lying at a distance of about 3 kiloparsecs (thus called the 3 kiloparsecs arm) and moving toward us (S indicates the direction to the sun) at about 54 kilometers per second; and (b) at about 2.5 kiloparsecs from the center, expanding much faster. It is believed that these four components resulted from an explosion at the center of the Galaxy, which gave rise to the expanding and rotating masses of gas.

relationship between it and the Milky Way. Since the center of the Andromeda galaxy is known to consist of a great number of stars closely packed into a comparatively small region (a few light-years in diameter), it is reasonable to assume that the same situation pertains also to the Galaxy. Inside the core the number of stars per unit volume is about 10 million times what it is in the neighborhood of the sun; or, put more succinctly, inside the core the stars are about 200 times closer to one another than in the rest of the sky. It is this enormous aggregate of normal stars that is responsible for the enormous amount of energy—produced by dust particles that have been heated by starlight—noted in infrared surveys of the galactic center. However, X-ray detectors on board an artificial satellite have found a similar source, which may be due to thermal emission of a very hot gas within the very center of the Galaxy.

The composite picture of the galactic center that

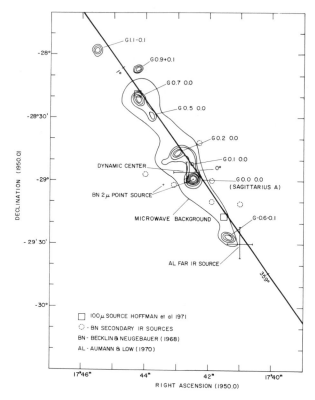

A Kitt Peak National Observatory radio and infrared map of the central region of the Galaxy, pointing out the positions of the more important radio sources in the direction of the galactic center (the "G" prefix indicates the galactic longitudes; latitudes show a plus or minus sign). The elongated contour is the result of infrared observations at a 100 micron wavelength.

emerges from these surveys is complex and open to speculation. The emission of large amounts of energy and the flow of gases, as evidenced by the two arms, seems to indicate that an explosion has occurred. Compared with other unusual objects, such as Seyfert galaxies or quasars (which we will discuss next), the galactic center appears fairly peaceful, but this may be just the calm before the storm. One cannot exclude the possibility that nuclei of ordinary galaxies, such as the Milky Way, pass regularly through periods of great activity—reflected by Seyfert galaxies and even quasars, with which they share the presence of strong radio and infrared sources, as well as a strong outflow of matter.

In addition to the more or less continuously distributed radio emission from the Milky Way Reber had noticed strong radio signals coming from the center of the Galaxy, as well as from other points along and even away from it. These points were at first referred to as "radio stars" and remained an enigma for a long time—even now they are not completely understood. None of them, with the exception of the sun, turned out to be stars and these strong centers of emission are now called radio sources. Some of these can be identified with well-known visible objects, such as the spectacular Crab nebula, but others, including the two most powerful, are at points in space where no conspicuous objects seem to be present.

To locate a radio source accurately is a difficult task at best, owing to the comparatively poor resolution. A single radio telescope can locate the position of a radio source no better than within one minute of arc (depending on the size of the dish). We have seen that the situation is somewhat improved by the use of twin telescopes or interferometers, but it still would be desirable to locate the optical image for positive identification.

A comprehensive survey using a double interferometer, consisting of four aerials each 320 feet long, was carried out in 1955, locating 1,936 radio sources over the entire sky. Only about thirty gave indications of being part of the Galaxy and some could be identified with nebulae. The balance were found to be distributed uniformly throughout the sky but with a distribution that increases with distance. This suggested that they might be of extragalactic origin, since sources in the Galaxy would be concentrated near the Milky Way, while galaxies are distributed uniformly. Since the intrinsic flux intensity of the emitting sources is unknown, their distances cannot be determined, and there is no direct way to find out whether they are extragalactic or not.

Sir Martin Ryle, the prominent British astronomer and Nobel Prize winner, and his co-workers from 1950 to 1955 carried out an analysis of the source distribution-distance, which confirmed the suspicion of their extragalactic origin. Since the intensity of the radiation varies inversely as the square of the distance, it is possible to determine how many stars within a spherical region will have more than a given brightness—under the assumption that the stars are uniformly distributed. For example, if one counts a number of stars of a particular brightness, he should find that the number of stars with at least one-quarter of that brightness is eight times as great. Deviations from that ratio—which were found—indicate either that the distribution is not uniform or that the emitted flux changes with the distance. Unless we are in a region of abnormally low density, which is unlikely due to the uniform distribution, the conclusion reached is that the radio sources are at very large distances, in some cases as much as 500 million light-years—beyond the reach of the largest optical telescopes, which, incidentally, is why so few radio sources have been identified optically.

Since Reber's time many galaxies have been discovered, and a greater number identified optically. These can be divided roughly into two groups, normal galaxies and peculiar galaxies, depending on their optical and radio characteristics. The normal (radio) galaxies, are clearly associated with their optically visible counterparts, are weak radio emitters, and form a kind of halo around the visible disks. It appears that most spiral galaxies, and

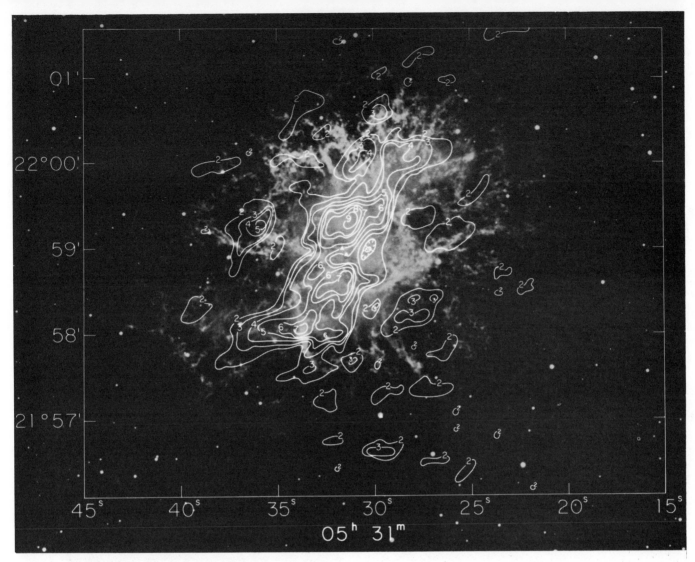

A high-resolution radio map of the Crab nebula made at the National Radio Astronomy Observatory at Green Bank with a resolution of 8 seconds of arc. This remnant of the supernova explosion of 1054 was the first radio source to be recognized as an emitter of synchrotron radiation. The radio contours are superimposed on an optical photograph of the nebula.

A distribution of radio sources resulting from the radio survey made by the University of Cambridge. The distribution is symmetrical, but from the number of sources of different intensity it appears that they increase in density with distance.

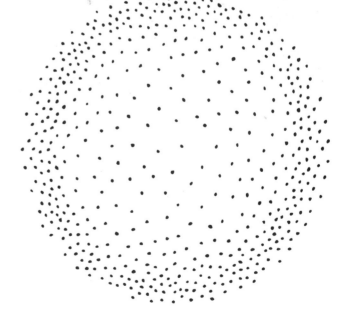

probably the irregular ones as well, are of that type. Peculiar radio galaxies, on the other hand, are strong radio emitters, and it is often difficult to pinpoint the optically visible galaxy associated with them. One of the most striking—and earliest discovered—peculiar radio galaxies is Cygnus A (radio sources are referred to by Roman letters, in order of strength). In 1951, when Walter Baade photographed the area with the 200-inch reflector, he found that what had first appeared to be one object in the center of two radio sources resembled two galaxies in close contact. When Baade suggested that this might be due to two galaxies in collision, at first he was not believed. He offered to bet Rudolf Minkowski, the son of Hermann Minkowski and a well-known astronomer, a thousand

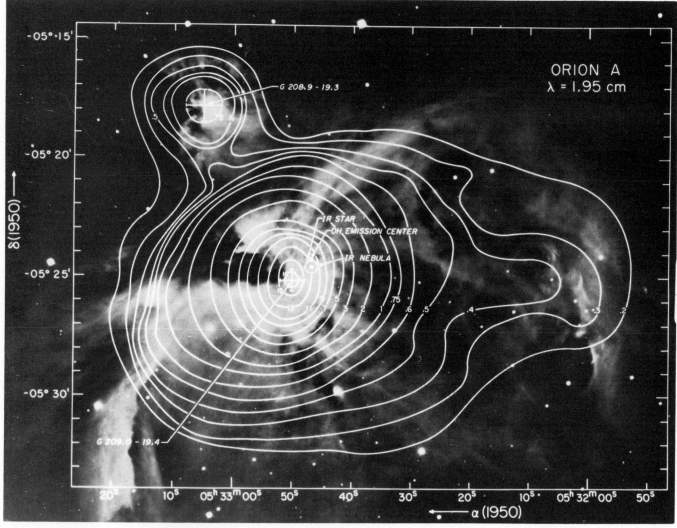

A radio map of the Orion nebula made at a wavelength of 1.95 centimeters with the NRAO 140-foot telescope superimposed on a photograph of the nebula. It shows two infrared objects (IR)—a star and a nebula—as well as an OH, or hydroxyl molecule, source.

dollars that the colliding-galaxy hypothesis was the only way the curious object could be explained, including the enormous amount of radiated energy. Minkowski refused, and the two astronomers finally settled on a bottle of whiskey; the evidence for collision was the presence of emission lines of high excitation. When two galaxies are "in collision," this does not mean that the individual stars are colliding—they are much too far apart. What does happen is that the gravitational attraction will perturb their motions and distort their structure. However, the gas and dust particles *will* collide with high-energy particles, and at these high speeds—hundreds to thousands of miles per second—the gas will heat to millions of degrees. As a result, the atoms are in a highly excited state and radiate accordingly.

When the spectrum was examined, it was indeed seen that the emission lines corresponded to a glowing gas; this confirmed Baade's conjecture. Several months later Minkowski walked into Baade's office with a bottle of

whiskey. The story does not end there, for, two days later, Minkowski, seeing the untouched bottle, drank it himself.

The collision theory had to be discarded later, since it could not account for the enormous amount of energy released at the faint outer regions, at a rate ten times the output by the colliding galaxies. Collisions between galaxies do take place, as Minkowski himself was able to demonstrate, but in rich clusters of galaxies having a comparatively high density; more or less isolated starlike objects—quasistellar radio sources—must generate their energy by other means.

Another remarkable object—only about 12 million light-years away—is Centaurus A (also known as NGC 5128). A dust lane that runs through its center is believed to be the remnant of an outburst, which produced the radio source. It is a peculiar elliptical galaxy, but because the outer parts give the impression of a spiral, it might in fact be two colliding galaxies—an elliptical and a spiral one. Also, the contours of the radio source show the characteristic

The normal radio galaxy (NGC 5457). This well-developed spiral galaxy, also known as M101, in Ursa Major is about 8 million light-years away, seen here through the 200-inch telescope.

Cygnus A *(center),* one of the most intense radio souces, looks like two galactic nuclei in contact. This has been interpreted as being either the result of two galaxies colliding or the fragments of a gigantic explosion.

The peculiar galaxy in Centaurus A (NGC 5128) about 12 million light-years away, as photographed with the 200-inch reflector. It appears to be a giant SO galaxy in collision with a spiral, seen edgewise. A strong absorbing band of dust and gas is at the center.

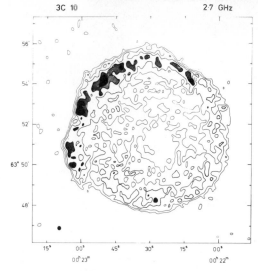

Contour map of Tycho's supernova remnant, provided at a wavelength of 11 centimeters by the One-Mile Telescope at Mullard Radio Astronomy Observatory (MRAO), Cambridge, England. The darkest areas indicate the strongest radio emission.

A contour map of the radio emission in Centaurus A, which clearly indicates the presence of two radio sources in the vicinity of the central source. The figures give the location and size of the source, with right ascension at the bottom and declination at the right.

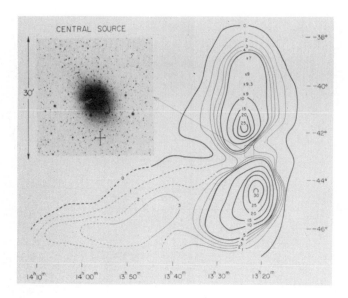

double source, but a smaller central source suggests the possibility of repeated "explosions" occurring within the galaxy. Cygnus A and Centaurus A are only two of the more striking examples of peculiar radio galaxies, of which there are quite a few known.

Several theories have been proposed to account for radio galaxies and the large amount of energy they produce. Regular galaxies can be understood in terms of the synchrotron radiation emitted by relativistic electrons (electrons at speeds close to that of light). These electrons are produced by collisions of high-energy particles within the disk of the galaxy, where the interstellar gas is concentrated. Collisions provide a continuous source of electrons, so that a normal galaxy can radiate for a long time. If this picture is correct, what is unknown is the source of the cosmic rays.

Peculiar galaxies, on the other hand, are more difficult to explain. In some cases, such as Cygnus A, the accepted explanation is the collision of two galaxies resulting in the production of very hot gases; it is still not clear, however, how the kinetic energy is converted into the energy of relativistic electrons that account for the intense radio emission. Another suggestion, made by the University of California husband and wife team Geoffrey and Margaret Burbidge, is the production of a chain reaction of supernova explosions within a galaxy, triggered by an initial supernova explosion. Intense radiation from the first explosion would cause nuclear reactions, which in turn would cause other stars to explode. In the process, electrons are produced, either directly by the explosions or indirectly by the production of cosmic rays in the interstellar gas.

Quite a different explanation has been put forward by V. L. Ginzburg in Russia. He suggests that the intense radio emission is associated with the formation of galaxies. The original gas cloud, the protogalaxy, contracts, releasing gravitational energy, which generates cosmic rays. Collisions with the interstellar gas—of which a large amount is present in the formation of the galaxy—is then responsible for the production of the large number of electrons. In this picture, radio emission is a comparatively short-lived process occurring in the early stages of the galaxy.

However, we still need a better understanding of the processes of radio emission if we are to gain a deeper knowledge of galaxies and the universe itself.

BRIGHTEST RADIO SOURCES (NORTHERN HEMISPHERE)		
Name	Intensity *	Identification
3C 461	2477	Cassiopeia A (supernova remnant)
3C 405	1495	Cygnus A
NGC 5128	1330	Centaurus A
3C 144	875	Taurus A (Crab Nebula)
3C 400	576	
3C 145	520	Orion A (NGC 1976)
3C 274	198	Virgo A (M 87)
3C 392	171	Supernova remnant in Milky Way
PKS 0321-37	115	Fornax A

* In flux units, a measure of the power received.

6. Novel Strains

The correlation of radio sources with optical objects remained one of the outstanding problems of radio astronomy. Many sources had been found to be either nebulae, remnants of explosions, or galaxies. The only known radio star was the sun itself, but in 1960 it appeared as if there might be others.

When the powerful 200-inch telescope was pointed toward the radio source 3C 48 (3C stands for Third Cambridge Catalogue of Radio Sources and 48 is the number of the source), no galaxy was found; instead there appeared to be a "star," a strange one, whose spectrum, consisting of broad emission lines, could not be identified. The puzzle was solved a few years later, when another "famous" quasi-stellar source, 3C 273, had been discovered and optically identified. It was indeed a remarkable object, with a "jet" exuding from its side. Yet there could be no doubt that this strange star shared the exact spot of 3C 273. In 1963 Cyril Hazard had managed to pinpoint its position by a very clever method; when the moon had come between the star and the earth—occulting the radio source—the signals disappeared. When the signals reappeared, they were double, indicating the presence of a double source—the two positions corresponding to the starlike image and the end of the jet. Another occultation confirmed the result and Quasar (as these quasi-stellar radio sources began to be called) 3C 273 was located.

Its spectrum was just as puzzling as that of 3C 48 and defied interpretation—that is, until Maarten Schmidt in 1963 at Mount Palomar Observatory had a hunch that proved to be correct as well as far-reaching in its consequences. We have discussed the shifting of spectra before whereby the spectral lines are displaced toward the red end of the spectrum; the spectra of galaxies also are red-shifted, indicating that they are moving away from us. Even for very distant galaxies this red shift is only a small fraction of its wavelength. Now Schmidt found that he could explain the spectrum quite readily by the elements commonly found in galaxies—but having very large red shifts, as much as 16 percent in the case of 3C 273 and 37 percent for 3C 48. This solved the problem of the spectrum but raised more questions. If the red shift was due to the shifting of lines of atoms in a gravitational field, then one would have to deal with very massive objects whose gravitational effects on nearby stars should be noted. On the other hand, if the red shift is due to the motion of the quasars, it would have to be at extremely large distances, about 1,500 million light-years. Since the apparent brightness is of the thirteenth magnitude, that

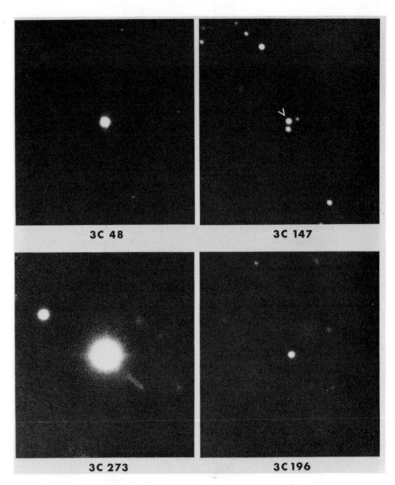

Four of the earliest-known quasi-stellar radio sources. 3C 48 was the first quasar to be identified optically. 3C 273 is of particular interest because of the "jet" pointing away from the nucleus, indicating a vast release of energy.

would imply—taking into account the decrease of intensity due to the inverse square law—an absolute brightness about one hundred times that of the brightest galaxy known. The generation of so large an amount of energy is one of the unsolved puzzles of quasars.

If the large red shifts are indeed due to large recession speeds, then it would be reasonable to expect to find quasars at even larger distances with very large red shifts. Indeed, such quasars have been observed whose red shifts may be as much as twice the original wavelength. This poses two additional problems: in the first case, lines will now appear that normally are in the untraviolet region and whose correct identification is difficult; second, the usual theory of red shifts as indicators of recession speeds breaks down and relativistic corrections have to be applied, implying speeds approaching the speed of light. For example, 3C 9 having a red shift of 2.012 recedes with a velocity of eight-tenths that of light.

An overexposed photograph of 3C 273 showing the jet—the horizontal arrow points toward the starlike component, B; the diagonal arrow points to the jet, or component A. The length of the jet is about 100,000 light-years, indicating that the explosion must have begun about one million years ago. The lower diagram, to the same scale as the photograph, shows the two radio signaling regions.

Quasar 3C 273's radio emission measured during its eclipse by the moon. The interval (center, when the quasar was covered by the moon) is about 30 minutes. The fluctuations at the beginning and end of the occultation are clearly the diffraction patterns produced by the moon's edge. ▼

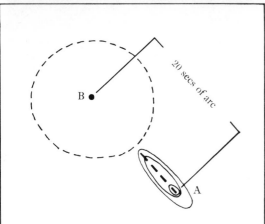

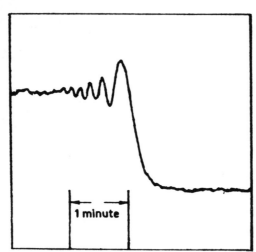

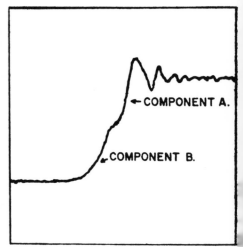

			NOTABLE QUASARS					
Object *	Right ascension			Declination			Apparent Magnitude †	Red shift ‡
3C 9	0h	17m	49.8s	+15°	24′	16.5″	18.21	2.012
PHL 923	0	56	31.7	− 0	09	16	17.33	0.717
PKS 0106+01	1	06	04	+ 1	19		18.39	2.107
PHL 3424	1	31	12	+ 5	32		18.25	1.847
3C 48	1	34	49.8	+32	54	20	16.2	0.367
PHL 1194	1	48	42	+ 9	02		17.50	0.298
PKS 0237-23	2	37	53.4	−23	22	05	16.63	2.223
MSH 03-19	3	49	09.5	−14	38	07	16.24	0.614
3C 138	5	18	16.5	+16	35	26	17.9	0.760
3C 181	7	25	20.4	+14	43	47.2	18.92	1.382
PKS 0922+14	9	22	22.3	+14	57	26.2	17.96	0.895
AO 0952+17	9	52	11.9	+17	57	46.6	17.7	1.471
3C 263	11	37	09.4	+66	04	25.9	16.32	0.652
PKS 1217+02	12	17	38.3	+ 2	20	20.9	16.53	0.240
3C 273	12	26	33.3	+ 2	19	42.0	12.8	0.158
3C 287	13	28	16.1	+25	24	37.1	17.67	1.055
3C 298	14	16	38.6	+ 6	42	21	16.79	1.439
3C 334	16	18	7.4	+17	43	30.5	16.41	0.555
3C 432	21	20	25.6	+16	51	46.0	17.96	1.805
PKS 2135-14	21	35	1.1	−14	46	27	15.53	0.200
PHL 5200	22	25	50.6	− 5	30	36	18.2	1.981
PKS 2251+11	22	51	40.6	+11	20	39	15.82	0.323
PKS 2344+09	23	44	3.4	+ 9	14	4	15.97	0.677

 * The letters correspond to the different catalogues, e.g., 3C = Third Cambridge; PKS = Parkes radio telescope in Australia; AO = Arecibo radio telescope; MSH = Mills, Slee, and Hill in Australia. PHL is a catalogue of faint blue stars, later identified as quasars.

 † A magnitude range between 15.5 and 18.4 makes it difficult to identify the source.

 ‡ From comparatively small values (0.2) to very large ones (2.2).

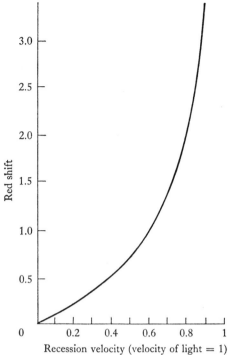

The red shift is an indication of the recession velocity of the object. For small velocities (compared with the velocity of light) the red shift is proportional to the recession velocity. But as the velocity approaches that of light (equal to 1 here), the red shift grows without limit.

The distribution of about one hundred quasars plotted in galactic coordinates. The symbols (note the key) indicate quasars of different red-shift ranges. N and S indicate the earth's poles, and the broken line is the projection of the earth's equator. ▼

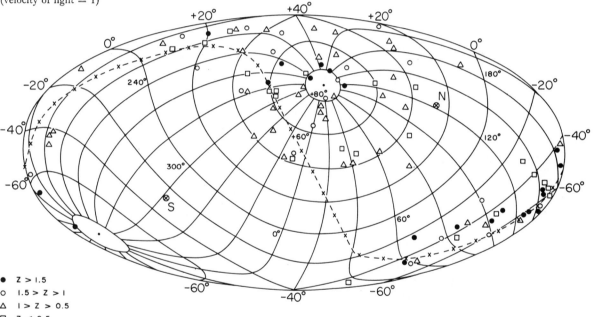

● Z > 1.5
○ 1.5 > Z > 1
△ 1 > Z > 0.5
□ Z < 0.5

During the years 1960 to 1965 more quasars were discovered, their red shifts measured, and spectra obtained. At present it is believed that the number of quasars is about one million; this includes those that are associated with radio emission and others that are "radio quiet," that is, observed only optically. The fact that not all quasars, indeed, only a few, are radio emitters poses another question, namely, what makes a quasar different from any other radio source? No definite answer has been given so far, although several facts do appear. They are starlike, that is, they appear as single objects, sometimes with large emanating jets, and they have luminosities transcending the brightest galaxies by as much as a factor of one hundred. The emission of radiation is not constant and may vary within years, months, and sometimes even

shorter periods. The most puzzling property, of course, is their anomalous red shift, which has important bearings in cosmology (which we will cover in the next chapter).

Several theories have been proposed to account for the huge amount of energy released. A model of a quasi-stellar source is likely to consist of three parts: a central region, or core, providing the energy source and part of the continuum radiation, a gaseous cloud generating the observed emission lines, and an outer halo responsible for the radio emission. The problem, of course, is to explain the energy production within the core. A possible explanation advanced by William Fowler of the University of California and Fred Hoyle was the existence of supermassive stars, some million times as heavy as the sun, whose collapse under the immense gravitational forces

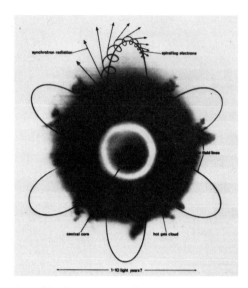

A model of quasi-stellar radio sources proposed by Maarten Schmidt and Jesse Greenstein in 1964. The observed emission lines are produced by an ionized gas cloud at a temperature of about 15,000° Kelvin and a density of 10,000 to 10 million particles per cubic centimeter. The cloud's mass is about 10 million solar masses, with a diameter of several light-years. Most of the radiation is generated from a smaller object within the gas cloud. High-energy electrons spiraling around the lines of a magnetic field would produce synchrotron radiation, which would account for the observed radio emission. (The model does not explain the energy production within the core nor does it give all observed features.)

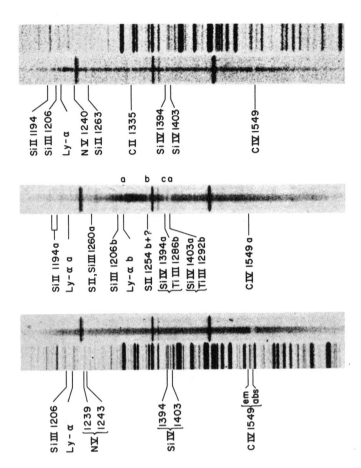

(Top) 3C 191 with sharp absorption lines, most of them arising from the ground states of the relevant ions. (Center) PKS 0237-23 (Parkes radio telescope catalogue, 2 hours 37 minutes, right ascension and minus 23° declination)—a rich absorption spectrum with many elements such as Ti III (triply ionized titanium); this quasar has the largest red shift known (2.223). (Bottom) PKS 0119-04. Its absorption lines are found on the long wavelength side of the emission lines; this might be due to gas falling into the central object. (The very narrow lines in all spectra are mercury lines from city lights.)

would result in the release of gravitational energy to be converted somehow into high-energy electrons producing the synchrotron radiation. The model actually consists of two parts, the still-burning superstar providing the luminosity and the collapsed superstar needed to supply the vast flux of electrons. But it is difficult to see how a collapsing object can emit energy amounting to a significant part of its mass unless the star collapses practically to its Schwarzschild radius, in which case it would become a "black hole" and could not radiate anymore.

Shortly after Einstein published his famous paper in 1916 on general relativity, the first rigorous solution of his equations was given by Karl Schwarzschild, a German astronomer. It corresponds to the gravitational field outside a spherical mass, at large distances from it, exhibiting the correct inverse-square behavior of Newtonian gravitation. It remains *the* "classical" solution of Einstein's field equations. Associated with that solution is a certain distance, the Schwarzschild radius, which, in fact, is a measure of the object's gravitational mass and determines the curvature of the space. The larger the mass, the larger the radius and the more curved will be the

underlying space. As light approaches the Schwarzschild radius, the large gravitational field will slow down its frequency of oscillation, the light frequency decreasing to zero on the Schwarzschild sphere so that no signals can penetrate the Schwarzschild sphere, nor can any light signals reach us from within it. Particles, too, as seen by a distant observer, would take an infinite time to cross (but from the particles' frame of reference the time would be finite). As long as the dimensions of actual "stars" are larger than the Schwarzschild radius—the usual situation—there is no problem; the Schwarzschild radius remains well within the region occupied by the star. However, if the star "collapses," by the aggregation of additional mass, we get a radius for the contracting object that is less than its Schwarzschild radius: no light signals will reach us and the star has become invisible, although its gravitational effect still exists for us; it has become a "black hole." Naturally, black holes cannot be seen, but there seems to be some evidence that at least one black hole is the companion of another star, Cygnus X-1. If this result should be confirmed, it would be another confirmation of the correctness of Einstein's theory of general relativity.

Another proposal suggests the occurrence of supernova explosions, but to arrive at the required amount of energy billions of stars must be involved.

A more attractive idea, proposed independently by the Russian astrophysicist I. D. Novikov and Yuval Ne'eman of Tel Aviv University, suggests that quasars may be remnants, or "lagging cores," of the original expansion of the universe (see Chapter VIII). Here, no attempt is made to understand the formation of the dense objects from the gas; rather this view concentrates only on what remained when the matter in the universe expanded. Coincident with a growing interest in the existence of black holes, these lagging cores may have been produced by the reverse process, resulting in "white holes." If this is the case, it is necessary to show that they can remain stable and continue to expand instead of reverting into black holes. More recently, Martin J. Rees suggested that quasars may be interpreted as massive black holes in galactic nuclei, which are fueled by capturing gas or stars from their surroundings.

An even more revolutionary proposal has been made by Hannes Alfvén, the Swedish astrophysicist and Nobel Prize winner, and the physicist Oscar Klein, who suggest that the mutual annihilation of matter and antimatter present in the universe might produce the required energy. Although there is no evidence that antimatter (matter consisting of antiparticles, such as antiprotons instead of protons, and so on) exists freely in the nature, that is, outside the laboratory, their mutual annihilation would produce radiation of extremely short wavelength, whereas quasars emit radiation of long wavelengths. Nor is it clear by what mechanism radiation by mutual annihilation is to be converted; if it derives from a magnetic field, then the bulk of the energy resides in the field itself and not in the particles, and the conversion could not occur.

It is not difficult to see that we are faced with a complex situation, which has been summarized as follows by George Gamow, the well-known physicist:

> Twinkle, twinkle, quasi-star
> Biggest puzzle from afar
> How unlike the other ones
> Brighter than a billion suns
> Twinkle, twinkle, quasi-star
> How I wonder what you are.

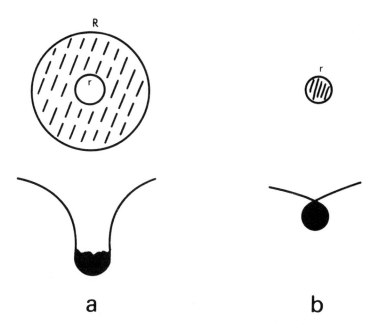

Schwarzschild singularity. (a) *Ordinary star:* The radius (R) of the star is larger than its Schwarzschild radius (r). The "throat" of the singularity defined by r is open. (b) *Collapsed star:* The radius has become equal to (or less than) its Schwarzschild radius (r). The "throat" of the singularity has closed and no light can leave. The star is invisible; it has become a black hole.

Late in 1967 radio astronomer Antony Hewish * and his graduate student Jocelyn Bell of Cambridge University were conducting an experiment to study the "twinkling" of radio signals from interplanetary space. When a beam of light—from a star or other pointlike source—travels through the earth's atmosphere, it is distorted so that the amount of light varies irregularly, resulting in the characteristic twinkling of starlight. Similarly, radio signals when passing through particles emitted by the solar wind will be bent and deflected, giving rise to scintillations of the radio signal. This effect is noticeable only if the source—light or radio—has a small angular diameter; for larger objects, such as planets or galaxies, the rays originating from different parts will be deflected along various directions; as a result they will average out and only a constant glow or steady signal is observed. It is therefore possible to determine whether the source is starlike—that is, a quasar—or extended like a radio galaxy.

While studying the printouts of these scintillations, Jocelyn Bell noted some rather disturbing interferences, which had occurred in the middle of the night—when, with the absence of the sun, such interferences should be at a minimum—and appeared to come from a distinct direction. More remarkable, however, was the fact that these pulses were quite regular. Also, the duration of each

* Antony Hewish shared a Nobel Prize in 1974 with Martin Ryle for pioneering research in radioastrophysics.

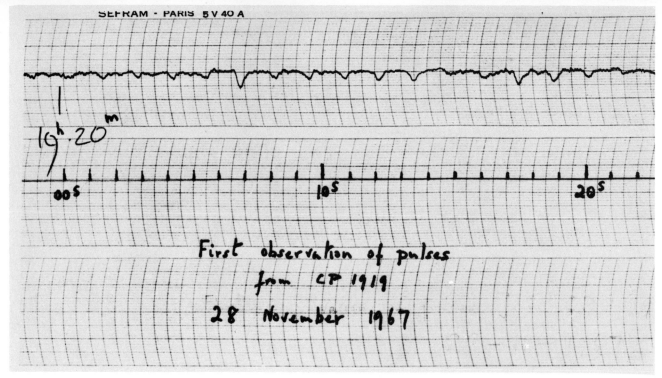

SEFRAM · PARIS 5 V 40 A

$10^h.20^m$

00^s 10^s 20^s

First observation of pulses
from CP 1919
28 November 1967

Typical pulsar records show a regular emission, though it varies in intensity. Fifteen distinct pulses can be distinguished during a twenty-second interval, or a pulse every 1.3 seconds. This is the emission trace of CP 1919, whose exact pulse interval is now established as 1.33730113 seconds.

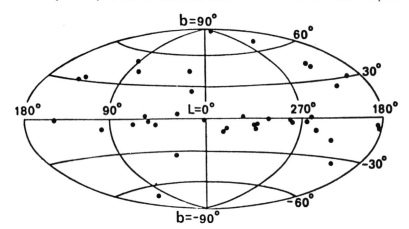

The distribution of known pulsars according to their galactic longitude (L) and latitude (b). Most pulsars lie in the galactic plane.

pulse was quite small—10 to 20 milliseconds—indicating that the size of the source was small, a few thousand kilometers.

The astonishing regularity of the pulses coupled with the small size of the source at first led the Cambridge group to believe that the signals might be coming from intelligent life on another planet. They had pinpointed three definite sources, which they named LGM 1, LGM 2, and LGM 3; LGM stood for "little green men." This theory, however, was soon discarded when they realized that the source was not orbiting as it would have been had it come from a planet of a star. Soon many more pulsars—as these mysterious objects came to be called—had been identified and their pulses studied.

Although the period and pulse width were quite regular, their amplitudes and shapes were uneven. Some of this irregularity may be due to variations in the source itself, but most is caused by the transmission of the pulses in the interstellar medium. The radio signal is slowed down—the longer wavelength components more than the shorter ones. From this "time lag" and the composition of the interstellar medium, the distances could be estimated. They turned out to be only tens to hundreds of light-years—distances of the brightest visible stars. However, searches at the locations indicated by the radio signals revealed no optically visible objects—at least up to the twenty-first magnitude. Thus, since they are comparatively close to us, they must be faint in the optical region; for example, the optical luminosity of pulsar CP 0950 (Cambridge Pulsar, right ascension 09 hours and 50 minutes) is less than a hundred-thousandth of the sun's luminosity, yet it is intrinsically a much stronger radio emitter than the sun.

The big question, of course, was to explain the nature of the pulsars and the mechanism that produces the pulses. The short duration of the pulses and the faintness of the pulsars indicate that the pulsars must be small or cold, or both. Two possible candidates fulfill these conditions: white dwarfs and neutron stars. We have seen that ordinary stars of masses comparable to the sun's upon

A schematic cross section of a neutron star. O and I denote the outer and inner solid crust respectively; L is the liquid interior and C the inner solid core. The outer crust is believed to consist of nuclei and electrons; the inner crust of nuclei, electrons, and neutrons. The liquid interior may be an ordinary fluid containing neutrons, protons, electrons, and muons (particles like electrons but much heavier), or it may be a superfluid made up of neutrons and protons. The inner core is more problematic and might consist of hadrons, which are heavy particles. The radius of the whole neutron star is only about 10 kilometers. ▶

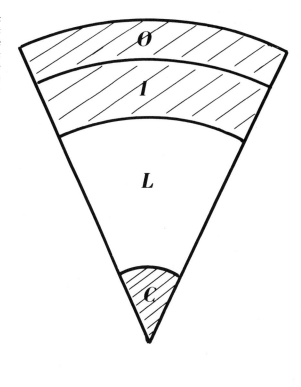

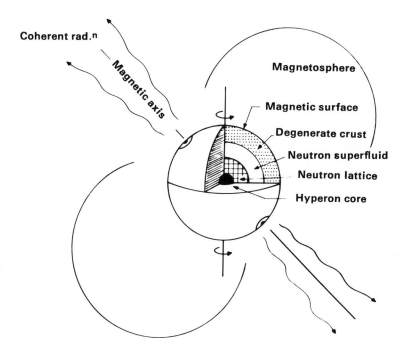

There is a strong magnetic field associated with the model of a rotating neutron star. The star itself consists of a core of hyperons—massive particles—surrounded by a crystal-type lattice of neutrons and a fluid of neutrons. The crust, as in white dwarfs, is a degenerate gas of neutrons beneath a magnetic surface. The star is surrounded by an envelope of plasma—hot conducting gases forming the magnetosphere. At places where the plasma breaks away, opposite a "dirty spot" on the star, a strong directed beam (coherent radiation) of radio waves will be emitted. It is this rotating beam that gives rise to the pulsar signals.

burning up their nuclear fuel, followed by contraction, can support themselves against the gravitational forces by becoming degenerate; degenerate material can withstand much higher pressures than ordinary gaseous matter. In fact, it is only the electrons in degenerate material that are confined. The nuclei still have plenty of freedom and are not appreciably affected by the great pressures—producing densities so great that a teaspoon of its material would weigh approximately a ton. This is the condition of a white dwarf, a star that, its nuclear fuel having been used up, has contracted until a new temperature equilibrium has been reached, slowly cooling and contracting until it is virtually dead. However, for a star with an original mass

exceeding about twice the solar mass, the collapse is more rapid, raising the temperature and finally resulting in a supernova outburst.

When the density is a million times larger than that of a white dwarf, the nuclei themselves are affected as well as the electrons. Now the positively charged nuclei begin to absorb the electrons, forming a degenerate gas of neutrons. At the surface of a neutron star is a shell composed of ordinary matter but at temperatures of several million degrees.

If white dwarfs resemble giant atoms, then neutron stars are like giant nuclei with densities of a billion tons per cubic centimeter. Both white dwarfs and neutron stars would be small enough to escape being detected optically.

With these two in mind then, the regularity of the pulses could be due to one of three causes: the stars pulsate like Cepheid variables; they form a binary system; or they rotate. Pulsations of white dwarfs had to be ruled out since none of them could have a period of pulsation as short as one-quarter second—the observed period of CP 0950. Neutron stars, however, would pulsate with much shorter periods than those observed. Clearly then, pulsars are not pulsating stars in the strict sense of the word. The second possibility, that they are binary systems revolving around each other, also had to be ruled out. Two white dwarfs orbiting around each other would have a period of nearly two seconds, while two neutron stars—being immensely dense objects—would radiate energy in the form of gravitational waves and, as a result, spiral closer and closer to each other, decreasing the orbital periods much faster than permitted by observation. Thus, by a process of elimination one arrives at a possible model—a rotating white dwarf or rotating neutron star.

Jeremiah P. Ostriker of Princeton University in 1968 proposed the "lighthouse" model of a rotating white dwarf. On its surface is a sort of "searchlight" that sweeps by the observer, who "sees" it as a "pulse." (An observer, of course, might "see" only some of the pulse-emitting objects and miss many others whose beams do not reach the earth.) Shortly afterward, Thomas Gold of Cornell University suggested that a rotating neutron star might be responsible for the lighthouse beam. He also noted that the presence of strong magnetic fields could be responsible for the emission of high-energy charged particles (such as high-speed electrons), resulting in a loss of angular momentum and a consequent slowing down.

No neutron stars had been observed; they existed only in a theoretician's imagination. But there was a way to differentiate between the two lighthouse models. Rotational forces cannot exceed gravitational forces if a star is to remain stable and not fly apart. This limits a white dwarf's period of rotation to a little over a quarter of a second; but rotating neutron stars—being more massive—could support larger rotational speeds. Thus, if pulsars with periods shorter than 0.25 second were to be found, rotating white dwarfs would have to be ruled out and only rotating neutron stars would remain as the sources of the pulses.

In 1968 a pulsating radio source, later known as NP 0532 was discovered in the Crab nebula by astronomers at the National Radio Astronomy Observatory. Its period or rotation was one-thirtieth of a second. Later work at the Arecibo Radio Observatory in Puerto Rico confirmed the results, showing that it was also gradually slowing down at a rate of 38 nanoseconds (billionths of seconds) per day. The energy released in the slowing-down process was found to be sufficient to keep the nebula glowing; thus another puzzle, the source of the Crab's energy, was solved. If one argued the other way, it could now be asserted that stars of radii of the order of 10 kilometers and masses approximately that of the sun—in other words, neutron stars—must exist, since the pulsar that supplies the energy for the Crab nebula has exactly these properties. Not long after, the pulsar was identified

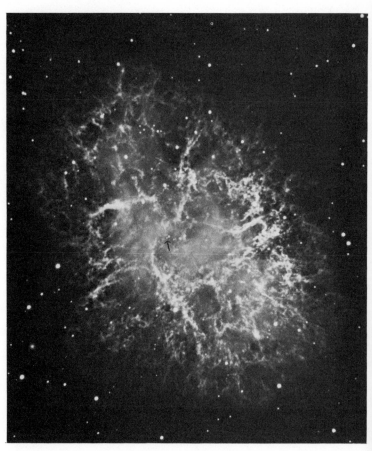

A Lick Observatory photograph of the Crab nebula, showing some of the individual stars. The south preceding star, identified as the pulsar, is indicated by the arrow.

NOTABLE PULSARS		
Designation *	Period (in seconds)	Pulse width (in milliseconds)
CP 0329 + 54	0.714518603	6
NP 0531 + 21	0.033094515	3
CP 0808 + 74	1.292241325	45
PSR 0833 − 45	0.089208370	2
CP 0834 + 06	1.273763151	35
CP 0950 + 08	0.253065037	13
CP 1133 + 16	1.187910980	38
HP 1507 + 55	0.739677616	13
PSR 1749 − 28	0.562551317	6
CP 1919 + 21	1.337301109	32
AP 2015 + 28	0.557954	10
PSR 2045 − 16	1.9615639	40

* The letters indicate the observatory and the numbers the pulsars' position. CP—Cambridge pulsar; HP—Harvard pulsar; AP—Arecibo pulsar; NP—National pulsar. CP 0329 + 54 is the Cambridge pulsar, 3h 29m right ascension, +54° declination.

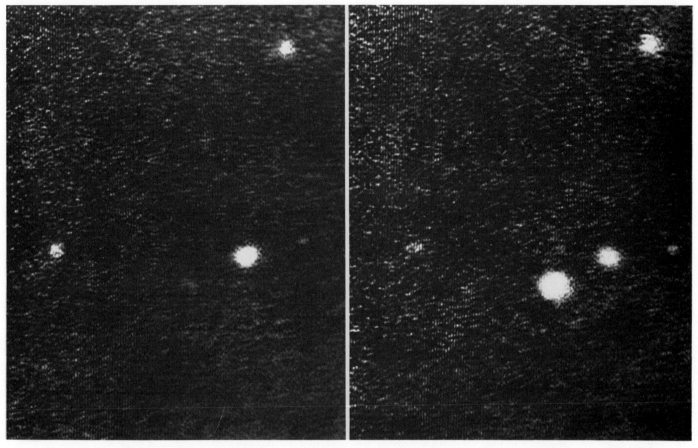

First pictures of pulsar NP 0532, the south preceding star in the Crab, taken at Lick Observatory with the help of a television system operating like a stroboscope, in conjunction with the observatory's 120-inch telescope. In the left photograph the pulsar is invisible; in the right it has appeared. The period of the pulsar was established by interrupting the light. If one took a disk containing six evenly spaced holes and rotated it at the rate of five revolutions per second, light from the pulsar would show through the holes every several revolutions. When viewed on a television screen, it would appear to be pulsing in slow motion. The exact period could be found by adjusting the speed of rotation. (The system was devised by E. Joseph Wampler and Joseph S. Miller.)

optically. It turned out to be a very blue star, called the south preceding star. (One of two stars near the center of the nebula was believed to be the source of the supernova. One was a little *south* and to the left, or *preceding* the other.) Although the star had always been considered somewhat unusual, the fact that it turned on and off thirty times per second had just not been noticed. With the help of a rotating shutter, operating like a stroboscope, its periodic flickering could now be demonstrated clearly.

Other facts also began to fall into place. As NP 0532 starts to contract, the magnetic lines of force—effectively "frozen" into the stellar material—occupy increasingly smaller areas. As a result, the magnetic field, compressed into these shrinking regions, increases immensely, reaching strengths more than a billion times that of ordinary stars. The magnetic field in the vicinity of a rotating neutron star has the characteristic dipole shape, but farther out it takes on a spiral form. It is this field that is responsible for the emission of strong but low-frequency (long wavelengths) radio waves.

Although it is believed that the supernova that was responsible for the Crab nebula resulted in a neutron star—whose rotation, and consequent loss of energy, keeps the nebula going—questions still remain to be answered: what is the origin of the pulses and why does the lighthouse theory seem to work so well? But at least a major breakthrough has been achieved by identifying pulsars with rotating neutron stars. It may even shed some light on other problems, such as the nature of quasars. Their spectra bear some resemblance to that of the Crab, and it is not unthinkable that quasars are collections of supernova remnants, each supplied by its own pulsar, which is also responsible for the generation of the high-energy particles and magnetic field. We have come a long way from the time when little green men were believed to be responsible for pulsar emission.

The two main "windows" through which celestial

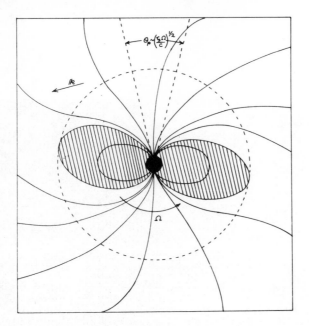

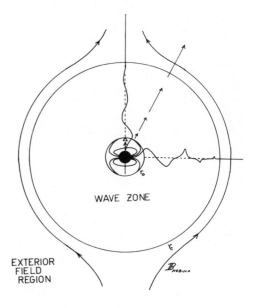

The near magnetic field of a rotating neutron star in empty space shows the characteristic "dipole" pattern (indicated by the shaded area), consisting of closed loops and lines of force going out in all directions. The velocity of the force is proportional to its distance from the star and reaches the speed of light at a distance that defines the "speed-of-light cylinder" (indicated by the dashed circle, which shows the cross section of the cylinder). Ω indicates the angular momentum of rotation, and the angle θ (defined by the two dashed lines and the equation showing its dependence on the angular momentum) determines the width of the beam—which accounts for the pulsar.

Between the near magnetic field seen in the center and the exterior field region lies the wave zone from which the electromagnetic waves originate. The two wiggly curves representing the wave zone show the form of the radiation parallel and perpendicular to the axis of rotation. The outer lines (B nebula) indicate the far magnetic field.

objects have been observed and their radiation of energy measured lie in the optical and radio wave region of the spectrum, with infrared radiation being another possible source. Until fairly recently a fourth source—X-ray radiation—could not be detected. X rays, so well known for their use in medicine, are relatively high-energy photons with very small wavelengths—from 0.05 to 100 angstroms, an angstrom being equal to one-hundred-millionth of a centimeter. They are readily absorbed by the earth's atmosphere, and their detection became possible only when rockets began to be used for astronomical research. Today, with the use of satellites and space probes, X-ray astronomy is one of the most important branches of the "new astronomy."

The first galactic X-ray source was discovered on a routine flight to detect solar X rays reflected by the moon. During its stay of some five minutes above the earth's atmosphere, the counters in an Aerobee rocket noted strong X-ray emissions coming from the galactic center in the region of Scorpius. Further flights confirmed this, and the X-ray source in Scorpius—later denoted as Scorpius X-1—was located. The remarkable fact about the source was that it seemed to be located in a neighborhood devoid of any visibly bright star, nebulosity, or even radio emission. What kind of "star" could produce an intense X-ray emission and still remain invisible when viewed through both windows?

Subsequently, Scorpius X-1 was identified optically as a faint blue starlike object resembling an old nova.

The search for X-ray sources continued. By 1970 dozens had been discovered with detectors on board rockets and balloons. But the real breakthrough was the satellite UHURU—Swahili for "freedom"—launched in Kenya in 1970. Although observation time for a rocket is limited, a satellite could monitor an X-ray source on a twenty-four-hour basis, and it was discovered that emissions from Centaurus X-3 varied regularly—with a period of 4.84 seconds. This figure is too large for a pulsar, but, coupled to the regular intensity variations, it led to a new phenomenon—the X-ray binary system. The X-ray light curve of Centaurus X-3 is like a typical eclipsing binary; its intensity variations result from the fact that during each revolution Centaurus X-3 is eclipsed by its companion. The X-ray source is therefore a compact star (white dwarf or neutron star), with, as its companion, a normal star with a mass—calculated from the orbital data—at least fifteen times that of the sun.

For a long time the "unseen" companion could not be found and only recently has it been identified with a faint star varying in brightness with the same period as that of the X-ray source. In accord with spectroscopic observations, it has been classified as a giant, with a luminosity about one hundred thousand times that of the sun (from the observed X-ray flux and distance it is found

Forward section of an Aerobee-Hi rocket instrumented by the U.S. Naval Research Laboratory. The instrument section is stabilized against roll of the rocket body by rotation of the entire nose at a point just above the black band. The doors have been thrown off, and the spectrograph unit is in the position it would be in during flight. The stabilizing mechanism makes it possible to scan a very small section of the sky.

A soft X-ray emitter studied with the satellite Uhuru. Perseus A, the Seyfert galaxy NGC 1275, belongs to a class of variable radio galaxies with an energy output close to that of our own galaxy. Like the quasar 3C 273, Perseus A has a core-and-halo radio structure, the core being about one light-year in diameter; but like other Seyfert galaxies, it lacks the optical output of a quasar by a factor of about a thousand—although it emits tremendous energy in the invisible infrared and X-ray regions. Thus Seyferts have been called invisible quasars. This small core contains millions of stars.

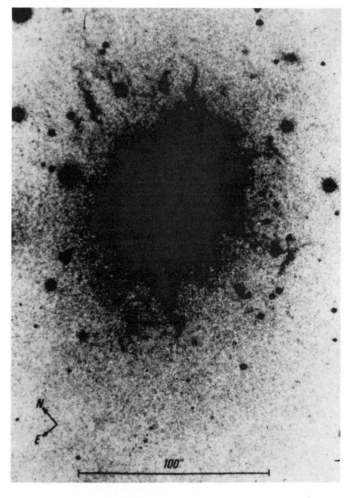

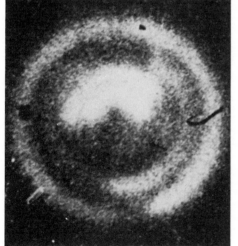

The first X-ray photograph of the sun, obtained April 19, 1960, with a pinhole camera aboard an Aerobee rocket. The image was smeared by rotation of the camera during exposure.

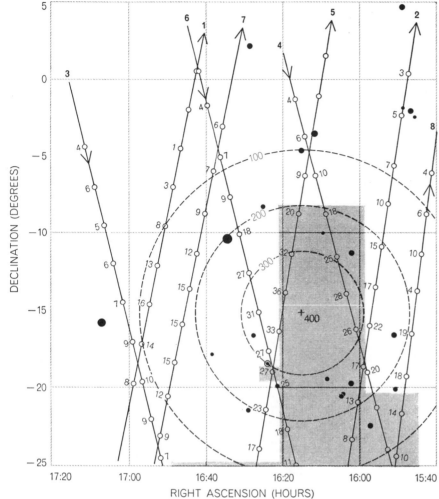

The diagram shows the location (the plus sign in the center circle) of the X-ray source Scorpius X-1. The eight diagonal lines indicate the passage of the X-ray counters on board Uhuru—in the direction of the arrows—each time it passed near the source; the numbers are the X-ray counts recorded per 0.09 seconds of flight time (the larger the number, the closer the source). The three dashed circles denote regions of equal X-ray intensity. The black dots represent stars—the larger the dot the smaller the magnitude (or the greater the brightness). The black dot in a small circle is a radio source. Evidently, no bright star, nebulosity, or radio emission can be seen in the vicinity of the X-ray source. The shaded area at the bottom and middle represents part of the region in the sky occupied by the constellation Scorpius.

A plot of thirty-three of the forty known X-ray sources. With the exception of two or possibly three X-ray galaxies (M-87, Sco XR-1, and the one at forty degrees), they all lie within the Milky Way, near the galactic equator. ▼

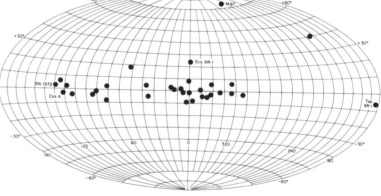

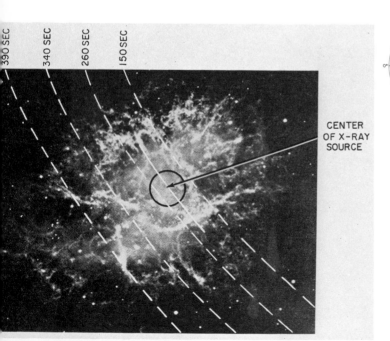

CENTER OF X-RAY SOURCE

◄

The X-ray source in the Crab nebula, found to be two light-years across. As the moon passed in front of the Crab on July 7, 1964, a rocket fired from White Sands watched it blot out the X rays. The arcs indicate the progress of the eclipse at various times after the launch.

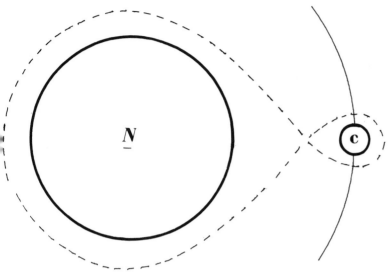

Possible mass transfer for a binary X-ray source—normal star N and its companion c. The broken figure 8 is called the Roche lobe, named for the French mathematician Edouard Albert Roche (1820–83) who first studied its properties. Beyond this boundary an expanding star will transfer matter to its companion in a binary system. In one possible mass transfer mechanism, the star N—not yet having reached its Roche lobe—loses mass in the form of stellar wind. Some of that mass (less than 0.1 percent) is captured by the companion, but the rapid fall associated with it is sufficient to transform the companion, a neutron star or black hole, into an X-ray source. In a second mechanism, the star would actually reach its Roche lobe, and matter would begin to flow outward toward the companion. It turns out, however, that in this case the rate of mass transfer (about a thousandth of a solar mass per year) will be too large to lead to the formation of an X-ray source, since a thick envelope, opaque to X-rays, will form around the collapsed star. Such an envelope will radiate mainly in the visible and ultraviolet regions of the spectrum, and the object will appear as a fairly normal star. Only if the normal component (a primary star if this were an ordinary binary system) has a mass not larger than a few solar masses, and if the rate of transfer is not very large so that the envelope will remain transparent to X-rays, will an X-ray source be produced by this mechanism.

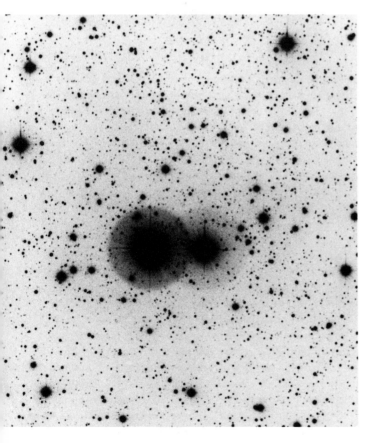

This photograph taken by Jerome Kristian with the 200-inch reflector at the Mount Wilson Observatory shows the supergiant HDE 226868 at the center. It is associated with Cygnus X-1 and is believed to be the normal star of that binary system. In addition, a radio source and an X-ray source have been observed at that location, indicating that they and the optical source are all the same object.

that Centaurus X-3 radiates energy at a rate of about ten thousand times the luminosity of the sun). It is nearly at the center of the Galaxy—some twenty-five thousand light-years away—and its faintness is due to the immense distance and obscuring stellar material.

Eight binary X-ray sources have been identified, with a visible component a giant or supergiant and an X-ray source a compact star.

Cygnus X-1, one of the strongest X-ray sources, gave rise to an even more interesting speculation, referred to earlier in connection with a black hole. Its companion, a spectroscopic binary with a period of 5.6 days, is a supergiant with a mass greater than fifteen times that of the sun. To be able to move such a heavy star with such high orbital speed, a compact star (Cygnus X-1) must

290

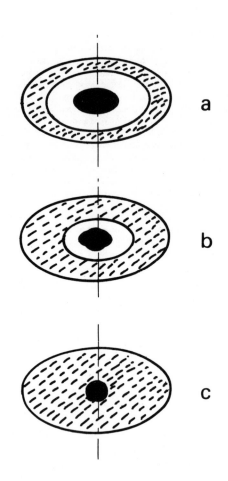

a

b

c

Three possible configurations of black holes. The difference depends on whether or not they rotate and on the amount of rotation—which, in turn, is determined by the angular momentum and mass as well as the gravitational constant and speed of light (also a constant). The hole (the central black area) is surrounded by an accretion disk (shaded area), which approaches the hole as the speed of rotation increases. For a stationary hole (a), the edge of the accretion disk is outside the "horizon"—here the size of the hole, which appears perfectly spherical. (Since the diagram is drawn from a perspective, circles will appear as ellipses.) As the speed of rotation increases (b), the edge of the accretion disk approaches the horizon and matter is sucked into it. The shape of the hole will be ellipsoidal but flat on top and bottom. For a rapidly rotating hole (c), the edge of the accretion disk has reached the singularity, which has a shape not describable by ordinary geometry, and matter continuously flows into the hole. Of course, the above is only a theoretical and idealized picture of what *may* go on inside a "black hole"—if such exists.

have a mass at least four times that of the sun (and it might be as much as eight times). This follows from the fact that angular momentum is conserved, as we have seen earlier. Now, on theoretical grounds it has been argued that the mass of a white dwarf or neutron star cannot exceed three solar masses; beyond that, gravitational forces outweigh the internal pressure and the star would collapse. Once a heavy star has started to collapse—and has been unable to get rid of its excess mass, which would enable it to build up counterpressures to stop the collapse—gravity would force all its matter into the Schwarzschild singularity and it has become a black hole. This is its ultimate fate, and, as we have seen, Cygnus X-1 might be the first example of that exotic novel strain.

Until it became evident that the mass of Cygnus X-1 was above the "critical mass" of white dwarfs or neutron stars, black holes were only a gleam in the theorist's eye—and even now it is not certain that they really exist. According to Einstein's general relativity theory, they are the physical counterparts of the Schwarzschild sphere that appears in the solution of the field equations. Their properties, as predicted from theory, are fairly simple. The size of the black hole, which is solely determined by its

mass, is quite small; typical masses lie between three and fifty solar masses, with circumferences (on account of the large space curvature one cannot talk about radii) between 60 and 1,000 kilometers. Most models assume that the hole is rotating and, as a result, will flatten out. The rotation creates a vortex, pulling in particles in spiraling orbits from surrounding space, forming accretion disks. It is there that X rays that are associated with sources like Cygnus X-1 would originate.

It is, of course, impossible to detect black holes directly. So far, most of the evidence is based on negative results: if a companion of a binary star cannot be seen and it is too massive to be a neutron star, it might be a black hole—or even a more bizarre object. The theory fits the observed results, but it is not conclusive. The formation of black holes should be accompanied by the generation of bursts of gravitational waves. Present detection equipment is not sensitive enough to observe these waves coming from objects outside the Galaxy, and this remains a project for the future. The case for black holes would be strengthened considerably if the properties of the X-ray emission could be predicted in detail and compared with observations from other sources, still to be found.

SOME CHARACTERISTICS OF X-RAY BINARIES				
Name	Period (days)	Luminosity (relative to sun)	Visible component	Distance (light-years)
Cygnus X-1	5.6	10,000	ninth magnitude blue supergiant, mass larger than 20 solar masses	10,000
Centaurus X-3	2.087	10,000	13.4 magnitude blue giant, mass larger than 16 solar masses	25,000
Small Magellan Cloud X-1	3.89	200,000	13.4 magnitude blue supergiant, mass larger than 25 solar masses	190,000
Vela X-1	8.95	1,000	Seventh magnitude blue supergiant, mass larger than 25 solar masses	80,000
3U 1700-37	3.412	1,000	6.7 magnitude blue supergiant, mass larger than 30 solar masses	90,000
Circinus X-1	15.0	?	?	?
Hercules X-1	1.7	10,000	thirteenth–fifteenth magnitude variable with 1.7 day period; about two solar masses	16,000
Cygnus X-3	4.8	10,000	no visible star, but infrared source with 4.8 hour period	25,000

VIII · THE EXPANDING UNIVERSE

1. A Paradox and Its Resolution

Heinrich Wilhelm Matthäus Olbers became interested in astronomy at the age of thirteen and pursued this "hobby" all his life. Astronomy was a sideline for Dr. Olbers, who was a general practitioner of medicine in Bremen until his retirement in 1822. Many professional astronomers would not mind trading places with him, for he made many important discoveries with the 3¾-inch refractor he set up in his house. His best-known work, on comets, included Olbers' comet, discovered in 1815 – a recurring reminder of his perseverance. And he and Baron Francis Xaver von Zach rediscovered Ceres after Gauss had calculated its orbit, thereby confirming the Titius-Bode law.

In 1823 Olbers wrote a paper, *On the Transparency of Space,* in which he posed a remarkable paradox. In trying to calculate the total amount of light reaching us from all the stars he found to his surprise that—contrary to the relative darkness observed—the night sky should be flooded with light. If we assume that the farther regions of the universe are very much like the areas we can see, it is reasonable to think of the sky as uniformly populated by stars—or even galaxies—of the same average brightness as those in our own neighborhood. The variation in brightness observed would simply be owing to the fact that on the average the brighter stars are closer, while the fainter are farther away, the intensity varying inversely as the square of the distance. Also, since the volume of space is larger the farther out we go, there would be more faint stars than bright ones—in agreement with observation.

One can thus think of space as a series of concentric spheres or shells surrounding us and containing ever-increasing numbers of stars. Each shell is assumed to be of the same thickness, and in order to calculate the light reaching us, it is only necessary to add up the contributions from the different shells. Now, the number of stars in each shell is proportional to its volume, which in turn is proportional to the square of its radius. On the other hand, the intensity of the light reaching the earth varies inversely as the square of the distance. These two opposing features, the increase in the number of stars and the decrease in light from each star, cancel each other out—and one would expect to receive the same amount of light from each shell, no matter how far. Adding the contributions from the various shells, one then finds that the total light received would be infinite for a universe that extends to infinity. Of course, one has to remember that a given star not only sends out light but also obstructs light from stars farther away (this obscuring effect will prevent some of the light from reaching us); nevertheless, the amount of light should still be 50,000 times greater than the strongest sunlight. It should flood the sky with light—even in daytime (when the sun would hardly be noticeable against such a background of shining stars and galaxies).

Apparently Olbers was not the first to have noted this paradox, commonly referred to as *Olbers' paradox.* In 1744 the Swiss astronomer Philippe Loys de Chéseaux of Lausanne carried out a more or less identical calculation in an appendix to his book on the comet of 1743. Some historians have been puzzled why Olbers did not mention Chéseaux's work, especially since a copy of that book was found in his library and both authors used the same star, Aldebaran, and Mars in calculating stellar distances and brightness. Despite this "evidence," it is very unlikely that Olbers was aware of Chéseaux's work. It was tucked away in an appendix, which Olbers might have overlooked, and

Heinrich Wilhelm Matthäus Olbers (1758–1840), born at Arbergen, a village near Bremen, Germany. Olbers, the son of a Lutheran minister, is best known for his work on comets, the discovery of asteroids Pallas in 1802 and Vesta in 1807, and of course for Olbers' paradox, first stated in 1826: he calculated that if the stars were uniformly distributed throughout space and the light was not absorbed, the night sky should be flooded with light and should shine with the brightness of the sun.

Olbers' paradox: The whole universe, uniformly populated with stars, can be considered to consist of an infinite number of spherical shells of constant thickness (d). The number of stars in each shell is proportional to the square of the distance (r) from Earth (E); the intensity of the light reaching Earth from a given star (P) varies inversely as the square of the distance and thus decreases as the distance increases. Those two factors cancel each other out; hence the total amount of light reaching Earth per unit of time would be independent of distance and should increase infinitely as the number of shells increases indefinitely.

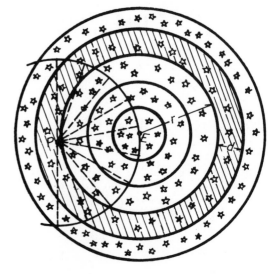

Aldebaran and Mars would be the logical choices for calculating stellar distances. More important, Olbers was known to possess the highest personal integrity and would hardly be guilty of plagiarism.

In arriving at his result, Olbers—and also Chéseaux—made several assumptions—some tacitly, without realizing that they were assumptions. First, Olbers assumed that the average density and intrinsic luminosity of stars do not vary throughout space. In other words, the universe is homogeneous and the intrinsic brightness of a star is independent of its distance. Second, he assumed that these quantities do not change with time. The light that reaches us now has been emitted some time ago, and the farther or longer it has traveled the more distant the past when it was emitted (we are dealing here with billions of light-years). Furthermore, quite naturally, he assumed that there was no systematic large movement of stars (and galaxies); he assumed that the universe was static as well as flat and infinite in extent. He also believed that the laws of physics applied throughout the universe, at all times, as they applied here on earth and, in particular, that the laws governing the propagation of light were equally valid in space and in the laboratory.

To resolve the paradox, both Olbers and Chéseaux suggested that an interstellar fog was responsible for absorbing the starlight. Although we now know that such interstellar matter does exist, it is too tenuous to absorb much light. In addition, as Hermann Bondi pointed out, after some time this interstellar matter would have become as hot as a star because of the light it absorbed and would then radiate as much light as it received—without fulfilling the desired purpose. Since the argument leading to the paradox was quite sound, one or more of the basic assumptions had to be fallacious and would have to be abandoned or modified.

The average separation of two stars or galaxies is much greater in measure than they are themselves—stars are more like pinpoints of light within a vast void. Only if one considers stars at tremendously large distances does their contribution give rise to Olbers' paradox. If for some reason either the density of stars or their intrinsic luminosity were to decrease with increasing distance, this would indeed cut down the total amount of light received. But this gives rise to a grossly inhomogeneous universe. This possibility must be rejected, on aesthetic grounds if no others, since it places the sun (or the Galaxy) in a privileged position. An ingenious alternative was suggested by the Swedish statistician C. V. L. Charlier who proposed that galaxies are grouped into clusters just as stars are grouped into galaxies and clusters. These clusters of galaxies would be grouped into superclusters, which themselves form super-superclusters and so on. In this way the overall homogeneity of the universe is

preserved, and if the distances between those higher-order clusters are sufficiently large, most of space is empty and the calculated amount of light received is reconciled with the observed result.

The paradox may also be averted if for any reason the luminosity depends on time or if the more distant stars are too young so that their light has not yet reached us. Recently, Edward Harrison has suggested a similar resolution based on a star's "luminous lifetime" being less than that time for which the whole sky would be ablaze with light.

By dropping the assumption of the stationary character of the universe and, instead, postulating that the universe is expanding, the paradox can also be avoided. If the stars and galaxies are receding from us, then the light that we receive is reduced owing to the increased distance *and* red shift reducing the energy received. It would be pleasing to say that this was the way the "expanding universe" was discovered, by a logical argument from a set of assumptions to a conclusion. But this was not the case; in fact, the earliest relativistic models of Einstein and de Sitter were stationary models.

Olbers's explanation of an interstellar fog had been accepted for a long time and drew the attention of later astronomers to the presence of interstellar matter, but the real nature of the expanding universe lay unrevealed until an explanation was proposed by Alexandre Friedmann in 1922.

The first indication of an expanding universe was Hubble's discovery of a systematic red shift. It has already been mentioned several times that such a red shift—unless it is of gravitational origin—is related to the motion of the source (or the observer). This effect, known as the Doppler effect or shift—named in honor of the Austrian mathematician and physicist Christian Doppler—is also operative with a train whistle. The same considerations apply in the case of light: the spectral lines of a receding object will be red-shifted (that is, their wavelengths will become large), whereas those of an approaching object will be shifted toward the blue end of the spectrum, or the shorter wavelengths. The important result is that the shift in wavelength is a measure of the speed of the object; for small speeds, compared with that of light, the speed is equal to the shift divided by the wavelength itself. (For speeds comparable to that of light relativistic corrections have to be taken into account.)

When Hubble measured the red shifts of different galaxies and compared these with the distances of the galaxies, he found that the red shifts were proportional to the distances: farther galaxies have larger red shifts than those close by, and the red shift increases linearly with their distance. Since the red shifts themselves are simply related to the speed of recession, this results in the

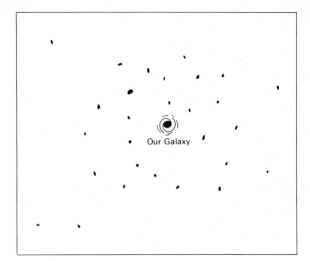

One way to avoid Olbers' paradox is to assume that the distribution of the stars is not uniform but decreases as the distance increases. This would put our galaxy at a preferred position and result in a universe centered around it.

A different way to circumvent Olbers' paradox while preserving the overall homogeneity of the universe was proposed by Charlier. In his "polka-dot" universe the galaxies (individual dots) are formed into clusters (circles of dots), which themselves are parts of clusters of clusters, and so on. Seen from any given galaxy, the view is the same as from any other, but as the size of the universe approaches infinity, the volume of the intervening space increases more rapidly than the number of galaxies. Thus, the total amount of light reaching a particular galaxy does depend on distance and will be finite, avoiding Olbers' paradox.

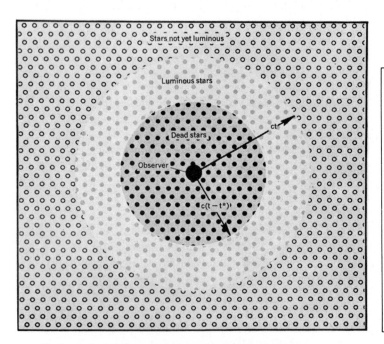

Harrison's dynamically static universe. Assume that the stars commence shining everywhere at a given time (t = 0). The observer then sees a luminous sphere of stars expanding radially at the speed of light (c). After a certain period of time (t*) the stars in the observer's neighborhood begin to die out. The observer is then surrounded by an expanding sphere of dead stars (black in the figure), beyond which lies a shell of still luminous stars of certain thickness (ct). Outside this shell lie stars that have not yet become luminous—light has not yet reached the observer.

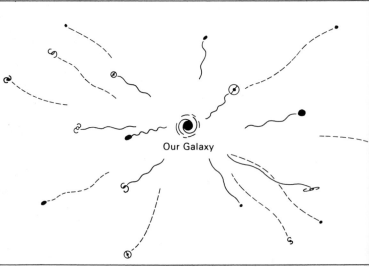

An expanding universe is now the accepted way to avoid Olbers' paradox. The universe is expanding and the galaxies are receding from us and one another. As a result, light received from a given distance will no longer be uniform but decreased and the most distant galaxies move away so rapidly that their light no longer reaches us.

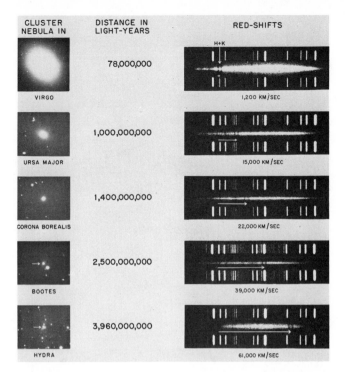

CLUSTER NEBULA IN	DISTANCE IN LIGHT-YEARS	RED-SHIFTS
VIRGO	78,000,000	H+K 1,200 KM/SEC
URSA MAJOR	1,000,000,000	15,000 KM/SEC
CORONA BOREALIS	1,400,000,000	22,000 KM/SEC
BOOTES	2,500,000,000	39,000 KM/SEC
HYDRA	3,960,000,000	61,000 KM/SEC

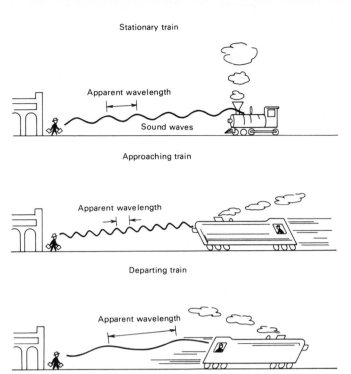

Stationary train

Apparent wavelength

Sound waves

Approaching train

Apparent wavelength

Departing train

Apparent wavelength

Relation between red shift and distance. At the left are galaxies at increasing distances. At the right are the spectra of these galaxies, showing the Doppler effect of two strong absorption lines for ionized calcium H and K (indicated by the vertical arrow). As the distances increase, these lines shift toward the right and can be located at the tips of the progressive horizontal arrows, which thus indicate recession speeds. These are listed below each spectrum. The two identical bands in each box are comparison spectra against which the shift can be measured. It is seen that the recession speeds increase with distance.

Doppler effect. The frequency (or wavelength) of sound waves (and similarly of light waves) changes with the motion of the source—here, the train whistle. As the train approaches the station, the whistle sounds at an increasingly higher pitch; more waves are "compressed" into a smaller distance, and hence the frequency increases (the apparent wavelength decreases). On the other hand, when the train is leaving the station, the pitch of the whistle grows lower; the apparent wavelength is increasing, and there is a corresponding decrease in the frequency.

velocity-distance relation, commonly referred to as Hubble's law. Not only does this relation confirm the expansion of the universe, but it also implies that the expansion is uniform; only the distance between galaxies changes and not their positions relative to one another.

The fact that every galaxy recedes from us might seem at first glance to indicate that we are at the center of the universe. But the opposite is the case. Every galaxy, including our own, is "running away" from every other galaxy, and, as a result, there is not a single galaxy that may be considered *the* center of the universe. The mutual recession of the galaxies and the expansion of the universe can be illustrated by a simple model. Consider a rubber balloon with buttons affixed to its surface. As the balloon is being inflated, the distances between the buttons increase, and they appear to move away from one another. In the same way, if we imagine the universe to be expanding, there will be a recession of all the galaxies from one another. An observer on any one galaxy will see all other galaxies receding from him. This avoids Olbers' paradox since now the farthest galaxies are receding fastest and have their light red-shifted so that we do not detect the light emitted.

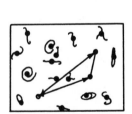
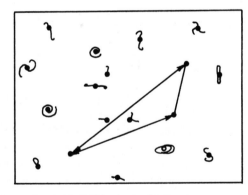

The expansion of the universe in accordance with Hubble's law implies that the relative distances of galaxies remain unchanged. If the two diagrams represent the universe and its content at two stages of the expansion, then it will present the same "view" at both times. In other words, taking the triangle, only the lengths (that is, the scale) and not the shape change during the expansion.

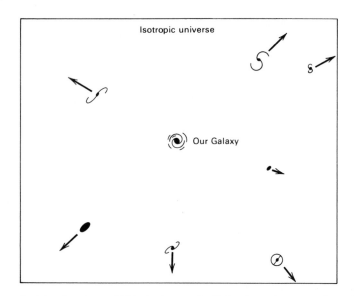 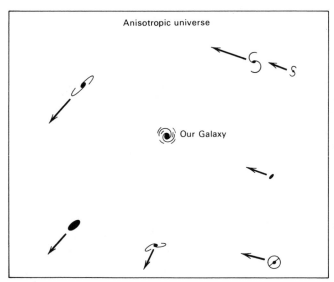

An isotropic universe *(left)* looks the same in all directions, whereas an anisotropic universe *(right)* presents a different view in some directions. The arrows indicate the recession of the galaxies, both in direction and in magnitude. As far as present observations permit, our universe is isotropic.

2. Models, Models, and More Models

The apparent uniformity of the universe, at least on a large scale, has given rise to a generalization, commonly known as the *cosmological principle.* According to this principle, all regions of space appear the same, and an observer at *any* point would "see" the same view of the universe, no matter where he is situated. Space is assumed to be isotropic, which, as will be seen later, is a severe limitation on the possible types of space-times. This isotropy, which implies also homogeneity in a wider sense (although the converse is not true), then leads to the description of the universe in terms of homogeneous matter and pressure distribution. (Although most of space is empty and matter only concentrated at individual locations or regions, one imagines matter spread out and distributed uniformly in this idealized picture.) Alternatively, Charlier's model, in which the same picture of the universe is presented to every observer without the underlying global homogeneity, also satisfied the cosmological principle.

The presence of local irregularities, nebulae and galaxies, makes it clear that the strict application of this principle can at best only apply to an overall description of the universe. The situation is somewhat similar to that which exists for a system of electrical charges that can be "spread" over a region to produce a uniform charge density, but in their individual neighborhoods preserve their own characteristic feature. Despite its plausibility it must be realized that the cosmological principle is not a principle in the real sense of the word, but an additional assumption, by no means proven by present observational data. Whether it should be taken literally to apply to arbitrarily large regions of space, or whether it describes some kind of homogeneous background representing a smoothed-out description of the actual galaxies, or whether it is only an approximation depends more on the preference of the investigator than on actual facts. What is certain, however, is that the development of modern theoretical cosmology would have been impossible without the cosmological principle, which provided a considerable simplification of the underlying equations and a limitation on possible world models. Keeping this in mind, we can then regard the cosmological principle as a reasonable working hypothesis on which further work can be based without prejudicing a different outlook.

Early models of the universe based on Newton's theory of gravitation proved unsatisfactory for two reasons. Taking the density as being constant throughout would give rise to a universe of infinite extent as well as infinite mass. On the other hand, if the gravitational potential were to tend to a definite limit at infinity, the mean density—calculated for a region that is large compared with the distance between neighboring stars (or galaxies) but small in comparison with the dimensions of the whole system—would have to decrease toward zero faster than the square of the distance increases, since only then would the product of mean density and surface area be finite. In this sense, the universe would be finite, although it would possess an infinite total mass that increases with the volume (as the cube of the distance). Radiation emitted by stars and heavenly objects possessing a large kinetic energy may overcome the forces of gravitation and, like projectiles attaining a critical velocity, escape and leave the universe altogether. These difficulties may be overcome by modifying Newton's law of universal gravitation and adding a repulsive element involving a universal constant—later referred to as the cosmological constant. The repulsive force, introduced *ad hoc,* may be thought of as due to an overall rotation—which, however, has not been observed—or to some new kind of retarding force.

As early as 1917 Einstein applied general relativity to the universe as a whole and in so doing founded relativistic cosmology. The problem that Einstein had set for himself was to see whether the existence of a uniform distribution of the fixed stars, as suggested by experience, and the absence of anything like a center of gravity of the total amount of matter could be reconciled with the general theory of relativity. After much travail he arrived at the remarkable result that the universe, considered as a continuum, was finite (closed) in its spatial dimensions—finite and without boundaries, in the same way the surface of a sphere is closed without boundaries. A light ray, for example, would return to its starting point after circling the universe, giving rise to a "ghost" image of the star that emitted it.

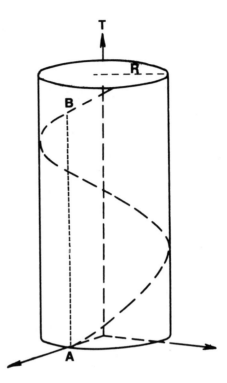

Embedded in a flat space (of five dimensions), the Einstein static universe appears as a cylinder (for obvious reasons only three of the five dimensions are shown). A ray of light traveling along a geodesic (indicated by the dashed curve) from A to B will return to its starting point having traversed a distance equal to the circumference of the circle. R is the radius of the universe.

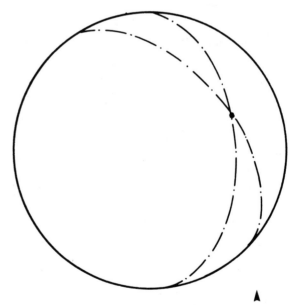

In a closed universe the curvature of space is positive, like the surface of a sphere. Light rays traveling along great circles can travel around the universe and return to their starting point.

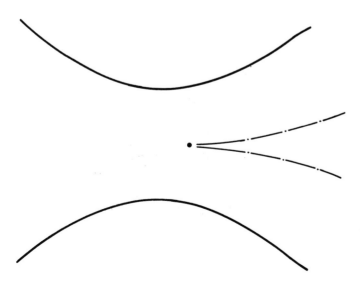

In an open universe the curvature of space is negative, like the surface of a hyperboloid of revolution. Light rays that travel outward in such a universe never return to their starting points.

Ernst Mach (1838–1916) was born in Turas, in the province of Moravia, then part of the Austrian Empire and now in Czechoslovakia. He received the coveted professorship at the University of Prague, where he remained twenty-eight years and spent the most fruitful time of his life. In 1895, at the University of Vienna, he occupied the newly established chair of philosophy dealing with the history and theory of the inductive sciences. Three years later a stroke paralyzed the right side of his body, and he retired and spent the closing years of his life at his home, near Munich, where he and his son, Dr. Ludwig Mach, continued to work. Mach's name has been popularized through the Mach number (indicating the ratio of the speed of a rocket or plane to the speed of sound). Mach criticized Newton's "conceptual monstrosity of absolute space" and thereby sowed the seeds for relativity. His insistence on measurable sensations as the sole contents of objects underlay his philosophical thinking. Mach at first endorsed relativity theory enthusiastically, but later he rejected it as too dogmatic. Einstein, nevertheless, acknowledged Mach's influence on his thinking and, in particular, credited him with shaping his early development.

Willem de Sitter (1872–1934). At the University of Groningen, the Dutchman came under the influence of Kapteyn. Although his chief interest was in mathematics, he became interested in astronomy when Sir David Gill invited him to become his assistant at the observatory at the Cape of Good Hope. He stayed there until 1908 when he was appointed director of the Leiden Observatory and professor of astronomy, a position he held for the rest of his life. While at the Cape, he commenced his study of Jupiter's satellites, whose masses and densities he determined. He was an acknowledged master in exact astronomy and recalculated all known astronomical constants. However, it was in cosmology that de Sitter gained universal recognition. He had become interested in Einstein's special theory of relativity as early as 1911, when it still attracted little attention. When Einstein proposed his general theory, de Sitter immediately grasped its cosmological implications and formulated what was to be known as the de Sitter universe. He and Einstein became not only close collaborators but also close friends, and their friendship endured until de Sitter's death in 1934.

The Einstein universe did not turn out to be a realistic cosmological model for two reasons. It assumed a quasistatic distribution of matter and therefore could not account for the Doppler shift of the galaxies, but it must be remembered that these were measured by Hubble only some time later. As a matter of fact, Einstein had to include in his equation an additional term, the cosmological constant multiplied by the gravitational potentials, in order to preserve the static nature of the matter distribution. He later discarded it, considering it the "biggest blunder" he ever made, but by that time it had become a fixture and modern cosmological models thrive on it. The second reason is that the Einstein universe is unstable; a slight disturbance would lead to continued contraction or expansion. As we shall see later, the Einstein universe is the limiting form of some expanding universes.

Despite these shortcomings, Einstein's idea of a finite but unbounded space is one of the greatest ideas of modern cosmology. It explained why stars should not "thin out" and disperse if space were infinite, and it gave physical meaning to Mach's principle. According to that principle, it is the presence of matter in the universe and the mutual action of bodies that determine the motion of a particle.

To incorporate Mach's principle into the field equations had been one of the aims of general relativity, and it appeared that Einstein had finally succeeded. However, at that time Willem de Sitter, the Dutch astronomer, found another solution to Einstein's modified equations. Basically, it is also a static model, but it can be brought into a form resembling an expanding universe. Consequently, in that form the model does account for the observed recession of galaxies. However, its most remarkable property is that it is completely free of matter (and radiation), which makes it unphysical. It must be discarded despite its other positive features. This has resulted in some unfounded criticism of general relativity. According to Mach's principle, it is the effect of all matter that is responsible for the space-time properties and thus

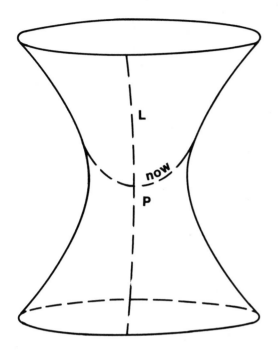

Alexandre A. Friedmann (1888–1925). During World War I he headed the air-navigation service and later returned to Petrograd. Although his main contributions are in hydrodynamics and meteorology, he is remembered for his "solution" to Einstein's field equations and the Friedmann universe. He died at the age of thirty-seven, a victim of typhoid.

Like Einstein's, de Sitter's universe can be embedded in a flat space of five dimensions, but unlike Einstein's, it is open and appears as a hyperboloid of revolution—light rays (L) traverse it without returning. P is the location of an observer on the curve of present time.

an empty universe with a space curvature, such as the de Sitter universe, should not exist. Yet here it is, a bona fide solution of Einstein's field equations. What must be remembered is that the solution of an equation such as the field equations does not necessarily reflect the physical situation; a solution requires postulating additional conditions, such as Einstein's boundary conditions. In Einstein's universe all the conditions are inherent, but in the de Sitter universe they are provided by Mach's principle—or rather by the fact that Mach's principle is not fulfilled; consequently the de Sitter universe must be discarded. In this sense Mach's principle acts as an additional criterion discriminating between physically acceptable and nonacceptable solutions of the field equations. But although the de Sitter model did not result in a physical interest, it had two important consequences. It was the first expanding model—although the expansion appeared as a result of a change of coordinates and was not due to actual physical processes—and it provided the mathematical apparatus used later by Bondi, Gold, and Hoyle when they formulated their steady state theory.

Although when observational data are limited to our own Galaxy there might be some justification for stationary universes, observed red shifts definitely indicate an expanding universe, which would avoid Olbers' paradox.

In 1922 Alexandre Friedmann had been studying Einstein's cosmological considerations when—according to George Gamow, who was then working with him in

Russia—Friedmann noticed that the field equations admitted nonstationary solutions, even under the stringent conditions of homogeneity and isotropy! It should be noted that Einstein at that time shared the general belief that the stars were, essentially, static and hence he did not look for nonstationary solutions. Friedmann's solution opened a new world for relativistic cosmology. Not only was there no need to introduce the cosmological constant, but the solutions applied equally well to "open" or "closed" universes.

For a space of constant curvature there are essentially three types of Friedmann models depending on whether the curvature is positive, zero, or negative. If the curvature is positive, space is closed and an "oscillating" model will result: starting from zero the radius expands to a maximum value, then decreases to zero, then starts to increase again, and so on. If the curvature is zero or negative, that is, if we have an open universe, the universe continues to expand, the only difference between the two cases being the rate of expansion. All three models start from a singular state—zero radius—connected with the initial explosion, or "big bang," the origin of the universe, which we shall discuss later on. But whereas in the oscillating model gravitation begins to take over, producing contraction, and later collapse, in the zero and negative curvature models the initial "explosion" was large enough to overcome and even outstrip gravitation. This is somewhat analogous to a projectile fired from the earth: if the initial velocity is smaller than the critical velocity, it

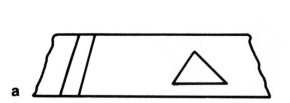
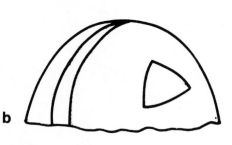
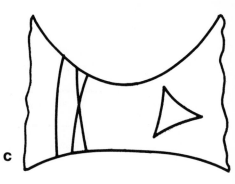

The three types of curvature: (a) *Plane surface*–zero curvature; only one geodesic (here a straight line) can be drawn through a point, parallel to another straight line; the sum of the angles in a triangle equals 180 degrees, and the surface extends to infinity. (b) *Spherical surface*–positive curvature; all geodesics (great circles) intersect and consequently there are no parallel lines; the sum of the angles in a triangle is larger than 180 degrees, and the surface is finite or closed. (c) *Hyperbolic surface*–negative curvature; many geodesics can be drawn through a given point without intersecting another geodesic; the sum of the angles in a triangle is smaller than 180 degrees, and the surface is infinite or open.

Friedmann models. The extent of the expansion of the universe is plotted against the time for the different types of curvature. The constant k may be used as a measure of the kind of curvature and to differentiate among the possible models. (A) Oscillating model–positive curvature, closed universe: k = 1; (B) Einstein–de Sitter model–zero curvature, flat universe: k = O; (C) hyperbolic model–negative curvature, open universe: k = −1.

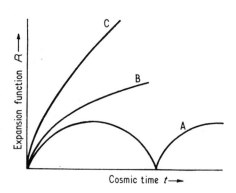

History of an oscillating model. The top diagram shows the universe as it is now, in an early stage of expansion. At the bottom the universe, having reached maximum expansion, is starting to contract but is still quite large. Later, it will contract further until it reaches zero volume (provided no other processes interfere).

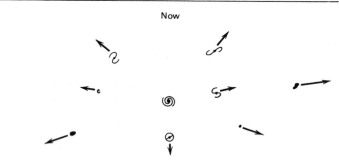

Now

Billions of years from now

will remain a captive of the earth's gravitational field; if equal or greater, it will escape. At present, observational data are not good enough to differentiate among these three models or even others that have been proposed.

Although Einstein had disavowed the cosmological constant and returned to the unblemished original form of his field equations—and the Friedmann universes—his point of view was not shared by everyone. Like mushrooms after a rain, a large number of models appeared whose classification depended on the curvature and the relative value of the cosmological constant. Perhaps the most interesting is the one proposed by the Abbé Lemaître, which begins like Friedmann's oscillating model. But instead of contracting, there is a nearly stationary period (in which repulsion and gravitational attraction almost balance each other), with the radius finally expanding repidly toward infinity. This by no means exhausts the possible models, since other factors may enter. For example, considering the presence of electromagnetic radiation as well as matter will give rise to a new class of models, depending on the relative amount of radiation present.

For a while all went well, but in 1948 it looked as if relativistic cosmology was in trouble. It appeared that the age of the universe as predicted by the Friedmann models

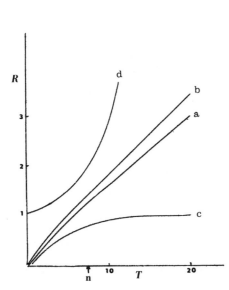

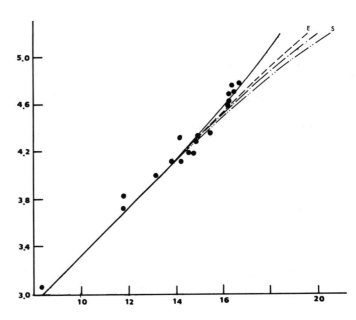

The radius (R) of the universe in arbitrary units measured against time (T) in units of a 1,000 million years for several expanding models. (Strictly speaking, R is only the time-dependent part of the radius and a measure of the expansion.) The "n" indicates the present time (close to 7,500 million years). (a) The Einstein-de Sitter universe; (b) the hyperbolic model, which is seen to expand at a larger rate than the Einstein-de Sitter universe, although at present the difference is fairly small; (c) the Euclidean, or flat, universe–the gravitational attraction balances the expansion, and the size of the universe remains constant (this is the limiting case, after which expansion is halted and contraction sets in, resulting in the oscillating model). All three models are singular, that is, they start from zero radius. (d) The steady state model has no initial value, but in order to compare it to the other three singular models its position at their starting point has been adjusted to the value of 1. It expands indefinitely, and after 10,000 million years will have reached nearly three times its original size.

Red shift and magnitude. The red shift, or speed of recession, is measured on the vertical scale and the apparent magnitude, which is a measure of the distance, on the horizontal scale, covering 18 faint clusters. (This, in fact, is the Hubble plot.) The three broken lines correspond to the theoretical predictions, and the unbroken line is the trend suggested by the 6 faintest, and farthest, clusters. Curve S represents a steady state universe, whereas curve E indicates an infinite Euclidean, or flat, universe. The central curve gives a universe expanding at the same rate; to its left the expansion slows down, but the universe is open and infinite. To the left of E the universe is closed and finite. The data are certainly not good enough to make a definite identification, and although the trend seems to be toward a closed universe, new data indicate that the universe might be Euclidean.

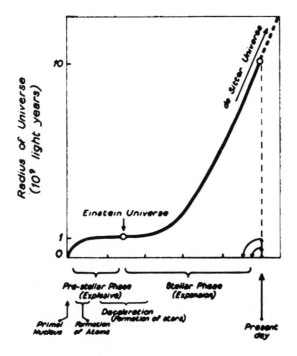

Lemaître's universe. The start of the expansion resembles the oscillating universe, followed by an almost static period containing the Einstein universe. Eventually the model expands very rapidly, approaching the expansion rate of the de Sitter universe. The time (in billions of years) is shown on the horizontal scale, measured backward from today. The vertical scale gives the radius in billions of light-years. According to Lemaître, the start of the expansion was caused by the primeval atom (Primeval Nucleus), followed by a pre-stellar phase including the formation of atoms, a Deceleration, and finally a stellar phase (Expansion) preceding the present epoch.

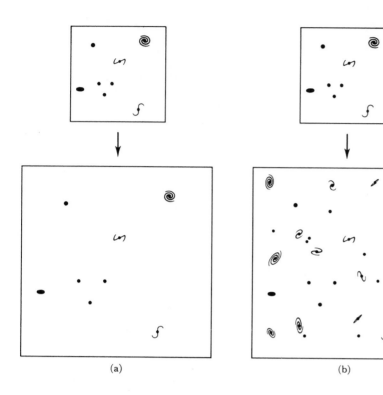

Evolving vs. steady state cosmology. (a) In an evolving universe the density of matter decreases, since the universe expands and the total amount of matter remains unchanged. (b) In a steady state universe the density of matter remains constant, and the expansion of the universe is compensated for by the spontaneous creation of matter. This continuous creation–a necessary ingredient of the steady state theory–is in contradiction to the accepted belief in the conservation of matter and energy, including radiation.

(a)   (b)

was less than the age of the Galaxy itself–clearly, an unsatisfactory situation. (As we have seen, these models start from the original expansion, and as a first approximation the age of the universe is equal to the present distance divided by the speed of recession.)

The difficulty could be avoided by reintroducing the cosmological constant, which would yield models such as Lemaître's.

Einstein, however, was adamant; in an appendix to his *The Meaning of Relativity* he wrote: "The age of the universe, in the sense used here, must certainly exceed that of the firm crust of the earth as found from the radioactive minerals. Since determination of age by these minerals is reliable in every respect, the cosmological theory here presented [the Friedmann models] would be disproved if it were found to contradict any such results. In this case I see no reasonable solution."

Others shared his view, and still others would save the original theory at any cost–even forsaking the cosmological principle, if necessary, and adopting a model in which the Galaxy occupied a special position.

At this time, Hermann Bondi, with Tom Gold, and Fred Hoyle independently, introduced a completely new theory, the steady state theory of cosmology. No longer was there any need to worry about the age of the universe, for it had neither a beginning nor an end. Every galactic observer would see the same picture of the universe, not only at a particular time, but at *all* times. In other words, the space t= constant is homogeneous and isotropic. This

ensures that the physical conditions in our locality are the same as in any other at the same time t= constant. The universe is homogeneous and isotropic not only in space but in time as well.

Since, however, our measurements refer to events that have taken place a long time ago–light having to traverse very large distances–it would be simpler to assume that both the physical laws and the state of the universe remain unchanged in time, implying a steady state universe. (It must be emphasized that "steady" is not "static." The situation is similar to that of a flowing river: a particular spot presents a steady picture, although water is continuously in motion.) Thus, the universe is not only uniform in space but also in time. This is the content of the "perfect cosmological principle," the basis of the steady state theory–which must be viewed as another assumption (even stronger than the "ordinary" cosmological principle) rather than the result of observation.

According to Bondi, it is only the perfect cosmological principle that permits us to justify the general validity of physical laws. If such laws are considered as generalizations of observations, it is then assumed that results based on terrestrial experiences can be applied to vaster regions of space and time, and ultimately to the structure of the universe as a whole. However, it is by no means obvious that this is the case, and it is certainly not uncommon in astrophysics to extrapolate existing laws into the past and future without demanding that they be unchanging for all time. Moreover, there is just one universe, and results cannot be compared with other similar systems, as is the case in the laboratory.

Viewed in this perspective, the perfect cosmological principle, and hence the steady state theory, then appears as an alternative to other cosmological models rather than the *sine qua non* of cosmology.

An immediate consequence of the perfect cosmological principle is that Hubble's constant becomes a true constant, and not only independent of position. Furthermore, in that case a constant curvature implies that space is flat. Nevertheless, it is not static. Change is going on all the time, but the overall picture does not change as in the river example above. Each star or galaxy comes into existence at a finite time; there is no zero radius or original explosion, and the universe is expanding.

Also, the density is constant in a steady state universe, but since the universe is expanding, matter must be continuously created. The question of where this matter is coming from has been ignored by proponents of the steady state theory, who say, with Newton, that they have not discovered the cause of this phenomenon and therefore frame no hypotheses. If we grant that creation does take place in some form or another, it is then assumed that this matter is created in the form of hydrogen atoms; since hydrogen is the most abundant element, it is likely the created matter should take this form. The actual amount necessary to keep the presently accepted value of the density at a constant value is quite small, amounting to one hydrogen atom per cubic centimeter every billion years. Nevertheless, one is faced with a violation of the law of conservation of matter and energy, in which the total amount of matter (or energy) in the universe is constant. One of the fundamental pillars of modern physics, it has withstood the challenges that have felled other conservation laws, and one would hate to give it up without additional experimental evidence. (Of course, matter can be transformed into energy, as evidenced by the atomic bomb, and the reverse process seems to occur with energy and radio sources, discussed in Chapter VII. However, now we are not speaking of converting radiation into matter, but of the actual creation of matter from nothing.)

The original formulation of the steady state theory by Bondi and Gold was a qualitative one and relied solely on the perfect cosmological principle. Later, Hoyle and co-workers introduced a creation field (C-field) into Einstein's field equations, insisting that the combined matter and creation field be conserved. Although Hoyle—like Einstein—rejected the use of the cosmological constant, it is interesting to note that the creation field is mathematically equivalent to exactly such a term. Thus, from a mathematical point of view the steady state theory

has to be ranked with other such cosmological models, except that the cosmological term now has some kind of physical interpretation.

Mainly because of the error in the age of the universe—but also owing to the forceful presentation of its discoverers—the steady state theory began to gain universal recognition. Then its *raison d'être* suddenly disappeared. In 1952 at a meeting of the International Astronomical Union Walter Baade announced that the galactic distances used in determining the age of the universe were too small by at least a factor of two (it is now thought to be even larger than five). The new distances were determined by the Cepheid variables from whose regular periods the absolute magnitudes, and hence distances, could be determined. However, before this could be done one had to find the absolute magnitude of at least one of the variable stars. Unfortunately the parallax measurements used in this exacting procedure were off by a factor of two; the velocity of recession, on the other hand, had been fairly reliably determined by the red shifts. As a result, scientists could now double the previous estimate of the age of the universe.

Although the steady state theory lost its claim to fame, its originators continued to extol its qualities—in particular, the absence of the original explosion. Recent observations disfavor Hoyle, but, more important, there is evidence that the big bang did occur.

3. The Big Bang

If the universe is continuously expanding—and its matter-energy content remains constant—then at some time in the distant past it must have been extremely small and dense. Projecting farther back, we arrive at the "singular state" of an infinite density and zero volume. Such a situation can be envisaged mathematically, but physically it is intolerable. Clearly, something quite unusual must have occurred if one takes the existence of the singular state seriously and not just as a breakdown of the mathematical equations.

The question of what happened at the beginning of the expansion has occupied cosmologists for quite some time, and it is now generally believed (although by no means proved with certainty) that some giant explosion—or a series of explosions—did occur. Several possible hypotheses or theories have been advanced, each possessing some merit, none completely satisfactory, perhaps because they attempt too much.

The Abbé Georges Lemaître in 1931 suggested that the universe started from one rather complex object, the

primeval atom. It must not be imagined as an atom in the usual sense of the word, since it contained *all* the matter of the universe. It was unstable, and as soon as it was formed it disintegrated into millions of pieces. The process of disintegration was similar to, although much more complicated than, the known radioactive decay of uranium or its fission. The decay products would include all the known atoms as well as others that disappeared long ago, having disintegrated into others. However, vestiges of that giant atomic explosion should still exist, traveling about the universe, and might take the form of cosmic radiation. The exact nature of cosmic radiation, which is continuously impinging on the earth, is still unknown, although it is now generally believed not to be cosmic in origin but to originate in the sun or neighboring galaxies.

Lemaître's theory is an attractive one, but he failed to work out the process of disintegration that would have to account for the abundances of the different atoms. Nor has he answered the question how the primeval atom was formed in the first place.

In 1946 a nearly diametrically different theory (later facetiously known as the $\alpha\,\beta\,\gamma$ theory, for a paper on it by Alpher, Bethe, and Gamow, although Bethe, who did not work on it, was included only for the title) was proposed by George Gamow. According to that theory, the universe started from a hot and very dense mass of neutrons (decaying into protons and electrons) submerged in a "sea" of high-energy radiation. Gamow called this mixture *ylem* (defined as "the first substance from which the elements were supposed to be formed"). As the universe was expanding—and cooling in the process—protons and neutrons began to stick together, forming deuterons, a form of heavy hydrogen. After that came helium, lithium, and so on, until all known elements were formed. The whole process took less than an hour and was carried out at temperatures of thousands of millions of degrees. Unfortunately, the theory encountered an insurmountable obstacle. The elements were to be built up step by step—by adding one proton or one neutron to each preceding element. This works until helium, consisting of two protons and two neutrons, is formed. But a collection of five nucleons (a nucleon is a proton or neutron) is unstable and immediately breaks up again into helium. Thus the $\alpha\,\beta\,\gamma$ theory could account very well

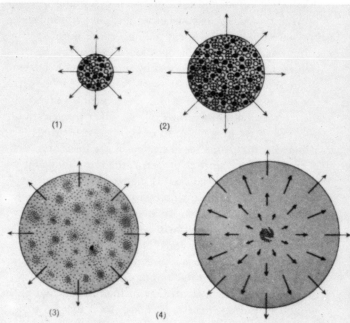

The present universe is believed to be the result of a giant explosion, the big bang. Lemaître suggested that it originally started from a giant atom—the primeval atom: (1) The primeval galactic atom just after its explosion. (2) Temperatures have decreased to about 1,000 million degrees and atomic nuclei are being formed. (3) After tens of millions of years, temperatures have decreased even further, and gas and dust accumulations are present, from which galaxies will be formed. (4) Today's universe, about 20,000 million years after the original explosion—the universe continues to expand rapidly. The arrows indicate the rate of expansion.

for the abundance of the light elements, such as hydrogen and helium—which, incidentally, form most of the universe—but it could not explain the formation of the heavier elements, since it could not overcome the five-nucleon barrier.

Gamow's hypothesis would probably have shared the fate of Lemaître's were it not for one interesting fact. Just as the cosmic rays could be the remnants of the primeval

George Gamow (1904–68). He spent his early years in his hometown of Odessa and at the end of the Russian Civil War enrolled at the Novorossia University in Odessa. However, conditions were difficult—the physics professor refused to lecture because he lacked any demonstration equipment—and Gamow went to Leningrad. To support himself, he managed to get a job as a lecturer in physics in the Artillery School of the Red October, holding the rank of colonel (at the age of twenty), which later led to some embarrassment and questioning by American security at Los Alamos, where he worked on atomic energy. He became attracted to Einstein's theory of relativity and received his formal education from Alexandre Friedmann at Novorossia University. An unexpected and welcome change in his career took place when he was recommended by a former professor—whose lectures he never attended—for a summer fellowship at Göttingen, the seat of the "new physics." His work on the penetration of potential barriers by α-particles in nuclei earned him fame in Russia and fellowships at Copenhagen and Cambridge, where he continued his work with Bohr and Rutherford. Upon his return to Russia in 1931 Gamow became a professor at the University of Leningrad, but since he was not a Communist, he found it difficult to adjust to the pragmatism of scientific thought that denied relativity, the uncertainty principle, and heredity; he also found it difficult to attend international meetings. After an unsuccessful attempt to row across the Black Sea to Turkey, Gamow—and his wife—were able to leave the country on the occasion of a Solvay Congress. He never returned and, after spending some time in Europe, went to the United States, first to Washington University and later to the University of Colorado. In addition to his work in nuclear physics, Gamow is known for his contributions in cosmology, especially his prediction of the big bang and the background radiation. The author of several popular and semipopular books on physics, which he illustrated himself, he made a difficult subject easy to understand.

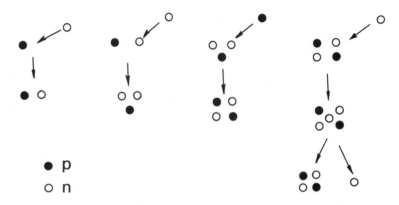

According to Gamow's theory, the elements are being built step by step. A neutron (n) combines with a proton (p) to form deuterium. An additional neutron yields tritium (a form of heavy hydrogen). Another proton then gives helium, a very stable nucleus. Now a difficulty sets in: a fifth particle produces another isotope or form of helium, which is unstable and decays immediately into helium and a neutron, arresting the building process. (The element lithium—three protons and three neutrons—could be formed by combining a helium with a deuterium nucleus, but the probability of its happening is remote.)

Dr. Robert W. Wilson (left) and Dr. Arno A. Penzias of Bell Laboratories with the Laboratories' horn-reflector antenna located at Holmdel, New Jersey, designed for Project Echo and Telstar space communication experiments. They found a residual amount of noise radiation that was later ascribed to the blackbody background radiation associated with the big bang. For that work Drs. Wilson and Penzias received the Nobel Prize in Physics for 1978.

atom, so, too, the original high energy—and high temperature—radiation would still be present, although, of course, at a very much lower temperature. Gamow calculated it to be 7 degrees K, whereas Ralph Alpher and Robert Hermann * in 1949 gave an even lower estimate of 5 degrees K.

A few years later, in 1965, Robert W. Wilson and Arno A. Penzias detected some radiation from their "horn antenna" that they could not account for. This particular antenna had been built to provide sensitive microwave-receiving systems for satellite communications. However, before it could be used it had to be tested, and it was then that Wilson and Penzias found it to be considerably

* It is told that Gamow wanted Hermann to change his name to Delter, but Hermann refused.

An artist's view of the big bang. The picture is rather idealized, since the galaxies were not formed immediately from the fragments as shown, but rather originated from the contraction of the protogalaxies formed from the cooling radiation.

The four stages of the universe: the early hot stage with temperature running into many degrees Inferno (one degree Inferno is a billion degrees Centigrade); the cooling, nonluminous plasma stage; the formation of protogalaxies and condensation of stars; the start of the expansion and dispersal of galaxies.

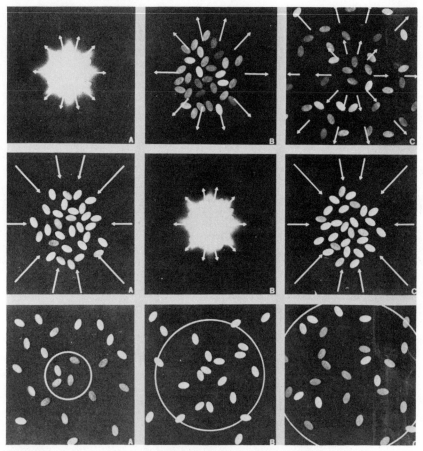

Oscillation or creation? *Top row:* Following the primeval explosion; galaxies condensed from an almost uniform hydrogen cloud, synthesizing heavy elements; expansion, under the original explosive influence. *Center row:* After a period of 25,000 to 60,000 million years, the universe, which has expanded, begins to contract; a new expansion begins; again followed by a contraction; and so on. *Bottom row:* Matter is continuously created, although the rate of creation is too slow to be detectable. As the universe expands; new galaxies are being formed; so that the overall aspect of the universe remains the same.

"hotter" (that is, absorbing more radiation) than expected. They dismantled it but were able to reduce the persistent day-and-night background radiation only by a few tenths of a degree to just under 3½ degrees K. It was almost a repeat of their colleague Karl Jansky's experience when he stumbled upon radio signals from the Galaxy while looking for interferences in telephone communications. Radiation from galactic and even extragalactic sources could be ruled out. When the intensity of the radiation was plotted against wavelengths, it was found that the data fit the curve one would expect from black-body radiation at 2.7 degrees K. The obvious explanation then is that this radiation is a residue of the primordial radiation originating from the fireball of the big bang. Originally, of course, the radiation was at an immensely high temperature, but during the course of time it dissipated or gave rise to pair-creation, and what we receive now are only the cooled-down remnants. This was a vindication of Gamow's hypothesis and agreed very well with his numerical prediction. Later experiments by P. J. Peebles and co-workers at Princeton bore out the existence of that background radiation; and its fireball origin now seems fairly well established.

Of course, one can only speculate on the nature of that primeval fireball. Matter and radiation at billions of degrees were concentrated in a comparatively small space, and out of that inferno came neutrons and other particles, forming various elements, and finally condensing into stars and galaxies. The history of the universe may be thought to consist of four phases. First came the early hot stage. It is this stage that now appears as the 2.7 degrees K background radiation. This was followed by a period of cooling and formation of nonluminous plasma (still hot and fairly dense). Then out of that plasma stars and protogalaxies condensed, which finally dispersed to form the universe as we now see it.

It is not surprising that in a subject as uncertain as the origin of the universe other hypotheses should have arisen. In 1974 Fred Hoyle proposed an ingenious explanation of the background radiation. In an obvious attempt to eliminate the existence of an original explosion—which would invalidate the steady state theory—he postulated the existence of "another space" smoothly connected to ours. The singular point of origin then is replaced by a point at which two branches of an extended curve of radial expansion connect. Nevertheless, the region of physical interest, although it is only a part of the extended universe, would contain all the galaxies even seen with our largest telescopes. The background radiation, on the other hand, would not be the result of an explosion at the interface of the two branches, but rather ordinary radiation generated on the "other side," thermalized at the

A radiometer, the instrument used at Princeton University to detect the primeval fireball. One of the horns is pointing upward to receive radiation from the sky. An amplifier and electronic equipment are included below.

boundary and then passed to "our" part of the universe where it is detected.

A starting mechanism, quite different from those proposed by Lemaître and Gamow, has been suggested by the Swedish physicist Oskar Klein. As mentioned earlier, there exist in nature antiparticles, which are in some sense the opposite of the corresponding particle. For example, the positron may be considered to be the antiparticle of the electron. (Both have the same mass, but the signs of their electric charge are opposite, negative for the electron and positive for the positron.) Accelerators have been able to create the antiproton, a negatively charged particle of the same mass as the positively charged proton; still other particles, charged or not, were found to have their corresponding antiparticle partners. This symmetry between particles and antiparticles is very satisfactory from an aesthetic point of view and has been useful in particle physics. An obvious question to ask is whether, in addition to ordinary matter, antimatter also exists, in which the chemical elements are built up out of antiparticles instead of particles. In all respects, antimatter would behave like ordinary matter and be indistinguishable from it. For example, it could be that some galaxies in the universe are composed of antimatter; the spectra observed would be identical to those of matter, and even the effect of a magnetic field would be the same, if one

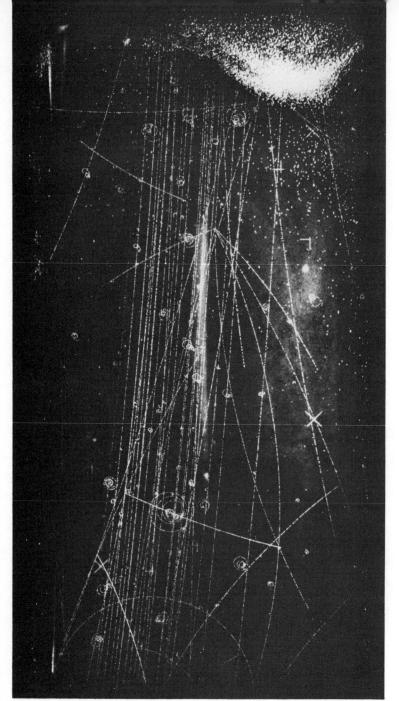

A proton-antiproton annihilation from a 3.3 billion electron-volt experiment in the 20-inch Bubble Chamber at Brookhaven National Laboratory, New York. The antiproton enters (diagonal running from upper left) and collides with the proton, which is at rest. The results of the annihilation are the tracks made by mesons (fanning out).

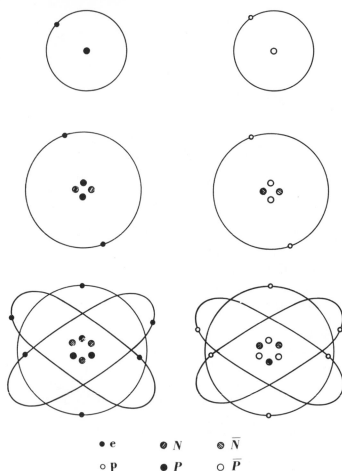

Constituents of atoms of matter and antimatter. *Top left:* Hydrogen consists of a proton with an electron revolving around it. *Top right:* Antihydrogen consists of an antiproton with a positron revolving around it. *Center left:* The helium atom has a nucleus consisting of two protons and two neutrons, with two electrons revolving around the nucleus. *Center right:* The antihelium atom consists of a nucleus composed of two antiprotons and two antineutrons, with two positrons revolving around the nucleus. *Bottom left:* The carbon atom has a nucleus consisting of six protons (only three are shown) and six neutrons (only three are shown), with six electrons revolving around the nucleus. *Bottom right:* In the anticarbon atom there are six antiprotons (only three are shown) and six antineutrons (only three are shown), with six positrons revolving around the nucleus. This correspondence can be continued for all the atoms by simply replacing protons (P) with antiprotons ($\bar{P}$) (which have a negative charge), neutrons (N) with antineutrons ($\bar{N}$) (both of which are neutral particles), and electrons (e) by positrons (p).

assumes that the direction of the magnetic field is also reversed.

When particles and antiparticles collide, they annihilate each other, resulting in the formation of other particles (and antiparticles) and the emission of high-energy radiation. According to this view it is therefore impossible to assume that the primeval atom of Lemaître or the ylem of Gamow contained antimatter as well as matter, since the resulting explosion would have been too big, even for the big bang. Instead, Klein assumes that in its initial state the universe consisted of an extreme dilute plasma of charged particles, or rather of an ambiplasma since it contained both particles and antiparticles. As this cloud began to contract, some of the protons and antiprotons collided, annihilated each other, and produced radiation. When the radius of the cloud shrank to about a billion

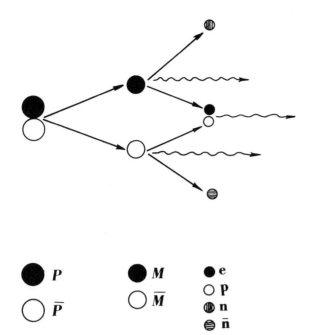

Particle annihilation. A collision of a proton (P) and an antiproton (P̄) results in their mutual annihilation. The particles are transformed into mesons (M) and antimesons (M̄), which decay rapidly and emit neutrinos (n) and antineutrinos (n̄), as well as gamma radiation (wavy lines). Only electrons (e) and positrons (p) remain, which may also annihilate one another, resulting in further gamma rays.

light-years, the radiation resulting from the pair annihilation became so strong that it overcame the effect of gravitation, and the cloud—which by that time had condensed into galaxies—began to expand. This, then, is the start of the expanding universe, according to Klein.

In its general features the theory is attractive, since it depends only on known physical principles and is in fair agreement with some observed facts, such as Hubble's law. However, there are two crucial questions that require a satisfactory answer. If, indeed, matter and antimatter were present, how were they separated and kept apart to form a stable world? The question may be answered, at least partially, by postulating the formation of a separation layer produced by the annihilation reaction between particles and antiparticles at the interface of matter and antimatter. (Such a layer is similar to the so-called Leidenfrost layer, formed when a drop of water is placed on a hot plate. If the temperature is quite high and the drop does not roll off, then it may exist intact for several minutes without boiling off, owing to a layer of insulating vapor at the interface.) More difficult to answer is the fundamental question how matter was separated from antimatter in the first place. In certain circumstances through the combined action of magnetic and gravitational fields by a process essentially similar to electrolysis—the separation of water into hydrogen and oxygen by an electric current—protons and antiprotons may collect in different regions, but the answer is still far from clear.

If it could be established that antimatter exists outside the laboratory, e.g., that there are antigalaxies composed of antistars containing antimatter, then there would be little doubt that Klein's theory is the correct one. The huge amounts of radiation produced by quasi-stellar radio sources may very well be the result of annihilation processes between matter and antimatter, but much more evidence is required before this explanation can be accepted. In the meantime the big bang continues to be the more favored explanation, despite its inherent difficulty regarding the formation of the primeval fireball.

4. The Search for Two Numbers

It was not until 1950 that observational cosmology had definitely established that the universe is expanding. Since then the abundance of new results may soon rule out many of the competing models and perhaps even pinpoint the correct one.

The crucial test of any model is the precise measurement of two numbers—the rate of expansion (the Hubble constant, H_0) and the deceleration (due to gravitational interaction) of the expansion (the deceleration parameter, q_0). Just as the future behavior of an automobile can be predicted if one knows its present speed and deceleration (or acceleration), so the future conduct of the universe is determined by these two parameters.

A first approximation of the Hubble constant, of course, is determined by the angle of the straight line determining Hubble's law (illustrated as Hubble's law, in the early pages of this chapter). However, it is the small deviations from that straight-line behavior (the illustrated plot in this chapter comparing red shift and magnitude) that are of interest, since only these can differentiate between the various models. It is here where precise measurements are of the utmost importance, since the distances involved are immense. Observations with the 200-inch telescope at Mount Palomar, using the corrected distances (recall that the original distances were off by a factor of 2 or more), have reduced the value H_0 considerably, the now accepted value being in the range 15 to 40 km/sec per million light-years.

The same magnitude-red shift relation also serves to determine the deceleration parameter (q_0). For all Friedmann models there is a simple equation that connects the apparent magnitude with the red shift, which also involves q_0. (A similar but more complicated expression exists for the more general models, for which the cosmological constant is different from zero.) In principle then, if the observations are sufficiently precise, the deceleration (and even the cosmological constant) could be determined from the magnitude-red shift relation. Different cosmological models lead to different theoretical expressions for the magnitude-red shift expression, and thus to different values of deceleration. For example, the steady state model requires that $q_0 = -1$ (it has a positive acceleration), whereas $q_0 = \frac{1}{2}$ gives the flat-space Einstein–de Sitter model; if q_0 is smaller than $\frac{1}{2}$ (but positive), space will be open with a negative curvature; the universe is closed with a positive curvature if q_0 is larger than $\frac{1}{2}$ (all these values of q_0 apply to models without a cosmological constant). The differences are greatly accentuated for objects with large red shifts, and present observations just do not go far enough to differentiate between the various models with a sufficient degree of certainty.

The magnitude red-shift relation is not the only way to differentiate between models and, in particular, between the types of curvature. If galaxies are distributed uniformly in space, their number for a given distance will be proportional to the enclosed volume. Ordinarily, the volume varies as the cube of the distance, but for closed universes this volume will change less than the cube of the distance; for open universes the opposite will be true. Thus, knowing the number of galaxies and hence the volume for a given distance as well as the distance makes possible, in principle, a determination of the spatial curvature—or at least its sign, positive for closed universes and negative for open ones. The quantity measured is the number of galaxies brighter than an apparent magnitude and plotted against that magnitude. The theoretical curves again involve the deceleration values and it should, therefore, be possible to differentiate between the various models. The difficulty with this approach is that even for

magnitudes as faint as 22 (the farthest the telescope can presently record), the variances in the number of galaxies for different deceleration values—between zero and one, the range of particular interest—are quite negligible (and are even masked by fluctuations). It would therefore seem impossible, at least for the present, to find the correct world model from galaxy counts alone—which would be more valid as corroborating evidence.

The fourth and last of the direct observational tests to distinguish between competing expanding-universe models involves the determination of angular diameters. Angular diameter depends on distance—which for an expanding universe will be different for different models—and types of curvature.

The diameters of galaxies determined from photographic plates usually refer to the size of the isophotal contours, or contours of equal brightness. However, for an expanding universe the surface brightness is not constant, varying with the red shift in a comparatively simple manner. But if the angular diameter of the isophotal contours of a given galaxy (say, M 31) is known, it is then possible to obtain its isophotal diameter from the red shift. At first glance, a practical solution would appear quite simple and could be read off a series of plates taken on the same night with identical exposure times for clusters with different red shifts. Unfortunately, comparing these with the theoretical curves in our plot cannot be done directly but involves photometric corrections. These depend on precise values for the galaxies' energy distribution and at present are not known accurately enough to determine deceleration values within 15 percent accuracy.

A somewhat indirect test, interesting for its own sake, concerns the age of the universe. If the universe—or, more precisely, its expansion—had a beginning, as required by the evolutionary cosmologies, then it should be possible to calculate the time that has elapsed and compare it with observations, such as the age of galaxies or even of the earth. However, if as postulated by the steady state theory there is no "singular point" denoting the start of the expansion, the question of age would not arise.

The calculation of the age depends on the particular model—including the amount of deceleration—and the Hubble time, which derives from the Hubble constant and can be found by a simple geometric construction. The age will always be less than the Hubble time, except for the flat Newtonian universe, where both are equal. Therefore, for each type of universe—open, closed, or flat—an expression for the age can be found from the underlying equations, dependent upon the deceleration and the Hubble constant.

Too brief an age would immediately eliminate all Friedmann models as being in contradiction with

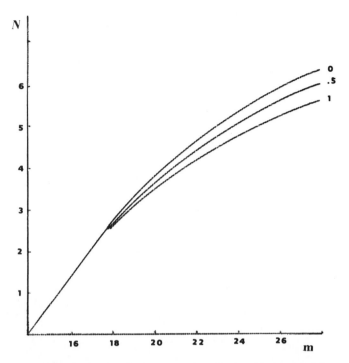

N represents the number of galaxies (on a logarithmic scale) that are brighter than a given apparent magnitude, represented by m and plotted on the horizontal axis; 0, .5, and 1 correspond to zero deceleration (that is, constant velocity) and flat and closed universes respectively. The curves start out as straight lines, confirming the power law for uniform distribution. Deviations occur only for galaxies of larger magnitudes, that is, fainter galaxies.

observation and rule in favor of the steady state theory, which predicts an infinitely long age. In fact, it was the earlier–and, as mentioned previously, wrong–determination of the age of the universe that brought about the steady state theory and gave it credence. However, present age determinations and, in particular, the Hubble time (which is the inverse of the Hubble constant) can be reconciled with most exploding models.

There is another way to distinguish between closed (or oscillating) and open (or ever-expanding) universes, which depends on the density of matter and radiation in the universe. If the density is sufficiently large, the gravitational interaction will be able to overcome the original expansion, slow it down, and eventually dominate, resulting in a contraction; in other words, the universe will be an oscillating one. However, if the density is not sufficiently great, the gravitational force will slow down the expansion but not reverse it and the universe will continue to expand. Thus, there exists a critical density that distinguishes between the two possibilities. Calculations based on simple considerations and models with zero cosmological constant show that this critical density is 10^{-23} grams per cubic meter (1 preceded by a decimal point and 22 zeros) or one atom of hydrogen (its equivalent in weight) per 10 cubic feet. However, the

density obtained by "spreading out" the matter concentrated in known galaxies over the whole universe is only 10^{-25} grams per cubic meter, which is smaller by a factor of 100. Even if one adds the radiation present, such as the background radiation, the result is only slightly changed. It thus appears that the universe is an expanding one. However, as in the previous considerations, the answer is complicated by several factors. In the first case, the value of the critical density depends on Hubble's constant, and, as has been seen, that value is by no means certain and different values may change the result (but only by a factor of about 4). More important, however, is the fact that the estimate of the actual density present is based only on the masses of galaxies and does not take into account the possibility of other matter being present. For example, if the universe were to contain a sizable number of black holes, their mass would increase the value of the density. Furthermore, the presence of X rays as observed by rockets indicates the presence of a large amount of interstellar matter. (The X rays are produced by interaction of radiation, presumably that of the primeval fireball, and electrons and protons–interstellar matter.) The amount of matter that would have to be present to account for the observed X-ray background is a hundred times larger than that condensed in galaxies–exactly that factor of 100 necessary to change from an expanding to an oscillating universe. Those observations are still quite preliminary and no definite conclusion can be drawn one way or another.

While astronomers have been busy looking farther and farther into space, cosmologists have been trying to improve their models. If the universe were to rotate, for example, the rotation would supply an additional parameter which, like the cosmological constant, could be adjusted to fit observation; but no overall rotation is observed. An anisotropic universe, too, would behave differently from a simple Friedmann model, but the isotropy of the background radiation rules this out. Inhomogeneities might be present, but they too can only account for small fluctuations and deviations from the overall homogeneous universe. A universe filled with radiation is another possibility, but although this might have been the case at the early stages, it is certainly not true now.

These are only a few of the many attempts to account for observational results that cannot be readily explained by the "simple" model. Other assumptions, such as a changing gravitational constant, are even more bizarre and only gained but a few adherents. In the meantime, the search for the two numbers goes on–with bigger telescopes and radio-telescope probing into space. Eventually they will tell us whether space is curved or flat, open or closed. Until then, it is anybody's guess.

IX · MAN AND SPACE

1. Rockets to the Moon

Travel to the moon—and the planets—is an ancient dream come true these last twenty years.

The earliest record of a journey, admittedly fictitious, is that of Lucian, a Greek satirist living in the second century A.D. In his book, *A True History,* he describes how a ship, encountering a fierce storm, is blown to the moon, where the crew, finding a strange assortment of inhabitants, became caught in a war between moon and sun people.

A more serious account is provided by Kepler's *Dream,* an allegorical work in which the author is not too much concerned about the actual mode of transportation—which he leaves to the spirits—but very carefully describes the hazards of space travel, especially the blast-off and final landing. Because the *Dream* had been misinterpreted, Kepler later added copious notes to explain his intention, which was to describe natural phenomena, such as climate and topography. He was followed by others, such as the poet Cyrano de Bergerac who in his book *Voyages to the Moon and Sun* concocted odd modes of transportation.

Jules Verne (1828–1905), among the earliest of the science fiction writers, saw space travel as an attainable goal. Although his launching device—a giant cannon shooting an aluminum projectile into space—was completely unrealistic, he understood the need for an escape velocity of more than 10 kilometers (6 miles) per second to overcome Earth's gravity. Moreover, his account *From the Earth to the Moon* was so realistic that many readers refused to believe it was fiction. For writers of science fiction, space travel has always been popular. Apart from providing entertainment, such literature performed an important service—it kept alive the dream of travel into space.

Rockets had been used by the Chinese as early as A.D. 1232 against the invading Mongols. Described as "arrows of flying fire," they appear to have been arrows with a flaming head propelled by small skyrockets, such as are

Jules Verne imagined the aluminum projectile fired into space by a 900-foot cannon.

still used in fireworks. The principle of rocket propulsion is simple; it is an application of Newton's third law of motion: to every action there is an equal and opposite reaction. The combustion process pushes the combustion gases backward and out of the combustion chamber, while a force of the same magnitude but in an opposite direction acts on the rocket, pushing it forward. Whether it is propelled by solid fuel containing its own oxygen supply or liquid fuel requiring mixture with the oxygen supply carried in a separate tank, the effect is the same. The resulting combustion produces gases, which are ejected with high velocities, to create the rocket's thrust.

"Arrows of flying fire" used by the Chinese as early as 1232. The flaming arrows were powered by small rockets utilizing sulfur or saltpeter as a propellant.

A rocket is based on the same principle as the recoil of a rifle, except that the recoil takes place continuously. As the propellant burns inside the combustion chamber (C), it generates hot gases that—like a stream of bullets—escape outward, thrusting the rocket in the opposite direction, or forward. To generate the explosion, an oxidizer (O) such as liquid oxygen is mixed with the liquid fuel (F) in the combustion chamber. (In solid-fuel rockets the propellant contains its own oxidizer.) The fuel tanks occupy most of the space in a rocket, and the payload (P) is concentrated in the nose cone.

In 1792 rockets were used successfully by Prince Hydar Ali of Mysore (India) against the British. This induced Sir William Congreve, a British colonel, to experiment with skyrockets to convert them into weapons of war. They were employed, under Congreve's direction, against Napoleon in Bolognea, and again against the French at Copenhagen, with devastating effects. The rocket had proved itself a powerful weapon and became the forerunner of the ominous intercontinental ballistic missile of today.

The fundamental laws of rocket motion—the basis of modern space vehicle design—were derived as early as 1898 by Konstantin Eduardovich Tsiolkovsky (1857–1935) who had become fascinated with space travel. The largely self-educated, unknown, and partially deaf Russian teacher of physics and mathematics starved himself to buy books and to carry out his basement experiments. He was the first to suggest the use of liquid propellants, and he introduced the idea of multiple-stage rockets. However, he did more than just expound his novel theories. He foresaw space explorations as an integral part of human development, believing "that not only the earth but the whole universe is the heritage of mankind." To advance his ideas, he wrote numerous articles, scientific and popular, and three

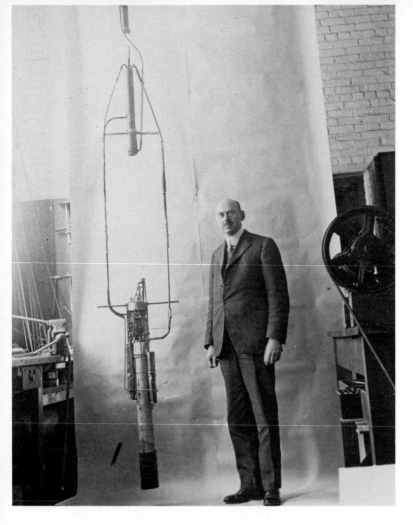

Robert H. Goddard with one of his early rockets in 1925. It used fuel pumps located near the base of the rocket but they were too inefficient to make the rocket fly. They had to be small and light and capable of withstanding the low temperatures of the liquid oxygen fuel. In a later model, for which Goddard used an old windmill frame as a launching tower, he managed to get his rocket up 90 feet. Parachutes added to the rockets ensured a soft landing; they were followed by the turbine-operated fuel pumps and motors that remain the basic ingredients of modern rockets. Born in Worcester, Massachusetts, Goddard began to think about rockets when he was seventeen and studied rocket fuels when he was a physics student at Clark University. Charles Lindbergh, impressed by his work, induced Daniel Guggenheim to give him a grant of $50,000, and Goddard moved his test site to Eden Valley in New Mexico. Unfortunately, only when the German V-2 rocket was examined in 1945 was it realized that Goddard's rockets were not only similar but more advanced. During his lifetime Goddard received 214 patents covering virtually every aspect of liquid-fuel rockets. Only after his death in 1945 was his pioneering work properly recognized by an award of a million dollars—half of which was turned over to the Guggenheim Foundation in appreciation of its original support—and by the naming of NASA's Goddard Space Flight Center.

A German V-2 rocket at the White Sands Proving Grounds in New Mexico about to be launched in May 1946. Burning a combination of alcohol and liquid oxygen, it is a preset missile with more than a ton of explosives for a payload. Guided by an automatic pilot, it could travel about 200 miles at nearly 4,000 miles per hour.

space novelettes, his *Outside the Earth* being the most remarkable of the fictionalized accounts of his scientific theories. Although his papers were well received, especially by Dmitri Mendeleev—the discoverer of the periodic table of elements—his work remained largely unknown during most of his life. Only in his later years were his works republished and read in the West, gaining for him the recognition and honors he so richly deserved.

Nor did the second pioneer of spaceflights, Robert Hutchings Goddard (1882-1945), ever see the fulfillment of his dream. Goddard, a rocket enthusiast since his schooldays and a professor of physics at Clark University, Worcester, Massachusetts, had experimented with rockets since 1906. In 1919 the Smithsonian Institution published his remarkable paper, *A Method of Reaching Extreme Altitudes,* resulting from work that was supported by a research grant of $5,000—even then a pittance, especially compared with today's billions for space projects. That paper contained the nucleus of space travel, as well as an allusion to the possibility of exploding some flashpowder on the surface of the moon (the light of the explosion would prove that extreme altitudes had been reached). This latter remark, seized upon by the press, caused the reticent scientist some embarrassment and induced him to conduct further experiments in comparative secrecy. In 1926 he launched his first successful rocket on "Aunt Effie's Farm." It reached a height of only 41 feet, in a total

flight of two and a half seconds, but it was a start. Goddard introduced a gyroscope to stabilize the flight of his rockets and added parachutes for perfect landings. More flights followed, some successful, but he never doubted the ability of rockets to gain extreme altitude and even enter outer space.

When World War II broke out, Goddard anticipated that the Germans would develop rockets for war. The fact that we did nothing, ignoring the pioneering work of "Goddard's rocket men," baffled the Germans; Hermann Oberth, a Romanian who later became a physics professor in Germany, had published at his own expense a small booklet, *The Rocket into Interplanetary Space,* in which he not only reviewed the results—obtained independently by Tsiolkovsky and Goddard—but revived the idea of a manned space station proposed earlier by the Boston clergyman Edward Everett Hale. To Oberth's amazement, his book became a best seller and started a chain reaction, with the mushrooming of rocket societies. From the "Verein für Raumschiffahrt" (Society for Space Travel), Hitler in 1937 recruited members of a top-secret laboratory at Peenemünde, a tiny village along the Baltic Sea. While the rest of the world "rocket-slept," the Germans furiously built rockets for war—notably the V-1, or buzz bomb (so called on account of the noise its engine made). It was actually a giant bomb propelled by a jet engine; the V-2 (Vengeance Weapon No. 2) was the first guided missile. The V rocket was not very accurate, having a scatter of five miles, but the cities of London and Antwerp bore witness to its destructive power—and man's perversion of a dream.

In 1945, at the end of the war, several V-2s and plans for future transatlantic rockets fell into the hands of the Allies, who had finally awakened to the practicality of rockets—in war or peace. Many of the devices used in modern rockets originated with the V-2, which may be considered the progenitor of rocketry. The V-2 was about 46 feet high and weighed about 12 tons, nearly three-fourths of it fuel and oxidizer. (Ordinary jet engines employing the rocket principle, of course, use air, of which one-fifth is oxygen. But rockets leaving the atmosphere must carry their own oxidizer; the V-2 used a combination of alcohol, made out of potatoes, and liquid oxygen.) The fuel was pumped into the combustion chamber at the record rate of one ton every seven seconds by means of steam-driven turbines only 2 feet in diameter, and the engine—weighing a mere 1,000 pounds and measuring 5 feet in length—was shielded from the hot gases by a protective film of the fuel itself. The rocket was guided by small vanes or rudders inserted into the rocket jet; changing the direction of the jet would then also change the direction of the rocket. These were controlled by an "inertial guidance system" that responded to the changes in direction and velocity from any preset course. Once the missile was on course and had attained the required velocity, the fuel was shut off and the V-2 coasted through space like a projectile or spaceship on course.

To increase the attainable speeds of rockets requires an increase in mass ratio (the ratio of the weight of the rocket when filled with fuel to its weight when all that fuel has been spent). To double the attainable speed, the mass ratio must be squared, at triple speed cubed, and so on. Even assuming that for a given payload the weight of the fuel and propellant chambers does not increase with

The mightiest Titan, Titan 3, developed for the Manned Orbital Laboratory in 1965. The four-stage rocket weighs more than 1,400 tons and is 125 feet long and 10 feet in diameter. Attached to its Titan 2 core are two 10-foot solid-fuel booster rockets.

the mass of the propellant, the result will be extremely large and heavy rockets. For the V-2 to attain a speed of 9,000mph it would have had to hold 45 tons of fuel instead of the nine needed to give it its velocity of 4,500mph. To lift 27 tons off the ground at that time would have been an engineering impossibility. Modern design and new materials have partially overcome this problem. The tanks of the Atlas rocket, for example, are so thin that they cannot stand up under their own weight but have to be pressurized internally. The step, or multiple-stage, rocket is another approach to that problem. If one rocket is mounted on top of another, we get a more favorable mass ratio from the combination, and it has been possible to attain very large speeds, although at great expense. The first American adaptation of the V-2 was a small rocket mounted on a V-2, which reached 250 miles. Unless more efficient fuels, such as nuclear ones, are discovered, the multiple-stage rocket will remain the answer to the problem of the mass ratios.

The United States followed the Project Bumper shots of the revised V-2 rockets with its own sounding rockets, such as the Aerobee and the larger Viking. The war in Korea brought some urgency to the missile program, resulting in a crash effort for the Atlas ICBM (Intercontinental Ballistic Missile) launched successfully at Cape Canaveral at the end of 1957. In the meantime two simpler IRBMs (Intermediate-Range Ballistic Missiles), the Thor and the Jupiter, were rushed into production. These were followed by the two-stage Titan and finally Saturn 5, the largest of them all, which was to carry

Apollo to the moon–closing the circle, with the rocket once again a peaceful probe into the unknown, though its fearful potentiality hovers like the Sword of Damocles.

2. Satellites

The International Geophysical Year (IGY), which was scheduled for the period July 1957 to December 1958, was to be a time of scientific cooperation among nations that wished to contribute to the knowledge and understanding of man's planet. The United States and the USSR, both well advanced in rocket work, undertook the attempt to launch and orbit an artificial satellite around the earth.

To fire a rocket is one thing, but to put a satellite into orbit is quite a different matter. In order to overcome Earth's gravitational pull a rocket must reach a speed of 7.1 miles per second. To reach these speeds, it must have the correct mass ratio, which can be achieved either by extreme power or two or more rockets in tandem (multiple stages), or by a combination of both. Once this escape velocity has been reached, a rocket-borne satellite will escape the gravitational pull of the earth and will become a satellite around the sun.

A second point concerns the nature of the orbit. Assuming for simplicity that the orbit is circular, the time to complete one revolution–the period–depends on its distance from the earth (a consequence of Kepler's third law). For example, at a distance of about 300 miles from the surface of the earth, it will take the satellite about one and a half hours to complete a revolution, having an orbital velocity of about 5 miles per second. (This orbital velocity must not be confused with the escape velocity mentioned earlier.) The larger the orbit, the longer will be the period, and the smaller the orbital velocity. A satellite at a distance of 22,300 miles from the earth's surface will take exactly twenty-four hours to complete a circuit, having an orbital velocity of only 1.9 miles per second. Such a satellite–when its orbital plane coincides with the equator–will appear to stand still. Such a satellite is called a geosynchronous satellite. (In theory, a satellite would revolve around the earth forever; space is full of floating debris of old satellites and rocket remnants. However, whenever a satellite strikes the earth's atmosphere, the aerodynamic friction will generate sufficient heat to burn up the satellite.)

We have been discussing satellite orbits as circles. Actually they are ellipses, with the earth at the near focus. The point in the orbit at which the satellite is closest to the earth is called the perigee (from the Greek *peri,* or "near," and *gaia,* "earth") and is like the perihelion of a

The Saturn 1 rocket lifts off its pad at Cape Kennedy to hoist into orbit one of the world's heaviest satellites, its own 29-ton second stage. Both stages weigh more than 1,100 tons. The purpose of its mission was to find out if supercold hydrogen fuel could be controlled for space use. A TV camera monitored the behavior of the 10 tons of fuel in the 90-foot-long tank during three orbits.

planetary orbit around the sun. After a complete revolution, a satellite will again return to its perigee. For most satellites the perigee is low enough so that the aerodynamic drag by the atmosphere is significant. As a result, such a satellite will lose some of its momentum and will not be able to cover the distance of its previous circuit. Eventually, the ellipse will evolve into a circle with a radius the distance of the perigee from the earth. However, that circle may not even be reached if the orbit instead decays into a spiral path along which the satellite falls toward its final burn-up. But, as with the circle, if the perigee is beyond the earth's atmosphere–and its drag–a satellite will be able to escape that fate.

To return to the Russians and the IGY, on October 5, 1957, the first man-made satellite began to circle the globe. It was the 184-pound *Sputnik I* (fellow-traveler around the earth). A month later it was followed by *Sputnik II,* weighing 1,120 pounds and carrying a live passenger, a dog named Laika.

A schematic flight plan of a three-stage rocket putting a satellite into orbit. At *a* the first stage has its burnout and separates, having reached an altitude of 36 miles and a velocity of 3,600 miles per hour. The second stage reaches burnout at *b* but continues until *c* (the apex of its parabola), where the third-stage rocket accelerates. At this point the satellite separates, and rocket and satellite continue on orbit.

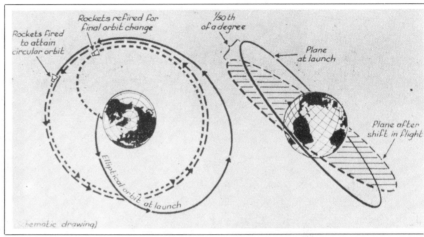

The type and size of orbit depends on the velocity (both magnitude and direction) and altitude at the point the satellite goes into orbit. Starting as an ellipse, it can reach circular shape by rocket firing and can be further changed (for example, for reentry) by additional rockets.

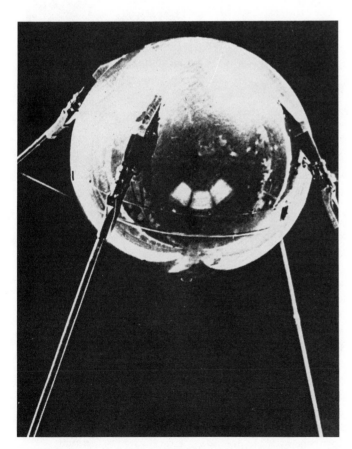

Sputnik I, the first satellite to be put into orbit, October 4, 1957, along with the upper stage of its launch vehicle. It weighed 184 pounds (the total mass of the orbiting system was about 2 tons) and consisted of a hermetically sealed aluminum sphere nearly 2 feet in diameter. It communicated via four whip antennae powered by batteries; its "pips" as it streaked across the sky have become famous.

What was to have been a scientific contribution to IGY now became a political issue—the space race was on.

On January 31, 1958, the first American satellite, *Explorer 1,* began its 90-minute circumnavigations of the earth. It was followed by several others, American and Russian, roughly in the ratio of three American to one Russian. During the five years following *Sputnik I,* about 90 satellites and probes, both manned and unmanned, had been launched.

From a purely scientific point of view, *Explorer 1* had been more important than *Sputnik,* for it included experiments that demonstrated the presence of the Van Allen radiation belts. These belts, whose existence had been predicted by James Van Allen, consist of deadly radioactive particles emitted by the sun and trapped by the earth's magnetic field—forming a zone of intense radiation, 250 to 6,000 miles above the earth's surface. Later, unmanned satellites and space probes were sent into space to bring back information on such vital subjects as temperature, radiation density, and other factors that would affect future manned spaceflights. Then and now these probes serve other important functions. There are spy-in-the-sky satellites equipped with powerful photographic cameras that can scan the whole of the earth's surface and report the presence of weapons installations as well as large-scale troop movements. The fine line between scientific and military uses of the space program becomes apparent in the use of weather satellites relaying back to Earth a global weather report. Vanguard 1 in March 1958 was the first of the kind, followed by TIROS (*T*elevision and *I*nfra-*R*ed *O*bservation *S*atellites) and many others. Another group of such sky workhorses

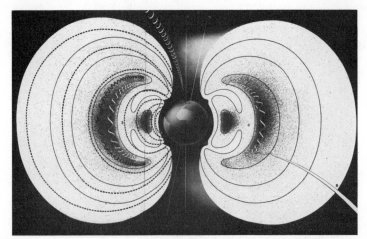

The earth is the center of an extensive region, the magnetosphere, in which its magnetic field is dominant. Reaching far into space—about 7 Earth diameters—it forms a barrier against charged particles coming from outer space and traps others. There are two regions in particular, known as the Van Allen radiation belts (shown shaded), where the radiation is extremely intense. High-energy cosmic rays, capable of passing through the magnetic barrier, collide with particles in the upper atmosphere. These, in turn, may produce neutrons that decay into protons and electrons. The protons are quite energetic and, being charged, will be trapped by the magnetic field. Another source of high-energy protons and electrons is the solar wind (B), and undoubtedly the electrons present in the outer zone are due to it. The two Van Allen belts are separated by a region (3) commonly referred to as the slot, where the intensity of charged particles is less than in the two radiation belts. The existence of the Van Allen belts was discovered by *Explorer 1*'s Geiger counters, which ceased to function whenever the satellite passed through the belts. This seemed unusual, since the cosmic ray counts are expected to increase with altitude. It was then found that the intensity of charged particles had increased so much that the instrument became saturated. Later satellites extended these studies and were able to map the shape of the belts and the magnetosphere fairly accurately.

Alouette, a wholly passive satellite built by the Canadian Defense Research Telecommunication Establishment. Its wide-band FM telemetry transmitter, receiver, and tape recorder are powered by solar cells and batteries.

Telstar, built by Bell Laboratories, weighing 175 pounds and measuring 34½ inches in diameter. The two rows of microwave antennae around the center receive signals sent up to the satellite, which relays them back to Earth. On the panel at left center, just below the antennae, is a radiation measuring device—an electron detector—that measures electrons in the range of 750,000 to 2 million electron volts. There are 3,600 solar cells on Telstar's surface that provide its power. ▶

are the communications satellites. These may be divided into two classes: "passive," such as Echo 1, which merely reflect radio waves; and "active," such as the famous Telstar, which receive radio signals, amplify them, and retransmit them to the ground.

Clearly, sooner or later man himself had to venture into space. Even the most sophisticated of computers cannot make independent judgments, but at best adjust to previously given instructions. But to put a man into orbit required more powerful satellites, since the payload (that part of the spaceship containing instruments and other equipment as well as the astronauts themselves) now had to be much larger. In addition, man had to be trained to withstand the hazards of space. He had to learn to adjust to weightlessness and to withstand the G force. This G force is a magnification of the earth's gravity that a

passenger would experience as a spaceship accelerates and decelerates, leaving and returning to Earth. Astronauts have had to withstand 7.7G, which means that their apparent weight was 7.7 times their ordinary weight on earth. Recovering an astronaut from the icy ocean first had to be simulated, and steps for his safe return had to be carefully worked out, including the training of technicians, engineers, and other supporting staff. Future astronauts spent hours in the training gym, pool, and the centrifuge, which simulated conditions they were to experience in space, including large G forces. Animals were sent into space—Russian dogs and American monkeys—to observe the effect of spaceflight on living organisms.

The first astronaut entered space on April 12, 1961. Yuri Gagarin completed one orbit around the earth in 108

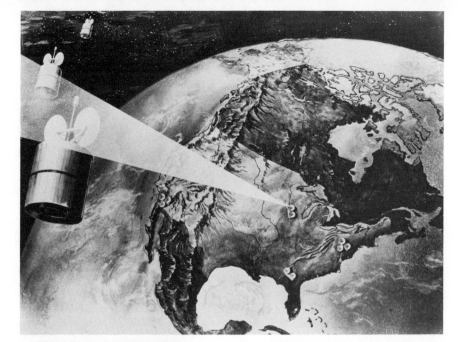

A proposed satellite communication system would use three stationary satellites 22,300 miles in space and seven Earth stations. The system would be capable of carrying 28,800 telephone calls simultaneously and would augment the Bell System's nationwide long-distance telecommunication network, as well as serve the contiguous 48 states and Hawaii. (Alaska and Puerto Rico would be served through Earth stations.)

Practicing for the real thing: Lunar Module pilot Charles M. Duke, Jr., holds a self-recording penetrometer, which will be implanted in the lunar surface to obtain data on the physical characteristics of the soil. Commander John W. Young and the Rover, used in the later *Apollo* flights, are in the background. Designed both for comfort and protection, the spacesuit carries its own air supply (the backpack) and protects against extreme temperatures and puncture by micrometeoroids.

Practicing flight procedures in a model of the *Apollo* command ship at the Johnson Space Center in Texas. *From left to right:* Jack Lousma, Dr. Owen Garriott, and Alan Bean. ▼

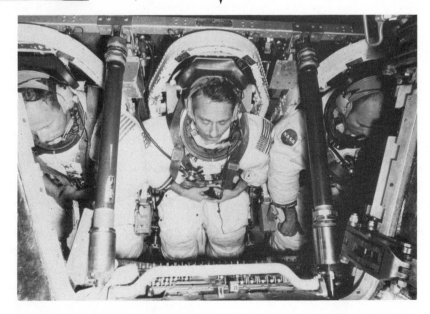

minutes of flight in his *Vostok* spaceship. Not quite a month later, on May 5, 1961, Alan B. Shepard followed, but not in orbit; his flight lasted only some 15 minutes, but he attained an altitude of more than 100 miles and was weightless for about 5 minutes. On August 6, Gherman S. Titov was the second Russian to orbit the earth—for the longest record, 26 hours and 16 orbits. On February 20, 1962, John H. Glenn became the first American to orbit the earth (three times in 5 hours). More and more manned spaceflights followed, each more daring and sophisticated; crews were sent into space (the first being three Russians in 1964), spacewalks occurred (the first by the Russian Leonov March 18, 1965, followed by American astronaut White on June 3), and dockings between ships—*Gemini* 6 and 7—were practiced, all in preparation for the grand finale: a landing on the moon.

EARLY MANNED SPACEFLIGHTS

Date	Ship	Crew	Date	Ship	Crew
April 12, 1961	*Vostok I*	Yuri Gagarin	June 3, 1965	*Gemini 4*	Edward H. White (spacewalk)
May 5, 1961	*Freedom 7*	Alan B. Shepard			James A. McDivitt (pilot)
July 21, 1961	*Liberty Bell-7*	Virgil I. Grissom	August 21, 1965	*Gemini 5*	L. Gordon Cooper
August 6, 1961	*Vostok II*	Gherman Titov			Charles Conrad
February 20, 1962	*Friendship 7*	John H. Glenn	December 4, 1965	*Gemini 7 **	Frank Borman
May 24, 1962	*Aurora 7*	M. Scott Carpenter			James A. Lovell
August 11, 1962	*Vostok III*	Andrian G. Nikolayev	December 15, 1965	*Gemini 6-A*	Walter M. Shirra
August 12, 1962	*Vostok IV*	Pavel Popovich			Thomas P. Stafford
October 3, 1962	*Sigma 7*	Walter A. Schirra	March 16, 1966	*Gemini 8*	Neil A. Armstrong
May 15, 1963	*Faith 7*	L. Gordon Cooper			David R. Scott
June 14, 1963	*Vostok V*	Valery Bykovsky	June 3, 1966	*Gemini 9-A †*	Thomas P. Stafford
June 16, 1963	*Vostok VI*	Valentina Tereshkova			Eugene A. Cernan
October 12, 1964	*Voskhod I*	Vladimir Komarov	July 18, 1966	*Gemini 10 ‡*	John W. Young
		Dr. Boris Egerov			Michael Collins
		Konstantin Feoktistov	September 12, 1966	*Gemini 11*	Charles Conrad
March 18, 1965	*Voskhod II*	Alexei Leonov (spacewalk)			Richard F. Gordon
		Pavel I. Belyaev (pilot)	November 11, 1966	*Gemini 12 §*	James A. Lovell
March 23, 1965	*Gemini 3*	Virgil I. Grissom			Edwin E. Aldrin
		John W. Young			

* *Gemini* 6 not launched.   ‡ First successful docking.
† *Gemini* 9 not launched.   § Last *Gemini* flight.

3. Man on the Moon

At only 240,000 miles from the earth, the moon is a convenient and natural space station and possible base for future penetration of the solar system. To reach the moon was not enough, the problem was to be able to leave it and return safely to the earth. This required careful planning and lengthy preparations. A whole series of American flights—known as Project Apollo—was to be devoted to that and related phases of the space program.

However, on September 13, 1959, the Russians had scored another first when the unmanned *Lunik II* crash-landed on the moon—a feat comparable to hitting the eye of a fly at 6 miles. And on October 4, *Lunik III* transmitted pictures of the far side of the moon, the side no one had ever seen because it is always turned away from us.

In 1967 *Apollo 3* was ready for its first test flight, when tragedy struck. While it was on the ground, fire broke out in the cockpit and seconds later, fed by the oxygen-rich atmosphere within, it was completely destroyed. Astronauts Grissom, White, and Chaffee, overcome by smoke, never had a chance; the escape hatches could not be opened in time and all three died within seconds. (Investigations showed that the fire was caused by faulty wiring, fed by excessive use of combustible material,

Apollo launches and their original projected landing sites, as indicated on a photograph of the moon's surface: *Apollo 11* (July 1969)–Sea of Tranquility; *Apollo 12* (November 1969)–Western mare region in Ocean of Storms; *Apollo 13* (April 1970)–flat highlands in Fra Mauro formation; *Apollo 14* (January 1971)–cratered highlands near Crater Censorius; *Apollo 15* (July 1971)–volcanolike projections in Littrow area; *Apollo 16* (April 1972)–Crater Tycho; *Apollo 17* (December 1972)–volcanic domes in Marius Hill area. Also shown are three proposed flights that were cancelled: *Apollo 18*–deep crater in Schröter's valley; *Apollo 19*–volcanic craters in Hyginus Rille; and *Apollo 20*–Crater Copernicus.

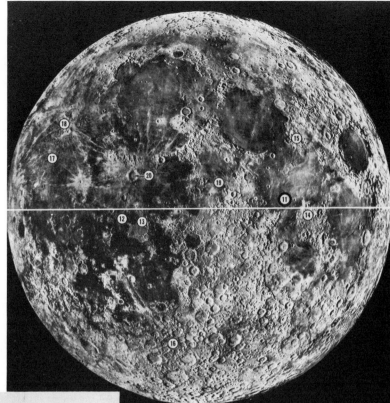

Diagram of the *Apollo 17* landing site shows approach views of Mission Commander Eugene Cernan (at the left) and Lunar Module pilot Harrison Schmitt. Prominent features are identified.

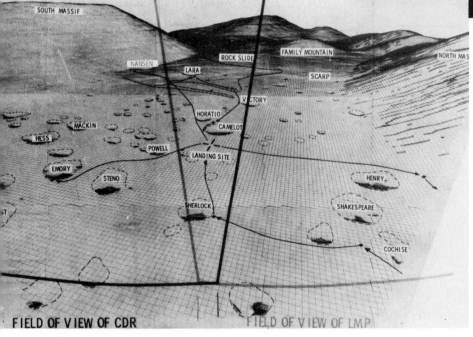

despite the obvious fire hazard of the pure oxygen atmosphere.) Only a few months later Astronaut Komarov in his *Soyuz I* spacecraft, following his eighteenth orbit and the start of reentry, plunged to his death when his parachute failed to open. (It is believed that *Soyuz I* was supposed to be joined by another craft which, however, was never launched.) The double tragedy caused some soul-searching in both countries and the feasibility–or at least the readiness for–further explorations began to be doubted. In the end, the project was continued but more slowly and only after the spacecraft had been redesigned.

The trip to the moon would be in stages. A powerful Saturn 5 rocket–itself consisting of three stages–would boost the command service module (CSM) into orbit. The first two stages of Saturn would overcome the earth's gravitation and the third would bring the CSM into lunar orbit. The command service module, equipped with engines of its own, would fire twice, once to maintain it in lunar orbit, and after leaving the lunar orbit to reenter the earth's orbit. The actual descent to the lunar surface required a third vehicle, the lunar excursion module (LEM), or "bug." Its modestly powered motors would counteract the much weaker gravitational field of the

As the two-week lunar day begins, *Surveyor 3* is shown sitting in a small crater on the Ocean of Storms. It was one of the five spacecraft built by Hughes Aircraft Company that successfully soft-landed on the moon between June 1966 and January 1968 to explore potential landing sites for the manned missions that were to follow. The photograph was taken by the *Apollo 12* astronauts during their second extravehicular run on November 20, 1969.

A geological map of the Copernicus Quadrangle. The central feature, of course, is the Copernicus Crater. The different shadings indicate the height or depth of the various formations. Letters (Ccp, Ccrr, etc.) indicate the different materials. The numbers give the elevations or depths (in parentheses) in meters.

moon during descent and takeoff, and its special undercarriage—making it resemble a bug—would absorb the shock during touchdown. After LEM's return to the mother ship, which would in the meantime continue to circle in its own orbit, it would be abandoned, becoming a satellite of the moon. The return trip would be carried out in the CSM, part of which would be jettisoned, leaving only the command module (CM) to make the final trip through the earth's atmosphere. Parachutes would provide a safe splashdown in the Pacific Ocean.

Each stage was carefully tested by various Apollo flights. *Apollo 8* was the first manned spacecraft sent into lunar orbit and, after ten orbits around the moon, returned safely to Earth. The next two flights were to test the LEM itself, including an all-important "dress rehearsal": the manned LEM had to make two passes over the lunar surface without landing. Although for a short but critical moment it looked as if there would be another tragedy when the bug began to spin wildly, it was steadied manually and the crew completed their test flight. The Apollo program was now ready for a manned landing on the moon.

On July 16, 1969, at 9:32 A.M. the giant *Apollo 11* rocket took off from its pad at Cape Kennedy in a perfect

Evidence of *Surveyor 3*'s hop-skip-and-jump as it landed on April 19, 1967. The "footprint" was photographed by *Apollo 12* astronauts when they visited the spacecraft. The dark shadow above the footpad masks the area where a trenching tool dug several furrows in the surface.

A close-up of the lunar surface by *Apollo 10* in May 1969.

Four views of *Apollo 11*'s landing site in the Sea of Tranquillity, received from earlier lunar flights: Ranger 9 returned its picture from about 5 miles above the surface before hitting the moon in February 1965; *Surveyor 5* soft-landed near the site in September 1967 and sent back this oblique view of the area; *Lunar Orbiter 5* photographed the site from an altitude of some 50 miles in August 1967 (the pattern is due to a film-processing problem in the spacecraft); *Apollo 10* astronauts made an almost vertical photograph from about 65 miles up in May 1969.

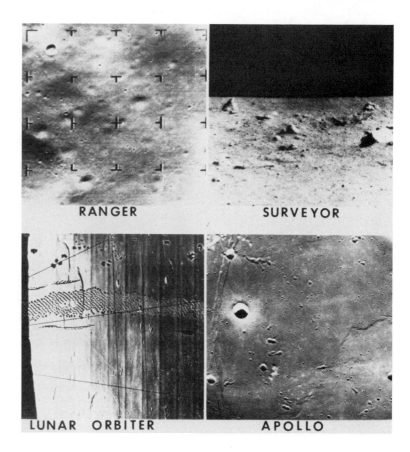

flight. (A few days before, *Luna V* had been launched, and it seemed as if the Russians might try to beat the Americans to the first landing. However, *Luna* turned out to be unmanned.) On July 19 the ship was in orbit around the moon, and the following day two of the three-man crew, Neil Armstrong and Edwin Aldrin, crawled into the LEM (which they had renamed *Eagle),* uncoupled it from the command module, and began their descent. At 4:17 P.M. the *Eagle* landed on Tranquillity base. A few hours later as Armstrong left the ship to take the first steps on the moon, the dream became a reality.

The next few hours were spent collecting samples of lunar rocks and soil, setting up shock experiments, and trapping rare gases from the solar wind. An American flag was planted and a plaque was left. With its engine ignited, the *Eagle* began its return flight. A smooth ride and a few hours later the two crafts maneuvered until finally they docked. Reunited with Mike Collins in the command module, the crew jettisoned *Eagle* into lunar orbit and began their flight back to earth. On July 24 the service module was discarded and reentry undertaken. A few hours later, what was left of *Apollo 11* splashed down in the South Pacific, some 950 miles southwest of Hawaii and 11 miles from the ship that was to pick them up.

Apollo 11 astronaut Edwin Aldrin, July 20, 1969, deploying the solar wind composition experiment, consisting of a piece of aluminum foil that traps inert gases. It was later dismantled and returned to Earth, where the gases were analyzed. The lunar landing vehicle is at the right.

Apollo 12 crewmen, from left: Charles Conrad, Richard Gordon, and Alan Bean (he received a minor cut over his right eye during landing) inside the quarantine van aboard the carrier U.S.S. *Hornet* following their splashdown and recovery in the South Pacific on November 24, 1969.

An *Apollo 12* astronaut approaches *Surveyor 3* in the Ocean of Storms. The Lunar Module that carried astronauts Conrad and Bean is seen in the background about 600 feet away.

Splashdown of *Apollo 17*, December 19, 1972—last of the Apollo moon landings. The Command Module floats in the Pacific Ocean about 400 miles southeast of American Samoa, while a recovery helicopter from the carrier U.S.S. *Ticonderoga* hovers overhead.

The first Soviet spacemen to visit the U.S. launch complex at Cape Canaveral (Cape Kennedy), with their American counterparts in front of a mock-up of *Apollo-Soyuz*, months before the launch in 1975. *Left to right:* Vance Brand, Tom Stafford, Alexei Leonov, Valeri Kubasov, and Deke Slayton.

Six additional manned flights were made to get more information on the moon. One, *Apollo 13*, nearly ended in disaster when an oxygen tank in the service module exploded. The crew moved into the attached LEM, which became their life raft bringing them back into Earth's orbit, where they jettisoned it and reentered the command module, making a splashdown only 4 miles off course. Scientifically the mission was a failure, but it was a triumph for teamwork, technology, and courage.

The last of the Apollo flights (*15, 16,* and *17*) employed a jeeplike vehicle, the Lunar Roving Vehicle (LRV), enabling the astronauts to cover as much as 40 miles from their landing site, in order to set up a network of seismometers and collect samples from as large an area as possible—during each of these missions nearly 200 pounds of soil and rocks were gathered. (One further but nonlunar Apollo flight was the successful docking of an *Apollo* and *Soyuz* spacecraft in outer space in 1975. This ended not only the Apollo program but possibly the competition in space between the United States and Russia.)

The Apollo flights and the exploratory flights that preceded them were unparalleled feats of technology, which brought back important information on the structure and evolutionary history of the moon. The seismographs that were installed on the moon by successive Apollo missions—many are still operating—indicate the occurrences of moonquakes, presumably the result of impacts by meteorites. While comparative quakes on the earth are measured in minutes, on the moon they last for several hours. Also, lunar signals build up relatively slowly, increase to a maximum, and then decay even more slowly. These and other unusual characteristics of lunar seismic signals have been interpreted as resulting from an intensive scattering of the seismic waves by the moon's heterogeneous layer; the layer covers the entire moon surface.

An analysis of seismic data of man-made impacts has established the existence of a lunar crust approximately 36 miles in depth. Below this crust lies the moon's mantle, but whereas the earth's mantle accounts for 69 percent of the earth's mass, the moon's mantle represents more than 90 percent of its total mass, making the moon, in effect, solid rock. The moon is spherical (if it were otherwise, its rock strength could not permanently withstand the effects of gravitational self-compression). Nevertheless, it would be wrong to think of the moon as a *solid* spherical rock; seismic data at greater depth (about 400 miles from the moon's center) indicate that lunar material close to the center tends to become plastic or even liquid. Also, whereas the surface temperature of the moon is seen to vary from −190°C to 127°C, the central temperature necessary to keep material molten must be around 1300°C.

And although the absence of a lunar magnetic field had been established in 1967 by a magnetometer on board *Explorer 35,* subsatellites of the *Apollo 15–17* missions, orbiting much closer to the moon's surface than *Explorer 35,* disclosed the existence of small local magnetic fluctuations strongly correlated with specific formations on the lunar surface. This shows that the source of the magnetic field has nothing to do with the interior but is a surface effect. This was confirmed by samples brought back: the carriers of the magnetic field were brecciated rocks (conglomerates of preexisting rocks) magnetized by impacts with outside particles. On the other hand, lunar crystalline rocks show a permanent magnetism, suggesting the presence of fields about fifty to five hundred times less intense than the present earth's magnetic field. It is not clear whether the mechanism that generated these fields in the past was due to the liquid core (and has now become extinct), to the greater proximity to the earth, to the solar wind, or to other unknown causes. Until we have further information on the origin of the moon and the solar system as a whole, the observed permanent magnetism of lunar crystalline rocks will remain a mystery.

Samples brought back from the moon's surface also provide some indication of the lunar internal structure and chemical composition. The average density of the lunar rocks is very close to the mean density of 3.34 grams per cubic centimeter. The rocks forming the earth's crust have an average density of 2.8 grams per cubic centimeter, whereas the mean density is 5.5 grams per cubic centimeter, allowing for a considerable amount of compression. A chemical analysis of the samples brought back, more than 800 pounds of rocks, shows that the most abundant element on the moon, as on the earth, is oxygen, followed by silicon and aluminum. However, oxygen forms about 50 percent of the earth's crust, whereas on the moon it is 60 percent; silicon is more abundant on the earth (26 percent) than on the moon (16 percent). The difference is even more marked with iron and titanium, which appear to be distinctly enhanced in the lunar crust, whereas the alkali metals, such as sodium, are less abundant.

More important, the effects of oxidation are conspicuous by their absence; consequently, the moon could never have had much water on its surface, since that would have left it in a much more oxidized state than is consistent with its grayish color (in contrast to Mars, for example, whose reddish color indicates the presence of a large amount of ferric oxide).

The absolute ages of solid rocks can be established from spontaneous nuclear disintegrations of certain chains of radioactive elements, such as the decay of uranium, which results in lead. Applying these methods to the samples brought back from various sites gave the mean age of rocks, ranging from 3 to 4 billion years. The "fines" (soil) collected at these locations exhibit an even higher age, 4.6 billion years, which turned out to be nearly the same for all localities. In contrast, apart from some rocks recently found in Greenland whose age may approach 4 billion years, the oldest sediments and volcanic rocks found on Earth date back a mere 3.5 billion years.

The most conspicuous feature of the moon's surface is the abundance of craters and maria (large basins that had been believed to contain water and, consequently, were called seas). Ever since Robert Hooke carried out simple experiments that showed that the craters could be the result of either volcanic action or impacts by foreign bodies, controversy raged over their origin, which even now has not subsided completely. However, based on the numerous photographs from the lunar surface, it is clear that the main cause of cratering is impact by asteroids and meteorites. This is not surprising if one remembers that the moon does not possess any protective magnetic or atmospheric shield, and that those objects have been undoubtedly more numerous in the past. Furthermore, the so-called lava flows are more than 3 billion years old, but the age of most craters is much less.

Piecing the various bits of information together, we can get a good idea of the origin and evolution of the moon. The age of the rocks and, in particular, the soil agrees very closely with that established for the oldest meteorites and is generally used to date the origin of the solar system as a whole. The formation of the sun and planets from the primordial nebula took place at about the same time, and the close agreement of the ages of meteorites and lunar soil strongly suggests that the moon originated as a by-product of the same events. That it ever was fluid throughout can be ruled out on account of its insufficient self-attraction, and the hypothesis that it is due to a condensation of gas at a temperature prevalent in the original solar nebula can also be ruled out. The chemical evidence on the composition of the lunar rocks clearly points to an accumulation of solid particles at low or moderate temperatures. However, we still do not know whether the lunar rocks acquired their characteristics before or after they became part of the moon.

What about the earth-moon system? Did the moon once form a part of the earth, or did the two come into being together as a gravitational system, or was the moon captured by the earth from a heliocentric orbit of its own? Osmond Fisher conjectured that the Pacific basin represented a scar in the terrestrial crust where the moon once separated from the earth, a suggestion which can be discarded in view of the fact that the moon originated long before the Pacific basin was formed. Furthermore, the total angular momentum of the earth-moon system is insufficient to cause fission into two parts. To decide whether or not the moon was captured by the earth is a more difficult question. The situation is similar to that of an artificial satellite sent out from the earth. Once it succeeded in leaving the earth's gravitational field it would remain in free flight, bypass the moon, and remain a member of the solar system. In order for the moon to capture the satellite it would be necessary to reduce the satellite's kinetic energy by the firing of retrorockets. In the case of celestial bodies, such a decrease in kinetic energy can be caused by the presence of other bodies or dissipative forces, such as those rising from mutual tidal interaction. For the moon to have come close enough to the earth to raise tides sufficient for capture, important markings should have been left on both bodies, yet none were observed on either. Unless we can assume that the rate of tidal friction in the past—in particular, 4.6 billion years ago when the hypothetical capture took place—was less than it is now (which implies that the moon and, in particular, the earth were less viscous than they are today), we are forced to conclude that the moon was never close enough to the earth to have been captured by it in the strict sense of the word, although, of course, the moon now is a satellite of the earth.

The fact that we are not in a position to answer these questions satisfactorily shows how much work still has to be done and how much has to be learned. It would also be quite unrealistic to expect an answer to these questions without taking into account the origin of the solar system as a whole, especially since we now know that the moon is an old and venerable charter member.

4. The Grand Tour

Travel to other parts of the solar system would require a more or less permanent station in outer space, manned and serviced by a space crew. Incoming flights would have to be able to dock, fuel, and take off on the next leg of their journey.

To study the problem of docking, as well as medical questions, such as living under zero gravity for a length of time, a number of space laboratories were sent up, starting in May 1973. It was a three-part program comprising a 28-day and two 56-day manned visits spanning eight months, beginning with an unmanned *Skylab* launched on May 14

and visited by successive crews on May 25, July 28, and November 15. Essentially, *Skylab* consists of the *Apollo* lunar-mission components: an orbital workshop, a modified Saturn 1B rocket, a multiple docking adapter for landing and takeoff, an airlock module for passage between components, and an *Apollo* telescope mount with its own solar batteries, as well as an instrument unit.

The different *Skylab* missions not only tested living conditions in space but brought back pictures that could not otherwise have been obtained.

Soon a new vehicle, the Space Shuttle, will join the long list of spacecraft. Riding piggyback on reusable rocket boosters, it will ferry crew and cargo from station to station and will also contain satellites to be released in space. Not only will the shuttle reduce the cost of spaceflights considerably, but it may become the space transport of the future. The first of the Space Shuttles, the *Enterprise,* named after the starship in the popular science fiction television program "Star Trek," made its public appearance on September 17, 1976. On August 12, and again on September 13, 1977, *Enterprise* successfully passed its first tests. Riding piggyback on a Boeing 747, the Space Shuttle glided freely from a height of 27,000 feet and landed perfectly five minutes later on a dry lakebed in southern California. With still other tests scheduled, the first space flight will be launched in 1979. The *Enterprise* will be flown by a crew of three and is designed to make at least 100 round trips into space before overhaul, lasting between 7 and 30 days. Although meant primarily as a means of ferrying satellites, it is also planned as the vehicle for putting Spacelab, a European space station, into orbit in 1980. Estimated at a cost of 5.2 billion dollars, the Space Shuttle will replace 21 of 22 launch systems now used and can carry over 30 tons of cargo.

In the meantime, following the successful moon program, Mars became the next major target.

Since Mars's mass is only one-tenth the earth's, its gravitational pull is much smaller and it can therefore retain only a very tenuous atmosphere—a fact that makes a landing by parachute too difficult; so special landing crafts, similar to the *Surveyor,* are necessary.

The first successful Mars probe was *Mariner 4,* which made a close approach to the planet on November 28, 1964. Although it was only a flyby mission, it brought back remarkable pictures, showing the surface of Mars to be full of craters. Successive flights confirmed these "Martian ruins." And the atmosphere turned out to be even thinner than expected, being composed mainly of carbon dioxide—hardly conducive to life as we know it.

Russian probes reached the planet at about the same time, depositing a pennant and a capsule, which, unfortunately, failed to operate.

On July 20, 1976, at 8:12 A.M., seven years to the day after the first men walked on the moon, *Viking 1* made an

Solar panels being mounted in 1972 for the Orbiting Astronomical Observatory—or the Copernicus satellite, named in honor of the 500th anniversary of Copernicus's birth. Its 82-centimeter reflecting telescope has a tracking accuracy of 0.02 seconds of arc. A smaller telescope can observe X rays with wavelengths less than a tenth of a millionth of a centimeter. Copernicus is particularly useful in detecting the ultraviolet radiation from hot and young stars.

America's second Shuttle Orbiter and the first destined to be sent into space takes shape at the Rockwell International plant in Palmdale, California. The craft is to begin a series of orbital tests in 1979; it will also be used in operational flights during 1980 and 1981. *Enterprise*, the first shuttle, successfully showed last year that it could fly in the atmosphere and land without power as an airplane does.

The various stages of the proposed Space Shuttle from launch *(left)* to landing. About the size of a large jetliner, the craft is launched "piggyback" on a large expendable propellant tank. Its three liquid rocket engines are assisted by two solid rockets, which are jettisoned *(left of center)* at an altitude of about 25 miles for later recovery (harnessed to parachutes). The tank is dropped *(center)* after orbital altitude is attained. In space the crew will carry out missions, such as launching satellites or servicing those already in orbit. Within 30 days the delta-winged vehicle is flown back to Earth, landing like an ordinary plane.

The Space Shuttle *Enterprise* on October 12, 1977, rides "piggyback" atop a 747 jumbo jet high above the Mojave Desert in California. Minutes later the craft separated and the *Enterprise* glided safely on its own. Escort planes fly nearby.

America's first women astronauts were among a group of thirty-five candidates selected for Space Shuttle missions in the 1980s. Introduced at a press conference at the Johnson Space Center in Houston, the women trainees from left are Dr. Margaret Seddon, Dr. Anna Fisher, Dr. Judith Resnik, Dr. Shannon Lucid, Sally Ride, and Kathryn Sullivan. In the foreground is a model of the Shuttle Orbiter.

A painting of the unmanned *Viking* in orbit about Mars, showing its searching lander and discarded capsule on the planet's surface. Four solar panels supply electrical power for the orbiter, and a white blanket protects its rocket motor from the sun. The antenna points to Earth. ➤

unmanned successful touchdown on Mars's Chryse Planitia, the Plain of Gold. The flight took nearly a year; the craft was launched from its pad in Florida on August 11, 1975, and went into orbit around Mars on June 19, 1976, in search of a suitable landing site. The flight was a crowning achievement for the project scientists, who had sweated through *Viking*'s earlier delays and scientific problems, and it was an important step in the exploration of the planetary system.

Pictures relayed back to Earth, each significantly superior to the best photographs ever taken of Mars, reveal a wild and remarkable landscape in which geological events figure prominently: ancient river valleys, immense volcanoes, great landslides, sand-dune fields, mysterious polygamical terrain, fogbound valleys and frosted craters (craters are one-tenth as frequent as on the moon),

The first photograph ever taken on the surface of Mars, obtained by *Viking 1* just minutes after it landed on July 20, 1976. The large rock in the center is about 4 inches across. At the right is a portion of the lander's footpad.

Viking 1 (at left) launched from Florida, August 11, 1975; it went into orbit around Mars on June 19, 1976. At top right, the lander separates from the orbiter; at bottom, it is on the surface, with its soil sampler extended. It takes 19 minutes for radio signals to travel the more than 200 million miles between Earth and Mars. ▼

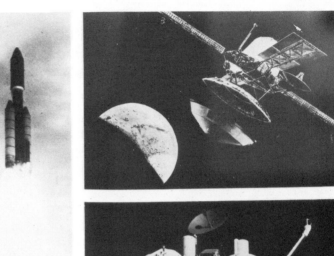

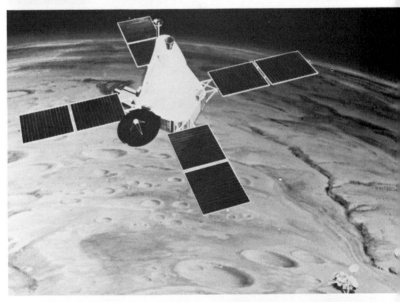

Mars's dramatic early morning lighting—3:30 A.M. local Mars time, August 3, 1976, looking very much like a scene in Death Valley, California. The sharp dune crests indicate windswept sand moving from upper left to lower right. The large boulder at the left is about 3 feet by 10 feet. A later close-up color photograph showed reddish soil and a sky tinged with pink. Project scientists say the soil color indicates that oxidation, somewhat like rusting, has taken place. The pink sky suggests the presence of many particles, such as dust and water vapor, in the rarefied air. Scientists also noted from the holes made by *Viking*'s soil scooper that the surface material has adhesion, that it is dense, and that it behaves somewhat like moist sand on Earth. The meteorology boom seen here, supporting *Viking*'s miniature weather station, cuts through the picture's center.

enigmatic mottled plateaus—a combination of impact, fluvial, aeolian, volcanic, and permafrost processes never seen on our own more restrained earth. Bitter cold sets in at night, −85°C, but temperatures rise in the late afternoon to a midsummer "warm" of −29°C. At the weather station, about 5 feet above the surface, temperatures are a little warmer. With the morning sun, a black sky is transmuted to a momentary, familiar blue-gray that turns pinkish salmon (owing to the red dust in the atmosphere that absorbs blue light while scattering red light from the sun). The soil is a deep rusty red, similar to Earth soil that has been affected by an interaction between surface minerals, liquid water, and air. The Mars soils are of three types: a volcanic ash; the Martian-like red soil containing iron (limonite); and a soil mixed with previously detected Martian elements, such as iron, silicon, calcium, aluminum, sulfur, and titanium. The rocks in the immediate vicinity of *Viking 1* are numerous and exhibit a great variety of form, color, texture, and size, all covered by a layer of fine red dust. We also know that a large fraction (5 percent to 10 percent) of the total magnetic material resides in the surface.

Everywhere are the ubiquitous channels that suggest an earlier, warmer, watery climate complete with floods and rain. The large channels believed to have been produced by floods could be as old as a billion years, but smaller streams and tributaries appear to have been cut by rain within the last 100 million years. *Viking*'s measurements of nitrogen and argon in the atmosphere also hint at a different climate, when perhaps the atmosphere was more dense and the surface pressure higher, allowing liquid water to remain at the surface. Nitrogen and argon are both products of the interior. Mars, like the earth, has vented a large amount of gases into its atmosphere through volcanoes and "slow leaks" at the surface. Much of this gas—or atmosphere—has escaped from Mars owing to its weaker gravity and minimal magnetic field. The presence of nitrogen—about 3 percent at the surface and never detected before on Mars—means that the Martian atmosphere has constituents similar to those on Earth, although in different proportions.

Viking 1 is equipped with a telescopic arm with which it scoops up soil samples to be analyzed in its miniature precision laboratory. Three different experiments were designed to determine whether life could exist on Mars. In one, the "gas exchange" test, large amounts of oxygen were given off when the soil was exposed to conditions simulating an earth laboratory. In the second test, the "labeled release" experiment, large amounts of radioactive carbon (carbon 14) came off the soil sample. Both results could be signs of living organisms at work in the Martian soil (all life, as we know it, is based on carbon compounds), but both can also be explained as chemical and not biological reactions. A third experiment, the pyrolytic release, also produced positive results. A significant amount of carbon dioxide (a waste product of microorganisms when they process nutrients) was released when the nutrient-enriched soil was incubated under Martian conditions with a Mars-like atmosphere and a lamp simulating the sunlight. Something in the Martian soil seemed to be "digesting" the nutrients. On the other hand, *Viking*'s gas chromatograph mass spectrometer (GCMS), which can detect the minutest amounts of organic compounds related to past or present life, found

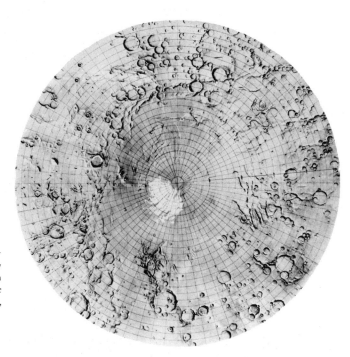

The first stereographic projection map of the south polar region of Mars prepared by the U.S. Geological Survey and the Jet Propulsion Laboratory. It is based on information received in 1971 from the orbiting *Mariner* 9 spacecraft. Shown are the polar ice cap, numerous volcanic craters, and other surface features. The chart, described as "highly preliminary," extends out to 65 degrees latitude.

nothing. It is difficult to reconcile these conflicting results, and more controlled experiments will have to be carried out before we can know definitely whether life exists on Mars. One possible theory, proposed by Carl Sagan of Cornell University, is the oasis theory, according to which microorganisms were blown from their home base (the oasis), where there is more water, to the site of *Viking 1*. They could survive but did not have enough water to reproduce and thrive.

On September 3, 1976, *Viking 2* landed safely on Mars's Utopia Plain. The terrain around the lander is relatively flat, with few of the huge sand dunes seen from orbit. The surface is littered with rocks and boulders, at least a third more so than at the *Viking 1* site. Apparently the Utopian Plain was not the site of an "oasis"—if such do exist—and Carl Sagan's theory is still uncorroborated. Experiments conducted by instruments from *Viking 2* have borne out the previous results from *Viking 1,* and further space missions will have to resolve the mystery of life on Mars.

One conclusion reached is that Mars's north polar cap is made of water-ice and not carbon-dioxide ice as had been thought; also that water apparently once flowed on the planet's surface in rivers and streams. These findings were reinforced by the discovery of krypton, xenon, and argon, heavy gases that further indicate that Mars once had an atmospheric density, which would have kept the surface water from dissipating. Whether this occurred 100 million years or 3 billion years ago is still anyone's guess.

While such projects continue—some more active than others—so too does the flight into the unknown.

Earth's other neighbor, Venus, is the bright morning and evening star of the ancients. Shrouded in a dense

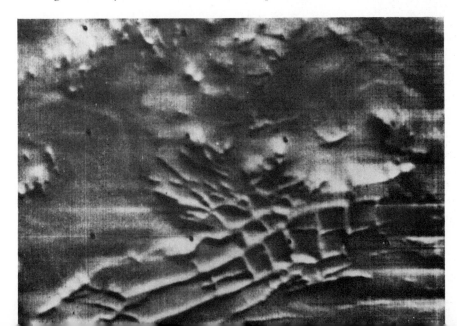

Martian "ruins" photographed by *Mariner* 9. At first glance this striking geometric pattern near the south pole of Mars resembles the ruins of an ancient metropolis. However, it is believed to be a complex of ridges probably created by a combination of fractures and erosions. The ridges are about 2 to 3 miles apart, and the total area shown is approximately 25 by 30 miles.

cloudy atmosphere, its surface cannot be discerned by optical telescopes. In October 1975 two Soviet spacecraft, *Venera IX* and *X,* landed on Venus and in their brief operational life sent back two photographs of a rock-strewn terrain. It appears that the surface temperature is extremely high, about 900°. Also it has been thought that the planet revolves around its axis once a month. But *Mariner 2*–in 1962 passing Venus by about 20,000 miles–and confirming radar measurements showed that Venus turns on its axis once in 243 days, an even longer time than its orbital period of 225 days.

The atmosphere near the surface of Venus is 10 times denser than the earth's and exerts a crushing pressure; it is seemingly composed mainly of carbon dioxide (93 percent to 97 percent), and the rest is nitrogen and the inert gases, with oxygen not exceeding 0.4 percent. An infrared radiometer did not penetrate the Venusian clouds, indicating that it did not find any breaks in the thick covering, and thus leaving the dark markings observed from the earth unexplained. On the other hand, the 19-mm band on a microwave radiometer recorded a very dark limb in the atmosphere at the edge of the planet, indicating high temperatures originating from the surface. These are attributed to the greenhouse effect in which "air" trapped under the clouds is continuously heated by the sun's radiation–like the air under the glass window of a greenhouse. The magnetometer experiment designed to measure the planet's magnetic field found no field in passing Venus at the point of closest approach, and there was also no change in the other radiation detectors. This does not necessarily mean that there is no magnetic field, only that–if it exists–it does not extend to a distance of 20,000 miles. In contrast, the earth's magnetic field can be detected at 40,000 miles, on the side toward the sun.

During its flight *Mariner 2* encountered only two hits by cosmic dust particles, indicating that its path was practically entirely free of this potential hazard. Moreover, solar and cosmic radiation were minimal, suggesting a not inhospitable space for prospective travelers. The predominant feature of the cruise was the overall presence of the solar wind. With a temperature of about 1 million degrees Fahrenheit and a velocity of from 720,000 to 1,800,000 miles per hour, it is more like a blast from a rocket nozzle than a wind.

Radar observations of Venus, made from the Arecibo Observatory in Puerto Rico, reveal a possible lava flow the size of Oklahoma, an impact basin much like those on the moon, and evidence of mountain-building processes similar to those that shaped the earth. Situated in the northern latitudes of Venus, the area appears to be a sharply defined feature on top of an older surface and to be the result of internal processes, such as volcanic eruptions, rather than that created by meteoric impacts.

Another major feature is a large basin about the size of Hudson Bay, extending about 1,000 miles north to south and 600 miles from east to west. The presence of rocky debris beyond the basin indicates that it was probably formed by the same kind of impacts that were responsible for the maria (seas) on the moon. Ridges extending for hundreds of miles suggest that some kind of internal forces are responsible for shaping the surface of Venus in somewhat the same ways volcanoes and shifting plates affect the earth's surface. The resolution of the radar pictures was so good that features as small as 12 miles could be distinguished. The *Pioneer* Venus missions of 1978 added to these data.*

Beyond Mars–and the asteroids, none of which is large enough to permit landing–is Jupiter, the largest of the planets, roughly 80,000 miles in diameter, covered by gases at −200°F. Landing on Jupiter is out of the question; it lacks a solid surface and takeoffs would be impossible on account of the extremely large gravitational pull. However, two successful flybys were launched, *Pioneer 10* in March 1972 and *Pioneer 11* in April 1973. Spacecraft operations were complicated by the 92 minutes of round-trip communication time and the need to send 10,000 commands to the spacecraft within the two weeks of closest approach–at a distance of 81,000 miles from Jupiter. *Pioneer 10* reached Jupiter on December 3, 1973, after a 620-million-mile journey, followed by *Pioneer 11* two years later.

In addition to photographing the planet's far side, *Pioneer 10* confirmed and mapped Jupiter's large magnetic field, the only planet–besides the earth–known to have a magnetic field. Evidence for its existence came from very high-frequency radio waves produced by electrons gyrating around the lines of forces (synchrotron radiation discussed earlier). Also confirmed were the latest expectations of Jupiter's atmosphere and surface, which is gaseous. As a result, the period of rotation is not the same for the whole planet; the various zones or belts spin at different rates–the equatorial belt at a rate about five minutes shorter than the rest. Most of Jupiter's atmosphere consists of highly compressed hydrogen, its presence maintained by the planet's huge gravitational pull. Ammonia and methane, as well as a considerable quantity of helium, make it unsuitable for the existence of life as we know it.

Recently it has been suggested by Soviet astronomers (although not confirmed from other sources) that Jupiter

---

* The *Pioneer* missions of 1978 found that the Venusian atmosphere appears to contain the gas argon-36 in proportions up to one hundred times greater than on Earth or Mars. The findings are important because that type of argon, an inert gas, cannot be created after a planet's formation. If Venus was formed in the same way as Earth and Mars, it probably would have the same concentration. The presence of large proportions of argon-36 means either that Venus was formed from substances different from those of the other planets or that the formation process itself was different.

Venus as seen by *Mariner 10,* 450,000 miles away, on February 6, 1974, as the craft swept by en route to Mercury. The predominant swirl is at the south pole.

Radar map of Venus assembled by computer from data gathered by the world's largest radio telescope at Arecibo in 1964 and 1967 when the planet was nearest to the earth—only 24 million miles away. It indicates that most of the planet's northern hemisphere is mountainous, whereas the southern hemisphere is relatively smooth. The two bright features located at −80 degrees longitude and 20 degrees and 30 degrees latitude are rough surfaces that may be mountain ranges. The map is about equal in detail and clarity to what the largest optical telescope could obtain—if it were capable of penetrating Venus's thick cloud cover.

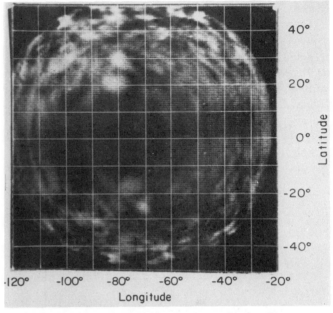

Drawing of *Pioneer,* designed to fly past Jupiter. Arrows indicate location of four radioisotope thermoelectric generators, representing the first use of nuclear electrical power on an interplanetary mission. Radioisotope heaters also protect equipment from the low outer space temperatures around Jupiter.

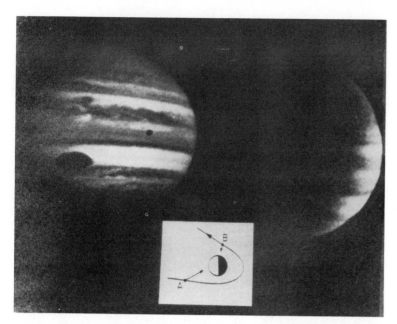

A double exposure shows the front *(left, or A)* and rear *(right, or B)* of Jupiter as photographed by *Pioneer 10* during its historic flyby in December 1973. Diagram shows the positions of the spacecraft when the photos were made.

Jupiter's north polar region as seen by *Pioneer 11* as it passed within 26,000 miles of the planet in May 1976. This view shows the breakup of Jupiter's regular banded cloud structure.

is not a planet but a budding star that will flare up in the distant future, reaching the brightness of the sun in 3 billion years. The reason for that speculation lies in the fact that Jupiter is radiating more energy than it receives from the sun, as revealed by the *Pioneer 2* space probe. Furthermore, its mass is nearly large enough—only 20 percent below—the mass of a star. If Jupiter were to increase its mass, say, by the capture of comets, meteors, and other interstellar matter, the gravitational compression would be sufficient to sustain nuclear reactions in the interior, which, it is believed, reaches temperatures on the order of 300,000 degrees on the Kelvin scale and continues growing.

During its flyby, *Pioneer 10* (and *Pioneer 11)* also crossed the orbits of some of Jupiter's moons. It came closest to Amalthea, Jupiter's tiny inner moon, at periapsis (closest approach to the planet). Amalthea, only 150 miles across and moving 1,000 miles per minute, affords a breathtaking view of the planet. If one could succeed in setting up an observatory on Amalthea, a wealth of valuable information could be obtained, but the prospects for such an undertaking are rather slim, especially since that moon lies within Jupiter's magnetosphere (equivalent to our Van Allen belt). The same can be said about Io, whose orbital position seems to be associated with Jupiter's radio

emission. However, Callisto and Ganymede, which were approached by *Pioneer 10* on December 3, are possible candidates for future space explorations, and even landings. They are about the size of Mercury and, since they are not as dense, have comparatively small gravitational fields and surfaces; this may make landings— at least unmanned—feasible.

Pioneer 11, now well beyond Jupiter, is expected to arrive at Saturn in 1979. It will pass 18,000 miles from the edge of the outermost ring and will swing in, under the ring plane, to a distance of 15,000 miles from the surface of Saturn. The decision to fly outside the rings rather than to pass inside them is based on the desire of the space agency to use Pioneer as a pathfinder for the Voyager spacecraft headed for Saturn encounters in 1980 and 1981.

Titan, which does have an atmosphere, might harbor life forms, but *Pioneer 11* unfortunately will not be able to enlighten us but will continue on its flight—leaving the solar system. Only when interplanetary flights—including return to Earth—have become a reality will we be able to get that information.

To explore the farthest expanses of the solar system, including a bypass of Uranus, Neptune, and Pluto at today's rocket speeds, would take about 70 years. Such a grand tour might remain a dream were it not for the fact

An artist's concept of Jupiter and its four main satellites, a future *Pioneer* target. *Left to right:* Europa, Callisto, Jupiter, Ganymede, and Io. (Unfortunately, Callisto—which is the largest and is meant to be shown farthest from Jupiter—appears out of proportion here.)

A drawing of *Pioneer 11* arriving at Saturn in 1979. The 572-pound spacecraft will fly outside the planet's innermost ring and then pass Titan (seen here almost centered in front of Saturn, which appears to have an atmosphere and might harbor some form of life.

▼

An artist's version of Europa's surface, near its north pole, featuring mountains covered with frozen gases. Europa is about the size of our moon and might make a convenient landing strip for a future spacecraft. Jupiter is seen in the background.

that a particularly favorable arrangement of the planets will occur at the end of the seventies. The outer planets will then be aligned so that each in turn will exert a gravitational pull on a probe—accelerating it well beyond its normal speed.

Taking advantage of that alignment, *Voyager 2* was launched on August 20, 1977. Having its sensors fixed on

the star Canopus, it scanned the heavens, comparing its orientation in space with its computer-stored star reference chart that guided it during the 29-month journey to Jupiter and 3-year trip to Saturn. *Voyager 1,* launched about 2 weeks later, arrived at Jupiter first, on March 5, 1979, because its flight path to the planet was more direct, while *Voyager 2* was scheduled to arrive July 10, 1979. Using Jupiter's gravitational energy, the two spacecraft will be propelled on to Saturn at speeds exceeding 32,000 miles per hour, and are scheduled to arrive at the ringed planet November 12, 1980, and August 27, 1981, respectively. If all goes well, *Voyager 2* may travel on to Uranus where it should arrive in January 1986. Perhaps if enough fuel is left, the spacecraft may be targeted on Neptune for a rendezvous with the outermost planet in

INTERPLANETARY EXPLORATION—UNITED STATES

Name	Launch	Mission
Mariner 1	July 22, 1962	Deviated from course; destroyed.
Mariner 2	August 26, 1962	First successful interplanetary probe to Venus.
Mariner 3	November 5, 1964	Shroud failed to jettison; communication with craft lost.
Mariner 4	November 28, 1964	Encounter with Mars; closest approach 6,118 miles.
Pioneer 6	December 16, 1965	Study of interplanetary phenomena at about 0.814 A.U.
Pioneer 7	August 17, 1966	Measurements over the solar cycle; aphelion 1.125 A.U.
Mariner 5	June 14, 1967	Planetary and interplanetary exploration; Venus flyby October 19.
Pioneer 8	December 13, 1967	Interplanetary phenomena at widely separated points.
Pioneer 9	November 8, 1968	To collect data on electromagnetic and plasma properties of the interplanetary medium.
Mariner 6	February 24, 1969	Mars flyby within 2,000 miles.
Mariner 7	March 27, 1969	Mars flyby within 1,900 miles.
Mariner H (8)	May 8, 1971	To study dynamic characteristics of Mars; mission unsuccessful.
Mariner I (9)	May 30, 1971	To study dynamic characteristics of Mars; entered orbit November 13.
Pioneer 10 (F)	March 3, 1972	Asteroid belt; Jupiter.
Pioneer 11 (G)	April 6, 1973	Interplanetary medium; asteroid belt; Jupiter.
Mariner 10	November 3, 1973	Measurements of Venus and Mercury.
Viking 1	August 11, 1975	Soft landing on Mars.
Viking 2	October 7, 1975	Soft landing on Mars.
Voyager 1	August 20, 1977	Measurements of atmospheres and surfaces of planets and moons, including Jupiter, Saturn, and outer planets.
Voyager 2	September 5, 1977	
Pioneer Venus 1	May 20, 1978	Orbit Venus to send back close-up shots of the surface; information about temperature, pressures, composition.
Pioneer Venus 2	August 7, 1978	Five separate probes through the atmosphere to send information about the surface.

INTERPLANETARY EXPLORATION—USSR *

Name	Launch	Mission
Venera I	February 12, 1961	Launched toward Venus, missing planet by 62,000 miles. Communication failure.
Mars I	November 1, 1962	Launched to Mars; contact lost.
Zond I	April 2, 1964	Launched toward Venus. Communication failure.
Zond II	November 30, 1964	Launched toward Mars. Communication failure.
Zond III	July 18, 1965	Deep space probe; photographed moon en route.
Venera II	November 12, 1965	Bypassed Venus by 15,000 miles. Communication lost as it approached planet.
Venera III	November 16, 1965	Impacted on Venus; failed to soft-land.
Venera V	January 4, 1969	Bypassed Venus.
Venera VI	January 10, 1969	Landed on Venus, but communication failed after 53 minutes.
Mars II	May 19, 1971	Orbiter returned data, but lander was smashed.
Mars III	May 28, 1971	Orbiter was successful, but pictures failed within seconds of transmission.
Mars IV	July 21, 1971	Supposed to go into orbit—did not, and data was returned.
Mars V	July 26, 1973	Was successfully placed in orbit and returned data.
Mars VI	August 6, 1973	Partially successful—lander signal ceased, other data was transmitted.
Mars VII	August 9, 1973	Data from main bus returned.
Venera VII	August 16, 1970	Landed on Venus, but communication failed after 51 minutes.
Venera IX	October, 1975 ⎫	Landed on Venus; sent back
Venera X	October, 1975 ⎭	2 photographs of terrain.
Venera XI	August, 1978	Soft landing on Venus; communication ceased after several minutes.
Venera XII	August, 1978	Soft landing on Venus; ground probe sent data for 110 minutes before falling silent.

* Not listed are space probes that did not reach outer space and were not reported by official USSR sources.

Planetary Voyager. A space project lasting more than seven years began with the launching in 1977 of two Voyager spacecraft. The probes are expected to reach Jupiter in 1979 and Saturn in 1981. A prime objective is to make detailed studies of several of their 23 moons, including Titan, Saturn's largest satellite. One of the spacecraft will then go on to Uranus (as shown in this illustration) for the first look at that planet.

September 1989. After their 13-year trek, the *Voyagers* will exit the solar system. Phonograph records on board carry pictures and sounds depicting the physics of our area of the Galaxy, character of earth and its diversity of life, culture, music, and thought, as well as messages from President Carter and Secretary General of the UN Kurt Waldheim. The *Voyagers* carry scientific instruments—including spectrometers, magnetometers, and television cameras—to carry out 11 different investigations of the atmospheres and surfaces of the planets and moons they will visit. Flight engineers will be able to communicate with the spacecraft for thirty years, long after they have left the solar system, provided, of course, no failures occur in the spacecraft communication systems.

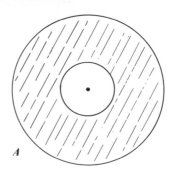

A

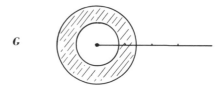

G

K

The habitable zone of three typical stars is indicated by dashed lines. The blank area within is too hot, whereas the one outside is too cold. An A-type star has a large habitable zone, but its comparatively short duration of stability makes the existence of life quite improbable. The sun is a G-type star; the line indicates distances marked in astronomical units—the habitable zone of the sun is shown to range from about 0.8 to 1.3 A.U., taking in the earth but excluding Venus and Mars. For a K-type star the habitable zone is quite small and near the star, but it is quite unlikely that a planet can be so close to its star without being drawn to it by its gravitational field.

5. Are We Alone?

More than two thousand years ago Lucretius wrote that in other regions of space there exist other earths, inhabited by other people and animals. When Copernicus demoted the earth from its central position, the possibility of other inhabited "earths" was proposed by Giordano Bruno—a suggestion that cost him his life. He and later proponents of extraterrestrial life were mostly speculating, but today the question of the existence of intelligent life—if still not answered—is at least treated with scientific exactitude.

We may begin by excluding life, as we know it, from any other planet of our solar system, since only the earth lies within the habitable zone of the sun. By this we mean the region around a star, such as the sun, which is neither too hot nor too cold and where water is in its liquid form, neither frozen solid nor in the form of steam. (According to some researchers forms of life might even exist in boiling steam.) The size of the habitable zone of a star depends, of course, on the temperature of the star—the hotter the star the larger the zone. Very hot stars, however, are rather short-lived and burn their fuel rapidly,

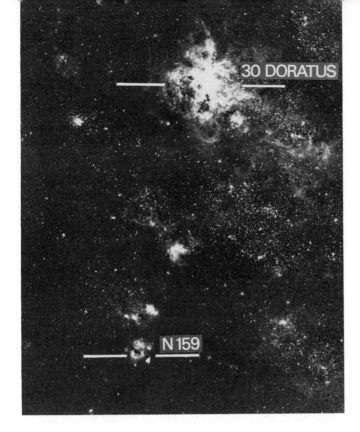

The Large Cloud of Magellan showing the region N159 near where the organic molecule carbon monoxide was detected by astronomers using the 13-foot Anglo-Australian telescope. The discovery of such organic molecules gives support to the theory that life exists in outer space. 30 Doratus is part of the constellation Dorado.

immensely larger.) Even so, numbers alone cannot predict the creation of life, even if the physical conditions are right.

However, if life exists somewhere in the Galaxy other than on earth, how can we detect it?

The most ambitious project to detect signals from outer space is Project Cyclops, designed in 1971 by a team of scientists from many universities and headed by Bernard Oliver (Stanford) and John Billingham (Ames Research Center). Cyclops envisions the building of 1,000 or more giant radio telescopes spread over an area of up to 10 miles in diameter and costing about $6 billion to $10 billion. Provided with their own computers, these telescopes would systematically scan the whole sky. Since one does not know the frequency used by the galactic transmitter, Project Cyclops proposes to scan each star over the entire frequency range—a process similar to turning the knob of a home radio-receiver slowly over the whole frequency range—until a suitable signal is discovered. Such a scheme might work if there were an intelligent community within 30 light-years of us *and* if it were to beam a powerful signal in our direction. Since there are only about 50 possible "habitable" stars within that range, such a search could be completed within a year. But, of course, the sample is too small.

For stars 30 to 300 light-years away there is a different problem. A signal from such distances is quite weak, and there may be difficulties in recognizing it. However, more

being a stable source for only 10 million years—too short a span for advanced life forms to evolve, if we may judge by terrestrial standards. Cool stars, on the other hand, have too narrow a zone, making the possibility of finding a planet there rather improbable. This leaves the medium hot stars—F, G, or K type—as the most likely candidates, like our sun, a G-type star.

This does not mean that every slowly rotating G-type star will provide an abode for life. In the first place, the star may have no planets revolving around it. As yet, no planet outside our own solar system has been seen—which is not surprising, since its tiny reflected light would be overwhelmed by the light from the star itself. Orbiting telescopes might in the future detect planets the size of Jupiter, but for the present we have to be satisfied with the possibility that other stars may have planets. In the second place, a large number of the known G-type stars are double stars, and the orbit of a planet around such a binary would be too irregular to receive the constant source of "starlight" for life to evolve. Finally, the planet would have to be of the right size; if it were too small, its gravity could not hold an atmosphere and thus it would be bathed by lethal radiation absorbed by such an atmosphere. On the other hand, if it were too massive— say, of the size of Jupiter—the large amount of atmosphere present and huge force of gravity would require life forms quite different from those with which we are familiar. Therefore, rejecting double stars and planets that are either too light or too heavy leaves about a billion possible candidates in the Galaxy alone. (If we include stars outside our Galaxy, the number, of course, becomes

An artist's conception of a high aerial view of the proposed Cyclops system (named after the mythical one-eyed giant). Consisting of 1,000 or more large radio telescopes over an area about 10 miles in diameter, it would make a systematic search of messages from outer space, as well as transmit its own.

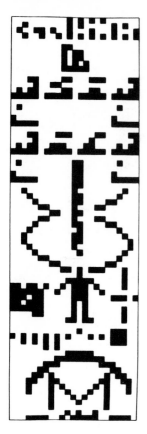

The Arecibo Message in pictures. Each consecutive line contains one group of 23 characters; the "1" in black. The symbols at top are the binary-system numbers 1 to 10 (starting from the right). Next are the atomic numbers for hydrogen, carbon, nitrogen, oxygen, and phosphorus, also in the binary system. This is followed by 12 groups denoting the formulas for sugars and bases in the nucleotides of DNA. The double helix of that molecule is indicated next, with the number of nucleotides appearing between the two parts of the helix. A crude figure of a human can be discerned next, its height at the right and the total human population of the earth at left. The rectangles and squares that follow represent the solar system—the sun the larger square at the right, with the square representing the earth displaced toward the human figure. Finally, the nearly semispherical outline represents the Arecibo telescope and the bottom line its diameter. A certain amount of ingenuity is required to decode the message, but it is assumed that if an alien civilization exists, it is more advanced than ours.

important, there is also the question of being at the right place at the right time. At a distance of, say, 100 light-years, there are 1,000 likely stars, each transmitting, we assume, at random. There is one chance in a thousand that there will be a transmission in our direction, and one chance in a thousand that we will be pointing our telescopes in that direction precisely at the time when the signal arrives in our neighborhood. The combined probability of both of these situations is one in a million—under the assumption that the frequencies used for transmission and receiving are in the same range. Detecting a signal from outer space may well be more the result of an accident than of a systematic search.

Another question is what kind of message to send—which would at the same time attract the attention of the inhabitant of a distant planet and be understood? Suggestions vary from emitting flashes that represent the prime numbers—3, 5, 7, 11, 13, and so on—to transmitting music by Bach, as was jocularly proposed by Lewis Thomas of the Sloan Kettering Institute in New York.

In 1974 the huge 1,000-foot antenna at Arecibo beamed a message in binary code toward the great cluster in Hercules. It consisted of 1,679 consecutive characters—like dots and dashes but represented by one of two specific radio frequencies—which, if broken up into 73 groups of 23 characters each (the only two factors contained in 1,679), resulted in a geometrical picture of the message (providing various facts about life on Earth). It is too early to say whether this message has been received and decoded by any intelligent being near Hercules.

Pioneer 10 and *Pioneer 11* carry identical plaques (of gold-anodized aluminum) bearing a message from Earth. Like letters in bottles tossed in the sea by shipwrecked sailors, they will travel past Saturn to the far side of the Galaxy and may someday land on the shore of an alien civilization. The plaques will survive virtually unchanged for hundreds of millions of years, and they may at some very distant future bear witness to a civilization that existed on a minor planet of a minor star at the outskirts of the Galaxy in A.D. 1973.

6. Whither?

We have learned a great deal about the universe, which is remarkable if one considers the size of the laboratory and the distances involved. We have a fair idea of the internal constitution of the stars, but we still do not know the origin of the solar system. We have learned to count stars, but we still do not know whether the universe is open or closed, evolving or in a steady state. We have discovered quasars and pulsars and speculate on black holes without knowing whether they exist. When we have found the answer to one question, we find that it raises new ones. We have built huge telescopes that reach into the vastness of space, but not far enough. We have built spaceships and sent men to the moon, and we have probed the farther extent of the solar system and even beyond.

Where do we go from here? Existing telescopes do not see far enough and cannot distinguish among the various cosmological models. Larger telescopes are too expensive and would not improve the situation markedly because of our atmosphere. But a large telescope on the moon or orbiting the earth at an even greater distance might overcome these difficulties. Orbiting telescopes, like those on the Copernicus satellite, would give us the answer to other questions, such as the nature of young hot stars. To see farther, we must go outside our global fishbowl. A Large Space Telescope (LST), planned for launching in 1980, equipped with a mirror 300 centimeters in diameter, would be the next step toward a series of space observatories.

Interstellar travel is another way of learning more about our "neighbors." But even reaching a "close" star like Proxima Centauri, which is only 4½ light-years away, is still impractical. However, it may be worthwhile to consider the problem a bit further. Material objects, like a spaceship, cannot be propelled at the speed of light and the human body cannot suffer such a large instantaneous thrust of several G's but must be accelerated gradually.

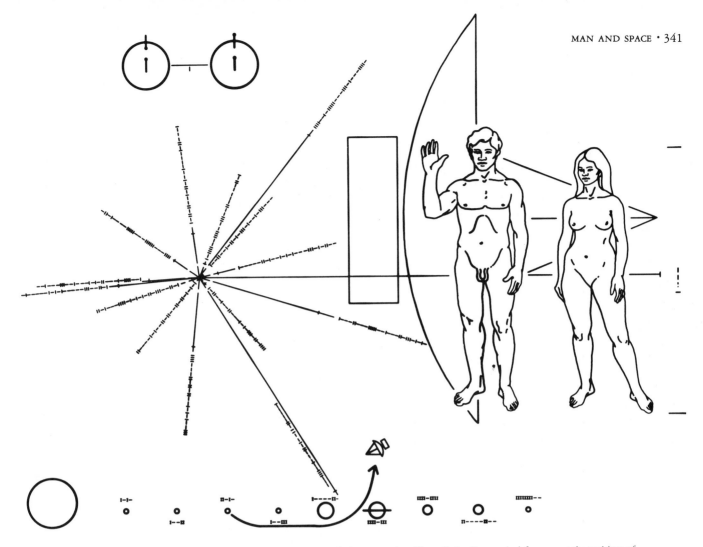

A replica of the gold-anodized aluminum plaque attached to the antennae of Pioneer 10 and 11. The radiating lines at the left represent the positions of 14 pulsars arranged to indicate the sun as the home-star of the launching civilization. The precise periods of the pulsars are specified in binary code to allow them to be identified. The hydrogen atom in two states is shown at top, marked with a "1" unity symbol (note the position of the two dots indicating the two different spin alignments). The energy difference between these two states provides the most precise standard of time known to science. Thus, the most abundant atom in the universe, the hydrogen atom, is used as a universal clock, and the regular decrease in the frequencies of the pulsars may enable another civilization to determine the time that has elapsed since launching. At the bottom, the trajectory of the spacecraft is show as it leaves the third planet (Earth) and swings by the fifth planet (Jupiter). (The diversion of *Pioneer 11* past Saturn had not been planned when the plaques were prepared.) The man's hand is raised in a gesture of goodwill. An attempt was made to give the images panracial characteristics. Their heights are shown relative to the spacecraft and are further identified by a binary number relating to the 21-centimeter spectral line (or 1,420 megahertz).

However, a flight plan may be feasible in which a spaceship could be accelerated with constant acceleration—say equal to that of gravity—so that an astronaut would feel exactly the same weight as he does on Earth. After reaching a velocity close to that of light, the spaceship would then coast freely and could be decelerated again with the acceleration of gravity until it reached its destination. Since it takes approximately one year to reach such a great velocity under this flight plan (during which time the spaceship has covered nearly one-half of a light-year), and an equal time to decelerate, it would take a little over 5½ years (one year each for acceleration and deceleration and 3½ years coasting freely) to reach Proxima Centauri—4½ light-years away. Moreover, at speeds close to that of light, the actual passage of time experienced by an astronaut would be much shorter than that of his counterpart left on Earth. This paradox, often discussed under the name of the *twin paradox,* has been

critically discussed by experts in relativity. Because of the relativistic time dilation, as seen from the earth, time on a spaceship traveling at speeds close to the speed of light will be slowed down; yet as experienced by the astronaut, time flows at a normal rate. Thus, a person, upon his return from such a space trip, will be younger than his twin on Earth. For example, a round trip to a star 100 light-years away would take a space crew 28 years traveling at 99 percent of the speed of light, whereas on Earth 202 years would have elapsed. Thus, such a trip could be made easily within the life-span of an astronaut, but he may be surprised at what he finds upon his return—he will have become a Rip Van Winkle. But to reach such high speed and to deliver a payload to its destination, his launch vehicle must be very much heavier than its payload, since the vehicle has to contain the necessary fuel for the trip. For example, for a round trip to Proxima Centauri the mass ratio required to accelerate a payload up to 99 percent of the speed of light is one billion, i.e., the takeoff weight would have to be one billion times the weight of the payload. Conventional fuels, of course, are out of the question, and it has been suggested that some kind of controlled fusion reactors will have to be used. Even so, the liftoff weight would be enormous. A stimulating proposal has been made by R. W. Bussard of the Los Alamos Scientific Laboratory. He suggests that the interstellar gas be used both as a source of energy (by nuclear fusion) and as a propellant mass needed for propulsion. Operating like a giant ramjet–the absorbing area has been calculated to be about 6 miles in radius–it would swallow up the gases present in the interstellar medium, generate energy by nuclear fusion, and expel the disintegration products, which would propel it forward. The advantage, of course, lies in the fact that hardly any fuel has to be carried on board; this permits a simpler construction and a larger payload. Such reactors are certainly not available today, but since no physical principles are violated, the suggestion may in some century be realized. In the meantime, we must be satisfied with theoretical calculations–and some day-dreaming.

A third area in which a major breakthrough might

occur–perhaps sooner than one would expect–is interstellar communication. The fact that we have not detected any alien civilization is no proof of its nonexistence. Martin Rees, the prominent British astronomer, said, "Absence of evidence is not evidence of absence." If there is another civilization somewhere in the universe, the chances are that it is superior to ours and will someday send a messenger probe–possibly a series of numbers representing the star's position. (It could be the star's constellation, but in order to be meaningful to us this would require a superior intelligence on the part of the sender, since the constellations are particular arrangements of stars as viewed from the earth and would be quite different when seen from a different–far distant– place. Whatever the form or content of that message, if and when it occurs, we should be prepared to detect it, for the opportunity may not come again. Project Cyclops would certainly be able to do so, but even present-day radio telescopes, if properly attuned, are capable of detecting it. We have the know-how and even some of the equipment, and need only make the effort.

The history of the universe is by no means complete; it may still be in its infancy.

Bibliography

There exists a large number of books dealing with the history of astronomy as well as with its particular aspects. The following are some titles suggested for further reading.

GENERAL BOOKS

Abell, G. O. *Exploration of the Universe.* New York: Holt, Rinehart, and Winston, 1969.

Brandt, John C., and Maran, Stephen P. *New Horizons in Astronomy.* San Francisco: W.H. Freeman and Co. Publishers, 1972.

Einstein, Albert, and Infeld, Leopold. *The Evolution of Physics.* New York: Simon and Schuster, Inc., 1961.

Holton, Gerald J. *Introduction to Concepts and Theories in Physical Science.* Reading, Mass.: Addison-Wesley Publishing Co., Inc., 1952, 1973.

Hoyle, Fred. *Astronomy.* New York: Doubleday & Co., Inc., 1962.

– – –. *From Stonehenge to Modern Cosmology.* San Francisco: W.H. Freeman and Co. Publishers, 1972.

Mitton, Simon, ed. *The Cambridge Encyclopedia of Astronomy.* New York: Crown Publishers, Inc., 1977.

Moore, Patrick, ed. *The Atlas of the Universe,* Skokie, Ill.: Inc., 1977. Rand McNally & Co., 1970.

Pannekoek, A., trans. *A History of Astronomy.* Totowa, N.J.: Rowman and Littlefield, 1961.

Rogers, Eric M. *Physics for the Inquiring Mind: The Methods, Nature and Philosophy of Physical Science.* Princeton: Princeton University Press, 1959.

Rudeaux, R., and de Vaucouleurs, G. *Larousse Encyclopedia of Astronomy.* Paris: Librairie Larousse, 1954.

Shapley, Harlow, ed. *Source Book in Astronomy, 1900–1950.* Cambridge, Mass.: Harvard University Press, 1960.

Young, Louise B., ed. *Exploring the Universe.* New York: McGraw-Hill Book Co., 1963. Second ed. New York: Oxford University Press, 1971.

BOOKS ON SPECIFIC TOPICS

Appel, F. *The Moon and Beyond.* London: Aldus Books Ltd., 1971.

Baker, David. *The Rocket.* New York: Crown Publishers, Inc., 1978.

Baumgardt, C. *Johannes Kepler, His Life and Letters.* New York: Philosophical Library, 1951.

Bell, Eric T. *Men of Mathematics.* New York: Simon & Schuster, Inc., 1937, 1961.

Bergamini, David. *The Universe.* Alexandria, Va.: Time-Life Books, 1969.

Bergmann, Peter G. *The Riddle of Gravitation: From Newton to Einstein to Today's Exciting Theories.* New York: Charles Scribner's Sons, 1968.

Bonnor, William *The Mystery of the Expanding Universe.* New York: Macmillan, Inc., 1964.

Bracewell, Ronald N. *The Galactic Club: Intelligent Life in Outer Space.* San Francisco: W.H. Freeman and Co. Publishers, 1975.

Burbidge, Geoffrey, and Burbidge, Margaret. *Quasistellar Objects.* San Francisco: W.H. Freeman and Co. Publishers, 1967.

Buttmann, Gunther. *The Shadow of the Telescope: A Biography of John Herschel.* New York: Charles Scribner's Sons, 1970.

Chapman, Clark R. *Inner Planets: New Light on the Rocky Worlds of Mercury, Venus, Earth, the Moon, Mars, and the Asteroids.* New York: Charles Scribner's Sons, 1977.

Charon, Jean. *Cosmology: Theories of the Universe.* New York: McGraw-Hill Book Co., 1970.

Clark, Ronald W. *Einstein: The Life and Times.* New York: Thomas Y. Crowell Co., Inc., 1971.

Cohen, I. Bernard. *The Birth of a New Physics.* New York: Doubleday & Co., Inc., 1960.

Cohen, Morris R., and Drabkin, Israel E. *A Source Book in Greek Science.* Cambridge, Mass.: Harvard University Press, 1948.

Defries, Amelia D. *Pioneers of Science.* New York: Arno Press, Inc., 1928.

Dreyer, John L. *Tycho Brahe: A Picture of Scientific Life and Work in the Sixteenth Century.* Magnolia, Mass.: Peter Smith, n.d.

–––. *A History of Astronomy from Thales to Kepler.* Magnolia, Mass.: Peter Smith, 1953.

Ferris, Timothy. *The Red Limit: The Search for the Edge of the Universe.* New York: William Morrow & Co., Inc., 1977.

Frank, Philipp. *Einstein: His Life and Times.* New York: Alfred A. Knopf, Inc., 1953.

Galileo Galilei. *Dialogue Concerning the Two Chief World Systems, Ptolemaic and Copernican.* Translated by Stillman Drake. Berkeley: University of California Press, 1953.

Heath, Thomas. *Aristarchus of Samos.* London: Oxford University Press, 1913.

Hodson, F.R., ed. *The Place of Astronomy in the Ancient World: A Joint Symposium of the Royal Society and the British Academy.* New York: Oxford University Press, Inc., 1974.

Hoffmann, Banesh. *Albert Einstein, Creator and Rebel.* New York: The New American Library, Inc., 1973.

Hubble, E. *The Realm of the Nebulae.* New Haven, Conn.: Yale University Press, 1936.

Koestler, Arthur. *The Sleepwalkers.* New York: Penguin Books, 1959.

Koyre, Alexandre. *The Astronomical Revolution.* Ithaca, N.Y.: Cornell University Press, 1973.

Lockyer, J. Norman. *The Dawn of Astronomy.* Cambridge, Mass.: The M.I.T. Press, 1964.

Lyttleton, R.A. *Mysteries of the Solar System.* Oxford: Oxford University Press, 1968.

MacNeice, L. *Astrology.* New York: Doubleday & Co., Inc., 1964.

Moore, Patrick. *Comets.* New York: Charles Scribner's Sons, 1976.

More, Louis T. *Isaac Newton: A Biography.* Magnolia, Mass.: Peter Smith, n.d.

Narlikar, Jayant V. *The Structure of the Universe.* New York: Oxford University Press, 1977.

Nathan, Otto, and Norden, Heinz, eds. *Einstein on Peace.* New York: Schocken Books, Inc., 1968.

Neugebauer, O. *The Exact Sciences in Antiquity.* Providence, R.I.: Brown University Press, 1957, 1970.

Nieto, M. *The Titius-Bode Law of Planetary Distances.* Elmsford, N.Y.: Pergamon Press, 1972.

Orr, Mary A. *Dante and the Early Astronomers.* Port Washington, N.Y.: Kennikat Press Corporation, 1956, 1969.

Page, Thornton, and Page, Lou W., eds. *Space Science and Astronomy: Escape from Earth.* New York: Macmillan, Inc., 1976.

–––. *Wanderers in the Sky.* New York: Macmillan, Inc., 1965.

Sagan, Carl. *The Cosmic Connection: An Extraterrestrial Perspective.* New York: Doubleday & Co., Inc., 1973.

Sambursky, S. *The Physical World of the Greeks.* London: Routledge & Kegan Paul Ltd., 1956.

de Santillana, George. *The Crime of Galileo.* Chicago: University of Chicago Press, 1955.

Schiaparelli, Giovanni V. *Astronomy in the Old Testament.* New York: Gordon Press, n.d.

Scientific American. Frontiers in Astronomy. San Francisco: W.H. Freeman and Co. Publishers, 1970.

Shapley, Harlow. *Galaxies.* Cambridge, Mass.: Harvard University Press, 1967, 1975.

Shipman, Harry L. *Black Holes, Quasars and the Universe.* Boston: Houghton Mifflin Company, 1976.

Singer, Dorothea W. *Giordano Bruno: His Life and Thought.* Westport, Conn.: Greenwood Press, Inc., 1950, 1968.

Singh, Jagjit. *Great Ideas and Theories of Modern Cosmology.* New York: Dover Publications, Inc., 1966.

Verschuur, G.L. *The Invisible Universe: The Story of Radio Astronomy.* New York: Springer-Verlag New York, Inc., 1974.

Weinberg, Steven. *The First Three Minutes: A Modern View of the Origin of the Universe.* New York: Basic Books, Inc., Publishers, 1976.

Picture Credits

Abbreviations

AAO   Anglo Australian Observatory

Ant   P. Brunet and A. Mieli, *Histoire des Sciences: Antiquités*, Ed. Payot, Paris. Used with permission of Payot

AO   Arecibo Observatory, Puerto Rico, part of the National Astronomy and Ionosphere Center, operated by Cornell Univ. under contract with the National Science Foundation

AP   Adler Planetarium, Chicago, Ill.

Ast   F. W. Hodge, *Astronomy Study Guide*, © 1973 McGraw-Hill Book Co. Used with permission of McGraw-Hill Book Co.

At   Patrick Moore, *Atlas of the Universe*, Mitchell Beazley Publishers Ltd.

ATA   Antikvarisk Topografiska Arkivet. Courtesy Royal Swedish Embassy, Tel Aviv

AtU   E. Br. and Tj. E. de Vries, *W. P. Atlas van Het Heelal*, Elsevier Amsterdam/Brussels MCMVIII

Bau   Courtesy Bausch and Lomb, Corporate Communications

Bell   Courtesy Bell Laboratories

BM   British Museum, London

BN   Bibliothèque Nationale, Paris

BNC   Biblioteca Nazionale Centrale, Firenze; photo Guido Samsoni

Bod   Bodleian Library, Dept. Western Mss., Oxford

BPK   Bildarchiv Preuss, Kulturbesitz, Berlin

BS   Bayerische Staatsbibliothek, Munich

CHP   Niels Bohr Library, Center for the History of Physics, American Institute of Physics, courtesy Joan N. Warnow, Assoc. Director

ConA   P. W. Hodge, *Concepts of Contemporary Astronomy*, © 1974 McGraw-Hill Book Co. Used with permission of McGraw-Hill Book Co.

ConU   P. W. Hodge, *Concepts of the Universe*, © 1969 McGraw-Hill Book Co. Used with permission of McGraw-Hill Book Co.

Cop   *The Heritage of Copernicus: Themes "Pleasing to the Mind,"* ed. Jerzry Neyman. © 1974 Massachusetts Institute of Technology. Reprinted with permission of the editor and publisher

Cos   J. Charon, *Cosmology*, © 1970 McGraw-Hill Book Co. Used with permission of McGraw-Hill Book Co.

CWO   Adapted from C. Lanczos, *Albert Einstein and the Cosmic World Order*, John Wiley & Sons. Used with permission of John Wiley & Sons

Dan   Royal Danish Ministry of Foreign Affairs, Press Dept. Courtesy Royal Danish Embassy, Tel Aviv

Dante   M. A. Orr, *Dante and the Early Aristotelians*, Gall and Inglis, Edinburgh

Dawn   J. Norman Lockyer, *The Dawn of Astronomy*, MIT Press, Cambridge, Mass.

DE   British Crown Copyright, reprinted with permission of Dept. of the Environment

DOG   *Discoveries and Opinions of Galileo*, Translated by Stillman Drake, © Doubleday and Co. Reprinted with permission of Doubleday and Co.

Ein   Estate of Albert Einstein, by permission of O. Nathan, trustee

Exp   Reproduced by arrangement with Holt, Rinehart and Winston, Inc., N.Y., from *Exploration of the Universe*. Brief edition by G. Abell, 1969

Fab   S. Toulmin and J. Goodfield, *The Fabric of the Heavens*, Hutchinson Publishing Group, London

FC   Det Nationalhistoriske Museum på Frederiksberg, Denmark

GS   U.S. Geological Survey National Center, Information Office, Reston, Va.

Hale   Hale Observatory photo, Hale Observatories, Pasadena, Cal. Courtesy Linda A. Chaffee, photo permissions

HBSO   British Crown copyright, reproduced with permission of the Controller of Her Britannic Majesty's Stationery Office

Hi   Abraham bar Hiyya, *Zurath Ha-aretz*, 1720

Him   R. Kühn, *Die Himmel Erzählen*, Droemersche Verlagsanstalt Th. Knaur, Nachf. Used with permission of publisher

Hist   J. L. E. Dreyer, *History of the Planetary System from Thales to Kepler*, Cambridge Univ. Press, London

HM   J. Kepler, *Harmonice Mundi*, Bologna

Hug   Courtesy Hughes Aircraft Co., Space and Communication group, El Segundo, Cal.

Inqu   Eric M. Rogers, *Physics for the Inquiring Mind*, © 1960 Princeton Univ. Press, figs. 14.4a, 14.4b, p. 225, 14.6 p. 228, and 14.11 p. 232. Reprinted by permission of Princeton Univ. Press

Int ast   C. Payne-Gaposchkin and K. Haramandanis, *Introduction to Astronomy*, © 1970, 1954, by Prentice-Hall, Inc. Reprinted by permission of Prentice-Hall, Inc., Englewood Cliffs, N.J.

JHA   *Journal for the History of Astronomy*, Dr. M. A. Hoskin, ed.

Kep   Archiv. Kepler Kommission, Bayerische Akademie der Wissenschaften, Munich, courtesy M. List

Kitt   Kitt Peak National Observatory, Tucson

Kunst   Staatliche Kunstsammlung, Kassel

Lar   *Larousse Astronom*, Larousse, Paris

Licht   Rudolf Thiel, *Und Es Ward Licht*, Rowohlt Verlag, Germany (1956)

Lick   Lick Observatory photo, Lick Observatory, Mt. Hamilton, Cal.

Low   Lowell Observatory photo, Planetary Research Center, Lowell Observatory, Flagstaff Ariz.

MC   D. W. Sciama, *Modern Cosmology*, Cambridge Univ. Press, 1971. Reprinted with permission of Cambridge Univ. ress, London

MM   National Maritime Museum, Haifa. Photo Sadeh, Haifa. Courtesy Arie L. Ben-Eli, director, and C. Melun.

MRAO   Mullard Radio Astronomy Observatory, Cambridge, England, courtesy B. Elsmore

NASA   NASA, Office of International Affairs, Washington, D.C.

NH   John C. Brandt and Stephen P. Maran, *New Horizons in Astronomy*, W. H. Freeman and Co., © 1972

NO   U.S. Naval Observatory, Washington, D.C. Courtesy W. Rhynsburger, Assistant Director, Northern Transit Circle Division

NRAO   National Radio Astronomy Observatory, Green Bank, W. Va., courtesy Wallace R. Oref, Public Education Officer

NRL   National Research Laboratory, Washington, D.C., courtesy H. Friedman

ON   Oesterreichische Nationalbibliothek, Vienna, courtesy I. Nemeth, Handschriftensammlung

Ph   *Albert Einstein: Philosopher--Scientist*, ed. P. A. Schilpp, Tudor Publishing Co. Used with permission of Tudor Publishing Co.

Phys   Adapted from *Physics: Its Methods and Meanings* by Alexander Taffel. © 1973, 1969, 1965 by Allyn and Bacon, Inc. Reproduced by permission of Allyn and Bacon, Inc.

Pion   O. Lodge, *Pioneers of Science*, Macmillan, 1893

Plan   Stuart J. Inglis, *Planets, Stars, and Galaxies*, 3rd edition. © 1967, 1972, John Wiley & Sons, Inc. Reprinted with permission of John Wiley & Sons

PS   V. H. Booth, *Physical Science: A Study of Matter and Energy*, The Macmillan Company, N.Y. © Verne H. Booth, 1962. Reprinted with permission of the Macmillan Company

PT   *Physics Today*, © American Institute of Physics

QU   Geoffrey Burbidge and Margaret Burbidge, *Quasi-Stellar Objects*, W. H. Freeman and Co. © 1967

SAAO   South African Astronomical Observatory, SACSIR, Cape Town, courtesy Sir R. Woolley, Director

Sci   G. Gamow, "History of the Universe," *Science*, cover vol. 158, Nov. 10, 1967. © 1967 American Association for the Advancement of Science

SG   *Stars and Galaxies*, ed. Thornton Page, © 1962 Prentice-Hall, Inc. Reprinted by permission of Prentice-Hall, Inc., Englewood Cliffs, N. J.

Short   Arthur Berry, *A Short History of Astronomy*, John Murray, London, 1898.

Sky   *Sky and Telescope*, Sky Publishing Corp. Reprinted by permission of Sky Publishing Corp., courtesy William E. Shawcross, Managing Ed.

SM   Science Museum, London

SPO   Sacramento Peak Observatory, Air Force Cambridge Research Laboratories, Sun Spot, N.M. Courtesy R. L. Faller, photographer

TAU   Tel Aviv University, Tel Aviv

TB   J. L. E. Dreyer, *Tycho Brahe*, Adam and Charles Black, London

TG   Tribuna Galileiana, Museo Zoologico de "La Specola," Firenze, courtesy Dr. M. Poggesi

Thor   Tycho Brahe, Astron. inst. Mechanica, courtesy Professor Victor E. Thoren, Indiana Univ.

U   G. Amaldi and N. Rudnick, *Our World and the Universe--The Universe*, Aldo Garzanti, Editore S.A.S. Milano

UG   Universitäts Sternwarte, Göttingen, Germany, courtesy Professor Dr. H. H. Voigt

USAF   Official U.S. Air Force photo

USIS   United States Information Service, courtesy, U.S. Embassy, Tel Aviv

VA   Victoria and Albert Museum, London

Wal   Andreas Cellarius, *Star Atlas*, 1661, courtesy Professor Dr. G. Walterspiel

World   Kingston Carp, *Our World in Space and Time*, Vantage Press, 1960. Reprinted with permission of Vantage Press

Yer   Yerkes Observatory, Univ. of Chicago, Williams Bay, Wis.

Pictures are listed according to page and position: t-top,
c-center, b-bottom, l-left, r-right, and combinations:
br-bottom right, tl-top left, etc. Pictures not listed here are
either in the personal collection of the author or in the public
domain.

CHAPTER I 8:Mus. Condé, BN 9tr:MM br:Griffith Obs.
bl:BPK 10t:Dean and Chapter Canterbury cl:MM b:Brit.
Crown Copyright SM 11b:Yer 12tl:Lick bl:Inst. Nac.
Antr. e Hist., Mexico br:BN 13tl, tr:VA br:Wal 14tl,
tr:Wal b:Yer 15:Hale 16l:VA r:World 19tl:BM
tr:Licht, Lademann, Copenhagen br:Met. Mus. of Art, NY
bl:Dawn 20t:HBSO b:Prof. A. F. Aveni 21b:Dr. E. C. Krupp
t:DE 22t:Prof. J. A. Eddy and US Forest Service b:Prof. J. A.
Eddy 23tl:Shur, TAU tr:Bod b:HBSO 24t:Dawn b:Dawn, Brugsch
25:Dresden Codex, Wm. E. Gates reproduction 26tr, b, 27tl:Yer
tr:ConA 27b, 28tl:Wal 29t:Lar 30t:ConA 31t:Exp 32l:U
33b:Exp 34t:Lick c:Exp
CHAPTER II 35:from Euclid Elements 361, 37c, 38, 401:Dante
r:Prof. E. E. Helm 41:Mon. Mus. e Gall. Patifcie, Vatican
42tl, tr:Inqu 42b:Exp 431:Dante 44t:HM Libre II b:R. Thiel
451:Wal br:Dante 47t:Wal b:Fabr 49:ON 56t:Ast cr:Cop
57:Hale 58tl:Dante b:Dante, H. Smyth 59:NH 60br:Ant.
61bl:Wal 621:Almagest 63tl:At bl:R. Thiel (Licht) tr, br:Dante
CHAPTER III 66:World 67t:Lerons 68:BS 72bl:Brit.
Library, London 73bl:Wal 75r:Silsilanāna 76l, r:Univ. Istanbul.
Library 77tl, tr:Hist b:MM 78cl:Silsilanāna tr:K.arui-Niyazov
br:Topkapi Saray Museum, Istanbul 79:Shahiashāhnāma 80l:BN
tr, br:Hi 82l:BS r:ON 83:BN 84br:P. Apian, Cosmographia
(1539)
CHAPTER IV 85:Kep 87t:London Library 89br:Fab
90:Hist 91t:Bibl. Comunale degli Intronati, Siena, photo Grassi
93tr:Brit. Library, London 94tl:Wal 96:Thor 97tl, tr:De Nova
Stella c:TAU, Kupo 98tl:Bod tr, bl, br, 99t:Kunst c:FC b:ATA
100t:Selskab. b:FC 101tl, bl, r:Dr. Wm. A. Blanpied, AAAS
102tl:BPK tr:Short 103b:Dan 104l:Bibl. Apostolica Vaticanana,
photo, Prof. O. Gingerich 105tr:Thor tl:Pion br, bl:Thor
106tl:NO tr:TB b:Hi 107:tl, tr:Thor 108tr:V. E. Thoren,
"New Lights on Tycho's Instruments," JHA, 1973 108cr:Thor
b:NM 109l:From "Astrolabe" by J. D. North, Copyright © Jan.
1974 by Scientific American, Inc. All rights reserved
109r:MM 110:Rheinisches Bildarchivs, Köln. Stadtmuseum 111t:Art
Centrum, Czech. Center of Fine Arts, Prague 111b:BPK
112l, r:ATA 113tl:Kep tr:Sky; photo Prof. O. Gingerich
c:Kep 114tl:Myst. Cosm. b:Cos 115l:HM, Libre V 116r:Prof. S.
van den Bergh, Star Atlas of Super Remnants, Dunlop Obs., Toronto
116l:Kep 118bl: R. Thiel br:Fab 119:Kep 120tl: D. T.
Whiteside, "The Keplerian Planetary Eggs," JHA, vol. 5 (1974
reprinted with permission of JHA 120cl:A. Koestler, The Sleep
Walkers, Hutchinson Pub. Group Ltd. 123, 124t:HM, Libre IV b:Hist
127l:Landesbildstelle Wurttembergische Landesbibl., Stuttgart
128t:Kep b:Yer 129l:TG 130:TG
131t:TG c:DOG b:BNC 132tl:BNC tr:Lick b:Exp 133tl:Sid.
Nuncius tr:Hale bl:Low br:Lar 134l:Pion r:Yer 135t, c:Lar
137:Low 138t:Lar c:Exp 139t:PS bl:BNC 139c, 140tl, cl,
bl:SPO bc, 141l:Lar r:NRL 142l, r:BN 144l:Wal 145:Louvre
146r:TG G. Carlo Oli, Italian Embassy, Tel Aviv, photo Alinari

CHAPTER V 148t:Gouvernement de France 150l:Photo SM r:Royal
Society, London 152t:Bau 153b:Royal Society, London 155tr:CHP,
Burndy Library 157tl:Plan 161t:Photo SM 162:U 163:Nat.
Maritime Mus., London 164:ON 167tl:Short tr:Yer bl:J. Maxwell,
A Treatise on Electricity and Magnetism (1892) 169cl:CHP, W. F.
Meggers Collection. 172tl:Ein, photo Viking Press tr:CHP, W. F.
Meggers Collection. 174l:CHP r:CHP, Segre Coll. 175:Prof. R. O.
Skinner, Relativity, Blaisdell-John Wiley and Sons, 1961 176r:
USAF 178:CHP 180b:Lick 181t:Ein, photo Viking Press bl: W. T.
Scott. Am.J.Physics 33, 712 (1963), Amer. Assoc. Physics Teachers
181br:CHP, T. J. See Coll. c:Weizmann Inst. Archives, Rehovoth,
Israel 182cr:CWO 184b:drawing by Augustus John, courtesy Trinity
College, Cambridge 185t: Ein,from O. Nathan, Ueber den Frieden,
photo courtesy H. Lang and Cie., Berne, Switzerland 188t:Ein, photo
Viking Press cr:TAU, V. Silver cl:Bell 189tl:Dan 190tl, c:Ph
tr:Prof. M. Klein, photo Ehrenfest 191tc:CHP, W. F. Meggers Coll.
tr:CHP, Segre Coll. b:Ein, photo Viking Press 192t:PT br:Prof.
J. Weber, Univ. of Maryland

CHAPTER VI 194b:G. E. Tauber, "What Is Light," The Book of
Knowledge, © Grolier, Inc. 195b:Exp 196t:Plan b:Hevelius Mach.
Coelestis 197tc:Phys 197b:Exp 198t:Yer cl:Photo SM br:NO
199tl:Int Ast tr:AAO br, 200t, br:Hale bl:F. Kahn, Design of
the Universe, Crown Publ., 1954 201tl:TAU, photo V. Silver
tr:TAU, photo A. Chai b:Aeronutronic-Ford 202tl:Publ. of Sir
William Huggin's Observatory (1899) tr:Kitt bc, 203t:SPO
c:Hale 204tl:Center for Astrophysics, Harvard College Obs.,
Cambridge, Mass. r:BPK bl:Lar, Ambroise Pare 205bl:J. A. Ruffner
The Curved and the Straight. JHA, photo J. A. Ruffner tl:Bod
br, 206tl:Low tr: Tapisserie de la Reine Mathilde, Ville de Bayeux,
France b:Low 207t, c:Hale b:Center for Astrophysics, Harvard
College Obs., Cambridge. Mass. 208tl. tr:Lar 209br, bl:TAU, photo
P. Wehinger 210tr:Iar 211tl:Yer tr:Photo SM br:Results of Astron.
Observations Made During the Years 1834-1838 at the Cape of Good
Hope (J. Herschel) 212:Yer 213:Lar 214:CHP, T. J. J. See Collection
215t:Pion c:P Moore, photo At 216t:Lar c, 217:Low 218c:Yer t:Low
b, 219tl:Lar tr, c:Low br:Lar 220t:C. Huygens, Systema
Saturnia, Pion b:Lar 221t:Short c:Hale b:CHP 222t:Low
c:Yer 223:Lar 224:UG, photo Hans Wilder 225tl:Short
tr:Lar 226br:R. L. Duncombe, Toro, the Imprisoned Bull, Sky
t:C. T. Kowal, Hale 227:M. M. Nieto, The Titius Bode Law of
Planetary Distances, Pergamon Press Ltd., Oxford, used with
permission of author and publisher 228t:Yer b:MM 229c:AP:Lar
231:Yer 232:F. L. Whipple, Earth, Moon and Planets, Harvard Univ.
Press

CHAPTER VII 235b:Yer 236tl:John Bayer, Uranometria, 1603
tr, bl:Lar br:Yer 237t, b, 238t:Lar b, 239t:Exp c, b:Lar
240t:CHP b:Center for Astrophysics, Harvard College Obs.,
Cambridge, Mass. 241:SAAO 242tl:MC tr:Lar c:CHP, W. F.
Meggers Coll. 243tl:Hale c:Obs. de Paris, Paris tr:Hale
244:Hale 245tl:Him bl, br:Hale 246l:Lar r:Plan 247l:Bau
r:Exp 248tr:Plan tl:CHP, H. Shapley Coll., photo D. Y. Martynov
249t:Plan 250t:Lar b:At 251:Hale 252t, 253t:Inst. för Astronomi,
Lund Obs. 252b:Cop 253b:Lar 254t:Yer c:A. H. Joy, Mt. Wilson
(Hale) 255t:Lar b:Hale 256t:Mme. Y. Georgelin, Obs. de
Marseille 257:Hale 258t:Kitt b:CHP, courtesy Mrs. W. S. Adams
259t:SG c:E. Hubble, The Realm of the Nebulae, Yale Univ. Press
260tl, tr, b:Hale 261l:Yer r:Plan, after H. Arp 262tr:Prof. Jan
H. Oort, Sterrewacht Leiden, Netherlands tr:Hale c:Exp
263t:E. Hubble, The Realm of the Nebulae, Yale Univ. Press b:ConA
274:NRAO 275tl, r, b:Hale 276tl:Thomas A. Mathews, et al,"Discussion of galaxies identified with radio sources," Astrophys. J.
140, 35 (1964), fig. 2, Univ. of Chicago Press 276r:MRAO
277:Hale 278tl:F. D. Kahn and H. P. Palmar, Quasars, Manchester
Univ. Press, photo Prof. A. T. Moffet 278r:MC, Prof. C. Hazard
279t:MC c, 280r:QU l:M. Schmidt, "Quasistellar Objects," Science
Journal 2, 77 (1966), Syndication International 282t:Prof.
A. Hewish, Radio Astronomy Obs., Univ. of Cambridge (MRAO)
c:TAU, Astrophysics 283l:Prof. A. Hewish, Radio Astronomy Obs.,
Univ. of Cambridge (MRAO) 284, 285:Lick 286l:r:Prof. J. R.
Ostriker, Princeton Univ. Obs., Princeton, NJ 287t, bl, br:NRL
288t:Dr. H. Friedman, NRL br, bl:NRL 289b:Dr. Jerome Kristian,
Hale
CHAPTER VIII 292t:photo courtesy Sky 294tl:ConU bl:E. L.
Harrison, PT br:ConU 295tl:Hale tr:ConA 296:ConU 298t:photo
courtesy A. K. Mach c:CHP 300b:ConU 301tr:Prof. A. R. Sandage,
Hale Obs. b:Lar 304t:Acad. Royale des Sciences, des Lettres et
des Beaux-Arts de Belgique c:AtU 305t:CHP, photo B. Gamow
b:Bell 306t:F. Kahn, Design of the Universe, Crown Publ., 1954
bl:Sci br:At 308l:Brookhaven National Lab., Upton, NY, Public
Relations Office 311:after A. R. Sandage

CHAPTER IX 312:J. Verne, Autour de la lune, J. Hetzel, Paris
(1872) 313l:Royal Asiatic Society, London . 314tl:NASA
cr:USAF 315, 316, 317c:USIS 318t:At 318cr,319t;Bell b:NASA-
USIS c, 321t, c:USIS 322t:Hug c:GS 323tl:Hug 323tr, b, 324t:USIS
bl:NASA br:Hug 325l, r:USIS 328tl:Cop c, b, tr:USIS 329tl:USIS-
NASA 329tr, c, b, USIS 330, 331tr, b, 333tr, tl, b, 334l, r, 335t:
USIS cr:P. Moore and D. A. Hardy, Challenge of the Stars,
Mitchell Beazley Ltd., 1972, reprinted with permission cl:USIS
338t:USIS-NASA 339t:AAO b:J. Billingham, "Project Cyclops," NASA
Ames Research Center, 1973 340:AO 341:USIS

Index